CW00687254

Mass-Observation at the Movies

Cinema and Society

General Editor

Jeffrey Richards
Department of History
University of Lancaster

Mass-Observation at the Movies

Edited by
Jeffrey Richards
and Dorothy Sheridan

Routledge & Kegan Paul

London and New York

First published in 1987 by
Routledge & Kegan Paul Ltd
11 New Fetter Lane, London EC4P 4EE

Published in the USA by
Routledge & Kegan Paul Inc.
in association with Methuen Inc.
29 West 35th Street, New York, NY 10001

Set in Century
by Columns Ltd of Reading
and printed in Great Britain
by T. J. Press Ltd.
Padstow, Cornwall

Library of Congress Cataloging in Publication Data

Mass-Observation at the movies.

  (Cinema and society)
  Bibliography: p.
  Includes index.
  1. Moving-pictues — Great Britain — History.
  I. Richards, Jeffrey. II. Sheridan, Dorothy.
III. Mass-Observation. IV. Series.
PN1993.5.G7M324 1987   791.43'0941   87–9509

British Library CIP Data also available
ISBN 0–7102–0878–2

For Len England

Contents

General Editor's Preface ix

Acknowledgments x

Introduction 1

Part 1   Cinema-going in Worktown 19

1   Research Programme for the Investigation of
    Cinema-going in Bolton 21

2   The Cinema Manager Speaks 27

3   Replies to the Bolton Questionnaire 32

Part 2   Cinema-going in Wartime 137

A   THEMES, TRENDS AND PREFERENCES 139

4   The Cinema in the First Three Months of the War 139

5   Letter and First Report from a Volunteer Film Reviewer 170

6   Report on Audience Preference in Film Themes 173

7   Report on Cinema Queue 188

8   Analysis of Joke Competition 191

9   'Fade-out' Competition Report 200

10 Social Research and the Film 209

11 The Hazards of Mass-Observing 217

12 Notes on the Effect of the War (January-September 1941)
    on the Film Industry 218

13 1943 Directive Replies on Favourite Films 220

14 The Film and Family Life 292

B   FEATURE FILMS   299

15   *The Lion Has Wings*   299

16   *Let George Do It*   331

17   *The Great Dictator*   350

18   *Ships with Wings*   364

C   NEWSREELS   381

19   Newsreel Content (28 January 1940)   381

20   Newsreel Report 2 (26 May 1940)   395

21   Newsreels (June 1940)   405

22   Newsreel Report 3 (6 October 1940)   409

23   The Faking of Newsreels   419

24   Interview with Kenneth Gordon   422

D   MINISTRY OF INFORMATION SHORTS   424

25   Fifteen Ministry of Information Shorts   424

26   *You're Telling Me* Film Report   433

27   Preliminary Report on Opinion about Ministry of Information Shorts   441

28   Report on Ministry of Information Shorts   445

    General Index   461

    Index of Film Titles   469

General Editor's Preface

The pre-eminent popular art form of the first half of the twentieth century has been the cinema. Both in Europe and America from the turn of the century to the 1950s cinema-going has been a regular habit and film-making a major industry. The cinema combined all the other art forms – painting, sculpture, music, the word, the dance – and added a new dimension – an illusion of life. Living, breathing people enacted dramas before the gaze of the audience and not, as in the theatre, bounded by the stage, but with the world as their backdrop. Success at the box office was to be obtained by giving the people something to which they could relate and which therefore reflected themselves. Like the other popular art forms, the cinema has much to tell us about people and their beliefs, their assumptions and their attitudes, their hopes and fears and dreams.

This series of books will examine the connection between films and the societies which produced them. Film as straight historical evidence; film as an unconscious reflection of national preoccupations; film as escapist entertainment; film as a weapon of propaganda – these are the aspects of the question that will concern us. We shall seek to examine and delineate individual film *genres*, the cinematic images of particular nations and the work of key directors who have mirrored national concerns and ideals. For we believe that the rich and multifarious products of the cinema constitute a still largely untapped source of knowledge about the ways in which our world and the people in it have changed since the first flickering images were projected on to the silver screen.

Jeffrey Richards

Acknowledgments

We are indebted to the following for their advice, support and assistance: Victoria Allanson, Dorothy Barber, Angus Calder, Arthur Calder-Marshall, James Power, Joyce Storer, Audrey Taylor, Alison Walker and Brenda Wright. This book is respectfully dedicated to Len England, pioneer of research into cinema and society. The British Academy kindly gave a grant to facilitate research for the book. We would like to thank the Trustees of the Mass-Observation Archive for permission to reproduce original Mass-Observation material.

Introduction

'. . . from the beginning film was of the highest interest to us. We were film-minded. . . .'

Tom Harrisson in 1973[1]

A glance through the lists of subjects studied by Mass-Observation will yield ample evidence of this 'film-mindedness'. Some fifty reports on the habits and preferences of the British cinema-going public were produced between 1939 and 1945. The raw material for these reports – observations, counts, interviews, questionnaires – fills fifteen storage boxes in the archive at the University of Sussex where the Mass-Observation papers are now housed. In terms of sheer bulk, the collection of papers on film is one of the largest collections on a single theme produced by Mass-Observation.

Very little of the film material found its way into print. The typed reports, several of which have been reproduced in this anthology, reached a certain kind of audience, chiefly at the Ministry of Information, but no popular works on film or cinema-going were ever actually produced by Mass-Observation. Only one of the twenty-five publications produced between 1937 and 1950 refers to film in wartime, and then only briefly. This was *Home Propaganda*, a pamphlet in the Advertising Service Guild's 'Change' series published in 1941. Mass-Observation's work on the subject tended to be directed towards people in the film trade itself or towards people with a professional interest in the role of film in home front propaganda. A good example of this is Tom Harrisson's article for the *Documentary News Letter*[2] (Item 10 in this volume) where he is critical of the lack of government interest in measuring the impact of films.

This anthology, therefore, presents a selection of writings on film from the Mass-Observation Archive which has hitherto remained unpublished. In general we have tried to keep editorial comment and interpretation to a minimum to allow the reader to draw his or her own conclusions.

The links between Mass-Observation and film-making were forged at a very early stage in Mass-Observation's history. Indeed, one of the most immediate influences behind the formation of this unusual and ambitious organisation was the documentary film movement itself. During the 1930s, the innovatory work in British documentary revolved around John Grierson at the GPO Film Unit in London. The Unit, which had the semi-official function of producing information films for the GPO and for other government departments, provided the apprenticeship for a number of young film-makers, many of whom were later to distinguish themselves as wartime and post-war directors and producers. One of these was Humphrey Jennings. Jennings joined the Unit in the mid-1930s and after two or three years of film work, he became involved in planning a form of *written* documentary. This notion emerged from discussions not only among the film-makers but among a wider circle of middle- and upper-class intellectuals, poets, writers and artists, who gathered at the home of Jennings's friend Charles Madge in Blackheath. Charles Madge was a well-known poet and was employed at that time as a journalist with the *Daily Mirror*.

A letter in the *New Statesman* in December 1936[3] galvanised Madge and Jennings into action. The writer pointed out that in all the excitement generated by the Abdication Crisis of that year, there was considerable scope for 'that anthropological study of our own civilisation of which we stand in such desperate need'. Madge and Jennings were swift to respond. A letter signed by Madge appeared in the *New Statesman* on 2 January 1937 which stated that a group had already been formed 'for precisely this purpose'. The aim of the as yet untitled group was to establish 'observation points on as widely extended a front as at present can be organised. We invite the cooperation of voluntary observers and will provide detailed information to anyone who wants to take part. . . . Only mass observations can create mass science.'

This letter attracted the attention of a third man who was to become crucial to Mass-Observation's fortunes. Tom Harrisson claimed that he read Madge's invitation in the Reading Room of Bolton Public Library. He had recently arrived in Bolton after spending over three years as an anthropologist living with the people of Malekula, an island in the New Hebrides. *Savage Civilisation*, the book he had written about this experience, had just been finished and appeared in 1937 in the Left Book Club series published by Victor Gollancz. Free to turn his attention to his own country, he was currently 'going native' in the pubs and cotton mills of south Lancashire. The idea of an 'anthropology of our own people' coincided closely with Harrisson's own work and he promptly presented himself at Blackheath to join forces with Madge, Jennings and their entourage. A third letter appeared in the columns of the *New Statesman*,[4] this time signed by all three men and under the heading 'Anthropology at Home'. Mass-Observation, they decreed,

> does not set out in quest of truth or facts for their own sake, or for the
> sake of an intellectual minority, but aims at exposing them in simple
> terms to all observers, so that their environment may be understood,
> and thus constantly transformed. Whatever the political methods called
> upon to effect the transformation, the knowledge of what has to be

transformed is indispensable. The foisting on the mass of ideals or ideas developed by men apart from it, irrespective of its capacities, causes mass misery, intellectual despair and international shambles.

So the cine-camera of the documentary film crew was to be replaced with the pen and paper, and on occasion by the paint-brush and the ordinary camera. The themes and preoccupations of films like *Night Mail, Housing Problems* or *Coal Face* were to find a new medium in Mass-Observation, and this time the subjects of the documentary were to be invited to take part.[5]

The earliest cinema work was carried out in Bolton. Leaving Madge and Jennings to co-ordinate the recruitment of volunteers from their base in London, Tom Harrisson returned north where he rented a small house in Davenport Street, Bolton. He was a charismatic and energetic man and quickly gathered round him a team of full-time and part-time investigators. Some of those who worked for longer or shorter periods included William Empson, Bill Naughton, John Sommerfield, Humphrey Spender, Julian Trevelyan, Woodrow Wyatt. Most of them were less well known, students on their vacations, local unemployed people, trade unionists, teachers, members of the Workers' Educational Association. They came sometimes for a few days, sometimes for months, living in the rather squalid headquarters in Davenport Street and directed each day by Tom Harrisson to observe and record the behaviour of the Boltonians at work and play. This was the 'Worktown' project.

Cinemas were of course prime targets for observational work on leisure, along with dance-halls and pubs. Going to the cinema in Bolton during the 1930s was a very popular pastime indeed. By a happy coincidence, the arch-chronicler of film, Leslie Halliwell, grew up in Bolton. In his autobiography he writes,

> For a film fanatic, Bolton was almost like Mecca. At one time there lay within my easy reach no fewer than forty-seven cinemas of varying size, quality and character. None was more than five miles from Bolton's Town Hall, and twenty-eight were within the boundaries of the borough.[6]

Harrisson was an enthusiastic film-goer himself. Some of his almost illegible notes on audience reactions to the films he saw in Bolton survive in the archive. He had also established some useful contacts in the film business quite early on. A letter from Stuart Legg dated 27 October 1937, evidently answering Harrisson's enquiry about film scripts, states dryly 'You will have a bad time trying to get hold of scripts. Though all studios keep their scripts they are regarded as part of the conjuring trick of film-making, and therefore secret.'[7] The value to Mass-Observation of having the scripts was that the observers could mark audience reactions against the relevant scene or piece of dialogue. Legg welcomed Mass-Observation's interest in film and was prepared to provide introductions but added a warning:

> Don't disillusion yourself about the potential value of the work to the trade: it is the most complacent industry in the world and if you want to raise any money from renters, etc., for research – why, forget it. . . . As to important research on the social effects of the film, there has never been any work done of the slightest importance.

Harrisson set about remedying the situation with formidable serious- ness. Papers in the archive show that considerable background research was undertaken. Notes from earlier surveys and references to other published accounts of cinema-going, notably from the American study *Middletown*,[8] which contains a short section on the role of 'motion pictures' in a small Midwest town, illustrate the kinds of influences which were affecting Mass-Observation's approach. The grandly titled 'Cinema Research Unit' (CRU) was established and plans were made to carry out in-depth studies of a selection of central Bolton cinemas where the managers could be induced to co-operate. The CRU seems to have been mostly the work of one person, John Martin Jones (or JMJ – all the observers were indentified by their initials). Very little is known about JMJ but it is likely that he was a student. His name appears on papers during late 1937 but not on later work. Under Harrisson's direction he produced an outline of proposed research (Item 1 in this volume) and was responsible for contacting cinema managers. The intention was to carry out a series of observations of performances, recording such information as the size, composition, appearance and behaviour of the audience, reactions to the films, overheard conversations and so forth. Information on the cinema itself – size, décor, types of programmes, seat prices, advertising, staffing, management policy, popularity – was also to be recorded.

Some fascinating reports have survived: interviews with cinema managers (see Item 2), an account of a publicity stunt – a children's party given by Binkie Stewart, 'England's Answer to Shirley Temple', a report on the extent of the advertising for Disney's *Snow White* (replica dwarfs on sale in Woolworths). One report (which has already been published) demonstrates the ease with which the Mass-Observers slipped from their 'objective' role of bystander into something a little closer to participant observation. A young male working-class Observer combines his observa- tion of the audience at a George Raft film at the Embassy cinema with a somewhat closer observation of the young woman companion he picks up on the street outside.[9]

The biggest cinema event during the Worktown project was the grand opening of the Odeon cinema with its seats for 2,000, its car park and its Balcony Café. Several descriptions of the opening night were made and two copies of the lavish programme were obtained for the files.[10] Odeon cinemas gave Mass-Observation a good deal of support. The Chairman, Oscar Deutsch, arranged for JMJ to interview the publicity manager, Richard Ford, in London. JMJ was provided with a pass so that he could attend performances free and Mr Abercrombie, the Bolton Odeon's manager, was instructed to help Mass-Observation in any way he could. Ford advised on the preparation of a survey of film-goers which Mass-Observation modelled on earlier surveys carried out by Sidney Bernstein in his London-based circuit of cinemas. Like the Bernstein questionnaire, Mass-Observation used the device of a competition to encourage response. The patrons of the three Bolton cinemas selected (the Odeon, the Palladium and the Crompton) were invited to answer a sheet of questions on their habits and preferences. The last section was left blank for general comments and two prizes of £1 each plus six double complimentary tickets were offered for the best entries. A total of 560 replies were received (see Item 3). It is difficult to know how many questionnaires were distributed although an estimate from a local printer mentions the figure of 29,000! It is unlikely that Mass-Observation could have handled this number. Some meticulous arithmetic was carried out on the replies but no summary of results seems to have survived (if it ever existed in the first place).

Observations in cinemas continued to be carried out by JMJ's successors during 1938 and 1939 but it looks as if Mass-Observation was concentrating much more on other work, particularly in Blackpool. Work had also begun on the first book to emerge from the project, *The Pub and the People* (although it was not published until 1943). There is no doubt that the high turnover of personnel, the chronic shortage of funds and what sometimes seems like the serendipity of the whole operation were hardly conducive to sustained and conclusive research. What is surprising under the circumstances is that so much was achieved.

During 1939, the imminence of war gave Mass-Observation a new direction. Harrisson was not slow to realise that the war offered a solution to at least some of Mass-Observation's problems. Until 1939, funds had come in unpredictable amounts from book royalties (the Penguin Special, *Britain* by Mass-Observation, had sold very well), from the monies advanced to him by Victor Gollancz for the production of four books on the Worktown project and from donations by wealthy benefactors. A contract with the government held the promise of a steady income to pay regular wages and the opportunity to earn official recognition. Harrisson set about persuading various government personnel that Mass-Observation was ideally suited to the job of monitoring civilian morale. Lord MacMillan, the first Minister of Information, had refused to employ Mass-Observation because of press and parliamentary criticism of the Ministry's overstaffing and excessive spending. But Mary Adams (who was a friend of Tom Harrisson) was appointed first head of Home Intelligence and succeeded in employing Mass-Observation after Lord MacMillan's replacement by Sir John Reith. She defended Mass-Observation against Ministry misgivings about its potentially subversive leftwingery and its lack of scientific and methodological rigour. Ian McLaine concluded:

> Mass-Observation became essential to Home Intelligence. . . . It is true to say that in the absence of the speedy and versatile work of Mass-Observation much would have gone unnoticed and unattended – especially in 1940 when Home Intelligence was having considerable trouble in creating its own machinery.[11]

During 1941 and 1942, Home Intelligence relied heavily on the reports supplied by Mass-Observation on the state of the nation's morale. A kind of morale 'barometer' was created based on indicators which only Mass-Observation could have invented: numbers of people carrying gas masks, dreams about Hitler, rumours, jokes, graffiti and, inevitably, the behaviour of people at cinemas, especially their response to government films.

By the late summer of 1940, Harrisson was running Mass-Observation on his own. Jennings was working with the Crown Film Unit (formerly the GPO Film Unit) after completing two projects with Mass-Observation: a book about the events on the day King George VI was crowned, *May Twelfth*, which presented short descriptions montage-style without editorial, and the film *Spare Time* which did not involve any of the other Mass-Observers but was shot partly in Bolton and has a characteristic Mass-Observation feel to it. Charles Madge stayed longer but he was uncomfortable with Mass-Observation's government work and much later described it as 'home front espionage'.[12] He left in mid-1940 to join the National Institute of Economic and Social Research. The film work had already become the responsibility of a new recruit, Len England (LE), who had joined Mass-Observation's ranks in 1939. He was fresh from school, about eighteen years old and brimming with enthusiasm. The greater part of the wartime film work that took place before 1943 was carried out or commissioned by LE himself.

During the first few months of the war, LE seems to have busied himself with a programme of self-education. He scoured film trade magazines and journals and exploited the sometimes tenuous links which Tom Harrisson had already made with key figures in the film industry. The results of these preliminary investigations were written up in a report, 'The Cinema in the First Three Months of War' (see Item 4). This was probably a joint effort with Tom Harrisson but it was LE who took it to Humphrey Jennings for his comments.

Meanwhile, observations in the cinema were under way and a dossier on audience reactions to the first wartime propaganda film, *The Lion Has Wings*, was being compiled. It was obvious, however, that the full-time core of staff at Mass-Observation's headquarters could not cover sufficient ground and in any case was almost exclusively London-based. It was decided to draw on the resources of the panel of volunteers (now numbering about 500 and actively keeping diaries or responding to monthly 'directives') for additional film work. In February 1940, LE wrote to selected volunteers inviting them to join a special panel of film reviewers. The replies and the subsequent reports testify to the extraordinary enthusiasm of people for the cinema (see Item 5 for an example of someone's first contribution). The most prolific reviewers were a male student at Manchester Polytechnic, a middle-aged woman teacher from Watford, a housewife and journalist from London, a young male clothing-manufacturer's assistant from Ipswich and a young male shop-worker from Greater Baddow in Essex. LE maintained close contact, advising on which films to see and offering tips on observing, including note-taking in the dark:

> Observer uses a notebook with pages turning from top so that a page once used goes underneath as extra support; writes on his knee, though a gas mask makes a useful table. Uses his left thumb to mark the place; as he writes a line he moves his thumb down half an inch and begins the next entry there. This removes both overwriting and leaving long gaps.

The reviewers were anxious to please: 'I would like my reports to be as near perfect as possible,' wrote one, 'so will you please point out any other faults.' Mass-Observers (and not only those in the cinema) continually ran the risk of being taken for spies as a letter from one unfortunate reviewer shows (Item 11).

Although Mass-Observation relied heavily on the regular reports of the special reviewing panel, the larger panel of volunteers was not forgotten. In 1941, the panel was asked about its cinema-going habits. Very sadly none of the original replies for 1941 has survived although the results were incorporated into the reports of that period. In 1943, fortunately, the panel was again quizzed about the cinema. They were asked to list the six films they liked best in the past year (see Item 13). The panel was a self-selected group of people, predominantly, but certainly not entirely, middle class. Publicity in popular newspapers enabled Mass-Observation to reach more working-class people, and during 1940 it ran two competitions in the *Sunday Dispatch* with the help of the paper's film correspondent Moore Raymond. In February, readers were asked for their views on the 'funniest incident' in a film and in April for the best 'fade-out'. The material was carefully analysed and written up as reports. LE also arranged with the film magazine *Picturegoer* that all their readers' letters be passed on to him. To ensure that readers wrote in with the right information, LE himself sent a letter to *Picturegoer*, signed 'Film Observer, Mass-

Observation', asking people to answer the following questions and send them to *Picturegoer*.

How often do you go to the cinema? Why do you go? What are your favourite pictures? And your favourite stars? What sort of humour do you like best and who are your favourite comedians? What type of film do you like best? Do you like single features or double features? Do you keep accounts of films you have seen? How many of you belong to fan clubs?

The letters continued to arrive at Mass-Observation until the *Picturegoer*'s offices were bombed in the London blitz.[13]

The greatest emphasis, however, was still placed on the investigations by the full-timers at Mass-Observation. Tom Harrisson was continually arguing with the authorities that his members of staff were engaged in work of national importance and should not, therefore, be called up. He was fighting a losing battle. By spring 1941, Len England was in the Army and the following year Harrisson began his training with the Special Operations Executive in preparation for guerrilla work against the Japanese in South East Asia. Most of the full-timers carried on sending in reports from the Forces, sometimes illicitly, and sometimes, as in LE's case, with the co-operation of Army personnel. Nevertheless, the greater part of the observational work took place between 1940 and early 1941. LE himself was responsible for a series of forty-five reports on film programmes between October 1939 and June 1940. Additional reports were carried out at the same time by the other investigators although film work was competing with a very wide range of other projects including assessments of the impact of other forms of government propaganda – radio, posters, speeches and meetings.

In September 1940, LE was able to report on an impressive list of film studies. At least two newsreels per week were being covered by full-timers in London and at least one other newsreel in the provinces by one of the film reviewing panel. He noted that newsreels were in general liked except for the obvious 'filling in' news with 'short and boring snippets'. The key issue was the credibility of newsreels in the public mind: did people believe the news stories? Did they care about the authenticity of the footage? A good deal of thought was given to the problem of film-makers' re-using old footage in the absence of action shots (otherwise known as faking) and some of the inside information provided by Mass-Observation's contacts, especially Christopher Brunel, son of film director Adrian Brunel, was very useful (see also the interview with Kenneth Gordon, Item 24). Mass-Observation was also concerned with the perceived popularity of well-known people: Churchill and members of the royal family for example.

Work on feature films revealed that comedies were preferred over dramas; topical films were well received providing they were not 'excessively realistic or particularly unpleasant'. Special surveys co-ordinated by LE were carried out on *The Lion Has Wings* and *Let George Do It*, a comedy starring the very popular George Formby. The jokes in the latter were submitted to careful analysis. Similar detailed work was carried out on Chaplin's film *The Great Dictator* in 1941 and on *Ships with Wings* in 1942 (see Part 2 of this volume) although by this time LE was no longer able to take part in the research. Direct questions put to people coming out of the film came to be used as much as observations inside the cinema. LE was compelled to refine his observational methods in order to standardise results. Audience response was marked out of five as follows:

(1) Three or four people respond
(2) Up to 20 respond
(3) Response fairly general
(4) Response very general
(5) Immediate response from whole audience

Applause was counted in seconds. Coughing was regarded as a sign of boredom. So was talking at the end of a sequence. Sections of the film itself had to be classified too. LE suggested the following:

(1) Action: violent (e.g. car chases, fights, sports)
(2) Action: 'normal' (e.g. letter-writing, kissing)
(3) Action: humorous
(4) Conversation: on plot
(5) Conversation: on love
(6) Conversation: on theory (e.g. on liberty, patriotism, war)
(7) Conversation: humorous[14]

Although Len England continued to carry out a good deal of his film work from the Army, he was forced to hand over some of the work (co-ordinating the film reviewing panel, for example) to a deputy. A young man called GG was recruited. Very little of GG's observations in cinemas seem to have survived but a series of letters from LE giving him instructions reveals a great deal about LE's approach. 'First of all,' he wrote in June 1941,

> You don't mind me being frank? – you must be a little bit less
> subjective. You and I know that *This England* is a complete flop by our
> standards: but we aren't interested in that as observers. What interests
> us is (a) the exact as possible story of the film plus such trivia as
> director, company, cast etc and (b) audience reaction to the film. Neither
> of these things are as easy as I tend to think they are, I'm aware of that;
> I've been doing it for a couple of years now, and it seems to come almost
> as second nature. But you might put your foot in it if you're not careful.

You say that the heroine has an appalling idea of what an American accent is: may I point out that Miss Constance Cummings is American born and bred, and that this is only her second big lead in British pictures? That shakes you.[15]

The formal relationship with the Ministry of Information demanded that reactions to the bricf information films known as 'shorts' were monitored (see Part 2, Section D). Mass-Observation frequently received direct instructions from the Ministry about which of these films to follow up. A letter from Nicolas Bentley (Home Intelligence) in September 1941, for example, which was sent out to members of the Ministry's own intelligence network, the Regional Information Officers, was also sent to Mass-Observation. A programme of captured German propaganda film was to be shown at selected cinemas and the Ministry wanted to know how it was received. The film covered the German advances on the Eastern Front into the USSR. Most of the work for the Ministry, however, consisted of repeated coverage of audience reaction to the output of the Films Division, from *Miss Grant goes to the Door* (how to deal with the German invader) to *A Few Ounces a Day* (how to cope with food rationing). Mass-Observation also checked on the distribution of the films to see exactly which cinemas were including MoI shorts in their programmes. More intensive work, involving several investigators travelling out of London to other towns, took place in late 1941 and early 1942 and focused on *Seaman Frank Goes Back to Sea, Newspaper Train, War in the East* and *Rush Hour* (see Item 28).

During this period, Harrisson was gradually handing over the direction of Mass-Observation to H. D. (Bob) Willcock, and although research activities continued to be as diverse as ever the film work seems to have become less important. This no doubt coincided with the end of the contract with the Ministry of Information. LE remained very interested in the cinema and in 1944 produced a report on the way family life was represented in film. Mass-Observation also recorded people's reactions to the release of films about the German concentration camps as part of a wider study of attitudes to the end of the war. After the war, LE covered a number of films in 1946 including *Chance of a Lifetime* and *London Town*,[16] and in 1948 the Conservative Film Association commissioned Mass-Observation to assess the impact of their political film campaign in Hull.[17] In 1950, Mass-Observation published two newspaper articles on the cinema: 'Why do they go to the pictures?' in the *Daily Film Renter* (10 July) and 'Do you cry in the dark?' in the *Daily Herald* (18 November). By now Mass-Observation had become a limited company and was looking much more towards the commercial world for research contracts. Len England became one of the Directors of the organisation in its new phase and was still actively involved as late as 1970 when the early papers were transferred to the University of Sussex to become the Mass-Observation Archive.[18]

Mass-Observation discovered a good deal about which films people liked and why, about what it was like to go to the cinema in the 1930s and 1940s, about the role of cinema in people's lives, about how the cinema responded to and depicted the war. In effect and invaluably they monitored the views of the man and woman in the stalls. They also seem to have followed faithfully the agenda for film research outlined by Tom Harrisson in an article for *Documentary News Letter* (Item 10). But they were never able ultimately to determine how, if at all, films influenced people's behaviour and attitudes, arguably the *raison d'être* of their MoI work. The detailed study they carried out on the reception of four MoI shorts (Item 28) suggested that three of these films at least had had no effect on people's views. This may well have informed the view that Harrisson expressed many years later at a conference at the Imperial War Museum:

> Morale is not, in my view – and I spent years studying it in those days – affected by things like films. Pints of beer affect morale; being healthy and all kinds of other things affect morale. But official films never really came into it in people's own estimate of what affected them in the crunch. Morale was completely unanalysed and basically misunderstood. From the beginning we were supposed to be dealing with a disease, or an illness, or a wellness – but nobody knew what it was. . . . We just gave war medicines; no one diagnosed. In my view, looking back, it was events and experiences and people's innate feelings that determined morale. Not only that – there were about 45 million morales in England, not just one. People did not really change at all in the war; they just had to do different things because there was a war. . . . Looked at in the short term, on the spot, in the war, neither films nor posters nor leaflets, nor any other form of *deliberate* propaganda directed at the home front really mattered at all. The war, morale and all that was going on at another level.[19]

There is some truth in this but it is perhaps too extreme a view. In his meticulous and invaluable study of the Ministry of Information, Ian McLaine has carefully assessed the question of morale and its definition and maintenance in wartime Britain. He demonstrates that there was a consensus about what morale was.[20] It was centred on behaviour and action, and good war morale was summed up by Dr Stephen Taylor, who had succeeded Mary Adams as Director of Home Intelligence, in his 1941 annual report. He defined it as 'conduct and behaviour indicating that they are prepared to go through with the war to final victory whatever the cost to the individual or the group'. He declared that morale depended on material factors – food, warmth, work, leisure, rest and sleep, a secure base, safety of dependants – and moral factors – belief that victory is possible, belief in equality of sacrifice, belief in the efficiency and integrity of leadership, belief that the war is a necessity and our cause is just. After an analysis of the British character – commonsensical, pragmatic, unimaginative, determined – he concluded 'There is at present no evidence to suggest that it is possible to defeat the people of Britain by any means other than extermination.'[21] Dr Goebbels seems to have taken a similar view, writing in 1942: 'The English show fantastic national discipline. . . . They are obdurate to a degree which in the long run gets on one's nerves. . . . The British people are like children: in addition they have the limitless patience of sheep.'[22]

The mandarins of the Ministry of Information seem at first to have underestimated the innate morale of the British people, fearing its fragility, seeking constantly to stiffen it, whereas the evidence suggests that from the first the British were determined not to be beaten, regarded their cause as just and were resolved to see it through to the end. At no stage between September 1939 and November 1942 did any questionnaire show less than three-quarters of the population expressing a belief in ultimate British victory. By 1942, the indications from Home Intelligence and Mass-Observation were that the public was tired of constant exhortation. This view concided with the inclination of the new Minister, Brendan Bracken, who substituted a policy of information and explanation. At the same time the exhortatory MoI five-minute shorts shown weekly in the cinemas were terminated and replaced by longer, more explanatory films, issued monthly.

If official films had little effect, then, the role of the commercial cinema was much more significant. It was a part of the leisure which Dr Taylor saw as a contributory factor to morale. For many, particularly the vast army of female war workers, it was as important as Harrisson's pint of beer. The average weekly audience at cinemas rose from 19 million in 1939 to 31.4 million in 1946, the peak year of attendance in British cinema history. Gross box office receipts trebled. In August 1940 a Mass-Observation questionnaire of 100 people about what would be the effect of a rise in cinema seat prices on their cinema-going showed that 69 per cent indicated there would be no change, 21 per cent said they would pay less and go in cheaper seats and 10 per cent said they would go less often.[23]

The feature film was not devoid of propaganda for the film industry as a whole came under the oversight of the Films Division of the Ministry of Information. At the outset of the war, the Films Division had prepared a memorandum outlining a set of agreed priorities for film propaganda: what Britain was fighting for, how Britain was fighting and the need for sacrifice if the war was to be won. Michael Powell's all-star thriller *Forty-Ninth Parallel*, the only feature film to be directly financed by the Ministry and a programmatic account of 'why we fight', was the top

British box-office success of 1941.[24] This film was a good example of two of the Films Division's axioms: 'Film propaganda will be most effective when it is least recognizable as such' and 'The film, being a popular medium, must be good entertainment if it is to be good propaganda.'[25]

An ideas committee was set up to liaise between the Ministry and the film industry, to propose appropriate feature film propaganda subjects and to vet forthcoming film projects to ensure that they were in line with official thinking. The industry co-operated fully and the Ministry was able to leave the commercial producers to provide the feature film propaganda, Laurence Olivier's *Henry V* was inaugurated after a suggestion from the Ministry and Anthony Asquith's *The Way to the Stars* and Carol Reed's *The Way Ahead* both originated as MoI packages (script, personnel, facilities). All three films achieved critical and popular success.

But it was also a fundamental belief of the Ministry that 'good quality films, even if not directly about the war, were good for the country'. The Films Division expressed 'a willingness to support all types of pictures, including entertainment of a dramatic and comedy kind, provided it was of the highest quality'.[26] In 1942 Ernest Thurtle, Parliamentary Secretary to the Ministry of Information, declared in parliament: 'British film production has necessarily fallen in quantity during the war but I think it can be fairly allowed it has risen in quality.'[27] The public agreed. In the Bernstein questionnaire of 1946, asked if British films had got better since 1939, 96 per cent said that they had. By contrast, only 26 per cent thought American films had got better; 56 per cent thought they had not changed.[28]

It has become an accepted part of film history that the Second World War was a golden age of British cinema, when the native industry finally attained its maturity. Roger Manvell wrote in 1947:

> The qualities which are uppermost in our cinema are humanity of characterisation . . . and a growing ability to create a cinematic poetry peculiar to British films. This poetry is the sign of a nation's artistic maturity. It occurs when dialogue, acting, photography and the movement of sound and image merge to create a deep emotional impression. It cannot, of course, be defined. It can only be recognized and acknowledged. It is to be found in . . . *In Which We Serve, The First of the Few, The Gentle Sex, Millions Like Us, San Demetrio-London, The Way Ahead*, and especially *The Way to the Stars*. These are war films; it is also present in films like *The Stars Look Down, The Proud Valley, Love on the Dole, This Happy Breed, I Know Where I'm Going* and especially *Brief Encounter*.[29]

Dilys Powell wrote similarly in 1947:

> The British public, always a cinema-going public, has become doubly so

during the war years. And with the increase in numbers, a certain
sharpening of public taste is to be observed. Themes which would once
have been thought too serious or too controversial for the ordinary
spectator are now accepted as a matter of course. . . . There is a desire
for solidity and truth, even in the sphere of entertainment. We have
seen how the semi-documentary film has gained a hold over British
imaginations. We have seen too how even in the film of simple fiction,
the demand has grown for knowledge and understanding. The British no
longer demand pure fantasy in their films; they can be receptive also to
the imaginative interpretation of everyday life.[30]

This view, the twin processes of documentarisation and democratisation,
has led some historians to see in Ealing's realistic war films a reflection
not just of a sea-change in British cinema but of that move to the left in
the national mood which led to the Labour victory in 1945.[31] This is part
of the truth but not the whole truth. Ealing's later war films seem to have
been less popular with the public than their earlier ones, notably *Ships
with Wings*, castigated by some critics as class-bound, romanticised and
outdated but a hit with film-goers, as Mass-Observation discovered (Item
18). If we look at audience preference as opposed to critics' choice, we get a
somewhat different profile of wartime cinema, but one which may well
have materially sustained morale.

The top British box office star from 1938 to 1943 inclusive was George
Formby. Mass-Observation paid particular attention to humour, analysing
in depth the Formby vehicle *Let George Do It* (Item 16), a picture which
produced, as Harrisson later recalled, in a fantasy scene of Formby
knocking out Hitler, 'one of the big laughs of the year in films'.[32] The
much-heralded return to the screen of Charlie Chaplin in *The Great
Dictator*, another Mass-Observation investigation (Item 17), also provided
much-needed laughter. The war saw Arthur Askey, Tommy Trinder, Will
Hay, Arthur Lucan and Kitty McShane and Frank Randle, among others,
all proving big box-office attractions in often cheaply made but eagerly
received comedies, just as on the wireless Tommy Handley made ITMA a
national institution. Humour was vitally important, bearing out the
statement of F. C. Bartlett, Professor of Experimental Psychology at
Cambridge, in *Political Propaganda* (1940):

In England, it is safe to say, two types of appeal must always be
prominent: to humour and to sport. If an English population loses its
capacity to laugh its way through depressing circumstances, its morale
will be on the road to destruction.'[33]

But from 1944 to 1947 inclusive, the top British box-office star was James
Mason, who eclipsed Formby to signal the arrival of a new and different
form of escape from reality – the critically excoriated but massively

popular Gainsborough melodramas. It was to these films rather than Ealing's realistic dramas that the public turned for solace in the last years of the war. Gainsborough melodramas were voted second (*The Man in Grey*), third (*Madonna of the Seven Moons*) and fourth (*They Were Sisters*) in the *Daily Mail* ballot for the most popular films of the war years. The top British box-office successes of 1945 and 1946 were *The Seventh Veil* and *The Wicked Lady*, both starring James Mason. It is clear that what cinema audiences wanted by 1944 was a complete alternative to war films.

Until 1943, however, they had been willing to watch and enjoy war films, but war films which met the cinema-goer's ever-present need for stars, stories, dramatic values and emotional situations. The top British box-office successes before the heyday of Gainsborough melodrama were, in 1940, *Convoy*, with Clive Brook and John Clements; in 1941 *Forty-Ninth Parallel*, with Eric Portman, Leslie Howard, Anton Walbrook and Laurence Olivier; in 1942 *The First of the Few*, with Leslie Howard and David Niven; in 1943 *In Which We Serve*, with Noël Coward, Celia Johnson and John Mills; and in 1944 *This Happy Breed*, with Robert Newton, Celia Johnson and John Mills. It is interesting to observe here the prominence of Leslie Howard and Noël Coward, whose contribution to the maintenance of national morale has never been properly appreciated. During the same period, the top American successes at the British box-office were *Rebecca* (1940), *The Great Dictator* (1941), *Mrs Miniver* (1942), *Random Harvest* (1943) and *For Whom the Bell Tolls* (1944), most of them quintessentially romantic Hollywood melodramas, several of them with English settings. The phenomenon of the war years was *Gone With the Wind*, which ran continuously throughout the war. What these popular successes tell us is that along with a desire to see depictions of the lives of ordinary people and a willingness to accept a measure of documentary realism, the pull of stars, romantic values, patriotism and glamour was just as strong as ever. The exponents of documentary realism were appalled that the British public still wanted Hollywood fictionalisations, even of England. The *Documentary News Letter* critic wrote with scarcely concealed disbelief of the reception of *Mrs Miniver*: 'You can sit at the Empire and hear practically the whole house weeping – a British audience with 3 years of war behind it crying at one of the phoniest war films that has ever been made'.[34] But the combination of Greer Garson and Walter Pidgeon, an idealised middle-class England, an essentially noble picture of genteel suffering and patriotic endeavour was genuinely uplifting and a 'good cry' has always been therapeutic. Mass-Observation's analysis of people's favourite 'fade-outs' testifies to that (Item 9). Herein lies the power of Hollywood and of the new high quality British films, and herein probably lies the key to the role of film in the maintenance of morale. J. T. McCurdy in *The Structure of Morale* (1943) wrote: 'The factors of morale are intangible because they are psychological and nothing psychological is truly measurable.'[35] Similarly involvement in a film was psychological, a combination of identification and projection, and absorption in something uplifting and affirmative was bound to be, however briefly, good for the spirits.

It was *Mrs Miniver* which provided the text for a seasoned film critic to reflect on the role of wartime cinema:

> Do you remember the scene in *Mrs Miniver* where Greer Garson read *Alice in Wonderland* aloud to the children in the air-raid shelter, the guns boomed outside, searchlights swept the skies, and the bombs whined and crashed nearer and nearer? The children listened entranced to the story, forgetting the air raid. The parents, you will recall, found a kind of courage too. . . . To many of us who have lived in England through six long years of war and gone about our ordinary family routine as well as we might, there is a certain parallel between the scene in *Mrs Miniver* and our memories of wartime nights' entertainment. For the men and women of this island . . . the pictures have been a sort of *Alice in Wonderland*. They have kept our spirits up. They have taken the worst strains off mind and body. No other form of relaxation has been quite so successful in helping people to bear the burdens they had – burdens of fear and loneliness, discomfort and overexhaustion; anxiety for husbands and sweethearts, and sons and little children. Consciously or sub-consciously, it was the firm determination of the people to keep on top, not to let themselves get depressed, so that they could stand the bombs and bad news when they came. So they went to the pictures and enjoyed the pictures and were all the better for the pictures.[36]

That is as comprehensive and as reliable a verdict as we are ever likely to get on the role of the cinema and national morale. It is not perhaps scientific but it makes sense.

Explanatory note

1 M-O used the following broad classifications to define interviewees:

A-rich people
B-the middle classes
C-artisans and skilled workers
D-unskilled workers and the least economically and educationally trained third of our people.

Usually the code was based on the impression gained by the investigator although it might also be based on information offered by the subject in a direct interview. M26B, therefore, means Male age 26 Middle Class. F50 D means Female age 50 Unskilled Working Class.

2 The M-O grading system for laughs is explained on p. 345 (Appendix 2a to Item 16).

Notes

1 From 'Films and the Home Front – the evaluation of their effectiveness by Mass-Observation', a paper given by Tom Harrisson at a conference at the Imperial War Museum, organised by the Inter-University History Film Consortium, 1973. Reprinted in N. Pronay and D. W. Spring (eds), *Propaganda, Politics and Film 1918–45* (London, 1982), pp. 234–48.
2 *Documentary News Letter* (November 1940), pp. 10–12.
3 The letter was written by a Mr Geoffrey Pyke in the *New Statesman* (12 December 1936). Mr Pyke did not become involved with Mass-Observation.
4 *New Statesman*, 30 January 1937.
5 For more details about the history of Mass-Observation, see Tom Jeffrey, *Mass-Observation: A Brief History*, Occasional Paper 55, Centre for Contemporary Cultural Studies, University of Birmingham, 1978. For a fuller account of M-O's methods, see N. S. Stanley, 'The extra dimension: A study and assessment of the methods employed by Mass-Observation in its first period 1937–1940', unpublished PhD thesis, Birmingham Polytechnic, 1981. See also Angus Calder, 'Mass Observation 1937–49' in M. Bulmer (ed.), *Essays on the History of British Sociological Research* (Cambridge, 1985); Penny Summerfield, 'Mass-Observation: social history or social movement?', *Journal of Contemporary History* (July, 1985), pp. 439–52, and Angus Calder and Dorothy Sheridan (eds), *Speak for Yourself: A Mass-Observation Anthology 1937–49* (London, 1984 and Oxford, 1985).
6 Leslie Halliwell, *Seats in All Parts: Half a lifetime at the movies* (London, 1985), p. 12.
7 Letter from Stuart Legg to Tom Harrisson in the M-O Archive, Worktown Collection Box 29, File F. Legg was a colleague of Humphrey Jennings at the time at the GPO Film Unit.
8 Robert S. Lynd and Helen Merrill Lynd, *Middletown: A Study in American Culture* (New York, 1929).
9 Calder and Sheridan, *Speak for Yourself*, pp. 39–41.
10 All the cinema material collected in Bolton is stored in Worktown Collection Box 29 at the Mass-Observation Archive.
11 Ian McLaine, *Ministry of Morale* (London, 1979), pp. 52–3.
12 See 'The birth of Mass-Observation' in the *Times Literary Supplement* (5 November 1976).
13 The letters from readers of *Picturegoer* fill two boxes (nos 4 and 5 of

the Film Topic Collection) at the M-O Archive.

14 From the Film Topic Collection, Box 2, File G, M-O Archive.

15 Ibid.

16 Film Topic Collection, Box 15, M-O Archive.

17 Film Topic Collection, Box 14, M-O Archive.

18 Further information about Mass-Observation and the Archive can be obtained from the Archivist, Ms D. Sheridan, The Mass-Observation Archive, University of Sussex Library, Brighton, BN1 9QL. *A Guide for Researchers* is also available.

19 Tom Harrisson, 'Films and the Home Front', p. 244.

20 McLaine, *Ministry of Morale*, pp. 8–11.

21 Dr Stephen Taylor, *Home Morale and Public Opinion*, INF 1/292, PRO.

22 Michael Balfour, *Propaganda in War 1939–1945* (London, 1979), p. 252.

23 M-O Film Questionnaire, 8 October 1940 (File Report 445).

24 On the relationship of the Ministry of Information and the film industry, see Anthony Aldgate and Jeffrey Richards, *Britain Can Take It: The British Cinema in the Second World War* (Oxford, 1986), and Vincent Porter and Chaim Litewski, '*The Way Ahead:* case history of a propaganda film', *Sight and Sound* 50 (Spring, 1981), pp. 110–16.

25 *Programme for Film Propaganda*, INF 1/867, PRO.

26 *Hansard*, vol. 381, columns 656–7 (7 July 1942).

27 *Kinematograph Weekly*, 30 July 1942.

28 Guy Morgan, *Red Roses Every Night* (London, 1948), p. 98.

29 Roger Manvell, *et al.*, *25 Years of British Films* (London, 1947), pp. 91–2.

30 Dilys Powell, *Films since 1939* (London, 1947), pp. 39–40.

31 See, for instance, William Harrington and Peter Young, *The 1945 Revolution* (London, 1978), pp. 35–44.

32 Harrisson, 'Films and the Home Front', p. 238.

33 F. C. Bartlett, *Political Propaganda* (Cambridge, 1940), p. 43.

34 *Documentary News Letter* (August 1942), p. 112.

35 J. T. McCurdy, *The Structure of Morale* (Cambridge, 1943), p. 128.

36 Morgan, *Red Roses Every Night*, p.67. The anonymous critic was almost certainly C. A. Lejeune.

Part 1 Cinema-going in Worktown

1   Research Programme for the Investigation of Cinema-going in Bolton

John Martin Jones's synopsis for the study of cinema-going in Bolton, drawn up in 1937, suggests a wide-ranging project, which might well have led to a book along the lines of *The Pub and the People.* But in the event only a part of the research was ever completed. The synopsis gives a good idea of Mass-Observation's aims and ambitions in this area (Worktown Box, 29D)

For an evocative first-hand account of cinema-going in Bolton at this time see Leslie Halliwell, *Seats in all Parts* (London, 1985).

At the beginning of 1937 it was decided to make a complete cultural study of a British industrial town, on the lines and methods hitherto used for the anthropological survey of primitive peoples. For various reasons Bolton was decided upon, and work has been in full progress since March.

No study of life in an industrial town, or for that matter in any community in Western civilisation, would be complete without a survey of the cinema and its place in the life of the people.

Although the cinema is comparatively new it has had in the short time of its existence a profound effect on the everyday life of all social classes. It has affected their education, fashions, morality, leisure and their social attitudes. The study of the cinema in the life of Bolton takes its place beside those of religion, politics and sport, with which it must be compared, and in the light of which its importance and influence can be assessed.

What new social patterns and behaviour forms has the cinema brought?

What gap has been filled, what place has been taken, and what old things have been ousted out by the films?

How does the cinema affect the different classes, what are their reactions to the new horizons that it opens up to them, how does it influence their everyday routine of life?

What types of film have the greatest appeal . . . why?

These are vital questions in the study of the culture of Bolton, and the following synopsis has been planned to answer them for the first time, by undertaking a complete survey of all aspects of the cinema, from the Commercial Chain House to the Amateur. A study of all the points raised in this synopsis will give a clear picture – the first attempted – of the role of the films in the life of a modern industrial community.

The Synopsis of Study is divided into four parts and a general summary.

Part One deals with the Cinema itself, the Commercial and Material Aspects of film presentation.

Part Two is a Study of the films, programmes and general problems concerning demand for different types of film, etc.

Part Three deals with the Place of the Cinema in Public Life, and the reactions and behaviour of the Public.

Part Four treats the unorganised film shows. It includes the single performance cultural or commercial shows, the films used in schools and the amateur film-maker and exhibitor.

The summary puts the facts ascertained above in their correct perspective in respect to the other aspects of life in the town. It analyses the effect of the films, estimates their influence and makes a comparative study with those things whose place they occupy or with which they compete.

Part I

Buildings. Architecture. With Illustrations.

Seating Capacities and Accommodation.

Comparison with population of Bolton – Question of redundancy.

Range of Prices and Position of seats in different price blocks.

Attendance at Cinemas – average price paid – Related to separate study of cost of living and unemployed.

Staffing. Pay and Hours.

Hours of performance.

Sunday Opening Question. Controversy in Local Paper. Opinions of individuals in and out of the Trade.

Private or Chain Cinemas. Effect on Programmes. Managers' Opinions.

Local Regulations – Police and Watch Committee.

Distributions of Advertisements. Posters and in Papers. Handbills and the Mailing of Programmes.

Other Publications issued by the Managements.

Receipts and Turnovers. Charges and Taxes.

Sidelines. Sale of Ices, Sweets, etc. Cafés. Advertisements in the Cinema or Programme.

Distribution of Free Tickets.

Part II

Programmes over a year. Their analysis.
British and Foreign Films. Effect of the quota.
Release dates.
Premieres and second showings. Reasons for Repeats. Periods between first and second showings, seasons. Immediate repeats in subsidiary cinemas of a chain.
Demand for Certain films. Correspondence in Local Papers. Contact of Public with managers.
Demand and appeal of stars. Through conversations, etc., and questionnaire.
Censorship of films. Local opinions. Church magazines, etc.
Films forbidden to children, locally and Nationally. Demand for types of films. War, sentimental, Crime etc.
News Reels. Educational Shorts. Advertisement Films and Slides.
Travelogues, etc. Analysis of contents.
Non cinematographic items in programmes. Organs. Music.
Changes in lighting effects during intervals.
Effect of the seasons on programme.
Attendances.

Part III

The reactions of the Public to specific films and programmes.
The public's sense of humour.
Appeal of Tragedy, Comedy, Pathos, etc.
Detailed study of behaviour at the cinema.
  During the Films. Noises and sitting positions.
  During the Intervals.
  Entering and leaving the Building and Hall.
  During the Anthem.
Behaviour of the Staff.
Full analysis of the ritual at the cinema. Entering, paying, ushering, disposal of coat and impedimenta.
Effect of the Season and Weather on the Public.
Social groupings according to seats, position and price.
A questionnaire will be issued, if possible with the co-operation of the managers, to obtain idea of the appeal of particular films, stars and plots, and also general public preferences.

The Public as a critic. Opinions of specific films, or types of film from conversations, and questionnaire.
Attendances at the Cinema. Sex and Age. Who goes in the families.
Class distinctions in percentages of attendances.

Part IV

Films in Schools.
Films under auspices of Societies, Churches, etc.
Existence of Local Amateur Cine Group?
Existence of Amateur film-makers?
Hire of films for private and public performance from substandard film libraries. Figures and lists. Analysis.

Summary

The Place of the Cinema in Local Leisure Pattern.
The Cinema as a Drug Habit.
Comparative Study with the Theatre and other forms of Amusement.
Cinema versus Church.
The Social place of the cinema.
Reaction of the Cinema on Local Patterns of Morality, Clothing, Manners and Outlook.
Influence of the Cinema on the standard of life.

At the present stage it is useless to go into cinemas and just make, or try to, reports on the audiences, staff behaviour, etc. I have been experimenting with ways of noting reactions of audience to incidents, and the best system I have been able to evolve is one where Observer has to learn a large number or letter groups to embrace every sort of noise and reaction, and which is likely to be too cumbersome. Also as a result of seeing the same film twice, and of being in the cinema a lot with the deliberate intention of studying ways of recording the audience's reactions I am coming to see the futility of it. As a result, and in view of the two favourable contacts that I have with both the Palladium and the Odeon I have evolved the following plan of work which will make a pretty complete study of two Bolton cinemas of completely different types. After we have done this it will be far easier to attack along a wider front, the material which we have collected on the one study being used both as a groundwork and direction indicator for further work, and also as a mild threat or spur to the other cinemas managers.

I am convinced that this is the best and safest method of approach. During one and the same week a study of both cinemas should be carried out, and a questionnaire issued with each performance for the whole week. In the Odeon that covers one programme and in the Palladium two.

The terms of the questionnaire have not yet been gone over, and I am waiting till I have read all the books and reports, and also till I have had a chat with the fellow at the Odeon place; but the results that I hope to get include the following: District covered by each cinema. Compare this with advertising. Amount of regular patrons. Frequency of attendance. Sex and age ratios. Study of the films and points which remain in the audiences' minds. General preferences. Favourite stars. Sunday opening question. Weather on cinema attendance. Do they come good or bad film. What alternatives have they to the cinema.

At the same time I wish to take full figures of attendance, maps of groupings in the seats at various times of the day, figures of half tickets sold, etc.

There will also come an analysis of the programmes, which can be used with the questionnaires to study the audiences reactions, incidents, etc.

The full data collected on this will provide enough publishable material to fill at least two chapters, if not more.

I further have the idea to introduce a questionnaire for children in various schools, provided the co-operation of the authorities can be obtained, as it should be done, fairly easily.

I shall be able to write down the more or less detailed plan of campaign only after having spoken to the man at the Odeon in London, who had written to me personally today, and also to the managers. Also when I have finished reading the books, had a break and got over my dose of examinitis.

Notes re questionnaires

On questions about stars, programmes should be studied for the past few months to find what stars have been shown there, and care should be taken not to include stars that have not been shown. Perhaps this will involve separate printing for the Palladium and Odeon questionnaires on this point.

The Cinema Manager Speaks

As part of the survey of cinema-going, interviews were conducted with cinema managers. On 4 December 1937, JMJ interviewed Mr Gregson of the Palladium and on 14 December 1938 he interviewed Mr Hull of the Embassy. The Embassy was a city-centre cinema with a poor reputation. According to Leslie Halliwell, 'It advertised itself as "Bolton's armchair cinema", but it was small and scruffy and the rumour ran that it was infested by rats.' (Worktown Box 29E).

(a) Interview with manager of the Palladium Cinema

Observer called round about 7.45. Gregson had a bad cold and was in office. Was very friendly and chatty. Made no hesitation at giving any of the information sought. Figures of staff-size of building, wages, etc. are on separate sheets.

Had a talk about the police and watch committee controls of the cinema. In Bolton Supt. Harrison is responsible to Chief Constable for seeing all acts regarding licensed premises are put into force, etc. Under him is Inspector Hodson. Says of Police: 'Couldn't wish for better people ... they'll assist you. They're very helpful is the Police in Bolton ... as long as instructions that they stipulate is carried out that's all they require. No one can grumble about the Police.'

Every week police make an inspection – usually come on Wednesday. Then they check over the vacuum cleaning of the seats and washing of the exposed floor. A CID man comes in the morning.

On and off an inspector comes round to try and catch you out – when you aren't expecting him. You never know when he's coming. Every year, during the second week in December there's a full dress inspection, with Chief of Fire Brigade, etc. That comes before the annual licensing. No charges are made to the cinema for inspection, which are done as a matter of routine.

In February of 1936 there was the only case that has ever happened in Bolton of a theatre or cinema being prosecuted under the cinema acts. That was at the Crompton Way when only half of the required secondary lighting – gas jets on the staircases – was lit, and when the centre door at the entrance was bolted. Inspector sent for the manager, and was kept waiting. Manager tried to act rather snotty, and got hauled over the coals and fined £40.

Incidental to this Insp. Hodson had had a blonde, whom Stockley, the manager, had stolen away from him, and so he had it in for him a little. Gregson is sure, however, that if Stockley had played up to Hodson, it would have ended with a severe reprimand from the Chief Constable, and no more – but he tried to argue back, and get away with it.

At present there is trouble about children going into balconies. This doesn't affect the Palladium, which has no balcony, but the Crompton, which is on the same circuit has a balcony, and is going to bring a test case in January at the licensing sessions. Law runs that at a performance where children predominate no children shall be allowed in the balcony. Custom has allowed that children with parents can go into the balcony. But as a result of a letter in the BEN [the *Bolton Evening News*] about Sunday opening, an inspection was made one Saturday afternoon, and a new policeman said this was not so. Case will be brought by the Crompton for the benefit of all other cinemas. Gregson pointed out that in the Grand children were allowed into the 2nd balcony, and that this is only supposed to apply in the cinemas.

There is never any trouble with the watch committee. On one occasion, some five years ago, a film was to be shown at the Palladium, and long before it arrived in Bolton the Catholic Women's Guild, which seemed to be conducting a nation-wide protest against it, complained to the Watch Committee. At latter's request it was shown to them privately. They said that they could see nothing wrong with it, except perhaps one dance where a woman doing the rumba waggled her tummy, and that it might be better to have that bit out. This was done and the film shown without any further trouble. Can't remember name of the film.

For Xmas Day and Good Friday the film must be U. and a synopsis of the film must be sent to Watch Committee for the special licences.

Children under twelve are not allowed in to see any film after 8.0 p.m. Said of girl letting children in to A. films . . . 'I know about the girl . . . she takes a risk when there's nobody about.'

Promised Observer plan of cinema and information of smaller sites on Monday.

(b) Interview with Manager of the Embassy Cinema

Asked for his opinions, Hull, a fair-haired, drunken-looking man of middle age, replied:

In a working town similar to Bolton they save their money, and that means they spend more at Christmas. Business increases from Christmas Week to the New Year. After that it drops from the level of the previous two weeks, but not from the previous 50 weeks in the year. That's why I say they save to spend at Christmas, because you get no big slump in your returns afterwards.

He said that Bolton people don't express their feelings about special programmes. In his first Christmas at the Embassy he played a very old thriller, *Mr Wong*,[1] on Boxing Day and did well. But Christmas Day flopped, it always does. Last Christmas he put on another thriller for Boxing Day, and again it did well. Again Christmas Day flopped.

Asked what was the attitude of Bolton people toward the Cinema he said that in the Cinema business it was very hard to tell. In 1936 trade was much better, and Cinemas did much better. In Bolton, Cinema is their first entertainment. 'Being in the centre of the town with 2nd and 3rd runs you would expect me to rely on passers-by, but I don't. My business keeps to a certain average all through the year. I'm not prepared to tell you what it is, but I don't have a losing week over a year. In Boxing Day week and New Year week we do exceptional business. I've spoke to several of my patrons, all working class, and they don't think they've been anywhere if they haven't been to the Cinema twice a week.

Business is better this year than last. If business is bad, the cinema is bad. You take any dispute concerning working people, in any mill or foundry in Bolton. During that dispute your evening takings drop, but your afternoon goes up. It proves that however hard up they are they still want the cinema, so they take the cheaper seats in the afternoon.

My average from June to this month, and that's not a good period in any case for the Cinemas, my average is something like £10 below 1936. (Manager showed Obs. part of return sheet which showed £58 increase over similar week last year.) Since those early figures the Lido and Odeon have opened, there are three to four thousand more seats in the town, yet I've had no drop. People are putting their pennies away to go. Last night I was boozing with two friends, both in the Cinema business, who had had the same experience. They're in different towns.

Week in, week out, I get 6,000 people or more who come here regularly twice a week.

If I get an exceptional picture like *Rosalie*,[2] its seventh run in Bolton, we always do well. 500 people were at the opening matinée of that film out of 600 seats. That's not bad for a seventh run. I've seen people out at the front say "Oh, we'll go and see this again." They won't only go once, but two and even three times to a good musical. Musical pictures in Lancashire go the best for any. Mystery pictures are nowhere. Give them anything they have to think about and they're lost. I ran *Firefly*,[3] 8th run, 50 per cent increase. *Maytime*,[4] 8th run, 50 per cent increase, same as with *Rosalie*, about 10 per cent increase. Until they had heard Donkey Serenade twice they wouldn't move from the Cinema. Just before it at the second performance the house would be full, afterwards it would be half empty. But bad musicals don't go. They flop dead. Cheap American or British musicals are no good. Mystery pictures don't go in Lancashire. You can cut them out. The finest mystery picture in the world I can't run it 3rd run. Another thing they like is old melodrama, especially in the cheap seats. They love it when the villain comes in and say "Aha, fair maiden, so you've gone that way." Spectacular films are another that go well. Anything spectacular. Like *Hurricane*.[5] There was nothing in it except studio effects, but it went very well. A clever film will not go. I had a very good picture, *The Divorce of Lady X*.[6] Couldn't run it 2nd run. *Bluebeard's Eighth Wife*[7] was another. Third run was no good. I've had good pictures in here and they've come out and said, "What made you put that rubbish on?" I've even had them come out and say, "How much did they pay you to put that on?" That was after *Bluebeard's Eighth Wife*. They don't want hidden humour. They're working all day, and they come up here at night all dressed up like dandies. They think they're on top of the Earth, you've got to make them think that they are. If there's anything crude they like it. Think it's a smasher. Look at *Escape from Devil's Isle*.[8] We were packed out, yet it was the crudest thing going. You could see everything coming.

Look at the film we've got running now. *The Baroness and the Butler*.[9] It's too clever. Some of them have come out and said, "It's a lovely picture, what's it all about?" (This was said of *Bluebeard's Eighth Wife*.) One woman came out and said, "but he'd no beard."

I get more fun out of people than out of films nowadays. Here's my staff. I have them on a five-day week. To-day there's a girl off. I bet you £5 to a 1/- that if we could find her now she'd be in the pictures. On Saturday night I've found them watching, when they're supposed to be working.

Five years ago I gave the Cinema three years. My view now is that it will always be here. Not only that, but they're building bigger places, 6,000 seats in this town since I've been here, but my business has increased. I believe people don't like the big barns, they like to be in a crowd. You go in a great barn of a place. You go in when there's a bad picture, and a few people dotted about, and you feel lonely. That's something you can't avoid. I go for best pictures. People don't. They go to a small place. There's a small place near here, next door to a 2,000 seater, it's taking more than the big place. I rang up a friend in a 2,000 seater, and when I asked him how he'd done over a certain film I found he'd taken less than I have.

Cinemas are a 20 per cent proposition any day. ABC and Gaumont paid that last year. The Odeons, and they're a new circuit, paid 15 per cent.'

Editors' notes

1 *Mr Wong* was probably *The Honourable Mr Wong*, UK title for the
   1932 Warner Bros thriller, *The Hatchet Man*, starring Edward
   G. Robinson.
2 *Rosalie* (MGM, 1937) starred Nelson Eddy and Eleanor Powell.
3 *The Firefly* (MGM, 1937) starred Jeanette MacDonald and Allan Jones.
4 *Maytime* (MGM, 1937) starred Nelson Eddy and Jeanette MacDonald.
5 *The Hurricane* (United Artists, 1937) starred Jon Hall and Dorothy
   Lamour.
6 *The Divorce of Lady X* (United Artists, 1938) starred Laurence Olivier
   and Merle Oberon.
7 *Bluebeard's Eighth Wife* (Paramount, 1938) starred Gary Cooper and
   Claudette Colbert.
8 *Escape from Devil's Isle* (Columbia, 1936) starred Victor Jory and
   Florence Rice.
9 *The Baroness and the Butler* (20th Century Fox, 1937) starred William
   Powell and Annabella.

All except *The Divorce of Lady X* were American films.

3   Replies to the Bolton Questionnaire

Why did people go to the cinema in the 1930s and 1940s and what did they make of the films they saw there? We have very little first-hand evidence of the views of cinema-goers themselves, which is why Mass-Observation's Bolton cinema questionnaire and the 1943 Directive replies (Item 13 in this volume) are so valuable. The Bolton questionnaire was issued in March 1938 to the patrons of three cinemas, which seem to have been chosen to represent the three different levels of cinema in operation.

The Odeon, Ashburner Street, opened amid great ceremony in 1937, was one of Oscar Deutsch's city centre art deco showplaces, an up-market cinema seating 2,534 people, at prices ranging from 6d. to 1/6d. It had a weekly change of programme, continuous shows from Monday to Friday and three separate houses on Saturday. There was a staff of forty-one, 15 male and 26 female, including page boys, chocolate girls, usherettes and doormen. There was an organ with a resident organist (Hubert Selby), and a cinema café, though Halliwell recalls that it was 'notorious for serving the toughest buttered crumpets for miles around'. The respondents' addresses and the greater literary fluency of the Odeon replies suggest a higher proportion of middle and upper working-class patrons at this cinema than at the other two.

The Crompton, Crompton Way, also opened in 1937, was a middle-range cinema of the 'mixed family audience' kind, with seating for 1,200, twice weekly programme changes, daily matinées and continuous evening performances. There was a special children's matinée on Saturday. Seat prices ranged from 3d. to 1/3d. Leslie Halliwell and his indefatigable 'Mum' attended the opening of the cinema and he recalled that 'both foyer and auditorium were very clean and functional, but gave the impression that there had been no money to spare for luxury trimmings or even for imagination'.

The Palladium, Higher Bridge Street, was a down-market cinema, frankly a 'fleapit'. It had opened on Christmas Day 1919 and had shown Bolton's first talkie (*The Singing Fool* with Al Jolson) in April 1929. But it had since gone down in the world and Halliwell recalls it as 'oddly dark and sinister'. It had seating capacity for 1,238, twice weekly programme changes, afternoon matinées, continuous evening perform-ances and Saturday matinées for children. There was a staff of twelve. Seat prices ranged from 4d. to 1 shilling. The Palladium's audience came in the main from the working-class city-centre area around the cinema. Both the Crompton and the Palladium were owned by Arthur Hall.

The cinema questionnaire offered two prizes of £1 for the two most comprehensive answers and six double complimentary tickets for the next six in order of merit. It asked for name, address and age, though an original plan to include occupation was regrettably not followed up. It asked seven questions: (1) Do you go to the cinema regularly? (2) How many times a month do you go? (3) Do you go regularly on the same day, if so which day? (4) Do you think you see people on the screen who live like yourself? (5) Which are the best films, British or American, or do you think both are the same? (6) Number the following types of films, putting number one for the sort you like best, and two for the second best and so on: crime, westerns, war, spying, historical, cartoons, nature and reality, travel and adventure, musical romance, drama and tragedy, slapstick comedies, love stories, society comedies. (7) Which of the following would you like more of in films? Number them from one to ten, number one being the one you specially want more of, and so on to number ten, the one you desire least: more humour, more religion, more politics, more action, more killing, more knowledge and educational subjects, more beautiful things, more beautiful people, more people like you or I, more royalty and aristocrats. A space was also left for the respondents to write any comments they liked about films.

We reproduce below these general comments on films. Spelling and punctuation have been tidied up for ease of reading. But the handwritten originals can be consulted in the Mass-Observation Archive. We have analysed the replies to the individual questions and give a summary of the results here.

There was a total of 559 respondents, 304 men and 225 women. They were distributed as follows: from the Odeon, 167 men, 182 women; from the Crompton, 57 men, 39 women; from the Palladium, 80 men, 34 women. 409 respondents said they went regularly to the cinema on the same day, frequency of attendance varying from once a month to twenty-four times a month. Nine respondents went twenty times or more a month. Of the 559 respondents, 351 (62 per cent) were aged 30 or under. Within that figure, there are interesting variations by cinema. Of the 30 Palladium women 24 (70 per cent) were 30 or under, and 60 of the 80 Palladium men (75 per cent). Of the 182 Odeon women 115 (63 per cent) were 30 or under, and 101 of the 167 Odeon men (60 per cent). Of the 39 Crompton women 18 (46 per cent) were 30 or under, and 33 of the 57 men (57 per cent). This indicates that the most working-class of the three cinemas gets the highest proportion of regular young attenders; the Crompton, characterised as 'mixed family' type cinema, the lowest.

Asked if they saw people like themselves on the screen, 363 said 'no' including 2 women who said forcefully 'No, thank goodness' and 'No and I don't expect to', and 196 said 'yes'. On the question of preference, out of the total of 559 respondents, 350 (63 per cent) preferred American films, 100 (18 per cent) preferred British, 104 (19 per cent) thought they were about the same and 5 did not know. The breakdown within the totals is interesting. Out of a total of 304 men, 200 (65 per cent) preferred American films, 46 (16 per cent) British, 54 (18 per cent) thought them about the same and 2 did not know. Out of 255 women, 150 (50 per cent) preferred American films, 52 (20 per cent) British, 50 (20 per cent) thought them about the same and 3 did not know. There is thus a slightly higher female preference for British films.

The individual cinema breakdowns provide further detail. Of the Odeon men, 107 (64 per cent) preferred American films, 32 (19 per cent) preferred British films, 26 (15 per cent) thought them the same. Of the Odeon women, 102 (56 per cent) preferred American films, 39 (21 per cent) preferred British, 39 (21 per cent) thought them equal. Of the Crompton men, 33 (57 per cent) preferred American films, 8 (14 per cent) British, 16 (28 per cent) thought them the same. Of the Crompton women, 23 (59 per cent) preferred American films, 9 (23 per cent) British, 6 (15 per cent) thought them the same. Of the Palladium men, 60 (75 per cent) preferred American films, 8 British (10 per cent), 12 (15 per cent) thought them equal. Of the Palladium women, 25 (74 per cent) preferred American films, 4 (12 per cent) British and 5 (14 per cent) thought them the same. A clear majority of patrons of both sexes and at all three cinemas preferred American films to British. But the audience registering the highest preference for American films was the largely working-class Palladium audience.

When it came to choice of film types, the first choice categories break down as follows:

1	Musical romance	171	30%
2	Drama and tragedy	99	18%
3	History	60	11%
	Crime	60	11%
5	Nature and reality	39	7%
6	Travel and adventure	35	6%
7	Love stories	23	4%
8	Society comedies	21	4%
9	Spying	16	3%
	Westerns	16	3%
11	War	10	2%
12	Slapstick comedies	5	1%
13	Cartoons	2	0%

There is some variation in choice between the sexes.

Men

1	Musical romance	74
2	Drama and tragedy	51
3	Crime	46
4	History	33
5	Travel and adventure	25
6	Nature and reality	17
7	Spying	14
8	{ Westerns	11
	{ Society comedies	11
10	War	9
11	Love stories	6
12	Slapstick comedies	4
13	Cartoons	2

Women

1	Musical romance	97
2	Drama and tragedy	48
3	History	27
4	Nature and reality	22
5	Love stories	17
6	Crime	14
7	{ Society comedies	10
	{ Travel and adventure	10
9	Westerns	5
10	Spying	2
11	War	1
12	Slapstick comedies	1
13	Cartoons	0

Women give a higher priority to history and to love stories than men and men give higher priority to crime than do women. But both sexes give musical romance and drama as their first two choices, with war, slapstick comedies and cartoons among the least liked.

There are some instructive variations too in the choice within individual cinemas.

ODEON

Men

1	Musical romance	51
2	Drama and tragedy	32
3	History	19
4	Crime	14
5	{ Nature and reality	11
	{ Travel and adventure	11
7	Society comedies	10
8	Spying	9
9	Love stories	4
10	Slapstick comedies	3
11	War	2
12	Westerns	1
13	Cartoons	0

Women

1	Musical romance	70
2	Drama and tragedy	35
3	History	21
4	Nature and reality	16
5	Love stories	14
6	Society comedies	9
7	Crime	6
8	Travel and adventure	5
9	Westerns	3
10	Spying	2
11	Slapstick comedies	1
12	War	1
13	Cartoons	0

CROMPTON

Men

1	{ Musical romance	11
	{ Drama and tragedy	11

Women

1	Musical romance	15
2	Drama and tragedy	5

	Men			Women	
3	Crime	10	3	Nature and reality	5
4	Travel and adventure	9		History	3
5	History	6	4	Travel and adventure	3
6	Nature	3		Crime	3
7	Love stories	2		Love stories	3
	Spying	2	8	Westerns	1
	Society comedies	1		Society comedies	1
9	Westerns	1		War	0
	War	1	10	Spying	0
12	Slapstick comedies	0		Cartoons	0
	Cartoons	0		Slapstick comedies	0

PALLADIUM

	Men			Women	
1	Crime	22	1	Musical romance	12
2	Musical romance	12	2	Drama and tragedy	8
3	Western	9	3	Crime	5
4	Drama and tragedy	8	4	History	3
	Historical	8	5	Travel and adventure	2
6	War	6		Nature and reality	1
7	Travel and adventure	5	6	Western	1
8	Nature and reality	4		War	1
9	Spying	3		Love stories	1
10	Cartoons	2		Cartoons	0
11	Slapstick comedies	1	10	Spying	0
12	Love stories	0		Society comedies	0
	Society comedies	0		Slapstick comedies	0

The most interesting feature to emerge from this breakdown is the prominence of crime the further down the scale you go. It is the first choice of Palladium men, narrowly misses being the first choice of Crompton men but as fourth choice comes a long way after musical romance and drama with Odeon men. It is furthermore noticeable that 18 of the 22 Palladium men preferring crime films come from the 15–20 age group. Conversely, society comedies rank lower the lower down the scale you go. In general, women's choices in all three groups tended to be closer to each other than to the men's.

Asked what they wanted to see more of in films, the respondents placed the categories in the following order:

1	More humour	1,605
2	More beautiful things	2,181
3	More action	2,246
4	More people like you and I	2,263
5	More knowledge and education	2,647
6	More beautiful people	2,916

7 More royalty and aristocrats	3,738
8 More religion	3,805
9 More politics	4,307
10 More killing	4,344

This breaks down as between men and women, as follows:

Men		_Women_	
1 More humour	797	1 More humour	808
2 More action	1,111	2 More beautiful things	818
3 More people like you and I	1,286	3 More people like you and I	977
4 More beautiful things	1,363	4 More action	1,135
5 More knowledge and education	1,403	5 More beautiful people	1,243
6 More beautiful people	1,673	6 More knowledge and education	1,254
7 More royalty and aristocrats	2,119	7 More royalty and aristocrats	1,619
8 More religion	2,138	8 More religion	1,665
9 More politics	2,238	9 More politics	2,069
10 More killing	2,265	10 More killing	2,079

Men give a higher priority to action than women. Women give a higher priority to beautiful things than men. But both are agreed about wanting more humour as top priority and both want least more royalty and aristocrats, more religion, more politics and more killing.

Within individual cinemas, the breakdown is:

ODEON

Men		_Women_	
1 More humour	421	1 More beautiful things	555
2 More people like you and I	662	2 More humour	586
3 More action	667	3 More people like you and I	712
4 More beautiful things	681	4 More action	825
5 More knowledge and education	770	5 More beautiful people	870
6 More beautiful people	905	6 More knowledge and education	893
7 More royalty and aristocrats	1,166	7 More royalty and aristocrats	1,130

8 More religion	1,217	
9 More politics	1,251	
10 More killing	1,365	

8 More religion	1,197
9 More politics	1,424
10 More killing	1,552

CROMPTON

Men		
1 More humour	140	
2 More action	188	
3 More people like you and I	191	
4 More knowledge and education	241	
5 More beautiful things	269	
6 More beautiful people	335	
7 More royalty and aristocrats	401	
8 More killing	414	
9 More religion	417	
10 More politics	437	

Women	
1 More humour	120
2 More beautiful things	124
3 More people like you and I	137
4 More knowledge and education	156
5 More action	183
6 More beautiful people	200
7 More religion	234
8 More royalty and aristocrats	251
9 More killing	289
10 More politics	298

PALLADIUM

Men	
1 More humour	236
2 More action	256
3 More knowledge and education	392
4 More beautiful things	413
5 More people like you and I	433
6 More beautiful people	433
7 More killing	486
8 More religion	504
9 More politics	550
10 More royalty and aristocrats	552

Women	
1 More humour	102
2 More action	127
3 More people like you and I	128
4 More beautiful things	139
5 More beautiful people	173
6 More knowledge and education	205
7 More religion	234
8 { More royalty and aristocrats	238
{ More killing	238
10 More politics	347

The general profile is on the whole repeated at individual cinemas with some interesting and perhaps characteristic variations. Almost all groups want more humour and are least interested in killing, politics, religion, royalty and aristocrats, though Palladium men give a higher priority to more killing than any other group and a lower priority to more people like you and I than the rest. Palladium men also give a higher priority to knowledge and education than any other group. Palladium and Odeon women give knowledge and education the lowest rating. Odeon women alone want to see more beautiful things most of all. This category is second for Crompton women and fourth for Palladium women.

In the space left for comments, there was a wide diversity of complaints and requirements. Twenty respondents expressed their appreciation of Hubert Selby's organ and called for more of it. Five respondents wanted less of the organ. Seventeen respondents wanted short slapstick comedies cut from the programme, something which accords with the low rating given to slapstick comedy in the audience preference section. Fourteen respondents wanted advertisements cut out, and 14 wanted an end to war films. Nine respondents called for one big film and full supporting programme rather than double-bills of two feature films. Seven respondents called for double-bills of two feature films rather than one big film and full supporting programme. Eight called for a ban on double-bills containing features of similar type. Eight respondents wanted more travel films, and 3 wanted fewer. Eight objected to the cutting of films. Seven respondents wanted films 'kept clean'. Six objected to trailers being shown. Five wanted audiences kept quiet. Five complained that credits were too long. Three wanted more stage 'turns'. One wanted no stage 'turns'.

Fifty-one respondents chose to write about why they went to the cinema and the reasons they gave were all variations on entertainment, amusement, relaxation, to be taken out of themselves, to escape the cares of the world and everyday life. But a further 26 mentioned that they valued films as a source of education, inspiration and knowledge; 15 more mentioned that they liked to see films with a good moral.

However, the greatest majority (86) chose to write about why they preferred American films to British films. The overwhelming complaint was that there was not enough action in British films. They were dull and lifeless. The settings were restricted and poverty stricken. The acting was stiff and artificial. By contrast, American films were slick, polished, fast-moving and often spectacular and American actors were natural and lifelike. Only 13 respondents declared that they wanted to see more British films. Ten respondents thought British films were improving. Five mentioned a dislike of 'Oxford accents' in British films, but 18 mentioned a dislike of American accents and American slang in films. Twenty-eight respondents called for greater realism in characters, settings and stories, something which reflects the comparatively high priority given to seeing more people like you and I.

Many respondents chose to name and talk about their favourite films and it is possible to construct a list of Bolton's ten most popular films according to this particular group of cinema regulars. They are:

Victoria the Great	38	(21 female, 17 male)
Stella Dallas	26	(19 female, 7 male)

A Star is Born	25	(16 female, 9 male)
Mutiny on the Bounty	19	(4 female, 15 male)
Charge of the Light Brigade	18	(7 female, 11 male)
Maytime	18	(9 female, 9 male)
Lost Horizon	14	(10 female, 4 male)
Action for Slander	11	(6 female, 5 male)
San Francisco	10	(6 female, 4 male)
Lives of a Bengal Lancer	9	(all male)

131 other films were mentioned mainly by 1 or 2 people; 37 of them were British, the rest American. Of the top 10, only 2 (*Victoria the Great* and *Action for Slander*) are British, the rest American. But interestingly only 3 of the 10 (*Stella Dallas, A Star is Born, San Francisco*) have American settings.

This list of popular films accords almost exactly with Leslie Halliwell's memoir of his childhood cinema-going in Bolton, *Seats in All Parts*. He recalls the popularity of *Lost Horizon* (the Theatre Royal was packed and had queues stretching both ways), *Lives of a Bengal Lancer* ('The whole town turned out to see this oddly-titled Indian adventure'), *Mutiny on the Bounty, San Francisco*, any film with Nelson Eddy and Jeanette MacDonald, the stars of *Maytime* ('A queue of Boltonians would form at the mere mention of their names.') and *Victoria the Great* ('most popular of them all'). The popularity of *Victoria the Great* might seem to be contradicted by the low priority rating given to seeing more royalty and aristocrats. But cinema-goers' reservations probably extended principally to more aristocrats, given the high proportion of them appearing as characters particularly in British films. This dislike of aristocratic characters would then be the converse of the desire to see more people like you and I.

What is striking about the list of Boltonian favourites is not so much the penchant for films which gave you a 'good cry' (*Stella Dallas, A Star is Born, Maytime*) and a 'good tune' (*Maytime, San Francisco*) but the strong patriotic note about the titles, the way the list conforms with the popular preference for musical romance, drama and tragedy and history, and the gender differentiation in choice. Some films are equally or almost equally popular with both sexes (*Victoria the Great, Maytime, Action for Slander, San Francisco*), but others have a much greater appeal either to men or to women. In general, the women seem to have been drawn to films about sensitive, long-suffering, self-sacrificing women, often tied to ungrateful or unworthy husbands or children, and the men to films about tough, *macho* he-men, who are good in a fight, stand up for what is right and love their country. This tells us something about the self-image of men and women in 1930s Bolton.

By contrast with films, individual stars are mentioned much less often and only a few get more than an odd mention: Jeanette MacDonald (7),

Laurel and Hardy (5), Gracie Fields (5), George Formby (5).

The national picture of cinema-going in the 1930s was that while a large proportion of the population at large went to the cinema occasionally, the enthusiasts were young, working-class, urban and more often female than male. The Bolton sample certainly shows a preponderance of people under thirty but more men than women responded. It seems likely that a majority of respondents will have been working-class given the overall composition of the cinema audience but this is not conclusively provable. What is clear is that their preference was for American films, though not necessarily always films about America. The reason is probably the one given by Peter Stead:

> In American films they saw their own reality, albeit related in strange accents, set in exotic surroundings and somewhat speeded up, but the sentimentality, the humour, the feel for family and community, the sexuality, and above all the celebration of the individual constituted a new and thoroughly intelligible, immediately recognizable and infinitely appealing version or interpretation of life.

On cinema-going in Britain in the 1930s in general see Peter Stead, 'The people and the pictures', in N. Pronay and D. W. Spring (eds), *Propaganda, Politics and Film 1918–45* (London, 1982), pp. 77–97, and Jeffrey Richards, *Age of the Dream Palace: Cinema and Society in Britain 1930–39* (London, 1984).

Palladium Cinema: Men

1 *William Wilson*, 7 Abraham St (aged 9), regular cinema-goer (12 times a month), preference – American films.
Comments: None.

2 *Stanley Kelly*, 57 Blackbank St (aged 10), regular cinema-goer (8 times a month), preference – American films.
Comments: None.

3 *Cyril Kelly*, 81 Wolfenden St (aged 11), regular cinema-goer (8 times a month), preference – American films.
Comments: None.

4 *William Shaw*, 29 Balcary Grove (aged 11), regular cinema-goer (twice a month), preference – American films.
Comments: None.

5 *Frank Richardson*, 52 Centre St (aged 11), regular cinema-goer (4 times a month), preference – American films.
Comments: None.

6 *Cyril Calderbank*, 63 Egyptian St (aged 11), regular cinema-goer (12 times a month), preference – American films.
Comments: None.

7 *Herbert Haddock*, 5 Hensor St (aged 11), regular cinema-goer (12 times a month), preference – both the same.
Comments: I like gangster pictures and Wild West films and cartoons. I don't like love pictures at all because they are not good ones. I like war films a good deal better than cartoons because there is more action in them.

8 *Joseph Cash*, 41 Clarence St (aged 11), regular cinema-goer (14 times a month), preference – both.
Comments: None.

9 *Harold Kirkman*, 11 Harwood St (aged 11), regular cinema-goer (10 times a month), preference – American films.
Comments: In my opinion of films, I say you do get some very good ones and some not so good. I should think the three Stoogies (sic) are really laughable and I hope you get more and also the Share the Wealth McClyde. I saw *Night Must Fall* and I sure think it did do in that film. I am your friend, Harold.

10 *Wilfred Hibbert*, 59 Arkwright St (aged 12), regular cinema-goer (8 times a month), preference – American films.
Comments: Dear sir, your pictures are good but the children like more crime and western films.

11 *Eric Ward*, 255 Halliwell St (aged 12), regular cinema-goer (12 times a month), preference – American films.
Comments: A good western all about Indians and scouts.

12 *Norman Greenhalgh*, 21 Lena St (aged 12), regular cinema-goer (6 times a month), preference – American films.
Comments: None.

13 *Vincent Broderick*, 22 Lark St (aged 12), regular cinema-goer (8 times a month), preference – American films.
Comments: None.

14 *Leslie Moran*, 59 George Arthur St (aged 12), regular cinemagoer (8 times a month), preference – American films.
Comments: None.

15   *Willie Catterall*, 14 Howarth St (aged 13), regular cinema-goer (12 times a month), preference – American films.
Comments: They are very good.

16   *Joseph Lovering*, 18 William St (aged 13), regular cinema-goer (8 times a month), preference – American films.
Comments: None.

17   *Walter Chadwick*, 89/14 Bridge St (aged 14), regular cinema-goer (8 times a month), preference – British films.
Comments: I think love pictures are too sloppy, such as Robert Taylor Pictures. Some pictures are far fetched such as *Tarzan, King Kong* and *Jungle Princess*, and [I] think they are not appreciated. More Popeyes, Mickey Mouse, Laurel and Hardy would be better liked.

18   *William Manning*, 2 Argyle St (aged 14), regular cinema-goer (6 times a month), preference – American films.
Comments: Dear Sir, I think that these last few weeks you've had some exciting and adventurous films, one of which I highly recommend, *They Gave Him a Gun*. I think the acting and the actors were all delightful, yours sincerely, W. Manning. P.S. I hope I'm the lucky one.

19   *Denis McDermott*, 60 Belmont Rd (aged 14), regular cinema-goer (6 times a month), preference – American films.
Comments: American films are, I think, 100% better than British ones. Not a matter of money but of brains.

20   *E. Fielding*, 27 Cooper St (aged 14), regular cinema-goer (5 times a month), preference – American films.
Comments: None.

21   *Paul Todd*, 101 Kay St (aged 14), regular cinema-goer (16 times a month), preference – both the same.
Comments: I have been to the Palladium a number of times and I think it should be praised.

22   *Joseph Pilkington*, 6 Chester St (aged 14), regular cinema-goer (6 times a month), preference – American films.
Comments: I do think you are right in not admitting children to Films Cert A-H. Please acknowledge my praise in pictures with child stars and comedians as characters.

23   *Arthur Walker*, 126 Waterloo St (aged 15), regular cinema-goer (6–7 times a month), preference – American films.
Comments: The reason why I do not like British films is they always seem to talk soft instead of ordinary, and all that I like about British is they have some extraordinary good comics. They are no use for Gangsters or mystery like American pictures. That only accounts for the pictures I have

seen. I would say a lot more, only there is not enough room for it, yours,
A. Walker.

24   *John Wood Molyneux*, 121 Vernon St (aged 15), regular cinema-goer
(8–10 times a month), preference – British films.
Comments: As you see I am only 15 years old but I hope this will make no
difference. My opinion is that the majority of films is too far fetched. If we
had more films about everyday things, I am sure that the number of film-
goers would increase. I also like films of Drama and Tragedy, for it is in
these films that a film star shows whether he is an *actor* or not. I am
certain that everybody appreciates these sort of films too.

25   *Ernest Rostron*, 8 Robinson St (aged 15), regular cinema-goer (13
times a month), preference – American films.
Comments: I must admit that I like travel and adventure. Such as Tarzan,
but the Tarzan pictures of to-day are too civil, the first Tarzan picture I
saw was very interesting because it was more wilder than they are today.
At one time Tarzan was unable to speak English, but today he acts like a
civilized being and that's what spoils them, I think.

26   *William Sharples*, 45 Clarence St (aged 15), regular cinema-goer (8
times a month), preference – American films.
Comments: I have no complaints to lodge and I am satisfied very much.

27   *Sam Foster* (aged 15), 4 Denvale Avenue, regular cinema-goer (8
times a month), preference – British films.
Comments: American films are good but show a great deal of vulgarness. I
myself think western films are very good. They include a bit of everything,
a bit of gunplay, a bit of fighting and robbery.

28   *George Nicholson*, 21 Prosperous St (aged 15), regular cinema-goer (8
times a week), preference – both the same.
Comments: One of the best pictures I have seen is *San Francisco* because
of the likeness of the earthquake and scenery.

29   *Denis Berry*, 52 Bangor St (aged 16), regular cinema-goer (4 times a
month), preference – American films.
Comments: None.

30   *Richard Quinlan*, 73 Cross St (aged 16), regular cinema-goer (6 times
a month), preference – American films.
Comments: In my opinion the American films are far more superior to the
British films. In the former the scenery and effects are more elaborate and
natural, whereas in British films the majority seem to be stunted and too
artificial. The players themselves in American films have a knack of living
the part they are acting, and the players in British pictures, mostly seem
to be 'acting' the part they are supposed to be living.

31 *Jack Holt*, 66 Wike St (aged 16), regular cinema-goer (8 times a month), preference – American films.
Comments: Not so many love pictures and uninteresting pictures. Give us more action and musical pictures.

32 *Edward O'Neill*, 1 Hensor St (aged 16), regular cinema-goer (10 times a month), preference – American films.
Comments: In films I see there is too much love in every picture, women change a man's mind. Instead of a man being tough he is made soft. If women were cut out of Western pictures more people would like them, and you would get more smiling faces.

33 *Richard E. Battersby*, 10 Snowden St (aged 17), regular cinema-goer (14 times a month), preference – American films.
Comments: I think that those cartoons advertising Horlicks etc. should not be shown in cinemas. People see enough advertisements outside.

34 *William Gregory*, 25 Denvale Avenue (aged 17), regular cinema-goer (8 times a month), preference – British films.
Comments: I hereby give my comment on films I think that murder films should not be shown. Because 1) It gives people a good idea how to commit murder. 2) It gives them an idea of what to do and what not to do. 3) It gives them an idea of what really lies behind people's minds. Murder films should be completely abolished.

35 *James Coleman*, 3 Arkwright St (aged 17), regular cinema-goer (12 times a month) preference – American films.
Comments: None.

36 *Ronald Fletcher*, 67 Johnson Fold Avenue (aged 17), regular cinema-goer (10 times a month), preference – American films.
Comments: In these days there is too much of the same thing in the pictures, most are based on the same subject. There is one thing, talking pictures are better than silent.

37 *Walter Rollinson*, 40 Crumpsall St (aged 18), regular cinema-goer (8 times a month) preference – American films.
Comments: In historical films I think they are modernized too much. *Example* Some of the Furniture and tapestry in houses and Mansions. Also the utensils that they use for meals. But they are very interesting. In crime pictures I think they are based too much on the same thing. Western pictures are very interesting because they are something out of the ordinary. By that, I mean the things we see in western pictures are not seen in everyday life. Such as horse-riding, the buildings, the scenery. I like the musical romance because of the singing and dancing and the humour.

38   *Ronald Sweeney*, 79 Morehall St (aged 18), regular cinema-goer (10 times a month), preference – American films.
Comments: Why do exhibitors insist on showing trailers? They are unnecessary because the films are always assured of publicity through the Press. After reading the reviews in the newspaper, cinemagoers object to seeing the big moments of a film in advance, and the inclination to see the show is lost. All this expense could be saved and extra value put into the actual films. Advertizing by film does not mix very well with our screen entertainment and can be very annoying. After all what are the hoardings for?

39   *Henry Smalley*, 3 Priory Place (aged 18), regular cinema-goer (8 times a month), preference – British films.
Comments: The trouble with your cinema is you get films that has been to other cinemas, therefore they aren't interesting, as parts have been cut out. Another thing is, before the programme starts, you show too many advertizements. Still I enjoy your programme every week and shall continue to do so as long as the price is still 4d.

40   *John McMunn*, 45 Bullock St. (aged 18), regular cinema-goer (6 times a month), preference – American films.
Comments: Sir, The best films I have seen in my opinion are 1) *The Bengal Lancers*[1] 2) *The Charge of the Light Brigade* 3) *Professional Soldier* 4) *On His Majesty's Service* (OHMS) 5) *Hell's Angels* 6) *Rose Marie*

41   *William Turnock*, 33 Buxton St (aged 18), regular cinema-goer (8 times a month), preference – American films.
Comments: As a complaint, I don't like many British films owing to there not being sufficient action, and the actors are not acting their part properly. 'Ace Films' of London are creating the proper spirit by showing films of American Colleges. As far as humour goes in the British films, I think that George Formby, the Famous Lancashire Comedian, just about tops the bill for his comedy is really exhilarating. As a special request (if it is in favour), I should very much like to see one of 'George's' early films *No Limit*, again. Yours sincerely W. H. Turnock.

42   *Jack Fletcher*, 12 Darbishire St (aged 18), regular cinema-goer (8–10 times a month), preference – American films.
Comments: More Sea Films. More films such as *Forever England* and Western Films such as *Hopalong Cassidy's Return*.

43   *James Hutchinson*, 78 Hulme St (aged 18), regular cinema-goer (8 times a month), preference – American films.
Comments: I like the American films best because they have more action and humour than our British films. Our own films are too dry, all the acting seems to be done in the same place.

44 *James Ridyard*, 126 MacKenzie, St (aged 18), regular cinema-goer (8 times a month), preference – American films.
Comments: I think Crime or Drama films get one excited waiting for the killer of [or?] the thief being caught. I also think Americans put more action in their films but the British are better directed.

45 *John Byrne*, 16 Dean St (aged 19), regular cinema-goer (12 times a month), preference – American films.
Comments: English films have no life about them. They have no tension about them, no life, when anyone sees an English film it's nearly always got a mist in it same as a foggy day. Why dont they spend a bit of money and get some proper scenery.

46 *William Harper*, 39 Harvest St (aged 19), regular cinema-goer (16 times a month), preference – American films.
Comments: Dear sirs, In my opinion, the films of today lack the necessary themes to give them a good basis. The acting and scenery improve with time. Excellent actors and actresses given unsuitable parts to play. The public of today are more critical and therefore more harder to please. More thought given to cast and theme and plenty of variety, and public would hardly quibble.

47 *Thomas Weatherall*, 40 Norwood Grove (aged 19), regular cinema-goer (12 times a month), preference – American films.
Comments: I like Western films, because there is plenty of excitement, action, killing. When you have spent a dull, dreary day in the spinning room you want to see some open air life as you usually get in Western films. Such films would pack your cinema, *The Plainsman, Robin Hood of Eldorado, Viva Villa, Hopalong Cassidy* series, Zane Grey's. Then you have drama and tragedy. Such films as *The Count of Monte Cristo* etc. Musical Romances as *Rose Marie, Naughty Marietta, You Can't Have Everything* etc. Slapstick Comedies as *O.K. for Sound, Alf's Button Afloat*, Laurel and Hardy, Wheeler and Woolsey. Historical as *Charge of the Light Brigade, Lloyds of London, Drake of England, Lives of Bengal Lancer*. Crime such as *G Men, False Faces, Counterfeit, Mary Burns Fugitive*.

48 *J. Gliston*, 16 Haworth St (aged 20), regular cinema-goer (6–8 times a month), preference – American films.
Comments: I would like more films of the Cagney type. Your programmes have been terrible up to about 3 weeks ago but you have made up for this the last 3 weeks by showing excellent films.

49 *W. Rimmer*, 13 Faraday [?] (aged 21), regular cinema-goer (8 times a month), preference – British films.
Comments: I would like to see more British Navy in Action and what the British Army do.

50 *George Shannon*, 8 Williamson St (aged 21), regular cinema-goer (4–6 times a month), preference – American films.
Comments: Dear sir, I'm regular film fan. American films are my favourite. Gangster films are a big favourite with the Public because they bring to light the reign of terror which swept America a short time ago. Gangster, Nature, and Reality are big favourites of mine. The latter are to give explanations to the Public not well up in knowledge. Western films are an attraction to children.

51 *H. Greenhalgh*, 21 Lena St (aged 21), regular cinema-goer (12 times a month), preference – American films.
Comments: I know that American are far-fetched but they are more enjoyable than British, but ours are simple and more realistic, such as the films George Arliss appears in.

52 *Albert Winstanley*, 532 Halliwell Rd (aged 21), regular cinema-goer (8 times a month), preference – American films.
Comments: I always regard the Cinema Proprietor's lot a difficult one. His patrons have a wide and varied taste and it is his first duty to satisfy them. Whilst some may prefer American gangster films or a romantic love story, others will prefer some educational film or an amusing comedy, whilst care has to be taken to cater for the younger children with perhaps a slapstick comedy or some Disney film. I do not think however that the average cinema performance can be improved upon. In almost every film show there is something to satisfy everyone, and as long as every film is kept clean, the cinema will always be a happy place of entertainment to every family.

53 *Fred Grundy*, 42 Oak St (aged 23), regular cinema-goer (10 times a month), preference – both the same.
Comments: Most English films would be more enjoyable and better entertainment if the people in it would put a bit more life into film. Westerns are allright for Children's Matinee only. There are some pictures which have a very good meaning and which are also good all round entertainment. viz. *You Only Live Once, They Gave Him a Gun*. War Films are interesting if treated as a picture but in my opinion people who have been through war have seen enough and the rest seem to get silly ideas in their head. It is no use having a good picture at any Cinema unless that Cinema is qualified to have attendants to keep quiet rowdy people. GOOD. SEATS MATCHING.

54 *Mr. W. Bannister*, 105 Kay St (aged 24), regular cinema-goer, (8 times a month), preference – American films.
Comments: Dear sir, I have seen some very good pictures in town when I go and some are very good. They are called: *Souls at Sea, A Star is Born, Top of the Town*, Paul Robeson in *Jericho, Another Dawn, The Gap* a film to prevent aeroplanes from bombing with searchlights in case of war.

55 *Albert Hill*, 27 Thorn St (aged 25), regular cinema-goer (8 times a month), preference – 'good and bad in both'.
Comments: Sir, There are good and bad films made by every Producer for the simple reason that everyone doesn't think alike. I am referring to Question No. 5. I dont think it is a fair one. But if you want my opinion on that one here it is. Britain has the biggest percentage of good films. We could do with more films like *Victoria the Great* because they cater and interest young and old persons. But I like a change sometimes, say, George Formby, Gracie Fields, Marx Bros. etc. Yours faithfully, Albert Hill.

56 *Leo Greenhalgh*, 67 Arkwright St. (aged 25), regular cinema-goer (20 times a month), preference – not given.
Comments: The picture *Mutiny on the Bounty* was indeed a great film, but why was it produced in America, when it possessed an English origin. Most of America's greatest films are based on English history. Why? Surely the British film industry can produce films, portraying our own British isles, than producing such as *For Valour*. When my fiancee and I saw the above, the people behind us and around passed such comments that it wouldnt be at all nice to write. So I think I am right in saying that films like *For Valour*, with such fools as Walls and Lynn, featured in it, should never be approved by the board of Film Censors.[2]

57 *John Thomas Longden*, 8 Ross St (aged 27), regular cinema-goer (8 times a month), preference – American films.
Comments: I go to the pictures mostly to be able to study the possibility of being taught what I am unable to afford 'i.e.', the ways and most of all the actions of certain characters of the past and present film stars. I also go because in my opinion the Pictures are the cheapest possible way of education and they give you the feeling that you are human beings after all. I have nothing to complain about any film, only some are more realistic than others and are fully looked forward to by yours sincerely, John T. Longden, March 18, 1938.

58 *Mr W. Platt*, 15 Haworth St (aged 28), regular cinema-goer (8 times a month), preference – American films.
Comments: None.[3]

59 *D. Garforth*, 29 Newton St (aged 30), regular cinema-goer (6 times a month), preference – American films.
Comments: Dear Sir or Madam, I would like to tell you that the films you have been showing have not been so good. I would like a little more thrills and comics. Otherwise I would have come more often.

60 *John Catterall*, 5 Orchard Avenue (aged 30), regular cinema-goer (6 times a month), preference – American films.
Comments: Films have at last grown up, they still have growing pains, but on the whole show a healthy tone. This has been brought about largely by

Education in its many forms and not in the least by the general (if somewhat indiscriminate) public. Whilst the cinema is a place where fairly intelligent people can go without any qualms, I think there is room for further improvement. Films can still make great strides on the aesthetic side. The younger generation which form the greater bulk of the cinema public dont go to the 'pictures' like their parents did. In those days, it was a means of escape from reality. Older folk can laugh now at 'super' picture palaces. Therefore, in conclusion, I would say films ought to aim at more sincerity, be less spectacular in short. More Art and less Artifice.

61 *Leslie Emms*, 111 Bennetts Lane (aged 30), regular cinema-goer (4–6 times a month), preference – British and American roughly the same.
Comments: I think it would pay a cinema to show some good old films than a lot of the new trash. Some of the present films are a waste of time, watching such as most gangsters, dance bands films. Such as *Mountain Music* etc., I class as rubbish. I am sure it would pay to have request weeks, booking such films as *Mata Hari*, Marx Bros. classics of fun, *Coconuts, Monkey Business* etc. etc. I would sooner see a good old one than a lot of new ones.

62 *Edgar F. Andrews*, 45 Beech St (aged 32), regular cinema-goer (8 times a month), preference – American films.
Comments: American films could slow down speed of speech to advantage and with clearer reception. British films could attend with better results to exactness of detail. Such films as the *Mutiny of Bounty* and *Last of the Bengal Lancers*[4] would I believe improve the public's following. With of course the continuance of good romance. Romance and Love I believe to be the attraction of regular filmgoers.

63 *Mr S. Lomax*, 36 Brougham St (aged 33), regular cinema-goer (8 times a month), preference – American films.
Comments: I think you are showing your first H film this week and in my opinion there is nothing horrible about it to turn parents with children away like you had to do on Monday Afternoon and so lose good money at the Box Office.

64 *Mr A. Wilson*, 36 Walnut St (aged 34), regular cinema-goer (7–8 times a month), preference – American films.
Comments: In regards to the double feature film one is apt to get too much of a sameness (viz.) two films may come together and both be serious, consequently the patron goes out in a serious mind. I think a better programme is one good feature, one comedy and one cartoon to relieve. That along with the News Reel constitute my ideal programme. Only *my* Ideal programme mind you but I am speaking as a 'man in the street', or better still, 'man in the cinema', yours etc., A. Wilson.

65 *Mr James Fogg*, 15 Everton St (aged 41), regular cinema-goer (4 times a month), preference – American films.
Comments: The films shown today are in my opinion perfect, as they cater for all classes of people.

66 *George Fletcher*, 12 Darbishire St (aged 42), regular cinema-goer (8 times a month), preference – American films.
Comments: When one has finished his or her's Labour at Home, or work it acts like a Tonic when one sees such a film like *San Francisco* or *The Street Singer*. The picture shown this week, *Thirteenth Chair*, held one in suspense all through, and was very interesting.

67 *Mr J. Smith*, 10 Albert St (aged 48), regular cinema-goer (8 times a month), preference – American films.
Comments: The majority of most films are sloppy and too much love in them. The most popular films are those dealing with human emotions and everyday life. War pictures keep many patrons away because it brings back many sad and unpleasant memories.

68 *Thomas Sharples*, 45 Clarence St. (aged 49), regular cinema-goer (8 times a month), preference – American films.
Comments: I must complement the Palladium on this last 4 weeks shows.

69 *Mr A. E. Mycock*, 18 Bernard Grove (aged 49), regular cinema-goer (8–10 times a month), preference – about equal.
Comments: I prefer British films because they seem to me the most natural and the talk is not slangy. Most of the actors appear to live unnatural lives on the screen. Cartoons such as 'Popeye' I consider a waste of time watching – they are certainly very unnatural and silly. I very much like the travelling newsreels, because they explain the various happenings better than written explanations. Please give us more travel and educational features.

70 *Robert Walsh*, 6 St John St (aged 50), regular cinema-goer (8 times a month), preference – American films.
Comments: None.

71 *James A. Walsh*, 22 Wentworth St (aged 50), regular cinema-goer (8 times a month), preference – American films.
Comments: British films are tame, the actors self conscious and wooden, the settings easily recognized as the work of novices. Experience dating from the first showing of Al Jolson in *The Singing Fool* goes to show that the man in the street likes pictures which advertise an American cast. One knows it will be a good picture. One often hears the remark, 'It's a British Picture, let's go elsewhere.' Comic shorts with too much horseplay and no point are a draw-back to box-office receipts. That is an undoubted

fact. English cowboys look foolish, they cannot mount and ride like the real Westerner and do not appeal. British Films are always a one-man show. In American Films the most important extras are worth watching, as well as the star performers. Walt Disney cartoons are always welcomed by young and old. Those are really first-class humour understood by all. Yours Faithfully. Film Fanner.

72   *Joseph Holt*, 23 Lena St (aged 55), regular cinema-goer (8 times a month), no preference.
Comments: None.

73   *Ernest Daniels*, 8 Norton St (aged 55), regular cinema-goer (16 times a month), preference – American films.
Comments: I like American Films. Reasons. Firstly the Artists taking part, no matter how different, seem to live the characters. Secondly. All American Naval, Marine and Air Corps films seem to be carefully supervised by an Ex Officer who has served and knows every detail of the procedure and routine. Thirdly they give a far wider series and to make a picture effective are not afraid to criticize and show defects of their own country. In regard to British Films they are very crude and limited in scope invariably. One I have in mind is OHMS,[5] taken with the cooperation of the Military authorities. A part of this Film was showing an inspection of troops and as they came by with colours and escort I saw a soldier and he was taking a principal part in the Film sat on top of a private car with his arm round a girl. At the latter end of the Film he watched the Colours coming out of Buckingham Palace without saluting until pulled up by a Sergeant.

74   *James Hope*, 35 Duke St (aged 57), regular cinema-goer (8 times a month), preference – American films.
Comments: Royalty, Aristocracy, beautiful people, and beautiful things help us to compare the 'other side' of Life. They give us something to realize and often make youth ambitious, which is the spirit of the British Race. A 'Western' or 'Detective' film is generally enjoyed as much as even the 'Ecclesiastic' loves his armchair and an Edgar Wallace thriller for a change. Love stories, Drama and tragedy have their lessons and Pathos of life. Most pictures to-day are worthy of our patronage as compared to the pictures of old. Travel and Adventure too, what better to thrill with pride the best of youth and age. Britons love those films. Give us more.

75   *Mr A. Wiggans*, 5 Baron St (aged 60), regular cinema-goer (8 times a month), preference – American films.
Comments: The Reason why I like American films is because British Pictures are too slow in their Actions. They want to put more pep into their Acting.

76   *Thomas Henry Smith*, 143 Kay St (aged 60), regular cinema-goer (8 times a month), preference – British films.
Comments: More Films by George Arliss, Charles Laughton and other Great English actors and actresses. One important item in the cinema is absolutely quietness from the audience.

77   *Thomas Byrne*, 3 Alpha St (aged 61), regular cinema-goer (8 times a month), preference – American films.
Comments: None.

78   *H. Holloway*, 51 George Arthur St (aged 61), regular cinema-goer (12 times a month), preference – American films.
Comments: Dear sir, those not marked I would not touch with a barge pole [i.e. more religion, politics, action, killing, royalty and aristocrats]. British pictures, there is neither life nor soul, no go, there is some good Historical Pictures. I like every thing that is good and beautiful on pictures and also with people, every action of Man denotes his characteristics. I may add I have been coming to the Palladium ever since it opened. You have considerable room for improvement. Pictures not as good as they used to be, but been better recently. Thanks for this opportunity to express an opinion. Good luck.

79   *Thomas Hough*, 61 Bush Fold Lane (aged 73), regular cinema-goer (6–8 times a month), no preference.
Comments: Sir, as a frequent patron of your theatre, I am pleased to state that your place seems to me to be clean and capably managed. However, I have one fault to find and it is this. At the end of the programme, while the King is being shown, I object to the curtain being drawn across the screen, blotting out the King before the music has finished. This is all. Good luck to you.

80   *John Ripley*, 43 Lyndhurst St (aged 70), regular cinema-goer (4 times a month), preference – British films.
Comments: We always enjoy your pictures and we think yours is the best in town and the cheapest.

Palladium Cinema: Women

1   *Irene Wilson*, 30 Haigh St (aged 7), regular cinema-goer (6 times a month), preference – American films.
Comments: None.

2   *Lily Hampton*, 73 Hulme St (aged 10), regular cinema-goer (8 times a month), preference – American films.
Comments: None.

3 *Eileen Torkington*, 29 Hampden St (aged 12), regular cinema-goer (8 times a month), preference – both the same.
Comments: I like Historical Films best of all the films I see because there is fighting, romance and action. I know History pictures dont suit everybody. But at school my best lesson is History.

4 *Beatrice Hamer*, 22 Haigh St (aged 13), regular cinema-goer (12 times a month preference – American films.
Comments: San Francisco. I enjoyed that picture because it showed that death and destruction destroyed that city through its vice and wickedness. It also showed how a bad man retrieved his character through a good woman.

5 *Kathleen Doherty*, 6 Wike St (aged 14), regular cinema-goer (8–9 times a month), preference – American films.
Comments: I think you should get more Films of Laurel and Hardy. They are not altogether soft but they make you laugh, and also Robert Taylor.

6 *Miss Hettie McDerby*, 473 Blackburn Rd (aged 14), regular cinema-goer (8–10 times a month), preference – American films.
Comments: I would like to see the cast of the films to be shown on the screen after the film and then any character you like in the film you will be able to find out the screen player who took the part. Also in western films the hero keeps firing without reloading their gun, and in crime pictures the hero always escapes no matter what sort of a tight corner he is in. I like to see and hear opera on the films and I like to hear great singers such as Jeanette Macdonald and Deanna Durbin whom I saw in *Three Smart Girls* and *San Francisco*.

7 *Edith Heaton*, 18 Turton St (aged 15), regular cinema-goer (8 times a month), preference – British films.
Comments: None.

8 *Miss Ida Heyes*, 141 Eskrick St (aged 15), regular cinema-goer (10 times a month), preference – American films.
Comments: You may be puzzled by an answer to question 4 (Do you think you see people on the screen, who live like yourself? Yes, but mostly children.) What I mean is that when you read descriptions of a child actress or actor's life in private, there is nearly always this phrase – So and so lives a normal, carefree life, just like any ordinary child etc. In regards to question 5. American films are certainly best. But British films are slowly but surely improving, and it is my belief that eventually we will surpass Americans. What I prefer are more 'singing' not 'crooning' pictures. These love pictures that we see are practically the same thing, but painted a different colour, as the saying goes, whereas, good singing or action pictures, such as *San Francisco* are a very rare occurrence. Another

point is that you can show such pictures twice over and still get a good house, but not so love pictures. I would also like a few more jungle pictures e.g. *Tarzan, Elephant Boy* etc.

9   *Ethel Rollinson*, 40 Crumpsall St (aged 15), regular cinema-goer (8 times a month), preference – none.
Comments: In western pictures the scenes are much the same to me; by this I mean when any of the actors are riding through the trees in search of anyone they seem to pass the same place every time. In Historical pictures one seems to get a better Idea of the costumes and houses than one can read in books. The thing I like about crime pictures is that they show people however good they do the crime they nearly always make one slip which goes against them more so than if they were told on. It also ought to teach people the lesson that 'crime does not pay'.

10   *Freda Douglas*, 66 Cooper St (aged 15), regular cinema-goer (6 times a month), preference – American films.
Comments: Dear sir, I never go to a British film if I can help it. I very much like the American crime and detective pictures. If the Americans would start making pictures, that would increase our knowledge of worldly things, mothers would not mind letting their children go more, yours sincerely, F. Douglas.

11   *Mary Greenwood*, 71 Boardman St (aged 15), regular cinema-goer (8 times a month), preference – American films.
Comments: Of the many Films I have viewed, I rather think that *After the Thin Man* with Myrna Loy and William Powell and *The Jungle Princess*, struck me as being very interesting. The former one for its action and humour combined, and the latter one for its scenery and romance. For humour, I think the 3 Stooges and Edgar Kennedy give good entertainment, whilst for thrills I admire Lloyd Nolan and Edward G. Robinson.

12   *Edna Millson*, 69 Marshall St (aged 16), regular cinema-goer (20 times a month), preference – American films.
Comments: None.

13   *Miss Gertie Richards*, 16 Chester St (aged 16), regular cinema-goer (8 times a month), preference – American films.
Comments: There should be more musicals and love stories combined together.

14   *Ivy Williams*, 81 Sidney St (aged 18), regular cinema-goer (12 times a month), preference – American films.
Comments: I think films of today are not enough realistic. I like films based on everyday life and ordinary people. I dislike lavish settings for films and heroine and heroes made up too perfectly to ever be seen in ordinary life. I have never seen a leading woman yet who looks real. Perfect

teeth, perfect flawless skin, spider-like eyelashes and a perfectly set, West end coiffure even first thing in a morning. I want more films of people like us who live and breathe, not beautiful statues or tailored dummies.

15 *Alice Gore*, 20 Victoria Grove (aged 19), regular cinema-goer (20 times a month), preference – American films.
Comments: None.

16 *Irene Allport*, 5 Castleton St, Tonge Moor (aged 20), regular cinema-goer (8 times a month), preference – American films.
Comments: None.

17 *Miss Josephine Hawkins*, 257 Waterloo St (aged 23), regular cinema-goer (12 times a month), preference – American films.
Comments: Personally I like films, which leave room for imagination. A film with a good story is worth patronizing. Far fetched films I do not care to see. A good, clean comedy is worth any-one's money, if it is only to banish the blues. Romance also, with good singing suits the majority of film goers. A good laugh, a cry and a little breath taking, in films suits me down to the ground.

18 *Agnes Ramsbottom*, 52 Centre St (aged 23), regular cinema-goer (12 times a month), preference – American films.
Comments: None.

19 *Annie Hill*, 27 Thorn St (aged 23), regular cinema-goer (7–8 times a month), preference – both if good.
Comments: Sir, I like films like *Top Hat, San Francisco, Penny Pool* etc. I saw *Day at the Races* tonight and liked it very much. A bit of everything in those sort. Get films like that and I for one, wont miss many, yours truly, Annie Hill.

20 *Emily McKenna*, 53 Virgil St (aged 23), regular cinema-goer (10 times a month), preference – both the same.
Comments: Pictures if interesting are a pleasure to watch but films like *Secret Lives* are terrible. Some Western pictures are allright but most of them are what I term as 'just filling out programme'. There are no Comedians today like Charlie Chaplin. Most of them are dry and try to get laughs by silly actions and childish prattle. Films such as *They Gave Him a Gun, You Only Live Once, Maytime, The King Steps Out, Charge of the Light Brigade, Nancy Steele is Missing, San Francisco* and many others are a treat to watch. Good Seats. View. Machine. are the main points to a really good night's entertainment.

21 *Lillian Hayter*, 7 Devonshire St (aged 24), regular cinema-goer (12 times a month), preference – American films.
Comments: I should like to see more coloured films shown. They help

people to see how their favourite actors and actresses really look like. I give praise to the News Reel, which helps to give us an insight of foreign affairs and shows the horrors of war. In conclusion I ask. Where have the PopEye films gone to? I think everyone enjoyed them.

22 *Mrs J. Holding*, 3 Lilly St (aged 24), regular cinema-goer (4 times a month), preference – American films.
Comments: When going to the cinema we go to be entertained and amused, and I think there is enough crime and tragedy in the world without seeing it on a screen. The one thing I have against the inferior type of American films is the way they speak. Give us more pure English – it is rather nerve-wracking to hear the way some children speak, especially small boys. Let us have more music, good music – why not light operas, Gilbert and Sullivan or something like that? People flock to hear a good singer in a picture and surely beautiful music is one of the best remedies to make us forget our troubles.

23 *Annie Cash*, 41 Clarence St (aged 26), regular cinema-goer (16 times a month), preference – American films.
Comments: The British Films are too slow and they seem always to be in the same place and the same rooms.

24 *Mary Ann Sixsmith*, 63 Lyon St (aged 27), regular cinema-goer (16 times a month), preference – American films.
Comments: In American pictures you get more action and more crime and they hold your interest to the end. In British pictures they seem very slow and gradually lose interest.

25 *Mrs Phyllis Cann*, 44 Bradford St (aged 30), regular cinema-goer (4 times a month), preference – American films.
Comments: I attend the cinema regularly as an amusement and also as an inspiration to my mentality. It is interesting to see people living ordinary lives such as you or I, also the screen reveals the lives of people we do not come into contact with. The network of humanity is a very interesting study. In my opinion the American productions are far ahead of the English, there is something snappy and altogether definitely conclusive about an American film, while most of the English films are slow and absolutely vague and lacking in interest.

26 *Mrs Nellie Barber*, 30 Haigh St (aged 31), regular cinema-goer (8 times a month), preference – British films.
Comments: My personal opinion is the British films are more solid but not as colourful as American films. I think a film which has a good meaning and the stars are good plain speakers are the best. One of these pictures I have seen and easily understood was *San Francisco*. It had good meaning, good talking and beautiful singing and was a pleasure to sit and watch.

27 *Bessie Lovering*, 18 William St (aged 35), regular cinema-goer (8 times a month), preference – American films.
Comments: None.

28 *Miss Annie Ferguson*, 59 Grasmere St (aged 40), regular cinema-goer (7 times a month), preference – British films.
Comments: None.

29 *Mrs B. Smith*, 53 Mona St (aged 46), regular cinema-goer (12 times a month), preference – American films.
Comments: American Films are far better than English films. The English films have good actors and no action. Americans have both.

30 *Emily Freeman*, 8 Prosperous St (aged 48), regular cinema-goer (12 times a month), preference – American films.
Comments: For myself I like a good musical comedy, because it helps you to forget everything, and makes you feel you are really enjoying yourself. I also like a good gangster film, that also holds you and takes you right out of yourself. As regards British Pictures candidly I think they are awful. I dont go if I know its British, because the talk is terrible and the people old and ugly. Give me American Pictures every time.

31 *Miss M. J. Downs*, 30 Mornington Rd (aged 50), regular cinema-goer (4 times a month), preference – British films.
Comments: My desire in pictures are ones of interest. *Either* Love, Adventure, Historical, Educational and certainly Witty or Humorous ones. But not Slapstick. They may appeal to some. *But* what a pity!

32 *Mrs Mary Jane Gibson*, 131 Halliwell Rd (aged 62), regular cinema-goer (8 times a month), preference – both the same.
Comments: Dear sir, it is our custom, hubby and I, to go to the Palladium twice weekly Monday and Thursday, providing the pictures suits me. If it does not, Hubby goes to the Palladium alone and I go just when there is a picture I like to see. I would walk a mile to see Kay Francis or Otto Kruger, Barbara Stanwyck or Franchot Tone, Joan Crawford or Robert Montgomery or any of that type of film star. My comment, Mrs. Gibson.

33 *Mrs Holloway*, 51 George Arthur St (aged 64), regular cinema-goer (8 times a month), preference – American films.
Comments: Sir, The pictures have not been very good of late, but would like to see better Pictures in the future.

34 *Mrs Nightingale*, 45 Hibbert St (aged 67), regular cinema-goer (10 times a month), preference – American films.
Comments: None [this return is missing].

Crompton Cinema: Men

1 *William Potter*, 10 Iona Place, Tonge Moor (aged 8), regular cinema-goer (12 times a month), preference – both the same.
Comments: I think that American Pictures are a bit above the British pictures. I think for crime pictures I would recommend American. But for war pictures I would recommend British.

2 *James Potter*, 10 Iona Place, Tonge Moor (aged 13), regular cinema-goer (10 times a month), preference – both the same.
Comments: For crime pictures, and gangsters, I prefer the American pictures. They also produce good comedies. But for war, spying etc. I prefer the British. The Americans also produce good Western pictures and cartoons.

3 *Leslie Potter*, 10 Iona Place (aged 14), regular cinema-goer (14 times a month), preference – both the same.
Comments: The American producers produce some excellent pictures. For crime, western, pictures etc. I prefer the American pictures. They also produce some good cartoons, such as Mickey Mouse, Donald Duck. But for war and historical pictures, I prefer the British. The producers also produce good comedies. The only complaint I have against pictures is that some pictures are cert A and I suggest that they should produce all pictures for children and grown ups and have all pictures passed as cert U.

4 *Master A. Green*, 7 Pole St (aged 15), regular cinema-goer (8 times a month), preference – American films.
Comments: None.

5 *Herbert Harwood*, 108 Pimlott Rd (aged 16), regular cinema-goer (8 times a month), preference – American films. (He made 2 separate returns)
Comments: None.

6 *Harold Neylon*, 17 East Way (aged 16), regular cinema-goer (4 times a month), preference – American films.
Comments: Night Must Fall. This film was rather too dramatic, although the acting was good. As you will see, I have said I like American films best. My reason is that most British films are devoid of humour and wisecracks. The best film to stand up to Laurel and Hardy style was *Okay for Sound* with Flanagan and Allen. This in my opinion was and is the best British film I am likely to see for some time. Actually the British film stars who are better than their Hollywood rivals are Flanagan and Allen, George Formby, Gracie Fields, Vivien Leigh and Jack Buchanan.

7 *Roland Stott*, 16 Huntroyd Avenue, Tonge (aged 16), regular cinema-goer (10 times a month), preference – American films.

Comments: More uptodate newsreel. I think all big pictures are well picked, all being good pictures but better like following-up pictures, cartoons, especially Popeye and Mickey Mouse (not forgetting Donald Duck and Pluto etc.)

8 *Joseph Barnes Jr*, 298 Crompton Way (aged 16), regular cinema-goer (10 times a month), preference – British films.
Comments: None.

9 *Joseph Stones*, 12 Pixmore Avenue (aged 16), regular cinema-goer (7–8 times a month), preference – American films.
Comments: Dear sirs, I am afraid there is just one complaint that I feel I must make. That is the missing of parts out of pictures. My dear sirs, I dont really think that is fair to the public. yours faithfully, J. S.

10 *L. Booth*, 1 West Way (aged 16), regular cinema-goer (8 times a month), preference – American films.
Comments: I think the public audience like to see films that include a little bit of everything such as *Charge of the Light Brigade*. This holds romance-action-drama and a little humour. I am sure that a larger percentage of people would rather see films like this than these slapstick as you call them and farfetched comedies which we are seeing a lot of now.

11 *Ronald Barton*, 9 Sherwood St, Astley Bridge (aged 17), regular cinema-goer (12 times a month), preference – American films.
Comments: Why I have put more action first. It is because there is too much talking in some films and not much acting. More humour second because we come to enjoy something to make us feel happy and forget the dark clouds that is hanging over us. I remain, yours, R. Barton.

12 *Joseph Lovatt*, 4 Back Lever St (aged 17), regular cinema-goer (8 times a month), preference – American films.
Comments: American Pictures Question No. 2 I have no alternative but to say 'American' for this answer. All American Pictures have twice more action than the English. English films lack both action and humour and will not in my opinion be able to compete with American Films until they obtain more 'go'.

13 *Sam Haselden*, 11 Firwood Lane, Tonge Moor (aged 17), regular cinema-goer (10 times a month), preference – American film.
Comments: I select American films to British, as I think British acting is slow. You can tell what's coming next. They take it in their turns so to speak.

14 *Frank Halliwell*, 101 Bradshaw Brow, Tonge Moor (aged 20), regular cinema-goer (7 times a month), preference – American films.
Comments: We want more first class films, such as *The Lives of a Bengal*

Lancer, The Charge of the Light Brigade, Think Fast, Mr Moto, Lost Horizon, Souls at Sea or *The Private Secretary.* Far too much time and money is spent on third rate films, whereas better entertainment could be had from a quarter of the number providing they were really good. I am waiting patiently for the time when I shall see Walt Disney's *Snow White and the Seven Dwarfs* which I think will be first rate entertainment. There is no doubt that this film will begin a new era in the colour cartoon industry which I think will be welcomed by the public in general.

15 *Henry Tong*, 27 Windley St (aged 21), regular cinema-goer (8 times a month), preference – American films.
Comments: I think the British films want more action and naturalizing. But for comedy I think the British Films are the best.

16 *Richard Lofthouse*, 142 Thicketford Rd (aged 21), regular cinema-goer (8–10 times a month), preference – American films.
Comments: Although several of the leading film stars are British, in my opinion British film productions are terribly lacking, compared with American. Our musicals haven't the same snap and dont go with the same swing. Dramas – Acting good as a rule but just that touch of amateurism about story and acting. What's the reason when our stars, both variety and otherwise, can lick the Americans lying down.

17 *Pat Morley*, Tonge Moor Rd. (aged 22), regular cinema-goer (8 times a month), preference – American films.
Comments: What is needed is more character actors, such as Laughton and Muni, and less so-called 'heart throbs', like Robert Taylor and Tyrone Power, to make people realize the full value of films.

18 *Mr H. Doran*, 39 Dimple Rd, Egerton (aged 24), regular cinema-goer (8 times a month), preference – American films.
Comments: As a regular patron of your cinema, I prefer two short films instead of a full-length Picture.

19 *Mr James Bradbury*, 10 Iona Place (aged 25), regular cinema-goer (8 times a month), preference – both the same.
Comments: Personally I think that British films have improved of late, and I would rather see one in turn. Americans are also good. For a musical film I prefer the American. My view is this, that if British films make the progress that they have done in the last 3 years, I think that they will be far ahead of the American films. J. Bradbury.

20 *Edward Jackson*, 52 Bow Lane (aged 25), regular cinema-goer (6 times a month), preference – both the same.
Comments: Sir, during the last twelve months, I should say 40% of the films were good, 30% moderate and 30% not worth watching. The moderate ones often lost interest halfway through, lack of action the

cause. Films like *Disraeli, Maytime* and *The Road Back* were the box office attractions, and it is these kind the public want. If I were to make a film and had the option of stars, I would choose my cast from the following. The misses J. McDonald, D. Lamour, M. Carroll, A. Neagle, B. Stanwyck and J. Gaynor. Messrs. R. Colman, L. Howard, G. Arliss, E. Flynn, H. Marshall and V. McLaglen. Action, humour and everyone a real star.

21   *Mr F. Foley*, 41 Egerton St (aged 26), regular cinema-goer (4 times a month), preference – British films.
Comments: Personally I think 50% of films shown are absolute tripe. We are shown people who look too bored with life to live, and who spend their time drinking cocktails, or spending untold wealth, all of which gives a very contented frame of mind to people living in manufacturing towns such as Bolton. But we have also had good films and I am glad to say about 30% of these have been British, such as *The 39 Steps, Victoria the Great, The Count of Monte Cristo*[6] etc. I take off my hat to America for the cartoons only, which everyone likes, and I would like to see them at your cinema. As regards your cinema, it is very comfortable but you have too long an interval between houses and they show advertisements for too long, making people bored, yours sincerely, F. Foley.

22   *William Hay*, 55 Tintern Avenue (aged 26), regular cinema-goer (6–7 times a month), preference – American definitely.
Comments: There is too much preamble to the average film. I go to the pictures to see the film and I dont care who is the 'recording director', who the costumes are by etc. and I don't care who distributes the film so long as it is worth distributing. Furthermore I don't like the programme being filled up by the lights coming on or the curtain being raised or lowered every now and then. Also 'forthcoming events' occupy too much time. Finally, generally speaking, American films are far superior in every way to the average British film. Briefly what I want at the cinema is 2 hours entertainment composed of a) newsreel b) a short comedy, cartoon, travel feature and c) the main picture. Cut out everything else and I for one will be more than satisfied.

23   *Kenneth Newton*, 743 Bury Rd (aged 26), regular cinema-goer (4 times a month), preference – American films.
Comments: Keep more on CLASS A films even if they have been shown in Bolton previously. People, myself in particular, do not always get the opportunity of seeing such films as *Mutiny on the Bounty* at first showing in Bolton and do not mind seeing it several weeks later at most convenient and homely cinema. Cut out the advertisements. It only irritates having to see same week after week. Pay instead for a small cartoon film etc. K. Newton.

24   *James Broadbent*, 5 Barrie Way, Tonge Moor (aged 28), regular

cinema-goer (4 times a month), preference – both the same.

Comments: Sir, this gives me an opportunity to complain about the cheap, pointless films, employing half a dozen actors and two rooms, slow-moving dialogue with a very uncertain climax. I still remember with a thrill that great sea drama *Mutiny on the Bounty*, real men, real acting, no stilted artificiality this, something that makes you proud of being an English-man. This was followed by that remarkable glimpse into the future, showing the futility and ultimate outcome of war – H. G. Wells' *Things to Come*. Then we have our own inimitable Jessie Matthews, for music and romance, rivalled only by that lovely American, Eleanor Powell, and who would not forget their worries watching that inspired actress Luise Rainer. Her superb performance in *The Great Ziegfeld* drew the admiration of everyone. For something portraying human pathos, nothing could be more searching than the films which have starred that coarse but loveable rascal, Wallace Beery. He does get under your skin. Give us more adventure, clean romance and musical comedy, but above all give us more action.

25   *Mr C. Hill*, 15 Norton St, Astley Bridge (aged 28), regular cinema-goer (10 times a month), preference – British films.

Comments: I have no complaints on the way you show your films. Get the best films. Show the best films, and you will get more patrons. Atta boy! C. Hill.

26   *Stanley Haslam*, 20 The Stray, Tonge (aged 28), regular cinema-goer (10 times a month), preference – both the same if good.

Comments: I like pictures like *Maytime* straight and good singing clear and musical. I like Spying Pictures because they convey the trend of how the Foreign Office takes its duties which otherwise we should not get an inkling. I like comedy because it brings a smile to the face of people round about us. It's so nice to see people whom have nothing to laugh at work or at home.

27   *Samuel Vaines*, 4 Moss Lea, Sharples (aged 29), regular cinema-goer (8–10 times a month), preference – American films.

Comments: I should like to see more British films not only for patriotic reasons but because I believe that a first class production with British artists can beat America's mainstay productions of the spectacular 'Eddie Cantor' type of film. *Cavalcade* was proof of this statement. The players were British and it was a first class production, although American. Also, on account of the radio, better education and a steady rise in the intellectual taste of the man-in-the-street, the average film-goer is beginning to appreciate a little more the art of correct speech; this we rarely obtain from American films. Although there is a type of person, who will enjoy any type of picture, I think much popularity is given to the film which deals with the ordinary man and woman, living an ordinary life in an ordinary home. What the average man understands he can appreciate with constructive criticism and what he cannot understand he receives with destructive criticism without appreciation.

28 *John F. Wood*, 200 Turton Rd, Bradshaw (aged 29), regular cinema-goer (4–5 times a month), preference – British films.
Comments: Pictures with a good plot, I consider the best – *preferably taken from books*. Films should be *as true to life as possible* in my opinion. Films of Society Life are *trash* in my opinion and serve no useful purpose. *Amongst the films I consider the best are*: 1) *King of Kings* (sacred picture) 2) *Nero* 3) *Ben Hur* 4) *The Count of Monte Cristo* 5) *Maytime* 6) *The Good Earth* 7) *David Copperfield* 8) *A Tale of Two Cities* 9) *Sorrel and Son* 10) *Blossom Time* 11) *Les Miserables*.[7]

29 *Frank Akin* 25 Cartmel St (aged 30), regular cinema-goer (3 times a month), preference – American films.
Comments: I would like to see British films brought to the standard of the *best* American films. Although I have seen good British films, there is usually some little point lacking which tends to lower British standard of production, one instance of what I mean was to be seen in *Victoria the Great* a fine film, but was marred by the scene of the arrival of Prince Albert, the boat was obviously a model and the 'sea' a wash tub, lacking reality. Britain must also improve the musical accompaniment to films, bigger orchestras. Although I have heard some good work by Louis Levy's bands in the big films. I have heard really marvellous orchestras on American films, which, if the film's story wasn't to your liking, you could sit back and enjoy the music, like listening to the Berlin State Orchestra at its best – pre Nazi. F. Akin.

30 *Walter Glynn*, 7 Lichfield Avenue (aged 30), regular cinema-goer (5 times a month), preference – American films.
Comments: They Gave Him a Gun. What a splendid moral this film had and yet I'll gamble that many people failed to see it on account of its title. Very misleading. My point is – if a film is badly titled, it should be given another one as soon as it arrives in the country or in the case of British films before it is exhibited. The Great British Public are film-conscious. Why not a short film each week on the lines of Inspector Hornleigh with a small prize to the first who detects the error. This film could be reserved for your slackest night. Give a Five Minutes talk each week (with illustrations of course) on a different Film Star. By way of Variety, General Knowledge Questions say once a month. Remember your film patron is an interested, intelligent, person and by showing the Best Films you will [be] helping to educate him or her into a useful citizen.

31 *Thomas Coulton*, 19 Fountains Avenue, Tonge Moor (aged 30),

regular cinema-goer (12 times a month), preference – American films.

Comments: Sir, you ask for your patrons' opinion, I am a patron of yours and you are getting a candid opinion. Recently you have shown one big picture and nothing else, not even the News Reel. I must apologise when I say nothing else, for I am forgetting the monotonous way in which the curtains drawn and redrawn across the stage takes place. I would suggest if I may that even a little comedy and short News Reel would be far more pleasing to your patrons than one big picture and occasional curtain drawing, I remain, your expectant patron, T. Coulton.

32 *Walter Glynn*, 7 Lichfield Avenue (aged 30), regular cinema-goer (5 times a month), preference – American films. (This is his second entry cf. 30.)

Comments: Book the Best Films. A Patron likes to feel when they come out after the show that they have had more than their money's worth. If we had more films like *Maytime* the World would be a much better place, because it made people think in a loftier, more inspiring way. A little Sentiment in a film is a Grand Thing. Historical Films or Films of Books by Famous Authors educate the people tremendously. The working classes who are the bulk of your patrons havent the time to read or delve into Historical Books. Hence the Cinema is indispensable. Short Films showing the beauties of the British Isles such as Abbeys, Old Churches and Cathedrals, Mountains and Rivers. Famous Beauty Spots etc. etc. Show the Cast *before* and *after* the Film. Avoid Old Films unless they are in good condition. Walter Glynn.

33 *John M. Berry*, 11 Oaks Lane, Tonge (aged 30), regular cinema-goer (10 times a month), preference – both the same.

Comments: I have taken the risk of appearing bloodthirsty in showing a preference for war films, but adventure and action films are more to a man's taste than the slower type of film. There are far too few historical films, which give tremendous scope for really good acting and dramatic interest. Until recently the working class public does not seem to have appreciated this type of film, because too often we got a mere costume film. *The Mutiny on the Bounty* has changed all that however, and was much appreciated by the general public. The Singing and Dancing film is not very desirable, as that sort of thing is better on the stage. Westerners are good supporting films. Slap-stick comedies are alright in moderation, but *not* Vita-phones. I think the questions are very well put, but some are difficult to answer 'yes' or 'no', e.g. British 'ordinary films' are better than American, but American 'super' films come first. I would like more sea pictures.

34 *Stanley Leech*, 40 Green Way, Hall-in-the-Wood, Bolton (aged 30), regular cinema-goer (4 times a month), preference – American films.

Comments: I like American films for the following reasons:
a) They are much better produced than British films.
b) The producers spend more money on the films than the British and consequently make a better job.
What I do not like is the American accent. American film actors and actresses are also inferior to the British variety.

35 *Harold Blackledge*, 13 Montrose Avenue (aged 31), regular cinema-goer (6 times a month), preference – American films.
Comments: The type of film that pleases me most is the one with a good moral in it, which like a good sermon is a help in our daily task.

36 *Mr and Mrs Smethurst*, 11 Knulshaw Crescent, Hunger Hill, Bolton (aged 31 and 32), regular cinema-goers (4 times a month), preference – American films.
Comments: None.

37 *James Hamer Howarth*, 169 Tottington Rd, Harwood, nr Bolton (aged 35), regular cinema-goer (8 times a month), preference – both the same.
Comments: Personally I would like to see more films of the *Maytime* type and less of the Laurel and Hardy stuff. You will of course gather that I like plenty of music and singing mostly. But to such as I good old songs made to come in with the picture would suit me down to the ground. The singing in *Maytime* was splendid but I can't say the same for them all. You must understand that the average man like myself likes to be able to understand what is being sung. Again I like Drama and Tragedy because I think it brings out the best acting or otherwise. Next comes History because one must understand it to come to an understanding of how things stand today in other countries in Europe. Travel and Adventure are fine as it helps us to understand the other man in other lands. A *good* spy picture is always fine to see, for the many intriguing positions which are created. To be frank about the sixth [i.e. society comedies] I have put this in to make the number up, yours, J. H. Howarth.

38 *Mr F. Loftos*, 16 Poplar Avenue, Bradshaw (aged 34), regular cinema-goer (6 times a month), preference – very similar.
Comments: There is in most Films too much of Society ways, I would like to see more scenes of the working class, such as Sydney Howard (*Up for't Cup*) for we get humour and pathos. In this Film there is portrayed the real Yorkshire humour. Let us have, also, more Historical Films (*Fire Over England, Mutiny on the Bounty*), two of the finest Films ever produced. To conclude, a word of praise for the Cinema, it is a great feature in our lives with its Films of various types.

39 *Jack Greenhalgh*, 7 Lee Gate Lane, Bradshaw (aged 35), regular cinema-goer (8 times a month), preference – American films.

Comments: In regard to films I personally prefer American because they certainly do have more Action, better scenery and as long as they make a good Film then expense seems to be only a secondary consideration and they also cater for all types of people. Jack Greenhalgh.

40   *Mr J. Lever*, 6 Tithebarn Crescent, Bolton (aged 36), regular cinema-goer (4–5 times a month), preference – both the same.
Comments: To the management, dear sirs, I don't like the films which are almost entirely dependent on one or two stars e.g. *Maytime*. Mind you, the scenes were very beautiful but at the same time with the picture taking such a long time it got quite boring, and if as I say there might have been some kind of humour I should have enjoyed it all the more. Here is what in my opinion is the Ideal programme.

1 News Reel.
2 Pathé Pictorial or a good Comedy.
3 A Drama with a touch of humour.
Yours Sincerely, J. Lever.

41   *Mr P. H. Frost*, 66 Eldon St, Tonge Moor, Bolton (aged 37), regular cinema-goer (5–6 times a month), preference – American films.
Comments: English Films are very tame, not enough realism in them, too much comedy. I am not saying they are all the same, for instance there is one being shown at one of your places this week, the *Tivoli, Action for Slander*, that is one of the finest I have seen and one of the best English.

42   *Ernest Idle*, 4 Colmore Grove, Tonge Moor (aged 37), regular cinema-goer (8 times a month), preference – depends on the subject.
Comments: I think a stage turn would add very much to what is as a rule a very pleasant evening.

43   *G. H. Holden*, 1 Howson Avenue (aged 38), regular cinema-goer (5 times a month), preference – both the same.
Comments: Films such as the following are in my opinion the standard for all producers to aim for.

1 *David Copperfield*	a masterpiece
2 *Little Lord Fauntleroy*	"
3 *Tale of Two Cities*	"
4 *The Thin Man*	
5 *After the Thin Man*	very entertaining
6 *Sorrel and Son*	splendid drama
7 *For Valour*	good comedy
8 *Maytime*	
9 *One Night of Love*	best musical pictures yet
10 *Time Marches On*[8] series	very educative.

44   *Edward Allen*, 13 St Bees Rd (aged 40), regular cinema-goer (5 times a month), preference – American films.
Comments: Please omit advertizing cartoon, and cut advertizing on screen to minimum. More *Mutiny on the Bounty* wanted and *Charge of the Light Brigade* and less of little bits to make up the 2 hours. Prefer Variety on the screen to empty comics.

45   *Thomas Madden*, 23 Dudley Avenue (aged 40), regular cinema-goer (2 times a month), preference – American films.
Comments: Life is drab, Life is full of worries, let's have a hearty laugh. Leave out the 'Wise Guys' who answer three telephones at once in an office and 'know it all'. They give sensible people a 'pain in the neck'. Although love stories may be good for the Box Office and suit the silly sloppy type who abound at present, why not educate them up to something better and nobler with such films as *The Good Earth, Mutiny on the Bounty* etc. etc. mixed of course with a good comedy now and then.

46   *Sidney Smith*, 30 Green Way, Hall-i-the-Wood, Bolton (aged 40), regular cinema-goer (4 times a month), preference – American films.
Comments: Our main requirement is comedy *that is comedy*, not the absurd stuff that we get now. If you cant give us the real thing, at least do not force on to us a poor imitation. Most supporting items, except news and cartoons, are very poor, and annoying to see. You should dispense with this obvious padding and let us have either longer main feature items or shorts of main feature quality. Cut out entirely the refreshment interval and next week's trailers, and if you must have cinema organs and advertisements, use them only in the intervals between programmes. Even the people who are musical do not care for too much organ music and many people dislike it intensely. Do something to stop people from talking while the show is on.

47   *Mr John Boardman*, 8, The Close (aged 40), regular cinema-goer (8 times a month), preference – American films.
Comments: None.

48   *George Horrocks*, 13 St Olaf St (aged 41), regular cinema-goer (4–5 times a month), preference – British films.
Comments: Give me British films, something we can understand and know what is said, good 'King's English', not 'twang'. Give us a few more Detective films. Keep us guessing who did it and how it was done right to the end, keep out the sob stuff, the dance bands, can get that at home on the wireless, I come out to the cinema for a change and expect something to clear the cobwebs off and feel like action, not to say I wish I had not turned out. GH.

49   *Arthur Harris*, 52 Alexander Rd (aged 43), regular cinema-goer (8 times a month), preference – both the same.

Comments: I've filled in thi form, I 'ope its' awreet.
An I've put in mi name an't'number o't'street
Tho' why yo should bother, blest if I know
It's a snug picture 'ouse – allus a good show.
If yo' reely ask me, I'd say 'bout a doubt
Lets 'ave some more fun, that's better nor out
T'world's ower full wi struggle an' strife
Summat to laugh at suits me an me wife.
Why send in t'form then? Well I allus bids
For any free tickets – an one o' them quids!

50   *Thomas Gill*, 514 Tonge Moor Rd (aged 43), regular cinema-goer (6–8 times a month), preference – British films.
Comments: As a regular patron of the Crompton Cinema, I think only the best is good enough for us. During the recent filming of *Maytime* proved that the best always pays. We have a very comfortable cinema in the Crompton led by an excellent management and staff, so I repeat again 'the Best always', wishing you all the best for the future, I remain, yours, Mr. J. Gill.

51   *John Foster*, 15 Drummond St (aged 45), regular cinema-goer (7 times a month), preference – American mostly.
Comments: I have seen the picture (*They Gave Him a Gun*) at your cinema tonight, 24/3/38 and I think from an actor's point of view, it is a perfect picture, but I think myself that it is time they let war pictures rest, and give us more of the things that do not reap up the things that bring back sad memories of 1914–18.

52   *T. H. Ward*, 35 Pimlott Rd (aged 45), regular cinema-goer (6 times a month), preference – British films.
Comments: Plain English speaking films and not cut ones are they which all patrons can follow. So wake up, British Film Industry.

53   *Mr Ashcroft*, 40 Maze St, Darcy Lever (aged 50), regular cincma-goer (6 times a month), preference – American films.
Comments: None.

54   *T. Shipperbottom*, 70 New Lane, Top O' th' Brow (aged 53), regular cinema-goer (8 times a month), preference – American films.
Comments: We want more with a bit of a kick in it. Not the love and the society bunkum which most of our own pictures produce. There are some of our own pretty good, but not many.

55   *Percy Pass*, 628 Tonge Moor Rd (aged 57), regular cinema-goer (4 times a month), preference – both the same.
Comments: Since your cinema opened, it is rather remarkable you have not shown us a Shirley Temple picture. I would like to see at your cinema

more picture successes that come to Bolton, even if we had to wait a few months after they are shown in town. Also in regard to the step lights in the balcony, which are at the bottom and face the audience in the balcony. I think they are in the wrong place. You cannot enjoy a picture on the screen with a light shining in your face at the bottom of the steps. The lights should be at the top of the steps and shining down.

56 *H. E. Hutchinson*, 646 Blackburn Rd (aged 60), regular cinema-goer (8 times a month), preference – American films.
Comments: Personally I think the best entertainment we get is the 2 picture programme with the newsreel and as there does seem to be the two pictures of quite a different character which makes it more enjoyable. H. E. Hutchinson.

57 *Mr John Fairclough*, 375 Tonge Moor Rd. (aged 68), regular cinema-goer (6–8 times a month), preference – both the same.
Comments: I like going to the Pictures at Crompton Way which I think they are best and have ever been. They are very comfortable and nice and cosy and clean. I dont think they cannot be beaten anywhere at the price it cost to go to them. I have no complaint to make in any shape or form. I am very well pleased with them all.

58[9] *John Stones*, 6 Furness Square, (aged 74), regular cinema-goer (8–12 times a month), preference – British films.
Comments: Dear sir, I think the pictures that are shown are very pleasing. The people that I have asked is very pleased and well praised by everybody, John Stones. Beautiful and Comfortable.

Crompton Cinema: Women

1 *Elsie Boardman*, 8 The Close, Tonge Moor (aged 13), regular cinema-goer (4 times a month), preference – both the same.
Comments: None.

2 *Annie Smith*, 11 Barrie Way, Tonge Moor (aged 14), regular cinema-goer (12 times a month), preference – American films.
Comments: Dear Sir, you give us some idea of the film by showing us various parts of the acts, in the cases outside, but on seeing the film some of the pictures shown outside never appear on the screen. For e.g. in *Lost Horizon* there were two pictures shown outside which we never saw in the film at all, which proves part of the picture has been missed out. If there not being shown in the film, why show them in the case outside. We'd rather miss a bit of the news and see all the film. Thank you!

3 *Betty Walker (Miss)*, 6 Barrie Way (aged 15), regular cinema-goer (8

times a month), preference – American films.

Comments: One good picture is a lot better than a few silly ones that don't mean a thing. We come to be entertained, not bored with silly slapstick (and more cartoons would be liked). Films like *Maytime* where one gets good acting, singing and a lesson. These sort of films attract people.

4   *Margaret Partington*, 5 Castlewood Square (aged 16), regular cinema-goer (4 times a month), preference – British films.
Comments: None.

5   *Marjorie Rothwell*, 12 Firwood Grove, Tonge Moor (aged 16), regular cinema-goer (10 times a month), preference – American films.
Comments: Only two complaints have I against this Cinema. 1st – If the film being shown the following week is a very good one, I think it would be better to show an advertizing trailer, to show the good points in that certain film. 2nd – Instead of the poor pictures shown like *The League of Frightened Men* etc. Why not show Shirley Temple pictures, these pictures suit almost everybody and are a big box-office draw.

6   *Gertrude Atkinson*, 49 Tintern Avenue (aged 17), regular cinema-goer (6 times a month), preference – American films.
Comments: I think that Crompton Way Cinema have had some fine pictures since it was built. yours. G. Atkinson

7   *Florence Cocker*, 4 Collis Rd, Deane (aged 17), regular cinema-goer (7 times a month), preference – American films.
Comments: When I say I would like more knowledge and educational subjects in the films, I do not mean these geographical films without a story. I think a good story is the main thing with good actors on the cast. If the story is true, so much the better. An historical picture such as *Victoria the Great* is educational and still first class entertainment. Even such imaginative a story as *Lost Horizon* gives us food for thought. People visit the cinema for pleasure, and expect light entertainment. Good stories with much humour mixed with crime and romance. When two long films are shown on the same programme, they should be totally different. Do not plunge your patrons in despair by two films of the sorrows of life, and the following week have them rocking with laughter, at, say, the Marx Brothers and Patsy Kelly on the same programme but in different productions.

8   *Mrs S. Greenhalgh*, 207 Tonge Moor Rd (aged 18), regular cinema-goer (8 times a month), preference – American films.
Comments: Nowadays people do not go to a cinema to see drama and tragedy, there is enough in our daily life. They either want something to cheer them up, or something really sensible with a good meaning to it

such as *Make Way for Tomorrow* and *Lost Horizon*. If it's to be a comedy
they choose, make it a sensible one, not ridiculous and too silly to laugh
it, for example, *A Day at the Races*, good talent, but story and silly actions
couldn't draw a smile.

9 *May Coulter*, 604 Tonge Moor Rd (aged 18), regular cinema-goer (8
times a month), preference – American films.
Comments: I think there should be more musical comedies than those far-
fetched films, also more true to history pictures.

10 *Marjorie Harwood*, 108 Pimlott Rd (aged 19), regular cinema-goer (6
times a month), preference – American films.
Comments: None.

11 *Edith Williamson*, 575 Tonge Moor Rd (aged 19), regular cinema-goer
(8 times a month), preference – American films.
Comments: There are a few of the pictures I prefer that have been shown
at the Crompton: *Mutiny on the Bounty, Maytime, Lost Horizon, The Great
Ziegfeld, Camille.*

12 *Miss Doreen Elton*, Railway Hotel, Bromley Cross (aged 22), regular
cinema-goer (8–10 times a month), preference – both the same.
Comments: None.

13 *Mrs M. Pickup*, 306 Ainsworth Lane (aged 24), regular cinema-goer (8
times a month), preference – American films.
Comments: None.

14 *Gladys Rothwell (Miss)*, Cemetery Lodge, Farnworth, near Bolton
(aged 26), regular cinema-goer (4–5 times a month), preference –
American films.
Comments: Whilst a 'flesh and blood' stage show always provides me with
a real thrill, I think the films take the honours for staging their
productions. With all the advantages at their disposal – magnificent
settings, elaborate 'stage sets', the finest actresses and actors, the film
would be able (and does) produce first class entertainment.

15 *Hilda Clarkson*, 44 Bar Lane (aged 26), regular cinema-goer (8 times
a month), preference – American films.
Comments: Whatever picture is being shown, I always look forward with
interest to the news each week. It is the only way of keeping in touch, and
realising what is happening every day and I consider it the best item on
any programme. Hilda Clarkson.

16 *Mrs F. Loftos*, 16 Poplar Avenue, Bradshaw (aged 28), regular
cinema-goer (6 times a month), preference – British films.
Comments: I think that double-feature programmes are better than one

big film and a lot of scrappy little American comedies. I like good clean humour in a story – such as that of Sydney Howard. I also like Dramatic, Historical and Romantic films, which must however have a good plot e.g. *The Passing of the Third Floor Back, The Barrets of Wimpole St., Mutiny on the Bounty, A Tale of Two Cities*, and last but not least *Maytime*. As a whole the cinema habit gives great enjoyment.

17 *Mrs Walsh*, 40 Laycock Avenue (aged 30), regular cinema-goer (6 times a month), preference – American films.
Comments: Too many films present a phase of life unknown to us.

18 *Mrs Norman Harrison*, 303 Crompton Way (aged 34), regular cinema-goer (8 times a month), preference – American films.
Comments: Would like more good Westerns, films of the *Covered Wagon* type, preferably with Gary Cooper or Randolph Scott as lead. Think there is scope for English films in historical drama, but that they lack the slickness of the Americans in modern stories save for the Jessie Matthews, Jack Buchanan and Tom Walls films. Personally would rather have two features instead of one and two or three shorts. Finally, think Gaumont Graphic the best newsreel.

19 *Mrs Annie Wright*, 5 Aldercroft Avenue, Top o'th'Moor (aged 35), regular cinema-goer (8 times a month), preference – American films.
Comments: None.

20 *Sarah Wright*, 10 Pegamold St, Tonge Moor (aged 36), regular cinema-goer (6 times a month), preference – both the same.
Comments: I like to be able to follow the plot or story of a picture without too much effort. Some pictures are so hard to keep up with that I feel I have done a hard day's work when I come away with trying to follow it and understand it. Such as *Night Must Fall* for example.

21 *Mrs M. Ward*, 35 Pimlott Rd (aged 39), regular cinema-goer (8 times a month) preference – British films.
Comments: Often a good show is spoiled by a cut film to allow time for often absolute rubbish to be shown. The patrons would much more appreciate the whole story than bits of it. M. W.

22 *Emma Miller*, 8 Colmore Grove, Tonge Moor (aged 40), regular cinema-goer (4 times a month), preference – mostly American films.
Comments: We like to see a film that is restful to us, and sends us home feeling a lot better in every way than before we saw it. We can enjoy almost any film, providing it is not too far-fetched or gruesome. Laurel and Hardy Films buck us up, also Gracie Fields. Anyhow I never fail to enjoy my weekly visit to 'The Crompton'.

23 *Mrs Perlberg*, 388 Tonge Moor Rd. (aged 40), regular cinema-goer (4–5

times a month), preference – 'some of each are good'.

Comments: We were bored stiff with Marlene Dietrich in *Garden of Allah* and with Greta Garbo in *Camille*. Most people have not read these books – the translation of them into films is quite poor in parts and ordinary people like us would prefer to see pictures of people we understand. *Magnificent Obsession* was 'good'. *Sabu* too.[10] We enjoy the newsreels most and the short travel and educational pictures. Also we would like to see the screen in the local cinemas better lit up. *Marx Brothers At the Races*[11] last Wed. was grand for humour and we had a good laugh. We certainly prefer topical shorts to an inane 'big' picture. B. Perlberg.

24 *Mrs Cotton*, 155 Thickford Rd (aged 40), regular cinema-goer (8 times a month), preference – American films.

Comments: British films are good but there are not many of them, *49 Steps*[12] being one of the best. Love stories with drama and a smattering of comedy and actors who speak good English. Two distinct houses are better. There is nothing more annoying than being disturbed by moving people, who always choose to move about when a tender lover scene is on the screen. Musical romance like *Maytime* is grand. *Ruggles of Red Gap* another type but very enjoyable. The programme should include a funny cartoon for the children. The newsreel is always welcome. Personally I dont care for turns on the stage. E. Cotton.

25 *Mrs Knowles*, 24 Tintern Avenue (aged 40), regular cinema-goer (8 times a month), preference – British films.

Comments: Two Feature Programmes. Why show two pictures almost alike and sometimes the same personnel? I think the Variety Turns on the films are O.K. Less Cheeky Pictures, more Wholesome Pictures better for everybody. On the stage, would like turns oftener.

26 *Miss D. Heaton*, 9 Florence Avenue, Astley Bridge (aged 41), regular cinema-goer (4 times a month), preference – American films.

Comments: As there is such a lot of gloom and sadness in the world, we come to the pictures for something bright and beautiful to cheer us up such as *Maytime*. You can talk of them when you get home.

27 *Mrs McCann*, 39 Platt Hill Avenue (aged 41), regular cinema-goer (20–24 times a month), preference – American films.

Comments: AMERICAN PICTURES are best. British pictures too dull and slow. Would like more Jeanette McDonald and Nelson Eddy pictures such as *Naughty Marietta* and *Maytime*, good acting and marvellous singing couple. More Freddie March pictures, especially costume ones, like *Anthony Adverse*. More Spencer Tracy and (Franchot) Tone films such as *They Gave Him a Gun* (great picture this). More coloured pictures because the colours are beautiful and I like beautiful things. I am very fond of those short coloured pictures 'travel talks' in place of Jazz Band pictures. Pictures in the last 2 years have been excellent.

28 *Mrs B. Williams*, 3 Minster Rd (aged 43), regular cinema-goer (8 times a month), preference – British 'for speech'.
Comments: Manager, Dear Sir, Your choice of films at Crompton Way Cinema are very good, and I can assure you, good films are the things to fill your House, hoping to see all the latest at Crompton Way, I am dear sir, yours very truly, Mrs B. Williams.

29 *Mrs Clara Hornby*, 659 Tonge Moor Rd (aged 45) regular cinema-goer (8 times a month), preference – both the same.
Comments: Dear sir, my opinion of the best films is anything like *Maytime* with beautiful singing and lovely scenery. They make one forget for a while the hum-drum of everyday life and I think that is what the public like. Mrs C. Hornby.

30 *May Hamer*, 41 Progress St (aged 46), regular cinema-goer (4 times a month), preference – American films.
Comments: Less American pictures and more British will stop American twang among children.

31 *Mrs Elizabeth Entwhistle*, 18 King St, Harwood (aged 49), regular cinema-goer (6 times a month), preference – both the same.
Comments: Sir, as I have not the best of health and get out of sorts, I think pictures with Shirley Temple would be a nice change.

32 *Mrs Leather*, 16 Valpy Avenue (aged 50), regular cinema-goer (4–6 times a month), preference – American films.
Comments: The present standard is good, keep it up. Improve if possible. One cannot understand the withdrawal of *Camille*. Perhaps the box office knows the reason, if that is so, the neighbourhood has need of education.

33 *Mrs Worthington*, 7 Florence Avenue, Astley Bridge (aged 50), regular cinema-goer (4 times a month), preference – American films.
Comments: As we come to the Pictures for entertainment, we like something nice to think about for many a day.

34 *Mrs A. J. Hyde*, 41 Cartmel Crescent (aged over 50), regular cinema-goer (6–8 times a month), preference – British films.
Comments: We like Crompton Way Cinema. Clean. Well kept. Talking Apparatus exceedingly good. Fare excellent. We have seen *The Good Earth* twice, also *Lost Horizon*. Like George Arliss, Grace Moore, Jeanette Macdonald. Unfortunately missed *Mr Deeds Goes to Town*. Is there a chance of it coming to your cinema? We all enjoy the news – enjoyed *Night*

Must Fall today and intend to see *Good Earth* again, and *Captains Courageous* and George Arliss in *Dr Syn* when it comes.

35 *Mrs A. Ashworth*, 113 Eldon St (aged 55), regular cinema-goer (5–6 times a month), preference – British films.
Comments: Having in mind the great opportunities the Cinema has for getting in touch with the ordinary public, far greater than the Press even, I often wish the producers would realize what a great responsibility theirs is. Young minds are influenced by good films and that is the reason I vote for the better type of Cinema shows, yours sincerely, Mrs A. Ashworth.

36 *Female*, no address (aged 56), regular cinema-goer (no), preference – British 'of course'.
Comments: Let's have more films of the type of *Vanessa, Prince and Pauper*.[13] Thrillers and War Pictures are alright occasionally but I go to the pictures to be amused or instructed anyhow, to be entertained and not to have a heart attack or to have my feelings harassed. A Well Wisher.

37 *Mary Ellen Stones*, 6 Furness Square (aged 74), regular cinema-goer (12 times a month), preference – both the same.
Comments: Please, this Cinema is a pleasure to come to. We come 8–10 times a month, me and [indecipherable] my husband. A pleasure to come. Warm, cosy and happy. Monday, Thursday, often Saturday afternoons. Also brings my grandchildren or sends them every week, also holidays from school, also many friends with sons and daughters that praises this beautiful picture cinema. Very much talked about, nearly a hundred people, more better they say [than] anywhere you go to.

38 *Mrs Burry*, 511 Tonge Moor Rd (aged 75), regular cinema-goer (10 times a month), preference – British films.
Comments: I do not know much about the subject. But I think the pictures are very instructional. It also gives us [indecipherable] an idea of what foreign countries are like. But I dont think the General public ever think of the cost, even to life and property, and expense, to give pleasure and instruction for a few coppers.

39 *Lena Ainsworth*, 33 Pegamoid St (aged 20), regular cinema-goer (12 times a month), preference – American films.
Comments: None [This return is missing].

Odeon Cinema: Men

1 *Leonard Allen*, 62 Lever St (aged 13), regular cinema-goer (13 times a month), preference – American films.
Comments: I think that films should be livened up. In comedies there is too

much soft stuff (i.e. falling in water, throwing pies). Drama is a bit too dramatic. If a person is doing an action he takes far too long.

2 *G. Halliwell*, 24 Leverhulme Avenue, Great Lever (aged 14), regular cinema-goer (12 times a month), preference – both the same.
Comments: I want more films like *Good Earth* and *Come and Get It* and *Dead End*. Comfortable seats (and the Odeon seats are comfortable) do not make up for bad films.

3 *Paddy O'Hara*, 287 Willows Lane (aged 14), regular cinema-goer (3 times a month), preference – British films.
Comments: None.

4 *Arnold Edge*, 280 Lever St (aged 14), regular cinema-goer (4 times a month), preference – American films.
Comments: None.

5 *Cyril Ashton*, 2 Carlton Place (aged 14), regular cinema-goer (4–5 times a month), preference – both the same.
Comments: I enjoy all the pictures at the Odeon.

6 *Ronald Carley*, 25 Carter St (aged 15), regular cinema-goer (9 times a month), preference – American films.
Comments: I have visited many cinemas in Bolton at different times and for comfort and good pictures I rank the Capitol and Odeon as leaders. The pictures got there generally suit my taste. I should like to see more stirring pictures such as the picture *Charge of the Light Brigade* or *Fire Over England*. These two films I rank first and foremost in filmworld.

7 *James Harrison*, 31 James St (aged 15), regular cinema-goer (8 times a month), preference – American films.
Comments: I like films such as *Frankenstein* and *Charge of the Light Brigade* and *Charlie Chan*. I don't like films such [as] Love and Historical.

8 *Frank Williams*, 86 Davenport St (aged 15), regular cinema-goer (8 times a month), preference – American films.
Comments: More pictures like *Saratoga* and *Lives of the Bengal Lancers* and *A Star is Born*. I do not like pictures such as Love and Musical Romance.

9 *Frank Stones*, 177 Egerton St, Farnworth (aged 15), regular cinema-goer (6 times a month), preference – American films.
Comments: Most of the English films are slow and have no action in them. American films are more life-like, and have plenty of action. The Americans have more sports and cartoons in their films.

10 *Clifford Brogden*, 26 Morley St (aged 16), regular cinema-goer (8 times a month), preference – American films.
Comments: I think that the American films are a good lot better than the

British. For one thing in the British pictures there is no proper acting at all, not only I think it but many others beside me. The best pictures you have ever had at the Odeon was *Victoria the Great* and *I Promise to Pay*, in both of these the acting was very good.

11   *Stanley Roberts*, 3 Eastwood Terrace (aged 16), regular cinema-goer (4 times a month), preference – American films.
Comments: British films do not seem to be in the same class as American films. The best film I have seen was *The Charge of the Light Brigade*. It was historical I would like to see at the Odeon more musical comedies.

12   *Alan J. Nowell*, 160 Plodder Lane, Farnworth (aged 16), regular cinema-goer (8–9 times a month), preference – American films.
Comments: In my opinion, films exhibiting scenes of war, crime and murder are apt to turn young minds, but are quite alright for older people. Comedy and humour in films are good all round.

13   *Jack Morris*, 37 Calvert Rd, Great Lever (aged 16), regular cinema-goer (12 times a month), preference – American films.
Comments: One complaint I would like to quote about any film is this. When a picture is just commencing the first thing flashed on the screen is the certificate. Secondly the name of the film. Thirdly the 'Director's' name, and this is followed by numerous names of Photographers, Cameramen, Dance arrangers etc. then lastly the cast. This could be cut down to 2 things. 1st Name of film. 2nd. Cast.

14   *Stanley Hardman*, 68 Rishton Lane (aged 16), regular cinema-goer (4 times a month), preference – British films.
Comments: I go to the Odeon because I am always sure of a good comfortable seat and a good clean show. That's the reason I go. None of the adverts induce me to go.

15   *William Brian Kenyon*, 789 Manchester Rd, Over Hulton (aged 16), regular cinema-goer (4 times a month), preference – both the same.
Comments: I visit the Odeon every week, as previously stated, and I can truly say that up to now I have not come away from the cinema disappointed. But the films I like most are Musical Romance Comedy and Love Stories. I really enjoyed such films as *Woman Chases Man, Café Metropole* and *A Star is Born*. They are films I would like to see more of. So I now leave it to you, and I would be pleased to have a copy of your monthly programme mailed to me.

16   *Master J. Bate*, 14 Regan St (aged 16), regular cinema-goer (20 times a month), preference – American films.
Comments: I visit the Odeon every Wednesday evening and the only complaint I can make is about the week's film, *Gangway*. There was only one real star in that picture and that was Nat Pendleton. He's American.

The English stars in it don't seem as though they're acting but trying to make fools of themselves.[14] Most of the filmgoers in Bolton who attend the Odeon would be greatly pleased if you got *Double or Nothing, Hurricane* and *In Old Chicago*.

17   *D. Bird*, 787 Chorley Old Rd, (aged 17), regular cinema-goer (4 times a month), preference – American films.
Comments: My reason for preferring American Films to British is that Hollywood as a whole (and what a hole it is) put more pep into their films. America particularly excels in making farces (This isn't a wisecrack, although in some cases it would apply very well.) What I really mean are such films as *My Man Godfrey* and another that I hope to see shortly *The Awful Truth*. In my opinion the best British humorous pictures are the Jessie Matthews ones which are brilliant satires on American life. My chief aversion are the films showing the injustices of American life, such as *Chain Gangs, Mountain Justice* etc. Of what interest are they to the British people? They are of course alright in America, but for goodness sake keep them there. What market would British Pictures get in America if they made these kind of films? They don't seem to get much as it is. Chief reason for visiting Odeon, however, is the pictures.

18   *L. W. F. Stark*, 779 Belmont Rd (aged 17), regular cinema-goer (4 times a month), preference – 'there is very little difference'.
Comments: When taking into consideration the difference between British and American Films, it should be remembered that American Films are usually more vivid than the British ones, but on the other hand, whereas the British speech is not displeasing to the Americans, the American dialect is very unpopular with numerous people in the country. I think that the amusing qualities possessed by such people as Alastair Sim, Eric Blore and Edward Everett Horton should be exploited more than they are.

19   *Ronald Edwards*, 239 New Brook Rd, Atherton (aged 17), regular cinema-goer (4 times a month), preference – American films.
Comments: Even though I enjoy looking for the little slips and mistakes I had to admit defeat in your picture called *Knight Without Armour* starring Marlene Dietrich. I must also add that never before have I been so thrilled by a film. *Knight Without Armour* is without doubt the best and most interesting film I have seen.

20   *Robert Hodgin*, 77 Crescent Rd (aged 17), regular cinema-goer (8 times a month), preference – American films.
Comments: I think that films require more stories. Too many of the films nowadays have the same story, which makes the film fan more prejudiced against going. So therefore if films were made with better stories I think the cinema would draw more crowds.

21   *Mr J. F. Ford*, 5 Bradford St (aged 17), regular cinema-goer (12 times a month), preference – American films.
Comments: Sir, give us less British films. They are slow-moving and usually have very poor supporting casts. Also I go to the cinema for amusement, so not so many tragedies or 'horror' films, if you please.

22   *C. Holt*, 290 Blackburn Rd (aged 18), regular cinema-goer (3 times a month), preference – mostly the same.
Comments: There should be more films of the type of *San Francisco* in which there was something of everything. The cast should be shown at the end of the film as well as the beginning. British films are quite as good as American as far as the leading parts are concerned, but more attention should be paid to the selection of the supporting cast. They also fall behind the American in staging brilliant spectacles in musical comedies.

23   *John W. Woodhead*, 37 Stanley Rd (aged 18), regular cinema-goer (6 times a month), preference – American films.
Comments: First of all I should like to thank the Films for the many entertaining hours I have spent watching them. I sincerely hope that the high rate of entertainment which has been reached in present-day Films will be maintained. Also, a word of praise for modern cinemas – their luxurious interiors certainly increase one's enjoyment of a show. *But must* we have:–

1 Worn-out film-plots?
2 Inane 'shorts'?
3 Depressing 'psychological', films.
4 Lady-patrons in front of us wearing eccentric head-gear?

24   *Roger H. Ashworth*, 36 Gilmour Rd (aged 18), regular cinema-goer (6 times a month), preference – British films.
Comments: I enjoy the musical interludes on the organ, but they should be longer. Historical films should be authentic in outline without too much divergence from the actual story. Dramatic films based on real life problems are preferable to much that is placed before the public to-day and in every case actors of real merit would command good audiences.

25   *Eric Baines*, 236 Folds Rd (aged 18), regular cinema-goer (5 times a month), preference – American films.
Comments: The English films in general are not 'a patch' on American films for variety and scenery. Question 7 [i.e. which of the following would you like more of in films?]: What more could people want than Action, Humour, and knowledge and Educational films? In my opinion the public go to a picture show to be interested and amused, and not to be depressed by Drama and Tragedy films. Some people, I believe, would like an occasional Religious or Political film.

26 *H. Lomax*, 25 Blake St (aged 18), regular cinema-goer (10 times a month), preference – American films.
Comments: The chief complaint I have to make concerning your programmes is the time spent on advertisements on the screen. This, I think, is a big fault as it wastes the time and patience of your patrons, besides giving your entertainment a certain cheapness, that you cannot stand the extra expense of giving us another picture and you fill in the time, and at the same time, earn a little money, by 'packing' in a lot of boring adverts. Your system of booking I find to be just the thing I have been waiting for, no queue in the cold or rain and a full programme assured. Your choice of pictures is also very excellent and I can honestly say I have never seen a poor picture at the Odeon since it was first opened, and I should like to thank you for getting them in Bolton so early. The organ interlude is marvellous.

27 *John Taylor*, 10 Wilmot St (aged 18), regular cinema-goer (8 times a month), preference – British films.
Comments: Dear sir, I would like to compliment you on the films you have had since your cinema opened. You have had real good common-sense films, not a lot of American ballyhoo, but good English films, especially *Victoria the Great*, a film that does anybody good to see.

28 *Harold Dunn*, 669 Tonge Moor Rd (aged 18), regular cinema-goer (24 times a month), preference – American films.
Comments: Dear sir, The trouble with most British pictures is that you can tell what they are going to do, by their actions, next. Give us a few more pictures like *The Road Back* and *All Quiet on the Western Front*. Also give us more of musical romances.

29 *A. Barton*, 11 Church Rd (aged 18), regular cinema-goer (5 times a month), preference – American films.
Comments: I think woman actresses get too hysterical. Also too many love scenes in otherwise good films. English pictures have too much Oxford accent in them whereas Americans use their own dialect.

30 *Alan Greaves*, 198 Ainsworth Lane (aged 18), regular cinema-goer (4 times a month), preference – American films.
Comments: None.

31 *Albert Horrocks*, 59 Arden St (aged 18), regular cinema-goer (4 times a month), preference – American films.
Comments: None.

32 *Ralph Denton*, 160 Folds Rd (aged 18), regular cinema-goer (10 times a month), preference – American films.
Comments: A love film is too sloppy at times and too soft. A Crime film wants more action, whereas a Western film has too much singing in it.

Sometimes I expect Gene Autry or Dick Foran to pull out a *throatspray* from their holsters instead of a gun. And at times like they are at present a spy film would be suitable.

33 *Walter Smith*, 38 Harold St (aged 18), regular cinema-goer (12 times a month), preference – American films.
Comments: What we want is more real life pictures like *Victoria the Great* but not necessarily historical.

34 *Robert Whiteside*, 6 Waggon Rd (aged 18), regular cinema-goer (12 times a month), preference – American films.
Comments: In my opinion films have good and bad points. Here is a bad one. When the picture commences the male star generally hates the female and yet at the end he falls for her. Why can't he go on hating them and instead of kissing her give her the best thrashing she ever had, yours truly, R. Whiteside,
Please excuse scribble, I'm supposed to be working.

35 *Fred Jolley*, 343 Manchester Rd, Westhoughton (aged 19), regular cinema-goer (12 times a month), preference – American films.
Comments: Dear sirs, you will note in question 5 [i.e. which are the best films?], I have answered American, but, if the British studios can produce more of the same calibre as *Farewell Again* and *Command Performance*, then it won't be long before I vote British, yours Fred Jolley.

36 *Walter Wilkinson*, 318 Deane Church Lane (aged 19), regular cinema-goer (8 times a month), preference – American films.
Comments: Films are the greatest boon of modern times. When one has a few idle hours one's thoughts usually go to the cinema.

37 *M. W. Smethurst*, 27 Leslie St, Tonge Moor (aged 19), regular cinema-goer (4–5 times a month), preference – American films.
Comments: None.

38 *Bernard Elmsley*, 'Peelholme', 374 Chorley Old Rd (aged 19), regular cinema-goer (6 times a month), preference – American films.
Comments: Mutiny on the Bounty was perhaps the finest film that I enjoyed. *After the Thin Man* in the American class was excellent. The enjoyment in these films was no doubt due to excellent acting, but the stories too were good. Cartoons are excellent if produced by W. Disney. A comfortable seat in a cinema is a good aid to the enjoyment of any film. The seating arrangements in Odeon cinemas are excellent.

39 *Thomas Trevor Fogg*, 66 Lakeside Avenue (aged 20), regular cinema-goer (8 times a month), preference – both the same.
Comments: I consider that all films, save those on purely educational subjects and comedy should have an interesting story, as it [is] this that

stays in the memory. In this the British Films excel. Next comes good scenery, a valuable asset to any picture. As good stories are found in drama, tragedies, love stories and crime, these are my favourites. Comedies are marred by involved plots, as these detract from the humour. I think the more lavish settings of American films balance the superior stories of the British.

40 *Mr E. Emmott*, 416 Bridgeman St (aged 20), regular cinema-goer (4 times a month), preference – American films.
Comments: Whilst there is no doubt that there have been a number of good British films, such as *Captain Blood, Mutiny on the Bounty* and *Victoria the Great*,[15] generally they lack action i.e. there are too many dull moments. Too many gangster films give the killers credit i.e. are apt to create a wrong impression.

41 *Mr Harold Collier*, 18 Grecian St (aged 20), regular cinema-goer (4–6 times a month), preference – American films.
Comments: Why don't we get more pictures like *The Good Earth* and *The Lost Horizon*, something which has a good story and most important of all, a good moral.

42 *Harold Walker*, 11 Regent St (aged 20), regular cinema-goer (10 times a month), preference – American films.
Comments: Regarding question 5 [i.e. which are the best films], I certainly am not a patriot, for in my opinion American films are far superior to British on every point: acting, direction, production, humour, yes, everything! (If I'm not mistaken, *you know it!*). As for your cheaply-made 'Quota' films – well –! Finally, I am eagerly awaiting the result of the combination of Hollywood and Our Gracie. Now what about question 7 [i.e. which of the following would you like more of in the films?] – I fail to see where either religion or politics should have any part whatever in films. In the same category I place 'people like you and I' and educational subjects for the simple reason that – we dont want what we know! or what we *should* know! no! first and last we want ENTERTAINMENT.

43 *Tom Lee*, 9 Market St, Atherton (aged 20), regular cinema-goer (12 times a month), preference – American films.
Comments: I think that your selection of pictures each week are quite good and I get a contrast each week, where in some 'Cinemas' you get the same morals each week, which certainly get stale. The 'Odeon' is quite good in both 'sound, seeing and selection', and is situated in a good position for people travelling from Atherton.

44 *H. Stevens*, 9 Rothwell St (aged 20), regular cinema-goer (10–12 times a month), preference – American films.
Comments: Could it not be possible for the organist to include in his

programmes more of the better known tunes? or alternately tunes which are in some way connected with the film showing or in films which are to be shown. Don't show in one programme 2 complete films for this is apt to lead to the majority of filmgoers becoming BORED with too much of one thing.

45 *Donald F. Atherton*, 259 Deane Rd (aged 20), regular cinema-goer (4–5–6 times a month), preference – American films.
Comments: The ideal length for a cinema programme is 2½ hours. I should like to see more British films and of a better quality. At present the only successful type of English picture is the musical comedy style of Jack Buchanan, Jack Hulbert and Jessie Matthews type. They produce too many historical films and too many old-fashioned films like *Lloyds of London*.[16] All advertising films should be done away with. I also prefer two big pictures to one big picture and a host of 'bits' such as travel talk, March of Time, miniature revues etc. We want more films in a light comedy vein with a dash of crime as well e.g. *Café Metropole*.

46 *Mr G. Harkinson*, 16 Moorside Avenue (aged 20), regular cinema-goer (4 times a month), preference – American films.
Comments: The criterion of the film world is *The Lives of a Bengal Lancer*, a film superbly acted full of action, colour and drama. A 'double length film' without a dull moment. Not enough use is made of our British scenery in English films. Unscientific 'cutting' of films is NOT appreciated by the modern critical public. Most of the so-called supporting films are a waste of time and money, why not have some short educative or travel film; why not boost our own country? The English film co.'s had better wake up before it is too late. We have the actors – but we lack U.S.A. technique and polish.

47 *Thomas Howcroft*, 2 Worsel St, Daubhill (aged 20), regular cinema-goer (6 times a month), preference – American films.
Comments: The main point about modern films seems to lie in the difference between English and American films. I think the trouble in the British studios lies in the inattention to detail, not only of background but of the 'small-part' actor. These people seem too stiff, as if they were members of a very inferior dramatic society. As an example take the landlady in Harry Roy's first picture *Everything is Rhythm* who spoke her lines as they were written and so lost all chance of being as a cinema-goer expects – natural.

48 *Samuel Hodson Jnr*, 206 Tonge Moore Rd (aged 20), regular cinema-goer (8 times a month), preference – American films.
Comments: I care more for the following types of films: *Lives of a Bengal Lancer, Mutiny on the Bounty, The Plainsman, Charge of the Light Brigade*. To each of these films there is a story – much more entertaining

to watch a film of this type than to see a lot of nincompoops in evening dress drinking champagne!

49   *R. W. Hurst*, 25 Merlin Grove (aged 21), regular cinema-goer (6 times a month), preference – American films.
Comments: Patriotic or no English films are deplorably behind their American competitors. Their slow-moving action, set off by the general excellence of diction, leaves a great deal to be desired. Speed up, you English producers, we have the talent as the American producers have shown us, why let them exploit it?

50   *David H. Profit*, 3 Lightburne Avenue (aged 21), regular cinema-goer (1–6 times a month), preference – American films.
Comments: Elephant Boy is undoubtedly the best film I have seen at the Odeon. I have not time, being a rather busy student, to go to the films every week. If I had I am afraid I should get tired of it. Frankly there seem to be very many more films of very poor quality than really good ones. Again when one sees a really first-rate film, the supporting programme is often poor. In these two respects, however, I have found the Odeon much better than other cinemas. I like to read the reviews of films before I see them and to know that if they are *worth* seeing. I thoroughly enjoy such films as *Lives of a Bengal Lancer, Mutiny on the Bounty, Under the Red Robe*, and though a different type, I thought *Love from a Stranger* excellent – in dialogue, photography and action. If there were more *really interesting* films like these I might become a regular 'once a week' Odeon enthusiast.

51   *James Brian O'Hara*, 916 Plodder Lane, Over Hulton (aged 21), regular cinema-goer (4 times a month), preference – 'good and bad of both'.
Comments: I consider that too many musicals are shown. As a rule there is no plot and little to interest. Films in general are too divorced from reality and thus the cinema instead of educating and uplifting the ordinary life of working people has degenerated into a mere mode of escape from man's day to day life. In a word it is pure 'dope' for the workers, deliberately encouraging lack of deep thinking.

52   *F. A. Wilcocks*, 38 Halk Lane, Hindley (aged 21), regular cinema-goer (4 times a month), preference – British films.
Comments: Films which are advertising stunts annoy most people that I know. I enjoy British films and most certainly object to American accents.

53   *Arthur H. Buckley*, 583 Bury Rd (aged 21), regular cinema-goer (8 times a month), preference – American films.
Comments: The chief fault with modern films is that the characters in the majority seem to exist in a land which is strangely different from our own, not the difference between America and England, more like between

Utopia and England. Lets have more ordinary films, true, even the ending. Show the joys and sufferings of the people who go to see the pictures and let's see a little more peace on the films and less of the American gangster killings, more humour and less tragedy, and *no* affectionate love scenes.

54 *H. Sewart*, 2 Ivy Rd (aged 21), regular cinema-goer (6 times a month), preference – American films.
Comments: Dear sir, I think the British films ought to buck up and provide something worth seeing. The American crime and detective films are very good, but if they would put more humour in them, they would be perfect, and I am sure they would increase the audience, yours sincerely, H. Sewart.

55 *James Glazebrook*, 53 York St (aged 21), regular cinema-goer ('as many as good films'), preference – American films.
Comments: The American companies govern the general run of films in the country; and why? Because they give the public what they want, not what *they* want to give us. You'll see everything from sport to thrills, acting to adventure in the American films and the sooner the British studios do the same, the sooner they'll be supported. The greater part of my cinema friends blame and condemn the British actors and actresses for their poor display; but to me this is not so, it is the directors who are at fault. For look how many British actors and actresses have made good in Hollywood. Yes! it's the directors who ought to take it on the chin, for their inability to handle the actors; the material; and wise money spending on their productions of which they have complete control. Admitting all this is really technical, it is in the minds of all who patronize your luxurious cinema.

56 *Jos. Douglas*, 12 French Grove, Darcy Lever (aged 21), regular cinema-goer (8 times a month), preference – American films.
Comments: Dear sir, I have had a bit of difference of opinion with a workmate who has never been to the Odeon or the Lido on account of the break in between pictures for the organ interval. Personally I like the organ and I think the majority of Bolton people are the same as myself and not like my workmate. Also I like a good Air picture like *Criminals of the Air* at the Theatre this week and from my knowledge of the Odeon programme, you have not had one, yours sincerely, Jos. Douglas.

57 *Mr J. Rigby*, 274 Wigan Rd, Deane (aged 21), regular cinema-goer (10–14 times a month), preference – American films.
Comments: A good variety of films has been shown lately at the Odeon. I think the William Powell style of film is very popular. *The Three Stooges* have a following but limited and many patrons are frankly disgusted at them. Historical films such as *Victoria the Great* are good – once in a while. 95% of patrons consider 'traveltalks' as mere fillups and a time

waste. English films as a rule are nicer to listen to and the photography is certainly good, but the technique of the actors is not up to American standards in most cases. The organ interlude is good and very popular but 4–5 minutes is not long enough.

58 *Norman Hodgson*, 278 Derby St (aged 22), regular cinema-goer (5–6 times a month), preference – American films.
Comments: My reason for coming to the Odeon is because I am a kind of scout for the family. When I get home my parents and the other children want to know what kind of pictures are on. I have been today to see *Stella Dallas*, result – all the family will go to see it this week. I think it is a mistake to put over a dud picture on every so often. For instance the Pictures shown at the Odeon the week before we had *Victoria the Great* was, you'll admit, very poor stuff. I, along with many friends I spoke to, could not sit the picture through. This has a tendency to make people wait till you have a good Picture before they come again. Now we have got the nicest and comfortablest cinema in the Odeon. All we want is good pictures.

59 *Joseph A. Laycock*, 23 Starcliffe St (aged 22), regular cinema-goer (6–7 times a month), preference – both the same.
Comments: I would rather see one *good* film than one average one and the rest of the programme filled in with *bits*. Not very keen on 'double feature' programmes, unless of widely varying types. Enjoy cartoons.

60 *Harold Johnstone*, 71 Bourne Avenue (aged 22), regular cinema-goer (8 times a month), preference – American films.
Comments: We have far too many films which glorify crime, spying, war etc. and have a bad influence on young people. Not enough films of Nature, Travel, Reality, Adventure, which tend to educate the film public in an interesting way. We have had some very good BRITISH films, and there is plenty of material in England itself for more good films.

61 *Mr D. Hall*, 47 Lena St (aged 22), regular cinema-goer (20 times a month), preference – American films.
Comments: The reason why I don't like British films is because they are altogether too dull, there's no action in them, and before they are half-way through, you are thoroughly fed up with the whole thing. The one being shown this week at the Odeon is the only British film I've seen that is anything like, and even then they have to try to copy the American picture.[17] Up to the present, I'm full of praise for the films being shown at the Odeon, apart from *Garden of Allah* which I think is awful.

62 *Cecil Whinham*, Chalet, Beehive, Lostock (aged 22), regular cinema-goer (10 times a month), preference – American films.
Comments: Having read the types of films, I think there is one or two types

been omitted which I would like to see: 1) Films of the Turf i.e.
Horseracing 2) Aviation.

63 *Mr G. Chapman*, 15 Holland St, Swinton, Manchester (aged 22),
regular cinema-goer (8 times a month), preference – American films.
Comments: I am taking the opportunity to debunk British films. For years,
famous American actors and actresses have been coming to this country to
make pictures with no better results than our own stars, while on the
other hand our stars have become famous over-night on going to
Hollywood, surely there are some of our film directors brainy enough to
see that the reason our films are second-rate is not the fault of the actors,
but the weakness of the story, which would take supermen to make even
the least bit interesting.

64 *Mr F. Cheetham*, 37 Crosby Rd, Bolton (aged 22), regular cinema-goer
(10 times a month), preference – American films.
Comments: Dear sir, My reason for saying American films are the best is
that to me watching ones I always feel as if the play on the screen is real
and I am there. I admit there has been one or two really good British ones.
(*But the Acting*) Why cannot our actors be real, and leave the 'old school
tie' talk out, speak natural. Believe me the best films we have made has
been spoiled by their silly 'Bia Jove' talk.

65 *George Livesey*, 108 Settle St (aged 23), regular cinema-goer (4 times a
month), preference – 'There's not much difference'.
Comments: There's a lot of sameness about pictures today, except from one
or two outstanding productions. A visit to the cinema, however, relieves
the monotony somewhat and helps one forget about worldly matters for an
hour or two.

66 *John Wilde*, 3 Grange Rd, Farnworth (aged 23), regular cinema-goer
(4 times a month), preference – American films.
Comments: Having good musical taste, I always prefer a musical film, a
film easy to watch and easy to listen to, along with a definite story of
romance enhanced by good music. The best film I have seen was *The
Moonlight Sonata* because it gave me a glimpse into the life of one of the
world's most brilliant pianists, which hitherto I should never have been
afforded.[18]

67 *Arthur T. Baker*, 203 Blackburn Rd, Egerton (aged 23), regular
cinema-goer (4–5 times a month), preference – American films.
Comments: None.

68 *Eric H. Hubbard*, 21 Ainsworth Rd, Little Lever (aged 23), regular
cinema-goer (4 times a month), preference – American films.
Comments: Too many third rate films being shown. All films should be
passed by the censor for their merits and not on their morality.

69 *Albert Bullough*, 193 New Brook Rd (aged 23), regular cinema-goer (4–5 times a month), preference – American films.
Comments: If we must have crime pictures, why can't we have some where the murderer is not so plainly known to the audience before the picture is twenty minutes old. Let's have some pleasant films, such as *The Thin Man*, where everybody came away feeling very pleased with each other. Let's have some really GOOD British films.

70 *Frank Marsh*, 28 Furness Avenue (aged 23), regular cinema-goer (3 times a month), preference – British films.
Comments: None.

71 *Robert Andrew Shaw*, 20 Alice St (aged 23), regular cinema-goer (6 times a month), preference – American films.
Comments: Dear sirs, First of all I should like to make a complaint i.e. First your films lately have been tiring and boring, simply because there is no action until late on in the picture. I should like to praise you on this week's picture *Gangway*, which I think is excellent, yours truly, R. A. Shaw. P.S. Hoping there is no ill-feeling.

72 *William Mannion*, 16 Philip St (aged 24), regular cinema-goer (10 times a month), preference – American films.
Comments: Our British pictures, it is sad to say, lack a great deal of polish. The good ones are few and far between. We will take, for instance, *Stella Dallas* besides good character acting on all sides, there was an equal amount of humour to hold one's interest. A British version would be either one or the other short of effort in production.

73 *Neville Douglas*, 3 Cobham Avenue (aged 24), regular cinema-goer (8 times a month), preference – American films.
Comments: Dear sirs, Maybe you have noticed I voted American films best? The reason really is I hate to hear an 'American gangster' with an Oxford accent and we get plenty in English pictures. The accent is noticeable in any foreign picture they take. Another thing, why do we want to see war on the screen, do we not read enough in the papers. For myself I enjoy them but there are old people too, who go to the pictures. Do they want reminding how their sons or husbands left them. Give us good comedians and we will appreciate this. Hoping there are others of the same opinion.

74 *Bernard Mitchell*, 26 Cambridge Rd, Lostock (aged 24), regular cinema-goer (4 times a month), preference – American films.
Comments: Although favouring the American films in theme, settings, music, and action, I deplore the American nasal drawl and slang words; give me a clear, clean and honest British voice anytime. One point that I do not like is the filming of 'close-ups'; to me it seems a mockery;

especially, when I hear the ribald laughter which accompanies such showing.

75 *James Pover*, 5 Bury St (aged 24), regular cinema-goer (8 times a month) preference – 'American films are still the better, English films are improving though.'
Comments: I honestly think you do your best to satisfy every taste for films as you always vary, but I think that English films have *still* a long way to go to satisfy as do the majority of American, although they are improving, I doubt whether anyone would prefer them.

76 *Harry Boylan*, 105 Valletts Lane, Smithills (aged 24), regular cinema-goer (12 times a month), preference – American films.
Comments: Well first of all, I have just seen *Gangway*. On the whole, it is a very good picture with a good story behind it and good clean humour, but I did not like the part in the American Bar. All that shooting which was on did not lead to anything and what's more, no one seemed to get hurt and I heard too much of Rod, Gat and McCoy, too much American slang.

77 *Harry Singleton*, 15 Keswick St (aged 24), regular cinema-goer (10 times a month), preference – American films.
Comments: More films like *Ben Hur, Victoria the Great, The Charge of the Light Brigade* and so on. Not 'Crime Films'. I know what is going to happen. *Musical Romance* are OK because they're always different in some way or other. You get *Talented Singers, Beautiful things* and *Colour*. Nobody wants war, that is why I haven't picked *War Films*. They're bad for youth that have an imagination. *Travel and Adventure* suit. They keep you interested. *Cartoons* are well liked by everyone. Old and Young. I don't like *love stories* because there's always a lot of kissing and crying. Who wants that? *Westerns* are impossible, such as a horse going into a blazing building and setting its master free, *Spy Films* are OK because you get brains and wit.

78 *Mr William Ramsden*, 5 Hough Lane, Eagley (aged 24), regular cinema-goer (12 times a month), preference – American films.
Comments: On comparing British with American films, I feel that on average the Americans are the best. The dialogue in British films is often just an recitation instead of being spoken realistically as in the American. The action in the British productions is slow and dull (particularly murder mysteries). Now in American, the action is always fast and furious and British comedies are more boring than funny. One good point in favour of the British films is the ability in portraying historic events, also pictures featuring dance bands and radio artists, now often seen, are of a higher standard than ever. This is my candid opinion which can be changed only by some first class British films which I hope to see in the near future. William Ramsden.

79   *W. E. Pugh*, c/o 236 Turton Rd, Bradshaw (aged 25), regular cinema-goer (8 times a month), preference – 'they vary'.
Comments: One of the items I enjoy when I go to the cinema is 'Traveltalks'. I should like to see them more regular, as I think they are an education to everybody! One of the best Films that I have seen for some time was *Maytime*. The singing and scenery was outstanding. I should like to see more of that type and I will say here that Jeanette Macdonald is one of my favourite stars. It is hard to say which are the best Films, British or American. America rather overdo their Films when it comes to shooting etc. With regard to the Detective Films some of them are not very true to life, they find the clues too easily. I am speaking from experience of that work in real life.

80   *John Miller*, 18 Clough St (aged 25), regular cinema-goer (4 times a month), preference – British films.
Comments: I think the picture this week was very good and so much in reality.

81   *Eric Barlow*, 123 Marton Avenue (aged 25), regular cinema-goer (8–10 times a month), preference – American films.
Comments: My Man Godfrey, The Lost Horizon, The Narrow Corner, The Go-Getter and *Mutiny on the Bounty* are films which have left pleasant memories and sustained my support of film theatres. The little bit of a man's philosophy plus the favourite actors has made for complete satisfaction. The fare provided by the above has left food for thought long after the theatre has been left. The spaciousness and beautiful decoration of our local Odeon cinema are also much appreciated.

82   *Frederick B. Longmill*, 'Holmehead', Longsight, Harwood (aged 25), regular cinema-goer (8 times a month), preference – American films.
Comments: The film *Victoria the Great* type is needed more. Cut out this cheap slapstick comedy stuff, also let us have less Gangster pictures and so provide for the younger generation as well as the Blood-thirsty.

83   *John Carlton Greenhalgh*, 31 Haworth St (aged 25), regular cinema-goer (8 times a month), preference – American films.
Comments: None.

84   *Arthur Ball*, 31 Raby St (aged 25), regular cinema-goer (4 times a month), preference – American films.
Comments: I think that a lot of the so called comedies of today are neither educational or entertaining, so why not substitute films with an educational value, say, on the lines of Traveltalks. Incidentally I think that Traveltalks are first class entertainment and I look forward to them when visiting the Odeon.

85 *George Barber*, 9 Bottom o'th'Moor, Harwood (aged 25), regular cinema-goer (10–12 times a month), preference – American films.
Comments: I have nothing else to say beyond that the Odeon is a smart place and uptodate and pictures good taste.

86 *E. A. Coldbreath*, 'Fern Lea', 43 Seedley Rd, Salford (aged 26), regular cinema-goer (6 times a month), preference – American films.
Comments: Why do English producers seem afraid to spend money on backgrounds to their films. Why not follow on the lines of the M.G.M. It would show the good qualities of a few of our own Film Stars.

87 *Reginald Grant*, 175 Kay St (aged 26), regular cinema-goer (6 times a month), preference – American films.
Comments: Films presented to the public are without doubt the most universally popular form of entertainment of the present day. Motion Picture Art is 200% better than say even a few years ago and the advent of talking apparatus is certainly becoming the main factor in the dearth of the provincial Music Hall. In my opinion the only improvement for the sustenance of this popularity is not so much in the production of films as the manner in which a programme is submitted on the Cinema Screen. News Reels are of course indispensable. If the fare in this type of film is second hand or old it is a sure method of losing patrons. The rest of the programme should be one good long film instead of dreadful 'bits and bobs'. Yes, indeed, the manager who presents this type of programme is the one who will always draw the crowds and money.

88 *Mr W. Turner*, 4 Curzon Rd (aged 26), regular cinema-goer (8 times a month), preference – American films.
Comments: English Pictures, drama and comedy lack in the background effects, acting too slow, but actors the very best.

89 *Mr George Winstanley*, 3 Blackledge St (aged 27), regular cinema-goer (20 times a month), preference – British films.
Comments: First of all a Cinema is a place mostly to entertain youngish people and I myself think that it keeps young people from loitering on the streets. I myself think that there is too much praise for some of these stars, and it makes them get swell headed. What we want is different faces, not just one or two heart throbs. Mr. Winstanley.

90 *Edward Critchley*, 159 Mayor St (aged 27), regular cinema-goer (4 times a month), preference – American films.
Comments: 'Films for the Public'. This must be the thought in the mind of many a Cinema Manager. He *must* please his public. In order to do this I would say 'Don't show British pictures merely because they are British; Give your public the best. That is the only way to draw the public – and keep them!'

91 *Mr A. Leicester*, 18 Greenway, Tonge Moor (aged 28), regular cinema-goer (6 times a month), preference – American films.
Comments: A film should be 100% entertainment value containing good clever wit and humour, drama and tragedy and a little sentiment, should have good photographic value and should enact scenes possible to happen to everyday people.

92 *Richard Harris*, 28 Abingdon Rd (aged 29), regular cinema-goer (8 times a month), preference – American films.
Comments: The first choice goes to films like *A Star is Born*. In my opinion this was a credit to the producer. I saw the film twice (about 8 weeks ago at the Odeon Cardiff and last week but one at the Odeon, Bolton), and I could see it again and enjoy it. It had all that was necessary to make it a good film, drama, tragedy and humour, all combined with good acting. R. Harris.

93 *G. Haslam*, 'Prior's Lea', 105 Smithills Dean Rd (aged 29), regular cinema-goer (4–5 times a month), preference – '100% British'.
Comments: Dear sir, I should like to see more films like you have had this last four or five weeks, something real and family like, not silly and sloppy stuff, which are mostly American. Films of everyday happenings and not those that will never happen and never will. A few on the style of *A Star is Born* and some of Charles Laughton's. And I think it has made things sound much better with the organ playing in the interval. From a picturegoer.

94 *Samuel Collier*, 236 Walkden Rd, Worsley (aged 29), regular cinema-goer (6 times a month), preference – American films.
Comments: American films seem to fit the various stars into the best stories. The British films seem to try to make a story round a star's personality. Only in films based on historical facts do they seem to have any theme whatsoever. Others seem to be all 'farces' or stage plays. American films attach great importance to minor details which so often can make or mar a film. They seem to try to cater more for the public, and show a star's versatility. They deal more to real facts, especially in 'gangster' pictures, so real that it is imperative to use phrases such as 'Any character in this picture is fictitious and do not intentionally apply to any living human.' Even so, they depict the facts which are absolutely genuine and true. My reason for placing 'more religion' into first place, was that for everything combined, my favourite pictures were *San Francisco – Mother's Boy*. My poorest picture that I can remember was *Gangway*, in other words JESSIE MATTHEWS.

95 *A. G. Taylor*, 115 Deansgate (aged 29), regular cinema-goer (5–6 times a month), preference – American films.
Comments: Question 16: Never go near sob-stuff, 'mighty acting' or

westerns. Question 7: Surely it is because the American producers, leave out religion, politics, education, ordinary folk and the 'aristocracy' of the silent days, that makes modern films to enjoyable. No, I dont ask for any more than a never ending stream of Astaire/Rogers, Bill Powell, Loy, Lombard, Loretta Young, etc. – in fact the type of film that a BRITISH studio has never yet produced.

96 P. C. Howcroft, 4 Bushell St, Deane (aged 29), regular cinema-goer (4–8 times a month), preference – British.
Comments: Sir, I candidly wish that more thought could be given to creating a good mood in which to receive the feature film by showing a pleasant cartoon or comedy of sensible proportions. The double feature (or less) programme is so apt to become boring and so spoil a night's rest and enjoyment, which, after all, is what we desire and pay for. Just recently, a good number of films from the U.S.A. have had a tendency to underestimate our intelligence by giving events or action terribly distorted beyond good judgment. e.g. gratis. Boyer's film *History is Made At Night*, giving instructions to captain, proceed full speed through fog, irrespective of humanity (just one of many). Boring?!

97 Arthur Jones, 6 Churchtown Avenue (aged 30), regular cinema-goer (6 times a month), preference – American. 'British films lack the stars and producers'.
Comments: Films founded on History or Adventure of Men and Women who will live forever and stars who by playing these parts bring to the screen the people whose lives we would never have known and whose Adventures and Lives have built Empires and made the World better for mankind. Films like *Rhodes of Africa, Ben Hur, Victoria the Great, Camille, Henry the Eighth, Christina* and *Lives of a Bengal Lancer*.[19]

98 E. V. Casey, 'Somerville', Wigan Rd (aged 30), regular cinema-goer (4 times a month), preference – both the same.
Comments: Principal pictures properly made do not need supporting by others of equal length but of inferior quality. Instead I would always like to see the programme completed by 4 or 5 'shorts' bringing some of the many wonderful things in the world to the screen; giving shots of news events from many countries; and when possible that rarity among films, the short comedy which is really funny and is a very long way from being extremely ridiculous. I think that simple announcements with detail of producer, 'stars' etc. are much more attractive than the impossible 'trailers' which often condemn what turns out to be a good picture.

99 Ledward, 430 Manchester Rd, Walkden (aged 30), regular cinema-goer (3 times a month), preference – American films.
Comments: I should like to see more films based on English Life and History, past and present. I think films with stories written round our

industries or colonies would be popular. I dislike super sentimental sob films. We could do with more *good* English films.

100   *John Ward*, 46 Cross Ormrod St (aged 30), regular cinema-goer (4 times a month), preference – American films.
Comments: Having visited the Odeon every week, since the opening, I wish to say that the choice of films for the public entertainment has been performed with great credit to the ones concerned. Although I select American films as the best, I must say that the Odeon has presented three excellent British films in name: *Victoria the Great, Action for Slander* and *Gangway.*

101   *Frank Wadsworth*, 20 Wardle St, Houlgh (aged 30), regular cinema-goer (8 times a month), preference – 'American for spectacular, British for talking.'
Comments: Would like to have more British Drama or Tragedy i.e. *Action for Slander*, though not of a 'high standard'. Would like to see *more spectacular* British pictures equal to American standard, but not to copy American slang and no inebriated hero roles acted like William Powell. A tip top D. and T. picture can keep me interested and absorbed and I do not mind if they are beyond real life possibility. As a pleasant change, Musical Romance is the ideal especially when one feels tired and jaded and *Maytime* is the standard required.

102   *James Lucas*, 26 Parkfield Avenue, Farnworth (aged 31), regular cinema-goer (12 times a month), preference – American films.
Comments: In my own opinion the quality of films being shown universally today compares very unfavourably with the films shown a few years ago, especially in the case of good musicals. How these have slumped in comparison with such as 1) *Sunny* starring the late Marilyn Miller or 2) *Viennese Nights* starring one of the finest casts I have seen or ever hope to see, its gorgeous scenes and wonderful melodies make it unforgettable. If only we could have more of these, instead of the weak musicals we are getting to-day which you have forgot all about in a week or so (O yes it is true).

103   *Joseph Morton Creighton*, 311 Lever St. (aged 31), regular cinema-goer (4 times a month), preference – American films.
Comments: A Star is Born: One of the best Pictures I have ever seen – to the management I say thanks a million. *Stella Dallas* – Another Great Show all the best to you and *keep it up*. Hubert Selby at the Wonderful Organ – OK.

104   *Douglas Barnett*, 210 Greenmount Lane (aged 32), regular cinema-goer (4 times a month), preference – 'impossible to generalize'.
Comments: A. Praise:– The individual acting for the most part is very good – indeed frequently the only saving grace of a film.

B. Complaint:– 1) Lack of imaginative and mature treatment of the story in a film medium: directors must forget all about the stage.

        2) *Very* poor stories in fiction films: usually because of bad psychology, rather than of improbable situations.

        3) When I go to a cinema, I do not like wasting time (a) listening to an organ (b) watching witless and badly photographed advertisements of proprietary articles c) having the next week's pictures spoilt for me by injudiciously chosen snippets in a 'trailer'.

        4) Finally, it gives me no pleasure to be deafened by a loud speaker which must evidently be operated by someone who is either tone-deaf or stone-deaf!

105 *Joseph H. Fullam*, 71 Swan Lane (aged 32), regular cinema-goer (10 times a month), preference – 'Little comparison'.
Comments: In my opinion many films are too long drawn out resulting in boredom, thus losing in entertainment values. Further when scenes are depicted of working class life, they are generally portrayed as a lot of buffoons, without manners or understanding, whilst historical or political films are usually a perversion of the truth. Let us by all means have entertainment of a light character with plenty of humour, so that after a monotonous day's work, everyone can be made to feel happier and brighter.

106 *Mr R. Gorton*, 69 Division St, Great Lever (aged 32), regular cinema-goer (4 times a month), preference – American films.
Comments: I like the Films – *A Star is Born, I Promise to Pay, History Is Made At Night, Action for Slander, Love from a Stranger.*

107 *Mr B. Bentham*, 219 Tonge Moor Rd (aged 33), regular cinema-goer (4 times a month), preference – American films.
Comments: None.

108 *John Crook*, 964 St Helen's Rd (aged 34), regular cinema-goer (12–16 times a month), preference – American films.
Comments: Musical Comedy Films apart from popularizing a tune or two lack a sincere plot and finish on a flat note. Historical Films are rather overdone and offer too much scope for many absurd mistakes in speech and accent. Political Films are of no interest to Industrial Workers. Dance Bands have no Box Office attractions; Radio is sufficient experience. Films of Local appeal: *Mutiny on the Bounty, Smiling Through, Lost Horizon*, all films starring William Powell, *The G-Men*, Shirley Temple. Something of Everything with Action as foundation.

109   *Mr E. Dalley*, c/o 74 Parrot St (aged 34), regular cinema-goer (12 times a month), preference – American films.
Comments: Drama and Tragedy appeals to general public. American Films are far superior and give a quicker action. A good second picture gives patrons better satisfaction and is far better than two or three 'make-ups', with the result that a real good 'Top Picture' loses its real value to manager and Theatre.

110   *Mr J. Fletcher*, 45 Walker Avenue (aged 35), regular cinema-goer (6–8 times a month), preference – American films.
Comments: The pictures I like are those comprising Good acting and good speaking (English), Good photography – nice scenes and settings, both indoor and outdoor. A feasible story running through and if musical a 'catchy' melody. *Examples of Pictures I prefer: Victoria the Great, Charge of the Light Brigade, Lloyds of London, Mutiny of the Bounty,*[20] *A Star is Born, Cafe Metropole*, something sensible and interesting.

111   *Walter Hurst*, 17 Bowness Rd (aged 35), regular cinema-goer (8 times a month), preference – British films.
Comments: I prefer historical pictures such as *Victoria the Great, Charge of the Light Brigade, White Angel*. They keep you interested. I like pictures such as Jessie Matthews puts before us. They make you feel comfortable and at home and I like pictures with a little tragedy, such as is being shown, *Stella Dallas*, that brings a tear to the eye. They make you forget everything.

112   *J. G. Whalley*, 67 Lonsdale Rd (aged 35), regular cinema-goer (4–5 times a month), preference – American films.
Comments: My opinion is that much more pace and action should be put into films. I go to the cinema to be entertained. I do not want to know who the dresses were by, who made the screenplay and so on. I think far too much time is wasted on this. What would be an advantage is give the names of the stars and all people who took certain parts *after* the film.

113   *Mr A. F. Macalister*, 70 Chorley Old Rd (aged 36), regular cinema-goer (8–9 times a month), preference – American films.
Comments: The first essential of a Good Picture is that it must be interesting, gripping – something that will make one laugh or cry at times; a story that enables folk to forget for an hour or so the worries and cares of existence. To make a film merely interesting is not enough. People go to school or the lecture theatre to be educated but to the cinema to be amused. One special request – Please don't show so many films advertizing proprietary articles. Many people find them most irritating.

114   *William Ward*, 25 Highfield Rd. Smithills (aged 36), regular cinema-goer (8 times a month), preference – American films.

Comments: 1) Crime 2) Musical Romance. The films I have chosen first appeal to me, because of the exercise of brain in trying to expose the correct solution in anticipation, and of course that morbid curiosity in all of us. My next preference is for that relaxation which people need after a day's work. An excursion into that world of make-believe which we each have a longing to explore but seldom do. It is also a pleasing sense of 'well being' to be amused.

115 *Arthur Wallwork*, Drywood Hall, Worsley, Manchester (aged 37), regular cinema-goer (6–8 times a month), preference – British films.
Comments: The play's the thing or so they say
And so we must have players.
All stars are stars by night and day,
If they wish to be stayers.
They start the film. They end it too.
But why? Oh why? The whole film through
Must patrons find nought else to do
But watch their bright and glorious star.
With chorus dim and distant far
In very sooth a film. Oh nay.
That, kind sir, is not a play.

116 *C. V. Bolton, FSMC*, 49A Leigh Rd, Leigh (aged 37), regular cinema-goer (5 times a month), preference – British films.
Comments: I do not like to see too many *Coming Shortlys* or too much time given to announcements for next month. I LIKE SENSIBLE FILMS NOT FAR, FAR AWAY FILMS. TRUTHFUL FILMS.

117 *Mr H. Moores*, 36 Craddock St, (aged 37), regular cinema-goer (8 times a month), preference – American films.
Comments: I would much prefer to see one long film rather than two short films and would be much obliged if the women would refrain from gossiping during the showing of the film.

118 *John Ashton*, 2 Carlton Place (aged 37), regular cinema-goer (4 times a month), preference – both the same.
Comments: I have no faults to find with any of the Picture Shows at the Odeon with regards Acting and Steadiness.

119 *Mr Joseph Bateson* 21 Exeter Avenue (aged 38), regular cinema-goer (4 times a month), preference – British films.
Comments: Please give us more British films and less, yankee doodle pip.

120 *Harold Kershaw*, Fleece Hotel, Bolton (aged 38), regular cinema-goer (12 times a month), preference – British films.
Comments: Praise.

121 *Mr Daniel Wynn*, 10 Leach St (aged 38), regular cinema-goer (8 times a month) preference – American films.
Comments: P.S. I like American Pictures because they always seem to end in a proper manner, I mean as an average person would expect it. They [indecipherable] to let themselves go properly when they are acting and they seem to have no end of scenery for making them, yours truly, Daniel Wynn.

122 *Mr E. Blackburn*, 34 Pleasant St (aged 38), regular cinema-goer (8–10 times a month), preference – American films.
Comments: American musical comedies are invariably very well set out with Good Background and Good Songs. A good Detective Mystery always appeals to me. British Pictures usually fail to come up to standard in the scenery and setting.

123 *Walter Ackroyd*, 116 Crompton Way (aged 38), regular cinema-goer (10 times a month), preference – American films.
Comments: We need more entertainment. Our Young when in British films are behind American. Not sufficient care taken about small parts. A good film can be shown twice in preference to a poor one – suggest 'top films' of one year would succeed on second showing. News and travel essential to every programme. A cinema succeeds by its programmes and people will always pay for the best.

124 *John Turner*, Vulcan Hotel, Great Moor St, Bolton (aged 39), regular cinema-goer (4–5 times a month), preference – both the same.
Comments: What we want is more pictures like *A Star is Born, Queen Victoria the Great* etc. But I have never missed coming to the 'Odeon' since the opening date; and I am quite satisfied with your programmes yet.

125 *E. Smith*, 23 Caledonia St (aged 39), regular cinema-goer (8 times a month), preference – American films.
Comments: None.

126 *William Rostron*, 31 Lavender Rd, Farnworth (aged 40), regular cinema-goer (12 times a month), preference – American films.
Comments: Sir, being a person who is always mixing with the picturegoers in general, I hear different opinions, but never a good opinion of the travel and adventure films. Public opinion seems to be for the 3 first numbered on the opposite page, preference being for drama and tragedy, which has some humour with it.

127 *Frank Poyner*, 58 Hulton Avenue, Little Hulton (aged 40), regular cinema-goer (7–8 times a month), preference – American films.
Comments: I would like more films similar to that of *Mutiny on the Bounty* starring Charles Laughton.

128 *Mr J. Parkinson*, 36 Walter St (aged 40), regular cinema-goer (8 times a month), preference – both similar.
Comments: My opinion regarding films is that there should be less crime and war picture and more of present day life pictures, of home life and a working man's daily life mixed in with a working man's variety. People want to forget about war, so why advertize it by showing films, but I would like to see a little education shown on films regarding gas masks etc. in event of war.

129 *L. Brooks*, 42 Bradford St, Haulgh (aged 40), regular cinema-goer (8 times a month), preference – both the same.
Comments: Pictures like *Stella Dallas* are a treat to enjoy. We would like more of them.

130 *George Edgar Shuttleworth*, 30 Chorley Rd, Swinton (aged 40), regular cinema-goer (2 times a month), preference – British films.
Comments: In my opinion the quality of *good films* is rapidly improving. I would like to see more films lasting say 2 hours, thus cutting out the necessity for padding. *My Ideal Programme*. NEWS. SHORT COMEDY – CARTOON – OR ORGAN. FULL LENGTH FILM. I would like to see more stories taken from English Literature, such as DAVID COPPERFIELD etc.

131 *William K. Collison*, 80 Green Lane (aged 40), regular cinema-goer (4 times a month), preference – British films.
Comments: Owing to the unsettled state of the world generally and the morbid and depressing news gleaned from daily papers, we require bright musical films and interesting travel. Crime and war pictures make one feel depressed whilst bright musical films make one feel that an hour at the cinema has been well spent and a tonic.

132 *Mr and Mrs Inglis*, 'Braeside', Bottom o'th'Moor, Bolton (aged 40), regular cinema-goers (4 times a month), preferences – British films.
Comments: Generally speaking there is a lot of room for improvement in the quality of the short films shown. We have seen some which are really an insult to one's intelligence, recent examples of these being Charlie Chase's Personality Bell film and a Roman Youth's Marriage Law. We would like to hear more of your excellent organ.

133 *Mrs James Fairhurst*, 19 Anson St (aged 40), regular cinema-goer (4–5 times a month), preference – both the same.
Comments: We think the average films you have already presented in Bolton have been of a very high standard and we have thoroughly enjoyed them. Yours respectfully, Mr and Mrs Fairhurst.

134 *Joseph Herbert Fogg*, 45 Abingdon St, Tonge Park (aged 40), regular

cinema-goer (4 times a month), preference – 'British for me'.

Comments I have a preference for the British films not merely because I am British but because the speech is so audible. Patrons must, as I do, miss quite a lot of Americanisms put over, partly because of their 'slang' and partly because there is too much speed of speech. Your recent *Action for Slander* is typically the style of film which holds my interest, and I feel that I have not wasted the evening. Let us see pictures which we can clearly understand, a good and thrilling story, and above all clearly spoken, which to me is essential to the picturegoer's enjoyment. I hate to leave a cinema with the word 'Trash' on my lips.

135   *H. S. Brown (Mr)*, 57 Church St (aged 40), regular cinema-goer (8–10 times a month), preference – American films.
Comments: The British film *Who's Your Lady Friend?* with Vic Oliver was as good, in my opinion, as any American film of the same type, but taken on the average the American Films are the best. They make the characters so real and life like, until you lose that sense you have of somebody just 'acting', as in lots of British films, and the absence of the 'Oxford accent' brings them more on working people's level.

136   *John Dootson*, 43 Grant St (aged 41), regular cinema-goer (12 times a month), preference – American films.
Comments: My reason for naming Musicals for my first choice is because I come across a good deal of people who are in the same opinion as myself. Musicals for instance always gives something interesting. I mean there never seems to be a dull moment when I see one, noting this week a speciality *Gangway*. So more musicals, from a regular attender.

137   *George Thomson*, 56 Smethurst Lane (aged 43), regular cinema-goer (4 times a month), preference – American films.
Comments: Good films help one to forget the workaday world. Not that the workaday world is uninteresting. Mind must have change and the films always give a mental balance if you choose wisely your subjects. Like Sandy Powell, use your head.

138   *Noel Charnley*, 91 High St (aged 44), regular cinema-goer (12 times a month), preference – American films.
Comments: I don't wish to know all the particulars of who made the film, dress designers, photography, sound production, continuity etc. I don't like wise-cracking Americans, who talk down their noses. I dislike sordid films and operating theatres. I hate the disgusting habit of spitting which American films often show. We want films with action, some love, beautiful scenery, a little mystery, beautiful women in beautiful gowns.

139   *F. Seddon*, 142 Deansgate (aged 44), regular cinema-goer (4 times a month), preference – British films.

Comments: The only complaint I have are adverts being shown. I might add here, you have the most comfortable Cinema in town, and if your programme as an experiment was changed, I and my wife would certainly visit you twice weekly.[21]

140 *Mr F. Pollitt*, 46 Carlton Rd (aged 45), regular cinema-goer (8 times a year), preference – American films.
Comments: Give us more of the pictures type *Three Smart Girls*, *Dodsworth*, with that insight into the little domestic scenes which happen in our own lives. Odd spots of physical jerks from Pa in the bedroom. Little domestic squabbles etc.

141 *F. H. Wilcocks*, 38 Hall Lane, Hindley (aged 45), regular cinema-goer (4 times a month), preference – British films.
Comments: Less advertising.

142 *Mr S. Weilding*, 78 Eustace St (aged 45), regular cinema-goer (4 times a month), preference – British films.
Comments: I think that British films are coming more into line, and are much easier to follow than American ones.

143 *G. A. Lloyd*, 39 Churchgate (aged 45), regular cinema-goer (5 times a month), preference – both the same.
Comments: No organ please. We get enough music with a 'tin-enough-sound' without an interlude.

144 *L. Adamson* 40 Welbeck Rd (middle age), regular cinema-goer (8 times a month), preference – American films.
Comments: The reason I have put *best* for American films. They are *brighter* and more perfect technique, than the British. Only a very few British are really good in my opinion.

145 *Mr J. S. Almond*, 9 Maple Avenue (aged 45), regular cinema-goer (4 times a month), preference – 'no choice.'
Comments: My biggest complaint is that on most of the big films, the large cast is generally reeled off on one long list. The audience, having no idea as to what the parts in the film are, are often at a loss, at the end of the picture, as to who has played these several parts. Couldnt the principal characters be given pictorially at the beginning?

146 *E. Kippax*, 18 Callis Rd, Deane (aged 45), regular cinema-goer (8 times a month), preference – both the same.
Comments: Music because it is the most beautiful on earth, along with Nature, beautiful people and scenery, also some humour. Natural things, because they are every day life, not far fetched. History because you get some knowledge knocked into you.

147 *Mr G. Gardiner*, Beaumonds Way, Rochdale (aged 46), regular

cinema-goer (6 times a month), preference – British films.
Comments: Most films assume a very low standard of intelligence. In fact many are an insult to the average mentality.

148 *Walter Rowley*, 178 Hamel St, Higher Swan Lane (aged 46), regular cinema-goer (8 times a month), preference – both the same.
Comments: I may say I have been to a few Picture Places in my time. But I find your Cinema is the one I prefer for comfort and good pictures. I may say I have a son, Doorman at one of your Cinemas, it is at Cosby, Northants. His name is Walter Rowley.

149 *Norman Jackson*, 5 Outwood Grove, Astley Bridge (aged 47), regular cinema-goer (4 times a month), preference – American films.
Comments: Sir, my opinion about the Films I have chosen [i.e. Musical romance, Travel and adventure, Society comedies, Slapstick comedies, Historical and Cartoons] is for the younger people. Of which they would in my opinion be more satisfied in seeing your Films. For the comfortable seats you can't improve, and your attendants are very obliging. Secondly, Those that I have missed out [Crime, Western, War, Spying, Drama and Tragedy, Love stories, Nature and Reality], people take it to heart, people get destructive enough without showing them on the Films.

150 *Percy Woodcock*, 99 Queensgate (aged 47), regular cinema-goer (12 times a month), preference – British films.
Comments: I would like to see longer news pictures and current events. Also coloured cartoons.

151 *W. T. Bickley*, 14 Crawford St (aged 47), regular cinema-goer (6 times a month), preference – American films.
Comments: I would like to make a Film that can happen and does happen in everyday life, such as *Madame X*.

152 *R. Rostron*, 178 Marland Hall Lane (aged 48), regular cinema-goer (3–4–5 times a month), preference – both the same.
Comments: A picture like *Stella Dallas* which you show this week is a credit to the Film Industry. At the present time, Drama and Tragedy pictures spoiled (in my opinion) are over done by showing of much press machinery, shouting etc. Society Comedies are another which is overdone, by far too much dancing and leg show, also follow my leader sort of game with the crowd. Most pictures of today do not carry a sort of 'Centre Focus', a laugh and a good ending. Both British and American.

153 *William F. Harwood*, 15 Penarth Rd, (aged 48), regular cinema-goer (8–10 times a month), preference – 'American with British actors.'
Comments: The films shown at this Theatre have been (with one or two exceptions) of a very high standard, judging by the comments I hear on leaving after the performance. Coloured Travel pictures and Technicolor

Comedies supporting a good Musical Romance or Historical Film is a good night's entertainment. American Racketeering and too much gunplay has not appeal for the regular cinema-goer, (*Knight Without Armour* was an exceptionally good film, also *Victoria the Great*) and *Action for Slander* was spoiled by some bad acting. Generally speaking people are satisfied and are getting their money's worth.

154 *Mr M. Pearson*, 22 Hindley St, Farnworth (aged 50), regular cinema-goer (6 times a month), preference – American films.
Comments: My candid opinion of the films, American (75 per cent) of your shows, up to the present time, is 'very good', and never yet have I heard a single complaint of any film, the management before its patrons. Yours faithfully, Mr M. Pearson.

155 *A. Fleet*, Palatine Club, Waterfoot, (aged 50), regular cinema-goer (6–8 times a month), preference – British films.
Comments: Films generally very good at Odeon but more such as *Ben Hur*, *Mutiny on Bounty*, *Cavalcade* etc. would draw better. Less Tinned Music when not in piece. Pictures that are restful but interesting, an advantage. More detail in Newsreel welcome. More adverts in outer districts either papers or posters. [Indecipherable] as many patrons come from outside districts as from the Borough? I personally visit the Odeon, Bolton, every Thursday if haven't seen picture before. I certainly admire theatre decoration; [indecipherable] and comfortable.

156 *J. Connor*, 2 Maple Avenue (aged 50), regular cinema-goer (4–8 times a month), preference – 'both good and otherwise'.
Comments: None.

157 *Robert Barlow*, 9 Bottom o'th'Moor, Harwood (aged 50), regular cinema-goer (once a month), preference – British films.
Comments: Education and Knowledge Films and History are educating. A good Humorous comedian is a tonic. Beautiful things and Beautiful [people] are as well necessary and Religion are to be placed properly. Action of killing, crime and spying, drama and tragedy, not a great lot of these, so they won't get on children's minds. Royalty we need as our Empire leaders. Aristocrats too uppish and too real especially for children gets them vain. Cartoons are alright.

158 *William Thomas Pedlar*, 250 Crescent Rd, Bolton (aged 57), regular cinema-goer (8 times a month), preference – British films.
Comments: I like pictures that are British because I hate the Yankee drawl as it gets on my nerves. You can understand a good British picture mostly on account of the quality of the speech.

159 *Mr F. Breakell*, Roper's Barn, Valletts Lane (aged 58), regular cinema-goer (12 times a month), preference – equal.

Comments: I do not agree with crime pictures, as although the criminal is usually found out it has an incentive to some people for excitement to take the risk of wrongdoing without thinking of the punishment. *Westerns* suitable for most young people who like adventure. *War*, why war pictures when everyone wants peace unless they show the horrors of war at its worst and the results. *Spying* only shows the cleverness of people and any spy is a sneak. Historical, Travel and Adventure Pictures are educational and gives most patrons a knowledge of past events, views of places, habits of people they will never be able to see. *Slapstick comedies* silly and not edifying.

160 *Mr E. Prince*, 217 Longfield, near Daubhill, (aged 59), regular cinema-goer (8 times a month), preference – American films.
Comments: I like the films like this week, something that can happen in real life.

161 *Henry Fox*, 42 Plover St (aged 60), regular cinema-goer (4 times a month, preference – British films.
Comments: None.

162 *A. E. Kirkman*, 61 Chalfont St (aged 60), regular cinema-goer (8 times a month), preference – British films.
Comments: I have no comment to make about the films shown. But I would suggest that more exits be put in on the second floor, say two on each side and so release congestion at the front doors and the temperature be seen to, as it gets very hot at the first evening performance.

163 *Mr Joseph Hopkins*, 64 Radcliffe Rd (aged 60), regular cinema-goer (8 times a month), preference – both the same.
Comments: None.

164 *James Lomax*, 67 Sloane St (aged 65), regular cinema-goer (12 times a month), preference – both.
Comments: I think such films as *Victoria the Great* and *Stella Dallas* speak for themselves. Nuff said.

165 *Arthur Rothwell*, 210 Halliwell Rd (aged 66), regular cinema-goer (8 times a year), preference – both.
Comments: Let us have British speakers for films, not *broken English*. Also, less *crime* pictures, there is enough crime in the world, without showing it in the pictures, yours, Arthur Rothwell.

166 *John William Farrington*, 57 Auburn St (aged 66), regular cinema-goer (8 times a month), preference – British films.
Comments: I want more films with humour, such as musical comedy, dramas on the bright side, cartoons, historical plays. Travel pictures are a treat. Can't go and see them. They are brought home to us. Other films which we can laugh at and be entertained. I do not like gangster shows, murder trials, poor cabaret shows which are not uplifting.

167 *William Heelis*, 95 Kay St (aged 67), regular cinema-goer (4 times a month), preference – British films.
Comments: Me and my wife as regular patrons to your beautiful Odeon. Congratulations to you of the splendid programme you have put on since the opening day and trust that you will keep up the same standard of quality. Also your splendid organ and organist (Mr Selby), which we enjoy. Wishing you, Mr Abercrombie, every success and good houses, yours sincerely, Mr W. Heelis.

Odeon Cinema: Women

1 *Miss Constance Thomas*, Prince Rupert Farm, Great Lever (aged 12), regular cinema-goer (4 times a month), preference – both the same.
Comments: I like the idea of Technicolor pictures because everything looks more real. The Odeon cinema is the most comfortable picture-house in town. The organ is very beautiful and when I get settled in one of the seats listening to the music, I feel that I could stay there forever.

2 *Joyce Howarth*, 53 Victoria Grove, C.O.R. (aged 13), regular cinema-goer (2 times a month), preference – American films.
Comments: I think the Historical Drama and Tragedy pictures that are shown at the 'Odeon Cinema' are the best. I did not like the musical romances which have been shown. The Historical films should be shown because when one leaves school one is apt to forget the builders of our Kingdom and our heritage. Then the Drama and Tragedy films convey a great amount of meaning, because of the splendid acting. But I also like a certain amount of humour. Because people don't go to the pictures to see other people's troubles.

3 *Mollie Ramwell*, 44 Wigan Rd, Deane, Bolton (aged 13), regular cinema-goer (4 times a month), preference – British films.
Comments: My favourite films are Gaumont British. Cicely Courtneidge in *Take My Tip* was very poor, although there was good dancing from Jack Hulbert. The story was also very poor indeed. In *Top of the Town* the acting and dancing were very good, and so were the scenes, but the story could have been better. *Gang Show* was a picture that was good in every way, and so was *Victoria the Great*. *Okay for Sound* was a very funny picture but it was apt to be rather too much so. Alice Faye, Claudette Colbert, Norma Shearer, and Renée Houston are very good, and I should like to see more of them. George Formby, Johnny Downs, Donald Stewart and Cesar Romero are also good actors. Arthur Tracy was very good in *Command Performance*, but the songs sung were too much alike. *Gang Show* is one of the best pictures I have seen.

4 *Joan Ackroyd*, 116 Crompton Way (aged 14), regular cinema-goer (7–8 times a month), preference – American films.
Comments: English films are definitely below the level of Americans, but sometimes – once a year – British produce a good film e.g. *Victoria Regina*.[22] American films have more scope about them. British film producers lack scope very much. Although I object to Americans trying to talk 'Oxford' in films about England. Surely there are more men like Gable, Flynn, Hunter in England instead of some half-baked college boys.

5 *Miss A. Parkinson*, 36 Walters St (aged 14) regular cinema-goer (10 times a month), preference – British films.
Comments: Give less killing, also no war pictures. Let us have more people like ourselves. Good Variety and Scenery pictures. Give us more of your wonderful Organ.

6 *Marjorie Wright*, 11 Meredith St, Great Lever (aged 14), regular cinema-goer (4–6 times a month), preference – both the same.
Comments: When I went to see Jessie Matthews in *Gangway* last week, I thought it was a very good entertainment, also I enjoyed *A Star is Born* better still. I thought Janet Gaynor was great. *Love from a Stranger* was very good, although I would sooner have dancing pictures and love stories.

7 *Miss B. Schofield*, 2 Cemetery Rd (aged 15), regular cinema-goer (4–5 times a month), preference – both the same.
Comments: I would like to compliment the 'Odeon' on the fact that since opening this cinema in Bolton, they have had some of the best and most entertaining films I have ever seen, and they have mostly been British films.

8 *Winifred Horrocks*, 30 West Rd, Great Lever (aged 15), regular cinema-goer (12 times a month), preference – British films.
Comments: I find that one of the best entertainments in town is the cinema. We have had some very good films in Bolton up to now, and I hope to see some more during this year.

9 *Lilian Golding*, 7 Salisbury St (aged 15), regular cinema-goer (8 times a month), preference – American films.
Comments: I think more pictures like the *Charge of the Light Brigade* should be shown because there was nothing impossible about it like the usual fictional stuff.

10 *Olive Bird*, 359 St Helen's Rd (aged 16), regular cinema-goer (16 times a month), preference – American films.
Comments: The films you have shown up to this date have had a pleasing effect on your patrons and so are often discussed afterwards.

11 *Edna Flanagan*, 177 Settle St, Great Lever (aged 16), regular cinema-

goer (5 times a month), preference – British films.

Comments: The film *The Prince and the Pauper* was interesting and worth seeing. In the film *Victoria the Great*, they should have shown more of her public life and less of her private life.

12   *Edna Watkins (Miss)*, 64 Blackburn (aged 16), regular cinema-goer (8–12 times a month), preference – American films.

Comments: In my opinion *Maytime* was an excellent film – with a like-wise cast and I'm sure the public would enjoy more of that type of films. Another film of great interest was A STAR IS BORN. The marvellous acting and casting, the true to life story and the touching, tragic ending all helped to make it an unforgettable film, as was *Stella Dallas*. Ronald Colman's acting in *Lost Horizon* was great. As was Greta Garbo's and Robert Taylor's in *Camille*. Also Marlene Dietrich and Charles Boyer in *Garden of Allah*, and *Rainbow on the River*. *Parnell* was disappointing, so was *Talking Feet*. *Jericho, Big Fellow* and *King Solomon's Mines* were swell.[23]

13   *Joyce Williams*, 50 Chalfont St (aged 16), regular cinema-goer (6 times a month), preference – American films.

Comments: Don't cut any out, we may read about scenes in a book, and not finding them, we feel cheated. Even if the film be exceptionally long, please keep the news in. We like to know what is going on in the world, even though we read the papers.

14   *Joan Marsden*, 122 Wright St, Horwich (aged 16), regular cinema-goer (8 times a month), preference – American films.

Comments: I prefer American films to English because they attend more to detail and production, their men stars act like real men. Not like the Englishmen actors who in my opinion are effeminate. They want to cut out the Oxford accent and speak more King's English.

15   *Stephanie Jackson*, 23 Mayfield Avenue (aged 17), regular cinema-goer (6 times a month, preference – American films.

Comments: I think that we get too many love pictures. There is nothing real about them. People in real life would not do the silly things that film lovers do. Myself and my friends come to the Odeon mostly because they get some of the best pictures ever made.

16   *Miss H. Bradley*, 37 Devonshire Rd, Atherton (aged 17), regular cinema-goer (6 times a month), preference – British films.

Comments: Thoroughly enjoyed the film *One in a Million* and would like to see more pictures as enjoyable as this one. I think Sonja Henie is the most charming and natural actress I have ever seen. Rest of the cast very good too.

17   *Miss Lucy Wyatt*, 93 Spring Lane, Radcliffe, Manchester (aged 17),

regular cinema-goer (6–8 times a month), preference – American films.
Comments: I would prefer the films if there were more co-star couples such as Ginger Rogers – Fred Astaire. My praise to the two coloured films I have seen at the Radcliffe Odeon, *Wings of the Morning* and *Garden of Allah*.

18 *Frances Parkinson*, 36 Walter St (aged 17), regular cinema-goer (12 times a month), preference – American films.
Comments: I think that some of the films of today are too far-fetched and there should be more films of true life. I do not like war pictures as it gives you a horrible outline of what it would be like if a war broke out today. The cartoons I like very much and think we should see more of POPEYE. I like the British films that star Gracie Fields and George Formby and I think The Three Stooges are gaining immense popularity.

19 *Miss K. B. Shaw*, 123 Bradford Rd, Farnworth (aged 17), regular cinema-goer (4 times a month), preference – American films.
Comments: Quite a number of good films have been shown lately; but we need more good moralled pictures that teach us lessons and help us to lead better lives, learning by other people's mistakes, not silly gangster pictures which are nothing but noise and leave wicked impressions on our minds, especially the minds of children. For a change a good laugh wouldn't do anyone any harm. Films like *Gangway* seem to suit all ages and classes. I certainly do not appreciate criminal ones, nor do I think they are good for children.

20 *Yvonne Naphtali*, 64 Church Rd, Kearsley (aged 17), regular cinema-goer (6 times a month), preference – American films.
Comments: May I take this opportunity of congratulating you on the films you have screened since the Odeon was first opened. You have shown films of every type to suit every person, and I am confident I shall always receive excellent entertainment whenever I visit an Odeon theatre.

21 *Brenda Edwina Jameson*, 82 Higher Swan Lane (aged 17), regular cinema-goer (4 times a month), preference – American films.
Comments: *Sabu the Elephant Boy*, I thought, was a most spectacular film, and of very great education value.[24] *Lilac Domino* was also an excellent film, but I thought that this masterpiece was utterly ruined by the voice of June Knight, and I am of the opinion that Grace Moore or Jeanette Macdonald would have been more suited to this role. The film *Victoria the Great* did not reach expectations, and although I am very fond of Historical films, I found it rather boring. The film *A Star is Born* was well acted but it was spoiled by the colour, which was too vivid.

22 *Edna Southworth*, 9 Brook Hey Avenue (aged 17), regular cinema-goer (4 times a month), preference – American films.

Comments: My opinion of films shown in the Odeon theatre are of the very best.

23   *Miss N. Dearden*, 33 Broxton Avenue, Daubhill (aged 18), regular cinema-goer (12 times a month), preference – American films.
Comments: I have not any complaint to make, as each film that I've seen so far I have enjoyed very much. Especially when I have seen the trailer, I have looked forward to it coming.

24   *Constance Badrock*, 906 Bury Rd (aged 18), regular cinema-goer (6 times a month), preference – American films.
Comments: Coming out of the cinema one often hears friends describe a picture as 'lousy', feeble etc. For years now I've looked forward to my visit to the pictures and I can truthfully say the cinema has never let me down. The critic may say I am easily pleased, but to think that for a few coppers, one can enter that world of make believe and leave behind all the worries and cares, well I say: 'Long live the Films!'

25   *Miss Joan Nicholls*, 58 Lonsdale Rd (aged 18), regular cinema-goer (8 times a month), preference – American films.
Comments: I think that American Films of English stories etc. are spoiled by the stars talking so American.

26   *Miss E. E. Holland*, 165 Green Lane (aged 18), regular cinema-goer (8 times a month), preference – American films.
Comments: None.

27   *Miss E. Docherty*, 33 Olaf St, Tonge Moor (aged 18), regular cinema-goer (16 times a month), preference – American films.
Comments: The kind of films that appeals more to me are Musical Romance, Tragedy and Drama, such as *Rose Marie, Stella Dallas, The Charge of the Light Brigade* and *A Star is Born*.

28   *Dorothy Cobb*, 20 Platt Hill (aged 18), regular cinema-goer (6 times a month), preference – American films.
Comments: Pictures like Janet Gaynor in *Star is Born*, also in Technicolor. Films like *Victoria the Great, Stella Dallas*. Less films like:– *Take My Tip*. More stars like James Cagney, Robert Taylor.

29   *Miss L. Dalley*, 34 Howcroft St (aged 18), regular cinema-goer (15 times a month), preference – American films.
Comments: The Odeon appears to be centre attraction for the best and varied films of real interest, humour, musical and drama, shown in Bolton.

30   *Lily Coughlan*, 23 Hengist St (aged 18), regular cinema-goer (12 times a month), preference – American films.
Comments: Pictures such as *Stella Dallas* appeal to me most. Touching stories that could happen to anyone in everyday life. I do not care for

farfetched films nor films about news reporters. I prefer the more sensible rules with people in them that really can act.

31 *Margaret Ward*, Hooper Green Farm, Westhoughton (aged 19), regular cinema-goer (8 times a month), preference – American films.
Comments: Pictures are a cheap as well as most entertaining occupation after a day's work. I can go and enjoy myself for two to three hours without feeling I am spending more than I can afford. Old and young enjoy seeing a 'picture'. The Picture Palaces are so comfortable, lovely seats etc. and of course the Organs are superb. The organ itself is an attraction.

32 *Hilda Hamer*, 3 Jauncey St (aged 19) regular cinema-goer (10 times a month), preference – American films.
Comments: I think on the whole American films are best, but I am not one of these people who will not go to a cinema if a British film is there, because I must admit there are some very good British films.

33 *Connie Brookes*, 131 Manchester Rd, Walkden (aged 19), regular cinema-goer (4 times a month), preference – American films.
Comments: The tendency today is towards old plots in a new guise. What is needed is more originality in all types of films.

34 *May Hodgkiss*, 26 Uganda St, Daubhill (aged 19), regular cinema-goer (4 times a month), preference – both the same.
Comments: The film *Victoria the Great* was the best picture I have ever seen. I hope there are more like it – starring Anna Neagle.

35 *Miss Joyce Waddington*, 5 Oaks Avenue, Bradshaw (aged 19), regular cinema-goer (8 times a month), preference – American films.
Comments: None.

36 *Margaretta Entwistle*, 628 Chorley Old Rd (aged 19), regular cinema-goer (10 times a month), preference – British films.
Comments: Drama – too much pathos. Why not have love stories more realistic. Alter theme of film story, too much of eternal triangle. Why not more Technicolor? Lately films are becoming more absorbing and scenes more real. Let's have more of it.

37 *Miss Edna Unwin*, 227 Deane Rd (aged 20), regular cinema-goer (16 times a month), preference – American films.
Comments: I think the films of today are too farfetched. Also there are not enough musical comedies, with singers like Jeanette Macdonald and Nelson Eddy. I saw *A Star is Born* with Janet Gaynor. It was to my mind a very good film. You got love scenes, excitement, and moments, which proved best in such a film. Why can't we have more of these kind of films? It was Natural (But in part farfetched). I suppose the films have to be

different to real life. I think we can do without war films. They are not pleasure, but agony to the mind.

38 *Miss C. Caffrey*, 329 Hulton Lane (aged 20), regular cinema-goer (3 times a month), preference – American films.
Comments: None.

39 *Miss Phyllis M. Burgess*, 40 Thornton Avenue, Heaton (aged 20), regular cinema-goer (6 times a month), preference – both the same.
Comments: From a technical point of view American films are better than English. Their photography and settings make their films more realistic than ours, and for this reason they excel in modern, sophisticated stories. But there are other outstanding stories such as *Fire Over England* for which only England can produce the right actors. Therefore, if British films could have the technical advantage of American, they would be perfect.

40 *Miss J. Bradley*, 51 Darwin Rd (aged 20), regular cinema-goer (8 times a month), preference – 'one is as good as the other'.
Comments: I like Musical Romance because you generally get good singing and a good story with lovely scenery. I also like Dramas because they keep you feeling interested with a certain amount of excitement. I dislike Society Comedies because they all seem senseless.

41 *Hilda Grimshaw*, 74 Randal St (aged 20), regular cinema-goer (8 times a month), preference – American films.
Comments: The organ interlude comes as a pleasant change from the third rate tit-bits generally musical, which are repeatedly shown. The news-reel is a necessary item of the programme. We enjoy the British Historical films, but the Dramas and Comedies create an artificial atmosphere. Two distinct performances are more sensible and convenient than the continuous method.

42 *Betty Pilling*, 22 Lime St, Church Bank (aged 20), regular cinema-goer (12 times a month), preference – British films.
Comments: None.

43 *Miss Linda Clare*, 32 Loxham St, Great Lever (aged 20), regular cinema-goer (8 times a month), preference – American films.
Comments: Charles Boyer was not suited for the part in *Garden of Allah*. I like seeing a good cartoon of the films. Some people think they're silly but there's a lot of clever work in them. Besides you get a good laugh. That's what we want these days.

44 *Miss M. M. Boardman*, 66 Crosby Rd (aged 20), regular cinema-goer (8 times a month), preference – both the same.
Comments: Let the same actors and actresses perform in sequence films. Too many stars are over-glamorized. Stars to keep the same type of roles.

45 *Phyllis Brook*, 59 Douglas St, Atherton (aged 20), regular cinema-goer (10 times a month), preference – American films.
Comments: Nowadays we seem to be hearing continually of many fine dramatic actors, who prefer to play in 'Slapstick Comedy' roles. Recently Leslie Howard turned comedian in *It's Love I'm After* and Carole Lombard still persists in playing such roles as she has had in *My Man Godfrey* and *Nothing Sacred*. This change seems to have turned out splendidly but what about all those promising young players who would show up to great advantage in such films? Surely we can leave the more difficult dramatic parts to our more polished actors!

46 *Miss L. M. Garstang*, 45 Fourth Avenue (aged 20), regular cinema-goer (4 times a month), preference – American films.
Comments: I have just seen *Stella Dallas* – one of the best films you have shown. Am looking forward to seeing Jack Buchanan next week in *The Sky's the Limit*.

47 *Nellie Bromiley*, 94 Auburn St (aged 21), regular cinema-goer (4 times a month), preference – American films.
Comments: I cannot make much comment about films but there are times when one feels envious at seeing all the lavish rooms and exciting things that happen but not being able to be present at the actual time. I don't think for one moment it is as thrilling to those taking part, as the audience when watching it.

48 *Phyllis Furber (Miss)*, 32 New Brook Rd, Over Hulton (aged 21), regular cinema-goer (4 times a month), preference – British films.
Comments: I like most films as they are, but I should prefer to see more Musical Romance Films with more good singing and good dancing. I think the Odeon always has the best films and the best programmes.

49 *Alice Speakman*, 38 Cartmel Crescent, Firwood (aged 21), regular cinema-goer (4 times a month), preference – both the same.
Comments: I like films with a good story in them. I loathe films that are long and unsatisfying. The British films have good detective and comedy films. But American Historical Films are better than British, and America has nearly all the best actors and actresses.

50 *Lucy Brabbin*, 11 Crowland Rd, Tonge Moor (aged 21), regular cinema-goer (8 times a month), preference – 'both are as good'.
Comments: I have nothing to grumble at about the average film. I hear music and see plays which probably I wouldn't do if there were no such things as talkies. On the other hand, those films which come below my idea of 'average' are those with the most killing in. *Give me* human stories.

51 *Vera Martlew (Miss)*, 109 Westbourne Avenue (aged 21), regular cinema-goer (6–7 times a month), preference – American films.
Comments: I prefer to see one good film at a show, than just a passable one; and a lot of little bits. It is much more interesting. If by any chance the show is double feature, I enjoy two films of different contrast, not forgetting the cartoons which are exceedingly clever.

52 *Miss Elsie Briggs*, 36 Mellor Grove, Smithills (aged 21), regular cinema-goer (4–5 times a month), preference – American films.
Comments: Less Silly Symphony cartoons please and let's have some real comedy acting instead. I think children and animals, especially dogs and horses, in pictures tend to attract people to see them – probably because they give a more natural performance. Why not revive more Operetta or Musical Comedy stage shows in pictures such as *The Student Prince, Betty, The Quaker Girl* etc. Incidentally, pictures taken from books by well-known authors – stories with good morals – always prove popular. I particularly like coloured pictures, especially when the picture has a fair amount of scenery in it, and think there should be more of these. American pictures are definitely superior to British. The action in the latter seems to be too slow. The fault lies in the direction mostly and not the acting I think.

53 *(Miss) Dorothy Broadbent*, 108 Devonshire Rd (aged 21), regular cinema-goer (6 times a month), preference – 'both the same'.
Comments: In my opinion, what is most lacking in Bolton is the absence of 'just released' films. By the time the films reach Bolton they are nearly 6 months old and have travelled nearly all over England. British films are certainly coming to the fore. Carry on England!

54 *Miss H. Cooper*, 132 Weston St (aged 22), regular cinema-goer (8 times a month), preference – American films.
Comments: The cinema is one of the blessings of this modern age. I think films should be purely for entertainment, to make us feel happier when we leave the cinema. Newsreels by showing us the true facts of world affairs perform a great service. We want more good shorts showing interesting places, and things of the world. Long live the Films!

55 *Betty Selby*, Hamer's Commercial Hotel (aged 22), regular cinema-goer (8 times a month), preference – American films.
Comments: Why don't you book more films on the lines of *The Thin Man, The Bride Wore Red, The Awful Truth* and *My Man Godfrey*, which contain 'laughable humour', are well-directed, snappy in dialogue and worth watching; and stop renting British films.

56 *Miss Hilda Asten*, 27 Canada St, Halliwell (aged 22), regular cinema-goer (6–8 times a month), preference – British films.

Comments: Sir, It wouldn't be fair to make any complaint about film stars in particular, because I have noticed if they do make a film that doesn't come up to expectations there's usually two or three that does, so why run the actors down, when he or she was probably playing a part they detested, and which would make it impossible to live the part. I have much praise for films, and everything and everybody that help to make them. I am only one but there are millions more who just for sixpence can see some of the most beautiful places on earth, hear the most glorious voices in song, and see some of the cleverest dancers in the world. Also a hundred and one things that must surely please the crankiest of people.

57 *Miss C. Barnaby*, 34 Newearth Rd, Walkden (aged 22), regular cinema-goer (4 times a month), preference – American films.
Comments: What is required in this time of crisis is:– more travel films or films depicting life in other countries. We should then be able to understand more clearly the difficulties confronting our ambassadors. At the same time we want to have our thoughts directed from these present worries by *brighter* films. There appears to be a growing tendency, in quite a number of cinemas, to show a *number* of *cut* films. We prefer to see one good film rather [than] a number of *bits*.

58 *Florence Lomax*, 99 Shepherd Cross St (aged 22), regular cinema-goer (4 times a month), preference – American films.
Comments: None.

59 *Miss Hilda M. Owen* 509 Bury Rd, Bolton (aged 22), regular cinema-goer (12 times a month), preference – both.
Comments: So far I think you have shown us a very interesting and varied programme, and feel certain you have succeeded in satisfying the great demand of such a critical public.

60 *Miss Edith Robinson*, 70 Higher Darcy St (aged 22), regular cinema-goer (4 times a month), preference – American films.
Comments: I should like to take this opportunity of thanking the attendants for the way they conduct their duties. I should be grateful if you would try to get a good musical comedy, as I think nearly everyone enjoys it.

61 *Mary Spires*, Royal Infirmary, Bolton (aged 22), regular cinema-goer (8 times a month), preference – British films.
Comments: Personally, I am all in favour of British films, though not so spectacular as American, they portray more everyday scenes, clean sense of humour and fine acting.

62 *Miss R. Falcon*, 'The Hollies', Breightmet (aged 22), regular cinema-goer (6–8 times a month), preference – 'Outstanding – British, average – American'.

Comments: Too many impossible things happen. Films would be better if based on real life – 'Truth is stranger than fiction.'

63 *Miss E. Lock*, 2 Callis Rd (aged 22), regular cinema-goer (8 times a month), preference – American films.
Comments: A large portion of films are too farfetched, impossibilities in real life.

64 *Monica Garstang, Miss*, 45 Fourth Avenue, Heaton (aged 22), regular cinema-goer (4 times a month), preference – American films.
Comments: My opinion is that a film should be either capable of bucking you up or in the case of the more serious picture you should come away feeling impressed by the moral of the tale. *Stella Dallas* was a wonderful picture, superb acting and quite true to life. *Gangway* was not very good, rather *too* light. *A Star is Born* was *very* unusual and interesting all through.

65 *Sally Wright*, 13 Markland St, off Soho St. (aged 22), regular cinema-goer (8 times a month), preference – American films.
Comments: Please get more American films, thank you, yours S. Wright.

66 *Ivy Benyon*, 58 Hulton Avenue, Little Hulton (aged 23), regular cinema-goer (6–7 times a month), preference – American films.
Comments: I would like to see more films like that of Anna Neagle's *Victoria the Great*.

67 *Miss Aileen Brown*, 91 Junction Rd, Deane (aged 23), regular cinema-goer (8 times a month), preference – American films.
Comments: I think *A Star is Born* was very good acting, the colouring was very good. *Victoria the Great* was splendid. *History is Made at Night* was very well done.

68 *Mary Hardy*, 14 Castle St (aged 23), regular cinema-goer (10–12 times a month), preference – American films.
Comments: I like English films when properly produced, but for one *Dark Journey* there are 3 third rate films, and the average film from America is much quicker moving than ours; but thanks to some English stage stars we have seen some ripping pictures lately, so show British, and we'll see British!

69 *Mrs C. Kean*, 216 Leigh Rd, Boothstown (aged 23), regular cinema-goer (8–10 times a month), preference – both the same.
Comments: I think that Cinema proprietors should only show light films and not those concerning war and death, because we see enough of it in the papers. The majority of people go to the Cinema for relaxation and entertainment, so I say the *lighter* the *better*.

70 *Martha Heap*, 3 Wardlow St, (aged 23), regular cinema-goer (4 times a month), preference – British films.
Comments: Too many films provide happy endings at the expense of reality and artistic merit. Many of the short films shown are of very poor quality and are only too obviously stop-gap. I should prefer more of sincerity, intelligence and humour in films and less of artificial situations and synthetic glamour.

71 *Ethel Scott*, 5 High View St, Deane (aged 24), regular cinema-goer (4 times a month), preference – American films.
Comments: I don't think the films of today are in comparison at all to the lives of over 60% of the people and I think they ought to be more natural and not as artificial and more like our everyday lives.

72 *Mrs G. Turner*, 4 Curzon Rd, Bolton (aged 24), regular cinema-goer (8 times a month), preference – both the same.
Comments: Why not more cowboy films.

73 *Miss Gertrude Bullough*, 17 Boughey St, Leigh (aged 24), regular cinema-goer (4 times a month), preference – British films.
Comments: None.

74 *Miss Constance Booth*, 268 St Helen's Rd, Bolton (aged 24), regular cinema-goer (8 times a month), preference – both the same.
Comments: In my opinion the film *A Star is Born* shown at the Odeon a week or two ago is one of the best I have seen. Perhaps it is because I know of another 'Norman Maine' in my own life. But whatever it is, I know that I have thought about that film a lot, in fact I went to see it twice, I thought it was great. Why even the title was an inspiration. It must have been to the Manager of the Odeon, or whatever it was, to give them the grand idea of giving that beautiful layette to the first baby born at Townley's Hospital after 2 o'clock. Even if he wasn't born a star, he was certainly born lucky.

75 *Mrs N. Cockshott*, 11 Horace St (aged 24), regular cinema-goer (4 times a month), preference – American films.
Comments: There is one thing I would like to say about the Odeon cinema and that is they don't show too many of these gangster pictures which I hate, full of things that never happened and never will. I only get one night a week out, so I take pot-luck, whatever the film is because I know I am sure of good sound entertainment at my favourite Odeon cinema.

76 *Myra Melling (Miss)*, 59 Essingdon St (aged 24), regular cinema-goer (12 times a month), preference – 'British if a good one but generally American'.
Comments: I like films well-acted which are convincing and makes one believe in the character and situations portrayed, whether they be tragedy-drama or comedy. Two good examples, *Action for Slander* and

Stella Dallas. One criticism, I object to the adverts of Ovaltine, Horlicks, and especially Lyons ice-cream. I feel it a waste of time even though they vary the adverts and try to fool us into thinking we are seeing a 'quickie'.

77   *May Harris (Miss)*, 138 Bury Old Rd (aged 24), regular cinema-goer (10 times a month), preference – American films.
Comments: Although I have stated that American are best, I only do so, because the American companies make more films and therefore win by majority, but when you do see a really good British Picture, it is really tip-top. What I do strongly object to is American films about British history. I think it is ridiculous to see some prominent British subject portrayed by an American actor with a strong American accent and using American slang. America needs to look to the technical side of their films and British wants to pull their socks up and they'd so be equal to their American films friends.

78   *Mrs Dora Ball*, 31 Raby St (aged 25), regular cinema-goer (4 times a month), preference – American films.
Comments: Films help you to understand things better, and give you a good idea about cities, countries, people and customs, of which otherwise you would know very little. Also when you are reading, you are better able to visualise what you are reading about, if you have seen the place on the pictures. They are the cheapest and best form of entertainment.

79   *Miss Irene Crook*, 12 Green Lane (aged 25), regular cinema-goer (3–4 times a month), preference – British films.
Comments: To qualify my answer to question 5, I would say that on the whole American films are more lavish and extravagant. But the best British films are better than the best American films. Also the worst British films (Slapstick Comedies etc.) are rather worse than the worst American films, if possible.

80   *Miss Doris Gaydon*, 59 Church St (aged 25), regular cinema-goer (6–8 times a month), preference – American films.
Comments: My friends and myself have one objection and that is to seeing a lot of small 'filling-in' films to support one big film. We prefer either one long film such as *A Star is Born* – or else two complete pictures.

81   *Margaret Gray*, Royal Infirmary (aged 25), regular cinema-goer (8 times a month), preference – British films.
Comments: The Odeon usually have a good show.

82   *Miss Irene Leyland*, 17 Saydale Close, Westoughton (aged 25), regular cinema-goer (6 times a month), preference – 'British now.'
Comments: Dear Sirs, When going to the Cinema I like to feel I am in a different world for the time being. That is, I like to see and hear the news of the world, a Walt Disney cartoon and a real fine picture, one that makes

you feel helped and gives you something to live for. A good society picture
or a drama with plenty of action. *Victoria the Great, Action for Slander*
and *A Star is Born* supplied these. Please let's have more like them.
I. Leyland.

83 *Mabel Melling (Miss)*, 59 Essington St (aged 25), regular cinema-goer
(12 times a month), preference – American films.
Comments: The attraction for me at the 'Odeon' is the well balanced
programmes e.g. comedy, news, organ and the big picture, as double
feature programmes are my pet aversion. Over boosting and over praising
a picture is harmful, as one is nearly always disappointed. The
programmes at the Odeon since *Victoria the Great* have been excellent.
Hubert Selby at the organ is great. Films that are human and an
appealing story such as *Stella Dallas* are always an attraction. The
comfort and warmth of the Odeon is an aid to enjoying the films.

84 *Betty Bates*, 14 Birley St (aged 25), regular cinema-goer (11–12 times
a month), preference – American films.
Comments: I have no complaint to make. If I don't think I shall like the
picture, I don't go and it is very rare that I am disappointed in a show. I
think going to the movies is an excellent night out.

85 *Mrs G. H. Haslam*, 'Prior's Lea', 105 Smithills Dean Rd (aged 25),
regular cinema-goer (4–5 times a month), preference – British films.
Comments: I think that it has been much better since the organist has
played between performances, but I should still like to hear more in place
of some of the silly short films. If we can't have two big films, I think that
it would be much better to have the top picture, news, a short travel film
(why can't they have English commentators instead of the Yankee slang?)
and a little more of the organ or better still a good variety act on the stage.
I am pleased to see that most of the films shown are British. Hurrah! for
good British films!

86 *Mrs A. Clitheroe*, 18 Atkinson Avenue (aged 26), regular cinema-goer
(8 times a month), preference – American films.
Comments: American films, on the whole, are far 'snappier' than British
pictures. The dialogue is usually much smarter, and the action quicker.
Dialogue in British films, except, say, the absolute tip-top ones, is often too
stilted and too 'stagey'. Such films as *It Happened One Night* and *The Thin
Man* series were bound to succeed, because of the cleverness of the
dialogue and the popular appeal of the stories. Especially do we want more
good, honest humour, not merely slapstick, and not too subtle for the
average film-goer to understand.

87 *Mrs V. Parker*, 55 Chorley New Rd (aged 26), regular cinema-goer (8
times a month), preference – British films.

Comments: Personally, I like the Travel and Educational best, because they show you places that you have never seen and perhaps never will and when done in colour are really *very* beautiful.

88   *Mrs Riding*, 146 Sapling Rd (aged 26), regular cinema-goer (6 times a month), preference – American films.
Comments: I make Saturday my day mostly because this gives me a chance of seeing which Cinema is showing the best Pictures. I like the Odeon very much. It is so comfortable and cosy. I have spent many happy times at the Odeom. This week's picture *Stella Dallas* is a great picture and one that we think and talk about. Not like the picture shown the week before *Victoria the Great*. I can't tell you the title of the Picture, as a matter of fact me and my husband went to sleep. Anyhow give us the best and we will be regular patrons at the Odeon.

89   *Nellie Greenwood*, 29 Horace St (aged 26), regular cinema-goer (4 times a month), preference – American films.
Comments: *History [is] Made at Night* (Very Good); *A Star is Born* (Very Good), *Okay for Sound* (Bad).

90   *Enid Wood*, 360 Deane Church Lane (aged 26), regular cinema-goer (8 times a month), preference – British films.
Comments: We want films containing people we can more readily identify with ourselves, to whom wonderful things happen, as they might happen to anyone. More real life stuff treated with imagination and insight. Situations that are real, and yet lift one 'out of oneself' more. I like to see films containing my favourite actor or actress – always *real* people.

91   *Miss V. Waldron*, Bridge Hotel, Horwich (aged 26), regular cinema-goer (12 times a month), preference – American films.
Comments: In my opinion of films, I think they should be a little less of war pictures as they would be more people visit the pictures if they were stopped.

92   *Edith M. Nicholson*, 10 Hughes St (aged 27), regular cinema-goer (7–8 times a month), preference – American films.
Comments: More films of the standard of *Charge of the Light Brigade, Victoria the Great, Lost Horizon* etc. are needed, and less of the second class films, which are shown as double-feature programmes.

93   *Mrs Linda Noake*, 8 Lynwood Avenue, Great Lever (aged 27), regular cinema-goer (8 times a month), preference – both the same.
Comments: Dear sir, I would like very much to see more tales of the sea and more silent good films as talkies. Thank you. Mrs. L. Noake.

94   *Mrs E. Skellen*, 5 Roseberry St (aged 27), regular cinema-goer (5–6 times a month), preference – American films.

Comments: When I go to the pictures I go to be entertained. For this reason I don't like seeing what producers fondly imagine are true to life films, simply because they are not true to life. I know far more about my own problems than film producers do or ever will do, so that when I go to the pictures I don't want to see these problems solved (to the satisfaction of the producers) in what are called true to life pictures. I like seeing historical romances i.e. *Charge of the Light Brigade, Captain Blood* or such films as *Queen Victoria* etc. Failing this, I like Musical Comedies or a really good Detective Picture because they take my mind off everyday things, and going to the pictures is a change and a tonic if I can see the films that I have mentioned.

95 *'Blackshirt'* (aged 27), regular cinema-goer (12 times a month), preference – American films.
Comments: The pictures you have shown during the last month have been very good. They teach people to live better. For instance after seeing *A STAR IS BORN*, it made me understand that beer drinking is a silly game. I now go to the pictures on Saturdays as well. Also the one this week *Stella Dallas* has a very good moral in it. If I win anything, send it to Miss Betty Smith, 27 Shipton St., Bolton, Thank you.

96 *S. Makin (Miss)*, 74 New Lane, Harwood (aged 27), regular cinema-goer (4 times a month), preference – American films.
Comments: The reason I like the Odeon Pictures: 1) You get all the sort of pictures I prefer 2) Also the sound of the talkies are perfect 3) So I thoroughly enjoy coming. Please excuse my scribble.

97 *Margaret Mary Stout*, 'Meadowcroft', New Brook Rd, Atherton (aged 27), regular cinema-goer (6–8 times a month), preference – British films.
Comments: Why waste your patrons' time with very second rate secondary films, often completely spoiling the impression left by the main and usually very excellent chief film? Surely people prefer a good news item, and educational film and then the chief film, and to get home a little earlier, satisfied that they haven't sat through a 'filler-in'!

98 *Mrs Ada Harris*, 326 Bolton Rd, Westhoughton (aged 28), regular cinema-goer (8 times a month), preference – American films.
Comments: I think the films help you to forget your cares and worries. You can relax and forget everything in your everyday life. There is nothing I enjoy better than a good film.

99 *Irene Berry (Mrs)*, 2 Austin's Lane, Lostock (aged 28), regular cinema-goer (4–5 times a month), preference – British films.
Comments: Should present life more as it is, without such an appearance of absurd wealth and luxury. I object to filling in programmes with inferior (American usually) rubbish and would prefer a shorter programme to this.

The acting in Films in general is excellent, but the quality of the stories is often poor. So called tragedies are ridiculous. Some films-such as the *Lost Horizon, David Copperfield, Bligh of the Bounty*,[25] *Quality Street* are magnificent.

100 *Mrs E. Walmsley*, 34 Platt St (aged 28), regular cinema-goer (12 times a month), preference – American films.
Comments: I do not care for films of Religion or politics, but I think *Love, Romance, Tragedy, Drama* and the *Cartoons* are fine. But on the whole I think the selection of films have been blended most admirable and as a regular patron, I trust they remain so.

101 *Miss G. Short*, 'Danescourt' (aged 28), regular cinema-goer (12 times a month), preference – American films.
Comments: I would like a few more pictures such as *A Star is Born*. A film like that lives in your memory a long time after you have seen it.

102 *Annie Barlow*, 9 Bottom o'th'Moor, Harwood (aged 29), regular cinema-goer (3 times a month), preference – British films.
Comments: I think the films best as numbered 1 to 13 inclusive in their, my, arranged order and from 1 to 10 also, as I have picked them out.

103 *Mrs Minnie Cocker*, 821 Belmost Rd (aged 29), regular cinema-goer (8 times a month), preference – American films.
Comments: I should like British film actresses to speak in a natural tone, instead of the mincing, affected, stagey manner they seem to adopt.

104 *Beatrice Hart*, 47 Rose St, Manchester Rd. (aged 29), regular cinema-goer (12–16 times a month), preference – Both.
Comments: Dear sir, The picture (*Stella Dallas*) was fine. It's something you are never tired of watching, in fact I've been twice this week, as you have a change of news and I like the cinema, as the attendants are very pleasing and civil. The organ is another attraction. The playing simply thrills everyone. You ask how many times a month do I go. Well, it's once a week I go to the Odeon and if there is any Picture that I enjoyed so much, go again later on in the week. You see, you give a change of news. I go to other cinemas, and the total is 12 or 16 times in the month. You see I'm not a good letter writer. P.S. I hope I've made it clear. I've just this one note.

105 *Clarice Tudge*, 3 Lime Grove, Walkden (aged 30), regular cinema-goer (2 times a month), preference – British films.
Comments: I enjoy the travel talks but sometimes the commentator talks too much and hinders appreciation of the scene. News also is good. But not too blunt propaganda as was given on Saturday 19th March. It was good for holders of armament shares. More films needed on the lines of *The Dark Angel, Love from a Stranger, Lloyds of London, Mutiny on the Bounty, The Barrets of Wimpole Street, The Good Earth*.[26]

106   *Dorothy Hamer*, 378 Crescent Rd (aged 30), regular cinema-goer (12 times a month), preference – British films.
Comments: One *good* film, with news or cartoon comedy is preferable to one mediocre and one so-called American comedy film in my opinion. And less background music to dialogue, please!

107   *Mary E. Ogden (Mrs)*, 1 Alfred St, Farnworth (aged 30), regular cinema-goer (8 times a month), preference – American films.
Comments: Complaints: 1) Two separate films featuring one or more of the same cast is to be avoided as one is apt to confuse the themes. 2) More 'full lengths' and less 'shorts'. 3) Cut out Slapstick Comedies and give us films that are really humorous. *To Cinema Owners* (some): Why the First Class Entrance with the 'No Class' Exits?

108   *Miss A. Bradley*, 51 Darwin St, (aged 30), regular cinema-goer (10 times a month), preference – British films.
Comments: I don't like comedies because they don't hold your interest like a drama or a romance does, and I think to really enjoy a picture you want something to occupy your mind, and take it off other things for a bit, that's what you come to the pictures for, a complete change.

109   *(Mrs) Edna Pearson*, 868 St Helen's Rd (aged 30), regular cinema-goer (4 times a month), preference – American films.
Comments: My film-going is based on a judicious selection of what I am led to believe are outstanding films. Story interest is of paramount import-ance. Film versions of novels and plays have an unfailing appeal, though I always feel that they suffer in adaptation. I realize, of course, that producers' license must be allowed for in the interests of wider 'box office' appeal.

110   *L. Makin (Mrs)*, 26 Kylemore Avenue (aged 30), regular cinema-goer (4 times a month), preference – British films.
Comments: *I do not* like films which begin quite interestingly and promisingly and then turn out to be advertisements for patent foods or washing powder etc. etc.

111   *Edna G. Bennett*, 357 Chorley Old Rd (aged 30), regular cinema-goer (4 times a month), preference – American films.
Comments: My preference for American films is based on the fact that they pay more attention to detail than British films do (E.G.) That fine film *Love from a Stranger* was spoiled by one glaring mistake – Upon winning the lottery, Ann Harding buys the latest creation in hats, and wears it again later in the film, supposedly months afterwards, a mistake no American director would have made. In my opinion British films have progressed wonderfully but given the choice to see a first class American

or a first class British film, I would still choose the American as yet. I would like to say how much I appreciate Donald Duck cartoons, I think he portrays a very common trait in human nature.

112 *Mrs Edith Race*, 537 Plodder Lane, Farnworth (aged 30), regular cinema-goer (3–4 times a month), preference – 'American. British fast catching up'.
Comments: There are no[w] so many first-rate actors that stars individually have not the same draw as formerly. Therefore show first class stories, dramatic or musical. Good acting will not compensate for poor material. Cut out the American short makeweight films. They let down a good programme. Why not more of the newsy topical stuff as shown in News Theatres? Your travel films are really good and must have a universal appeal. Finally, though not a comment on films, do not let anything endanger the popular organ interludes.

113 *Mrs Haslam* 124 Pen St (aged 30), regular cinema-goer (18 times a month), preference – both the same.
Comments: I think the films *Love from a Stranger* and *Action for Slander* are two of the best I have ever seen. I hate newspaper gangster films, shouting and shooting all the time. Fair gives one headaches.

114 *Mrs D. Molyneaux*, 23 Ormrod St (aged 30), regular cinema-goer (4 times a month), preference – American films.
Comments: I have put American as my choice of Films because I think that they are always well ahead in acting and have a lot finer talented actors than British actors, and everybody I know would sooner walk a mile to see *Scarface* than walk a yard to see *The Frog*.[27] P.S. Hoping the Odeon management will stick to American films.

115 *Lilian Whittaker*, 85 Ashworth Lane (aged 30), regular cinema-goer (8 times a month), preference – both the same.
Comments: Reserve films with Good Music, a little bit of love and a laugh. Then reserve me a seat.

116 *Mrs D. Barnett*, 210 Greenmond Lane (aged 31), regular cinema-goer (8 times a month), preference – American films.
Comments: I personally like to be entertained at the Cinema if possible in a light, witty, humorous way – either, obviously artificial but *brilliant* comedy e.g. *My Man Godfrey* – or human, natural comedy well acted e.g. *Call It a Day*. I appreciate particularly, good acting. I have no preference for American or English films – *Storm in a Teacup* was good: it was well-done. *Fire Over England* was mediocre, although Miss Robson gave a brilliant performance – the story was hardly authentic and anyway weak. Generally, I think, Americans do most films better than the English.

117 *Mrs E. Howarth*, 19 Rothwell St Flats (aged 31), regular cinema-goer

(8 times a month), preference – American films.

Comments: I much prefer seeing American films, as you get the real thing. They spare no expense when making a film to get the real scenery and it isn't faked like the English films, and then look at the lovely scenes you get in some of the pictures made in American films, they must cost thousands of pounds where the English pictures always remind me of someone being hard up, afraid to spend. Give me the American films every time. British are only learning yet how to make films. E. Howarth.

118   *Mrs Ethel Parker*, 43 Third Avenue (aged 32), regular cinema-goer (4 times a month), preference – British films.
Comments: Should like to see more British Films, particularly of light musical type with good story.

119   *Mrs Minnie Parker*, 24 Roseneath Rd (aged 33), regular cinema-goer (8 times a month), preference – British films.
Comments: My idea of your pictures since the opening of the Odeon. I think you have done fine with your programmes. Hoping you still keep giving the good pictures you have been giving. Also the good time we get with the organist Hubert Selby. Wishing him luck and hoping that you will keep him at the Odeon. Bolton.

120   *Doris E. Lindley*, Tickle Farm House, Stoneclough (aged 33), regular cinema-goer (4 times a month), preference – American films.
Comments: In my opinion – a musical Background – almost throughout a picture has a tendency to interfere with the dialogue. In some cases nearly blots out the voice altogether, as in the case of Miss Neagle in *Victoria the Great*. In the early days of the talkies, silence was asked of the patrons so that the picture might be enjoyed to the full, but with the passing of the years more and more chatting goes on during the performance. Is it asking too much that the patrons be once again reminded that silence is golden.

121   *Mrs Gray*, 'Highleigh', Regent Rd, Lostock (aged 33), regular cinema-goer (8 times a month), preference – 'American except gangsters.'
Comments: None.

122   *Miss Ormrod*, 64 Croston St (aged 33), regular cinema-goer (4 times a month), preference – British films.
Comments: The films have been very enjoyable but it would be a change to have an organ interlude sometime instead of Donald Duck. He gets rather boring. A 'Travel Talk' picture would be quite interesting too.

123   *Olive Ward*, 25 Highfield Rd (aged 33), regular cinema-goer (8 times a month), preference – American films.
Comments: I like the Musical Romance type of film best because 'It's Romantic, it's Superb, it's Colossal.' To find yourself singing the catchy tunes the next morning, then you know you get the utmost pleasure out of

the films. They just relive in your memory. Crime (Gangster) pictures always give me such a thrill – they are well worth seeing. Saturday at the 'Odeon' saves one from Boredom. Olive Ward.

124 *Miss Edith Worthington*, 68 Ainsdale Rd, Great Lever (aged 35), regular cinema-goer (8 times a month), preference – British films.
Comments: I prefer to be entertained when I visit the Cinema, something to cheer and brighten, but nothing silly, and to come away feeling that I have also learned something of music and history. Life is serious and tragic enough for most people without paying to see more of it. So carry on! and help to come away feeling better for our visit.

125 *Mrs M. Shepperd*, 45 Danesbury Rd (aged 34), regular cinema-goer (12 times a month), preference – British films.
Comments: Personally I could do without any of those films similar to the Mexican film showing this week (14–19th March). I might also suggest a speeding up in the time between shows in London and the South and the dates they are released in the provinces. Though I must admit the Odeon gets the big pictures as soon as any local cinema. Why not have two big pictures and cut out the short stories or travel films in its place.

126 *Mary Emily McGuiness (Miss)*, 25 Rothwell St (Flat) (aged 34), regular cinema-goer (8 times a month), preference – American films.
Comments: Films shown at the Odeon in my opinion are up to standard. From what I gather from Bolton people need no more variations.

127 *Mrs Margaret Cooper*, 16 Kirk St (aged 36), regular cinema-goer (4 times a month), preference – both the same.
Comments: I don't as a rule like historical films but I thought the film *Victoria the Great* was wonderful and am glad I did not miss seeing it. In the film *Action for Slander* I was held by the dramatic tenseness of the card game. I don't like films which are full of singing and are really meant for the stage such as musical plays.

128 *Gladys Louise Connor*, 2 Maple Avenue (aged 36), regular cinema-goer (10 times a month), preference – British films.
Comments: I should like more films like *The Count of Monte Cristo* and *The Song of the Forge* and *Victoria the Great* and *Catherine the Great*. I certainly like the Odeon Picture House for real comfort and the good music from the organ. I look forward to my visits there and usually have the same seat which is very nice idea and good service. G. L. Connor.

129 *Miss G. Roscoe*, 51 Longfield Rd (aged 36), regular cinema-goer (10 times a month), preference – both.
Comments: I think your films are first class and I have enjoyed each one of them so far.

130 *Eleanor M. Dobson*, 61 Beaconsfield St (aged 36), regular cinema-goer (4 times a month), preference – British films.
Comments: I don't care for the silly humour one gets in some pictures, but the witty types, such as one gets in the society comedies. My preference for British pictures is because of the acting, culture and wit which far exceeds the American.

131 *Mrs Jennie Winstanley*, 3 Blackledge St (aged 36), regular cinema-goer (20 times a month), preference – American films.
Comments: First of all I myself is hard to please but I must say most of the films shown lately are bunkum. I call it easy money for most of the stars. Modern people of today want wit, humour, something that won't slip out of their minds easy. I like pictures sincerely and I recommend them, if they are suitable, as I know the cost of upkeep for cinemas needs plenty of patronising to keep going. Mrs Winstanley.

132 *Mrs E. Smith*, 23 Caledonia St (aged 36), regular cinema-goer (8 times a month), preference – American films.
Comments: Since the Odeon [h]as opened, I have enjoyed all your pictures and feel at home. Also I like the organ very much.

133 *Mrs Dyer*, 328 Bolton Rd, Westhoughton (aged 38), regular cinema-goer (16 times a month), preference – American films.
Comments: None.

134 *Anne Nelson*, 21 Chorley New Rd (aged 38), regular cinema-goer (4 times a month), preference – 'some of each'.
Comments: I think there ought to be more films with a good story first and the actors a secondary consideration, viz. *Over the River, The Beloved Vagabond*. The actors should be put IN the story NOT a story round the actors. Some of them are *painful*. There are heaps of splendid books that could be suitably filmed.

135 *J. A. Watkins (Mrs)*, 4 Durham St (aged 38), regular cinema-goer (6–8 times a month), preference – American films.
Comments: I think that *A Star is Born, Maytime, Stella Dallas, Lost Horizon, Camille* and *Garden of Allah* are 6 of the best tragic or dramatic films of late. *Parnell* was very disappointing, not the acting but the whole picture in general. *Jungle Princess* was a very interesting film. *Night Must Fall*, the acting was marvellous but it was so horrifying that all real enjoyment was missing. *Rainbow on the River* and *Wee Willie Winkie* are two excellent pictures which show how children can hold an audience's attention. Last year's *The King Steps Out* was great. *Shall We Dance* was a very delightful Musical Comedy.

136 *Mrs Hewitt*, 63 Church St (aged 39), regular cinema-goer (3 times a month), preference – American.

Comments: I would like to see more films like *Victoria the Great, Charge of the Light Brigade, The Lilac Domino* etc. I think they were fine.

137   *Mrs A. P. Marshall*, 77 Kirkby Rd (aged 35–45), regular cinema-goer (6–8 times a month), preference – both the same.
Comments: Very fond of spy pictures, drama or anything that could actually take place, no far-fetched ones or things that is impossible. I like nature studies, travel pictures and as comedy such as cartoons (Walt Disley [sic] etc). Advertisements on screen are entirely out of place unless short and snappy. Programme should not be too long. One big picture and short comedy or Travel Educational [indecipherable] and News. I specially look for this and in general opinion.

138   *Miss B. L. Brown*, 16 Fountains Avenue, Tonge Moor (aged 40), regular cinema-goer (3 times a month), preference – both the same.
Comments: I thoroughly enjoyed *Stella Dallas* because it was a natural film. On the whole, I think the Odeon show the best films and seats are the most comfortable. The staff and management are always courteous.

139   *Gertrude Crompton*, 46 Kimberley Rd, Astley Bridge (aged 40), regular cinema-goer (4 times a month), preference – American films.
Comments: I like to see good Society Pictures and we certainly get it at the Odeon. You get education from them.

140   *Mrs L. Brown*, 15 Smithills Croft Rd (aged 40), regular cinema-goer (4 times a month), preference – British films.
Comments: Well satisfied with recent programmes.

141   *May Crawshaw (Mrs.)*, 14 Heaton Avenue, Harwood (aged 40), regular cinema-goer (4 times a month), preference – both the same.
Comments: I like when going to the Cinema to see one long picture, with a little humour and a little pathos as long as it brings out the qualities of the actor, and a little love not overdrawn. Also a travel coloured picture, or a Mickey Mouse, and for a change, short musical revue. Then of course a good news reel with pictures of Royalty and not too much war news. I dont mind the ice cream advert, but hate to sit in semi-darkness watching adverts of housing estates, furniture, permanent waves etc.

142   *Mrs N. Smith*, 39 Harper Green Rd, Farnworth (aged 40), regular cinema-goer (4–6 times a month), preference – American films.
Comments: The reason I would rather have American films at present is because the action is quicker and they seem to have a more human note with them. Hoping to see British pictures as good in the near future. They are certainly improving.

143   *Mrs G. Lingard*, 31 Danesbury Rd (aged over 40), regular cinema-goer (4–6 times a month), preference – American films.

Comments: I like plenty of action to hold my attention and distract my mind from everyday worries. Also I should like them to speak plainly and not gabble too fast. Also not too noisy.

144 *Mrs May McPherson*, 144 Hall Lane, Farnworth (aged 41), regular cinema-goer (8 times a month), preference – American films.
Comments: I like 'Westerns' (and I think they suit every man and child and no doubt most women), for three reasons, because the scenery is beautiful and what is nicer than a large herd of cattle on the trail with wonderful horses alongside and then again I think they are inexpensive as they require no elaborate costumes.

145 *Mrs McDowell*, 148 Mornington Rd (aged 42), regular cinema-goer (4 times a month), preference – American films.
Comments: General tone of films are highly satisfactory.

146 *Mrs B. Hutchinson*, 15 Rawson Rd (aged 42), regular cinema-goer (6 times a month), preference – American films.
Comments: I went a few weeks ago to see *Victoria the Great* and thought it one of the best pictures I had ever seen. There should in my opinion be more of this kind and of the *Stella Dallas* kind. They were, I thought, very human and therefore interesting from start to finish. Yours sincerely, B. Hutchinson.

147 *Mrs Smith*, 3 Wilfred Rd (aged 42), regular cinema-goer (8 times a month) preference – American films.
Comments: What is the use of seeing a very good picture, if it is to be followed by a soft comic, only fit for kiddies to laugh at.

148 *Miss F. Redfern*, 40 Bradford St (aged 42), regular cinema-goer (6 times a month), preference – 'British win on voice and comedy'.
Comments: Films can make us happy or sad, whilst others make us simply mad. So give us plots, dramatic and gay, and we are sure to come another day.

149 *Mrs Baldwin*, 19 Luton St (aged 42), regular cinema-goer (6–8 times a month), preference – American films.
Comments: Sir, I think a few more comedies in these troublesome times would be good entertainment for most of us.

150 *Mrs G. V. Hunt*, 81 Hawthorne Rd, Deane (aged 43), regular cinema-goer (4 times a month), preference – 'fair selection of each'.
Comments: I think the average (middle-aged) person, and I think we deserve consideration, would prefer a good, commonsense drama, not too farfetched, preceded by a light humorous comedy. *Stella Dallas*, for instance, created an excellent moral. *Victoria the Great* was perfect.

151 *Mrs A. Lee*, 3 Briarfield Rd, Farnworth (aged 43), regular cinema-

goer (8 times a month), preference – American films.

Comments: To whom it may concern, I can honestly say, although I know I'm only one out of hundreds, that the Odeon without doubt gets some of the finest pictures I've seen in Bolton for some time. As a regular picturegoer I think I should know, as I have never been bored yet.

152   *G. Richards (Mrs)*, 'Green Acre', Chorley Old Rd, Horwich (aged 45), regular cinema-goer (4–5 times a month), preference – American films.

Comments: Musical films are usually good entertainment. One does not expect anything true to type – just good singing and pretty or spectacular scenes: things do not need tiring concentration. A really good story film from a book is often spoiled by breaking the thread of the story too long – for a dance or showy part. I do not care for your organ too much; it is rather loud. Sentimental, sweet tunes sound better than hot jazz.

153   *Miss J. Speirs*, 83 Bury New Rd, Breightmet (aged 45), regular cinema-goer (8–10 times a month), preference – American films.

Comments: Although I have had to confess to a preference for American Films, I think there is a marked improvement in British films during the last two years, and I am hopeful of the time when British films will lead the way. American films are more 'polished', the action is quicker, and the producers have found the secret of appealing to the film goer. Now a grouse against the management. I am one of many to deplore the fact that the Saturday evening performance is not a continuous one. We may be in the minority but we have become accustomed to continuous shows and they suit us better. It would be helpful to patrons if prices and times of showing the star picture were clearly stated in advertisement, whether newspaper or poster.

154   *Mrs Ethel Bradley*, 15 Green Avenue, Great Lever (aged 46), regular cinema-goer (4 times a month), preference – American films.

Comments: The films that are most like human life give people food for thought. So where you sit in Odeon, you get a clear view of screen, which is very satisfactory.

155   *Mrs Sugden*, 179 Willows Lane (aged 46), regular cinema-goer (4 times a month), preference – both the same.

Comments: None.

156   *Mrs Ellen Tyas*, 93 Longsight, Harwood, (aged 47), regular cinema-goer (4 times a month), preference – both the same.

Comments: I have been a frequent visitor ever since the Odeon opened. It is about the only pleasure I get as it is most comfortable and you can always rely on value for your money. I have seen the picture this week,

Stella Dallas. I think it is marvellous and lot of other films I have seen and have never found cause for criticism. So I think if you follow the films of the Odeon you cannot go far wrong.

157 *Mrs Kirkman*, 69 Astley St (aged 48), regular cinema-goer (6 times a month), preference – both the same.
Comments: A good clean film, plenty of humour and beautiful dresses.

158 *M. Gladwin (Mrs)*, 385 Bury Rd (aged 48), regular cinema-goer (8–10 times a month), preference – British films.
Comments: I like British pictures best because nowhere is there more beautiful scenery than in Britain. I like those showing customs, manners and traditions of our land whether country or in society. American pictures have no traditions, only glamour and artificiality. British pictures give us decently spoken language, American-slang, phrases which I detest. I like *historical* pictures that are as near authentic as possible e.g. *Victoria the Great*, also *biography* touched with romance and drama, as recent as possible e.g. *Pasteur*.[28] Please give us more *customs of other countries* – Japan, China, such as *The Good Earth*. I also like pictures from well-known *novels*, especially those with an uplifting moral e.g. *Lost Horizon*. The discussion in town after *that* picture's visit shows that spiritual uplift is beginning to attract in pictures. Nature pictures are interesting to *all* types of picture minds.

159 *Mrs Mabel Bromilow*, 9 Chapel St (aged 49), regular cinema-goer (8 times a month), preference – both the same.
Comments: I think all war pictures should be stopped as it makes people miserable instead of happy. I would not see a war picture free. I like to come home smiling after an evening's entertainment at the cinema.

160 *Mrs Southworth*, 9 Brook Hey Avenue (aged 49), regular cinema-goer (4 times a month), preference – British films.
Comments: My opinion of films shown in the Odeon theatre are Al.

161 *Mrs J. Whaley*, 24 Chilham St (aged 50), regular cinema-goer (8–10 times a month), preference – British films.
Comments: I think crime films should not be shown.

162 *Mrs E. A. Kay*, 45 Kendal Rd (aged 50), regular cinema-goer (3 times a month), preference – American films.
Comments: Better scenes and orchestration in English films.

163 *Mrs J. Ward*, 26 Hardman St, Farnworth (aged 50), regular cinema-goer (4 times a month), preference – both the same.
Comments: Dear sir, I should like to see more Musical Comedy and little more Gaumont News, thank you, Mrs J. Ward.

164 *Mrs Whitehead*, 310 St Helen's Rd (aged 51), regular cinema-goer (8 times a month), preference – both the same.
Comments: None.

165 *Mrs J. Webster*, 43 Orm St (aged 52), regular cinema-goer (12 times a month), preference – both the same.
Comments: The most comfortable cinema in Bolton. Keep your Organ recital going, and your pictures O.K.

166 *Mrs T. Wilson*, 51 St John St (aged 53), regular cinema-goer (6–7 times a month), preference – American films.
Comments: Whilst, on patriotic grounds, I would like to be able to say that I enjoy British films, I am afraid that, generally speaking, this is not so. My comparisons are:– British, 'wooden' actors, inferior settings, weak script. Verdict: A pain in the neck! American: actors 'natural', settings lavish and thoughtfully produced, script snappy with humour, 'just right'. Verdict: Gets my ninepence every time! One criticism of all films, British and American. Why such long preliminary announcements. I am interested in knowing only the actors and producers and authors. The rest is so much wasted screening time. It would, however, be a good idea to give this abbreviated 'cast' at the end of the film as well as the beginning, in order that I may check the name of any smaller-part actor who has impressed me.

167 *H. Stansbie (Mrs)*, 35 Doyle Rd (aged between 50 and 60), regular cinema-goer (4 times a month), preference – 'American generally, Some British are very good'.
Comments: The travel picture tonight (Tuesday) was beautiful and I should like to see a similar film as a regular feature. It is, however, objectionable to see the part of a British monarch or a member of the aristocracy played by an American, doing all the wrong things and speaking with the wrong accent. Also to see the parts of butlers and ladies' maids taken by people who do not understand the running of a gentleman's house, and doing things that would not be tolerated for a moment. Films like *Victoria the Great, Action for Slander, Fire Over England, Love from a Stranger, Disraeli, Lost Horizon, Dark Journey, Dodsworth*, which can be seen and enjoyed a second time, are the ones I like best. The organ is not a favourite feature of mine. It is too noisy.

168 *Mrs Florence Stewart*, 64 Radcliffe Rd (aged 56), regular cinema-goer (12 times a month), preference – both the same.
Comments: None.

169 *Mrs S. Hammond*, 17 Rock Terrace, Bromley Cross (aged 56), regular cinema-goer (8 times a year), preference – not given.
Comments: I loved the picture of *The Great Victoria*.[29] I like films that show real Home-life stories. I detest stories of killers, thieves, and

underworld stories of drug addicts and pick-pockets, and I certainly would not encourage my children to see them. Of course, I like a good comic. My husband and I are hoping soon to be able to go oftener. My husband's choice is always a good rollicking comic.

170 *Mrs Hodgkins*, 26 Uganda St (aged 56), regular cinema-goer (4 times a month), preference – British films.
Comments: The film *Victoria the Great* was very good, also the film *A Star is Born*.

171 *Mrs Ogden*, Tickle Farm House, Stoneclough (aged 57), regular cinema-goer (4 times a month), preference – not given.
Comments: As an old theatre patron, I am glad to get this opportunity of what has been in my mind for a very long time. I think if we had less such as Walt Disley [sic] cartoons etc. as these should be left for such as children's matinees and put some of the good old plays of 30 years ago, for instance *Woman and Wine, Span of Life, One of the Best, His House in Order, White Heather, The Prodigal Parson*. I am confident you would fill your house, satisfaction being supreme on both sides.

172 *Mrs Fox*, 42 Plover St (aged 58), regular cinema-goer (4 times a month), preference – both the same.
Comments: None.

173 *Mrs Leach*, 64 Radcliffe Rd (aged 58), regular cinema-goer (16 times a month), preference – American films.
Comments: None.

174 *Edna Aspinall*, 142 Manchester Rd, Westhoughton (aged 58), regular cinema-goer (12 times a month), preference – both.
Comments: Dear sir, There is no need for complaint as I think you do your best to please everyone which is rather difficult, as we people are so different in what they like. I went to see *Stella Dallas* on Monday which I thought a very fine picture and *Victoria the Great* was A1. I must give credit to the organist who is a fine player and it is a treat to listen to the music.

175 *Clara Barlow*, 9 Bottom o'th'Moor, Harwood (aged 59), regular cinema-goer (1–2 times a month), preference – British films.
Comments: These as I have filled in need no comment from me. You ask me my opinion, so I have numbered them as I think I like them. It would not do for everybody to be alike.

176 *Mrs Hodgson*, 278 Derby St, (aged 59), regular cinema-goer (6 times a month), preference – American films.
Comments: Myself and family have not missed a week since the Odeon opened. We like the place and have enjoyed some of the programmes very much and am sorry to say now and again we have not. The mistake is

when we get a very good picture. You now and again show a poor one. I'm sure there is enough people in Bolton to pack the Odeon every night, so give us the Best.

177 *Mrs Louie Hopkins*, 64 Radcliffe Rd (aged 60), regular cinema-goer (12 times a month), preference – American films.
Comments: None.

178 *Mrs Lily Hornby*, 9 Blackledge St (aged 60), regular cinema-goer (18 times a month), preference – American films.
Comments: First of all, I myself is not very hard to please. But I must say most of the film shown lately are Bunkum. I call it too easy gotten money, for most of the stars. You know modern people of today wants wit, humour, something that wont go out of their minds, something which they can remember. I love pictures really and I am one for recommending them if they are suitable, as I knoe the cost of the upkeep, as I know cinemas wants patronising. L. Hornby.[30]

179 *Mrs Rothwell*, 210 Halliwell Rd (aged 63), regular cinema-goer (8–10 times a month), preference – both the same.
Comments: I do not like war pictures. People who lived through the last war do not wish to be reminded of it.

180 *Mrs Annie Whittle*, 40 Salisbury St (aged 65), regular cinema-goer (6 times a month), preference – American films.
Comments: I go to the cinema primarily for relaxation and entertainment. A lot of American films are alright for Americans but not for us as the meaning is lost to us, i.e. various rackets. Like to see musicals but get fed up with that foot-tapping, a bit, alright, a lot, bored. Like to see films with good singers and beautiful natural scenery. Think films like *Three Smart Girls* are excellent, for their spontaneity and freshness. Think British musicals are excellent but the rest a long way off American. As yet waiting for the time to come when British films will portray ordinary people like the Americans do, not impossible if talent and not something else is rewarded.

181 *Jane Melling (Miss)*, 59 Essingdon St (aged 67), regular cinema-goer (8 times a month), preference – 'A good British is equal to a good American.'
Comments: Going to the cinema is my chief relaxation and I always look forward to same. Sometimes a picture gets great publicity and when I see it I am disappointed, for instance *Lost Horizon* was much over-rated. *Action for Slander* came very quietly and I thought it was great. *Victoria* was sublime – as criticism. This week *Stella Dallas* is very good. I also greatly enjoy listening to the Odeon's grand Organ and Hubert Selby's fine playing. So carry on, Odeon. Keep showing the kind of films you have been showing lately and you will have it filled to capacity.

182   *Mrs Lillie Williams*, 30 Crescent Avenue, Over Hulton (aged 78), regular cinema-goer (4 or 5 times a month), preference – both the same. *Comments*: I go to the films to be entertained, amused, to forget everyday worries. Find it a success and would go oftener if I could afford it.

Editors' notes

1 The correct title is *The Lives of a Bengal Lancer*.
2 *For Valour* was one of a series of farces starring the Aldwych team of Tom Walls and Ralph Lynn.
3 He submitted two entries; neither contained comments.
4 He refers to *Mutiny on the Bounty* (1936) with Charles Laughton and Clark Gable and *The Lives of a Bengal Lancer* (1935) with Gary Cooper and Franchot Tone.
5 *O.H.M.S.* (1936) was directed by Raoul Walsh and starred Wallace Ford, John Mills and Anna Lee.
6 *The Count of Monte Cristo* was an American film but with a British star (Robert Donat).
7 All these titles except *Sorrell and Son* and *Blossom Time* are American. By 'Nero' he probably means Cecil B. DeMille's *Sign of the Cross* in which Charles Laughton starred as Nero. *Ben-Hur*, the silent film epic, was re-issued with musical soundtrack in the 1930s.
8 He means *March of Time*.
9 The Mass-Observation total for Crompton male cinemagoers is 57, as they count Walter Glynn once. His two returns, which contain different comments, are printed separately here (nos 30 and 32).
10 She probably means *Elephant Boy*, starring Sabu.
11 The correct title is *A Day at the Races*.
12 She means *The Thirty Nine Steps*.
13 *The Prince and the Pauper*, starring Errol Flynn.
14 The British stars were Jessie Matthews, Barry Mackay and Alastair Sim.
15 *Captain Blood* and *Mutiny on the Bounty* were American films, though with British subjects and some British actors.
16 *Lloyds of London* was an American film.
17 This is *Gangway*, with Jessie Matthews (cf. no. 16).
18 *Moonlight Sonata* starred Paderewski.
19 'Henry the Eighth' is *The Private Life of Henry VIII* with Charles Laughton and 'Christina' is *Queen Christina* with Greta Garbo.
20 He means *Mutiny on the Bounty*.
21 Odeon film programmes ran a whole week; many other cinemas changed their programmes on Thursdays, running each programme for three days.

22 She means *Victoria the Great*.

23 *'Big Fellow'* was in fact called *Big Fella*. All three films starred Paul Robeson.

24 *Elephant Boy* is the correct title. Sabu was the star.

25 *Mutiny on the Bounty* with Charles Laughton as Captain Bligh.

26 All these films except *The Good Earth* had British settings but only one (*Love from a Stranger*) was British-made.

27 *Scarface* (1932), an American film directed by Howard Hawks, starred Paul Muni and George Raft. *The Frog* (1937), a British film directed by Jack Raymond, starred Gordon Harker.

28 *The Story of Louis Pasteur*, starring Paul Muni.

29 The correct title is *Victoria the Great*.

30 This return is more or less the same as no. 131, from Mrs Jennie Winstanley, 3 Blackledge St.

Part 2 Cinema-going in Wartime

4   The Cinema in the First Three Months of the War

When the war began, all cinemas were immediately closed as potential air raid hazards. But they were soon reopened after an outcry not only from the film industry but from public figures such as George Bernard Shaw, who in a letter to *The Times* (5 September 1939) called the cinema closures 'a masterpiece of unimaginative stupidity'. Cinemas would be needed, he argued, for the entertainment of troops on leave, evacuated children, etc. Cinema in general came under the aegis of the Films Division of the Ministry of Information but here too there was in the initial months considerable confusion and uncertainty. This Mass-Observation report (FR 24) paints a graphic picture of the cinema and cinema-going at this time. It also shows Mass-Observation deploying the techniques of interview, observation and analysis to chart reactions to film and beginning to articulate a theory of film and its social role in wartime.

Our National Panel figures suggested that cinema-going was more affected than anything else by the black-out, even in November when the results were obtained. Twenty per cent of the men and 17 per cent [of the] women said that their cinema-going was reduced by the black-out; on the other hand, a small number said cinema-going was increased by the black-out. As with dance halls, sports meetings, music halls, church services, all the problems of black-out, transport, evacuation and expense have come into operation. Like the pub and the dance hall, the cinema offers a modification on the rhythm and tempo of everyday life which is likely to have special function in wartime. Unlike the pub and the dance hall, the cinema (as at present organised) does not give sociability in any direct form, but, like in sport, the participants are spectators, part of a crowd, and more passive than a sports crowd. Finally the modern cinemas give a luxurious release from the physical features of mass life.

Therefore the cinema is perhaps half way between jazz, already dealt with, and sport, to be dealt with below, having the advantage of offering another interpretation of topicality, personal wish, romance, or the world beyond one's vision, but having the disadvantage of presenting this in a somewhat impersonal atmosphere. The biggest thing that cinemas can do, and to some extent have done to people, in the first three months of the war is to show them the war which they cannot see and hardly believe in. But here, as in every other institution which caters for the masses, the films have become embroiled in a labyrinth of red tape and restrictions which have prevented them from fulfilling much of their possible function. It is impossible here to go into all the amazing confusions and upsets which the film industry has suffered since 3 September, but it is necessary to outline one or two of them so far as they affect the films that got across to the masses, the audience's response, and thus the effect upon morale and the course of the war.

The film industry at war

There is no doubt that in an emergency the national importance of all cinemas would immediately increase; even in the crisis of September 1938, the value of the cinemas was clearly evident, not only for disseminating information but in providing an antidote for worry and nervous strain. Indeed the psychological value of the cinema in combating 'jitters' may well be its strongest claim to be regarded as a public servant.

This optimistically, Mr Richard Ford of the Odeon Education Department addressed the British Association just before the outbreak of war. Everyone in the cinema industry believed, and had some reason to believe, that the cinema could do big things in war and would be encouraged to do so, but like several other of the newer institutions, their independent and unpolitic growth, their own energetic self-satisfaction had brought them on the one hand to underestimate the mass of people a little, and, on the other, to overestimate the people who were to be responsible for the co-ordination of war help. One finds only faint traces of suspicion about these people; for instance, in the same article in the *Cinema* which quoted Ford's remark with the headline:

THE CINEMA AS PUBLIC SERVANT
ESPECIALLY AS WAR TIME SEDATIVE

there was the following aside:

But the haphazard growth of the cinema business is one of the primary causes of its unstable career. In 1914 the investing public, the men of affairs, and even the respectable middle class, probably regarded the cinemas much as we regard pin-table saloons at the present day. This attitude persisted during the 1920's and may still be found to-day among elderly people.

Unfortunately for the cinema elderly people took charge of the war. Many in our cabinet are far from cinema fans. The principal responsibility for the film industry in wartime went to a large film department set up in the Ministry of Information – jazz, sport, theatre and music hall did not have sections or even representatives. The achievements of the film section as far as we can learn, from scores of interviews with people in all parts of the film industry, from our own experiences with the Ministry and our intimate contacts with people in it, are staggeringly little in the first three months of the war. The most severe restrictions prevented film units from taking films about the countryside in Britain, the most severe censorship prevented the showing of films from the front, and so every sort of film production and organisation had to get sanction from the Ministry.

Great difficulties were here encountered. The official GPO Film Unit, headed by a Civil Servant, was allowed to take pretty well all the film it wanted, but was unable to go ahead with production plans for shorts, and so in the first three months of the war was able to produce one film dealing entirely with life in wartime London. Executives and directors in the GPO Unit lived for these three months in the same sort of state of endless frustration as did poster experts and opinion researchers in the Ministry of Information. Delay after delay broke for a time the heart of the industry which expected in war to have a great opportunity to give its great and unique form of service. The key people, responsible for the major indecision, were almost literally the people who had been running the Conservative party before the War. In a reply to a question in the House of Commons, Sir Edward Grigg gave the names and salaries of the film department of the Ministry of Information as follows.

Director: Sir Joseph Ball (unpaid)
Deputy Director: G. E. G. Forbes (£1,150 – £1,500)
Hon. Adviser: Lt. Col. A. C. Bromhead (unpaid)
Other posts:
  Sir Edward Villiers (£800)
  D. K. Clarke (£600)
  J. G. Hughes Roberts (£700–£860)
  R. Nunn May (£750)
  R. Ferguson (£500)
  J. Reeves (£500) (not yet taken up duties)
  W. Sellard (£450–£600) (not yet taken up duties)
  Oliver Bell (unpaid) (on temporary loan from Film Institute)

But obstruction was not of course confined to the Ministry. The War Office put numerous obstacles in the way not only of film but also of hapless amateur photographers. And above all the Director of the Board of Trade, Mr Oliver Stanley, son of the Earl of Derby, kept the industry in consternation for just under three months. A full story of his activities would be worth a volume in itself. Briefly the position was summed up by the editor of a trade paper who is also one of the moving figures in the all-powerful Ciné-Technicians Union. He told an observer (22 Nov.):

Well, I had better tell you the whole story from the beginning. Two years ago it was discovered that the film business was a racket – the Trafalgar film business showed that up – and this gave the industry a nasty jolt. At that time the Quota Act was due for revision, but the film industry was divided in itself and the few attempts at creating a unified front didn't meet with much success, though the ciné-technicians did something towards it. The New Act didn't help us at all to get out of our tail spin. It wasn't much better. By the old Quota Act 25 per cent of the films shown in this country were British though this was actually over the Quota necessity limit. But under the New Act only 15 per cent need be British. The result was a slump and in the first year after the Quota instead of the usual two hundred only one hundred British films were made. Then production began to increase until the beginning of the war put an end to everything. Everything was cut short, partly because all the cinemas were closed, and in the second place Mr Stanley in the Board of Trade, proposed to repeal the Quota Act. There was immediate agitation with interviews, letters to the Press, collaboration from all parties. Finally a Committee in the House of Commons was appointed and Mr Stanley promised he would do nothing without consulting this committee. But the Government has made no decision either way, and nobody knows what is going to happen. The result is that there are no investments going into films and there is no future. The effect on the employees is disastrous – carpenters, small actors, and such like are now 90 per cent unemployed. Before the war the government said 'the film industry should continue as it seemed a material asset', and with this in view they made many of the key grades into reserved occupations. Now we are reserved for an occupation that doesn't exist. Some of the film workers, it is true, have got jobs in ambulances and so forth but in a number of boroughs people in reserved occupations are refused. Many of us earn too much when we are in work to qualify for the dole and our position when we are out of work is very bad. What is needed is for the government to say exactly what its intentions are.

This is exactly what Mr Stanley would not do. It was not until the actual day of this interview that he announced that the Quota would remain. This meant that the greatest terror in the film industry which had paralysed it for the preceding eleven weeks had gone – the terror that the Quota would be removed and the market flooded with American films or that there would be new and more stringent measures passed by Stanley.

One of Stanley's main subsidiary arguments was that men could not be spared to work the Quota in wartime but experts in reply claimed that twelve clerks could do the job comfortably. Whatever the facts – the position is extremely obscure as it has all gone on in Mr Stanley's mind and very few replies have been received from him to repeated inquiries from the film industry – the effect on the film industry was that in the first few months of the war it was paralysed by doubt for the future. Natural paralysis. Neither the industry nor the Board of Trade had any carefully worked out plans, adequate co-ordination of interest, or adequate contact with public opinion and public demand. Therefore, instead of being able to cash in on the war and influence the public morale, the film industry has produced in the first three months of the war only one film, *The Lion Has Wings* which was anywhere near the mark. Not only has this lost their money and lowered the whole national income, it has lost their prestige and put them under a new initial handicap.

Effects on Hollywood

The effect on Hollywood was equal bewilderment. For one thing they feared the complete loss of their important English market and the whole position has engendered ill-will from the American industry which doubts whether it will be able to get films into England at all, and even if it does so is afraid that even if they are topical they may suffer the same fate as the anti-Nazi *Professor Mamlock* which has been cut to pieces and, even then, banned before being seen by the Hove Watch Committee. So, while at Elstree and Denham nothing has happened, in Hollywood it is worth less than nothing from the British point of view. 20th Century Fox, Charlie Chaplin, and Warner Brothers have cancelled films with pro-British or Anti-Nazi themes. Reporting from Hollywood to the British Film Institute Journal, *Sight and Sound*, Ezra Goodman said:

> The screen capital is experiencing a local war of nerves. The spark that has set off the European conflagration has also kindled a worried look in Hollywood's collective eye. For war, which exerts a profound effect on each of us, usually deals a severe blow to the arts. And the screen, as an international and widespread medium, is no exception. Already Paris and to a certain extent London studios are reported to have been closing down so that men and materials might be utilised for the more pressing needs of national defence. And although Hollywood has not gone so far as yet to shutter its sound stages, the war has caused extensive economy and production curtailment. Bagdad on the Pacific is viewing the European situation with alarm. The loss of the major portion of its world market has proved a severe blow to American production. With the British and French movie houses cut off for the time being, Hollywood has been deprived of a vital source of income and has to re-adjust itself

accordingly. Expenses and production budgets have been heavily cut, and the prevailing opinion is that as long as current conditions exist, the average top budgets will run to only half a million dollars, compared to the previous figure of approximately one million dollars for super-specials.

While America was cutting out anti-Nazi films, British producers were groaning to produce them. In the meanwhile Charles Laughton went off to Hollywood and transferred his Mayflower Company lock, stock and barrel to Los Angeles. Off went Alfred Hitchcock, Herbert Wilcox was there already; Victor Saville is now in Hollywood, Korda has gone over there too, clutching a copy of *The Lion Has Wings* in the American Clipper. David Niven, however, has come back – to fight, not film. No wonder a Union official high up told an observer:

I am very afraid of a repetition of 1914. Then the British were flourishing and probably the premier industry in the world. But by 1922 we were dead and there was no protection for us. Agitation started then and continued until 1927 when the First Quota Act was passed, renewed in 1937 for another ten years. In 1926 nowhere in the British Empire was a cinema handle turning.

Renewed life in the industry

Oliver Stanley having at last cleared the air, the position improved slightly. George Formby announced that he was making a start on a comic film about his capturing a submarine. *Hell's Angels* and *All Quiet on the Western Front* are being taken off the shelf and new bits put in which could not be used before because of German feeling. MGM went ahead with *Waterloo Bridge* which is going to be all about air raids. British National announced four films to be produced between the end of November and June:

Laugh It Off a topical musical comedy with Tommy Trinder, Jean Colin, Geraldo and his Band.
This German Freedom Diana Wynyard and Clive Brook playing together for the first time since *Cavalcade* in a story of the German Freedom Radio Station.
Black-out Conrad Veidt in a contraband story of the present war.
Gas Light Diana Wynyard in a screen version of the stage success.[1]

This German Freedom, directed by Brian (Desmond) Hurst who had been largely responsible for *The Lion Has Wings*, is proving difficult because actors have to be found to play Hitler, Goering, Goebbels, and Streicher in special circumstances. Francis Sullivan is almost a certainty for Goering, and it is Goebbels who has proved the greatest difficulty. Fierce-faced comedian, Alfred Drayton, was tipped for bald-headed Streicher but, as someone has pointed out, you 'cannot have Streicher accidentally collecting laughs in the middle of the picture'.[2] In addition, Michael Balcon has announced forthcoming production for a film about the convoy system. All these pictures will have a straight film story against the background of this actual war and our German enemy. So far practically all the films planned for production and announced are along these lines.

From the experience of jazz one might suspect that the reaction towards war is almost too violent. Certainly if all these and other productions are successful in 1940, the theory of the cinema as 'escape' will be exploded. Long before, Mass-Observation had collected information which raised profound doubt as to whether people really went to the cinema to escape. It is rather, we believe, that people go to the cinema to see situations and surroundings which they have heard of or dreamt about and have not been able to see themselves. And in a war which has peculiar ambivalence between the Home Front and the Front Line as well as a rigid censorship which largely ignores popular interest, they can portray uniquely the actuality and the dream intermixed. The bomb and the hero. The submarine and the spy. Only *Picture Post* can approach the pictures at this, and it can only perform a fraction of the film's 'exciting' function. We have always questioned – and especially once in a heated argument with Mr Richard Ford (above) – that the films are simply sedatives. They are partly sedatives. They can invest the sordid circumstances of war with noble qualities and thus can make reality at the same time more 'real' and more acceptable. Before examining this situation in its actual context of the films shown and audience response in the first months of the war, we must just touch on the exhibition side of the industry which can, and sometimes has, intervened between production and public with some of the same attitudes as Oliver Stanley.

The exhibition of films

Exhibition and distribution to the troops, which would appear to be a fairly straightforward matter, was the subject of some upsets quite early on. To combat this, Sir Adrian Baillie was appointed a liaison officer. Like the Ministry of Information film officials he is a strong Conservative and MP for Tonbridge; aged 41.

He was appointed to the job on 21 October, he resigned from it on 10 November. The sequence of these events (as reported by the *Daily Mail* on 11 November):

Oct. 20   *Daily Mail* reveals BEF are not getting films.

Oct. 21   Sir Adrian Baillie appointed.

Oct. 23   Sir Adrian starts work.

Oct. 24   NAAFI announce first film show 'behind the lines'.

Oct. 25   Announced General Film Corporation to send *new* films to BEF is to be formed.

Oct. 27   *Daily Mail* reveals red tape still holding back films. NAAFI announce all films must go through them.

Nov. 6   Film chiefs appoint two committees of 15 members each to assist Sir Adrian.

Nov. 10   Sir Adrian finishes.

Sir Adrian stopped because, he said, the problem was solved but in mid-November the press reported that the troops were still getting one or two year old films and it might be some time before they got new ones.

The troop confusion was small as compared to the distribution and exhibition inside Britain. At the outbreak of the war every cinema was forcibly closed by Order in Council. As air raids failed to materialise and the public and the vested interests grew more and more restive the Government retreated and started to allow local authorities to exercise their own discretion. Outside the Embassy Cinema, Notting Hill Gate on 7 September a notice written in white chalk on a blackboard announced:

***   Embassy Cinema   ***
Notting Hill Gate.
CLOSED
Until further notice
Nearest cinema open
Aberystwyth
239 miles.

At that time Aberystwyth had the distinction of being the only town in Britain showing films of any sort. Then on 11 September cinemas in reception areas were allowed to open; on 15 September cinemas in evacuation areas were also allowed to open until 10 with the exception of the West End of London where all were to shut at 6. Sir John Anderson made considerably more speed in making a decision than his colleague Stanley. But he was up against the pressure not only of the industry but also the public whose possible anger alarms any politician. So he preserved simply his own area of London as a Presbyterian sanctuary and it was not until 4 October that any West End cinemas were permitted to remain open in the evenings; even then the cinemas were divided into two groups, each group taking its turn to stay open till ten for one week, then back to six the next. This is still the position at the time of writing (25 Nov.) though an announcement on 4 November allowed cinemas to open until 11 o'clock in the evening. But by the time all these arrangements had been made several major London cinemas had given up the struggle and had closed down for the duration. Many other cinemas claimed losing as much as £1,000 a week. Many offered half price to men in uniform and most cinemas stopped matinee prices by arrangement with the CEA.

Confusion was increased by distributors of films changing the terms of booking along the following lines.

Lack of exploitation of situation

To the cinemagoer very little of all this was apparent. All that they saw was first no films and a complete black-out, then gradually more and more films, several of them with a topical story. This topical interest was curiously little exploited by the exhibitors who always tend to show less perspicacity. Observers were able to collect only a few examples of cinemas which captured the new spirit and exploited the new background. The Tooting Granada had posters for *The Spy in Black* – 'The Story the Papers didn't dare to print', and the Granada[3] at Clapham Junction advertised the Ritz Brothers Comic Horror film *The Gorilla* with 'See "The Gorilla", even crazier than Hitler'. On 7 November the *Liverpool Echo* carried the following:

> NOW ... THIS SENSATIONAL STORY CAN BE TOLD ... OF ENEMY
> MENACE IN ITS GRIMMEST FORM ... OF U-BOAT 29 ... LURKING,
> WAITING ... THE BRITISH FLEET IN PERIL.
>
> CONRAD VEIDT
> CONRAD VEIDT
> in
> THE SPY IN BLACK
> THE SPY IN BLACK
> THE SPY IN BLACK
> with
> SEBASTIAN SHAW
> VALERIE HOBSON
> Marius Goring

> Deep Mystery, Intense Drama, Glorious
> Romance, Hair-raising Thrills are all
> packed into this Grim Drama of the
> U-Boats.
> It takes you Spell-bound Behind the
> Scenes into the Secrets of the Most
> Menacing Espionage System ever to

> threaten the World. Who is the spy in
> Black? . . . Where is U-Boat 29? See and
> Thrill to a Terrific Drama as Topical
> as To-Day's Headlines!

The Sunday Graphic (5 Nov.) had the following film note:

> Outside a cinema playing *Good-bye Mr Chips* the other day a man
> paraded dressed as Hitler and carrying a placard saying 'Unfair. They're
> paying more attention to Mr Chips than to me.'

An observer noticed (1 Nov.) a somewhat elaborate topical poster outside
the Cameo, Charing Cross. His report reads:

> Prominently displayed outside the theatre was a drawing headed 'The
> Stream of Life'; on the right hand side of this was traced the progress of
> man, Man himself running down the centre and offshoots being labelled,
> some by the names of animals, others with names of Germans in
> authority (e.g. 'donkeys' on one, 'Goebbels' on another). On the left side
> were eight or ten squares showing fairly accurate outline drawings of
> Nazi chiefs; the majority of these were given their right names but
> Ribbentrop was called Brickendrop. Underneath was a swastika with
> Hitler's head at one point, a dagger at another, a bleeding hand at a
> third. This seemed to attract little attention and those that did inspect it
> were not amused.

Number of 'spy' films

It was fortunate or perhaps foreseeing that both American and British
producers had a series of new films dealing with the spy situation,
including the following:

Confessions of a Nazi Spy

A detailed account of the facts of the round-up of Nazi spies in America.
The first half of the film deals purely with the organisation of the spy ring,
with its agent in Scotland, the almost fanatical leader of the American
Nazi party, Dr Kassel, and the neurotic but sincere young German who
writes to a German newspaper and asks to be made a spy. But the Scottish
agent is arrested and the first indications of the position are given to the
American police. The neurotic tries unsuccessfully to obtain blank
passports and is arrested; under cross-examination he breaks down and
admits that he gets his orders from the political leader of the German ship
Bismarck. When next the ship docks the police go on board and although
the leader himself is not on board his mistress and confidante is, and she

too breaks down under cross-examination and gives away Dr Kassel. Kassel himself is interviewed with success, and the chain of evidence is complete. But here the Gestapo intervenes. Kassel disappears and is finally discovered on the *Bismarck* which refuses to stop or release him. Another key witness suffers the same fate. But despite these setbacks four spies are found guilty and the whole system is exposed; the film ends with a short glorification of the American democracy.

Spy in Black

Long Hope is a small island in the Shetlands. To it comes a U-Boat, lands its commander, and awaits his return with valuable information for he has gone to the schoolmistress who is reputedly a German spy. In her house where he stays a day or two he not only has a magnificent view of the complete English fleet but also is introduced to Ashington, a lieutenant in the Navy who is prepared to sell secrets, and tells the Commandant that a party of destroyers will be passing a certain point at a certain time. This information is passed on to the U-Boat and arrangements are made for the destroyers to be met with the complete German submarine fleet in English waters. But the same night the Commandant discovers that the schoolmistress is no German spy but an English one and that Ashington is her husband. In a last desperate effort to save his ships he manages to get control of a packet boat and hurries off to the appointed base. But before he gets there his own U-Boat sinks the packet boat and he goes down with the ship.

(It is important to note that in this film the Germans are not only made human but also honourable gentlemen who are only serving their country in the same way as their enemies).

Nurse Edith Cavell

Nurse Cavell owns a nursing home in Belgium before the war. The Germans occupy the town but she carries on. Then a refugee from the Germans needs her help and she gives it him and hides him in a secret room in the nursing home. Soon she is at the head of a 'committee' who help prisoners to escape, getting them forged passports, hiding them in barrels on barges and seeing to their safety. But finally a German spy discovers this by posing as an escaped prisoner, and Nurse Cavell is arrested and condemned to be shot. To this verdict there is much opposition led by the American ambassador on the grounds that she has not been spying but only helping prisoners to escape. But despite this, and despite the demonstration of one of the firing squad who refuses to do his duty, she is shot, her last words being the famous 'patriotism is not enough'.

Q Planes

A series of test flights all end in sudden silence and the complete disappearance of the plane in question. The secret service puts Captain Hammond on the job but he is not able to stop an air pilot going up with a new and very secret engine attached to his plane and suffering the same fate as all the other machines, namely paralysis by means of a ray directed from a ship which later takes the plane and pilot aboard her for further examination. But comparison of Lloyds list with the positions at which these disappearances had taken place leads Hammond to suspect a certain boat and he goes in a destroyer to seize it. But meanwhile the pilot of the last flight has not only gained his liberty but has also captured the ship and so all ends well with the middle European country which was after the planes well and truly defeated.

An Englishman's Home

Victor Brandt, a spy from a country which is hostile to England succeeds in establishing himself with the Browns, a typical English family whose head does not believe even in the possibility of war. Brandt sets up a wireless by means of which enemy aircraft can be directed to this country but also falls in love with the daughter of the house and plans to elope with her. But on the very evening before this, the enemy decides to move and the planes are heard overhead in the middle of Mr Brown's great birthday celebrations. From these planes men are dropped by parachute to defend the wireless stations against attack and the Browns' house is consequently siezed. Brown loses his temper, shoots a German and is therefore shot himself. But an English plane bombs the house, the ray is cut off, the invaders turn back, and England is saved.

Espionage Agent

(Not as yet shown in this country.) A famous diplomat marries a spy and consequently falls from favour but tries to build up his position by unmasking the espionage system which is responsible for the sabotage that is rampant everywhere. After a long chase and other thrills the two are successful and all is well.

Exile Express

A girl from a middle European country is applying for naturalisation but is informed by agents of her country that she will not be allowed to obtain it unless she gives them the secret of a new poison which her doctor employer has discovered. She refuses but that night the doctor is murdered but he first destroys the key to the formula. The spies thus try all they can to get hold of the girl to make her give the required information but all effort is foiled by the reporter who dogs her tracks.

Trapped in the Sky

A new aeroplane invention is tried out but the first test is a failure through sabotage. In an endeavour to discover who is the culprit a captain gets himself court-martialled and then, in his disgrace, is approached by agents of foreign countries who are interested in the invention. By pumping them he finally finds out that the real sabotageur is the inventor himself who has been bribed heavily. He frightens him into admission and the invention is taken up by the United States Government.

Smashing the Spy Ring

A G-Man is murdered while investigating a spy ring. But the detective in charge of the case helped by the dead man's sister helps to find the murderers but is only saved in the nick of time when he is trapped in a laboratory and keeping the foe at bay with bottles of acid.

Secret Journey

In an attempt to get a secret formula from an agent of a foreign country the hero makes friends with the agent's son, while the heroine makes love to him. They get the formula but hearts are broken in the process.

They made her a Spy

A girl's brother is killed by spies, and she decides to catch them. She gets on to one man and he in turn reveals that the spy-in-chief is a man high up in political circles. He is cornered and all is well.

All these films were ready or released just before the outbreak of war. To a psychologist this simple fact would give a good picture of the mentality of the sort of people producing films at that time and of the general atmosphere of inferiority and paranoia which the American democracies were unconsciously feeling towards aggressive Germany. This inferiority so accentuated by Munich (see our Penguin Special *Britain*) was released by the fact of war and we at last showed ourselves able and ready to stand up to this sinister enemy with his humanity-eliminating Gestapo. These spy films with their inevitable atmosphere and representation of war where the spy feature in a *military* context was the major theme [sic]; witness, for example, the report of a power loom turner of Huddersfield:

13 Oct. Came home on bus. Seated in front of me a little boy and girl.
They sounded to be going to the pictures. The little girl said something,
then the boy turned to her and loudly and indignantly said 'It isn't, it's a
war picture.' The girls said 'sh-sh'. The young woman next to me said
'It's all war pictures or else cowboys'. She smiled. 'I've an aunt at
Chester and she has a boy and he goes to see all the cowboy pictures and
when he had scarlet fever my aunt had to play cowboys with him. . . .'

Where the spy theme was only used in general, in its more sensational and
less relevant-to-war aspect, the films did not do nearly so well in box office
takings up to the end of November.

The Lion Has Wings

Apart from these films, only one other film dealt specially and clearly with
the war. *The Lion Has Wings* was the first film of this war. It opens with
the commentator saying 'This is England where we believe in freedom'
and while he speaks photographs of the English countryside are thrown on
to the screen. Then it is shown how the people are cared for, how the
children are looked after; but all the while Germany is preparing for war
and a vivid contrast is made between our peaceful life and their warlike
one. But we also are ready as indeed the Hendon Air Pageant showed
clearly as long ago as 1937. We fought against the evil but all in vain.
Germany marched into Austria, into Czechoslovakia, threatened Poland.
And at 11 o'clock on 3 September, the Prime Minister declared to the
whole country that England was now in a state of war. The war machine
began to move, and soon orders were received by one squadron that they
were to bomb two warships entering the Kiel Canal. This feat is
successfully accomplished and as they are seen returning the commentator
announces that although the shots of the actual raid have been
reproductions, nevertheless 'the men that you see now leaving their planes
are the actual pilots who bombed Kiel'.

  The film now turns to a mythical air attack on England and its defeat by
the RAF. The word comes through that an attack is to be expected and
from then on every move that the Germans make is charted on a special
map 'somewhere in England'. But before further details are given a flash-
back reveals how England faced the danger of invasion four hundred years
ago. Queen Elizabeth addressed the troops in stirring tones, the word was
passed from mouth to mouth, and the country was united against the
menace of the Armada.

  In the present again steps are being taken to repel the invader. Round
the all-important map are many high officials in various defence
departments and from them orders are issued to all parts of the country.

Searchlights and anti-aircraft guns are manned, squadrons are sent up and, by keeping in touch with General Headquarters, manage to find the enemy planes and turn them back; only one German flight gets through and that has but to look at the balloon barrage to realise that their quest is hopeless. The raid is over, the counter measures have been a complete success.

One of the Wing Commanders who had been at GHQ goes home tired out and falls asleep while his wife speaks to him of the sacrifices of the women of England. And on his sleeping form the picture fades and ends.

Under any circumstances this film would be excellent propaganda for it is well made and it contains as well as some extremely funny moments where Hitler is contrasted to a Derby bookie some superb photographs of the RAF in action which possess considerable popular appeal. Yet added to all this is the introduction of a 'human interest' by means of the appearance of several well-known actors in small parts which link each separate incident and make it a combined whole. Ralph Richardson, for instance, is an air pilot who is seen first during the Hendon display, appears later entering his house during the Prime Minister's speech, then finally helping those in the control room who were responsible for the defeat of the air attack. The part that Merle Oberon plays as his wife is even smaller, lasting three minutes in all; she is shown listening to Mr Chamberlain's speech and then at the very end delivering a speech on the sacrifice of womanhood. But, despite the brevity of their parts, they serve their purpose admirably and while this idea is not entirely new – it has been used in travel films before – nevertheless it is a first-class method of adding vitality to what otherwise might have been a colourless account.

The film was made with secrecy and even more haste. Indeed it is surprising that the censor allowed as much as he did to pass him for not only is the inside of a bomber shown but also the control room of the General Headquarters of the RAF. The haste is understandable for obviously the sooner such a film could be released the greater would be its topical value. In this direction Korda must have been much helped by the existence of previous pictures of which large portions would be of value. In the first place there was his own much boosted but never finished epic *The Conquest of the Air*, in the second *Fire Over England* which provided a long complete sequence, while finally – a fact which only Graham Greene in the *Spectator* was brave enough to point out – many of the scenes were taken from a film called *The Gap*, made to point out the weaknesses of our air defences. Some portions, of course, had to be taken especially and for this three directors were employed each working independently so as to save time. Three weeks were spent in the cutting room and a commentary was added by E. V. H. Emmett of the Gaumont British News.

That the film will be a success can be determined not only from the fact that a West-End audience clapped and cheered, an incident rare enough in itself to cause comment, but also from the fact that even a trailer evoked very considerable response as the following report from an observer at the Paramount Theatre, Tottenham Court Road, indicates:

> Observer missed many details owing to man throwing fit in front of him. But shots included two of Hitler; each time there were two or three hisses and one raspberry. Another shot showed an A.A. man getting ready to 'give the nasties what for'; this was greeted by a very loud laugh. Pictures of the RAF were greeted in silence and there was a good deal of comment after it had finished.

Of fifteen different reviews of *The Lion Has Wings* that an observer analysed only three showed any real hostility to the film. *The Times* remained rather aloof, confining itself to a brief commentary on the film with occasional mild criticism; *The Sunday Dispatch* complained it was a 'hotch-potch of brilliant ideas and dull languid stuff that should have been left on the cutting room floor', while Graham Greene in *The Spectator* although enjoying the first half, could not, as mentioned above, reconcile himself to the new significance of the excerpts from *The Gap*. Many of the others criticised the detail. Three complained of the *Fire Over England* sequence as being irrelevant, another three ridiculed the sentiment at the end and *The Daily Telegraph* joined *The Sunday Dispatch* in commenting on the ragged quality of the film. But at least four papers from *The Observer* to *The Daily Mirror* emphasised its value as propaganda and only *The New Statesman* questions whether '*Journey's End* officers and Bruce Bairnsfather men are our best propaganda types'. And what are three mild doubters against so many? *The News Chronicle* deemed the film worthy of the place of honour in their middle page, and *The Daily Mail* says 'The most magnificent picture of the British spirit and of British courage that has ever been produced. Marvellously done.'

Other propaganda films

In fact the film has an enormous reaction value, but, as we shall see in a moment, all films dealing with war have produced a high degree of reaction. The March of Time was also fortunate or foreseeing with its topical release of *The Battlefleets of Britain*, a twenty-minute account, first and very briefly of how England went to war, then of her might on the sea, with the type of ship described, then a short description of the work of the China Squadron, the Mediterranean fleet, and the Home Fleet, all of which was very well received by the public and by public-conscious Winston Churchill too. Also emerging in November were *Our Fighting Navy*, produced by Butchers unit, which shows the British Navy 'in all aspects of its lawful occasions', target practice, torpedo discharges, dropping of depth charges, and the air arm, brought up to date with pictures of the First Lord and special emphasis laid upon the *Courageous*. *The Cavalcade of the Navy* is another topical picture which traces the history of the Navy from Carthage and Alfred the Great to modern times and is again brought up to date, this time by the introduction of a sequence showing the Prime Minister making his speech. This film has the distinction of being in colour throughout and runs for well over half an hour. The Air Force is represented chiefly of course by *The Lion Has Wings* but another short with the self-evident title of *Raiding Air Fighters* is doing good business while a film made at the beginning of the year called *Wings over Empire* has been booked well, though it deals more with civil flying than with the RAF. There are thus three films dealing with the Navy, two directly and one indirectly with the RAF, and none with the Army at the end of November. This is approximately equal to the general publicity aroused by the three services, the Navy largely through its energetic Minister, the Air Force with the assistance of thirty-one journalists, twenty-one of whom are at home stations, costing £20,000 a year. Finally a film called *'Arf a Mo, 'Itler* compares this country with Germany since the Great War of 1914 to 1918, laying particular stress on our help to the weak and undernourished, on our determination, and on our sense of humour but there are also a number of shots of the training of militiamen.

All the documentary topical films since the war have had, or are having, a great success in evoking a high degree of audience response. And perhaps the increase in such films will increase the amount of cinema response and turn the cinema-goer from a passive creature into someone more alert and civilised because the new film subjects are more near to everyday life in wartime. In peace time the cinema practically never approached the problems of life other than the psychological problems.

Do It Now

A nice example of alertness came by when the GPO Unit released as soon as the cinemas opened, a documentary film about ARP, which they had brought up to date by having an ARP Warden address the audience from the screen at the beginning of the picture. This film was entitled *Do It Now* and told the public what to do and what not to do in the case of war, air raids, etc. It showed an air raid alarm sounding and immediately everybody rushing down the streets, people scurrying into shelters, people putting on gas masks and policemen running hard and blowing whistles, deserted cars and bicycles in the street, and men frantically knocking at a door trying to get in, people mopping their brows as they took off their gas masks coming out of the shelters.

All these items evoked loud laughter. Some of the situations were intended to be funny, others were not. But in any case they went too far and by trying to pass it off with 'if the war does happen' and make it all seem rather fun they made the film seem only foolish. For that was not the way that the public did behave when the worst did happen and by the time the film was released everybody knew that it was not the way that people had behaved. Before the war the GPO Unit might have got away with it but even so the hidden effect on most of the spectators would have contained disbelief and lack of sympathy. The film showed, for instance, a sequence of a woman ordering food to hoard and she keeps on making the shop assistant go up and down the ladder to get more and more and more sugar. The exaggeration of a well-off producer who seldom went into a small shop and certainly had not observed the real behaviour in them before the war. The rumour-mongers with their heads together was equal fantasy. Good fun before the war, perhaps, such sequences produced an audience response of ridicule and even contempt by mid-September, and such a film would probably never have been effective in getting people to take the precautions that it recommended, the purpose for which it was produced. We have already seen how few people did take these precautions anyway.

Reactions to Confessions of a Nazi Spy

Compare with the reception of the GPO film the reception of one of the more successful spy films released near the beginning of the war. Note how the laughter is entertainment, is not uncomfortable laughter against unflattering representations of situations which one can identify with oneself. The observer compares the audience reaction with the main sequences of the film.

A First National Picture. (no subtitles)	Immediate murmur as censor's pass is put on screen.
A silhouette man speaks to the audience pointing out that truth is stranger than fiction and that all this is truth (NB throughout picture there are interruptions from this commentator).	N.r. (no response)
A Scottish village. A postman delivers letters to some woman and comments on the fact that she gets so many from abroad.	A good deal of whispering.

A German meeting in New York where Kassel is addressing an enthusiastic audience. He speaks of the necessity of German culture in USA and at the end of his address all stand and salute.

One snorts at the sight of the swastika at the back of the hall; a few titters are caused by the gestures of Kassel. One laughs at the remark 'we are proud of our great Fuhrer'. Toward the end there is louder laughter at gestures and the 'heil' raises general laughs.

A neurotic sensitive man, Schneider, is carried away by this, talks of the value of Nazism, then gets himself enrolled as a Nazi spy.

Some comment as he speaks on Nazism. General silence as he becomes a spy.

The German reception of Schneider's application. It is decided to employ him but to set the s.s. *Bismarck*'s leader to investigate when the ship lands.

A good deal of coughing and whispering.

Leader on the ship gives lecture to crew shows power in various ways, but also shows he is power of Gestapo who are travelling with him.

General silence but laugh at crew giving Hitler salute.

Old lady, having beauty treatment from Hilda, Leader's friend, tells how she longs for the Germany of old. And is betrayed.

N.r.

A shot of the Captain's study with Hitler's picture on the wall. Three men in the room all salute.

Laugh at Hitler salute, also at picture, very loud when it is brought to a close-up.

Commentator talks to background of shots of Germany in 1933 with the first exposition of the doctrine of racial purity.

N.r.

Back to German bund in America. A Legion man complains that Kassel is not talking as he should about the Bill of Rights and others also object. There is a free fight and objectors are thrown out.

Some laughing at the introductory passages and a good deal of clapping at the objectors.

Schneider gets his first assignment and though he quarrels with his wife manages to get two things that are required of him, thinking he will be paid for information.

Titter when Schneider tells friend he gets information from Hitler himself. Some coughing and talking at full details of how he gets information.

Leader meets Schneider who gives vent to his complicated schemes for a variety of things. He is paid, but very little.

Some comment at the beginning. Dies out as Schneider first sees visitor, swells and dies again as money is produced. Laugh at 'heil Hitler's which finish interview.

One man complains of Hitler though he is in Nazi party. He is taken to inner room then put on board ship and returned to Germany.

Murmurs through his complaint, but silence as he is captured and shipped. One woman tut-tuts. (Old woman in front of obs. now asleep; remains so for rest of picture.)

Kassel leaves for Germany. Shots of Germany and her leaders while commentator runs the country down.

Sundry snorts at shots of ranting Germans.

Kassel meets German leader (may be meant to be Goebbels himself), is told that he is appointed leader of the new American Nazi group whose job it is to 'encourage faction.'

Snort at vast picture of Hitler on the wall. Otherwise silence.

Long shots of various ways that propaganda was spread through the USA.

General silence throughout. Laugh when commentator says 'stupidities of Germany'.

Woman in Scotland is arrested and much information is discovered.

A good deal of comment.

Back to America where information from Scotland has been sent. Military authorities hand matter over to Federal Bureau in shape of Detective.

The detective is Edward G. Robinson. There is an immediate and widespread murmur.

Detective points out that the USA is already fighting Germany, or rather that Germany is fighting USA.

N.r.

Kassel returns to be greeted by a Horst Wessel camp. Inspects troops including boys and girls 'who have

Laughs at introductory 'heil'. Snorts at boys lining up and comments as they repeat the right been trained in revolver practice', then gives address.

answers. Some laughs throughout scene.

Schneider goes to café and is told to get blank passports. A man in inner room is trying to back out but thinks better of it when he is informed of Gestapo's presence.

For both parts of the scene there is very general silence.

Schneider tries to get passports by posing as under-secretary. Gets frightened and keeps on sending parcel which contains them to different spots to be collected by him. But he is caught in the end all the same.

Some comment all through the scene and a good deal of laughter as he keeps changing place where he is to fetch parcel. Much comment when he is arrested.

Detective cross-examines Schneider. Plays on the fact that Schneider thinks a lot of himself and finally gets a full confession (Commentator describes part of the process).

Silence at first then some comment and rustling. At end silence again and then more rustling.

Bismarck comes to shore and Hilda is arrested and taken to Detective's.

Some comment on the arrest of Hilda.

She is cross-examined without success but the entrance of Schneider shakes her and she then makes a mistake about the Christian name of the Leader.

Murmurs at first then silence, laughs at mistake over name. A very loud laugh and one clap at Detective's remark 'New York is very much part of the United States.' (Obs. may have missed some remark or gesture.)

Detective goes to Kassel's and inspects room, foils Kassel's attempt to burn code.

Silence at first but comment when code is found.

Kassel is cross-examined and breaks down when Hilda enters. He raves, calls her 'stupid cow'. He recovers himself, but then talks about 'our Fuhrer'. Then confesses.

A lot of comment at this but Hilda's entrance stops this; and titter at 'stupid cow'. Some laughs at 'our Fuhrer'.

He tells all he knows (not given in full of course but there is a good deal of talk).

Silence at first but some talk later.

Kassel is allowed home, tells Gestapo (who he finds there) that he gave nothing away. They leave and are promptly arrested.

Murmurs at arrest of Gestapo.

Three more spies arrested in various places.

Slight laughs at these arrests.

Back to Germany. Commentator on march into Austria. Brief shot of Hitler in car riding over frontier.

Immediate hiss but not very general.

Kassel returns to wife, hears that Gestapo spies have been released on bail but goes to case which telephone call summons him to. Captured by the Gestapo.

General silence. One says 'oh' when the release on bail is announced, another 'oh's' as he is caught. Then much comment.

Detective discovers that Kassel is on the *Bismarck* and charters a seaplane. But captain refuses to stop.

Much comment on these scenes and one or two laughs at the seaplane.

Kassel gets to Germany. Is promised that he will be safe if he formally denies all that he has said in America. Final remark from the German: 'You'll be safe for the present.'

Someone tut-tuts at the beginning and there is a general murmur at 'for the present'.

German sees Detective and hints at international difficulties if Hilda is not released immediately.
Departs with a flea in his ear.

Loud and long laughter at the German's discomfiture, one person starts to clap.

German gets in touch with his Government; starts off confidently but is told off.

Titters throughout.

To the court in Washington.

One of the key prisoners vanishes and is taken to Germany. American ambassador calls on him at Southampton but for some unspecified reason he refuses to be taken off.

N.r.

Courtroom again. Prosecutor gives long speech on the evils of Nazism in the USA.

Silence at the beginning but soon coughing and murmurs.

Fade-out to Germany and the march into Czechoslovakia, full shots of Hitler and of thousands of marching soldiers.	Immediate hisses and 1 or 2 jeer at Hitler.
Goebbels(?) is seen pointing out the necessity of getting propaganda into America.	N.r.
Back to courtroom. The speech goes on emphasising the necessity of American prevention of such measures and saying 'America is democracy'.	General silence but one laughs at 'America is democracy'.
Conviction indicated by newspapers, then short judge's speech.	N.r.
Detective and prosecutor discuss the case afterwards. Detective compares Germany to a madhouse and calls them an insane race.	Fairly loud laugh at 'madhouse' and 'insane' remarks.
Waiter says 'They seem to forget that this ain't Europe'. Prosecutor: 'The voice of the people'. Detective: 'Thank God'.	N.r.
The End	Slight applause.

Another observer briefly reports before the war and before general release (30 August):

Edward G. Robinson tells German lawyer to get out of his office.	Applause.
Each appearance of Hitler.	Hissing, not very loudly and with subsequent laughter.
German (meant to be Goebbels?) addresses staff – says 'Japan is our ally' at list of triumphs.	Laughter.

Once the war had begun, response to all these films was greatly increased. There is not the space here, though there will be at a later date, to analyse exactly the elements and conditions which make for audience response in wartime (and in peace time).

But the increase in response in all its aspects, in clapping, hissing, laughing, verbal comment, and conversation after the film is distinct. It is equally an increase in favourable reaction to things and people that people dislike; this is by no means confined to story films and documentaries Take newsreels, for example. Observers covered all the main newsreels. If we compare fifteen news reels in the latter half of August and fifteen war time newsreels, in both cases selected we find the same striking tendencies.

Newsreels

The commonest pre-war figure in newsreels was Neville Chamberlain; in wartime up to the end of November he never appeared as a prominent feature and only three times very briefly in passing and got no response on any occasion. Halifax was as common as Chamberlain, but he has not appeared in observed newsreels since the outbreak of war. The third most popular personality in August was Sir Neville Henderson who has now disappeared, and fourth came the King. The Queen was much less frequent. Now the Queen is easy first as a wartime newsreel character. The emphasis has absolutely changed from political figures to the royal family. In pre-war observations 23 per cent of the leading characters were royal; in wartime this has gone up very nearly to 80 per cent, and the response to them had changed dramatically. Whereas previously only 13 per cent of their appearances were greeted with applauses and response of any kind, during the war they received 38 per cent response, invariably applause, except once when the Duke of Windsor was hissed though he also got much longer response than anyone else whether royal or common. The Queen, now much the commonest newsreel figure, gained a much lower audience response, but the commonest political figure, Churchill, got the highest wartime response. Hitler who had generally been received in silence, even in the last days of August, now received 100 per cent hissing though a National Panel observer at Troubridge (Wiltshire) noted on 30 October in his diary:

> After tea, cinema and saw *I was a Prisoner of Nazi Germany*. When Hitler appeared a large percentage of the audience (not including myself though I felt like it) booed and with Goering hissing. I cannot explain the difference.

Roosevelt and Baldwin and Lloyd George, the three characters who got most audience response before the war, were not featured in any of the post-war [wartime] newsreels. In general politicians have retreated from the newsreels. When politicians have appeared since the war [started] then reception has mainly been silent; many things can alter this tendency as the war goes on and the main thing that would obviously alter it would be if the leaders inspired the followers to have more personal and confident feeling about them.

In the newsreels observed before the war, sequences dealing with soldiers were received with a high degree of response but almost always laughter (nearly 90 per cent). The situations then produced were amusing, wholly, or seemed funny to the audience – gas drill or a tank chasing geese. Since the war the response of laughter has decreased but applause is very frequent, often arising spontaneously from a cinema and at the very sight of anything military in newsreels – especially the RAF, tanks, battleships ploughing the waves, soldiers marching with a swing.

The biggest laugh at any remark recorded in any film since the outbreak of war was in the Crazy Gang film *The Frozen Limits*, a Gainsborough picture. In the picture the Six Wonder Boys are destitute in a fair side-show but discover a notice on the bit of newspaper wrapped round their fish and chips which proclaims a gold rush in Alaska. There is no date but they know it is recent because an adjacent news item contains a statement by Chamberlain to the effect that we must arm and be ready. As one of the Boys says, 'He hasn't been talking like that for long.' This invariably aroused a tremendous laugh from the whole belly of the audience. It turns out of course that the paper really referred to Joe Chamberlain.

One of the Crazy Gang, Bud Flanagan, also appeared in a newsreel. The incident was remarkable in that it was unlike anything normally in newsreels and contained the elements of a really surrealist fantasy.

And in another newsreel the Crazy Gang suddenly appeared as wrestlers and indulged in slapstick of various types finishing with a slow-motion fight between Nervo and Knox. The Crazy Gang are in fact becoming quite a good substitute for real information in this war. Their music hall show was the first new live show since the war and is running as a smash hit with the direct take-off of Hitler occupying new territory and its plugging of two of the now best-selling jazz tunes 'Franklin D. Roosevelt Jones' and 'Run Rabbit Run' (equals 'Run, Adolf, Run'). The rabbit killed in the Shetland raid and claimed by the Nazis as a seaplane was stuffed and sent down to the Palladium to help the Crazy Gang have fun. Indeed the newsreels have needed such substitutes. Mass-Observation data show great dissatisfaction with these in the first two months of the war and still in November they remained very uniform and highly formalised. It was left to *The Lion Has Wings* to show any shots of the Kiel Canal raiders and usually they had to rely – due to censorship and other military restrictions – on, for instance, shots of the *Royal Oak* when refloated some years ago with highly varnished 'heroic' and 'major disaster' commentary to carry the thing over. Here is the whole contents of a typical newsreel on 17 October:

Pictures of *Royal Oak* in dock in peace.

Static pictures of the Bletchley train smash.

French troops.

French showing American journalists the Maginot Line.

British journalists being shown Air Force *behind* the lines, mostly facetious shots of airmen eating, but including the widely produced press photo of an aeroplane protectively covered with branches.

Here is another on 11 November:

Pictures of the City of Flint from all angles but never close up; then a shot of the American ambassadress. 1 min.

Dutch-Belgian Peace Plan. Pictures of Leopold and Bernard (taken pre-war?). ½ min.

Armistice Day shots with long verse commentary of the most sententious sort (see last section of this book) entitled a Tribute by British Movietone News. 5 mins.

This is all the news reel you get on 11 November, but it is a lot better than you get at the Gaumont, Haymarket, on 18 Nov.:

> *Churchill on the War.* For most of the time Churchill is simply talking to the audience, but there are rapid cut-ins to the Navy, Goering, Hitler and Poland. The last two minutes are entirely Churchill's face close-up. 5 mins.

That is the end of the news. If you went to a special news theatre you sometimes did better, got a longer 'news', though seldom anything dramatic or any real news. Over everything shown in the newsreel lay the dead hand of Civil Service and military caution and censorship. The best and liveliest newsreel seen so far was at the Eros News Theatre, Piccadilly Circus, on 20 November containing Paramount News and British Movietone. For historical purposes it is set out here. It is not difficult to see how much the treatment of the national situation or any of these subjects could be vitalised and how dull their impact at present is.

THE EROS NEWS

(The first three shots Paramount, the remainder Movietone)

	(1st showing)	*(2nd showing)*
Shot 1. *Bratislava.* ½ min.		
The election of Father Tisot	Rustles	Comment

Shot 2. *London.* ½ min.		
King and Queen inspect a canteen	Sudden silence	Some talking
Shot 3. *Brussels.* ¾ min.		
Funeral of Burgomaster Max	N.r.(No response)	N.r.
Shot 4. *The Convoy System.* 2 mins.		
The forming and protection of British convoys	N.r.	N.r.
Shot 5. *Edith Cavell.* ½ min.		
Remembrance day in Paris	N.r.	N.r.
Shot 6. *The Poilu Remembers.* ½ min.		
French soldiers march past the tombs of those who have died in this war	Some unrest and coughs	N.r.
Shot 7. *The Guards in Paris* ¾ min.		
The Welsh Guards marching through Paris, and being welcomed by the girls	N.r.	
Shot 8. *And Still They Come* ½ min.		
More British soldiers landing in France	N.r.	N.r.
Shot 9. *Petrol Supplies.* ½ min.		
The piling up and camouflaging of petrol in France	N.r.	N.r.
Shot 10. *Building their own Railway.* ½ min.		
The BEF built their own railways	N.r.	N.r.
Shot 11. *The C-in-C lays Wreath.* ¼min.		
Lord Gort lays Cenotaph wreath in France	N.r.	N.r.

Shot 12 *Dominion Leaders in*
France ½ min.

Eden, Casey, and Khan inspecting the lines with the Duke of Gloucester	N.r.	N.r.

Shot 13 *The Allied Air Forces.*
1 min.

Imaginary shots of the air battles on the Western front interspersed with real pictures of shattered planes and captured pilots.	One tries to clap at sight of winning machines	Man says 'of course it isn't real'

The audience response, as one notices, is almost entirely negative. Notice the comment of the man at the last shot in the second showing. Compare the typical impact of *The Lion Has Wings, Confessions of a Nazi Spy* with the dramatic newsreel shots interspersed. For instance, here is a diary entry of a school teacher at Watford who went to see *Confessions of a Nazi Spy* on 9 November:

> The whole audience listened and watched quite absorbed. At the end, two young workmen behind, perhaps 30 years of age, were discussing the film. I caught the following remark 'That's facts, you know; that isn't imagination'. I had forgotten that in the cinema there is a collection for Haig's fund, usually by women connected with the British Legion. The tin boxes were sent round by men in khaki uniform. A young man at my left had left his seat for a few moments and had missed the box. When told about it he seemed amused and said 'So I saved a penny by going out'. His companion said 'it's disgusting that they go on collecting'.

Censorship demands the cutting out of films of the balloons shown over Downing Street (8 September), the supply of anything which even by a million-to-one chance might be of use to the enemy. But whether or not this is necessary the effect on newsreels is to deaden them and thus to deaden the response of the people which pins itself more easily to uninterfering personalities like the royal family. A famous documentary director said to an observer (24 November) 'they are bastards on the Ministries, the RAF are the best because they are the most modern but nearly everything we get isn't through the Ministries but through private contacts and officials that we are friendly with'. This situation, unsatisfactory from the point of view of public morale, had apparently got through to the Government by the end of November for they made a new post in the Ministry of Information film department, 'Director of Documentaries', appointing A. R. Hyatt who had some time previously been boss of GPO film. But at the end of November there were still no documentaries at all and anything and everything that came out was with official sanction and with every sort of difficulty of photographing, censorship, distribution and exhibition.

Conclusion

The film can in fact be immensely potent as 'propaganda', that is to say, as enlightening, encouraging and instructing the mass of people who do not adequately understand what is happening to the country and who want to understand. It is in the interests of the authorities that they should be independent so far as is compatible with war tactics and more than ever before the film is ready to be obliging and 'socially conscious' in its realistic way. But the first three months of the war has damaged its structure, personality, and prestige. It shows signs of revival but most of the signs are still only plans and there are signs too that these plans are being framed on a rather short view of mass reaction to a developing war. The film has made so many major assumptions about human beings and mass reactions that it inevitably gets on tricky ground when there are so many rapidly changing external factors to complicate the situation. From our own observations we should say, tentatively and roughly, that among the best draws in film at the moment are:

1 Exciting [?] in low falutin language – not Movietone verse on the dead of the last war but the rapid in and out cutting of German orators with bookies in *The Lion Has Wings*.
2 Interesting leadership, again speaking simply not in the long words of Anthony Eden or with long close ups of Winston Churchill but with the benevolent good humour of Sir Charles Bressey criticising the lay out of London in Elton's recent film *The City* which has been shown during the war and has been exceptionally well received though it has the important advantage of showing brilliantly lit London streets which excite people tremendously.
3 Recognisable situations with a humorous twist to take the edge off the impression registered in the mind. Not bad humour like that in the GPO ARP film but good humour such as the expression on the painter's face as a bus runs over his white lines in the same unit's *The First Days*.
4 Patriotism and the presentation of 'desirable sentiments' such as patriotism and heroism, and general build-up for Britain (propaganda) but not laid on heavy. By 'laid on heavy' we mean the incident in *The Lion Has Wings* when Merle Oberon asks Ralph Richardson if we are prepared. He replies in a stirring voice that we have never been better prepared. This even produced audible barracking on one occasion which is very rare in cinemas – 'never been prepared, you mean' and 'Oh God what

propaganda'. Compare the Crazy Gang's handling of the same situation.
5 Music and a theme song may help to attract people to the incident and
Gracie Fields or George Formby singing can register advice, for instance,
or instruct on anything a good deal more strongly, we believe, than Lord
Halifax or Mr Hore Belisha.

Postscript

[In an interview with Len England, Humphrey Jennings made a number
of criticisms of the first draft of *The Cinema in the First Three Months of
the War* of which the most substantial are the following (Cinema Box 4,
File A, dated 28 November, 1939.]

> You should get Control of Photography Orders 1 and 2 from the
> Stationery Office. The point is that anybody in uniform can photograph
> anything he likes; you get into awful difficulties over this when
> policemen for instance see people photographing balloons and don't stop
> them because they are in uniform. . . . Remember *The March of Time* is
> still functioning and is doing a great deal of work in England. And they
> have done a lot of propaganda for us. It is not only a question of *The
> Battlefleets of Britain* but also an early one about England that they did
> about peace and propaganda. . . . These five films that you mention (i.e.
> the British National Films production schedule) were all planned pre-
> quota and Corfield was going ahead with them in any case. The man
> was a fool of course but he was going to. And don't leave out the Old
> Mother Riley one because that is the one he is going to make all the
> money on [*Old Mother Riley Joins Up*, 1939]. . . . Remember that at the
> beginning of the war Walter Mycroft went on making films as if nothing
> had happened. In fact the two [studios] that you mention [as stopping]
> were the two that did continue to function. Denham and the Associated
> British [Elstree Studio] went on. The others stopped: Twickenham,
> Teddington, Sound City, M.P., Rock's, the vast Amalgamated which has
> never been used, Ealing and Pathé studios. . . . You ought to mention
> Basil Dean. He was put in charge of Ensa films and after a time gave a
> list of the films that he had sent over. They were all over a year old and
> about ninety per cent of them came from the ATP studios in which he is
> a big shareholder. You will find it all in back numbers of the
> *Cinema*. . . . You must find Shaw's letter to *The Times*. He asks what
> agent of Nazi Germany has decreed the closing of all cinemas and it was
> that letter that did more than anything to make the government alter
> its mind.

Editors' notes

1 *Laugh It Off, Contraband* (formerly *Black-out*) and *Gaslight* were all
    released in 1940; *Freedom Radio* (formerly *This German Freedom*) in
    1941.
2 *Freedom Radio* was eventually directed by Anthony Asquith, not Hurst,
    and did not feature the Nazi leaders.
3 A footnote here reads:
    The Granada circuit is run by Mr Sidney Bernstein who is the only
    man in the film industry who has taken the trouble to find out what
    the public really wants. Every year he issues questionnaires to his
    patrons asking them to vote on film stars, films, etc. These
    questionnaires accept all the basic and traditional dogma of the film
    and so seldom touch on the fundamental problem but they give
    Mr Bernstein a particular insight which has constantly enabled him
    to respond rapidly to public opinion.

5   Letter and First Report from a Volunteer Film Reviewer

A first report and covering letter giving personal details from a new volunteer film reviewer, a 27-year-old housewife from Northwood, Middlesex. It was from the raw material of viewers' reports that the file reports were compiled. (Film Topic Box 1, File B.)

Northwood,
Middx.
Jan. 25th, 1940.

Dear Mr England,

Thank you so much for your letter admitting me as a helper in the films section of M.O. I enclose my first report, and here is an account of my personal film-going habits.

I am a very keen film-fan, going once or twice a week, and have been known to go three or even four times in one week. My main interest is in the acting and the personalities of the players. I don't care a hoot about the story, providing the acting is good, and the actors well cast. Bad casting annoys me extremely. I have a long list of favourites any of whom I will go a long way to see. I take *Film Weekly* regularly, and always keep the casts of films so as to refer to them, and look up the names of any players which interest me. I like spotting small-part players and watching their careers progress, and I am always interested in Warner Bros. pictures as they have such excellent supporting casts.

The types of films which interest me most are historical ones (but the history *must* be authentic), comedies, travel and adventure, and 'family' ones, such as the Jones Family series. I am very keen on French pictures, which I consider vastly superior to either British or American ones, especially in photography. I saw *Carnet de Bal* five times, *L'Equipage* three times, and several others twice. Unfortunately I cannot go to many Continental films now, as I have a small baby and my time is very limited.

The cinemas I go to mostly in this area are the Rex, Northwood Hills, a Shipman and King theatre; the Langham, Pinner, an ABC theatre; and the Embassy, North Harrow. Sometimes I go to others in Harrow, Watford and Rickmansworth. At the Rex, where the prices are 6d, 9d, 1/-, 1/6 and 2/-, I go in the 9ds, at the others where there are no 9ds, I go in the 1/-s. I usually go in the evenings.

My husband is in France, and I am living with my family. This consists of my father (60) who occasionally goes to a news theatre for a 'good sleep' as he puts it; my stepmother (38) who is rather high-brow and only goes to good, well-reviewed films; and my two step-brothers aged 13 and 11, who are film-mad, with a decided preference for gangsters, crime, and lots of shootings and sudden deaths, etc.

I do not know anyone in the cinema industry, nor have I any specialised knowledge. The nearest I have ever got to a film studio is to see a few sets in a field not far from here (we are about six or seven miles from Denham).

I hope this data will be of some use to you.

Yours sincerely,

S. P.

Report 1, January 1940

Since the war started one small cinema, the Ritz, has closed down in Northwood. This was never very popular and showed old films or B pictures many months after their general release. It is now a canteen. The closing of this cinema has left only one to serve the districts of Northwood and Northwood Hills – The Rex, Northwood Hills, the next nearest being the Langham Cinema at Pinner about three miles away. The majority of the films at the Rex lately have been comedies and crime pictures, and all the films shown since the war started have been of a much lighter nature than before. We have many soldiers billeted in this area, and the local cinemas are well patronised, the Rex being full or nearly full every time I've been. The audiences are very appreciative, especially in the newsreels – hissing Hitler, cheering the King and Queen, clapping Winston Churchill, and other celebrities, and any special shots of RAF pilots, or ships' crews, etc. We seem to get lots of laughs in the wrong places these days, especially in intense love scenes, for which I suspect the soldiers. As far as I can see the black-out has not made any difference. I always go in the evening myself, and as I have said our local cinema is nearly always full, and once or twice recently there have been queues. (There was a long queue for Will Hay in *Where's That Fire?*). None of my family or friends have cut down film-going, in fact one or two go more often, as it is the only available entertainment. I think quite as many children go in the evenings now as before.

Matinée prices have been suspended in all cinemas in this area, but advertising has only been cut in one or two instances, one Watford cinema and three Harrow ones no longer advertising in Northwood.

At all cinemas round here the regulations about carrying gas-masks have been entirely relaxed, and at only one – the Langham, Pinner – is the notice still flashed on the screen about Air-raid warnings. At the Rex, Northwood Hills, there is a large collecting box in the foyer for cigarettes for the Troops.

6   Report on Audience Preference in Film Themes

Compiled by Len England and dated 17 March 1940, this report (FR 57) sought to assess audience taste in film subjects six months into the war. Interestingly, cinemas had sought to cater for an interest in war subjects by reviving old films about the First World War, including *Hell's Angels* (1930), *All Quiet on the Western Front* (1930) and *I Was a Spy* (1933), some of which were very strongly anti-war. Anti-war sentiments were also to be found in *Things to Come* (1936), Alexander Korda's lavish film of H. G. Wells's vision of the future which begins with the outbreak of war in 1940. It too was revived.

Questionnaire

In the middle of December 1939, 200 people were asked among other film questions 'Do you like a different sort of picture now to what you did before the war?' While nearly three-quarters said that the war had made no change at all in their tastes (see Appendix 1) nevertheless 34 per cent of the women over thirty who form the bulk of the cinema-going public objected to 'war films'; against this only 2.5 per cent said that they would like more war films. In only one case, however, did anybody suggest that they objected to 'war and topical films' so that it may be assumed that the bulk of this objection may be to actual scenes of battle and not to the mention of the war situation. This is borne out by the exceptionally high response to *Laugh It Off*, a film about the army at home, and the equally exceptionally low response to *Tommy Atkins*, a film about the army in the trenches; these films, however, will be dealt with in more detail later in the report.

Pre-war films

In the first six months of the war only one feature film made since the outbreak was generally released; this was *The Lion Has Wings* with which all the normal processes between planning and release were so speeded up as to make it possible for a film planned in September to be released at the end of November. Yet in these same six months 13 per cent of the films released were of a topical nature (see Appendices 2 and 3)[1], containing themes of spies or wars. Nearly 25 per cent of these films had a spy element and among the films made pre-war and not yet released are the following: *Traitor Spy, Spy for a Day, Television Spy, Espionage Agent, Enemy Agent* and *Spies at Work*. In many of these films the spy element was of secondary importance, taking the place of the gangster element: in *Trapped in the Sky* for example, the story centred on the efforts of a man to steal a new and secret aeroplane invention: it was indicated that he was working for a foreign country, unnamed and very much in the background. Almost the same plot was used in *Spies of the Air* where the whole emphasis was upon discovering who was the spy, the political aspect being practically ignored. The point remains, however, that producers both in America and England produced these themes in order to 'cash in' on European unrest.

Next in order of popular topical themes are the services. Five out of twenty-seven topical films released between September 1939 and February 1940 concerned army, navy or air force, four of these being British. The fifth, a French film dubbed for English audiences, was called *Double Crime on the Maginot Line* and was primarily a murder mystery with an army setting; yet the main response points indicate that the interest of the film lay not in the story but in the shots of the Maginot Line itself. Of the four British films two concerned the navy, one film primarily serious, the other a comedy with Sandy Powell as an AB. *French Leave* was a re-issue of an old film about the British army while the fourth, an Old Mother Riley film, dealt rather incidentally with the ATS. In the same period *The Lion Has Wings* was released concerning the Air Force, but this was made after the beginning of the war.

Three films in the period dealt directly with life under the Nazi rule. Two of these, both American, *Confessions of a Nazi Spy* and *I Was a Captive of Nazi Germany* followed very much the same lines; both of them linked together the incidents of the film with a commentary describing the changing events in Germany and both emphasising that they were recounting true stories. The third of these films, *Professor Mamlock*, was not licensed for general exhibition until after Russia's march into Poland. It was released with English sub-titles and no dubbing.

Emphasis on war and patriotism is the main feature of seven other topical films dealing some with the last war and some with war in other parts of the world or in the Empire. *Thunder Afloat* was the story of the American navy in the last war, *Nurse Edith Cavell* is a sufficiently expressive title. *Beau Geste* and a re-issue of *Under Two Flags* both concern fighting in the foreign legion, while *North of Shanghai* deals with the Chinese war and *Conspiracy* tells of the rise of a dictator and his downfall. Finally Hollywood produced in *Gunga Din* and *The Sun Never Sets* two glorifications of the British Empire.

The Frozen Limits, while primarily a comedy about a goldrush in Alaska, contained many passing references to topical points and depended in part upon a confusion between Joseph Chamberlain and the present Prime Minister.

Though no full observation has been made in the matter, it appears that in these six months repertory cinemas have kept clear of any topical subjects, a fact which is borne out partly by an interview with a manager of a Classic cinema and partly by checking the programmes of such cinemas in London, Ipswich and Chester. In no case was any war or topical film noted. Yet at two West End cinemas war films were revived with success – *All Quiet on the Western Front*, a violently anti-war film, and *Hell's Angels* – while in some suburban cinemas *I was a Spy, Things to Come* and *British Agent* were seen as secondary features.

Wartime films

There is much difficulty in discovering what films are being made at any given time. There is no record at all available of what effect the war has had on the type of film in Hollywood, though it is known that one of the films being made is *Waterloo Bridge*, the climax of which is an air raid. In England, however, some check can be made. Since the outbreak of war twenty-seven films have been completed; of these seventeen, or over 60 per cent, have topical themes. Easily the most popular theme is the services, which form the basis of nine out of the seventeen films. Five out of the nine concern the Navy or the war at sea; *Sons of the Sea* tells of spying plots at Dartmouth, *For Freedom* recreates in narrative form the story of the Graf Spee, *Let George Do It* is a new George Formby comedy describing how he defeats a gang of spies who signal to the enemy the positions of defenceless merchantmen and finishes with his antics in the control room of a U-boat. The titles of the remaining two, *Contraband* and *Convoy*, tell their own story.

The army is represented by three films all concerned with life behind the front line. As yet the RAF is represented only by *The Lion Has Wings* but two more films are being planned.

Three of the remaining films deal with life in Germany, one, *Gestapo*, tells of a concentration camp, another, *Pastor Hall*, is a story based on the life of Pastor Niemoller, while the third, *The Siegfried Line*, is a Crazy Gang comedy.[2] Another three deal with the Home Front; the effect of the war on family life is dealt with in *The Briggs Family*, the first of a series of films, and the effect on coalmines in *The Proud Valley*. The third film in this category is a version of Shaw's *Major Barbara*, a story of armament manufacture.

Comparison of pre-war and wartime films

The basis of comparison between pre-war and wartime films is not strictly accurate as the former conclusions are based upon films released whether American or British, the latter upon only British films; nevertheless an examination of Appendix 3 will show that British topical films maintain a fairly constant proportion of the whole.

Before the war the main emphasis was upon spy films which embraced nearly 25 per cent of the total of topical films; since the war only one film has been made in which the spy interest is the main one, and even in this (*Law and Disorder*) much of the action takes place with the principals in the army.

Before the war five films were made about the services, three connected with some form of army life and two with the navy. Since the war, out of approximately half the total of topical films, nine concern the services. Even inside this category emphasis has shifted from the army to the navy. Before the war, also, three out of the five films concerning the service were humorous; now while all three of the army films are in the main humorous ones, only one out of the five of those connected with the navy are comedies.

Before the war not a single film about Germany was made in this country;[3] the fact that *Professor Mamlock* was not passed by the censor may possibly indicate official opposition. Whatever the reason there is no such absence now, as three films about Germany have already been made and a fourth at least is scheduled. In other films there are many passing references to Hitler and Germany while in George Formby's *Let George Do It* a dream sequence includes George engaging in a hand-to-hand fight with Hitler himself.

Naturally, with a European war there is no need to go elsewhere for scenes of battle, though Hollywood is reported to be preparing a 'non-political' film about Finland. On the other hand, before the war the Home Front was only considered in one film, *An Englishman's Home*, and in this it was a minor element while since the war already three films have dealt exclusively with this aspect.

In brief, since the beginning of the war the number of topical films has proportionately more than trebled, but the categories within this heading have changed in size. Spy films and films about wars outside Europe have become much less frequent while films about the forces have become more numerous and at the same time more serious. Films about Germany and also the Home Front have also increased in number.

Wartime shorts

Appendix 5 gives a list of short films produced since the war in this country.[3] It will be seen that the main alternation in category from full length films is that the shorts concentrate far more on the Home Front and deal directly with such problems as evacuation. The positions of army, navy and air force are practically the same as in features, the army being slightly more popular in shorts than in full length films.

The most important thing to notice about this list is that it is 100 per cent war subjects. It must be emphasised that this cannot be guaranteed complete but the observer has been unable to track down a single documentary made since the war in this country which has not some aspect of the war as its main theme. While obviously a documentary must be very much more affected by current events than a fictional film, nevertheless there are still subjects, such as nature study, in which the war has had little effect.

Audience response to types of films

It will be seen from Appendix 2 that not all the pre-war topical films could be seen by observers, though the important ones were covered from two to five times. But of those covered, it may be said that the best response to the film as a whole, as opposed to individual situations within a film, was to those concerned with the forces. Obviously much of audience response depends upon the popular appeal of the film in question whatever its subject matter; but whereas a B feature spy film often caused much restlessness in the audience, the type of 'forces' film was very well received.

Audience response to spy types

It has already been mentioned that many of the spy films which make the largest category among topical films released so far this war, have the spy element forcibly included to make the film topical. It is therefore very difficult to judge the effect of spy films on audiences. *The Spy in Black* was very well received yet espionage was not the main factor in this story. The beginning of *Spies of the Air* showed how landladies, taxi-drivers, ticket collectors, all could be in the Secret Service and details were given of how spies are always at work everywhere; at all these scenes, however, there was a great deal of coughing. Finally, in *An Englishman's Home*, though spying was of some importance, the main emphasis was upon fear of air raids and this will be dealt with later.

'Services' films

Six out of the twenty-seven topical feature films listed concerned the services and of these three were humorous. As well as these, two more films of a humorous nature concerning the army have been observed at West End cinemas. From these five films it may be deduced that the services are a very popular subject.

One of the box-office successes of the first six months of the war was *The Frozen Limits*, a Crazy Gang film. In this at its West End showing, five points were noted where there was laughter from the whole body of the house, at its local showing only three such points were noted. In *Laugh it Off* there were twelve such points. In *Frozen Limits* less than 50 per cent of the laughter points received more than three seconds laughter, in *Laugh it Off* very nearly 75 per cent received this amount. There follows an extract from an observer's report on *Laugh it Off*:

Tommy leaves her with the remark 'be a man, good girl'	Laughs (2)
Tommy gets to depot with other recruits and marches with other recruits	Laughs (5)
Sergeant Major is discovered to be a man he had played joke on in railway station	Laughs (5) *Boos* (2)
Tommy tries to humour him without success	Laugh (3) cont.
Tommy talks to an officer as man to man	Laughs (4)
Tommy gets ATS girl annoyed with him, but she also blows up the Sergeant Major	Laughs (5) *Claps 6 secs*
Tommy produces his catch phrase 'You lucky people'	Laughs (5)
Tommy is given fatigue. Peels a mountain of potatoes	Laughs (5)
Washes plates, scrubs floors	Laughs (3)

It will be noted that not only are the laughs high but also that there are boos and claps. In no other film has booing been heard except for the appearance of Hitler, while applause for 6 seconds at the discomfiture of the Sergeant Major is the highest recorded, except for the return of the Exeter men and for the ending of *The Lion Has Wings* at a Cricklewood showing. All this was at the Paramount theatre, Tottenham Court Road, where response is usually low.

Laugh It Off is only the extreme example of the popularity of 'service' jokes, a point which has been proved also, incidentally, in music hall studies. In Streatham, where much of this study was done, the Old Mother

Riley pictures and those of Sandy Powell have not been shown until recently, when both comedians appeared in military films. While in neither was the volume of laughter great, in Sandy Powell's *All at Sea* not one joke misfired, from over twenty recorded. In *Old Mother Riley Joins Up* forty-one comic situations or remarks were noted, thirteen of which, or 35 per cent, caused no laughter at all; but of the fourteen jokes connected with the army, only two, or under 15 per cent, were not laughed [at] at all, a very much smaller percentage. The reception of *Spy for a Day*, not yet generally released, was also very good.

These four films not only deal humorously with the life in the forces, but also deal mainly with the lighter side of such life, though *Spy for a Day* does concern actual fighting in parts. *Laugh it Off* is the story of a new recruit who enjoys army life except for the sergeant major; finally he is given a commission. *All at Sea* tells a very similar story: Sandy Powell joins the navy by accident, 'wouldn't change his job for worlds' but also falls foul of the sergeant who is finally worsted. *Old Mother Riley Joins Up* is mere farce, but the discomforts of army life are only pointed out by two Mayfair girls who join up and dislike their surroundings.

Yet a short film made since the war, *Tommy Atkins*, the first of a series, has as its background the trenches of the last war, as its main point, an attack, and as the basis of its humour narrow escapes from death, or, in one case, death itself. Out of thirteen jokes noted in *Tommy Atkins* only three, or less than 25 per cent, got any laughter at all, each one of these getting response from less than one-fifth of the audience. For instance:

One goes over, gets shot. Falls back, makes a joke and slumps   N.r.

After attack. One comes back wounded, goes back to help a   N.r.
friend

Another complains that a bullet has ruined his tin hat   Titter.

The film consisted of incidents, supposedly true, submitted to an evening paper.

Of three serious service films, two were observed. One *The Lion Has Wings* has been more fully dealt with elsewhere; it is interesting to notice, however, in the present connection that in the five showings observed, not one of the common response points was directly connected with the RAF. Also the scenes at the end dealing directly with RAF at work were not as well received as the earlier ones. The other film *Double Crime on the Maginot Line*, a French film with English dubbing, was greeted mostly by bored silence though shots of the Maginot Line caused some comment, particularly one of a tank passing through a corridor.

The evidence to prove that serious films about army life is scanty but it must still be borne in mind that a fairly large percentage of people interviewed object to 'war films' [sic]. There are indications that humorous films about military life are received exceptionally well, however, and films about actual fighting in this period have not been numerous. Possibly, therefore, it is the serious film about the services that is sometimes meant when objection is expressed to 'war films'.

'Germany' films

Of the three films about Germany released in the six months since the beginning of the war, two have been American, one Russian; both American ones were reconstructions of actual events, one, *Confessions of a Nazi Spy*, describing the break up of a Nazi ring in Germany, the other, *I Was a Captive of Nazi Germany*, telling the adventures of a German woman who was imprisoned to a background of Hitler's rise to power. The Russian film *Professor Mamlock* is the story of a German Jew who turns Communist and is shot for his faith; this too is to the background of the Nazi's rise to power. This film was shown throughout the country merely with English sub-titles and no dubbing and this handicap was sometimes too great for its success; a report from Watford mentions that there was continuous talking throughout the showing 'the audience thinking that because the dialogue was in Russian, talking on their part did not matter'. On the other hand, an observer who saw the film both at its West End showing at the Academy and also in the suburbs found the degree of response exceptionally high. Out of forty-eight response points only three times were there signs of boredom in the West End showing, at ten in the suburbs; while the latter figure may seem rather high, it must be remembered that many of the response points consisted of little action and much unintelligible dialogue. Also at the local showing there were seventeen response points which caused comment, that is nearly 40 per cent of the total; this is an exceptionally high figure. Finally, Miss Cohen, managing director of the Academy cinema, told an observer:

> The degree of response was so great from the moment the picture opened, that it could not have been greater even through the war. I can perhaps say that no picture has possibly had such a unanimous response from our audience as *Professor Mamlock*.

The response to *Confessions of a Nazi Spy* was even greater. Here forty-eight response points were noted, eighteen or nearly 25 per cent were commented on; while this [was] slightly lower than in *Mamlock* it includes clapping and booing to some small extent – an extreme form of response not noted in the Russian film. On the other hand, only three points caused signs of boredom as compared with ten out of a smaller total in *Professor Mamlock*. It must be mentioned, however, that *Confessions of a Nazi Spy* was released in November, only three months after the war had started and also had the advantage of being the first directly anti-Hitler film shown in this country; *Professor Mamlock* was shown in January and to some extent covered the same ground.

The response to both these films is higher than that recorded for any other serious film seen since the war. [In the case of] the third film in this category, *I Was a Captive of Nazi Germany*, though signs of boredom were not many (20 per cent of the total response points), signs of interest were even fewer (less than 10 per cent of response points); for the most part an audience that is usually responsive sat quite silently. *In observer's own opinion* this was due partly to the lack of atmosphere created by the film, but mainly to the fact that the incidents related were very petty; the captive was only allowed to change her underclothes once a fortnight, for example, and this was regarded as a very shocking point. In *Professor Mamlock* a man had been beaten and kicked, in *Confessions of a Nazi Spy* men had been shown in a state of utter terror. Probably a great part of the audience had seen one of these films already and in a comparison *I Was a Captive of Nazi Germany* must have suffered.

Other subjects

In the other categories of topical films, 'last war', 'other wars' and 'Empire', such analysis is difficult, partly because fewer films have been observed, and partly because the main interest in these films lies in the sequences containing actual fighting, a matter which will be discussed later.

In general, then, the most popular topical subjects have been comic films about the army or navy and films about Germany. All this is, of course, subject to the value of the film.

Individual sequences

In these topical films, some sequences constantly recur and are of some interest; most important of these are air raids, scenes of actual fighting, Hitler salutes, and anti-war speeches.

The main body of a cinema audience consists of women and the most probable way in which the war will affect them is by means of air raids. One of the films released between September 1939 and March 1940 was *An Englishman's Home*, a story of how a spy entered a British home and fell in love with the daughter; nevertheless he did his duty, used the house as an aerial base to guide enemy ships, and caused the father to be shot before the attack was finally circumvented. The main purpose of the film was to show the necessity of National Service and slight alterations had to be made to make it acceptable, to an audience of people already at war.

Nevertheless in this it was not entirely successful. At the immediate beginning of the war, according to the picture, fleets of enemy aeroplanes numbering thousands cross the coast and drop men by parachute at the same time bombing cities with little opposition. This film was seen five times, twice at its West End showing at the Paramount, Tottenham Court Road, once at Hanwell, once in Streatham, and once in Ipswich. Twice the 'air raid' caused a great deal of laughter and jibes, twice it was received in complete silence, and once an observer reports signs of hysteria (WRL). But on four out of five occasions the shots of the myriad aeroplanes caused adverse comment or remarks such as 'how silly' or 'they've brought enough of them, haven't they?' The fact that the actual scenes of the air raid were well received on only three occasions may therefore be due to the utter unreality of the previous scenes. That 'real' scenes of horror still cause shocked comment can be gathered from the newsreels containing shots of dead Russians and from the scenes in *Professor Mamlock* and *Confessions of a Nazi Spy* already mentioned.

Almost the same applies to *Things to Come*, a revival of which was seen by an observer in March. Here again shots of thousands of planes crossing the coast caused some laughter, but the actual shots of air raid panic, of gas-masks being issued, of people running for shelter, and so on, were received in silence and with interest. In *Things to Come*, however, the effect was more magnificent, less real; the emphasis was not on individual death but to a much larger extent on the falling of large buildings and so on.

Finally, in *The Lion Has Wings*, while there was no air raid the sound of the warnings in the crisis sequences caused much interest.

In brief, air raids have caused little comment though much interest. In every case, however, there have been some circumstances which have divorced the action on the screen from reality. In *Waterloo Bridge*, however, a film that is now being made, the main action centres on the bombing of London, and it is probable that this will not make the mistake of large fleets of aeroplanes which merely cause laughter.

Scenes of actual fighting

In no film generally released since the beginning of the war has there been a scene of actual battle, though in *Beau Geste* and *Gunga Din* there were scenes of fighting against Arabs and Indians, while in *Nurse Edith Cavell* one scene showed the nurse exploring battlefields for wounded British soldiers. There have, however, been many revivals of old films which do contain war sequences. Locally, *I was a Spy* and *Things to Come* have been observed, while *All Quiet on the Western Front* and *Hell's Angels* were seen in the West End.

In every case the first response from the audience was astonishment and comment and less signs of horror were noted than at the newsreels which have shown pictures of Russian corpses. For instance, at the showing of *Hell's Angels*, out of a total of 44 response points, 9 or over 20 per cent caused comment; comment was heard practically continuously in the scenes of a Zeppelin over London while later there was nearly as much at the bombing of the ammunition dump. The only other response noted was laughter at obvious jokes, signs of boredom at two sequences, while finally, there was one cry of 'oh' at the sight of an airman struggling in a blazing machine. In *All Quiet on the Western Front* there are shots of a man struggling with barbed wire; a bomb explodes and only his hand is left on the wire; yet even this caused no comment or sign of horror.

Both of these films were observed in the West End and while both cinemas were crowded, the audiences were obviously specialised; at *Hell's Angels* for instance, the observer noted only three women in the whole audience. At a local cinema, however, a revival of *I Was a Spy* was witnessed and while there is not a great deal of fighting in this film, nevertheless a long shot showing British planes bombing a church parade caused interest at first and after a time talk and coughing. Precisely the same thing occurred in the battle scenes of *Things to Come* where the scenes after the first air raid were regarded with very little interest. Here, however, in contrast to *All Quiet on the Western Front*, a shot of a man hanging from the barbed wire raised 'Oh' from well over half the audience.

At each cinema there was a mixed audience, at *I Was a Spy* the theatre was full and standing; there is even some evidence that people came solely to see *I Was a Spy* as an observer noticed three separate people who entered the cinema at the beginning of that picture and left at the end of it, without waiting for the other.

Hitler Salutes

In five films observed since the war, a sequence has contained the Hitler salute; altogether, including more than one sequence in the same film and films observed more than once, observations were made to the reaction of twelve showings of the Hitler salute. On every occasion except one the reaction was laughter although on only three occasions was the incident obviously funny. One film, *Traitor Spy*, had been made before the war and had been brought up to date by the introduction of occasional references to Germany and one short scene in which the spy is shown with his superior officer; on each observed showing, there was immediate laughter, though the scene was very brief. Similarly in *The Lion Has Wings* a rather short scene showing German airmen preparing to go up and saluting their officer caused laughter on four out of five observed showings and much comment on the fifth. Similarly with the other films.

Anti-war speeches

In many of the films observed in the first six months of war there have been speeches and scenes deploring the futility of war, the films having been made before the outbreak. In particular must be noted *Idiot's Delight, The Silent Battle* and *Things to Come*, the last being a revival.

It seems a general rule in cinema – insufficient evidence is as yet to hand to prove this – that speeches meet with very much poorer response than action shots. Yet in *Idiot's Delight* out of thirty-one response points thirteen or 40 per cent caused signs of boredom. In three long scenes the pacifist case is put forward by an earnest young man and a cynical mistress of a financier; not once in one of these scenes did the observer hear a single remark or cough. In *The Silent Battle* the opening sequences depict a French soldier being demobilised after the crisis of 1938. His sweetheart says to him 'I'm proud of you because you went to fight'; he replies 'I'm not, I was as crazy as the rest of the world. War is senseless and disgusting. But what else can we do?' Again the film was not well received with nearly as large a percentage of response points causing boredom as in *Idiot's Delight*. Yet the scene containing the anti-war sentiments was received in complete silence.

In *Things to Come* the opening scenes and their reactions were observed as follows:

Fade in '1940'	Laugh (1)
Shots of warning of wars cut with preparing for Christmas	Talk (1)
Cabal and Passworthy at home; Cabal points out the futility of war	N.r.
Christmas party	Talk (1)
More anti-war talk from Cabal	N.r.
Passworthy leaves; chatter on doorstep	Coughs (1)

It will be noted here again that anti-war speeches were received with much more interest than anything else.

Effect of the war on cinema-goers' taste

A questionnaire was made from two hundred interviews with boys at Merchant Taylors' school in 1937 and again in December 1939. In many cases the results here tally with the larger and more general Bernstein questionnaire and in practically every question there is hardly any change in 1939 from the opinions offered in 1937; only in the popularity of certain stars is there any striking differences, a matter in which the success of recent pictures in which they have appeared plays a large part. From this it appears that the war has had but little effect on people's tastes and Sam Eckman, managing director of MGM, said in an interview recently (*Picturegoer*, 23.3.40):

> You'll hear people say that filmgoers want comedy films now. Certainly they do – but they wanted comedy films before the war as well. They don't want an unrelieved diet of comedy films at any time. Here are the figures on *Thunder Afloat*, a film about U-boats. You'd think, perhaps, that with so many very real U-boats cropping up in the news, filmgoers wouldn't want to go and see more of them on the screen. Well, you'd be wrong. *Thunder Afloat* isn't a super film, but it's done much better than average business. . . .

This theory is borne out by observations in cinemas where there has been no adverse comment to the most violent war films and a very high degree of interest shown to many topical films. Against this is the questionnaire figure of 18 per cent wanting less war pictures. Possibly the solution lies in the fact that war pictures are consistently at the bottom of the Bernstein polls and many of those questioned said that they had always disliked war films. The objection to war films may be basic and not affected by the outbreak of an actual war.

Note on newsreels

Full details of newsreel responses are given elsewhere. Since then, however, it has been noticed that the response has considerably decreased to all factors, although the return of the men of the *Exeter* received the longest applause noted for any newsreel. Many showings of the King and Queen have caused no response at all, the Duke of Windsor who has been clapped more often than anyone else has only been applauded once and very feebly, while even the appearance of Hitler at Brenner caused no hissing as it has done on every previous occasion.

At the same time, in the newsreels themselves there has been less comic reconstruction. Nothing has been noted in this direction except the Pathé 'Nastie News' and even this, in January and February a weekly feature, appears now only at irregular intervals, sometimes not for weeks at a time.

Appendix 1: Questionnaire

Q. Do you like a different sort of picture now to what you did before the war?

	Class B				Class D				Total
	MU 30	MO 30	WU 30	WO 30	MU 30	MO 30	WU 30	WO 30	
Less war	8%	8%	16%	36%	16%	12%	16%	32%	18%
More war	4%	–	–	–	–	4%	12%	–	2.5%
More 'fun'	–	–	8%	8%	–	8%	4%	4%	4%
Less propaganda	16%	8%	4%	–	–	4%	–	–	4%
No change	72%	84%	72%	56%	84%	72%	68%	64%	71%

N.B. (1) Main objection to war films comes from women over 30 who form bulk of cinema's audience.
(2) Most of those in favour of more war are women under 30 in class D.
(3) Most of those objecting to propaganda are men under 30 of class B.

General Conclusions

1 Questionnaire shows 18 per cent of cinema-goers dislike war films.
2 13 per cent of films released since outbreak topical, majority spy films, then services.
3 60 per cent of wartime films topical, majority services and Germany.
4 Wartime short films practically all war subjects about Home Front.
5 Best response to released films has been to comic films about the services.
6 Good response also to films about Germany.
7 Air raid scenes caused no horror.
8 War scenes liked (but by special audiences).
9 Nazi salute caused almost invariable laughter.
10 Anti-war speeches listened to very attentively.
11 War made very little difference to taste.
12 Newsreel response now less than before.

Editors' notes

1 All appendices except Appendix 1 are missing.
2 *Gestapo* was re-titled *Night Train to Munich; Siegfried Line* was re-titled *Gasbags.*

3 The suspicion that films about Germany ran into official opposition
  before the war is confirmed by a study of censorship records. Films
  overtly critical of Nazi Germany were not permitted by the British
  Board of Film Censors. See Jeffrey Richards, *Age of the Dream Palace:
  Cinema and Society in Britain 1930–39* (London, 1984), pp. 125–8.

A typical piece of mass observing, done by Len England. His report, dated 24 May 1940, is in Cinema Box 3, File D.

Cinema visited was the Regal, West Norwood. This is situated in the main Norwood road but stands back from the rest of the other shops leaving a wide open block of pavement in front of it. It is a square building perhaps 80 feet high. On the top, one at each side, are two flagpoles with union Jacks flying from them. In the middle of the roof is a large sign 'REGAL' in red built-out letters, and a similar sign is on the right-hand side. The whole building is of brick with white facing, now turning brown with age. In the front centre, flanked by two Corinthian columns, is a large decorated window. At each side there are smaller windows flanked by neon tubing, which used to light the cinema before the beginning of the war. Over the entrance is a large semi-circular awning of steel, while to each side of the entrance there are shut doors leading to other parts of the building. Above these doors, inset in panels, are notices in blue on a yellow background such as 'always the best programme', 'Complete change on Sundays', 'Louis Mordish at the Organ'. All these notices are not changed weekly with the film, but immediately on each side of the entrance a large panel, four foot by two, advertises the pictures showing during the week.

Inside the foyer the box-office is by the entrance on the right; above it is a plan of the seating in the cinema. On the opposite side of the foyer is a timetable showing when each picture is showing. Otherwise the foyer is empty except for a row of chairs at the back; on the right stairs lead to the gallery. By the stairs a door opens into the stalls. On the other side doors are marked 'Private' lead into the manager's office, etc.

Films showing the week that obs. went were *Drums Along the Mohawk*, a Technicolor film with Henry Fonda and Claudette Colbert of the early days of American independence, and *Contraband* with Conrad Veidt and Valerie Hobson, a spy thriller about contraband control in the present war. All advertisements for the films stated simply:

Henry Fonda
Claudette Colbert
in

DRUMS ALONG THE MOHAWK
in Technicolor

Conrad Veidt
Valerie Hobson
in
CONTRABAND

As well as the notices on each side of the cinema a large advertisement
covers the whole of the side wall of the shop on one side of the theatre. On
the other side a similar notice deals with the films being shown the
following week.

When obs. arrived at the cinema there was a long queue outside; the
cinema had not yet opened and people were waiting to go in. The queue
stretched across the front of the building, down the side wall of the shops,
and in front of one or two shops partially blocking the doorways. There
were about a hundred people in the queue, mainly working-class women,
some old men, and a few children. Soon after obs. arrived the doors opened
and the queue moved slowly forward; but as it did so more people joined on
the end. By the time obs. reached the box office it had reduced in size to
about the length of the cinema. In the main the queue is two deep but here
and there three or even four people, when friends, stand in line together.

Most of the women are wearing coats and hats, everyday clothes, a fair
number, perhaps 25 per cent, have shopping baskets with them; most of
these are empty as if the women were going to do their shopping after they
left the pictures and before going home. The men were nearly all wearing
caps and chokers, all old as if they were retired or unemployable. A few
better-dressed younger men in lounge suits and trilbys.

Most of the people in the queue are quiet; even when they are with
friends they speak very little. What little is said is about domestic affairs,
shops, food, stories of friends and relations. Obs. only heard one comment
about films; as one working-class woman passed the advertisement board
outside the cinema she said 'Oh, I didn't know it was in colour.' No war
talk at all. Two men behind obs. are talking of a third. They see a friend
leaning on a lamp post watching them; they call to him, he replies and a
conversation begins though they are about thirty yards away from one
another.

For a few moments it drizzles with rain. A few of the women have
umbrellas with them but they make no attempt to put them up. Some look
at the sky and decide that it will not be much; others turn their collar up
or hunch into their coats. Then the rain stops again and collars are turned
down.

An old man in a frayed blue suit stands by the queue playing a violin
almost tunelessly. When he has finished he takes up his cap which has

been lying in front of him and goes to the front of the queue. He walks down the queue, holding his cap out, waiting for people to throw money into it. A few people look in their bags or feel in their pockets and throw a copper in the cap; most look straight ahead as he passes trying to ignore him. He goes right to the end of the queue, in all collects about a shilling or one and sixpence. He takes the money out the hat, counts it; then goes back to near the front of the queue, and plays with his cap a little in front of him so that those who wish can throw money in it. All those in queue in front of obs. had already been canvassed once and obs. did not see one person put any money in the hat.

Two cinema officials wish to get through the queue to get to the back of the building. They speak to a man, he pushes himself back a little, they squeeze through, thank him, and move on.

People passing in the street look incuriously at the queue; a few stand and watch, leaning against a wall or by a lamp post. Some of those in the queue look out towards the street and the people but most look ahead.

As the queue moves forward those men behind obs. who had been talking to a man by the kerb have to talk louder to make themselves heard but they do not stop for some time. They are exchanging trivialities, 'What are you doing with yourself?' 'Seen Bert lately?' and so on.

As the queue gets near the box-office it forms one deep; there is no pushing or argument. The large posters outside the door attract some attention and people read them, straining their necks to read the top words. But only one comment is made as mentioned above. As the people reach the box-office they put their money on the counter and a ticket slides out of a machine at them. Most have the exact money, which they put down without a word. Some say 'Sixpenny please', or 'Two please' if they are paying for someone else. There is little delay and the movement forward is at a continual rate.

A commissionaire in a green uniform with white gloves and a white peaked cap stands by the box-office saying nothing. In the middle of the foyer a man in a check suit stands smoking a pipe and watching the crowd; probably the manager.

Inside the cinema is still light and people come straight in, are shown by usherettes to the right block of seats; they very soon find a place and settle down. There is still hardly any talking and very little movement.

The lights go down and the picture begins. There is a little comment and then silence.

8

Analysis of Joke Competition

Mass-Observation was particularly interested in humour and in jokes. In this report (FR 198), dated 13 June 1940, Len England analysed the results of a competition run by *The Sunday Dispatch* seeking the three funniest film incidents since the coming of sound. The results demonstrated the long-term impact of memorable situations on the film-goer as well as indicating the most popular sources of humour.

Preliminary

In the *Sunday Dispatch*, 4 February 1940, a prize was offered for readers' 'three funniest film incidents or wisecracks since talkies began'. By the kindness of Mr Moore Raymond, film critic, the entries to this competition were handed over to Mass-Observation for analysis.

631 entries were received, 305 from men and 326 from women. Each entry voted for three different jokes and the total number of votes recorded was 1865; regionally these were divided as follows:

483 votes from London (26% of the total)
395 " " " 21%
173 " " " 9%
299 " " " 16%
432 " " " 23%
 83 " " " 5%

[The ditto marks under 'London' are an error in the original – details of the regions should appear here. – Ed.]
These votes referred to 900 situations in 489 different pictures. Of the 900 situations 579, or 64 per cent, were mentioned only once. No one situation gained even 2 per cent of the total of votes and only 4 gained over 1 per cent.

Biggest laugh

The four that were most popular were as follows:

Ruggles of Red Gap. Charles Laughton, a model butler, drinks steadily with no appreciable result. Suddenly he yells 'Yippee' at the top of his voice.

Bachelor Mother. David Niven and Ginger Rogers are trying to feed a baby. Niven is reading a modern book on the subject, but turns over two pages and reads 'The food is put on a piece of gauze and rubbed into the baby's navel'.

Modern Times. Charlie Chaplin is a worker on whom a patent feeding machine is tried out. The machine goes wrong and rams all the food into his mouth at the same time.

Libelled Lady. William Powell is trying to fish with the aid of a manual on fishing. He gets a fish on the line but only succeeds in falling in.

A further 22 situations were mentioned more than 10 times. Briefly the laughs were caused as follows:

The Awful Truth. Irene Dunne and Cary Grant as husband and wife stand in night clothes, one each side of a bedroom door.

Andy Hardy Gets Spring Fever. Andy is rehearsing a play and the property moon is wobbling; he says: 'How can a man make love when the moon is doing a rumba?'

Bachelor Mother. An old man thinks he has a grandchild but the paternity is doubted; he says: 'I don't care who is its father. I'm its grandfather.'

The Cowboy and the Lady. Gary Cooper imagines he is in the house he will build for his wife; he pretends to sit on chairs, walks through doors, none of which exist.

The Frozen Limits. An old man (Moore Marriott) gets up in the middle of the night and walks to an outhouse. Audience assumes it is a lavatory but he returns with wood for the fire.

The Frozen Limits. An old man walks round a town in a nightshirt. The Crazy Gang all make themselves up to look like him and there are seven men all exactly alike walking round the town in nightshirts.

Fra Diavolo. Laurel and Hardy get drunk.

A Girl Must Live. Renée Houston replies to sanitary
inspector who has asked her out 'You can't make a
convenience out of me.'

Henry VIII (Charles Laughton) stands at the door
of the bedroom of Anne and Cleves and says: 'The things
I've done for England.'

The Hardys Ride High. Andy Hardy goes to a debutante's
flat but leaves in a hurry very embarrassed.

It's in the Air. George Formby in a runaway aeroplane shouting
'Mo-other'.

The Kid from Spain. Eddie Cantor as a toreador.

The Lady Vanishes. Two men (Basil Radford and Naunton Wayne)
who go through the wildest adventures thinking only of the
Test Match that they are missing.

Modern Times. Charlie Chaplin, after screwing nuts all day,
continues to screw when he comes off duty.

My Man Godfrey. Mischa Auer pretending to be an ape.

Night at the Opera. The Marx Brothers and a great many other
people squeezed into one small room.

Old Bones of the River. Will Hay washing a black baby.

Queen of Hearts. Gracie Fields being thrown about in an apache dance.

Roman Scandals. Eddie Cantor in a runaway chariot.

A Slight Case of Murder. Edward G. Robinson's casual treatment
of dead bodies.

Up for the Cup. Sidney Howard tries to get into the press box
as representing *Old Moore's Almanac*.

Whoopee. Eddie Cantor showing his operations.

The general conclusions that can be drawn from these incidents can often
be substantiated by statistics that will be given further in the report. The
most obvious point is the widely accepted one that humour must concern
events of everyday life. Despite the fact that well over 50 per cent of films
produced in this country concern the upper classes, almost without
exception the incidents mentioned here are working class or classless. The
biggest laugh from Will Hay is created when he deals with the domestic
matter of bathing a baby and with George Formby in a runaway aeroplane
the humour, as has been mentioned more than once in the entries, lay in

[his] despairing call for 'Mo–other'. The reference to the Marx Brothers is to a situation that happens to everybody in a modified form. Finally, practically the only satirical reference among all the entries is to a film which made fun of gangster films, which to many people are part of everyday life.

Three out of the four main incidents depend indirectly for their humour on a pompous or superior men being brought suddenly to earth. A larger number of the entries concerns what is possibly the reverse side of this theme, the little man struggling against the rest of the world. Eddie Cantor, mentioned three times in these 26 situations, is always finding himself in great trouble, both Charlie Chaplin and George Formby are always getting into trouble through no fault of their own. Andy Hardy is struggling with the difficulties of adolescence.

Films that do not deal with everyday affairs or comedians who do not portray the man in the street are hardly mentioned at all. Harold Lloyd with his speciality of climbing down skyscrapers is mentioned only once, and W. C. Fields and Jack Hulbert with their rather more superior manner are not popular.

A large number, almost 50 per cent, of the comic situations most frequently mentioned are played by actors and actresses who are not primarily comedians. Charles Laughton (twice referred to) David Niven, Cary Grant, Gary Cooper, Mickey Rooney have all appeared successfully in tragedy. It seems likely that this can be explained as follows. On the music hall professional comedians are making more and more use of some particular mannerism or phrase which they use so persistently that the audience finally laughs every time they use it. The whole point of the laugh lies in the constant repetition of one action or phrase and this is impossible in the films where no comedian is seen more than five times a year. The humour therefore depends far more upon situation and far less upon actors. And in situation a tragic actor can distinguish himself as well as a professional comedian.

Type of situation

Each situation mentioned in the competition was catalogued under one of the categories used for music hall jokes. Easily the most frequently mentioned type of joke was 'ill-health' which gained almost double the references to its nearest neighbour 'sex'. The third category is 'domestic affairs'. These three are also the three most frequent categories in music hall analyses.

Throughout the whole list there is similarity between the lists for film and music hall. Lavatory humour is less popular in the films but this is due to some extent to the stricter censorship in the cinema. The 25 different lavatory situations are voted for 70 times, a higher proportion of votes per situation than any other category except sport. This seems to indicate that lavatory humour when it is passed by the censor is very popular indeed.

Art rising to fifth place in films is more popular than in music halls; practically all the situations mentioned in this connection are to burlesques of opera singing, etc. Clothes, on the other hand, are less popular. But it must be remembered in this connection that it is an accepted principle that comic clothes create an immediate short laugh; in a competition for the longest laugh in talkies these laughs, though frequent, may have been forgotten.

A very large proportion of the sex references are to verbal jokes. In the whole competition less than one in ten of the jokes mentioned are wisecracks or remarks. But in the sex category well over one third of the total are verbal jokes. This again may be due to film censorship; but it is interesting to note that one of the most popular forms of stock humour, the comedian being made love to by a glamour girl, is not mentioned at all in the competition.

The 'alcohol' jokes almost all take the form of the drunk doing very suddenly an unusual thing. The *Ruggles* incident, the most popular of all, is an example of this and nearly all the other situations mentioned are very similar to this. On the music hall on the other hand drunk jokes usually consist of silly remarks or attempts to climb up lamp posts, etc. On the films in almost every case superficially the drunk looks sober; when he suddenly does an absurd thing the surprise element comes into play.

Sex difference in humour

In no category is there any really marked difference between the tastes of men and women. Men laugh more at jobs and alcohol and sport jokes while women laugh more at domestic affairs. This serves merely as a further indication of the fact that humour must be connected with everyday life very closely. The woman in her home is all day concerned with domestic affairs; the man is at his job, goes to the pub, and is more interested in sport.

There is however a more marked difference in the comedians that are liked by men and women. Of the 66 references to the Marx Brothers in all their films, 53 are from men and only 13 from women. On the other hand out of total references of 22 in *Henry VIII*, 17 were from women and in the Hardy films the percentage is almost as high. Eddie Cantor and George Formby are both more popular with women and Mae West creates more laughs – this is not to say she is more popular – with women. There is indication possibly here that women like a quieter form of humour while men laugh at more absurd and outrageous matters. But from neither men or women is there any mention of laughs from slapstick. Laurel and Hardy, the best exponents of slapstick, are mentioned frequently but almost always for remarks or for such situations as Laurel making a snowstorm with paper so that a St Bernard dog will regard him as a lost traveller and give him the brandy that he carries. The more frequent Laurel and Hardy situation where one inflicts bodily harm on the other is mentioned only on two occasions.

Regional differences in humour

Here again there is no really marked difference in tastes; indeed the figures are surprisingly constant, the percentages mentioned on page 1 being kept to within a unit or two throughout each category. London is more clothes-conscious than the more industrial North, the [?] is more interested in sport and in domestic affairs. The North, while having no more liking for sex jokes than the South, prefers the American wisecracks, a point which is not easily understood. Ireland is unusually interested in art jokes; it has already been said that most of these jokes refer to music and Ireland is known for its music which to them is more a part of everyday life than to those in England. Lavatory jokes are more popular in the South than anywhere else.

Few 'regional comedians' are mentioned except for George Formby and, to a lesser extent, Gracie Fields; both of these are popular all over the country and Formby now rarely has a Lancashire background to his comedies. Duggie Wakefield is mentioned two or three times from the North, Max Miller's only mention is from the South, but neither English or American comedians who gain the most votes are 'local'. Will Hay for instance has been an Irish porter, an English schoolmaster, an African coloniser, Laurel and Hardy have been everything from undergraduates to legionnaires. Few Scots comedians are mentioned and the American gagmen, Ned Sparks and his fellows, are also rarely mentioned.

Date of jokes

There is no indication in this competition that the public forgets stars and films as soon as they are a few months old. The most popular films were released in the following years:

Ruggles of Red Gap	1935
Bachelor Mother	1940
Modern Times	1936

Libelled Lady	1936
Awful Truth	1938
Andy H. Spring Fever	1939
Cowboy and the Lady	1938
The Frozen Limits	1940
Fra Diavolo	1933 (reissued 1939?)
A Girl Must Live	1939
Henry VIII	1934
Hardys Ride High	1939
It's in the Air	1938
The Kid from Spain	1932
The Lady Vanishes	1939
My Man Godfrey	1936
Night at the Opera	1936
Old Bones of the River	1939
Queen of Hearts	1936
Roman Scandals	1934
Slight Case of Murder	1938
Up for the Cup	1933
Whoopee	1931

Of these 24 [23–Ed.] films, 12 or 50 per cent are over three years old and 5 [4–Ed.] are over six years old. Eddie Cantor who is mentioned three times in the list has not been seen on the screen in this country for three years, and the Laurel and Hardy film that is mentioned is one of their very earliest features.

To a small extent more recent films are more popular than earlier ones; of the 66 Marx Brothers references, for instance, 50 are from their last three films. But with other stars, notably Eddie Cantor and Ralph Lynn, it is their earliest films that gain nearly all the references. It is probable that *Bachelor Mother* and *The Frozen Limits* owe their very considerable popularity to the fact that they were released only a few weeks before the competition began. But it is equally probable that they would still keep a fairly high position for some years.

Nationality of films

Of the 489 films mentioned, 324 or 65 per cent were American, 161 British, 3 French and 1 Australian. The average ratio of British films released to American is 1 to 4, that in this competition is 1 to 3. This shows a slight tendency towards British films, natural as British films are concerned more with the domestic life that is known to their audience.

Comedians as stars

From box-office receipts in this country the most popular comedians are George Formby, Gracie Fields, Will Hay, Gordon Harker, Will Fyffe, in that order. But the votes for British comedians are very different in this competition; they are as follows:

Will Hay	66 votes	(3rd on box-office list)
George Formby	59	(1st on box-office list)
Crazy Gang	54	(not mentioned)
Gracie Fields	30	(2nd on box-office list)
Gordon Harker	5	(4th on box-office list)
Will Fyffe	1	(5th on box-office list)

The popularity of Gracie Fields does not depend entirely upon her humour but she is alone in this respect. The difference between Will Hay and George Formby is slight but the Crazy Gang reach third place though they are not even mentioned in the box-office list. Even excluding *The Frozen Limits* which was released in 1940 after the box-office figures had been made up, they receive 22 votes which is very much more than Gordon Harker or Will Fyffe. Of the five votes noted for Gordon Harker three occur in films in which most of the humour was provided by Alastair Sim, and in the Will Fyffe comedy *Said O'Reilly to MacNab* the situation referred more to O'Reilly than MacNab.

'Cinematographic' sequences

Of the 900 situations only 22 were of a type that could not have been expressed in any other medium, that is, that depended for their laughs on trick photography or montage; a further 28 situations were from cartoons, all but two of these from Disney. Most of these situations are mentioned more than once and at least three of them (George Formby in his plane, Eddie Cantor in a chariot, and Gracie Fields in an apache dance) appear among the most popular situations. Only 6 of the situations thus mentioned are voted for only once, and of these two are in the *Topper* films which are frequently quoted. A great many of the cartoon situations are dependent entirely upon their medium.

This seems to indicate very definitely that the cinema is not taking sufficient advantage of its unique possibilities and is depending too much upon the technique of the stage. Its few ventures into the realm of trick photography have met with an exceptionally high response.

Unintentional humour

Eight jokes mentioned were not intended to be humorous. These consist mainly of remarks with double meanings, the most popular being that in *Hell's Angels* when a glamour girl invites a man to her rooms and, though wearing very little at the time, goes out 'to change into something comfortable'. Other situations mentioned were: in *King Kong* two monsters are fighting and one knocks the other out with a perfect uppercut; in *An Englishman's Home* German aeroplanes are coming over England being guided by a beam. The beam is cut off, they immediately turn round and steer for home. In *Snow White* the witch kicks away the skeleton of a man.

General conclusions

From all this several 'rules' for humour emerge. The first and most obvious one is that all film humour must concern matters which are common knowledge to the whole audience; despite this, as has already been mentioned, over 50 per cent of British films deal with the upper classes. The second point is that film humour lies mainly in situation; words and particular characteristics of actors are of less importance. The fact that it lies in situation provides the film industry with a possibility of exploiting their particular medium far more vigorously than they do at the moment. The main subjects are ill-health, sex, domestic affairs and food, as in other branches of humour. There is no indication that audiences have short memories or that they forget stars who do not make frequent appearances. Those comedians who are regarded as best box-office do not always provide the loudest laughs.

Yet despite all this it must still be remembered that no situation gained even 2 per cent of the total, the universally popular joke is still not found. The 'rules' above show what factors are most likely to produce the results. They do not solve the problem of what else is needed.

'Fade-out' Competition
Report

In a report (FR 393), dated 23 August 1940, Len England analysed the
results of another *Sunday Dispatch* competition on the most memorable
'fade-out' in films.

Preliminary

On 31 April (sic) 1940, a competition was set in the *Sunday Dispatch*,
awarding prizes for what readers thought the best 'fade-out's in films they
had seen. By the kindness of Mr Moore Raymond, film critic, the entries
were handed to Mass-Observation.

577 people entered the competition, 257 men and 320 women. Each
entrant named three fade-outs, and 354 different films were mentioned.

Popular fade-outs

The most popular fade-outs were these:

Three Comrades (76 votes). Two of the comrades, already dead, beckon the
third to join them. Arm in arm the three comrades march through the
skies.

Dark Victory (61 votes). The heroine walks slowly upstairs to die, bravely
and alone.

Goodbye Mr Chips (59 votes). Mr Chips in his old age murmurs the names
of the boys that he has known, as he dies.

Wuthering Heights (48 votes). The hero climbs the hill, faithful to a tryst
with a lover who is dead.

A Tale of Two Cities (42 votes). Carton says 'It is a far, far, better thing,'
etc. The camera pans as the guillotine knife falls, and shows the clear sky.
Then a scripture text.

Modern Times (41 votes). Charlie Chaplin and his girl walk off down the
road together.

Queen Christina (40 votes). The exiled Queen stands at the prow of her ship, like a figurehead, looking into the future.

Lost Horizon (34 votes). The hero struggles back over the mountains to the dream city of Shangri La.

The most evident fact from these eight fade-outs is that they are all connected with tragedy. The first five are directly connected with the death of a principal character, and the other three show people facing the future with hope as their only asset. The first humorous film ending that is mentioned is twenty-sixth on the list with only 14 votes. Even more striking is the number of films mentioned with a 'spiritual' ending. There cannot be more than two or three films a year that end with the characters who have been parted in life meeting again in Heaven. Yet in the first twenty films on the fade-out list, four are thus concerned; *Three Comrades*, already mentioned, is the most popular fade-out of all, *Smiling Through* is ninth on the list and is followed by *The Castles* and *Maytime*.

A breakdown analysis shows these points even more clearly.

Categories of fade-outs

The fade-outs mentioned were divided into four types:
(a) Love, including romantic love, mother love, self denial, etc.
(b) Uplifting, including a patriotic speech, a message of hope, and so on.
(c) Tragic.
(d) Comic.

The numbers in the table indicate the references made to each category. Percentages for men and women are worked out separately as more women than men entered the competition.

	Men	*Women*	*Total*
Emotional	121 (17%)	196 (23%)	317 (21%)
Uplifting	220 (31%)	209 (25%)	429 (29%)
Tragic	273 (38%)	316 (38%)	589 (38%)
Comic	104 (14%)	117 (14%)	221 (14%)

The most important point that emerges from this table is that nearly 40 per cent of men and women alike prefer fade-outs that are tragic. No exact figures are available on the number of films made yearly that are tragic, but a small random sample showed that out of 100 films 32 were comedies, and only 12 were tragedies; and of these 12, only 2 had tragic endings. In other words, in only 2 out of every 100 films is the fade-out tragic; but 40 in every 100 people prefer these fade-outs to any other.

Obviously a comic film is not going to take a great deal of care about its fade-out as there is no necessity here for a climax. But nevertheless if 32 per cent of films made are comedies, it is rather surprising that only 14 per cent of the total vote for popular fade-outs is for comic endings.

In these two categories the votes of men and women have exactly equal percentages. But women seem to like emotional endings much more than men. *Stella Dallas*, for example, ends with the mother walking away from the wedding of her daughter, having watched it from the crowd; this fade-out is mentioned 11 times by women and only once by a man. It is, of course, only natural that themes of mother love and so on should be far more popular with women than with men, but under this heading are included sentimental endings of almost any type. Men much prefer uplifting endings; *A Tale of Two Cities*, for example, is mentioned much more often by men than by women. This is possibly due to the narrower outlook of women that had already been shown in the report on the joke competition; women are more bounded by the four walls of their own home, but within these walls they can experience the emotions of love. Men with a slightly wider outlook can appreciate fade-outs with a wider significance.

There is a most remarkable neglect of any films with social content; admittedly the number of films that are made with the intention of driving home an idea to the audience is small, but it is surely not as small as would appear from the competition. The only film of this nature mentioned more than five times is *Blockade*, an ordinary adventure film about the Spanish Civil War which ended with an impassioned speech on the idiocy of war, and with the queries, 'why must it go on' and 'where will it end?'. The rather similar ending of *Things to Come* ('All the universe, or nothing. Which shall it be?') is not mentioned at all. *Fury* does not appear at all, *Winterset* only once, and *Dead End* five times. A simple message (e.g. Everything will be all right in heaven, While there's Life there's Hope) will apparently impress the audience, but a more complex one, a complaint against some part of the existing system, for instance, is not at all well received.

The fade-outs have been submitted to further break-down analysis to give a fairer idea of their actual content as well as of the emotions on which they play. For this thirteen categories were used as follows:

1 Death. Fade-outs on dead bodies.
2 Bereavement. Fade-outs on those suffering loss of friends, etc.
3 Supernatural. Fade-outs with the spirits of the dead.
4 Hope. Fade-outs with characters looking forward to a better future.

5 Deep emotion. Fade-outs of people weeping, etc.
6 Self denial. Fade-outs on lovers parting, mother leaving her children, etc.
7 Embraces. Fade-outs of lovers kissing.
8 Pathos.
9 Horror.
10 Patriotism.
11 Comedy.
12 Abstract. Fade-outs on purely inanimate objects.
13 Nature. Fade-outs on flowers, animals.

The numbers and percentages referring to these different types of ending are as shown in the table.

	Men		Women		Total
Death	152	22%	181	23%	333
Bereavement	8	1%	20	3%	28
Supernatural	128	19%	165	20%	293
Hope	95	14%	68	9%	163
Deep emotion	32	5%	52	7%	84
Self denial	31	4%	50	6%	81
Embraces	21	3%	35	4%	56
Pathos	28	4%	29	4%	57
Horror	40	6%	15	2%	55
Patriotism	15	2%	28	4%	43
Comedy	88	13%	100	12%	188
Abstract	14	2%	19	2%	33
Nature	7	1%	6	1%	13

There is a most striking similarity between the percentages for men and women. The largest variation is 5 per cent, and in 7 out of 13 categories the variation is not more than 1 per cent.

The emphasis upon supernatural endings, already commented on, is even more clearly brought out in this table. Twenty per cent of the votes are for fade-outs with the spirits of the departed living happily in that world though they could not in this. The number of films with such endings cannot be ascertained, but a survey of 100 films does not reveal a single one, while further investigation by inv. revealed only one film, not mentioned in the competition, with a spiritual ending; this was the Douglas Fairbanks silent film, *The Man in the Iron Mask*.[1]

In this analysis, as well as the others, the emphasis on death is pressed home. Fade-outs actually on the bodies of the dead is the largest category of all; the second largest category, supernatural, presupposes the death of the characters; fade-outs of bereavement, that is somebody mourning another's death, add another 2 per cent to the total; horror endings are presumably mostly connected with death; and even abstract fade-outs are often symbolic of death; *The Spy in Black*, for instance, has a very popular ending with the German's cap floating on the water to indicate that he had been drowned.

Two categories that have surprisingly few votes are Patriotism and Embraces. A very large number of films must end with the hero and heroine in each other's arms, but none of these are presumably sufficiently out of the rut to be memorable. The lack of patriotic endings is less understandable when it is considered how popular 'uplifting' endings are. Uplifting fade-outs constitute 30 per cent of the total, patriotic only 3 per cent, nearly all of these being for *Shipyard Sally* in which Gracie Fields was seen singing 'Land of Hope and Glory' with the Union Jack as the background.

Abstract and nature endings seem to be a little too subtle for the audiences to understand. *The Spy in Black*, already mentioned, was fairly popular. The only other film mentioned at all frequently is *Eternally Yours* where the mating of two rabbits is symbolic of the marriage of their two owners.

Dates

As with the joke competition, there is no evidence to support the theory that audiences have short memories. The production dates of the first fifteen films on the list are as follows:

Three Comrades	1938
Dark Victory	1939
Goodbye Mr Chips	1939
Wuthering Heights	1939
Tale of Two Cities	1935
Modern Times	1936
Queen Christina	1934
Lost Horizon	1937
Smiling Through	1932
A Star is Born	1937
San Francisco	1936
Bengal Lancer	1935
Gunga Din	1939
Spy in Black	1939
Dawn Patrol	1938

Over half these films are more than three years old, one of them eight years old.

Stars, directors, nationalities, etc.

Fade-outs are not so much the merit of the star as the director, but in the list of the fifteen most popular fade-outs only one director is mentioned more than once. This is Edmund Goulding who directed both *Dark Victory* and *Dawn Patrol*.

Ronald Colman appears in two of the first fifteen films (*Tale of Two Cities* and *Lost Horizon*) and also in *The Prisoner of Zenda* which is very popular. Ronald Colman, however, almost invariably appears as the despairing hero who dies gallantly and tragically at the end of the film – in each of his last six films he has died or walked into the night – so the probability is that it is Colman's type of film that is so popular. Norma Shearer also appeared in two of the first fifteen films (*Marie Antoinette* and *Smiling Through*).

In the joke competition it was found that approximately 50 per cent of the films mentioned were of British production; in the fade-out competition only two out of the first fifteen were made in this country. In the analyst's opinion, the reason for this is that while humour is, to some extent, regional, sentiment and emotional treatment of death and tragedy are not. It is almost universally acknowledged that technically Hollywood is much superior to Britain, and therefore their treatment of fade-outs is more appreciated.

General conclusions

The most memorable fade-outs are those connected with death and with life after death, particularly those which treat the theme in an uplifting manner; the hero or the heroine dies bravely and unafraid, or the future world is depicted as a joyful spot where those parted in this world meet again. On these points men and women agree.

Comic endings are not at all memorable, nor are fade-outs with social content that have a bearing on real life. The usual ending of lovers embracing is not often mentioned, nor is the more subtle, symbolic fade-out.

There is no indication that audiences have short memories for many of the very popular films are four or five years old. No star or director is frequently mentioned. Less than 15 per cent of the films mentioned are British.

List of films in order of their 'fade-out' popularity

Name of film	Total	Men	Women
Dark Victory	76	31	45
Goodbye Mr Chips	59	27	32
Wuthering Heights	48	24	24
Tale of Two Cities	42	23	19
Modern Times	41	23	18
Queen Christina	40	11	29
Lost Horizon	34	17	17
Smilin' Through	29	6	23
A Star is Born	29	13	16
San Francisco	26	14	12
Lives of a Bengal Lancer	24	8	16
Gunga Din	24	15	9
Spy in Black	22	13	9
Dawn Patrol	22	10	12
Story of Vernon and Irene Castle	20	7	13
Maytime	19	7	12
Prisoner of Zenda	18	9	9
Five Came Back	16	9	7
Sign of the Cross	16	6	10
Suez	16	3	13
Shipyard Sally	15	6	9
When Tomorrow Comes	15	7	8
Cavalcade	14	5	9
One Way Passage	14	7	7
Q Planes	14	8	6
Algiers	13	5	8
Great Ziegfeld	13	6	7
Invisible Man	13	8	5
Marie Antoinette	13	4	9
Snow White and the Seven Dwarfs	12	5	7

Stella Dallas	12	1	11
Angels with Dirty Faces	11	9	2
Huckleberry Finn	11	5	6
Juarez	11	4	7
Nurse Edith Cavell	11	5	6
Women, The			
Captains Courageous	10	4	6
Four Daughters	10	8	2
French Without Tears	10	2	8
Young Mr Lincoln	10	6	4
Blockade	9	6	3
Mayerling	9	2	7
Only Angels Have Wings	9	7	2
Ask a Policeman	8	4	4
Hurricane, The	8	6	2
Informer, The	8	6	2
Poison Pen	8	3	5
You Only Live Once	8	7	1
After the Thin Man	7	2	5
At the Circus	7	4	3
I am a Fugitive from a Chain Gang	7	4	3
Lion Has Wings	7	2	5
Man in the Iron Mask. The	7	5	2
Ruggles of Red Gap	7	2	5
Three Smart Girls Grow Up	7	2	5
The Barretts of Wimpole Street	6	1	5
Eternally Yours	6	3	3
Four Feathers	6	3	3
Great Waltz	6	3	3
Les Miserables	6	2	4
'M'	6	3	3
Oh Mr Porter	6	3	3
Old Maid	6	1	5
Stanley and Livingstone	6	5	1
Bringing up Baby	5	2	3
Circus, The	5	3	2
Citadel, The	5	3	2
Dead End	5	3	2

Farewell to Arms	5	2	3
Fifth Avenue Girl	5	2	3
I met a Murderer	5	3	2
Love Affair	5	1	4
Plainsman, The	5	1	4
Stagecoach	5	3	2
Stars Look Down	5	4	1
Tovarich	5	–	5
Where's that Fire	5	4	1

Editors' note

1 *The Iron Mask.*

10   Social Research and the Film

In an article for *Documentary News Letter* (November 1940), Tom Harrisson deployed the findings of Mass-Observation to argue the case for regular and systematic analysis of the public reaction to films. The published version differed little from the draft (FR 446), except from the occasional judicious toning down, for instance, 'It is staggering to find that the Films Division of the Ministry has no machinery whatever for detailed checking up of the effect of its films' became 'It is . . . interesting to find that the Films Division of the Ministry appears to have no adequate machinery to provide it with much evidence . . . on the influence its films have had and are having.' The postscript on five-minute films which Harrisson added to his article is omitted here, as it is identical with the report produced later in this collection (Item 26).

In recent numbers of *Documentary News Letter* there have been numerous references to the apparently *ad hoc* policy for Ministry of Information films, and several references to the apparent failure of the Films Division to check up on what it is doing. Moreover, recently the Select Committee on National Expenditure stressed the need for the Films Division to consult the Home Intelligence Division of the Ministry on the sort of films and treatment needed, *before* embarking on the making of propaganda films. It is clear that the short-term function of the Films Division is to affect public opinion. The *only* test of its value is, therefore, the *effect* of its films on the people who see them; the only justification of its output, a demonstrable need for every film. The Films Division has the immense responsibility of producing films with effects favourable to the continuation of the war and our victory. These films may either have a general effect on temper, temperament, determination, etc., or deal with specific subjects.

It is therefore interesting to find that the Films Division of the Ministry appears to have no adequate machinery to provide it with much evidence, either by observation, interpretation or questionnaire, on the influence its films have had and are having. Apparently the only substantial data available to the Division are reports from cinema managers.

It is not worth elaborating for readers of this publication the difficulties which would face any cinema manager who, while carrying on his ordinary jobs, attempted without training to observe the reactions to specific points, including the sequences of short films, sandwiched in full-length programmes. And it is the detailed breakdown which is so important in checking on propaganda. A small incident in a film may produce unforeseen effects. For instance, *Miss Grant goes to the Door* (best liked of MoI shorts), apart from terrifying some rural spinsters and widows, was incidental propaganda for a 'people's war'. The whole solution of her problem depended on her getting a revolver (from the fortunately placed corpse). The sight of this untrained hand wielding the weapon, however ineffectively, at once played on the secret wish to have some weapon of protection in times like this. Trivial examples of this sort can be multiplied. And it is really amazing that any informed propaganda unit can have produced for *general* distribution a film like *Call to Arms*, which was calculated to alienate many sorts of working-class or other feelings. The Films Division with its highly intelligent personnel, in its very high building, tends to be easily out of touch with the rather simpler reactions of industrial Lancashire and rural Somerset. One of the reasons why Social Research has come into being is because, under modern economic and administrative conditions, it is difficult for any 'high-ups' to keep in close or sympathetic touch with 'low-downs'.

But if the Films Division of the MoI needs social research, the whole film industry needs such machinery at least as badly. For in wartime, war becomes by far the most important item in our lives, and the subject of many feature films. The effect of these films, extensive and expensive as they often are, may often prove greater, if less direct, than short or five-minute documentaries. *The Lion Has Wings* was, for instance, a powerful contribution towards Chamberlainish complacency; *Let George Do It*, a detailed analysis of enemy espionage, has given rise to persistent and sometimes hysterical rumours that broadcasters, ranging from Vic Oliver and Charlie Kunz to Edward Ward and C. B. Cochran, have been arrested (interned, shot, hung) for sending out code messages over the radio.

So much for the general considerations. I am suggesting with diffidence that the Films Division is operating in a vacuum at present. Can it *prove* that it is not doing more harm than good? I am also suggesting that the commercial film industry and the independent documentary concerns must consider and accurately measure the effect of their films, not only in the terms of aesthetics, box-office and techni-colour, but also in terms of morale, behaviour and social conduct.

Having, I hope, broadly stated the case for research on film effects, film people will ask what sort of potential machinery exists for checking, and how accurate is it? Here I must ask that my answer be treated with the utmost caution. I am heavily biased, because for some three years now part of the energies of Mass-Observation has been directed to studying film effects. And as I can find exceedingly little other definite British research on this subject, except for occasional local questionnaires, and

Sydney Bernstein's annual popularity polls, I am forced to start out rather from our own experience. I should mention that we are already adequately employed!

The only thorough film research ever undertaken was sponsored by the Payne Fund, through the Motion Picture Research Council, in the USA, 1929–32. Many of the best sociologists and social psychologists in America took some part in producing the twelve volumes of research results. But these were concerned exclusively with children, and there is nowhere adult data for comparison. The method used in the survey was almost entirely that of direct questionnaires to children, probing hundreds of problems, such as the most popular film scene, film attendances, the effect on conduct and emotional life, relation of films and crime. It was found that, sometimes, even a single picture had the effect of altering children's attitudes, e.g. *Birth of a Nation* caused antagonism towards negroes; *All Quiet on the Western Front*, objection to war. A high proportion (66 per cent) of children imitated their favourite film stars in emotional and sexual circumstances. Children who went frequently to the cinema were found to be less favourably disposed to school, home and other normal environments than those who went only occasionally. In brief, it was established that the film exerted an immense influence on American children.

From these investigations it has generally been assumed that the effect on adults is similarly immense. *But no scientific evidence on this subject exists.* In a small way, Mass-Observation has attempted to assess the influence of the film on several occasions. While we would not, under any circumstances, claim a general validity for our results, several different studies, separate in time, place, subject and method, have given pretty similar results. For instance, in March, 1939, we made a study of one thousand voluntary ARP wardens in a typical borough, and among other things sought to discover what propaganda had influenced them to join ARP. In their view, the following was the relative importance of the different propaganda channels in determining their attitude to ARP:–

	per cent
Press	26
Talk and Friends	24
Posters and displays	19
Radio	11
Leaflets, pamphlets and books	10
Meetings	3
Films	1
Miscellaneous	6

Shortly after the declaration of war, we asked our nation-wide panel of voluntary observers (*not* a typical cross-section of Britain) to ballot on what they considered the main influence in determining their general attitude to the war and their understanding of the events leading up to it, with the following result:

	in importance
Friends and 'own opinion'	1st
Press	2nd
Radio	3rd
Leaflets, pamphlets, etc.	4th
Posters and displays	5th
Films	6th

The numerous subtle *indirect* impacts of the film probably add up to an important total; in a fashion survey a couple of years ago we found Joan Crawford was fourth most important factor in determining the headwear of Cockney and Lancashire girls. But the *direct* effect of films, specifically presented as propaganda or with the object of producing an immediate effect, would seem to be small when compared with the generalisation often made by interested parties. Further research into this subject is clearly of importance.

It is easier to make continuous studies of newsreels than of documentary films, and we have watched what we believe to be a pretty steady decline in the prestige, never high, of newsreels, in the past year. At the end of 1939 just under two-thirds of all persons asked said they liked newsreels, and expressed sentiments distinctly favourable to them; by August, 1940, only just a quarter of those questioned held this point of view. In 1939, 12 per cent spontaneously criticised newsreels for having no news; in 1940, 35 per cent spontaneously made this criticism. These results have no *absolute* validity, but a comparative value.

The investigators, the question, the areas and class proportions were the same each time; and the questioning was spread over several weeks in order to avoid the dominant influence of any one newsreel. A whole wealth of criticism was revealed, some of it very unfair to the newsreel companies. At the same time, we have found repeated cases where the newsreels have alienated people by their political bias, by their treatment of emotional topics, by the commentaries (which are often unsympathetic to ordinary people), and have shown by numerous indications that they are sometimes out of touch with the feeling of the moment and even, sometimes, with the permanent feelings of housewives or labourers.

A newsreel at the beginning of the present blitz preceded pictures of bombed London (presented in a manner hardly calculated to elevate the provinces) with:

Britain's Day of Prayer
More Canadian troops arrive

'Dead' Guards VC is prisoner-of-war
New Zealand band plays popular airs for London
US ambulances for Great Britain
Duchess of Kent visits a hospital

The prestige of newsreels seems to have fallen most sharply among middle-class people and among men; there is some parallel evidence that the prestige of Ministry shorts has not risen lately, and that they are more appreciated among the middle classes than among the working classes (the greater part of the population). Incidentally, people who see favourable reviews of Ministry shorts often find difficulty in locating the cinemas where they are showing, and our own investigators have wasted much time and energy in this way.

So far we have been dealing mainly with verbal responses, *public* opinion. If we are to understand fundamental attitudes, to the film or anything else, we must penetrate below the superficial words. The film, in its environment, the cinema, offers almost ideal material for the student of *private* opinion. The large numbers of people provide adequate quantities of types, of all classes, ages and sexes. The darkness provides the privacy in which people can react as individuals and even perhaps hiss a Minister they would only dare glare at in the flesh. Moreover, films provide an immense range of human situation, and present to the audience a great variety of emotional problems.

Watching audience responses in cinemas gives the same sort of information about what is really going on in people's minds as we get from intimate war diaries, or dream studies. For instance, while public opinion polls and press letterbags showed a heavy increase in Chamberlain's popularity after the beginning of the war, and while this popularity was superficially maintained until within a few days of his resignation, newsreel observation showed a steady and accelerating decline in favourable audience response whenever he appeared on the screen, though it is the 'done thing' to be loyal to your Prime Minister in public, especially in wartime. Similarly, direct opinion testing would always show a big hand for the King. But in the early months of the war newsreel (and other) studies showed that his popularity was at a low ebb.

Since the bombing of Buckingham Palace the King's popularity has risen, as instanced by one-seventh of appearances applauded at the outbreak of war to over one-third of appearances applauded since the blitz. The Duke of Windsor, who is not often seen, has the highest score of all, maintained throughout the war. Before the Dakar incident General de Gaulle had a 100 per cent favourable response and, in more than half of our observations, was clapped for over five seconds; mass-observers await with interest his next newsreel appearance.

Clearly, much depends on the methods of measuring audience response.

We have devoted a good deal of effort to developing an accurate measure; but as well as being accurate, it must also be practicable under the special conditions for observation, which are far from a laboratory. Observer variation, the rapid sequence of film events, the difficulty of getting scripts as a check on observation, and the darkness in which the observer must write and record, are all difficulties. We have tended, therefore, to observe a few films in detail, rather than many films in brief.

Six main types of audience response are observed, each response graded into categories according to the approximate extent of response amongst the audience, and the duration is stated in seconds. Testing with different investigators has shown that this method provides information which is reasonably reliable for practical purposes. In studying *Let George Do It*, for instance, with six investigators working separately, recording audience response to fifty sequences in the film, the degree of consistency was striking. Moreover, in this as in many other investigations, we found a striking similarity in the responses of widely different audiences.

The emotional background for laughter seems, on our detailed studies of films, music hall and pantomime, to be remarkably stable, but the *detail* of treatment for successful jokes on familiar themes is very changeable, especially under contemporary conditions. The living stage comedian is immediately sensitive to this and can modify his jokes accordingly from evening to evening. The film comedian, or the documentary film producer who wants to make the point with a touch of humour, is at a disadvantage here in having less contact with public opinion, and therefore more need for a well-based understanding of probable trends. To refer once more to *Let George Do It*, the 'topical' jokes in that film were not popular and received little more than half the volume of response given to non-topical jokes in the same sequences. The conditions for their particular topicality had changed while the film was being made and distributed. We have made five separate investigations into joke reactions, in Blackpool, in London music halls, in a last Christmas pantomime, in a Sunday newspaper competition and in Formby films. In every case, much over half of the successful laughter points came from themes of ill-health, deformity, sexual abnormality, or potential death (including war) situations. This was as true of Blackpool in 1937 as of a music hall in 1940. Even in 1937, in Blackpool, war was running only a little behind ill-health as the most successful joke subject.

I might fade out this article by mentioning an analysis we made of the replies received by the *Sunday Dispatch* (courtesy of film critic Moore Raymond) in a competition where they asked people to name which 'fade-out' of a film they liked best. Usually, press information of this sort is of little value, because those who reply are influenced by what they think the paper will or won't like as indicated by its published attitudes on the subject. In this case there was no attitude or indication of opinion to influence the readers; they simply wrote on postcards their ideas of the perfect ending. The most popular fade-outs were these, in this order of frequency:

Three Comrades. Two of the comrades, already dead, beckon the third to join them. Arm in arm the three comrades march through the skies.
Dark Victory. The heroine walks slowly upstairs to die bravely and alone.
Goodbye Mr Chips. Mr Chips in his old age murmurs the names of the boys that he has known, as he dies.
Wuthering Heights. The hero climbs the hill, faithful to a tryst with a lover who is dead.
A Tale of Two Cities. Carton says 'It is far, far better thing', etc. The camera pans as the guillotine knife falls, and shows the clear sky. Then a scripture text.
Modern Times. Charlie Chaplin and his girl walk off down the road together.
Queen Christina. The exiled Queen stands at the prow of her ship, like a figure-head, looking into the future.
Lost Horizon. The hero struggles back over the mountains to the dream city of Shangri La.

Here we see down into the heart of stolid, shy old British emotion. The tragic ending wins every time, provided it looks into the future and brings some message of heroic hope. It is because Winston Churchill feels like the readers of popular Sunday papers that he is able to call out so much in British people that Chamberlain, Halifax, or Attlee could never command.

On the basis of our own experience, plus the existing techniques available from propaganda testing and market research, and the Payne Fund studies, it would seem to be a relatively simple matter to set up an independent bureau, recognised and supported by all the interested parties. This bureau would be concerned entirely with research, establishing and using accurate and agreed criteria, observational, verbal, statistical and qualitative, to measure the effects of all sorts of film, and to predict the needs of existing and potential film audiences. Its job would include:

1 Keeping a regular check on opinion about films in general, different types of film and their prestige in particular.
2 Reporting on public reaction to all relevant films, especially shorts, which are not measurable by any box-office index.
3 Discovering what symbols and subjects are suitable or require film treatment at any time. (e.g. At the time of writing Indian troops are a particular popular symbol not being used on the films; acute boredom is caused by shots of arms workers, the history of the crisis before the

outbreak of the war, and the Duchess of Gloucester inspecting things, subjects repeatedly used.)

4 Providing information on the varying situations which produce 'undesirable' effects, the general trend of reaction to war themes, etc. (e.g. from September, 1939 to August, 1940, there was a steady 17 per cent disliking all themes connected with the war unless humorously treated, a higher proportion objecting to horror shots of any sort).

5 Producing general factual criticism, from the public opinion point of view, on all propaganda films; and providing comments on the elementary social factors which seemed to have escaped the attention of the industry (e.g. films such as *Call to Arms* and *Mr Borland Thinks Again* have been generally distributed, though their application was particular. Mr Borland was concerned mainly with silage, a word that was not explained until the last minute of the film).

The Hazards of Mass-Observing

A letter from a very keen volunteer observer, a middle-aged teacher, recounting a recent experience in a cinema (Film Topic Box 1, file B).

Watford, Herts.
May 4th, 1941.

Dear Mr Harrisson,

I regret to have to report further trouble with my note-taking in a cinema. Last Monday, two women objected to my writing and reported it to the Manager. Later he sent for me and asked me to explain. He told me that many complaints were made in the cinema, some caused by people trying to photograph newsreels. His difficulty was that he had never heard of Mass-Observation. He kept my paper, saying he would send it later.

Yesterday brought a detective who wanted to know all about the incident. He, too, had never heard of M-O but was most interested to hear of it. I gave him all the bulletins I could see, as well as all the copies of *US*, which had just been returned from a friend. Luckily, I happened to find the letter in which Mr Paul Rotha had asked for audience reaction on the MoI short *You're Telling Me*; and he asked for it. He asked whether M-O were a political organisation. I said 'no; though questions were asked on political subjects.'

The result of this interview seemed satisfactory, the man saying that he wished all his cases were settled so easily, so I do not anticipate any further enquiry.

I think it would be inadvisable to go on with the newsreel reports, except where I can memorise the headlines. I am sorry about this, because I have really enjoyed helping you, and it has made my cinema going so much more worthwhile. Would you like me to continue sending the weekly newspaper cuttings?

With best wishes and continued success,

yours sincerely,

(Miss) E. J. A.

12   Notes on the Effect of the War (January–September 1941) on the Film Industry

This handwritten set of notes (Film Topic Box 2: file 2H) from Len England, dated 15 September 1941, and sent from Doncaster, shows that although he was now in the forces, his interest in films and in particular the aspects concerning M-O continued unabated.

1 Newsreels seem again to be losing popularity and the degree of response to them is small. There has of late been in them very little of outstanding interest, no action pictures of any sort except from Russia (see below). Most frequent pictures are of our desert troops, and these are all very similar.

2 Gerald Sanger of BMN[1] in an article in *Sight and Sound* (Autumn number) defends the newsreels on a charge of reconstructing, distinguishing between this and faking: he defines reconstructing as showing a ship firing and pretending it is firing at a German, and faking as showing shots of London and pretending they are of Hamburg. Reconstruction seems to be becoming increasingly popular. One recent Pathé newsreel (seen at Clifton, Wellington, 1.8.41), showed what was patently a reconstruction of bringing a relief to a sick woman in the desert, and followed it with shots from Russia. These purported to show, for instance, bombs dropping and exploding: the camera was exactly focused where the explosion took place *before* the event. There were also shots of planes crashing which were in my opinion definitely faking.

3 MoI shorts seemed to have fully retained their popularity. An MoI show at the camp was very well received, and *Merchant Seamen* was excellently received in Wellington. *Target for Tonight* is one of the few films that are eagerly looked forward to here.

4 There is evidence that the managers still do not realise the value of these shorts. They are shown very irregularly here, and often one is shown two consecutive weeks. This causes a great deal of annoyance.

5 Producers have at last woken up to the natural antipathy to war and Nazi films, and are now concentrating on light stuff which entirely ignores the war. In Hollywood a cycle is beginning of big musicals, and this seems to be popular taste.

6 The majority of war films being made are of the adventure-thriller type

with little direct propaganda. Most popular is the Englishman-chased-in-Germany that has produced *Pimpernel Smith* and *Mantrap*,[2] two highly publicised pictures. Also glamourised accounts of our gallant airmen in such films as *Dangerous Moonlight* and *Ships with Wings*. Many films have substituted the fifth columnist for the criminal and otherwise remain unchanged. Some have laid heavy emphasis on the keynote of freedom, and have drawn analogy from the past. See very particularly *This England, The Sea Hawk, Penn of Pennsylvania, Son of Monte Cristo* and *Lady Hamilton*.

7 Shortage of man power is telling seriously on English production. Actors are being called up, and young men are very difficult to find. The market is restricted, but the best films are being well received in America, and cinemas where they are left are well filled.

8 Gallup's survey on American cinemagoing (see *Observer*, 1.8.41) seems to bear a close resemblance to conclusions made by M-O of this country.

Editors' note

1 British Movietone News.
2 *Mantrap*. He probably means Fritz Lang's *Manhunt* (1940), in which a big-game hunter (Walter Pidgeon), planning an attempt on Hitler's life, is pursued through Germany and later England by Nazis.

1943 Directive Replies on Favourite Films

The November 1943 Mass-Observation directive included the question: 'What films have you liked best during the past year? Please list six films in order of liking and give your reasons for liking them.' The replies provide a fascinating cross-section of cinema-going preference during 1943. 104 women replied, of whom 56 said they did not go often or at all to the cinema or had not seen six films during the year. The reasons varied: war duties, family commitments, dislike of the medium. 116 men replied, 47 of whom said that they did not go often or at all to the cinema or had not seen six films, again for a variety of reasons, though mainly in this case dislike of films. About half the respondents then were regular cinema-goers, many of them keen and knowledgeable, not to say opinionated. The most popular choices of film are revealing. Among women, the favourite films were *The Life and Death of Colonel Blimp* (28), *In Which We Serve* (26), *The Gentle Sex* (19), *Mrs Miniver* (17), *Random Harvest* (15), *Desert Victory* (11), *Thunder Rock* (10), *The First of the Few* (9), *Bambi* (8) and *Fantasia* (8). The men's choice was: *In Which We Serve* (28), *The Life and Death of Colonel Blimp* (21), *Desert Victory* (15), *Thunder Rock* (14), *The First of the Few* (10), *Random Harvest* (10), *Bambi* (10), *Mrs Miniver* (9), *Gone With the Wind* (8), *The Gentle Sex* (7), *The Magnificent Ambersons* (7). There is comparatively little difference between the two lists. When they are conflated, they produce the following list of the most popular titles of 1943: *In Which We Serve* (54), *The Life and Death of Colonel Blimp* (49), *Desert Victory* (26), *Mrs Miniver* (26), *The Gentle Sex* (26), *Random Harvest* (25), *Thunder Rock* (24), *The First of the Few* (19) and *Bambi* (18). The principal difference between men and women seems to be Leslie Howard's tribute to the ATS, *The Gentle Sex*, which attracted 19 women but only 7 men. *Fantasia*, which made the women's list with 8 listings, attracted 6 men and *The Magnificent Ambersons* which attracted 7 male choices, attracted 5 female. *Gone With the Wind* attracted 8 male votes and 5 female. *Mrs Miniver* drew 17 women but only 9 men. Like *The Gentle Sex* it was perhaps seen as a 'women's picture'.

How does the Mass-Observation choice accord with the nation's choice of the most popular films of the year? The trade paper *Kinematograph Weekly* published annual league tables of the popular box-office successes and they make a fascinating comparison. The picture is somewhat distorted by the variable release pattern of films and the M-O returns include films released both in 1942 and 1943. But the picture that emerges is quite clear and unequivocal. The Mass-Observation respondents' choice mirrors almost exactly the choice of the nation. The top British box-office successes of 1943 were *In Which We Serve* and *The Life and Death of Colonel Blimp*. *The Gentle Sex* was among the top seven British box-office hits. The other hits of 1943 include *The Adventures of Tartu* and *The Lamp Still Burns*, which were only released in November and therefore could not figure prominently in the directive returns, and the Gainsborough melodrama, *The Man in Grey*, which was released in August, and had attracted nine votes overall from the panel. The top documentary of 1943 in the national returns was *Desert Victory* and the top cartoon, *Bambi*, both of them figuring in the M-O list. The top box-office success of 1943 from any source was the Hollywood drama, *Random Harvest*, placed sixth on the M-O list. But it is interesting to note too the prominence on the M-O list of *Mrs Miniver*, the top box-office success of 1942, and *The First of the Few*, the top British success of 1942.

The one real surprise of the M-O list is *Thunder Rock*, which was not a box-office hit and gives us one of several hints about the composition of the M-O panel. *Thunder Rock* was a film of ideas, detailing the conversion of an isolationist intellectual (Michael Redgrave) to commitment to the struggle against Fascism. Its prominence, together with the comparative popularity of such films as the political thriller *Mission to Moscow* (10 votes), Orson Welles's flawed masterpiece *The Magnificent Ambersons* (12), the Gauguin biopic *The Moon and Sixpence* (9) and a scattering of foreign-language films suggests a rather more intellectual tinge to the sample than applied to the national cinema-going constituency, with whom these titles were not successes. Equally the relative absence from the M-O list of such popular national successes as *Hello, Frisco, Hello* and *The Black Swan*, both lavish Hollywood extravaganzas, coupled with the marked preference for British films over even the most popular Hollywood titles suggests a middle-class bias. For British films were traditionally more successful with middle-class audiences. Similarly there is some disparity between the cinema-going habits of the M-O respondents and the nation as a whole. The Wartime Cinema Survey of 1943 discovered that 70 per cent of the population went to the cinema at least once every two months, 45 per cent went at least once a month. The 50 per cent of the M-O sample who had seen more than six films, representing a minimum regular two-monthly visit, is lower than the national average. But the Wartime Survey also found that the most regular cinema-goers were young, urban, working class and female and the weighting of the M-O sample towards older, more middle-class, better-educated people would explain the shortfall. Despite all these reservations and qualifications what is remarkable is not the difference between the M-O respondents and the nation but the comparative unanimity between them, pointing to the genuine cross-class appeal of the cinema.

Men

1 Insurance clerk, aged 35, Newport.
Colonel Blimp: I liked it because it attempted to depict a character against a background of recent English history. It was amusing yet the motif was serious and thoughtful. It was a cartoon of 30 years of recent life.

2 Clerk, aged 34, Belmont.
Afraid I haven't seen six during the year. However, these have appealed to me, and I have enjoyed seeing them.

(1) *Target for Tonight*
(2) *In Which We Serve*
(3) *Watch on the Rhine*

(1) I liked this best because it was the real thing. Documentary films have a great appeal to me. The atmosphere of a bombing raid was very well put over, and I consider this to be one of the films which is the best ever.
(2) I thought this a great work, chiefly because the characters were very true to human life, each was representative of a class of type. The dialogue was excellent.
(3) If this was meant to be an anti-Nazi film, it failed but the entertainment was grand. Here again the dialogue was excellent, but it was a film of the play rather than an actual happening. Atmosphere was not well conveyed.

3 Consulting engineer, aged 69, London.
Any film which we have seen in which Deanna Durbin, Monty Woolley and Chas. Laughton have occurred, singly or together.

4 Assistant entomologist, aged 28, Horley.
Fantasia, fantasia, fantasia, fantasia, fantasia and *fantasia*. Has there been another film without any propaganda in it worth spending 10d. on during the last 12 months? (NB I exclude propaganda, because like excretion, it is not meant to be entertainment). *Fantasia* is very nearly art.

5 Writer, aged 20, Danbury.
I haven't seen six films even, this year, but two outstanding ones that I remember are *Gone with the Wind* because it took one back to days that if war-torn, were different, and *The Life and Death of Colonel Blimp*, because it provided a diversionary glimpse of an English character that has its faults better known than its virtues, and which provides good, sensible entertainment.

6 Accounts clerk in RAF (Orkney), aged 23.
During the past year the general standard of film quality seems to have

gone down. The outstanding ones only number about a dozen and of these six are listed below. I unfortunately missed *Casablanca* and *The Magnificent Ambersons* otherwise I think they may have come in the first six too.

Easily top of the list comes *In Which We Serve*. I liked it most because everything was right. The spirit of the Navy was captured excellently and there were so many deft touches in the action and dialogue which revealed how completely and intimately Coward knows the Englishman at war. It was obviously a film of things as they are, and not just a string of hashed up ideas from the back-room boys of the film world with false heroics and sentiment. Nothing was sacrificed to suit public taste, the language was not emasculated and the love interest was inobtrusively fitted in. The direction was superb and the acting on the part of the whole cast of remarkably high standard, while the production was equally good, not a wrong detail anywhere (I can vouch for this, having talked to a number of Navy men about it). The explanation of its general excellence and dramatic unity is undoubtedly that one man was completely in charge; the same quality was noticeable in *Citizen Kane*. Coward wrote the script, did his own production and direction and selected his own actors – the result a coherent and beautifully rounded-off conception of the film as a whole, instead of the usual effect of strain and jerkiness in a film where the author has conceived his story in one way, the director in another, the producer in a third and the actors individually at the behest of the director and the producer, to say nothing of the alterations in the script to suit the box-office, whatever may be the result on the story. Altogether, the finest piece of work to come out of the British Studios for a long time past.

Next in the war films I'd put *The First of the Few*. Again a really first class job of sensitive direction and action, especially by Leslie Howard and David Niven. The word best expressing the quality of this film is the French 'sympathique'. This is not translatable into English, the nearest equivalent one can get is much more than sympathetic, conceived in the right spirit. The best explanation of it is by quotation of two passages where it was most in evidence. First where Leslie Howard has been overworking at the office and his secretary and David Niven try to get him to ease up a little, and even more so where Howard and his wife were looking at the dawn and he tells her that he has known all along about his failing health. Even the touches of humour in the story have been introduced with a certain wistfulness.

The third war film of outstanding quality was *The Moon is Down*. There have been so many bad films before this about the occupied countries that I feared this might be just another, especially after reading the book, the quality of which I felt to be almost impossible of interpretation in celluloid. Steinbeck created a story of feeling, a study of atmosphere rather than a story of adventure or even narrative. The film managed to capture much of this atmosphere and although the Norwegian town was rather too pretty-pretty for reality, the essential character of the main actors was most skillfully portrayed except for the local Quisling. The book was notable in that it recognised that all Nazis are not mindless robots, without feeling, that they are not all bestial but can be victims of their own system in spite of their better judgement. In the film, too, Col. Lanser, the local CO, was not the typical regimented unthinking Hun who can't understand why people resist overwhelming force and ruthless terrorism. He realised the inevitability of events from the moment he appeared; by doing so, aided and abetted by his young lieutenant, he elevated what would have been just another film to the level of a work of art worthy to be put beside Steinbeck.

Of the 'away from the war' films, I enjoyed *Road to Morocco* most in the musical comedy class. I am a Crosby fan and I think Bob Hope is one of the few real comedians America has produced. His sense of satire and fun is devastating and Crosby is the perfect foil, as well as pleasant to listen to. The film abounded in ingeniously contrived and comic situations which gave the artist full play.

Maltese Falcon was a top-scorer in my selection of crime films. Humphrey Bogart revealed an astonishing versatility in acting which his gangster roles had hitherto obscured, and the fat man master criminal and Peter Lorre were both excellent. The story was in the best traditions of Charteris or Beeding, much removed from the usual who-dunnit. Lloyd Bacon's direction was first-class in many sequences.[1] It was what I call an intelligent film.

Sixth place goes to *Tales of Manhattan*. It was original and interesting and good performances were put up by Ginger Rogers and Charles Laughton particularly – I saw it too long ago to remember the others, but all the episodes were well done, just what a film of short stories should be like.

7   Musician, journalist, author, aged 52, Brighton.

I see only 3 or 4 a year, so have next to nothing to say. I forget, too, whether I saw them last year or the year before. *Foreman goes to France*[2] is one of the very, very few that I recall at all. Good simple British style in that, I thought. (I don't go to see any war films at all, if I can avoid 'em). *Fantasia*. Disney: but desperately tasteless in parts – e.g. Beethoven. Mickey as Apprentice Sorcerer was A1. Saw *Ruggles*[3] again. Old film. Cd. see it any number of times. One of only four I ever wanted to see twice. I like its simple broad farce and Laughton's real acting – character. Afraid I remember no others.

8   Wireless operator in Royal Corps of Signals, aged 26, Kent.

1 *Thunder Rock*

2 *Fires were Started*
3 *Strange Incident*
4 *Desert Victory*
5 *Journey into Fear*
6 *Life and Death of Col. Blimp*

(Some revivals seen during the year – *Petrified Forest, Citizen Kane, Alexander Nersky, 49th Parallel, The Long Voyage Home* – would rank as high as those 1943 ones in the list above.)

1 *Thunder Rock.* Because it's a serious film, with an idea – and plenty to think about. Technically interesting too (camera, music) and convincing in its 'illustrative' sequences: e.g. foreign correspondent Redgrave trying to fight English apathy.
2 *Fires were Started.* The best wartime documentary yet: never have ordinary people been more convincingly done (Humphrey Jennings' M-O training?) and the film is nevertheless 'poetic' in its treatment.
3 *Strange Incident.* Grim stuff about a lynching in Nevada in 1885; most intelligently done, with no false Hollywoodian touches.
4 *Desert Victory.* Factual stuff (sometimes with vivid beauty of desert photography) expertly edited – with outstandingly good music – and manages to be soberly inspiring even on a third seeing.
5 *Journey into Fear.* Orson Welles at his technical trickery again. Only a spy thriller – but it out-hitches Hitchcock so exciting is it in photography and typical Orson Welles touches – intelligent filmcraft at its best.
6 *Life and Death of Col. Blimp.* At last a British film that's able to compete with Hollywood efficiency and technical competence. Plenty of pleasantly subtle touches and a quite intelligent story and all so expertly done that I should like to see it again.

10   Architect, aged 36, in Pioneer Corps.

1 *Fantasia* (Walt Disney) parts of it a great work of art.
2 *Dumbo* the flying elephant (Walt Disney) in parts even better than *Fantasia*, more consistent as whole.
3 *Tales of Manhattan*
4 *Random Harvest*

Not: *Colonel Blimp* – good in parts but not as good as a film and very bad as the story of Blimp.
In Which We Serve certainly the Nazis have made similar ones during the war. Noel Coward I disliked profoundly.
Battle of Stalingrad or *Desert Victory* very interesting but I imagine that the claims of reality they make is not accomplished though probably nobody could stand it to have more reality as they showed us.

11 Sgnt. in Royal Corps of Signals, aged 25.

I have only been to the films 17 times this year. The films I liked best were:

1 *Dumbo* (because of Disney's humour and colourful imagery).
2 *The Moon and Sixpence* (because it really showed an insight into the artistic temperament).
3 *Palm Beach Story* (funniest film I saw this year).
4 *Desert Victory*
5 *Nine Men for the Desert Army*[4] both good propaganda films
6 *This Land is Mine* (because of Charles Laughton's acting and the fine representation of the Nazi occupation of a small country).

12 Clerk in clothing mill, aged 35, Macclesfield.

1 *The Life and Death of Col. Blimp.* – typical English character.
2 *In Which We Serve* – a good war film, well-produced.
3 *Yankee Doodle Dandy* – a first rate American musical.
4 *The Man in Grey* – a good romance, well filmed.
5 *The Man Who Came to Dinner* – a good straight comedy.
6 *The Pied Piper* – another good war film.

From the fact that four out of the above are English films, you will see that I appreciate English technique, and I certainly think that the restraint and good taste of English films are superior to most of the American. This especially applies to plays. In 'musicals' and pure 'shows' Hollywood reigns supreme. But personally I much prefer plays to those types of films.

13 Aero-examiner, aged 40, Yeovil.

Only been to the films 5 times this year. Four times because I wanted to see the films and once to kill time.

1 *In Which We Serve*
2 *Queen Victoria*[5]
3 *Stalingrad*
4 *Desert Victory*
5 Don't know but it was absolute tripe.

14 ?? Skipton.

(a) *Thunder Rock.* Very good acting – intelligent and a play with depth and psychological insights. Production also excellent.
(b) *Fantasia.* Music very good, choreography excellent, direction also good.
(c) *I Married a Witch.* Cleverly amusing and witty, very well cast especially the witch and father.
(d) *Keeper of the Flame.* Good acting.
(e) *You were never lovelier.* Enjoyable music, I like Rita Hayworth.

15   Research physicist, aged 21, Streatham.

I have not been to the cinema for 6 months and I am not sure which films come within the year. I only go to films when the title conveys some idea to my mind and I have some idea what it is about (preferably not the war). Those that recently impressed me are:

1 *Greek Testament* – not much story but lovely pictures of Greece and a café in Bute Street, Cardiff, only a few doors from where I typed page of this.
2 *Gone with the Wind* – light on the American Civil War.
3 *Major Barbara* – rather an improvement even on the play, especially if one had read or seen the latter.
4 *Pygmalion.* Much the same about this.
5 *Dr Jekyll and Mr Hyde.* Vividly illustrates Stevenson's book.
6 *Brewster's Millions* – a hilarious farce. I am not sure about the order but these are nearly all the films I have been to within the year.

16   Proof reader's assistant, aged 21, Leeds.

I am not a regular film goer. I try to see the films which I think will interest me. Nevertheless I have missed films which I would have liked to have seen such as *The Glass Key, This Gun for Hire, Bataan, H. M. Pulham Esq.* and number of others simply because I haven't have the leisure to see them. During the past year I have seen no picture as good as *Citizen Kane* or *All That Money Can Buy* or *Fantasia* which I saw last year. However, here is my list as well as I can remember what I have seen.

1 *The Magnificent Ambersons* because of its general high standard of intelligence and its clever direction.
2 *Thunder Rock* for very much the same reasons.
3 *Bambi* because like all Disney films except *Victory Through Air Power* it was so beautiful to look at and so innocent in its theme.
4 *Gone With the Wind* partly perhaps because it was so much better than I expected it to be but also because it was by Hollywood standards a well-produced, well acted and well photographed film.
5 *Now Voyager* because it was well produced, well photographed and well acted (particularly by Bette Davis) and because its dialogue was for a film exceptionally good.
6 *Escape to Happiness* largely for Ingrid Bergman's acting.

17   Retired clerk, aged 67, Letchford.

How Green was My Valley wh. portrays the miner's hard life.
Strauss Jr. Blue Danube and other beautiful music.[6]
Bambi sympathy with the animal world.

18   Estate agent, aged 26, Conisborough, near Doncaster.

I don't see many. I think the outstanding film was *In Which We Serve* though Noel Coward was a little too much to the fore. *Mrs Miniver* and *War Against Mrs Hadley* giving a convincing picture of reactions to the war in England and America were memorable. Then there was *Desert Victory*. All these are connected with the war. I can hardly remember the titles of other films seen. Pictures are an anodyne and the ones I would see I often can't get to see. Perhaps *They Died with Their Boots On* would make no. 6.

19 Proprietor in family jewellery business, aged 49, Leicester.
I have only been to the cinema four or five times this year, yet the only two films I can recollect are *Colonel Blimp* and *The Tales of Manhattan*. Both were excellent and held my interest from start to finish. I would say that the brilliant character-drawing and acting, the crisp dialogue, the 'snap', intelligence and composition of these pictures as a whole were reasons for making them a satisfying entertainment. But obviously I cannot answer this question properly.

20 Fitter, aged 23, Glasgow.

Desert Victory
Life and Death of Colonel Blimp
Next of Kin (reissue)
Squadron Leader X
All That Money Can Buy
George Washington Slept Here

I liked *Desert Victory* and *Next of Kin* because both were very plausible. I like the documentary type of film so long as there is no time spent trying to make 'hate propaganda' against the enemy.

Squadron Leader X gave the enemy some credit for intelligence and was also very exciting in parts during the actual combat.

Life and Death of Colonel Blimp was both in colour and was 'different'. I liked it – why I cannot say.

All That Money can Buy was a film with a moral. The photography was good and the film gave the public credit for some intelligence.

I like Jack Benny, his original jokes and his antics, hence I enjoyed *George Washington Slept Here.*

21 Warehouseman (unemployed), aged 24, Northampton.
Main films liked during this year are:

Those Kids From Town true to life
The Scarlet Pimpernel one against many
Fantasia original and clever
St Martins Lane acting and good plot
The Amazing Mrs Holliday again true to life

22   Wireless operator in Royal Signals, aged 22, Weston-super-Mare.

I haven't been to six films this year: on consulting my diary I see have been to *100 Men and a Girl*, *49th Parallel* and *Desert Victory*. Each of these was quite memorable in its way, and it isn't often that I grace a film by my presence twice which is true of *100 Men and a Girl* – but that is because of the music it contains. *49th Parallel* had some very notable acting, especially the scenes of the Brotherhood community, but I had been expecting a quasi-historical film and not a present-day war story.

Desert Victory was the best of the three films and convinced me with its great sincerity and vivid scenes. Many of the 'shots' remain in my mind still.

23   Commercial traveller, aged 35, Leamington Spa.

Once per month I go to the films. This is when my car is greased at a neighbouring garage, and I find it convenient to sit in the warmth and comfort of a cinema until the operation is complete. I cannot remember 6 films I have seen. I saw *Dear Octopus* this week. I liked it. It had not one damned Yankee accent in the whole film. The usual strident idiocies of Hollywood were absent. I did not, as usual, feel like vomiting. And even the news short did not as usual give the impression that Americans only were fighting the Germans. If you want an opinion about films you will have to go to others. My opinions are perhaps illformed, but they are definite, if given vent to, they make me swear.

24   Retired man, aged 67, Liverpool.
Haven't been for 4 years.

25   Nurseryman, aged 53, Newick, Sussex.

Five Graves to Cairo for excellent acting by everyone.
Bambi because I am an ardent Disney fan and adore his stuff.
A Day on the Russian Front (an M of I film) brilliantly conceived and daringly procured realism.
Mission to Moscow for its insight into pre-war mentality
The Jungle Book for its vivid colour photography.
The Goose Steps Out because I am tickled to death by Will Hay's humour.

26   Retired electricity supply engineer, aged 63, Worthing.
I have not thought any worth a 4-mile trip to the 'germ exchange', Miss Lejeune suffers for me and tells me all about it in the *Observer*.

27   Army dental surgeon, aged 26, Slough.

1 Leslie Howard's *First of the Few*
2 Coward's *In Which We Serve*
3 Ida Lupino in a waterfront film about a small gangster versus two foreign-born Americans.[7]

4 *Road to Morocco* (Bing Crosby and Bob Hope)

5 *Casablanca* (Ingrid Bergmann)

6 Deanna Durbin in a film about Chinese refugees and an eccentric old shipping magnate.[8]

These are the only six I can recall but I didn't enjoy the latter ones very much. I'm sure there were others I enjoyed more which I can't remember.

28 Sub-Postmaster, aged 55, Newcastle-upon-Tyne.
Haven't seen many films this last year, tho I am a film fan without being very intelligent about them.

1 Ralph Richardson in that Dutch picture.[9]

Speaks well for my observation that I cannot remember six films. I saw Walt Disney's aeroplane picture a few days ago. I didn't like the Sevensky man, was it because he is a Jew. Was he convincing the converted. He was selling the Americans central control of an aircraft which we have.

29 Solicitor, aged 24, London.

Carnet de Bal. There was an emotional mood about the film which held the various episodes together. It dealt with an emotional subject which most people are interested in – the feeling that things that happened in the past were more romantic than things which are happening now – and it dealt with it artistically and at the same time in a way which one felt to be true to life.

Holy Matrimony. It is good comedy, and amusing skit on many things – burial in the Abbey, art dealers, the Press, the courts, the law, the unartistic public, and it was well acted.

The Magnificent Ambersons. It held your interest – with original photography – particularly the lighting – and original directing and acting. It presented a drama and an environment vividly and interestingly.

Journey Into Fear. Most of what I have said about the films before apply to this, though in a lesser degree, the story being, to my taste, less important and the social criticism missing, but an atmosphere of suspense was cunningly created; it was a thriller without being altogether unrealistic.

Watch on the Rhine. I didn't think this was a particularly good film but it is practically the only other one I can think of. Bette Davis' acting is always worth seeing.

30 Teacher, aged 51, Woking.
I am not in a position to judge the year's films, as I rarely go to the pictures nowadays. I can't stand pep war films nor the blaring noise.

31   Technical researcher, aged 20, Chingford.

The six best are (as I remember them, but not in order of merit):

Casablanca. A political thriller, with an insistence on little things; the war is merely the setting.

Tales of Manhattan. Ingenious interweave of tales, diverting, neither patriotic, nor thrilling. They gave me the illusory feeling, while I saw them, that they were 'true to life'.

The Man in Grey. A clever piece of story building from scant but fascinating material. I have often wondered to whom that muddied glove on the street pavement belonged, and it is this inquisitiveness that is satisfied, romantically enough, in this film. Once again, it is 'escapist' and we forget the present to dwell in the past when young ladies were taught just what to say to men who asked their hand in marriage, even though the latter were scoundrels.

Five Graves to Cairo. A film vividly in the present, portraying Rommel in all his splendour, and his shrewdness as well. We can stand it now, because the Egyptian battle is long over, and Rommel is showing a few bedraggled feathers beneath his fine plumage. The film makes one really believe one is present in the headquarters from which the affairs of momentous importance were directed. Gave me a thrill.

The Moon Is Down. A frankly patriotic film, anti-Nazi propaganda. But not as crudely put as many are. The Nazi-lieutenant is a human being, wanting, as so many of us do, his little joy amongst all this horror. His choice of his love was unfortunate. I rather liked him. The Nazi Colonel-commandant was an understanding man. I couldn't help feeling he would have made a good mayor for the little Norwegian town if only he had been from there instead of Germany. This film presented the Nazis as many of them are – just rather warped editions of ourselves. And perhaps not even warped.

32   ?? Portsmouth.

1 *The Life and Death of Colonel Blimp*
2 *One of Our Aircraft is Missing*
3 *The Silver Fleet*
4 *Dangerous Moonlight*
5 *The Man in Grey*
6 *Kings Row*

It has surprised me that the first three films which I remember with pleasure have all been produced by one company 'The Archers'. All these films I enjoyed for the same reason. They were all absolutely true to life. I could believe everything about them. They all seemed to possess a magical quality which I have never seen in an American film. *No. 1.* I consider this the best film that I have ever seen. I specially liked its modern sequences with the speed of modern life and compared with the slower, older sequences. The flash-back technique also appealed to me. *No. 2.* This film intrigued me from the first scene; before the Credit Titles; a scene in which an aircraft crashed into a pylon. I think this film had perhaps the most novel presentation of Credit Titles that I have ever seen. *No. 3. The Silver Fleet* appealed to my emotions somehow. The actions of the chief character seemed to portray *real* heroism, not the cheap, flashy stuff of the American films. *No. 4.* My fourth film is included not so much for the actual visual aspect; but for its beautiful background music – 'The Warsaw Concerto'. I have seen this film twice for its music. One scene from *Dangerous Moonlight* sticks in my mind: 'The Warsaw Concerto' was playing, to the accompaniment of bombs bursting: the scene had a shivering montage effect, and was very moving. *No. 5.* I don't know quite how the *Man In Grey* appealed to me, but I do remember it with pleasure. *No. 6.* The last choice is included for one reason: the pleasurable thrill of horror when one of the characters found that both of his legs had been amputated.

33   Civil Servant, aged 29, Stoke-on-Trent.
I have not seen any films for nearly 3 years.

34   Cost clerk and Special Constable, aged 33, Doncaster.
Rarely go to the pictures and don't suppose I have seen 6 pictures this year. I can't at the moment recall a single one. Going further back, I very much enjoyed:

Dangerous Moonlight. Liked music, general atmosphere & acting.
Blossoms in the Dust. Liked the Technicolour, realism and acting.
Dr Jekyll and Mr Hyde. Liked the ACTING, general air of tension, and psychological soundness of the plot.
In passing, am often struck by the improvement in the quality of film entertainment and the decline in the theatre.

35   Assistant personnel manager, aged 37, London.
I am afraid I cannot answer this question as I hardly ever go to the films.

36   General Handyman, aged 38; Birmingham.

1 *Dear Octopus.* A human and uplifting story.
2 *Hello, Frisco, Hello.* For its colour.
3 *Tarzan Triumphs.* Adventure excitement.
4 *49th Parallel.* Community life and showing false ideals.

37   Chemist, aged 42, Ashtead.
I have not seen 6 films in the last year. I have not been aware of 6 worth seeing.

I saw *In Which We Serve* and enjoyed it for its production and the excellent technical quality of the photography. Noel Coward spoiled it. I never once was able to forget that I was watching Noel Coward, an actor, and not a naval officer.

Perhaps the only films certain to please me are Disney's Silly Symphonies. Disney, in my view is the first man to go up to a ciné camera and say 'Here is a new instrument, it has possibilities for a new mode of artistic expression. Let's *invent* a new mode of expression.' This, I feel, he has done and I never feel it so strongly as when I see his imitators. Perhaps as an infrequent visitor to the cinema my opinion is not particularly valid but I do not like Technicolour. The producers do not yet seem to have recovered from their initial astonishment that the photographic reproduction of colour is a technical possibility and have not yet ceased to indulge their childlike wonder. If colour is to be used for colour's sake to produce an artistic effect something very different from a Technicolour film must be produced. Apart from Disney and the producers of the documentary film, who must be a class apart because of their different object, film producers, I feel, are still hide-bound by the tradition of stage craft. The stage and the screen are, I think, as the poles apart.

38   Headmaster, aged 45, Oxted.
Haven't been to six films this year – shame!

39   Public health official, aged 26, Birmingham.
Bambi. A most charming film with pleasant music. Although a cartoon film animals most natural and beautifully coloured.
Dangerous Moonlight. A very moving film in which 'Warsaw Concerto' predominates, and acting of Anton Walbrook.
Kings Row. A well balanced film, well acted, with interesting plot.
Heaven Can Wait. A comedy in technicolour an unusual theme with amusing plot.
Lamp Still Burns. Mainly for good acting [by?] the heroine who breaks all hospital's rules and even answers back the Matron!
Dear Octopus. A rehash of the play but quite well acted and a change from most American films.
Generally, I found the non-war films most enjoyable and refreshing and hated the usual Yank spy film or the American hero winning the war!

40   REME Captain and engineering student, aged 20, Wallington.

1 *In Which We Serve*. A most impressive picture of navy work, probably more vivid than strictly accurate. Good characterisation of the varied types.
2 *Little Foxes*. Interesting study of period of American social history. Good dramatic acting of Davis.
3 *First of the Few*. A clear simple dramatisation of something topical and

important. Accurate, restrained performance by Howard.

4 *Dear Octopus*. A beautifully detailed sketch of family life, full of pleasant humour and irony.

5 *Bataan*. Perhaps the best American war film. Not very much big drum beating, which is a relief, and excellent character drawing of the American soldiers.

6 *Gentle Sex*. Very interesting to one who has quite a number of ATS to work with, both as a documentary of their training, and for the study of the effect on different types of girl.

41   Psychologist, aged 26, New Forest.

Have there been any good ones this year? Can't remember any.

42   Chemist, aged 42, Manchester.

I am hard put to to answer this. I may have seen 10 films this year, I don't think more, and I can't even remember the titles of some of them. The names of the stars I hardly ever remember. However I will do my best, and hope my memory does not let me down. Incidentally the two worst films I've seen this year are *Somewhere on Leave* and *Rio Rita*.

1 *In Which We Serve*. Very well produced and acted. No histrionics. Appeals to the emotions and to the patriotism of the audience. The love scenes and feminine interest are natural and subordinated, or integrated, into the main story. Sound effects not overdone. No theme song.

2 *First of the Few*. Wonderfully restrained acting of Leslie Howard. Careful combination of fact and fiction throughout the narrative of the film and the sequence is not choppy. Excellent pictures of flight, and a touch of humour. Again the feminine theme naturally introduced and not sentimentalised.

3 *Tomorrow is Another Day*. (I'm not quite sure of the title.)[10] To my mind gives a very true picture of occupied France and the resistance movement. The acting of the German troops was likelife, and the feeling of underground activities very well expressed. The ending, which could hardly be called happy, but better hopeful, was dramatically correct, and the whole film well balanced.

4 *The Petrified Forest*. Another Leslie Howard picture, a distinct change from the spate of war themes, and a cameo of meticulous acting by Leslie Howard and Bette Davis. Not having seen the play but heard contrasts over the radio, I was anxious to see how the film technique would tackle the theatre's subject. I was agreeably surprised to find what a good job they had made of it, the atmosphere of an almost constant scene was neutralised by skilful use of side shoots, and close ups, and the dialogue faithfully reproduced Sherwood Anderson's words. And they didn't botch the whole by altering the ending.

5 *Bambi*. A delightful picture of animal life and excellent coloured

drawings of nature. The theme of birth, growth, manhood, and fatherhood wonderfully reproduced, and with a piquant humour, touch of tragedy, and final triumph, made it a treat for young and old.

6 *Cargo of Innocents.* The American counterpart of *In Which We Serve.* Much more bombastic, the war incidents more improbable, in fact the main incident impossible, but with a great deal of humour running through it. Pathos restrained, fine acting by Robert Taylor, Charles Laughton, and the destroyer's captain, the interest kept up right to the end, and the 'lovelies theme' started, but then dropped, and thank God not re-introduced. And no theme song.

43   Sales manager, aged 33, Blackburn.

The six films I have enjoyed during the year are as follows and are in order of merit.

(a) *Fantasia*
(b) *Black Sheep of Whitehall*
(c) *Random Harvest*
(d) *Silver Fleet*
(e) *Desert Victory*
(f) *The Young Mr Pitt*

In the first place I am not a film fan. I go to the cinema as a diversion and when something outstanding is showing. I have been let down many times. Nevertheless I do enjoy an occasional visit to the cinema and my reasons for picking the above half dozen films from those I have seen during the past year are:

Fantasia. This effort on the part of Disney forms, for me, a nucleus of everything that a film should contain. It contains the very best music, the photography is superb, the interpretation by the artists of the particular musical score is, to say the least as interesting and alluring as the music itself. Who, for instance would imagine the 'Casse Noisette' suite, specifically written for the type of Art portrayed by Disney's artists. Imagine 'The Dance of the Hours' deliciously satired as a romantic, humorous Ballet in which the Ballerina is an animal the entire opposite to the sylph-like human ballerina – a hippopotamus. Take again Beethoven's Pastoral Symphony – the ecstatic music of the master is coupled with a delicate yet beautiful satire on Greek Mythology. Bach's Toccata and Fugue played by a fine orchestra and lit in a manner which beggars description – how these bows flashed and wove around the screen in thousands of patterns and yet when all the art had been taken away the sonorous Bach was living and teeming with interest. Yes, Disney did something which from my own experience baffled the public, they did not seem to be able to absorb the real significance of the film. Who could have devised the small intermission where a huge Symphony Orchestra becomes so human as to start a small 'jam' session. Fantasia was sheer Art from beginning to end – and in spite of the fact that it was drawn and painted and photographed, it was above all – Very Human. I have seen the film twice – I want to see it again and again – like most good things it grows on acquaintance, it betters with keeping. It is definitely a classic.

Black Sheep of Whitehall. I place this second because I do love humour, I also like to be slapdash to a point. Will Hay in this picture caused me to laugh and laugh, and still laugh. He did me a whole world of good, I remember the story as almost impossible, the situations fantastic, but it was jolly funny. And I can never forget that Will Hay is a first class astronomer. I take my hat off to all good comedians – the power and the gift to amuse one's fellow men is a very great and wonderful talent. The presentation was passable, the photography fairly good. But it was damn funny.

Random Harvest. I went to see this film because I had made several attempts to read the book and it had failed to interest beyond three chapters. I was curious to see what Hollywood or Elstree could make of it. They made a good job. Ronald Colman's acting as the shell shocked officer with imperfect speech was exceptionally good acting and the filming was also of very high standard. The settings too had received considerable thought, whilst the sequence of the story was not what was expected. The story was good, the filming and presentation good, and the acting good. In all, a very enjoyable picture. An orchestral arrangement of 'Swan Lake Ballet' as incidental music was worth the money I paid to see the film. I still cannot get beyond the third chapter of the book.

Silver Fleet. A war film of real interest. Notable for the acting of Esmond Knight the blinded actor. His portrayal of the Gestapo officer was really outstanding. The story was good, the photography passable, the production scrappy, nevertheless the acting of Ralph Richardson and Esmond Knight place it as one of the best of the year.

Desert Victory. This film was of course purely documentary. The production and editing had been carefully executed, but above all the photography – I am no mean photographer myself and I confess to feeling really awed when, as I watched this film I realised that I was to all intents and purposes in the battle line behind the lenses. It dawned on me that focusing had to be done, that light had to be read, that angle and composition and all the many little things that go to make a good photography had to be done. On the screen was the result of REAL photography. From beginning to end, the whole thing was to me an amazing example of photography. Yes, the troubles, and trials, the fight, the heat, the mud, the fire, shells, bombs, and barrage did interest me, but I must confess that I had read and re-read all about the battle and I was genuinely awed by such brilliant photography, under such appalling conditions.

The Young Mr Pitt. I always enjoy Robert Donat's acting, but in this film he did not reach the standard which I am accustomed to expect from him. The record of the historic fight between him and Fox, the meetings in the House of Commons gave to me a fair glimpse of the character of the Young Mr Pitt. I am interested in History and for that reason I thoroughly enjoyed this film. The production could have been better, there was far to much use of obviously false backgrounds. I think English films can learn quite a lot from America about false backgrounds. However, that is another story. The cast was representative, especially Fox, who according to cartoons by Gilray had a protruding bottom lip. Detail work and dialogue were well chosen and the historical data was paramount throughout. There you are sir. You have my half dozen. In a film I must have the following qualities. Good photography, production, acting, and the accompanying music must be well arranged and inserted at the right places. There is only one film in which I have found all these things contained, and that is FANTASIA.

44   Office worker, aged 48, London.

Thunder Rock
Land of Promise (Palestine)
Here is Tomorrow (American Co-ops)
Early Each Morning (LCS Milk)
Mission to Moscow
When We Build Again (Town Planning)

45   Research physicist, aged 37, Castle Bromwich.
Best undoubtedly –

1 *The Gentle Sex*
2 *Operational Height*
3 *Stalingrad*
3 A whole series of Donald Duck

I cannot remember any others. Most films we see seem to be moronic musicals, padded out too much, with poor tunes, censored sex, quickfire humour that misfires. O for the legs of yesterday!

46   Clerk, aged 29, Oswestry.
I am virtually a non-picture-goer. The question is therefore quite beyond me.

47   RAF Officer, aged 35, Bourne.
The only ones I remember seeing are, in order of preference:

In Which We Serve
The Foreman Went to France

48 Telephone Engineer, aged 30, London.
Have not seen 6 films.

49 Bombardier, aged 25, London.
Millions Like Us – saw it last night, and consider it the best film since
Bank Holiday. Presents Britain and life as it is – we must have truth and
integrity in our films.
Gone With the Wind – much better than I expected; the best adaptation of
a book I've seen, beating even *South Riding*.
In Which We Serve – Coward is a genius. See notes on *Millions Like Us*.
Rebecca – damn' fine entertainment in Hitchcock's best style. Keeps one
interested, and was obviously made with care and thought.
The Meanest Man In The World – Jack Benny kills me.
The Road To Morocco – So does Bob Hope. And Bing, of course, is
Bing – perfect as always.

50 Army [?] aged 30, Pembroke.

1 *The Green Eyed Woman*
2 *The Glass Key*
3 *The Major and the Minor*
4 *Dangerous Moonlight*
5 *Desert Victory*
6 *The Fleets In*

51 Vicar, aged 42, Bourne.
Have only seen 3 films this year

(a) *Mrs Miniver*
(b) *Colonel Blimp*
(c) A Flanagan & Allan (can't remember the name, but it was tripe).

52 Farm worker, aged 31, Macclesfield.
I have seen about five or six films this year:

Life and Death of Col. Blimp – much fairer than I expected.
Mission to Moscow – good propaganda, though too much window dressing
of Communism to suit American ideas of respectability.
Story of Stalingrad – contemporary history.
Five Graves to Cairo – feeble plot, unrealistic acting.
Manila Calling – good clean drama for fourteen-year-olds.

53 Medical student, aged 18, London.
Fury (reissue) magnificent photography, building up of the atmosphere of

mob passion and individual reaction. Fine acting and direction, psychological truth. (1)

1 *Thunder Rock*. Well acted. Good story, convincing, original, sincere and intelligent. (4)

The Grapes of Wrath. (Before *Thunder Rock* and equal with *Fury*). Magnificent photography, psychological truth. Examination of a situation of Economic depression which was and may again become a world problem and illustration of consequences. Shows clearly the need for State action in preventing and alleviating Economic Crises. Terrific emotional impact (same with *Fury*).(1)

In Which We Serve. Very fine piece of dramatic reportage. Good photography, direction, acting. Sincere. Emotional impact. (2)

Life and Death of Colonel Blimp. Charming story and technicolour, Humour, Characters seem real. (3)

First of the Few. Gripping story. Humorous too at times. (4)

Pastor Hall. True to life. Shows up and illuminates the crisis of our age. Emotional impact. (4)

How Green was My Valley. Fine study of S. Wales, and its people. Characterisation. Good photography, fine plot. (2)

54   Technical supervisor, aged 37, Birmingham.
I go but rarely to the cinema and then only when I am fairly sure of liking the film. I find most films jejune and silly. I doubt if I have seen many more than six 'big' films in the last year, so instead, I give you a list of three which I thought the best.

1 *Thunder Rock*
2 *Tortilla Flats*
3 *The Life and Death of Colonel Blimp*

55   Timber merchant, aged 44, Leeds.
A question I put to myself with regard to this is: how do you value the different answers without knowing which possibilities the answerer had in the year, and how many films he has seen altogether? (f.i. certain films can't be seen anywhere, or other films the time is unsuitable, etc etc) As far as I remember I recall: *Mr Jordan*[11] – *Man Who Came to Dinner* – *Colonel Blimp* – *Citizen Kane* – *Mrs Miniver* – *Tales of Manhattan*.

Mr Jordan was in some ways a perfect film – theme, fantastic but earthbound enough to be more than a mere trifle; *Man To Dinner* a witty comedy, a type I very much prefer in films; *Colonel Blimp* got me interested and captivated me (and what a fine actor played Blimp); *Citizen Kane* was interesting enough as an experiment; *Mrs Miniver* could have done with a little less sentiment; *Tales of Manhattan*: some excellent short stories, of which I would like to see more.

56   Insurance Broker, aged 45, Cheadle Hulme.
(I have not seen six films during the year.) The following seem worth
mentioning: *One of Our Aircraft is Missing* and *The Moon and Sixpence*.
Both were well produced and in each case the plot was sufficiently
plausible to pass muster.

57   Clergyman, aged 65, Portrush (N. Ireland).
I have not seen more than six films during the past year. *Let The People
Sing* entertained and amused me immensely. I was bored with *Gone With
The Wind*.

58   Chartered Accountant, aged 39, Bristol.
I haven't been to a cinema since August 1942. I have very little free time
for amusements of this nature, and I invariably go to a theatre, when I can
get an 'evening off'.

59   Tax Inspector, aged 30, [?]
Mrs Miniver: a picture, faithful throughout, of people who at first sight
were just ordinary people, yet their sense of values made them extraordinary. Nostalgic and inspiring. Contained some of those fine, really
human heroisms of the war I should like to remember always.
Major Barbara: pure Shaw on the screen. Stimulating, but humour as I
like it. Characterisation, in the Shavian manner, really splendid.
How Green Was My Valley: certainly a romantic portrayal of life in a
Welsh mining valley, but a successful attempt to paint a picture. Standard
of acting and characterisation among the best I've seen, especially the
father. I enjoyed the handling through personal narrative – a novel
treatment very suitable to the themes.
Next of Kin: a sound piece of craftsmanship and intelligent propaganda.
Random Harvest: frankly romantic and exceptionally well handled with
not a false note. The best 'escape' film of the war.
The Foreman Went To France: in its way, a useful little documentary of
the war. Inspiring in its heroism of ordinary people and its emphasis on
the best in the British character. And, in places, very good photography.

60   BBC employee, aged 29, Reading.
Having been inside the cinema only about six times in all during the last
twelve months I am only naming two films which stand out in my
memory: *Gone With The Wind* and *Colonel Blimp*.

61   Retired banker, aged 69, Co. Antrim.
I have no interest in films. *Gone With The Wind* was good for 2/3rds. The
cast 1/3rd aery faery. Films of the Nature type, which I like, are not
popular here. A Lady who went to see *Mrs Miniver* told me it was the
nicest film she had ever seen. She simply cried the whole time and was
going back every night it was here.

62   Biologist, aged 30, Birmingham.

I have not seen 6 good films, the following are those that are worthy of being put in a list of the 6 best:– *Bambi, Desert Victory, In Which We Serve, Pygmalion, Gone With The Wind.*

I see I've answered this wrongly, giving no reasons and not putting them in order as I now do:–

1 *Gone With The Wind.* Just first; chiefly so I think because I had previously avoided going to it under the impression that I could not stand a 4hr. film especially when it was based on a novel of which I had not heard the best criticisms. Indeed, I didn't read the book because it too seemed inordinately long.

  So I went prepared to be bored and instead was amazed to find that the 4hrs. (there was no interval as at some cinemas) seemed no longer than 1½ – 2. The film is not a 'great' one but as a piece of ordinary filming it is excellent and the technicolour hardly ever obtrudes itself by means of the 'purple sunset' etc! First class entertainment.

2 *Pygmalion.* This is something more than entertainment, a far better film based on a far better 'book'. If I waited till tomorrow I should probably put it first in my list. This is the sort of film that makes the average 'good' American effort seem childish! Many American films, of course, are only too obviously in the infant class without comparing them with anything else. One might almost put them lower than the infant class, into a special mental decay group. It was good entertainment, but it was also something to 'chew on'. To remember, and think about long after most films have gone with the wind.

3 *Desert Victory.* The best bit of war reporting I've seen.

4 *Bambi.* Not one of Disney's best efforts but, of course, enjoyable. Perhaps a little disappointing after *Pinocchio* and *The Reluctant Dragon.* Inclined to be too 'pretty pretty' with unreal backgrounds.

5 *In Which We Serve.* If only Noel Coward could have been content with writing the script, composing the music and producing it, I would have put it higher in the list, but I found myself unable to believe in him as the captain while his frequent 'draw nearer men' little talks gave me a pain. Otherwise it was very well done and the lesser parts excellently portrayed. It may or may not be true to life but it all seemed very real to me.

63   RAF pupil pilot, aged 19, London.

1 Disney's *Bambi* (All Disney's productions come first on my list)
2 *Casablanca*
3 *Millions Like Us*
4 *In Which We Serve*

64 Doctor, aged 59, Sheffield.
Have scarcely seen any.

65 Student draughtsman, aged 18, Wigan.

1 Disney's *Fantasia*. Completely original, with typical Disney colour and ideas. But especially because original.
2 Orson Welles' *The Magnificent Ambersons*. (I didn't see his *Citizen Kane*, which the reviewers think is better.) I like his sense of the dramatic, and his use of the camera and lighting.
3 *Action In The North Atlantic*. Because it was, mainly, an action film of the Merchant Navy; the romance near the beginning was permissible by contrast and to show how the men and their wives feel at parting.

These are the only ones I've seen which are worth remembering. (There probably have been others, but I haven't seen them. They don't come to Wigan! (Both (1) and (2) I saw in London.) At the bottom of the list, *Dixie* with Bing Crosby and Dorothy Lamour. The only two excuses for the film would have been Bing's voice, which wasn't well used enough, and Lamour's legs, which (to my amazement!) weren't used at all. My only reason for remembering it is that it's only five days since I saw it.

66 Civil engineer, aged 21, Nottingham

Gone With The Wind
The First Of The Few
Forever And A Day
The Great Mr Handel
Mr Bunting Goes To War
The War Against Mrs Hadley

67 Company secretary, aged 48, Leeds.

1 *Random Harvest* (Splendid acting)
2 *The Man In Grey* (A page of history)
3 *Mrs Miniver* (Very sincere acting)
4 *Scarlet Pimpernel* (Seen four times (Superb))
5 *Wake Island* (Most realistic)
6 *In Which We Serve* (Most moving acting)

68 Doctor, aged 40, Cambridge.
As I go often to the pictures, I have seen a lot but I have not kept notes and don't think it worthwhile to list them.
Blimp was very good. *Thunder Rock*
In Which We Serve   *They Met In The Dark*
Victory in Desert[12]
Tartu[13]

But this is neither a representative list nor in proper order. I don't even know what were 1943 and what older films.

69   Steelworker, aged 30, Kilburnie.

The Moon and Sixpence
An example of what genius has meant to people who came in contact with them and a fair sample of a genius.
Thunder Rock
Always the ordinary man has been striving for this better land; here we have a sample of some peoples attempts.
The Man Who Came to Dinner
I enjoyed this for its upsetting of all our ordinary standards of what is done and its ridiculing of what people are attempting to be.
Random Harvest
The acting in this situation was very good and the plot feasible.
Yankee Doodle Dandy
The music and songs were tuneful.
Nine Men
That might be what it would have been in the African Campaign.

70   Factory manager, aged 37, Leek.
I have not had time to see a film during the past year.

71   Clothing manufacturer, aged 21, Ipswich.

1 *Random Harvest* (Splendid acting)
2 *Mrs Miniver*
3 *Thunder Rock*
4 *In This Our Life*
5 *The Man in Grey*
6 *Shadow of a Doubt*

72   University student, aged 20, Matlow.

Citizen Kane – originality, greatness of theme
The Magnificent Ambersons – originality, acting
Now, Voyager – good acting, larmoyant story
World of Plenty – importance of subject, directness of presentation
How Green Was My Valley – all-round Gallic excellence

73   Retired policeman, aged 60, Wirral.
Very seldom see films. I wasn't too impressed with Noel Coward's *With Whom We Serve*,[14] but it is a matter of chance what I see when I do go.

74   Headmaster, aged 50, Billingshurst.
I have not been to any.

75   Park keeper, aged 48, Eltham.

I do not visit cinemas nowadays. I still have a hangover from an operation which gives me continual headaches. At times I cannot even listen to the radio.

76   Architect, aged 48, London.

Doubt if I have seen more than six. 1 *Desert Victory.* 2 *In Which We Serve.* 3 Forget the title. But George Formby in the Home Guard. Had a good laugh.[15]

77   Accountant's clerk, aged 17, London.

1 *The Magnificent Ambersons.* (Orson Welles) Because it was done by Orson Welles.
2 *La Fin du Jour* (Louis Jouvert)
3 *Shadow of a Doubt* (Joseph Cotten, Teresa Wright)
4 *In Which We Serve,* (Noel Coward)
5 *The Human Comedy* (Mickey Rooney) Because of two marvellous scenes – the scene of the girls in the rain in transparent macs and with transparent umbrellas and the scene when the shop-window dummy comes alive and frightens the small boy.
6 *The Major and the Minor* (Ginger Rogers) and *Journey Into Fear* (Orson Welles, Joseph Cotten)
(I also *resaw* three films during the year which would have come in this list – *Pygmalion, Rebecca* and *Quiet Wedding.*)

78   Technical artist, aged 31, Sidcup.

Wake Island
Nine Men
Crash Dive
So Proudly We Hail
Black Swan
Bombardier
Not necessarily in order of preference – all have plenty of action. *Life and Death of Colonel Blimp* was good also. I suppose I saw about 20 films in all in 1943.

79   Non-combatant Corps, aged 37, London.

I go to far fewer films than I used to – only to those comparatively few that I expect to enjoy. Often these do not leave London, so that unless they are showing these during my 3-monthly week's leave, I miss seeing them at all. Thus ones I should like to have seen are the 2 Orson Welles' ones since *Citizen Kane* (the best I have seen of recent years), the documentary of Fire Fighting in the Blitz, the Battle of Britain, etc. In fact I can think of only *Casablanca* and *The Maltese Falcon* (both straightforward thrillers) as being two that I have enjoyed. I might add (?) *Land of Plenty* (Food documentary) as an also-ran. . . . I expected much from this picture and was disappointed.[16]

If not too late, the following two films should be added to my reply to question 6 of the November Directive –

Life and Death of Colonel Blimp
? (Film about the life of the artist Gauguin).[17]

80   Chief electrician, aged 38, Blackburn.
Sorry but I can't remember all the films I have seen, I feel pretty sure however that I haven't seen any outstanding films comparable with *The Great Dictator, Professor Mamlock, It Happened One Night, Mr Deeds Goes to Town*, except my first choice.

1 *The Man Who Stayed To Dinner*[18]
The unusual theme, the dialogue, the excellent acting.
2 *Desert Victory*
The stark reality portrayed. I don't know where or how the film was made but I was deeply impressed by the reality of it. I react violently and very adversely to Jingo patriotism but this certainly got under my skin.
3 *Hellzapoppin*
Because it was so utterly crazy, what more can I say.
4 *When We Were Married*[19]
The barbed humour of the theme and dialogue and the excellent characterisation.
5 *Ladies In Retirement*
Superb acting and a plausible plot and no happy ever after end.
6 *The Foreman Went To France*
The impressive scenes portraying the refugees on the roads.

81   University lecturer, aged 55, Aberystwyth.
I do not think I've seen six films during the year. I certainly can't remember six titles. I have enjoyed the following, but not in the order given. I should find it difficult to say in what order I would place them.
(a) *Mrs Miniver* – interesting photography but the hidden propaganda just damned impertinence – all the upper-class characters were such nice people and all the lower class such perfect bloody fools. cf. the station-master.
(b) *How Green Is My Valley*[20] – excellent example of what complete ruin some picture producers will make of a book. Much of this was just sheer nonsense. I know some Welsh mining valleys, schools, and houses, and miners. Much of the film is just tosh. I was so bored I could scarcely keep awake. High-grade slush.
(c) *The Silent Village* – I believe that was the title. Welsh Lidice. This was good. Quiet, impressive, real. No melodrama.

(d) *In Which We Serve* – some good acting of lower-class service and artisan parts.

(e) A technicolour film showing an episode in the life of Capt. John Morgan as Governor of West Indies. I can't remember the title.[21] Good straightforward blood and thunder. Most enjoyable. Nice change. And the aristocratic wench turned out quite nicely in the end.

(f) Film in which principle parts taken by the woman who played Mrs Miniver, and Ronald Colman. He was a shell-shocked officer who had lost his memory. Quite interesting to while away an hour or so. But I've forgotten the title.[22]

I also saw *Hellzapoppin*. Not very funny. I prefer Tommy Handley on the wireless any day. I believe I've seen one or two more but I can't in the least recollect either their titles, or what they were about.

82   University student, aged 19, ?

I am not a film fan and only 6 films stand out in my memory:

(1) *Citizen Kane*
Though I did not understand the enigma of 'Rosebud' the photography and acting of this film were superb. The characters were new, for American films, and rang true.

(2) *We Dive At Dawn*
Refreshingly English. Perhaps because of this the characters were all far more homely than is usual, even with British films.

(3) *Random Harvest*
A very fine story, the good qualities of the book being retained by good acting.

(4) *The Moon Is Down* (or, the film of that book)
The acting of Sir Cedric Hardwicke made this film. He seemed the true Nazi who had fought before – not overdrawn, which is rare for Hollywood.

(5) *Tales of Manhattan*
Good but nowhere near the two above. The incident where the new conductor's coat splits and everybody starts laughing until the celebrity took his off, and then they divested themselves, struck me as ludicrous and infuriating. Perhaps Yanks laughed, certainly nobody in the House I went to did. Charles Laughton was very good in this film.

(6) *First Of The Few*
Leslie Howard was the backbone of this film (excuse mixed metaphor). It was his acting which raised it from a hum-drum string of facts to a very human story. Released in 1942 I only saw it this year.

Apart from the first *Disney* I have ever enjoyed – of Pluto and a bone – and the newsreels of low-flying over the Low Countries, and the March of Time film of *Our Soviet Ally* and a MoI film *Up Periscope* I have seen nothing of note. I should like to make it clear that I am not a regular picture-goer.

83   Lieutenant RA, aged ?, Scotland.
Tales of Manhattan: Excellent story of an unusual kind; good acting and production.
Bataan: Good acting; excellent subtle propaganda.
Kings Row: I was able to appreciate the dilemma in which the hero found himself towards the end of the story.
I cannot mention six, as out of the few films I have seen, these are the only ones I have really enjoyed.

84   Schoolboy, aged 14, Welwyn Garden City.
During the last nine months I went to only one cinema show. I used to go to the pictures very often, until one day I got so fed up with this artificial form of amusement, that I have sworn not to go to any more cinemas if I can help it, until my opinion alters. I saw one film – *My Learned Friend* – last week, and this only strengthened my opinion. . . . I do not know exactly how old *The First Of The Few* is, but if it is less than a year old, I would place this film first.

85   Soldier, aged 22, Salford.
It is difficult to put them in strict order of preference as I don't usually compare say a thriller with a comedy film. I can enjoy both equally but in a different way. Roughly classifying into comedy, musical, war, story or character films.
   The best war film I have seen this year was *Nine Men*, liked because it was so true to life, clearly presented and with a purpose.
   Another war film, *Col. Blimp*, for character portrayal and human interest, and again for presentation and colouring.
   In Which We Serve, for its acting and presentation, but too much of Noel Coward and his pep talks.
   For documentaries *A Day In Soviet Russia* takes pride of place for its realism combined with a demonstration of human nature at its best.
   Bambi for its sheer beauty and the fascinating presentation of the parallel between animal and human life.
   Watch on the Rhine and *Thunder Rock* for a purposeful story, good acting and good presentation.
   Story films. *Shadow of a Doubt*, skilful suspense, good psychological presentation and good acting.
   Road to Morocco for the pleasure of seeing Bob Hope and Bing Crosby and for a good laugh.
   Mrs Miniver and *Random Harvest*, good story, human interest, good acting and presentation, and Greer Garson.

86   Technical chemist, aged 61, Luton.
I saw a film a few months ago. It had aeroplanes in it and was quite good, but too much repetition.

87   'Independent', aged 57, Andover.
I have not seen many films during 1 year, perhaps not as many as six.
Here is a list of last six films I have seen. I select them by reviews etc. and
only go when there is something I expect to like. It is not often I am
disappointed.

The First Of The Few is just the type of film I hope to see after the war,
just light without heroics showing how men can be truly great without
bullying others just seeing their duty and doing it in spite of every
obstacle.
The Fair Sex[23] after war we shall want to show women and those at home
in a similar film how they are helping to light and happiness in distant
parts of the world. Alas for L.H.[?]
The Moon Is Down a real attempt to understand the mentality of German
invalids and showing that Germany is no mere fiends dressed as humans.
Blimp The German refugee trying to explain himself to authorities was
one of the most moving scenes I have seen. Thank God we can still
understand.
For Which We Serve[24] moving film showing both sides of sailors life
without too much heroics.
For Ever And A Day I went to see the Brains Trust but I found this quite a
good film.

88   Secretary, aged 30, New Maldon.
I have not seen 6 films this year. I like films but have no time to go. I saw
and liked: *In Which We Serve, The Great Mr Handel, The Foreman Went
To France. Flemish Farm* I did not like, although it had good points.

89   Agricultural worker, aged ?, Kenton.
The Lamp Still Burns (English)
After the nasty, gory, war films from America, this was like drinking clear
water, listening to English accents, a film removed from war, with a good
plot, and finally a message to the public.
Its That Man Again (English)
The humour, not so slick as American, is or was, good clean English
humour, with an aroma of English about it.
Tales of Manhattan (American)
Noticeably produced by a Frenchman, with a very large foreign cast, this
film was a dazzling display of stars at their best or their second best.
Stormy Weather (American)
I liked this film because it showed off the coloured Americans, in a part
best suited for them, 'Show Business', and secondly, showed them in an
intelligent light, something rare in the average film from USA.
La Fin du Jour (French)
One of the brilliant films brought over here before the war, with all the

subtlety of the French Direction. Polished, finely acted by a group of the most accomplished French actors and actresses, it left one with subdued respect for a finished article.

Thunder Rock (English)

A thoughtful plot, well acted, tense with drama, and a good cast.

Peter The Great (Russian)

A good product of the Russian School, well acted, good photography (something rare in Russian films) and life-like.

Gentleman Jim (American)

A typical Hollywood film, enjoyable in an easy way, without the use of one's concentration. A film which the Americans excel – a story around the hero (American) with plenty of wise-cracks, fast movement, powdered ladies, and rich old Colonels etc. etc. Alright for boys of 14!

90   Civil servant (Retd), aged 59, Weymouth.

I am not a patron, and therefore no judge. I should be if they were more of an uplifting and enlightening type than is normally displayed outside the cinema.

91   ?? Sutton.

I am not at all keen on cinemas. I always go when there is an educational or historical picture something you can bring away and think about.

92   Electrical engineer, aged 33, London.

Unluckily I have not had the opportunity this year to see many films but of these:

1 *Thursday's Child*. It seemed an almost credible situation and was well worked out and dealt with ordinary English people.
2 *Blossoms In The Dust*. The whole theme was enjoyable and it is always nice to see a film of someone who had a purpose and sticks to it whatever happens.
3 *The Gang Makes Good*. We liked this largely because we did not expect it to be much of a film. It was the second one and turned out the better.
4 *Fires Have Been Started*. Having lived through the London blitz we naturally enjoyed this film. We were impressed with the way things were done and with the lack of heroics.[25]
5 *Map Reading*. The army film on map-reading. This was the best educational I have ever seen and greatly impressed me by its humour.

   I can't think of any others, except perhaps *The Magnificent Ambersons*, though this I did not think quite as good as *Citizen Kane*.

93   Engineer, aged 55, Wolverhampton.

I haven't seen six films in the year. Of the three (I think it is) I have seen the order is (1) *Desert Victory* (2) The ATS film (title forgotten)[26] (3) *In Which We Serve*.

94   Engineer, aged 20, Manchester.

World of Plenty
Peter The Great (Russian film)
The Underworld (French film)
Citizen Kane
Fantasia
Papageno (fairly old German film)

I am afraid I have no time to give the reasons for liking them.

95   Author, aged 51, Kinnersley.
I have not been to the 'films' this past year.

96   Railway draughtsman, aged 63, Manchester.
I have not attended a Cinema for many months, perhaps for over a year.

97   Research technologist, aged 36, Birmingham.

Bambi
Colonel Blimp
Shadow of a Doubt
Gentle Sex
Tortilla Flat
The *Brains Trust* films

Each the best of its kind in a class that appeals to me.

98   Chemistry teacher, aged 23, Huddersfield.
I see a great many films in the course of a year and have difficulty in placing the date of those of three months or more ago. The only film that really stands out in my memory of films seen this year is *Fantasia* though I am not sure of the year of its general release.

99   Engineering student, aged 20, London.
1 *Thunder Rock* – due to its time sequence it made the following of the story more difficult than the usual film in which everything is made easy and very, very obvious. Also it was not afraid to raise controversial issues.
2 *Things To Come* – even now it is a very interesting film. The technical production is excellent, the whole attitude of the film is unique and a very refreshing change from the ordinary.
3 *Bambi* – excellent technical production and music and different story. The cartoon at its best.
4 *My Sister Eileen* – The usual American comedy with acting, production and story much above the usual.
5 *Carnet De Bal* – Good acting and the different systems and styles of French production.
6 *Wuthering Heights* – Excellent acting.

100   Substation attendant, aged 31, Fleet.
I have a strong idea that I've only seen one film in the last year – *In Which We Serve*, and I cannot remember if that comes within the last year.

101   Farm worker and ex-librarian, aged 24, Worcester.
I have only seen about 3 or 4 films this year. One that amused me, tho' its cynicism was a little shallow, was *Heaven Can Wait*. At any rate it wasn't exactly what I expected. The touch that was missing was the suggestion that the whole of Henry Van Cleve's world was silly; therefore, the producer might say, why not be silly with it? But that wasn't quite the point.

102   Clerk, aged 41, Nottingham.
Not a film fan except for naval items.

103   Retired railway official, aged 67, Leeds.
I have only seen two or three films during the past year. I am not very fond of films, holding the opinion that about 90% of the films shewn are worth neither filming nor seeing. The film I saw worth mention was Disney's *Fantasia*.

104   Quantity surveyor, aged ?, Newquay, Cornwall.
I seldom go to a cinema as we are 6 miles from the nearest.

105   Education inspector, aged 36, Ramsgate.
I can only remember seeing five films this year. They were, in order of preference:

Tales of Manhattan
The Moon And Sixpence
Mr Handel
In Which We Serve
Escape To Happiness

Of these we saw the second and third off our own bat, so to speak, the others because recommended. I enjoyed them all, but I would only see the first-named again, and that with no special keenness; though, to be sure, it was a very good film, interesting throughout and not without moral implications.

I can find no common factor in 'the films I have regarded as outstanding' (which do not include any of the above) and I do not regard myself as being in any sense a film fan. Pre-eminent among all the films I have seen was the silent *Such Men Are Dangerous*, with Emil Jannings taking the part of the mad Czar Paul. Then comes the American film *These Three*, a study in perverse childhood. Third is another Jannings, *Masquerade*, or some such title with Lya da Putti and about trapeze artists (silent).[27] Then a completely trivial French film, *Le Roi S'Amuse*, which I liked as a veracious and unflattering picture of political life in the Third Republic. Fifth I would place *The Private Life Of Henry VIII*, sixth *Dreyfus*, and seventh *Little Friend*.

106 Technical author, aged 36, Coventry.
I have not seen 6 films in the last year. Of those I saw, only *The Gentle Sex* was outstanding. This was well cast, and produced with imagination. Its continuity and completeness were excellent, it had no dull moments, and yet had no need to resort to cheap drama for its effects.

107 School teacher, aged 35, Bishop Auckland.
(This list shows how long we, in this isolated hole, have to wait for our bloody entertainment. The films I would like to see, and have listed especially, are, in order –

1 *Mission To Moscow*, for its exciting reality.
2 *The Magnificent Ambersons* and
3 *Journey Into Fear*, for Orson Welles' direction.
– and God knows if they'll ever come.)

1 *Road to Morocco*. Dislike the actors in it, but its craziness and its songs, made it a real escape from reality.
2 *Moon And Sixpence*. Story and acting (technicolour at end, horrible). Story dates, for us, back to nostalgic days.
3 *Amphytrion 38*. French film seen in London – contrast between classical theme, and its modern debunking treatment. Enhanced by being seen on holiday in London, and happy memories of its language.
4 *Thunder Rock*. Memorable for its brave attempt to put over an intelligent point of view – outstanding photography.
5 *Major and Minor*. Ginger Rogers at her best.
6 *Col. Blimp*. In spite of technicolour, and the glamourising of that pest, the Colonel, it was an amusing film.

108 Schoolmaster, aged 36, Reading.

1 *Tortilla Flat* 2 *Moontide* 3 *Casablanca* 4 *Escape To Happiness* 5 *The Silver Fleet* 6 *The Watch On the Rhine*

1 Because it was real, and not Hollywoodified. The people were simple, or just plain crook, or just plain necessitous. The dialogue was a welcome change, being simple too, and the faith of these rude creatures was also affecting. I suppose their drama was no more deep than that of the glamour folks, but it seemed unforced, more like a Russian film, where the most inconspicuous individual is allowed to be plausible and indeed an individual. And of course the performance of Spencer Tracy was a masterpiece, I thought. Allen Jenkins appealed as usual, and I thought Frank (Ralph?) Morgan good.
2 I forget who directed it, but I suspect there was a lot in that. Again,

freedom from glamour. The thing done with restraint, Thomas Mitchell in an unsympathetic part. Claude Rains not too mushy as the wise adviser, the romance of two outcasts and the haunting tune of the record, 'Remember'.

3 I enjoyed this because I thought it a good tough yarn, and also it dealt with the war, but not in the usual Hollywooden manner, I thought; the parts of Paul Henried and Ingrid Bergman afforded the usual amount of romance that a sentimentalist like me cannot cure myself of liking, and Bogart was a winner. And there was Claude Rains doing his stuff again. One thing always strikes me as the epitome of twentieth century ruthlessness, cynicism and general hopelessness. When they have shot down the Veidt character and the two have got away in the plane, and the police come, Rains says 'Arrest the usual suspects.'

4 More romance and glamour, but well acted I thought by Leslie Howard and Ingrid Bergman. The shot where the child gets run over had me out of my seat. Again there was restraint and a slower pace in the story that gave one time to be really moved.

5 Good show by Ralph Richardson, and the boy. The modest key again appeals, and the minor characters were all plausible, especially one remembers the grocer, who looked like a quisling but was the goods. There were some good tense moments as when the Richardson character pretended to have killed the man in his house. Myself I thought Esmond Knight over-acted, and over-brutalised the Nazi gauleiter or whatever he was.

6 A fine performance by Paul Lukas, but the Davis character for once disappointed me. The American characters were admirably isolated, the villain not overdone, and the whole thing took on the air of inevitability that made it seem impressive. The sad things men suffer, the brave things they do, hardly ever earn the fanfare that some purveyors of mass entertainment would have us believe.

109 Farm worker, aged 23, Aberdeen.

I can think of only five films I've enjoyed to any great extent in the last year or so; four, strictly speaking, with a fifth thrown in for acting. Only very roughly in order:

(a) *Strawberry Blonde*
(b) *The Magnificent Ambersons*
(c) *Action In The North Atlantic*
(d) *King's Row*
(e) *The Scarlet Pimpernel*

Reasons –

(a) I don't remember SB very clearly now. After I'd seen it I didn't know what to make of it, then in two or three days, mulling it over, I realised it was one of the most attractive things I'd seen for a long time. I still don't know why; I guess I am just a sentimental sort of a guy and that was the way it struck me. It was a bit sentimental, and it had a dreamy quality, and it was unbelievably quiet and unpretentious; its being a period piece gave it a very peaceful air. Also, it had a theme-song that kept coming back like a fugue, which (research reveals) riled some people no end, but which tickled me a lot. Escape – yes. But it just happened to be right for me.

(b) I can dissect TMA much more surely. I liked it because it kept your wits sharp, never let you go to sleep, kept giving you something new to make you think or startle you. For the most part purely technical tricks, I suppose, but the reason I revelled in it all was that I saw behind it a lively mind, and it was a pleasure to follow the workings of that mind as it made the whole thing up and presented a real world as it might have existed. And the people in the film were real people, and they did what real people do, too. It's true to present situations absolutely, 100 percent true to life, leaving nothing out and presenting all the trivia with as much emphasis as the essentials, is to defeat one's own ends, since art is surely a selection of essentials and their presentation in a vivid form. But I think this film has nearly all the merits and next to none of the faults.

(c) One of the main reasons AITNA attracted me was that it missed out a good many of the film cliches which become so nauseating after the first few hundred times. It wasn't dominated (and ruined) by a totally irrelevant and hackneyed 'love-story': this alone is enough to make me shriek aloud in favour of any film. It didn't have a reporter or other pansified hero who showed up everyone else in the cast, beat up a dozen Japs (Germans, thugs, cops, dope-fiends, & etc. ad nauseam) single-handed and alone survived in the end, or did any of the other impossible things which are still, remarkable to relate, au fait in the picture business. i.e. with an occasional slip it was tolerably life-sized. Also, you became interested in every character in it. I don't seem able to give any reasons why this was an outstanding film: it's rather an honest film, which fulfilled its purpose, disdained to make ridiculous concessions, and avoided many of the mistakes which abound in most films, and which any reasonable film-goer would wish banished forever.

(d) This again I liked because the situations and motives and dilemmas, although bigger than life-size, were essentially the sort of ones we find in everyday life. True, it was a bit sugary, but what the hell. And also, it erred rather on the side of explicitness. A case-history in a psychiatry text-book has its own definite value, but it can hardly be considered as art, and presumably any film except a documentary or a purely educational one is aiming at being a work of art in its content, as apart from its technical qualities. However, this I think was well and honestly done once more, and I didn't go to sleep.

(e) I saw this in one of its many revivals, since I hadn't seen it before. I don't want to praise it as a film: indeed, especially towards the end, I thought it was a deplorably melodramatic and unconvincing piece of work, and I left it with a strong feeling of dissatisfaction. But I do think Leslie Howard's acting was among the best I've seen for a long long time, and that of all the screen actors I can think of, he managed to convey to the audience the most pleasant and highly likeable character.

A few general remarks. Probably I saw several films in the past year or so which would oust one or two of those mentioned from the list. I just can't remember them. But I go to the films very rarely nowadays, and indeed, through the summer I wasn't able to go for months on end, having no time off, tho' there were several films showing which I'd like to have seen. I find that whereas formerly I went to the pictures as a matter of course every week, or to escape from the usual fit of depression of a Saturday afternoon at the beginning of the war, now I enjoy myself much more by going only to those I know I'll enjoy a lot, and rigidly avoiding all second-rate or slightly below par. The system might not work for others, but it suits me fine.

Another point of possible interest. For years my father had said that he never liked to see a picture made from a play if he'd seen the play first. I could never understand this, probably because I hadn't seen the plays. But I've been theatre-going for all my worth for several years now, and occasionally, now, I see a film adapted from a play. And I'm bound to agree with him. In every case the film seems very inferior. The latest example was *The Petrified Forest*. I missed the film when it first came over, but saw it a month or two ago. Quite apart from the merits of the film qua film, and especially some of the acting, which was far from bad, it was sad to see that such an intelligent play, full of life and shrewdness and keen thought, had been so imperfectly translated. (Yet my sister, whose tastes often differ from mine, preferred it to the play.) On this score I didn't have the heart to see the film of *Watch On The Rhine*, much as I enjoy watching Bette Davis and Paul Lukas as a rule, because I had such fond memories of the play. Similarly, I'm often scared if a novel I've read is filmed: it rarely seems right, somehow.

110 ?? London

At practically every occasion on which I visit a cinema I have to digest some miserable propaganda film about the war. As a result of this I see so few films as to be unable to give any useful opinion.

111 Plant pathologist, aged 31, Newton Abbot.

I go to the cinema but rarely and even then forget most of the films I see. Here are my choices:

(i)   *Thursday's Child*   (ii)   *Marx Bros Go West*
(iii) *The Moon And Sixpence*   (iv)   *The Light Of Heart*
(v)   *Itma*   (vi)   *The Great Mr Handel*

112   Headmaster, aged 55, Llangollen.
(Note: I only go to films once or twice a month).

(1) *The First Of The Few*: The acting of Leslie Howard.
(2) *The Silver Fleet*: Sobering reminder of occupied Europe.
(3) *Here Comes Mr Jordan*: good amusing fantasy.
(4) *Mrs Miniver*: Smooth Hollywood fairytale on 1940 Britain.
(5) *Random Harvest*: 'Human drama'; successful suspension of disbelief.
(6) *Holiday Inn*: Sheer entertainment value, and rest-cure.

I have seen few if any of the notable recent films – e.g.

Magnificent Ambersons
Journey into Fear
In Which We Serve
We Dive at Dawn
The Gentle Sex, etc. etc.

113   Radio operator (unemployed), aged 31, Newport.
I have enjoyed the following six films during the year. Do not attach very great importance to the order of liking.

(1) *Tarakanova*, a pre-war French film seen in London, about a plot against Catherine II of Russia, with love interest; not what I usually like, but including a lovely performance of the part of the 16-year old pretender, Princess Tarakanova, by Annie Vernay, a fine actress and a very lovely girl. She is dead, I understand.
(2) *The Silent Village*, a short film showing how Cwmgiedd, near Swansea, might have been treated by the Nazis if it had been Lidice in Czechoslovakia. Played with complete sincerity and conviction by the inhabitants of Cwmgiedd, without any professionals.
(3) *Thunder Rock*, about a journalist who despairs of the modern world and retires to a lighthouse, but is reconverted to hope by the ghosts of six people drowned near the lighthouse 100 years before. A tract against political despair and apathy, very needful at the present time.
(4) *Wuthering Heights*, revival of a pre-war film of Emily Brontë's novel. Without following the novel slavishly it captured the spirit of it completely, I thought.
(5) *The Moon is Down*, occupied Norway, from a novel by John Steinbeck. Patriot mayor, bewildered but resolute, local quisling, fanatical young

Nazi, homesick and miserable young Nazi, colonel anxious to avoid trouble. Thoroughly convincing.

(6) *Watch On the Rhine.* Into a wealthy Washington home, remote from war and bloodshed, comes long-lost daughter, her three children, and her German husband, a member of the underground liberation movement. Resulting complications teach Washington a thing or two. I also saw the stage play in London; film was better, I thought.

114   Lance-Corporal (Army?), aged ?, Colchester.

I can only think of two films, which I liked very much during the last year. The best one I have seen this year is: *In Which We Serve.* I like this film, because it is a realistic story. It is very life like and also very well acted. The other film I referred to is: *The Life And Death Of Colonel Blimp.* Well acted, it gives a good view of an English character. Unfortunately this film is often misunderstood.

115   Architect's assistant, aged 25, Ealing.

I have not seen many films, and I remember very few of those that I have seen.

(1) A French film at Studio One. I forget the name but it was about a home for aged actors. I always enjoy French films. The acting is sincere and small details are so true to life that I always feel I know the people. I can almost smell the continental odours of cigar smoke and 'Toillette' or 'ABORT' that pervades the continent.[28]

(2) *The Man Who Came To Dinner.* Brilliant wit and sincere acting.

(3) *Desert Victory*, a special army showing. Astounding pictures of battle. Made you feel that at last the army was a worthwhile thing.

(4) *In Which We Serve.* I remember, but can best remember that the Capt. was too perfect to be real. The best humans have some small failings.

(5) *The Weaker Sex.* I enjoyed it at the time but it has not impressed me permanently.[29]

Have seen perhaps a half dozen others but can't remember anything about them.

116   Motor driver, aged 44, ?

As I have not kept a record of the films I have seen during the past year, my list may be faulty owing to bad memory, but I have particularly enjoyed:

Desert Victory
Fires Were Started
Battle Of Britain
Shadow Of A Doubt
The Man Who Came To Dinner
In Which We Serve

Women

1 Economist in Civil Service, aged 42, Newcastle.
I haven't seen many good films in the past year partly because we don't get them up here and partly because being unable to go out in the evenings my film-going is confined to such films as I can manage to see on my half days after I have finished with meetings which usually leave me free about 4.30. From memory I should place the following in the first six places but not necessarily in this order. *In Which We Serve*, a wonderful film despite the somewhat class-conscious acting of Noel Coward – both Shorty and the Chief PO were excellent[30] – so were their wives and the PO's mother – the various Xmas parties were awfully well done. *Lost Horizon* – a lovely film which I had never seen, also very exciting in parts with some magnificent photography – I liked the heroine very much and thought the hero and his brother quite good though never quite true, the two lamas were excellent and so was the plumber and his mate.[31] *Random Harvest* sentimental and too drawn out but a good picture. *Mrs Miniver* also very sentimental and quite impressive in parts such as Mrs M entirely American and loathsome family but a picture that has remained in my memory. *Five Graves to Cairo*, a rattling good picture which carried you along with it. *Watch on the Rhine* – I thought the husband's acting particularly good but all the parts were excellently taken.[32]

2 Legal clerk, Norwich.
Impossible to get to cinema this year owing to job, house and other work and the blackout and lack of transport at night.

3 Housewife and former teacher, aged 28, Wallington, Surrey.
Have only been to the cinema twice this year so can make no comment.

4 Teacher, aged 46, Watford.
As I keep a record of all films I see, it is very difficult for me to make a short list of only six.

Without exception, the British films I have seen have been interesting and enjoyable; from them I have learnt much about such subjects as desert fighting, submarine warfare, spy catching, airplanes.

Of the American films, I liked the amusing *The Bride Came COD* and *Cargo of Innocents* and was pleased to see *The Petrified Forest* for the first time. But my six chosen films are British:

1 *The Gentle Sex*: something quite new, that the USA cannot film and extremely well done.
2 *The Life and Death of Colonel Blimp*, for its colour and the acting of the cast, and its interesting history of an army man, followed by the Home Guard exercise.

3 *Undercover*: for its unusual milieu Jugoslavia, the scenery and the story.

4 *Quiet Wedding*: (reissue) for its Englishness, its fun, and the priceless acting by Bernard Miles, Roland Culver and Sidney King.

5 *Dangerous Moonlight*: for its lovely music.

6 *The Foreman Went to France*: for Tommy Trinder in a splendid part, for newcomer Gordon Jackson, and Clifford Evans, and for its scenes in France.

5   Housewife and mother, aged 32, Newport.

I am sorry to report that I have not been able to visit any pictures for the past three years. But if the children had not kept me from going I would have liked to see:

1 *Gone With The Wind*
2 *In Which We Serve*
3 *Desert Victory*
4 *Mrs Miniver*

6   Civil Servant aged 37, Purley.

Single parent of small twins

I haven't seen 6 films this year. In fact the only film I think I saw was *Bambi*, which I enjoyed mainly for its technical skill. I have to make a special effort to see anything now because at the weekend M (nanny) is 'off'. I have the twins to look after and in the week the last programme starts too early and anyway I don't like missing the limited time I have for the twins. I wanted to see the film about the Greek resistance but missed it. On the whole tho I prefer to use my very scanty opportunities for plays and concerts.

7   LCC social worker, aged 33, Purley.

Sister of above

I don't think I saw 6 films during the year. I go very rarely because the programmes of the last performance in Croydon and Purley start before I get back from work and its very expensive going in London. However, I saw and enjoyed a Russian film at the Tatler called I think *Suvoro*.[33] It told the story of this general's career and was pleasantly free from the sort of propaganda one used to connect inevitably with Russian films. There were a few memorable shots including one of an old soldier sitting in the middle of a group of villagers and recounting tales of his campaigns. I saw the film last Spring.

I also saw and enjoyed *Bambi*, the Disney film about the baby deer. Its colouring was lovely and I was very much moved by the hunting scenes – they made me weep. I cannot remember weeping at the cinema for years before that.

Of quite a different kind but exceedingly good was *The Road to Morocco*.

I liked the humour in this and was sorry not to be able to catch more of the Americanisms. I go so rarely to the cinema that I don't understand American very well. I found the Camels commentary in this film most refreshing.

I saw *This Land Is Mine* and liked it very much indeed. I think it was a French production but am not quite sure.[34] If it was British it was unlike most British and American films in showing people's characters in their strength and their weaknesses instead of showing good people as perfect and the bad ones as wholly evil.

8   Optical factory worker, aged 34, Bowden, Cheshire.

I doubt if I have been to 6 films. I only remember *Mission to Moscow* which I thought worthwhile but a bit amusing – Churchill with wall and Stalin with pipe etc. Oh, I also saw – attracted by the title – *Colonel Blimp* – and of course it wasn't Colonel Blimp. It whiled away an evening but I don't like colour and I can remember that the cinema was cold. I believe I saw *Pygmalion* and *Major Barbara* both for the third time. I liked them both for Shaw's ideas and Howard's acting, but I can't assess them against *Mission from Moscow* which is different use of the cinema.

9   Housewife, aged 29, Reading.

Have only seen 5 films in the last 12 months. Much of the best was *The Keeper of the Flame*, then *Bambi*. The others were unimportant – *Bedtime Story, Presenting Lily Mars* and another. My sister said that the best she saw was a US film on Food Production and Distribution.

10   Teacher, aged 32, Thornaby on Tees.

1 *Russian Fairy Tale* – Children's Theatre Moscow (Tatler, Charing Cross Road). It was quite different from any film I had ever seen. It was just right for children, the colour, speech, attitude, happy ending.

2 *The Gentle Sex* – I liked the documentary mingled with the story. The characters were real and natural and the humour grand. It is present day material presented in a very pleasing manner.

3 *Mission to Moscow* – Very good representation of historical events, true as to facts, realistic, coherent and educational.

4 *In Which We Serve* – Enjoyed the unusual technique, the extremely good acting and the general high level. Again a real subject dealing with present-day events. We are living in most stirring times and it is good to see them being recorded.

5 *Desert Victory* – reasons similar to No. 3. The continuous war atmosphere was rather tiring but it was convincing and very well produced.

6 *Dear Octopus* – a charming story well acted and a welcome change. I like stories about families when they ring true.

11 Civil servant, aged 23, Dorset.
I doubt if I have been to the cinema 6 times altogether in the past year. Of the poor variety of films I have seen *Women aren't Angels* (Robertson Hare and Alfred Drayton) stands out in my mind as the one I would like to see again – several times. It was most amusing and delightfully near the bone sometimes.

Mr Handel[35] was bearable but not memorable. *The Human Comedy* was a dreary pain in the neck. I suppose shots of Yankee soldiers singing hymns were just to inform us that the Americans are just big boys at heart.

12 Aerodynamic researcher, aged 47, Farnborough.
Would go if I could get a seat. But films going here means standing outside for 25 minutes and then inside for another half an hour. Too tired. Don't go.

13 Housewife, aged 38, Lincoln.
Documentary and MoI.
(I like books and films which tell the facts in the form of fiction.)

14 Housewife and mother, aged 49, Accrington.

1 *Mrs Miniver* – I like Greer Garson and find her a tonic as well as restful. I feel all the picture was in tune.
2 *Gone With The Wind* – All the characters were very well played, especially Scarlett and Rhett. I didn't like the war scenes. Otherwise it was perfect.
3 *Pride and Prejudice* – again Greer Garson and Laurence Olivier played splendidly and kept to the spirit of the book. All characters were good.
4 *The Pied Piper* – a moving picture with touches of real humour.
5 *Sing As We Go* – an old film re-shown. I never miss Gracie Fields. She lifts me to a high plane as well as entertains me with her thorough affinity with human joys and sorrow. This so alive.
6 *Bambi* – a Disney film. Presentation lovely. It's the perfect children's picture second only to *Snow White*.

15 Teacher, aged 34, Masham, Yorks.

1 *In Which We Serve*. Seemed true to life – unemotional but moving. Not obviously out for Box Office receipts. Well acted, good technique.
2 *The Gentle Sex* – I thought the psychological reactions of the girls interesting – probably true. It seemed natural and was distinguished by straightforward unaffected acting. A film about life as it is now for many girls.
3 *Colonel Blimp* – magnificent acting – again, about life as we know it. Colour effects were good. Psychologically interesting.
4 *Tomorrow We Live*. Revealing – about way French peasants feel. The film seemed to speak truly. Well acted.

5 *The Magnificent Ambersons*. Technique profoundly interesting – lighting effects unusual. Good acting.

6 *The First of the Few*: distinguished by Leslie Howard's restrained acting. Informative if Mitchell bomber did come into existence like that.

16 WAAF, RAF Hopton.
The six films which I have liked best this year are:

1 *The Life and Death of Col. Blimp*
2 *The Gentle Sex*
3 *The Man in Grey*
4 *Desert Victory*
5 *The Amazing Mrs Holliday*
6 *Immortal Sergeant*

Reasons for liking:

1 *Col. Blimp*. I like a film that is long and this is the longest film I have seen for some time. I thought the technicolour excellent. The story and characters portrayed most true to life.
2 I liked this film for its realistic portrayal of service life which I know so well.
3 A dramatic well produced film.
4 From *Desert Victory* I learned a lot which I should never otherwise have known of the fighting in Africa.
5 Deanna Durbin's singing.
6 An amusing realistic story.

17 Poultry farmer's wife, aged 52, Arborfield, Berks.
I live in a village 6 miles from Reading and though I like a good film I am not a cinema fan. Each week I read the film reviews in the 'Observer' and make a note of any I'd like to see. Then I look at the local paper to find out whether any of these come to Reading. Usually there isn't even one a month that I want to see. I enjoyed all the war films – *Next of Kin, In Which We Serve, Mrs Miniver* etc. and there was a really good thriller *Shadow of a Doubt. Mission to Moscow* was terribly disappointing after having read the book. A real Hollywood shameless travesty of history. Sorry I can't be more helpful.

18 Housewife and part-time worker in Assurance office, aged 46.
I seldom go to see a film as I have little time and enjoy a play more – I saw and enjoyed *Col. Blimp* also *Fantasia*. The latter I saw twice.

19 Guardian's Committee Clerk, aged 47, Bury St Edmunds.
I have seen so very few films since the war and I think nothing outstanding. Nothing I went to see a second time, anyhow. Perhaps *Wuthering Heights* was the best. It is a good novel and not American. *Gone*

With The Wind was too long drawn out and without the genius of *Wuthering Heights. Madame Du Barry*[36] had interesting colouring. I understand it pays cinema proprietors better to put on 'tripe' and they get full up whatever the programme.

20 Teacher, aged 34.
Can't think of six films.

1 *Heaven Can Wait.* Witty, light tone, no heavy morality. Lubitch direction, charming colour, unexpected happenings. No sickly sentiment.
2 *The Man in Grey* – just romantic escape from wartime. Good story. Enjoyed costumes, setting 'Becky Sharp' theme.
3 *Alibi* 1942 film seen 2nd time. Wit. Plot. Acting. Caste.

21 Market gardener and housewife aged 42, Corfe Castle, Dorset.

Stalingrad Fights – Inspiring.
Fantasia – good Disney.
Dear Octopus – Good characterisation.
Millions Like Us – True to life story.
The Life and Death of Colonel Blimp – Clever production and thoughtful play.
Tales of Manhattan – Amusing and ingenious.

22 Teacher, aged 51, Chepstow.
The films I have liked best are:

1 *Col. Blimp* for its splendid characterisation and its almost perfect Technicolour putting American colour to shame.
2 *The Moon and Sixpence* for the excellent acting of George Sanders and the portrayal of a man who wouldn't be denied his creative instinct.
3 *The Shadow of a Doubt* for its psychological approach and its really thrilling episodes.
4 *Random Harvest* for its stars Ronald Colman and Greer Garson and its tender love stories.
5 *The Man in Grey* for its unusual plot and again its good acting.
6 *The More the Merrier* because of its utter craziness cleverly pursued in the part of Jean Arthur.

23 Companion/help, aged 56, Bristol.
I have not seen any films during the past year.

24 Mother and part-time typist, aged 27, London SW3.
All these are fine films. I couldn't say which I liked best.

1 *Nine Men* – Crown Films.[37] 'Realism' of characters. Superb acting and photography of exciting story.

2 *Desert Victory* – Army Film Unit. First class 'documentary' shooting and editing.

3 *World of Plenty* – Rotha. Vivid dramatisation of essential though hitherto abstract subject of postwar feeding.

4 *In Which We Serve* – Coward. Brilliant conception of behaviour. Patterns of different classes united in common loyalty.

5 *Soviet Russia at War* – Highly interesting subject, shot and edited with realism and skill.

6 *Lone White Sail* – sensitive and beautiful interpretation of class conflict.

24.1 'Home duties', aged 39, Llangollen.
Only been to one which I didn't enjoy. It's only very rarely that I can go but should like to see *Gone with the Wind, Fantasia, Dumbo* and *First of the Few?* (the one with Leslie Mitchell and Walton's music, Spitfire Fugue).[38]

24.2 Housewife, aged 54, Gateshead-on-Tyne.
I've seen no films at all. But I heard from 4 thinking people (1 man, 23, in Buxton) that *Random Harvest* was most enjoyable.

24.3 Farmer's wife, aged 50, Wrexham.
I have not been to the pictures for four years except to an odd news theatre – I can't say why, I just have felt no inclination.

24.4 Housewife, aged 30, Norwich.
Only saw three rather feeble ones – no that's not right – one was exceptionally good – *Mr Pitt the Younger*[39] – and am in no position to judge.

25 Welfare officer and former nurse, aged 38, Glasgow.
The films I liked best this year.

1 *In Which We Serve*, as truly British, I could visualise it happening to me, or any of my friends and the reactions would have been the same.
2 *The Gentle Sex*.
Again truly British (of a world wide subject that in a crisis Women are 'made to obey') and the reactions were human.
3 *Yankee Doodle Dandy*.
I loved its energy and generosity.
4 *The Road to Morocco*.
Lavish and Rich, its fun.
5 *Charlie Chaplin's Return*.[40]
I laughed again and was delighted that I could do so. I love Charlie's antics.
6 Disney's *Flying Gayloot*.
The irrationalities of Nature evil and machine, and man's struggle to overcome the same.

7 *I Married A Witch.*
Was excellent.
8 (Russian) *The New Teacher.*
Comedy characterisation was good. How I laughed.
9 (French) Cannot recall name, but it was a home for retired actors, this
film was choice as no detail was missed.[41]
10 & 11 I saw *Lady Hamilton* for first time, I liked the style, and
Wuthering Heights, its beautiful childhood scenes.

26 'Provincial lady', various village activities, former teacher, aged 62,
Chew Magna, Nr Bristol.
Have not seen many – Best: *In Which We Serve* and *The First Of The Few.*
Both inspiring and without eyewash or false notes or 'heartiness'.

27 Housewife and local food office clerk, aged 32, Sheringham.
I don't think I've seen 6 pictures this year. All I can remember are *The
Jungle Book* and the *Arabian Nights* – visited for the sake of Timothy my
7 year old son. I don't go a) because I don't [want?] to go, b) because I can't
leave my baby.

28 Housewife, aged 53 years, Burnley.
Films 1 *Life and Death of Colonel Blimp*, 2 *Escape to Happiness*, 3 *Random
Harvest*, 4 *We Dive at Dawn*, 5 *Tales of Manhattan*, 6 *The Gentle Sex.*

1 *Life and Death of Colonel Blimp* was a grand film, interesting on
   account of the period of time it covered. Films of the immediate past are
   always attractive to me probably because they bring back memories.
   This film also seemed to be well-produced. The story was easy to believe
   in, though there were many unexpected 'twists' in it.
2 *Escape to Happiness*: I liked the hero and heroine in this picture, the
   acting was realistic and restrained.[42] Various charming pictures added
   to the attraction.
3 *Random Harvest*. Here again I liked the main characters and the way
   they acted their parts. One noticed that the whole thing was a breach of
   the law of the land though this does not worry film-makers or the
   public. Some beautiful scenes and photography added to the attraction.
4 *We Dive at Dawn* – the 'submarine' picture. I liked this much better
   than *In Which We Serve* though the latter was more boosted locally. The
   main character, in his serious moments especially was convincing and
   likeable – e.g. on duty at the periscope. The story was free from the
   melodramatic quality of the film *In Which We Serve* and the effect
   produced was not so theatrical.
5 *Tales of Manhattan* was a comprehensive and attractive film, with no
   connection with the war. I enjoyed it immensely for its variety and
   contrasts.
6 *The Gentle Sex*. Though dealing with the present war this film was a

change from the usual style. It was interesting and instructive as well as varied.

29 Publicity writer and BBC reporter, aged 30, Northampton.

(a) *The Gentle Sex* – for its human presentation of us as a people, and its splendid direction. (Alas, why couldn't we have protected Leslie Howard better?)

(b) *Heaven Can Wait* – a film for adults, artistic, delicately treated and yet delightfully modern – psychological depth and attention to relevant detail – beautiful colour, and photography, original creation.

(c) *Tales of Manhattan* – perhaps because it reminded me of 'Carnet de Bal' – liked the Latin touch about certain scenes, particularly the scene where the maestro removes his dinner jacket . . . we wouldn't have thought of that just like that, would we?

(d) *Casablanca* – for its superb acting and its fundamental truths – excellent photography and character studies.

(e) *Desert Victory* – yes, no more war fiction, please – Don't forget that American studios took the hint 18 months ago . . .

30 Stenographer and press agent, aged 36, Birmingham.

To the best of my recollection I haven't seen six films during the past year, but only five. This really means I have been to the pictures only five times (which is quite up to my average annual film intake) and I can't list any of the supporting films I have seen because I simply don't take enough notice of them to remember anything about them. The five things I have seen, in order of liking, are:

Pygmalion
In Which We Serve
Desert Victory
Random Harvest
The Gentle Sex
– afterthought, just come to me,
We Dive At Dawn

1 *Pygmalion*: I had of course seen before on its original production. This was part of the general revival of Howard's films following his death. To my surprise I realise that this was not only the best film, but the best show of any kind, I have seen during the year, with the exception of the Sadlers Wells production of *Figaro* and *Barber of Seville*. Reasons for liking: 1) the rare and highly stimulating flavour of Shavian dialogue emanating from (of all improbable places) a cinema screen. Good Lord one thought, here's *mind* manifesting itself in what we have come to accept as a mindless medium. 2) Howard's own playing and direction, which made me mourn more than ever his loss to the screen. This again is a quality of mind, for he hadn't a fraction of the obvious animal or

sensuous charm which makes up 99.9 per cent of American film actor's personality. 3) Wendy Hiller's playing of her own part, just as brilliant as Howard's with not an inch of film-space conceded to Hollywoodism; and the same can be said of all the minor parts – especially Wilfrid Lawson as Doolittle. But the best thing about it remains that taut, mental-muscle-stretching tussle of Higgins' and Eliza's personalities at the last – more exciting, to my mind, than anything else I have ever seen on the screen.

2 *In Which We Serve*. I have a small snob fear about confessing that I thought this was extremely good, because one or two of my brainier friends thought it was rather bad. Nevertheless, I was extraordinarily moved by it – the more extraordinarily so, considering that I had heard a great deal of praise of it before I went and might have expected too much. I was a little uncomfortable about Coward's own playing of the Captain's part, but I honestly think if I had never seen him before or known nothing about him, I should have accepted it as a fine piece of character acting. The Coward voice in which so many cheap and base wisecracks have been fired off was a little out of tune with the rest of the picture. But the rest was really excellent, and I don't care who hears me say so. I think Coward is one of those people, like Dickens, who can't draw a gentleman. But he has real genius with the common people, and I think as a whole this film knocks all the other semi-propaganda war films I have seen or heard of into a cocked hat. From the little I know of the Naval officer class I shouldn't say the snob-stuff was a scrap too thickly laid on.

3 *Desert Victory*. Was first-rate, and couldn't have been bettered in its class. An eyeopener, too, as far as the making of war films is concerned. I had had no notion that the cameras got anywhere so near the line of battle as that. There was a pleasing sort of modesty about it too – considering it told the story of an out-and-out victory it didn't bang the big drum to an embarrassing extent, I thought.

4 *Random Harvest*. Good of its kind – even very good – but for me too much sicklied o'er with the anything but pale cast of Hollywood. Hush, too too hush. But I respect both Greer Garson and R. Colman as actors.

5 *The Gentle Sex*. Mm – yes Pretty good. A little too neat and trim and obvious perhaps, but with some nice touches. Successful, I should say, in that it made even me, over age and ineligible for half a dozen reasons as I am, wish for quite a few minutes that I could join one of the Women's Services.

6 *We Dive at Dawn* had exactly the same flavour, but far less of it, as *In Which We Serve*. Good but not startling.

31 ATS Sergeant, aged ?, Edgware.
I found it rather a difficult job to select six films out of the many I have

enjoyed – and once I decided on six – the placing in order of liking seemed well-nigh impossible. Anyway the reasons for my liking them are much the same for each – I admired the stars, the acting was good, the story enjoyable, and in two of them children were portrayed.

1 *Random Harvest* 2 *Man in Grey* 3 *Dear Octopus* 4 *Pied Piper* 5 *Blossoms in The Dust* 6 *Thunder Rock.*

You will notice that three of these are British films – I always have a soft spot for well-made home productions. I enjoy the acting of the stars Greer Garson, Margaret Lockwood, Barbara Mullen, Monty Woolley, Ronald Colman, James Mason, Michael Redgrave etc.; and the babies in *Blossoms in the Dust* and the children in the *Pied Piper* were delightful, as was the grand humour portrayed by Monty Woolley as the Pied Piper.

32 Housewife and farmer, aged 40, Tayvallick.
I've hardly seen six films during this year.

1 *We Dive At Dawn* – Easily the best film I've seen for many years.
2 and 3 *Dumbo* and *Fantasia* – About equal in different ways – *Fantasia* has enormous possibilities but I think I enjoyed *Dumbo* more.
4 *Casablanca* – A long way below the above. But quite a good story and well-filmed.
5 *Flying Officer X* – Quite good thriller stuff.
6 *In Which We Serve* – I call this a bad film, but put it in because the only others I've seen (*I Married An Angel* and something with Bob Hope in it) were even worse.

33 History teacher, aged 43, Taunton.
I find that most of the good films I've seen 'recently' I saw in 1940. Taunton has been badly served recently. I've liked – though I hesitate to put them in any particular order.

(a) *Gone with the Wind*
(b) *Here Comes Mr Jordan*
(c) *The Pied Piper*
(d) *Moontide* (? I mean the Hollywood version of *Quai des Brumes*)[43]
(e) *Colonel Blimp*
(f) *Assignment in Brittany*

Reasons

(a) Beautiful acting.
(b) A fantastic tale that gives one a real 'escape'.
(c) So 'real', except perhaps for the end.
(d) I can watch Jean Gabin for hours – whatever he does.
(e) Good acting – (though I think the title either foolish or misleading).
(f) Good drama – and acting too.

I've seen very few films recently that one remembers mainly because of good production.

34 Housewife, aged 57, Coventry.
Haven't seen six films.

35 Social sciences student, aged 19, Edinburgh.

1 *First of The Few* – historic interest. Photos of flying and aeroplanes superb, and good acting and convincing story.
2 *Moon and Sixpence* – original and artistic interest and Romance.
3 *Fantasia* – imagination, music, no war interest.
4 *Gone with the Wind* – convincing and vivid character studies – good acting.
5 *Major and the Minor* – sheer undiluted fun – no war interest.
6 *Kings Row/Amazing Mrs Holliday/Mrs Miniver* – natural acting, family life and children, always some interest besides romances.

36 'Home duties', aged 55, Matlock.
I cannot help you with films as I know little about them. I dislike impersonations and impressions in any form. I [faked, hated?] photography. Also I dislike to see the dead impersonated on the films and all for commercial gain. Their private affairs are turned and twisted to suit the public and I do not think it should be allowed. There are many who frequent cinemas put a wrong construction on some of the actions of the people who are gone and cannot defend themselves and their reputations suffer. I cannot think either Queen Victoria or Prince Consort would have liked the general public to see their private domestic life, and they would be hurt at such a display . . . if it is possible to hurt the departed. The days of privacy and reverence appear to have gone and everything is sacrificed to commercialism gain and publicity noise and display.

37 College lecturer, aged 55, Norwich.
I go very seldom. I can't remember whether the ones below belong to this year or earlier.

1 *In Which We Serve*: documentary, convincing, moving.
2 *Mrs Miniver*: story not *too obtrusive*.
3 *Random Harvest*: liked it and now can't remember it.
4 One whose title I forget but it looked back upon a brief invasion of a bit of England.[44]
5 *The Mountains Wait*: Norway, informing and moving.

But *Target for Tonight* seen earlier tops the bill. But I am no film fan.

38 Housewife, aged 43, Harrogate.
The films – I'm afraid I don't share the popular taste. I always like a good laugh – but feel like swearing when English family is presented as the Minivers. Wealth – to me fabulous – wealth every time. The great

majority of us are poor and we have plenty of tragedy and comedy that could be filmed to advantage. I think that is why I was so impressed with *How Green Is My Valley*.[45]

39 Housewife, aged 62, Orpington.

I haven't been able to afford to go to the pictures *and* smoke, so gave up the pictures – I fancy smoking may have to follow suit.

40 Housewife, aged 45, Bristol.

I have attended the cinema less than usual this year and forget the films I saw during the first 6 months of the year. I remember with pleasure

(1) *For Whom The Bell Tolls* (just seen)
(2) *First of the Few*
(3) *In Which We Serve*
(4) *Kings Row*
(5) *The Magnificent Amberleys*[46]

41 Housewife, aged 61, Wallington.

Have only seen two films since 1939. Too busy and can't afford to catch colds or flu.

42 Canteen worker, aged 49, Manchester.

1 *Colonel Blimp*
2 *Mission To Moscow*
3 *The First of the Few*
4 *In Which We Serve*
5 *The Gentle Sex*
6 *Salute John Citizen*

All the films hold your interest from beginning to end, and deal with actual facts, they deal with the immediate past in which we are all still living. We all know actual people similar to those acting. One cannot say this of the usual Hollywood films.

43 Shop assistant, aged 36, Dewsbury.

Do not think I have seen six this year. I can only remember –

1 *Mrs Miniver* – very sentimental and untrue to English life and yet it seemed to touch the spot. Besides Greer Garson is one of my favourite actresses – I can tell what she says.
2 *The Gentle Sex* – Went to see this because I had heard it on the wireless. Very good although very indistinct. It was nearly the end of the picture before I had sorted them all out – the Czech girl stuck out a mile above the others for being the part. I liked it because it showed what our young ladies are doing and have to put up with.[47]

3 *In Which We Serve* – Very much Noel Coward but still a thrilling and I felt authentic picture.

All these made me feel I know nothing of the war – I live in a backwater and apart from slight and general inconveniences have no knowledge of the war. That is the value of such films, I think, apart from the story. It brings the war home to such as I am.

44 Civil Servant, aged 52, Morecambe.

This is a difficult question to answer with any certainty as, for one thing, films seen recently stand out in one's mind more than those seen in the early months of the year. Also one's opinion varies with mood, I *think* the following list comprises those which have given me most pleasure. But on another date I might put them in a different order – or even change some titles for others not included:

1 *Dangerous Moonlight*. (Seen for the second time) I liked this chiefly because it is not just a story, but really deals with a very real and vital present day problem – viz what *is* the duty of the artist in war time? Also I enjoyed the music. Also Anton Walbrook's acting. When I first saw this film, too, the technique of starting at the end of the story was fairly new. It seemed to me then to be a clever and well constructed film, and the impression remains although the novelty has gone.

2 *The Great Mr Handel*. Again the music gave me great pleasure. Also the film brought to life a great man who was not much more than a name attached to his music before. It seemed to be true to life – the characters were human – and there was a pleasant and not exaggerated humour throughout. I also appreciated the *absence* of any sensational love story.

3 *The Life and Death of Colonel Blimp*. This again appealed to me as being very true to life; and like *Dangerous Moonlight*, it was an attempt to understand a problem or, rather, a character. It was more than just entertainment. I enjoyed, too, the English scenery, and the restrained use of technicolour – and of course the humour.

4 *In Which We Serve*. Another film which seemed to me very true to life. All the characters were just ordinary men and women with normal human interests. There is pathos, tragedy, strong emotion in it, but no exaggerated sentiment, and no 'glamorous' film stars stepping out of its story to show off their 'charms'. It was a novel and brilliant idea too, making the *ship* the focus of the whole story. Quite out of the ordinary.

5 *Mrs Miniver*. This gave me a good deal of pleasure when I saw it – I can remember writing to all my friends what a great film it was, but I do not think I should enjoy it so much now. At the time I saw it there had not been such a spate of war films and it was interesting to view the blitz – or rather the way people lived through it – as a whole, and from the standpoint of a spectator. It seemed to me, too, a fairly good

representation of ordinary, natural people – though not so good as *Salute John Citizen* which I had seen late in 1942.

6 *Dear Octopus.* I'm not sure whether this ought to be included. I saw it only a few weeks ago and it may be for that reason that it stands out in my mind more than others seen earlier. I enjoyed the absolute detachment from the war – simplicity and homeliness of it – the naturalness of the characters – The cleverness with which a story was made at all out of such very slight material – *and* I was in sympathy with the theme.

45 Speaker for Townswomen's Guilds, WI, British Legion, Co-op Guilds, etc; aged 73, Leigh-on-Sea.
Mrs Miniver.

46 'Landed gentry', aged 45, Chelmsford.
Have only been twice to the cinema in the last 15 months. I preferred *Col. Blimp* to *You were never Lovelier?* (Fred Astaire, Rita Hayworth, not sure of its name)[48] because it was a more intelligent production with one or two witty touches. I have also see two MoI Rural Shows, one poor, the other with *Tobruk* and *Malta Convoy* good.

47 Housewife, aged 57, Ilford.
I do not go to the cinema, so cannot make any remarks.

48 Newsagent, aged 43, Barry.
I have seen very few films this year. Those I have seen were of two types and can't be compared. Two informative films were *Mission to Moscow* and *World of Plenty*. *Mission to Moscow* I particularly wanted to see because I have the book and I wondered how it would shape as a picture. I was agreeably surprised. It was a good film of the book. *World of Plenty* too I enjoyed but I wondered how many would care to see it. I saw it last Bank holiday Monday while on a visit to London. Since then it has been put on as a second feature for general release.

Two other pictures of quite different type of more entertainment value were *Random Harvest* and *Coney Island*. *Random Harvest* I thought extremely pleasing. Greer Garson the actress and Ronald Colman, both English, were not over glamourised. It was a very charming picture, dignified and one of the most pleasing that has come out of Hollywood. I saw recently *Coney Island*. This is typically Hollywood but as I hadn't seen a musical film for some time I enjoyed it. The colourings were very beautiful not harsh like the early colour pictures of even a year or two ago. The music was pleasing. The colourings attracted me most, the music next and the story last, although it was the usual one written about the American backstage. But I was in the mood to see light entertainment that evening. I'm not a regular filmgoer.

49 Housewife, aged 37, Blackheath.
Haven't been to a cinema this year. Have not had the time. There have been quite a few films I wanted to see.

50 ATS Sergeant, aged 22, London.

Thunder Rock – Adult thinking and subtle production.
The Silent Village – Natural – very moving and restrained.
Now Voyager – Excellent sympathetic escapist story excellently acted and produced (escapist not used detrimentally).
Col. Blimp – Rattling good story – very well acted.
The Sky Is The Limit[49] – Top in its class – Astaire's dancing – Benchley's brilliant comedy.
Casablanca – Good unpretentious but achieving what it set out to achieve.

51 Farm worker (poultry maid), aged 36.
I find I have only been to 4 films this year and give them in order of preference.

Went The Day Well?
This was a good story, with enough credibility to make it enjoyable. The characters were well presented and not too much 'film-ised', and the backgrounds were telling and natural. There was some very good acting, and the whole film was intelligent and amusing, and not much exaggerated, and it went along at a good pace.

Victory Through Air Power
I regard Walt Disney as one of the prominent artists of our time, and always enjoy seeing his productions. This one was full of original ideas in the presentation of facts, and the use of colour was very good. The matter of the films was interesting, though there was too much of Sevasky(?).

  A Thriller, I can't remember the title, it was something like *Fall of Paris*, and the stars were Elizabeth Bergner and I think Gary Cooper. It was quite exciting and fairly well acted, especially in the smaller parts, and I always like looking at Bergner, but it was rather sentimental and quite impossible.[50]
Random Harvest
Some good acting and some decorative scenes and dresses, but I don't like Ronald Colman, and have a poor opinion of his acting. This film was *very* sentimental in places.

52 Journalist, aged 33, London.
I have had no time to see many films this year, except for a news programme every fortnight between duties. Doubt if I have seen 6 feature programmes. *Col. Blimp* impressed me greatly – perhaps the best I have ever seen – technically, for its movement, its Englishness and its colour. Also liked *Mrs Miniver* quite well, but it didn't strike true. *Victory*

Through Air Power had immense punch and impact on me – possibilities of the technique v. great. But it promulgated a faulty military philosophy.

53 Art student, nursery assistant, aged 17, Northampton.
So far during 1943 I have seen only 16 films, including 'second' pictures, obviously not always of my choice. Some of the 16 were re-issues, or second time I had seen them. Here is my 6; I have not put *Fantasia* at the top, where it belongs, as it was the 5th time I had seen it, and I hope to see it many times more, just as I go to see *Hamlet* every time it is performed.

(i)   *Mayerling*: Exquisite acting, perfect settings and period atmosphere, appropriate and moving music, in a rarely lovely story. Near the top of my complete film list.

(ii)   *Thunder Rock*: Unusual presentation; forceful production; high standard of sincere acting in a thought-producing tale.

(iii) *Bambi*: Delightful naïveté, beautifully sincere presentation. Such a change from the pseudo-sophisticated usually shown at cinemas.

(iv)   *Magnificent Ambersons*: An original presentation, with emphasised authenticity of period style. Remarkable photography, with highly polished acting from the whole cast. In a class apart.

 (v)   *The Shape of Things to Come*:[51] Still a good film, in spite of its age Clean-cut direction, good acting, in a provoking prophecy. The music an integral part – yet still good music by itself. Excellent settings and costumes.

(vi)   *Stradivarius*: The restrained acting of these French players is so unlike Hollywood and true to life that an interesting but by no means remarkable story gives an unusually good film. Sincere and moving.

54 Housewife, aged 49, Barrow-in-Furness.
I feel rather like Tommy Handley in his 'yer that's right sketch. I feel I've forgotten titles and cannot remember films by their names. I enjoy going to the pictures, but they rarely make an impression on me after I leave – I don't go much now. The last one and the one which made the most impression on me was one about the building of the Canadian Pacific railway over the Rockies. It was not alone the magnificent photography but because an uncle of my father's travelled to Canada to help in a party of experts from England.[52]

Penn of Pensylvania. I've a liking for 'pioneer' people and they were Quakers, and my forbears up to my Gran's time were Quakers. Also I'd read a book called 'Down Ryton Water' about the same time and although of the Mayflower Pilgrims, it made the time and people 'live' for me.
Yankee Doodle Dandy. Tuneful singing, good photography and acting, decent story and acting.
Random Harvest. I like R. Colman and Greer Garson and enjoyed the production and setting even more than the story and acting.

Sorry I cannot think of more 'titles' I've not been since summer. A few I've seen I enjoyed but cannot recall. One about Nazi occupied Norway – I *think* called *They Shall Rise Again* had a good propaganda slant with good story and photography, and a quite amazing Sky film with a German pilot getting by accident to England was good if improbable.[53]

55 Housewife, aged 34, Potters Bar.
The Gentle Sex. The masterly direction of Leslie Howard inspired me. I was interested, of course, also because it is a film about my own sex.
Battle of Britain, and *Desert Victory.* Its truth make it outstanding. Seldom do we get a chance to *see* History.
How Green Was My Valley. A lovely change from war films though very pathetic. Very moving.
Crash Dive. American Technicolour. Good plot and well handled.
Colonel Blimp. I liked this story, particularly the last part. Very unusual film of a man's whole life.
Some of these films are old but here in Potters Bar we have to put up with old ones, as there is no competition.

I would like to stress the point that most films we see here are cut. Why? It completely spoils the film and sends *us* elsewhere. Of the six films listed only two were seen in Potters Bar, *The Gentle Sex* and *How Green Was My Valley.* *The Gentle Sex* was badly cut, and so, I should imagine from the gaps in continuity, was the other.

56 Housewife, aged 51, Axbridge.
Have only seen one film – *Bambi*, by Walt Disney – and have enjoyed it immensely – metallic voices my only objection – colours and amusing incidents excellent.

57 WAAF, LACW, aged 33, Leicester.

1 *Colonel Blimp.* I liked this film because its propaganda was subtle and good, because the Edwardian scenes, in Germany, particularly the duel, were delightful and showed a pleasant touch of humour and because of the splendid character acting of Livesey and Walbrook.
2 *Random Harvest.* The charm of Greer Garson and the unusual theme of this film appealed to me.
3 *Watch on the Rhine.* A splendid film with an unusual psychological angle. Bette Davis as usual superb – and the old American country house made a charming background. The woman who played the part of Bette Davis' mother was also excellent.[54]
4 *Fantasia*, which I saw again when I was in town at Studio 1 and which I still think is one of the greatest film experiences ever made.
5 *King's Row.* Though melodramatic this film was sufficiently well acted and well cast to 'put it over'. Betty Field's acting as the deranged Cassie was poignant and eerie and the old grandmother was delightful.[55]

6 *Dubarry was a Lady*. This was a silly film which I only went to to fill in an idle hour, but I include it because I thoroughly enjoyed it. It had a peculiar insouciant lunacy of its own and would be worth including if only for the deliciously funny impersonation of Charles Boyer at the beginning. It was colourful and had some peppy tunes and good cracks in it.

58 ATS, War Office psychologist, aged 29, Leeds.
This is a hopeless question, as I very seldom go to the films, and if I do I rarely remember what I've seen. I know I've seen and enjoyed *Casablanca*, and I can't remember a single other film except *Yankee Doodle Dandy* – which I saw by mistake and didn't like.

59 Company secretary, aged 45, Warlington.

1 *Colonel Blimp*. Because it has everything films can yet show, with supreme regard to quality and decent restraint on quantity. High-light: the best bit of acting since George Arliss's *Old English* dinner scene i.e. Anton Walbrook's long monologue.
2 *In Which We Serve*: Because it made me feel I would die for the Senior Service – and I'm hanged if I would die for any other employer. . . . Superb photography, a joy in itself.
3 *Wuthering Heights*: I carefully avoid love-story films, but this one just 'got me'. Nearer real-life love affairs than anything I have seen on stage or film before. Two real artists.
4 *We Dive at Dawn*: Second-cousin of *In Which We Serve*.
5 *I Married a Witch*: Not really good but different – as Vic Oliver used to say, for which much thanks.
6 *Dangerous Moonlight*: An authentic wedding of two artists – music and film.

60 Schoolgirl, aged ?, Dowlais, Glamorgan.

Random Harvest
Escape to Happiness
In Which We Serve
Mrs Miniver
The Moon and Sixpence
Life and Death of Colonel Blimp

Could not say why.

61 Housewife, aged 49, Sevenoaks.
I have not seen a film for 3 years.

62 Schoolmistress, aged 27, Burnley.
Favourite films:

1 *Colonel Blimp*
2 *Mrs Miniver*

3 *Gone With the Wind*
4 *The Gentle Sex*
5 *They Dive at Dawn*[56]
6 *The Pied Piper*

In most of these films there is a really beautiful actress with a good voice; and I am very susceptible to beauty of face and voice! Also in *Colonel Blimp* and *Gone With the Wind* I enjoyed the colour; in *The Pied Piper* I enjoyed the children and the little French tune that belonged to them. In *Mrs Miniver* and *Gone With the Wind* I enjoyed Greer Garson and Vivien Leigh, who were the main portions of these pictures respectively.

All these pictures have a moral tone that is above the general standard for films. They do *not* assume 1) that wealth and show are all-important 2) that sexual love is the biggest thing in life, and the only thing for women.

63   Teacher, aged 39, Burwash Weald.
Films. I've been to only one film in the year: *Gone with the Wind*. It was a great film – good acting and the film was true to a really great book.

64   Charities organiser, aged 26, Glasgow.

1 *Fantasia*
2 *Millions Like Us*
3 *Shadow of a Doubt*
4 *We Dive at Dawn*
5 *Shining Victory*
6 *The Magnificent Ambersons*

Fantasia I liked because of the beauty of the music and the ingenuity and genius with which Disney matched actions and pictures to the spirit and phrasing of the music. There was a great deal of this film which I disagreed with violently, but there were so many moments of pure joy that it more than compensated for the bits I disliked and even these were interesting. It is a film I can see over and over again without being bored. *Millions Like Us* I enjoyed, because it really was true to its title. These were real people, people one knew and liked, not film actors and actresses. It was like spending an evening with a delightful variety of people and enjoying with them all the humour of everyday-life now and in the delicious glimpse of the joys of holidays in the pre-war world. I loved the quiet charm of the heroine.
Shadow of a Doubt I enjoyed, because once more the people were real, and not just conventional hero, heroine, villain etc., though they were more exaggerated types than the people in *Millions Like Us*. I enjoyed the tense excitement of this film, its humour and the cleverness with which the

story was built up and the way insight was given into the minds of the characters by clever photography.

We Dive At Dawn I enjoyed too, because of the variety and reality of its characters, its excitement and humour and the realistic picture (or so I imagine) it gave of life on a submarine.

Shining Victory I enjoyed, because it presented in a very convincing way the clash of viewpoints between the impersonal and scientific way of thinking and the sympathetic, idealistic way. Although it was rather sentimental in bits, it did present real problems and real people and an atmosphere of devotion to work and thought which is unusual in the film world.

The Magnificent Ambersons I enjoyed, because it had a new and entertaining way of building up the story, the characters were unusual and well acted and the photography was pleasing. I was charmed too with the inventor and his daughter and their attitude to life.

65 Social worker, aged 41, London.

I tend to like films dealing with the everyday occurrences of life in wartime; films which make the significance of our everyday lives more vivid. I prefer a good British film to a Hollywood production, which, though usually more lavish and sometimes technically superior, is usually more artificial in character. I have seen a good number of films during the year which I have definitely enjoyed and appreciated. I think I would perhaps give my preference to the following:

1 *The Gentle Sex*. This gives the impression of being very like real life. The girls seem like real people, and their experiences in the ATS very much what would be likely to happen in actual fact. I like the way in which we see them all, and know something of their background, before they join up, and the way in which we may observe the development of their characters in Army life.
2 *Millions Like Us*. Much the same applies here. In this film, we also get the contrast between the life of a certain family in peacetime and in wartime. No attempt is made to give the film a conventional happy ending, which again seems more realistic. It is obviously not intended as unmitigated propaganda – as witness the scene in the Employment Exchange when Celia goes to register, and this to my mind strengthens its 'patriotic' appeal.
3 *In Which We Serve*. Here we have 'real-life' characters transported to the still less familiar atmosphere (to the ordinary civilian) of the Navy at sea – with scenes at home to link up their heroism in times of special danger with their ordinary lives as part of the nation at war.
4 *We Dive At Dawn*. Much the same applies here – in fact, I have the events of the two films somewhat confused in retrospect.

5 *Desert Victory*. An excellent documentary. Particularly thrilling was the atmosphere of suspense when the men were waiting at El Alamein for the signal to attack – then the crash of the barrage suddenly breaking out, and the skirl of the bagpipes as the Highlanders marched into battle. As a rule, I prefer a film with a certain amount of 'story' attached, but of course this particular one would have been spoilt by the introduction of a love interest or other fictional element.

6 *Mission to Moscow*. Skilful blending of fact and fiction – helping to make more vivid the impressions created by reading the rather 'heavy' book of the same title, and giving a vivid picture of wartime Russia.

66   Teacher, aged 47, London.
The only film I have seen, is *My Friend, Flicka*. Perfectly delightful.

67   Doctor's assistant, aged 40, Soutborough.
No films seen.

68   Typist, aged 15, Tottenham.
I very seldom go to the pictures but will endeavour to answer the questions to the best of my ability.

The film I enjoyed most of all this year was *The Four Feathers* because it was very exciting. I think it was rather 'far fetched' in places, but then it was only a story and as such I think it was very good. The colouring was very beautiful and also the scenery. The acting was very good too.

The Day Will Dawn was a very good film. It was rather frightening, especially if you have anybody abroad, etc., but the acting was very good, and I think it was a good idea to show the people what really is happening in the world today. *Secret Mission* and *The Pied Piper* which I enjoyed immensely were on the same lines, also Leslie Howard's *The First Of The Few*. Leslie Howard seemed very fitted for the part.

Rebecca was another good film, which takes ones mind completely off the War, and I think it is good to see these sort of films, to liven one up.

69   Foreign correspondent, secretary with US War shipping administration; aged 36, Glasgow.
I don't go to the pictures very often and after a fortnight's steady effort can remember only *two* films seen in the last 12 months, viz.
The Little Foxes. I think Bette Davis' a wonderful portrait of character.
The Remarkable Andrew. Clever plot.

70   'Household duties', aged 45, Leeds.
Haven't had much time for films.

71   Office worker, aged 42, Sunbury-on-Thames.
Haven't seen a film for years. In any case only like historical portraits, and good presentations of such.

72 Housewife, aged 37, Huddersfield.

The Petrified Forest. For the marvellous performance of Leslie Howard. (I know this is an old film but I only saw it today.)

In Which We Serve. For the excellent portrayal of the British character.

Mrs Miniver For the beauty and charm of Miss Greer Garson, and again the pride it made me feel in being British.

How Green Is My Valley.[57] I thought this was a beautiful film. It was so natural and human, true to life. It made one realise what life in the coal mines is like, for both the miners and their relatives.

The Gentle Sex. I enjoyed this film of life in the ATS – and of course the voice of Leslie Howard. I think it was the report of comradeship between the girls that appealed to me.

The First of the Few. Because it was British, and because Leslie Howard in any part is a joy to watch and hear.

I would place them in the following order of liking.

1 *How Green Was My Valley*
2 *The Petrified Forest*
3 *Mrs Miniver*
4 *In Which We Serve*
5 *The Gentle Sex*
6 *The First of the Few*

From which it will be gathered that I am a great admirer of the late Leslie Howard, and that I prefer British films.

73 WRNS, aged 23, Plymouth.

On the whole films to my mind are getting worse and worse. They seem to be nearly all propaganda and badly directed. I really cannot say that I have enjoyed many during the year but I doubt if I've seen more than 20 altogether this year. I cannot put them in any order or remember them very clearly but I quite enjoyed:

I'll Walk Beside You
Cargo of Innocents
Tales of Manhattan
Katia

Can't think of any others.

74 Welding researcher, aged 24, Sheffield.

I've only been to the pictures 9 times this year – as against about 70 pre-war. Reason – present-day films don't hold my interest sufficiently – I find films about the war boring – with one exception.

(1) *In Which We Serve*
(2) *Tales of Manhattan*

(3) *The Man Who Came To Dinner*
(4) *Thunder Rock*

Those 4 films I thoroughly enjoyed because of their psychological interest – the others I saw aren't worth mentioning. For me to enjoy a film, it has to be either of psychological interest, Beauty (e.g. *Fantasia*) or Comedy.

75 Housewife, aged 41, Petersfield.
Films, I have seen more films than usual: I must have been about a dozen times to the cinema, in the 12 months, a very high total for me: no doubt I shall increase it in London. I forget the titles of some, but I enjoyed most of the following:

Went The Day Well?
Mrs Miniver
The Gentle Sex
The Lighthouse[58]
Random Hall[59]
Gentleman Who Came to Dinner[60]
Holy Matrimony
Fortyninth Parallel
Foreman Went to France

76 Nurse, aged 60, Steyning.
I go only to some special film. Order of liking: *Fires Were Started* (Reality) *Thunder Rock*. Not specially good acting, but it did show up what happened before the war, and how the newspaper correspondents were muzzled when they tried to tell the people what was happening in the world. *Desert Warfare* for its reality.[61] No women in that for unreal romance. This is also true of *Fires Were Started*. *Millions Like Us*. Reality again. I did not have to keep thinking 'that couldn't have happened' as I do over so many radio plays or description of Hollywood pictures. I don't go to Hollywood pictures, but see some on the same programs of the other ones that I go specially to see (and there are some horrible ones, to which I generally close my eyes). For instance, when I went, in rather a tensed mood, to see *Millions Like Us* a long preview was shown of a picture with Deanna Durbin being kissed, as it was stated for a draw. In that preview she was shown kissing or being kissed by about 6 different men. THAT was the box-office view of what would draw the crowds. There are other films I would have liked to have seen but have not been able to go. *Battle of Britain* is one, *Thursday's Child* is another.

77 Schoolmistress, aged 57, London.
Have not seen a single film.

78   Office worker, aged 27, Whitchurch.
I don't think I've seen 6 films this year.

79   WAAF secretary, aged 27, Altrincham.
The Gentle Sex, Maltese Falcon, Life and Death of Colonel Blimp, Casablanca, Dumbo, Fortyninth Parallel, Next of Kin. [No order given.]

80   Housewife, aged 68, Coggeshall.
Being old and cold, I rarely go a journey to the cinema. I went to one during the year, *Colonel Blimp*, and thought it excellent.

81   Housewife, aged 37, Birmingham.
I am not a picture goer, the one outstanding picture I have seen was *Journey for Margaret*. It was real, it characterised real people the same as ourselves.

82   Housewife, aged 46, Bradford.

(a) *One of Our Aircraft is Missing*
(b) *In Which We Serve*
(c) *Colonel Blimp*
(d) *Silver Fleet*

(a) The acting throughout was superb; wellcast; no superfluous women; no romance; good story; lots of humour; Bernard Miles one of my favourite actors – so are Eric Portman and Hugh Williams.
(b) I like 'episodic' films and these 'episodes' were true to life; good acting, with Bernard Miles again; the Navy is my 'pet' Service; this film would have tied with (a) if Ralph Richardson had taken the Noel Coward part.
(c) I am not fond of technicolour films, though I must admit that the colour in *Colonel Blimp* was the most pleasing of any I have yet seen. The presentation of the story was unnecessarily involved. There was no need to have the Home Guard scenes both at the beginning and the end of the picture. The three periods were uneven in merit – I much preferred the German scenes pre-1914. The girl in the Berlin scenes was exquisite – not so good as Mrs Blimp. Again there was no 'oomph' or 'it'.
(d) Ralph Richardson, for me, would redeem the most inane of films. Esmond Knight blinded, slightly repelled me, but the story was plausible, and the Nazis not too much over-drawn.

The only other films I have seen are *Casablanca* and a horror *The Black Swan*. I saw the former on the recommendation of my sister (I should have been warned); because my son adores Ingrid Bergman; and I was deceived by the cast – Conrad Veidt, a favourite of mine, and Sidney Greenstreet. I was disappointed – banal in the extreme. *The Black Swan* was the only 'possible' when I had to find entertainment for my 17 yr. old niece. Never have I suffered anything so putrid. The technicolour was monstrous, the story of the novelette style, the acting unspeakably bad. The thought of it makes me go hot under the collar.

83   Housewife, aged 30, Sheepscombe (Gloucs.)
Have only been to two films this year. 1 *The Reluctant Dragon*. 2 *The New Moon*. Always prefer musical comedy film with good singing. Nelson Eddy for preference. Occasionally like a really humorous one. No opportunity to visit films. Have 3 children (one under 2 years), 2 eldest (aged 7 and 8½ years) have only been to the pictures twice in their lives: 1 *The Blue Bird* 2 *Fantasia*.

No convenient buses to fit in with film times . . . nearest picture house 5 miles away.

84   Housewife and part-time factory driver, aged 26, Hemel Hempstead.
Films come to this district rather late, and I don't very often go, but as far as I can remember these six are the last I have seen –

In Which We Serve: I like all Noel Coward's work.
Desert Victory The best war film produced.
Target for Tonight and *One of Our Aircraft is Missing*: enjoyed these as I am interested in flying.
Maryland: because it deals with horses and racing.

85   Clerk, aged 31, Manchester.

1 *How Green Was My Valley* for sheer poetry and the lovely Welsh feeling of it, its homeliness and yet its beauty.
2 *The Life and Death of Colonel Blimp* for catching a complete prewar atmosphere for its café abroad, and Roger Livesey's great acting.
3 *Watch on the Rhine* for a completely moving and intelligent film about Nazism – a very rare thing.
4 *When we are Married* for its lovely 'Yorkshireness' and quiet mirth and homeliness.
5 *Dear Octopus* a lot of talk to good purpose and its attitude to life as spoken by its characters.
6 A mystery film with Theresa Wright and Joseph Cotton, I cannot remember the name, directed by Alfred Hitchcock I believe . . . for its excellent holding qualities.[62]

86   Housewife and ex-science teacher, aged 54, Saxmundham.
Living in the depth of the country with no transport save a bicycle. I have only seen ONE film this year *In Which We Serve* which I thought was a marvellous film from every point of view, as a production and ideologically.

87   Nursery assistant, aged 37, Oxford.

(1) *Colonel Blimp*

(2) *In Which We Serve*
(3) *Thunderbird*
(4) *Kasdja*[63] and the *Carnet de Bal*
(5) *Journey for Margaret*
(6) *Random Harvest*

ad1) Very good, true picture of the official English attitude towards the various problems of this war: e.g. the old – the young generation of soldiers; the attitude of non hatred . . . very good colour-technic; non-sentimental ending; propaganda that doesn't clash with reality too much.

ad2) Well acted, gives a vivid idea of navy life, of the difficulty of the wife of the seaman whose heart is only half hers and who identifies himself with his ship. Restores our sense for proportion.

ad3) Well acted. The psychological conflict of the hero masterly translated into film language.

ad4) Nice, oldfashioned pictures, one takes in for its stories and as they are well acted they have your attention without rousing your readiness to criticise.

ad5) Children are always a great attraction to me in a film; especially if they are not affected and allowed to be natural. And the children in this film act well. The spirit of the home they are being brought after the catastrophes suits my own views on dealing with children and I consider it was good propaganda for this purpose.

ad6) *Random Harvest*: The idea of the man who loses his memory is attractive for a film subject and the heroine's acting was excellent.

88 Retired teacher, aged 59, Cudham (Kent).
A few war films I have seen have been impressive – can't remember the names. The only other 2 which I have seen which have struck me as good or unusual –
Col. Blimp
First of the Few (Leslie Howard as Mitchell).

89 Typist, aged 20, Reading.
I find it difficult to remember the names of some of these films and I'm not sure always if I saw them this year or last.

1 *Thunder Rock*. because it was a beautiful and intelligent film. And one wasn't 'let down' at all – anywhere.
2 *Fires Were Caused*.[64] (I think I've got the name wrong). It was a short, 'official' film, but very sincere, moving *and* human. About the work of the AFS. Photography was good and the actors were perfect.
3 *Desert Victory*. Very impressive.

4 *Life and Times of Colonel Blimp.* Amusing and it had that mysterious quality 'charm'. I liked the musical background too.

I can't think of any more. Not because I don't generally like films, but I don't often go.

90 Mother's help, aged 48, Haltwhistle.
Have not been to *any.*

91 Secretarial student, aged 16, Wirral.

(i) *Casablanca* with Paul Henreid and Ingrid Bergman – because it portrays the spirit of France so well, and all the minor characters are played wonderfully too. (I belong to the Assoc. of Friends of the Free French, knowing and loving France myself.)

(ii) *Watch on the Rhine*, with Paul Lukas and Bette Davis – superb acting, and different from the ordinary war film full of Nazi atrocities, without being fantastic.

(iii) *The Great Waltz*, with Louise Rainer and Militza Korjus – off the subject of the war, and very well acted and produced, plenty of beautiful music of the lighter kind, and a fitting tribute to one of our greatest waltz composers.

(iv) *Random Harvest*, with Ronald Colman and Greer Garson – also not to do with the war, and a very good story wonderfully acted.

(v) *Lost Horizon* with Ronald Colman – fantastic, but marvellously filmed, and full of glorious scenery; an original story, with a certain amount of moral behind it.

(vi) *Mrs Miniver* with Greer Garson and Walter Pidgeon – one of the best of our propaganda films in spite of being over-done in parts. Very good acting by the main and minor characters.

92 School medical inspector, aged 44, Northallerton.
I find I have been 65 times to the cinema during the last year. We have three picture-houses so I had a choice each time. I have classified my liking of them.

A very much enjoyed
B enjoyed
C quite liked
D forgotten what they were about, or they left me cold.
I have classified them as followed:
A = 14
B = 20
C = 17
D = 14   Total 65

This is the list of the 6 which I think I liked the best.

(1) *In Which We Serve*
(2) *Thunder Rock*
(3) *Tales of Manhattan*
(4) *The Gentle Sex*
(5) *The War and Mrs Hadley*
(6) *My Gal Sal*

I liked these because they were well photographed, well produced, had each an interesting theme particularly *Thunder Rock* and were extremely well acted right down to the minor parts. I think *In Which We Serve* is by far the best of the War Pictures. I suppose the reason is Noel Coward's superb sense of 'theatre'. I preferred *The War and Mrs Hadley* to *Mrs Miniver*, which I also saw and enjoyed because it was Americans about Americans instead of Americans about British and not quite right in detail. The acting of Charles Boyer, Charles Laughton, and the negroes in *Tales of Manhattan* was superb. *My Gal Sal* was an excellent production of the Musical Comedy type and gave an insight into the theatrical life of a time.

93 Housewife, aged 39, Otley.

(1) *Magnificent Ambersons* and *Mission to Moscow*
(2) *Colonel Blimp*
(3) *The Silver Fleet*
(4) *This Land is Mine*
(5) *Casablanca*
(6) *Alexander Nevsky*

Actually I could make the list much longer. *In Which We Serve, They Dive At Dawn* (because of Eric Portman), *Went The Day Well, The War and Mrs Hadley, Siege of Leningrad, The Human Comedy,* and *Pride and Prejudice* are a few memorable ones but the seven listed above are the ones that I liked best – they are the ones I saw more than once – or wanted to see again.

Now for the reasons.
I've bracketed *Mission to Moscow* and *The Magnificent Ambersons* together because they are the two of the list that I would have minded most not seeing. I liked the *Magnificent Ambersons* not so much because of the story which is rather trite in its essentials but because of the direction or production. The acting like the title was magnificent, the pace was good. It combined the best of the theatre with the best of the film. Also I liked the theme – it was good to get away from tanks and submarines and coastal commands (a film I also enjoyed). Also there was nothing pretentious or bogus about it. It was art holding up the mirror to nature so to speak. I saw it twice and would willingly see it again.

1 *Mission to Moscow.* I liked because I am always glad when the case for

Russia is put by the Capitalist. It also had the true authentic note – Beautifully acted, good propaganda in short all the good parts of a documentary and yet an artistic whole. I saw that twice and I wouldn't mind seeing it again.

2 *Colonel Blimp*. Once I forgot how I enjoyed this very much. Again not so much the story but the acting and direction – I saw that twice.

3 *The Silver Fleet*. I went to see that principally because I had seen Googie Withers in *They Came to a City* and because I like Ralph Richardson. I enjoyed the story – quite impossible really but while in the cinema the illusion held. There were no loose ends. A little sentimental but I can take it – that kind anyway (*The Human Comedy* is a kind of sentimentality which I can only stand if I grit my teeth – the H.C. had good moments but it was too syrupy somehow). I thought Richardson's performance particularly sincere and moving and Googie Withers was good though I preferred her as J. B. Priestley's Alice.

4 *This Land Is Mine*. I thought this a very good 'occupied Europe film'. Well directed and well acted in the main though I thought the mother overdrawn. It was a fair picture and tried to show that people are not just black and white – even a so-called Quisling may be acting from sincere motives, and even if he isn't his fault may be in his environment, not in his inherent evilness. I would like to see it again. Laughton was excellent.

5 *Casablanca*. I enjoyed this as one enjoys 'escapist' fiction. It was well done, a particularly good performance by Claude Rains and I always like Humphrey Bogart. I saw it once, wouldn't mind seeing it again.

6 *Alexander Nevsky*. I saw this twice. I think I liked the strangeness about it. Most people thought it childish (my small son aged 10 liked it immensely) but I rather liked the slow place. I thought the acting good – rather Shakespearian and the music and photography I thought wonderful. There was something inevitable and majestic about it all. A real *Gotterdammerung* feeling. Grand opera translated into the medium of a sound film and after so many slick competent American films this was an interesting change.

94   ?, ?, Ilford.

I'll Walk Beside You. Good clean sentiment, charm and humour.

Thunder Rock. Thoughtful and thought provoking.

The Passing of the Virginians. Interesting study of a type somewhat akin to a Britisher, such charm and humour.[65]

Kings Row. Good because of commonplace types studied and displayed by unusual photography. Important in showing need of psychological approach to injured people.

The Life of Handel or something like it.[66] Favourite music.

95   Housewife and clerk, aged 41, Sheffield.

We go to a cinema so seldom that I'm not much help here. I saw *Bambi* and loved it. Wd like to see it again, because it was good propaganda for animals and against man with his blasted gun. I saw *San Francisco*, having seen it years ago. It was good entertainment still, but the havoc didn't upset one so much as we have seen plenty of that round our towns lately. We saw *Springtime in the Rockies*, in colour, and thought it beautiful. The acting was quite good for the light entertainment it was – it just took us away from blackout and such for an hour or so. Recently I saw *Two Yanks in Trinidad* which infuriated me because the Americans didn't think there was a war before Pearl Harbour.

96   Housewife, aged 45, St Ives.
I have seen only three films this year

The Gentle Sex
The First of the Few
Desert Victory

I liked them all.

97   Housewife, aged 57, near Ware.
The few films I have seen recently have all been war films, *Bomber Command, Target for Tonight*, Noel Coward's *In Which We Serve*. I liked this best, chiefly I think because I am fond of the sea and all things connected with it. My father a Merchant Navy man had as a small boy sailed before the mast and I never tired of listening to his tales of the sea. I am however looking forward to seeing Leslie Howard's last film *The Lamp Still Burns*, when it comes to my district.

98   Clerk, aged 32, Westcliffe-on-Sea.

1 *The Life and Death of Colonel Blimp* – Fine acting, good story.
2 *Dangerous Moonlight* – Fine acting, good music.
3 *Mrs Miniver* – True to life.
4 *Bambi* – Amusing and sentimental.
5 *The Amazing Mrs Holliday* – Good singing, amusing.

99   Secretary, CAB, aged 50, Epsom.
Have seen only –

In Which We Serve – Admirable.
Mrs Miniver – deplorable, could hardly sit through it.
I Married a Witch – delightful fantasy, but felt that René Clair has become too much 'Hollywood'.
Fantasia – Parts of which I adored, and others hated and think it is all most unsuitable for children.
Thunder Rock – Very impressive, though having seen the play, was rather disappointed in treatment of film, felt that the play was the most

encouraging and heartening moment since the war – did not have that reaction from the film.

100   Clerk, aged 25, Hitchin.

1 *The Moon is Down* The anti-Nazi film which rang most true to me of all anti-Nazi films I have seen.
2 *Mrs Miniver* and
3 *The Gentle Sex* both because they show so well and unaffectedly the English spirit.
4 *The Great Mr Handel* although I know it was too sentimental and childish, because I love Handel's music and it was one occasion to hear it.
5 *The Petrified Forest* a very old film which came quite without special reason to Hitchin, which is wonderfully acted and gives a counter-balance to the optimistical films of today.
6 Walt Disney's *Fantasia* because of its uniqueness.

Editors' notes

1 The director was John Huston and not Lloyd Bacon.
2 *The Foreman Went to France.*
3 *Ruggles of Red Gap* (1935).
4 This is *Nine Men* (1943).
5 *Queen Victoria* was the first half of *Victoria the Great* (1937) and the second half of *Sixty Glorious Years* (1938) spliced together and re-issued as a patriotic morale booster.
6 He probably means *The Great Waltz* (1938).
7 *Out of the Fog.*
8 *The Amazing Mrs Holliday.*
9 *The Silver Fleet.*
10 *Tomorrow We Live.*
11 *Here Comes Mr Jordan.*
12 *Desert Victory.*
13 *Adventures of Tartu.*
14 *In Which We Serve.*
15 *Get Cracking.*
16 *World of Plenty.*
17 *The Moon and Sixpence.*
18 *The Man Who Came To Dinner.*
19 *When We Are Married.*
20 *How Green Was My Valley.*
21 *The Black Swan.*
22 *Random Harvest.*

23 *The Gentle Sex.* By L.H. he probably means Leslie Howard.
24 *In Which We Serve.*
25 *Fires Were Started.*
26 *The Gentle Sex.*
27 *Variety.*
28 *La Fin du Jour.*
29 *The Gentle Sex.*
30 Shorty and the Chief Petty Officer were played by John Mills and Bernard Miles.
31 The heroine of *Lost Horizon* was Jane Wyatt; the hero and his brother, Ronald Colman and John Howard.
32 The husband in *Watch on the Rhine* was played by Paul Lukas.
33 *Suvorov* (1940), directed by V. I. Pudovkin, starred Nikolai Cherkassov.
34 *This Land Is Mine* was a Hollywood film directed by Jean Renoir and starring Charles Laughton.
35 This is *The Great Mr Handel.*
36 This is *Dubarry was a Lady.*
37 *Nine Men* was an Ealing Studios film, not Crown Film Unit.
38 *The First of the Few* starred Leslie Howard as R. J. Mitchell. Leslie Mitchell was a newsreel commentator and broadcaster.
39 *Young Mr Pitt*, with Robert Donat.
40 She may be referring to *The Great Dictator* here.
41 *La Fin du Jour* (1938), with Louis Jouvet and Michel Simon.
42 Hero and heroine of *Escape to Happiness* were Leslie Howard and Ingrid Bergman.
43 *Moontide* was indeed the Hollywood version of *Quai des Brumes.*
44 This is *Went the Day Well?* with Leslie Banks and Elizabeth Allan.
45 *How Green Was My Valley* (1939).
46 *The Magnificent Ambersons.*
47 The Czech girl she refers to, played by Lilli Palmer, was a Polish girl.
48 *You Were Never Lovelier* is indeed the correct title.
49 *The Sky's the Limit.*
50 This is *Paris Calling*, with Elizabeth Bergner and Randolph Scott.
51 The film was called *Things to Come*, the original Wells book *The Shape of Things to Come*. The film was first released in 1936.
52 *The Great Barrier* (1937), with Richard Arlen, re-issued in 1942.
53 These films are probably *The Day Will Dawn* and *Squadron Leader X.*
54 Bette Davis's mother was played by Lucile Watson.
55 The old grandmother was played by Maria Ouspenskaya.
56 *We Dive At Dawn.*
57 *How Green was My Valley.*
58 She probably means *Thunder Rock.*
59 *Random Harvest.*
60 *The Man Who Came To Dinner.*

61 *Desert Victory.*
62 *Shadow of a Doubt.*
63 *Katja.*
64 *Fires Were Started.*
65 *The Vanishing Virginian* (1941), with Kathryn Grayson.
66 *The Great Mr Handel.*

14 The Film and Family Life

Len England contributed periodic reports on film trends as he had observed them. His report on *The Film and Family Life* (FR 2120), dated 13 June 1944, was one of the fullest. In 1940 he had noted an upsurge of 'Victorianism' in films and theatre (FR 485), affectionate recreations of the life, leisure and music of the nineteenth century and the Edwardian era, and he attributed it to a desire to escape the troubled present. In 1944, he noted a cycle of supernatural films (FR 2190e), showing 'the dead in heaven still looking very much the same as they always had been and taking a deep interest in their loved ones below'.

Every week something like 7,000,000 people in this country go to the cinema. There they spend two or three hours, watching moving pictures of every type of life, every known and unknown country, every period of history. The films that they see are of various types; cowboy, detective, comedy, social, etc. All these themes recur at regular intervals and in a regular pattern. So also does the 'family film'.

Nearly thirty years elapsed before the film producers realised that the 'escapism' which they were convinced was good box-office could be found just as well in the life of the family next door as in the adventures of cowboys and Indians, and glamorous blondes, and Keystone Cops. The advent of the talkies made domestic, less vigorously moving scenes reasonably easy to cope with, and the 'family film' was born. Shirley Temple, Mickey Rooney, Deanna Durbin shot to the top of the tree, and round about 1938–9 there was a definite cycle in 'family films'. Since then, throughout the war years, steadily both England and the USA have turned out films about everyday people in everyday life.

One of the first of these films concerned a young American boy called Andy Hardy who lived in a 'typical' American town called Carvel. The film was a great success, so great in fact that the producers had the idea of making another film about the same people and in the same surroundings. In this way the family series was born, and today, some eight or nine years later, the fourteenth Andy Hardy film is being shown in England. Other companies realised that this was far too good an opportunity to miss and there appeared on the screen a number of other film families whose adventures were told in series of films. For instance:

Blondie: still running after eight years, based on an American strip cartoon that has been running twice that time. A middle-class suburban family, father (Dagwood) who is usually doing the wrong thing, mother (Blondie herself), baby (baby Dumpling) who grows up as the boy who plays his part grows up. They live in a small American town, and their adventures are mainly of a rather domestic nature – losing a job, finding a house, having evacuees, etc.

The Aldrich Family, The Higgins Family, The Jones Family. The similarity between these three is very marked, though now only the Aldrich family is making films. The usual set-up of these families is a crochety, yet rather humorous, grandfather, father, mother, a daughter who is at her flirting age, and a son of fourteen or so who gets himself in trouble in every way, girls included.

Old Mother Riley. The taking over by the films of a music hall character. Old Mother Riley and her daughter Kitty usually start off their adventures in a slum area of some town with a background of pubs, pawnshops, washtubs. Various circumstances affect them, and they find themselves in society, in Parliament, in the ATS, owning a circus, sent abroad, and so on and so forth. Old Mother Riley is the biggest money-maker of all British films. In some parts of England cinemas that nothing else can fill are packed to the doors by Old Mother Riley.

Gert and Daisy. Another music hall turn taken over by the films. Here the films tend to be rather more episodic and keep far more to the brass tacks of life. The main incidents here are the fixing up of a local marriage, collecting salvage for the local driver, opening a special tin of pineapple, etc.

These are the main 'series' of films. Others have been started without much success, and there have been a steady stream of light-hearted family pictures not directly concerned with film families.

Parallel to this development there have been a large number of films dealing with family life on a more serious plane, and these too must have undoubtedly had their influence. Most famous of these films is *Mrs Miniver* which was the biggest box-office success of 1942, and the only war film to date to be a smash hit; it describes the impact of the war on an 'average' middle-class family in England, the raids, the marriages and deaths, the local people, the alteration of outlook. *Salute John Citizen* did a very similar thing from the British standpoint – *Mrs Miniver* was made in Hollywood. *Millions Like Us* tells the story of another British family, mainly centring on the girl who gets called up into munitions and marries an airman. *The Sullivans* is the story of five American brothers, their happy family life and their death together in an American warship. *How*

Green Was My Valley showed life in the coalfields of Wales, and *The Grapes of Wrath* was concerned with a wandering family through America. *Love on the Dole* showed England in the slump and in the slums. Noel Coward's new film *This Happy Breed* tells of twenty years in the life of a 'normal' family in Clapham. The total number of such pictures is very much smaller than that of the less serious ones, but there is nevertheless a steady flow of them.

In all these films, light-hearted and serious, there are certain definite characteristics, all of which tend to standardise the impression of the family provided by the cinema. Of these the most important are as follows:

(i) The characters in these films tend to type into father, mother, grandfather, son, daughter.

The *father* is usually rather irate and apparently bad-tempered, always offering advice that is usually not accepted and turns out to be right, usually getting sat on by the rest of the family but coming out on top at the end, very fond of his wife and kids and always doing his best for them.

Practically every character actor in Hollywood has played such a role. Witness Thomas Mitchell in *Gone With the Wind,* Lionel Barrymore in *You Can't Take It With You*, Jed Prouty as Mr Jones, James Gleason as Mr Higgins, Charles Coburn in *Heaven Can Wait*, Walter Brennan in *Slightly Dangerous*, Eugene Pallette in *The Ghost Goes West*, Victor Moore in *The Ghost Goes West*,[1] William Demarest in *The Miracle of Morgan's Creek*, Charles Winninger in *Three Smart Girls*, and so on and so on and so on.

Judge Hardy (Lewis Stone) does not fall into this category. But the main feature that is always cropping up with him is the good advice that he gives his son in their 'man-to-man' talks. Wilfred Lawson in the otherwise 'normal' family of *Thursdays Child* portrayed a father, cruel and rather forbidding but believing that he was doing right by his family.

The *mother* is less steadily characterised, but tends to be fluffy and talkative and seemingly frivolous. She is found to have a decided will of her own and usually gets her own way. Her children find that nine times out of ten her advice is right.

The late Mary Boland and Spring Byington are the two perfect examples of this type of woman. They hardly ever play any other kind of part.

The *grandfather* is not so common a character but tends to be crotchety, rather doddery, yet still capable of getting himself into trouble of all descriptions. Charley Grapewin and Harry Davenport (Grandpa Higgins) play a great many roles in this character.

The *children* usually include one adolescent boy who is getting into scrapes of every description mainly through trying to act older than his age – Andy Hardy, Henry Aldrich. His sister is usually older and is usually flirting and bringing in strange men – Andy Hardy's sister, the sister in *Millions Like Us*. A younger brother is often getting into all sorts of unlikely mischief, or alternately making wisecracks at the expense of his brother and sister.

This formation of family is by no means limited to the light film. In some way or other it very often fits its way into the more serious efforts. Rarely the whole family, but nearly always certain of the stock characters appear.

(ii) There is a very strong tendency in all these films for everything to come right in the end. This is natural and to be expected in the light films, but is not at all unusual in the serious films too. In the light film troubles invariably disappear; the dud shares that father bought turn out to be O.K. after all; the girl with the phenomenal voice does get to the ear of the maestro; the entry for the competition is the winning one; the man who bought a horse instead of a house manages to get rid of it again.

The serious film, however, tends very steadily along a similar line. The violinist who runs away in *Escape to Happiness* comes back to find his wife waiting and his child recovering and likely to live after being knocked down in a car accident. *Mrs Miniver* loses her daughter-in-law. Mr Sullivan his five sons, but everybody is inspired by the cause in which they died and feels triumphant. Even the Joads of *The Grapes of Wrath* look forward to a better future. The picture that is uncompromisingly black is *Love on the Dole*; the son gives a girl a baby, gets thrown out of home; the daughter has her fiancé killed in a strike meeting, and becomes a bookie's mistress to keep the family from starvation.

(iii) Rather linking with (ii) is the tendency in these films to ignore the less pleasant aspects of life. Occasionally a film family may find itself hard up, or one member may be attacked by illness, or father may lose his job, but such a catastrophe is a major event and all interest is then centred on it until the difficulty is cleared up. The only family character to be affected seriously by money troubles, for example, is Old Mother Riley, and these troubles never stop her getting her pint of wallop or dressing daughter Kitty in luxurious clothes. The Minivers 'an average middle class family' owned their own motor launch as well as a high-powered car. The Hardys seem to have two cars, and none of the American families seems to be without one, and a refrigerator, and a dog, and other luxuries.

Unemployment is considered only in such serious films as *Love on the Dole, How Green Was My Valley, Shipbuilders*. If Blondie's husband loses her job, it is funny only, and rarely if ever do any of the other film characters get into such a scrape at all. Sickness is hardly ever mentioned, and all the houses that are shown are roomy enough for all.

The troubles that do occur with these families are nearly all *emotional* (yet usually exclude the main trouble – the eternal triangle). The golden voice, the phenomenal child, the rich philanthropist do not turn up in real life like they do in films.

(iv) However fanciful these stories get, the opening sequences are invariably well within the bounds of possibility. Whatever the film family is doing, it is something that every other family can do; one is discussing its next door neighbour or listening to the wireless over the evening meal; one is saying goodbye to father as he makes off to work in the morning; one is dreaming of winning a film competition; one is wondering what they can give for a salvage drive; one is getting the daughter ready to take the new boy friend out.

The exaggeration in such sequences is minute, and the sequences are always long enough to build up the correct atmosphere of reality. The audience not merely find on the screen individual characters that resemble people that they know, but the whole set-up is drawn to make the screen family act *as a whole* like the family next door. Later the unlikely things happen. The daughter's new boy friend is a millionaire; the prize competition is actually won; father gets lost on his way to work. But by this time the original picture has been created.

The regular cinema-goers of this country are thus given a fairly steady picture of the 'film family'. It is housed in reasonably comfortable surroundings whatever its official class or status, it is reasonably unaffected by the normal troubles of family, money, quarrels, illness, employment. It is a family that is fairly closely connected, usually a large family, but one in which the parents, whatever their idiosyncracies, are very fond of their children. The family, if foolish, is never wicked and usually finishes up repentant. Whatever goes wrong comes right in the end. And above all whatever else the family is it is *not* humdrum; whatever the set-up is at the beginning, however normal and drab, exciting and unusual things happen before the end.

Marriage is always particularly romanticised, *The Grapes of Wrath* and *Love on the Dole* being again notable exceptions. The married people always have enough to live on, and a house of their own to live in. Domestic quarrels do not go beyond the comic stage and are usually very smoothly patched up. If mother-in-law is at first unpleasant, difficulties vanish by the end of the picture. There is never, of course, the hint of anything really unpleasant, a serious rift that cannot be patched up (unless a child star is required to do the patching later) or a miscarriage or even incompatibility. The moral is definitely that even if the path of true love does not run smooth all will still be well in the end.

Will all this have any effect on the public? No accurate survey on this point has yet been made, and it is really quite impossible to judge to any degree of accuracy. Certain points, however, do indicate that the influence of the cinema is very considerable. Witness for example:

(i) The studies of [an] American sociological group which discovered that the youth of America founded its ideas of sex, crime, travel, etc., almost entirely on what they saw at the movies.

(ii) The importance of the films in popularising songs and fashions. Old melodies like the notorious Tchaikowsky Piano Concerto reach unparalleled heights of fame through a single film, and new ones – the Warsaw Concerto – become famous overnight. The influence of Hollywood on clothes is now greater than that of Paris, and hair styles of such as Veronica Lake are copied by millions.

(iii) The whole psychology of the film fan which kept two very large film weeklies [going] before the war, which causes the mobbing of Robert Taylor or Clark Gable on their arrival in this country, which drives the poor to buy presents for people in Hollywood they are never likely to see. Here again research has gone nowhere near far enough to produce any hard fact, but there seems little doubt that the influence is very considerable.

(iv) Psychologists say that the whole set-up of the cinema, the dark, the reasonably comfortable seats, etc., are all conducive to a mild sort of hypnotism.

It is reasonable to suppose that the average man who goes to the pictures every week is influenced more than somewhat by the films that he sees on the screen. It is just as reasonable to suppose that of all films that he sees those that influence him most are the 'family films'.

It can be argued that the really successful films are nearly always the 'Cinderella' stories – the poor little girl who marries the Prince Charming who has wealth and position and good looks. It seems reasonable to believe that the reason for this is that in the opening sequences the audience can fairly easily identify itself with the hero or heroine, and follow them more easily in imagination in their subsequent adventures. If the people in the film at the start bear only slight relationship to the people in the audience, then the cinema-goer is watching a character in a film rather than a personification [sic] of himself.

Now all this applies very specifically to the family film. Emphasis has already been laid on the regularity with which the opening sequence of such films is always concerned with everyday events that could happen to everybody. Then, just as the girl in the audience sees herself as the Cinderella of the screen and personifies [sic] herself with the heroine for the rest of the film, so the average audience imagine themselves as the ideal family of the screen. As the film starts they realise that these people are like the people next door – their own family even – and what they do is done in the home town too. The story moves on and the improbabilities that creep in are not realised. The audience feel at first 'I am like them'; with a normal slick production that impression will be maintained throughout the whole film.

And the effect of all this? The *Daily Telegraph* (29.5.44) reviewing *This Happy Breed* criticises its portrayal of suburbia:

> The characters live economically in a vacuum. No one is ever out of a job, or fed up with his job; no one ever comes back grumbling about overtime or the boss's temper. Other people may worry over income tax or the butchers bill or the price of a new dress. At 17 Sycamore Road nothing so vulgar as money is ever mentioned.

The family life of films in other words is one in which the unpleasant and monotonous rarely happen, and if they do are remedied immediately and successfully. The minor troubles of life do not occur, and no petty matters interfere with the things that really count. Life has its up and downs on the films but it is not so *difficult to live*. Coupled with the exceptional realism of such films and consequent personal identification, this can only have the effect of increasing the wishful thinking attitude of the average audience. Seeing the film characters face problems very similar to their own, they feel that their own can be just as easily solved. They may very well take the same course of action as the film characters only to find out that things work [out] very differently indeed.

Perhaps this seems not very serious but the course of action taken by film characters could lead to very serious results in actual practice. The film shares that father buys may turn out ultimately to be a gold mine; in real life the purchase of dud shares may ruin the whole future of a family. Love at first sight with the handsome hero works excellently on the screen; the steady monotony of suburban life, however, is a little different to the glamour of the film romance. The couple who marry impetuously in the film manage to get on very well; in real life they may find an unexpected doctor's bill or hire purchase payment throws a spanner in the works.

The realism of such family films only increases such danger. They look like life, but they are not like life. People take subconscious advice from what they see on the screen, and act on it with possibly serious results. The whole set-up of the family film is designed this way, and the effect of such films in this respect must be entirely deleterious.

Love on the Dole faced the real facts of this situation. It was one of the biggest box-office failures for years.

Editors' note

1. Victor Moore was not in *The Ghost Goes West*.

15 *The Lion Has Wings*

The Lion Has Wings, the first feature film of the war, was made by producer Alexander Korda in six weeks flat, following the outbreak of the war. An out-and-out propaganda piece, it blended documentary and newsreel footage with staged dramatic scenes and feature film extracts to show how and why Britain was fighting Germany. Three directors were utilised (Michael Powell, Brian Desmond Hurst and Adrian Brunel), three Korda contract stars employed (Ralph Richardson, June Duprez and Merle Oberon) and footage was cut in from Korda's production *Fire Over England* (including Queen Elizabeth I's speech to the troops at Tilbury on the eve of the Armada), *The Gap* (an instructional film on the state of Britain's air defences) and an uncompleted MGM feature on the RAF, *Shadow of the Wing*. The Ministry of Information provided technical facilities and in due course received part of the film's profits. The film was trade-shown on 12 October 1939 and went on general release on 3 November. It attracted so much business at the box-office that *Kinematograph Weekly* named it along with *Pygmalion* and *The Citadel* as one of the top three British box-office successes of 1939. Retrospectively it has received a bad press for its over-obvious propaganda, its mixture of styles and its outdated class attitudes. But even at the time it provoked criticism. Tom Harrisson, writing in the *Documentary News Letter* (November 1940) called it 'a powerful contribution towards Chamberlain-ish complacency'. There were even stories that it was being shown in Berlin as a comedy. The Mass-Observation report (FR 15) was compiled by Len England and is dated 26 December 1939.

On the making and the background to the film see Ian Dalrymple, 'On the Lion Having Wings', *The Ciné-Technician* 6 (1940), pp. 10–13; Anthony Aldgate and Jeffrey Richards, *Britain Can Take It: The British Cinema in the Second World War* (Oxford, 1986), pp. 21–5.

Summary of story of *The Lion Has Wings*

(1) England at peace

Shots of the British countryside; new buildings being built before the war; the training of the young with physical culture and special schools; hospitals; the English playing games, rowing, cricket, tossing the caber.

(2) Comparison of English Life and German

The English about their daily duty, the Germans marching in their thousands; the Germans listen to Hitler speaking, the English do 'Boomps-a-daisy'; German cavalry march past, girls on English beaches ride donkeys; a vast German meeting (sound track of sheep baaing); Hitler speaking, English bookies at the Derby, cut with one another, the King and the whole Royal Family doing the 'Chestnut Tree' at the King's Scottish camp.

(3) History of the German rise to power

Hitler speaking; shots of Dolfuss and his funeral; German march into Austria; signing of Munich; march into Czechoslovakia; march into Memel; quotations from *Mein Kampf* read by the commentator.

(4) England's preparation

Shots of the Navy; of march past of the Guards watched by the King; tanks being tried out somewhere in England; long shots of the RAF at Hendon (1937) with various manoeuvres, formation flying, smoke screens, etc. Ground shot of Ralph Richardson and Merle Oberon as husband and wife watching the performance. Richardson talks to a German airman.

(5) England's manufacture of arms

Making of Wellington bombers; of A-A guns; of shells; of bullets, especially machine gun bullets.

(6) History of the crisis

The story told very rapidly chiefly in posters of Hitler's claims on Poland; Mr Chamberlain's speech, heard in various houses, finally in Oberon's house. Richardson enters as 'God Save The King' is being played. Oberon asks him if we are prepared; he replies better than ever before, and then has to go to his station. The air raid warning. Brief shots of air raid havoc in Poland. Connecting shot of an aeroplane under cover in a field in Britain.

(7) The raid on the Kiel Canal

News passed to a certain squadron that they are to bomb Kiel; planes are got ready, bombs loaded, one marked: 'One for Adolf'; pilots are given full details on the map by squadron leader; one complains that he will have to postpone a party till next day; further details outside; planes leave, routine on board shown; also the good spirits of the crew as one asks Sparks to get Mr Middleton on the wireless; a ship is sighted and a message of good luck is given; the German navy is sighted and bombs are dropped; shots of bombs hitting; the actual pilots are seen on their return.

Connecting shot of balloons going up.

(8) Details of an imaginary air raid on England

The German pilots are given their orders; a spy gets the news through to Britain; the RAF works out details in a control room with charts on which the exact position of the Nazi planes can be seen; outside the army on the watch making jokes, one complaining that all his life he has wanted a dark room and now in the black-out he can't use it, another warning them that the Nasties are coming over and they must give old Adolf a kick in the pants.

(9) Elizabeth and the Armada

(Flashback) England at night being warned of the approach of the Armada; Elizabeth speaking to her army; brief shot of the navy going out to meet the Armada.

(10) Imaginary air raid (contd)

Flight A goes into action; air battle; Flight B goes into action; searchlights and anti-aircraft guns; return of Flight A; one Nazi squadron through but will not face the balloon barrage; on its way back it is engaged by B Flight and some are brought down. All clear.

(11) Woman's part in the war

Richardson returns and goes with his wife to the river. She talks of the sacrifices that are called for from women and they have never complained. Richardson falls to sleep while she is talking.

FADE OUT: THE END.

Observers' reports

The Lion Has Wings was observed five times at different cinemas, at the Leicester Square Theatre, at Tottenham Court Road, at Cricklewood, at Streatham, and at Worktown [Bolton]. Here is a typical report.

> Observer: LE. Date 9.12.39.
> Weather Conditions: fine and warm.
> Time: 3.00 to 4.15.
> Place: Gaumont, Streatham.
> Audience: 6d. and 1s. seats entirely full, large number standing by 3.30.
> Equal numbers men and women; sprinkling of children.

	Action:	*Response:*
(a)	Pictures of the English countryside. The Commentator says: 'this is England where we believe in Freedom'	General whispering at first but gradual silence
(b)	Houses and new buildings in England	Whispers (2)
(c)	Care of the young. Schools and hospitals and physical fitness	Murmurs of sympathy at children in hospital, then much louder (2) at the sight of baby in bath
(d)	The English playing games; rowing, swimming tossing the caber	Laugh (2) at caber tossing
(e)	Shots of German soldiers marching in perfect time	Laugh (2)
(f)	Continued contrast between England at play and Germany preparing for war	Comment (2) and one or two laughs
(g)	Shot of 'Boomps-a-daisy'	Laugh (2)
(h)	First sight of Hitler	One 'Oh' 2 or 3 hiss
(i)	Comparison between the horses used in England for recreation and in Germany for military uses	Laughs (4) at German horses with bumping riders
(j)	Further shot of Hitler	2 or 3 hisses

(k)	Shots of a German assembly; sound of sheep baaing	Laughs (3)
(l)	Shots of Hitler speaking cut with bookies at the Derby	Continuous laughs (3)
(m)	The King at his Scottish Camp	Immediate clapping (5) for 3 secs
(n)	King, Queen and Princess do 'Chestnut Tree'	Continuous laughs (4) At end claps (4)
(o)	History of the German rise. Hitler speaking in 1933	Titter at speech
(p)	Shots of German people, the civilians	N.r. [No response]
(q)	Austria. Dolfuss speaking, then his funeral	Comment (1) at Dolfuss
(r)	March into Austria	N.r.
(s)	March into Czechoslovakia. Brief shot of Mr Chamberlain at Munich	N.r.
(t)	Memel	N.r.
(u)	Extracts read from *Mein Kampf*	N.r.
(v)	'The same as the last war'. Shots of the Kaiser	Comment (1)
(w)	Shots of the navy	Coughs (3)
(x)	And of the army, culminating with the Guards on parade	Claps (4) for Guards
(y)	Very brief shot of the King reviewing Guards	Claps (3)
(z)	Tanks and mechanised units	Comment (1) at end
aa)	The Air Force. Shots taken at Hendon 1937 of formation flying	N.r.
ab)	Ralph Richardson (R) seen as pilot officer	One or two comment
(ac)	More shots of the plane manoeuvres. Commentator mentions that we have much expanded since	N.r.

(ad)	R meets his wife Merle Oberon (O) and makes a pun	Titter at joke
(ae)	Details of how a plane is made	Coughs (1) increasing
(af)	Details of how A-A guns and bullets are made	Coughs (2) at beginning, comment at bullets, more coughs at end
(ag)	Short history of the crisis	N.r.
(ah)	The PM's speech as heard in various homes, finally in that of O	N.r.
(ai)	R enters just as 'God Save the King' is being played on the wireless	No sign of discomfort whether to stand or not
(aj)	At end R asks 'What was that?'. O asks him if we are prepared, he replies never better and then goes off to his station	One person laughs at 'What was that?'
(ak)	O. watches him go. Then the sirens go and she rushes off to the Hospital where she is a nurse	N.r.
(al)	Brief shots of air raid havoc in Poland	N.r.
(am)	Brief shot of planes camouflaged in a field	N.r.
(an)	News comes through that a raid is to be made on the Kiel canal	N.r.
(ao)	The planes are got ready for action	Coughs (1)
(ap)	RAF man chalks 'One for Adolf' on a bomb	Laugh (1)
(aq)	Officer gives directions to pilots as to where they are to go and what they are to do	N.r.
(ap)	One airman says that his party will have to be put off until the next day	Laugh (1)
(as)	Further details to the pilots	Talk (1)
(at)	The planes leave	N.r.
(au)	The wireless operator of leading plane is asked to get Mr Middleton	Laugh (1)
(av)	Further detail of plane organisation and discipline	Coughs (1)

(ax) The ships are sighted; the bombs are got ready including the one marked 'Adolf'   One laugh at 'Adolf'

(ay) The bombs are dropped and score direct hits   Comment (3)

(az) The planes return   N.r.

(ba) Commentator announces that although scenes have been reconstructions the men getting out of the planes are the actual pilots   Claps (5) for about 4 secs

(bb) Other preparations are made. The RAF stand by in their tents. One has the 'Hitler wanted' sign on it   Laughs (1) at 'Wanted'

(bc) The balloon protection and the anti-aircraft   N.r.

(bd) Shots of Berlin. The chief of air staff gives his orders. Commentator notes the difference between the way that orders are given in England and Germany   Laughs (2)

(be) A spy carries through the message and all England is warned to expect an air raid   Coughs (1)

(bf) The Fighter Command stands by in special Control Room   Coughs (1)

(bg) One man on the watch complains that he has always wanted a dark room and now in the black-out he has to watch the birds   Titter

(bh) News comes through. Sergeant says that they must stand by for the Nasties and to give Adolf a kick in the pants   Laughs (2)

(bi) Back to the days of Elizabeth when the Armada was repulsed in the same way by the united front under Queen Elizabeth   Coughs (1), slight murmur as Flora Robson appears as Elizabeth

(bj) The planes take off against the raiders   Comment (1)

(bk) Pilots are told to get ready to meet the enemy. One is half sleeping and has to be called again   Laugh (1) at mistake

(bl) They see the enemy and go into action   N.r.

(bm) A second flight goes out to intercept a second part of the raid   Coughs (1)

(bn)	Searchlights and anti-aircraft go into action. Tracer bullets bring one plane down	Tracer bullets cause comment
(bo)	The first flight returns	N.r.
(bp)	The third part of the enemy raid advances on London. But they see the balloon barrage and turn back only to be caught by a British squadron	Coughs (1). One says 'ssh'
(bq)	Then all clear signal	Comment (1)
(br)	R returns to his home	Rustles (1).
(bs)	O. comes home and they go down to the river. .. R. says 'Isn't this perfect?'	At the remark 'Isn't this perfect?' the lights failed. Laughs (4)
(bt)	O. speaks of the sacrifice of women all through the ages, trying to make a better world for their children	Throughout the scene the lights were flickering and the sound very bad as well so no real indication of the reaction of the audience was given
	THE END	Two clap

A comparative table of all five reports made on *The Lion Has Wings*.

	LE 30.10.39 Leicester Square Theatre	*BC* 27.11.39 Paramount, Tottenham Court Road	*HN* 2.12.39 Queens, Cricklewood 7.30.	*LE* 9.12.39 Gaumont, Streatham 3.0.	*AH* 16.12.39 Lido, Bolton 2.10.
(a)	N.r. [no response]	Coughs	N.r.	Whispers (1)	N.r.
(b)	N.r.	N.r.	N.r.	Whispers (1)	N.r.

	LE 30.10.39 Leicester Square Theatre	BC 27.11.39 Paramount, Tottenham Court Road	HN 2.12.39 Queens, Cricklewood 7.30.	LE 9.12.39 Gaumont, Streatham 3.0.	AH 16.12.39 Lido, Bolton 2.10.
(c)	Murmurs of sympathy	Murmurs of sympathy	Laugh	Murmurs of sympathy	Murmurs of sympathy
(d)	Laugh at Scot	Laugh at Scot	Laugh at Scot	Laughs (2) at Scot	N.r.
(e)	Slight hiss	N.r.	Laugh	Laughs (2)	Laughs
(f)	N.r.	N.r.	N.r.	Comment (2) and laughs	N.r.
(g)	N.r.	Laughs	Loud laughs	Laughs (2)	General laughter
(h)	Slight hiss	Slight hiss	Much hissing, few boos	Slight hiss	Boos 5 secs (children)
(i)	Titter	N.r.	Laughs	Laughs (4)	Laughs
(j)	Hisses	Hisses	Hisses	2 or 3 hisses	Boos
(k)	N.r.	Laughs	N.r.	Laughs (3)	Comment
(l)	Loud laughs	Loud laughs	Loud laughs	Laughs (3) continuous	Boos (children)
(m)	Loud clapping	Claps	Loud claps	Loud claps (5) 3 secs	One faint clap
(n)	Laughs, claps	Laughs	Laughs, claps 2 secs	Laughs (4) claps (4)	General laughter

	LE *30.10.39* *Leicester* *Square* *Theatre*	*BC* *27.11.39* *Paramount,* *Tottenham* *Court Road*	*HN* *2.12.39* *Queens,* *Cricklewood* *7.30.*	*LE* *9.12.39* *Gaumont,* *Streatham* *3.0.*	*AH* *16.12.39* *Lido,* *Bolton* *2.10.*
(o)	N.r.	N.r.	Hiss	Titter	N.r.
(p)	N.r.	N.r.	N.r.	N.r.	N.r.
(q)	One man applauds	N.r.	N.r.	Comment (1)	N.r.
(r)	N.r.	N.r.	N.r.	N.r.	N.r.
(s)	N.r.	N.r.	N.r.	N.r.	N.r.
(t)	N.r.	N.r.	N.r.	N.r.	N.r.
(u)	N.r.	Coughs at end	N.r.	N.r.	N.r.
(v)	N.r.	N.r.	N.r.	Comment (1)	N.r.
(w)	N.r.	N.r.	N.r.	Coughs (3)	N.r.
(x)	Loud claps	N.r.	Comment	Claps (4)	N.r.
(y)	N.r.	Slight claps	N.r.	Claps (3)	N.r.
(z)	N.r.	N.r.	N.r.	Comment (1)	N.r.
(aa)	N.r.	N.r.	Comment	N.r.	N.r.
(ab)	Slight murmur	N.r.	N.r.	Slight comment	Slight comment
(ac)	N.r.	N.r.	Comment	N.r.	N.r.
(ad)	N.r.	N.r.	N.r.	N.r.	N.r
(ae)	Comment	N.r.	Comment	Coughs (1)	Comment
(af)	Coughs	Coughs	Comment	Coughs (2), comment at bullets	Comment

	LE 30.10.39 Leicester Square Theatre	BC 27.11.39 Paramount, Tottenham Court Road	HN 2.12.39 Queens, Cricklewood 7.30.	LE 9.12.39 Gaumont, Streatham 3.0.	AH 16.12.39 Lido, Bolton 2.10.
(ag)	N.r.	N.r.	N.r.	N.r.	N.r.
(ah)	N.r.	N.r.	Comment	N.r.	N.r.
(ai)	N.r.	Cough	N.r.	N.r.	N.r.
(aj)	N.r.	Coughs	N.r.	N.r.	N.r.
(ak)	Cough	Comment	Laughs	N.r.	N.r.
(al)	N.r.	N.r.	N.r.	N.r.	N.r.
(am)	N.r.	N.r.	N.r.	N.r.	N.r.
(an)	Coughs	N.r.	N.r.	N.r.	N.r.
(ao)	N.r.	N.r.	N.r.	Coughs (1)	N.r.
(ap)	Slight laugh	N.r.	Laugh	Laugh (1)	Laughs
(aq)	N.r.	N.r.	N.r.	N.r.	N.r.
(ar)	Slight laugh	Slight laugh	Laughs	Laugh (1)	Laugh
(as)	N.r.	N.r.	Coughs	Talk (1)	N.r.
(at)	N.r.	N.r.	N.r.	N.r.	N.r.
(au)	Slight laugh	Laugh	Laugh	Laugh (1)	Slight laugh
(av)	N.r.	N.r.	N.r.	Coughs (1)	N.r.
(ax)	N.r.	N.r.		Laugh at 'Adolf'	N.r.
(ay)	N.r.	N.r.	Cheers, claps	Comment (3)	N.r.
(az)	N.r.	N.r.	N.r.	N.r.	N.r.
(ba)	Loud claps	N.r.	Loud claps 5 secs	Claps (5) 4 secs	N.r.
(bb)	N.r.	N.r.	N.r.	Laugh (1) at 'Wanted'	N.r.

	LE 30.10.39 Leicester Square Theatre	BC 27.11.39 Paramount, Tottenham Court Road	HN 2.12.39 Queens, Cricklewood 7.30.	LE 9.12.39 Gaumont, Streatham 3.0.	AH 16.12.39 Lido, Bolton 2.10.
(bc)	N.r.	N.r.	N.r.	N.r.	N.r.
(bd)	Laughs	Laughs	Loud laugh	Laughs (2)	Boo
(be)	N.r.	N.r.	N.r.	Coughs (1)	N.r.
(bf)	N.r.	Coughs	N.r.	Cough (1)	N.r.
(bg)	Titter	N.r.	Loud laughs	Titter	Laughs
(bh)	Laughs	Laughs	Loud laughs	Laughs (2)	N.r.
(bi)	Comment	Coughs	Much comment	Comment (1)	N.r.
(bj)	N.r.	N.r.	N.r.	Comment (1)	N.r.
(bk)	N.r.	N.r.	N.r.	N.r.	N.r.
(bl)	N.r.	N.r.	N.r.	N.r.	N.r.
(bm)	N.r.	N.r.	N.r.	N.r.	Comment
(bn)	N.r.	N.r.	N.r.	Comment at tracers	Comment
(bo)	N.r.	N.r.	N.r.	N.r.	Comment
(bp)	N.r.	N.r.	N.r.	Coughs (1)	N.r.
(bq)	N.r.	Coughs	N.r.	Comment	N.r.
(br)	N.r.	N.r.	N.r.	(see special report)	N.r.
(bs)	Comment	N.r.	Comment		N.r.
(bt)	Coughs	N.r.	Comment		N.r.
THE END	Some claps	Some claps	Claps	Two claps	N.r.

These comparative reports omit remarks overheard by observers either during the performance or after it. There follow these remarks arranged in chronological order through the film.

At (a)   Girl (18) says 'That looks like Lyme Regis' at shot of seaside
         (LE, Gaumont)

At (m)   Woman says 'That's nice isn't it?' (HN)
         Woman says 'Got it all off pat hasn't she?' (of Margaret Rose)
         (BC)

At (x)   Boy says 'Grenadiers are better than Germans, aren't they?'
         (AH)

At (aa) Boy says 'Look at them' and later 'Look at that smoke screen'
         (AH)
         Woman says 'It's marvellous, isn't it?' (LE, Gaumont)

At (ae) Comments are 'Lord, how can they do it?'
                      'Gosh, it's marvellous!'
                      'Crikey, what super things' (HN)

At (ak) One or two say 'The sirens' (LE, Gaumont)

At (ao) Boy says 'Ooh, bombers. Watch them start off. Go on. Get in.
         Start off.' (AH)

At (as) Argument between two girls as to which pilot is Derrick de
         Marney (LE, Gaumont)

At (bj) Boy says 'Ooh they're off' (AH)
         Girl says 'Marvellous how it's done isn't it?' (LE, Gaumont)

AT (bm) Girl asks 'What is cornflower red?' (code signal of the planes)
         (LE, Leicester Square)

Comments overheard immediately afterwards by HN:

> 'That was a good film'
> 'Marvellous wasn't it?'
> 'A bit too much'
> 'I enjoyed it much better than ...'
> 'Damn clever'

Questionnaire

In a questionnaire on film-going habits 200 people, equally divided into
sex and age groups and into Classes B and D, were asked whether they
had seen the film *The Lion Has Wings*. Of this 200, 110 had seen the film
(Table 1).

Table 1

	Class B	Class D	Total both classes
Men under 30	15	15	30 (60%)
Men over 30	13	12	25 (50%)
Women under 30	14	16	30 (60%)
Women over 30	12	13	25 (50%)
TOTAL	54	56	110 (55%)

Of this 110, 43 people liked the film very much indeed, that is 39.1 per cent. Fuller details are given in Table 2.

Table 2

	No.	Dislike	Doubtful	Like	Strong Like
Class B					
Men under 30	15	2	6	4	3
Men over 30	13	–	2	4	7
Women under 30	14	1	2	7	4
Women over 30	12	–	1	5	6
Class D					
Men under 30	15	5	2	5	3
Men over 30	12	3	1	3	5
Women under 30	16	1	–	6	9
Women over 30	13	2	2	3	6
TOTAL	110	14 (12.7%)	16 (14.5%)	37 (33.6%)	43 (39.1%)

In a further analysis class was ignored and the results in Table 3 were obtained.

Table 3

	No.	Dislike	Doubtful	Like	Strong like
Men under 30	30	7	8	9	6 (20%)
Men over 30	25	3	3	7	12 (48%)
Women under 30	30	2	2	13	13 (43.3%)
Women over 30	25	2	3	8	12 (48%)

Again, taking no notice of class or sex the figures are as shown in Table 4.

Table 4

	No.	Dislike	Doubtful	Like	Strong like
Under 30	60	9	10	22	19 (31.6%)
Over 30	50	5	6	15	24 (48%)

With Table 4 divided into classes, the result is as shown in Table 5.

Table 5

	No.	Dislike	Doubtful	Like	Strong like
B Under 30	29	3	8	11	7 (24.1%)
B Over 30	25	–	3	9	13 (26%)
D Under 30	31	6	2	11	12 (38.7%)
D Over 30	25	5	3	6	11 (44%)

Finally, regarding sex only, the figures in Table 6 were obtained.

Table 6

	No.	Dislike	Doubtful	Like	Strong like
Men	55	10	11	16	18 (33%)
Women	55	4	5	21	25 (44%)

With Table 6 divided into classes, the result is as shown in Table 7.

Table 7

	No.	*Dislike*	*Doubtful*	*Like*	*Strong like*
B Men	28	2	8	8	10 (25.7%)
Women	26	1	3	12	10 (38.5%)
D Men	27	8	3	8	8 (29.6%)
Women	29	3	2	9	15 (51.7%)

Of the 110 people who had seen the film, 65 gave reasons why they liked or disliked the film (Table 8).

Table 8

	No.	*Gave reasons*	*Did not give reasons*
B Men			
under 30	15	7 (46.7%)	8
Men			
over 30	13	9 (69.2%)	4
Women			
under 30	14	10 (71.4%)	4
Women			
over 30	12	5 (41.7%)	7
D Men			
under 30	15	10 (66.7%)	5
Men			
over 30	12	9 (75%)	3
Women			
under 30	16	9 (56.2%)	7
Women			
over 30	13	5 (38.5%)	8

These 65 who offered further criticism gave their reasons for like and dislikes shown in Table 9.

Table 9

Criticism	Class B				Class D				No.	%
	M U 30	*M O* 30	*W U* 30	*W O* 30	*M U* 30	*M O* 30	*W U* 30	*W O* 30		
Propaganda										
(approval)	1	3	1	–	–	–	–	–	4	6
(disapproval)	–	3	3	1	3	3	2	1	16	24
Details of film										
England prepares										
(approval)	1	–	–	–	–	1	–	–	2	3
(disapproval)	1	–	1	–	–	–	–	–	2	3
Hitler – bookie										
(approval)	1	–	–	–	–	–	–	–	1	1.5
Kiel raid										
(disapproval)	1	1	1	–	–	–	–	–	3	4.5
Fights										
(disapproval)	1	–	–	–	–	–	–	1	2	3
Flying										
(approval)	–	–	1	–	–	–	–	1	2	3
(disapproval)	–	–	–	–	–	–	1	–	1	1.5
German skill										
(underestimated)	–	2	–	–	–	–	–	–	2	3
German men										
(villainous)	–	1	–	–	–	–	–	–	1	1.5
British airmen										
(inefficient)	–	–	–	–	1	–	–	–	1	1.5
TOTAL										
Details	5	4	3	0	1	1	1	2	17	25.5
Technical										
excellence	1	–	1	–	–	–	1	–	3	4.5
Story										
(disapproval)	–	–	2	1	1	2	1	2	9	13.5

Criticism	Class B				Class D				No.	%
	MU	MO	WU	WO	MU	MO	WU	WO		
	30	30	30	30	30	30	30	30		
Stars unnecessary	1	–	–	–	–	–	–	–	1	1.5
Stars not seen enough	–	–	–	–	1	–	–	2	3	4.5
Taken from: The Gap	1	1	1	–	1	–	–	–	4	6
Fire Over England	1	–	–	–	–	–	–	–	1	1.5
The Londoners	1	–	–	–	–	–	–	–	1	1.5
Newsreels	–	–	1	–	–	1	1	1	4	6
News (app)	–	–	–	–	–	–	1	–	1	1.5
Old material	1	–	–	–	–	1	1	–	3	4.5
TOTAL Story critics	5	1	4	1	3	4	4	5	27	40.5
Information Revealed organisation	–	1	1	1	–	2	–	–	5	7.5
Did not reveal organisation	–	–	–	–	–	1	–	–	1	1.5
Could not believe it	2	2	1	2	1	1	–	–	9	13.5
TOTAL Information	2	3	2	3	1	4	–	–	15	22.5
Emotions roused Interest	–	–	1	–	–	–	–	1	2	3
Security	–	–	1	–	–	–	1	–	2	3
Thrills	–	–	–	–	1	–	3	–	4	6
Terror	–	–	–	–	–	–	–	1	1	1.5
TOTAL	–	–	2	–	1	–	4	2	9	13.5

Misc. Not understood, M 20 D, too long, M 20 B, liked because friends did not, M 20 B.

Briefly dividing this into approval and disapproval produces Tables 10 and 11.

Table 10

	Class B	APPROVAL *(Total criticisms 92)* Class D
Propaganda	5	–
Details of film	3	2
Story	–	1
Technical excellence	2	1
Information	3	2
Emotional pleasure	2	6
Total	15 (16.5%)	12%

Table 11

	Class B	DISAPPROVAL *(Total criticisms 92)* Class D
Propaganda	7	9
Details of film	9	3
Story	11	15
Information	7	3
Emotional disapproval	–	1
Total	34 (37.4%)	31

These points can best be expanded by quotation:

Well, the beginning of the film was fairly amusing, and it was fairly good propaganda. The bloke who did the Hitler-bookie bit was certainly a genius. For the rest of it I thought it was pretty lousy really. The Control Room was fairly good propaganda, I suppose, but the fights were just absurd. To tell you the truth I can't remember much about it so that's a fairly good indication of how good it was. (M 20 B)

I didn't think much of it. It didn't get anywhere very well and I'd seen it all before. The stuff in the aeroplane was good but the rest was all old. Ralph Richardson and Merle Oberon weren't necessary at all. And again it was too efficient. If we know all about what happens as soon as the plane leaves Germany, how is it that some get over Scotland? Part of it is cribbed from *The Gap* and part of it from *Fire Over England*. And it's hopeless to say that what they showed you at first was England; it was the sort of England that you meet with once in a lifetime. It went on too long and it didn't say anything new. (M 20 B)

It was good propaganda. But one thing about it to my mind was the absolute immunity of the British fighter and the extraordinarily easy manner in which the German fighter was blasted out of the sky. Mind you, I believe the Fighter Command is very good. Another thing I noticed was that it had a lot of shots taken out of *The Gap*. And in the Kiel Canal Raid some of it looked very authentic but they didn't show the losses. (M 30 B)

As can be seen by far the largest criticisms were on the propaganda element in the film:

I don't think that England will ever like propaganda but it was very well done not like the German wireless. (M 20 B)

You got too much propaganda stuffed down your throat. (M 20 B)

Yes, damn clever propaganda. A real success. Lousy really. (M 20 B)

It was an awfully good picture and it acts as a very good piece of propaganda. (M 40 B)

Quite good, the propaganda was not too heavy. (M 45 B)

Not bad propaganda but it was spoilt by being left in British hands. (M 30 B)

It was quite good but more for propaganda than amusement. (M 40 B)

I didn't think much of it, it was more of a propaganda picture. (M 50 B)

It was too much propaganda. (F 20 B)

It was very well done but there was too much propaganda. (F 20 B)

Propaganda, but quite an enjoyable evening in its way.

It was very good propaganda but they thrust it down your throat. (F 20 B)

Rotten, too much propaganda. (F 25 B)

Propaganda pure and simple, don't think so? (F 40 B)

It was propaganda but it was quite good all the same. (M 20 B)

It was too much propaganda. I think it un-British to shove propaganda down your throat like that. They should regard us as more intelligent than that. (M 20 D)

It could have been a lot better, but it could have done with a bit less propaganda.

Always the best as usual, we British. (M 25 D)

I didn't think much of it, it was a propaganda film. (M 40 D)

It was all right but it was a sort of propaganda picture. (M 50 D)

We don't want to see that but we might send a copy to Germany. (M 30 D)

Well, wasn't it sweet of old England. I nearly cried my eyes out. (M 40 D)

As a film it was marvellous, but as a theory, as a story it was too much propaganda. (F 20 D)

I didn't like it at all, it was all propaganda. Nobody wants to see that sort of thing, it's not entertainment. They get enough of that on the news. (F 25 D)

Propaganda. (F 50 D)

About details of the film the following are typical remarks:

It was interesting but I thought that at Kiel they might have been shot at by a gun or a ship. (M 20 B)

It was magnificent but there was one thing I didn't like, and that was the portrayal of the Germans as swarthy villains. (M 50 B)

It rather underestimated Germany. . . . (M 30 B)

As for the Kiel raid bit I thought that that was rotten with just one bomb dropping on a ship. (F 20 B)

I don't like to see our chaps half asleep and having to issue orders twice. I was disappointed. (M 20 D)

It showed you England getting ready, I enjoyed that. (M 50 D)

We've seen it all in the news pictures except for the Kiel Canal bit. (M 30 D)

I think it was very nice but there was too much flying in it. (F 25 D)

Only three commented on production and such things:

Technically it was surprisingly good. (M 20 B)

I thought it was well taken especially the reconstructed scene in the aeroplane. (F 20 B)

As a film it was marvellous but as a story. (F 20 D)

There were more opinions about the story:

One thing I thought was very bad. On in the same show was a GPO film on London called *The Londoners* and vast chunks of it appeared again in *The Lion Has Wings*. (M 20 B)

It reminded me of *The Gap*. (F 20 B)

It was very good but there was not enough story. (F 20 B)

A bit too newsreel wasn't it? (F 25 B)

Topping but the love element might have been cut out; that was stupid. (F 50 B)

The story was terribly silly. (M 25 D)

Terrible, it was the same as *The Gap*. (M 20 D)

Ralph Richardson and Merle Oberon you only see three or four times. (M 20 D)

There was no continuation, it was just a collection of snapshots. It could have been good with a story. (M 30 D)

. . . the story was just sort of bits like the Kiel Raid. (F 20 D)

It was quite good. A lot of news reels put together of course but good all the same. (F 25 D)

I was disappointed in it, it was more of an illustration than anything. I thought it was going to be a drama. (F 40 D)

I liked it but Ralph Richardson and Merle Oberon didn't have much to do. (F 60 D)

I didn't care much about the love bit. (F 50 D)

There were so many well-known people in it for such an ordinary picture. So many good people spoiled it; it would have been better with less-known people. (F 40 D)

I liked it as a newsreel. (F 20 D)

Here are some quotations as to what people thought about the amount and the quality of the information provided by the film:

I'm afraid I couldn't believe half of it. (M 20 B)

It was fine to see how it all works. So many don't know. (M 45 B)

You've got to take the first half with a pinch of salt. (F 20 B)

It showed the workings of how things were done in England. (F 25 B)

I was disappointed, it was much too optimistic. (F 50 B)

It was thoroughly up to date and it showed you what people were going through. (F 50 B)

I was thinking that looks very beautiful but with my experience of government departments I didn't believe it. But it emphasises the bravery of the RAF. (F 40 B)

It was very good as far as explaining the organisation goes. (M 40 D)

There was no plot but there was a little education in it. (M 60 D)

Well, there was a lot held back, they only gave you a glimpse of what happened. But I think it was O.K. (M 30 D)

A few merely remarked how the film affected them:

It makes you feel much safer. (F 25 B)

Quite an enjoyable evening in its way and quite interesting. (F 20 B)

Quite thrilling. (F 25 D)

Lovely and exciting wasn't it? (F 20 D)

I was thrilled to death. (F 25 D)

I think all people who are nervous should go and see it. (F 25 D)

I enjoyed it to a certain extent but not entirely as I don't care for that sort of war pictures. It was all terrifying. (F 60 B)

Finally a few miscellaneous remarks:

Well everybody said it was so bad that I liked it. It does happen like that doesn't it. (M 20 B)

Not bad. I thought it was so complicated. (M 20 D)

Mighty hard to guess what those bullets were. (F 25 D)

As propaganda . . . for persons of our generation it was very good. But apparently the younger people didn't think so much of it. (M 50 D)

Actual summing up of the picture ranged from:

Tripe (M 20 D)

Pretty awful (M 20 B)

Utter tripe (M 20 B)

to:

A bloody fine picture (M 25 D)

Magnificent (M 50 B)

Most people, however, answered 'very good', 'good', 'very nice', etc. Many who had not seen the film offered comments on it:

It's good as far as I've heard, though there wasn't enough tail in it. (M 25 B)

I dodged it. It was all flag-wagging wasn't it? (M 50 B)

I didn't want to see that, it's a lot of tripe. (M 30 B)

I heard it was rather good. (M 40 B)

I heard it was the usual tripe. (M 35 B)

I have heard about it. All about the war, but I don't want to be reminded of the war. (M 40 B)

I've heard it's not as good as it's cracked up to be. (F 20 B)

A good picture was on somewhere else. (F 20 B)

No, I heard it was a propaganda film. (F 35 B)

I haven't but they all say that they made Germany such a terrible looking lot and us too damn fine. (F 40 B)

I thought it was a war film. Apparently it isn't. Some propaganda I should think. (F 50 B)

I wouldn't have gone because it's propaganda and about war. You've got enough of that in the papers. (F 40 B)

I don't go to any British propaganda films least of all about the war. (F 45 B)

I heard it was well worth seeing but I daren't face the black-out. (F 45 B)

We didn't think it would appeal to us with a lot of aeroplanes. [?]

I didn't go and see it, my wife said she couldn't go and see it. [?]

I never went. There was nobody much in it was there. (F 20 D)

I didn't go as it was a war picture. I know it was propaganda but I didn't go (F 60 D)

As well as from the questionnaire one observer collected a few individual opinions:

> No, I haven't seen it but all sorts of people have told me I must go as a duty. (M 20 B)

> No I haven't seen it and I wouldn't go and see it. It was only made to stir up patriotic feeling in a country that doesn't want war. (M 40 D)

> My father [says] 'oh it's magnificent, you must go and see it.' He hasn't seen it himself but he thinks it right to talk like that. (M 20 B)

> I must see that. I don't like aeroplane films but I feel it's my duty. (F 50 B)

Press reviews of *The Lion Has Wings*

Reviews of *The Lion Has Wings* were taken from the following papers:
Daily Telegraph (31.10.39 and 6.11.39) (*DT*)
The Times (31.10.39) (*T*)
Manchester Guardian (31.10.39) (*MG*)
News Chronicle (31.10.39) (*NC*)
Daily Mirror (3.11.39) (*DM*)
Daily Sketch (31.10.39) (*DS*)
Observer (29.10.39 & 3.11.39) (*O*)
Sunday Dispatch (5.11.39) (*SD*)
Sunday Express (5.11.39) (*SE*)
Sunday Pictorial (5.11.39) (*SP*)
New Statesman (3.11.39) (*NS*)
Listener (23.11.39) (*L*)

Analysing these under the same categories as the questionnaire:

No.	Dislike	Doubtful	Like	Strong like
12	–	2	3	7 (58%)

Analysing their criticisms under the same headings as the questionnaire:

Propaganda (approval)	6 (50%)
(disapproval)	2 (16.6%)
Details of film	
Hitler – bookie scene	2 (16.6%)
Kiel raid	1 (8.3%)
Flying scenes	2 (16.6%)

Story

Fire Over England (disapp.)	1 (8.3%)
Old material (disapp.)	1 (8.3%)

Technical skill	1 (8.3%)

Typical quotations from the Press:

The film indicates so clearly Britain's case for entering the war that no plans should be spared to ensure its wide circulation in neutral countries. (*NC*)

The effectiveness of the film would of course be greater if it gave a less misty explanation of the purposes for which the Lion is using its Wings. But for that fault Mr Korda is not to blame. (*NS*)

If you want to see an exciting, amusing and intensely interesting picture don't miss *The Lion Has Wings*. (*L*)

Admirably the film expresses the attitude in which Britain has approached the war. Convincingly it shows her determination and her ability to fight it to a finish. (*DS*)

If anybody had told me that I would sit in my seat for an hour and a half and enjoy every minute of what is frankly a propaganda film I'd have eaten my hat. . . . It is not only a wonderful pictorial tribute to the RAF but a film you'll enjoy as much as I did. (*DM*)

The Dominions will love it. For us at home – a film to give you courage and confidence on the darkest days. (*SE*)

The Lion Has Wings is in many ways a fine piece of work, but it is a hotch-potch of brilliant ideas and dull, languid stuff that should have been left on the cutting room floor. (*SD*)

Considering how rapidly the whole thing was rushed through, I do not see what else [than a hotch-potch] could reasonably have been expected. (*DT*)

War audiences may not want war films in general but I believe they will welcome this one. Its chief effect is to send people home from the cinemas quickened and in an odd way reassured. (*O*)

Altogether it was a better work than we had dared to hope. (*MG*)

On the whole it is stirring and good-humoured propaganda. (*T*)

Advertisement of *The Lion Has Wings*

Quotation from *Kine*, 7.12.39:

W. J. Rawkins attracted large numbers of potential patrons to the Savoy, Burnt Oak, by means of a model RAF Display which he presented in one of the spacious alcoves of his lobby to publicise *The Lion Has Wings*.

Above a realistic balloon barrage was suspended model airplanes in formation flight. On one side of the floor, amidst model shrubs and trees was a miniature anti-aircraft battery and every type of Army transport lorry. On the opposite side, partially hidden by foliage, lay field ambulances and a fire-fighting unit, each complete in detail. The whole scheme was shrouded in fine white silk net which gave a truly cloudy effect and was surmounted by a Royal Air Force pilot's wings 20 feet in length.

A similarly effective display was to be seen last week at the Regal Edmonton where, to advertise *The Lion Has Wings*, E. C. Hurry had suspended two small red-painted model aeroplanes (made, I suspect, by himself and his staff) before a vigorous picture of Wellington twin-engined bombers in action in the clouds, so that one gained the impression of a hefty aerial combat in progress.

Of course, *The Lion Has Wings* lends itself admirably to a variety of stunts, and although those cited above are interesting, many exhibitors might have gone further. One of those who did so was Stanton Jeffries, the Odeon Musical Director, who is temporarily in charge of their Edgware Road theatre.

The aeroplane in this case was a scale model of a Hampden twin-engined bomber, lent by Handley Page Ltd. The title of the film was also emphasised by a stuffed lion loaned by a Piccadilly taxidermist. The display was surmounted by a larger reproduction in colour of the RAF badge.

A civic send-off was given to the picture by the Mayor and Mayoress who attended in state and later in the week Air Vice-Marshal Sir Charles Longcroft and Lady Longcroft, attended with the Paddington Air Defence Cadet Corps.

Quotation from *Kine*, 24.12.39:

Although last week Croydon showed three concurrent runs of *The Lion Has Wings* what might be termed the lion's share of the business fell to Eric G. Bowker. One reason of the interest displayed by Odeon patrons was the presence on the opening night of fifty members of the RAF, an event which was fittingly splashed with pictures and editorials on the amusement pages of the local papers. The visit apparently caused quite a stir, because Mr Bowker told me that each succeeding night patrons enquired: 'Are the RAF coming again tonight?'

A number of Air Force Officers and men also attended the Odeon, Balham, where Captain Harold Arnold also acted as host to the Mayor and Mayoress of Wandsworth at a gala presentation of the Korda picture.

Incidentally the Odeon managements seem to have corralled most of their local mayors wherever *The Lion Has Wings* has been shown. The Mayor and Mayoress of Chingford were present at the Odeon at the invitation of A. W. Street who also entertained a number of officers and men of the Forces stationed in the area.

The Major and Mayoress of Guildford, with members of the Corporation, officials and leading townsfolk, also attended the premier Guildford presentation. A display of model aeroplanes arranged by Manager W. Mills in collaboration with the local Model Aero Club afforded patrons a foretaste of the contents of the film.

Quotation from *Kine* 28.12.39:

The concurrent screening of *The Lion Has Wings* at the Odeon and Carlton cinemas, Norwich, provided S. Newbury and H. F. J. Smith respectively with a good field of exploitation. Special space was jointly taken in all the local Press prior to and during the week's screening. A large lion's head with wings attached mounted on three-ply and pushed through all the main streets of the city with a special 12-sheet poster carrying the title of the film with times of screening at both cinemas drew considerable attention.

Group Captain Vincent, RAF, attended the opening performance at the Odeon, accompanied by a party of officers of a Norfolk aerodrome.

In the foyer at the Odeon a series of photographic enlargements of modern aircraft was displayed on loan from the Air Ministry which also lent RAF ensigns. These were draped over the tabs.

The display of model airplanes, exact replicas of those used for the instruction of pilots, was also a prominent feature of the local store.

Quotation from *Kine*, 4.1.40:

Details of the exploitation of *The Lion Has Wings* continue to arrive but the subject matter of the film necessarily limits the efforts of the showman to the obvious course of inviting Civic and Service personalities to the presentation. This course was adopted at the Colchester Regal, by Manager Alex Thompson, who supplemented his publicity by the exhibition of a striking device which occupied a prominent position in the foyer.

The picture was showing simultaneously at four Southampton kinemas and at two – the Regal and the Plaza – it was given a civic send-off by the Mayor who expressed the gratitude of the public to the management of Odeon theatres for securing the film for early screening.

A distinguished audience, including the Mayor, attended a special screening at the Odeon, Newport, Mon., where R. N. Parrington obtained considerable editorial support for the presentation.

A preview of *The Lion Has Wings* at the Regal, Rotherham, was also attended by a large civic party augmented by numerous service guests. The parade of the latter outside the theatre attracted the interest of considerable crowds. The publicity obtained by F. W. Morris from this function was all the more valuable as pictures appeared beneath the advertisement of the presentation in the *Advertiser* on a page devoted to news of local men in the Services.

The Air Ministry were most helpful in loaning RAF pennants and bunting, two large gilt RAF crests, and also several large aerial photographs showing the various types of aircraft used in the Service, to Q. E. Cheeseman who was presenting *The Lion Has Wings* at the Majestic, High Wycombe, Bucks.

In addition, they loaned a special illuminated display cabinet which carried a moving band on which was written: 'The King and Queen paid their first visit to the Cinema since the war commenced to see *The Lion Has Wings*. See it yourself at the Majestic'.

All this material was erected in the vestibule a week prior to playdate with the bunting, pennants and crests draped around the walls.

From the local model aircraft club, Mr Cheeseman obtained the loan of 30 working models of airplanes, which were grouped around the pay-box and hung from the ceiling and made everyone stop and examine them.

On the opening night there was a civic reception and performance, at which the Mayor and Mayoress and members of Council and their ladies were present. June Duprez, the Korda star, made a personal appearance and gave a delightful speech from the stage.

The affair being the first civic performance to be held in the town, Mr Cheeseman reaped first-class publicity, all the town talking about the occasion.

Miscellaneous data on *The Lion Has Wings*

Extracts from a letter from Christopher Brunel, son of Adrian Brunel, director, and himself an assistant cameraman on the film (2.12.39):

> I don't know how much it cost; it seems that this is a very closely guarded secret and even my father has no idea how much. A lot of people worked for nothing, and I know that Alex Korda did a lot to help

the film. United Artists distributed it so . . . Korda will get his money back that way. In passing a point of interest (and a cause of a great deal of discontent in the industry) is that the Government gets paid, I think it is, 50% of the profits (this is, of course, apart from Income Tax, etc.) for giving 'technical facilities' in the production of the film. The opinion is that if after getting this money from the film, the Government does not help the industry the industry will not be sorry if there is a Red revolution!

The shooting took about three weeks. There were three units working – Michael Powell's doing most of it such as airplane scenes, control rooms; Brian Desmond Hurst's doing the Merle Oberon – Ralph Richardson stuff together with some other bits such as civilian observer posts; my father's doing a lot of crisis scenes and about the Dutch spy on the quayside. . . . I think I am right in saying that Micky Powell went and did some of the flying stuff – I don't mean the inside-the-bombers stuff – as soon as the film was proposed, before the story was written; anyway some of the shooting took place before they had finished writing it.

The cutting took about 3–4 weeks; immediately the first feet had come from the labs. the cutting started and so it is difficult to say how long the cutting took. It is correct to say, though, that from the time the last shot was taken to the time the film was ready for exhibition was about 3–4 weeks.

I think some use was made of *The Gap* but I don't think any of *The Conquest of the Air*. No doubt both films were viewed while the *Lion* was being planned. All the control room stuff (although I believe there was a lot of it in *The Gap*) was shot specially for *The Lion* the set being constructed at Denham with technical advice from the Air Ministry. I think that Vincent Korda, the Art Director, actually visited the real thing. . . .

As far as I know very little of the Kiel raid is the real stuff; I have only seen the film once so I can't remember well, but I think there is a shot from the air of one of the German ships, rather a misty shot – this is genuine; also a shot of a bomb hitting a German ship; this may or may not have been authentic. That was all except for the scenes AFTER the raid. I imagine the time taken in the film was considerably reduced. Both Ralph Richardson and Merle Oberon were, I am pretty certain, already under contract. With regard to the supporting parts such as Anthony Bushell, Robert Douglas, Derrick de Marney, Milton Rosmer, some of them might have been under contract (I believe Anthony Bushell was) but most of them were obtained at a flat rate (by special arrangement with the agencies – £5 a day I believe) or else gave their services free – on account of the patriotic theme of the film. . . . There were a lot of other big names used but since cut out – Gibb McLaughlin,

Miles Malleson (who also worked on the story) Nellie Wallace, Ronald
Shiner. I think the introduction of the 'human interest' parts were only
valuable in so far as they enabled the use of Ralph Richardson and
Merle Oberon – both big box-office stars.

Quotation from *Kine* 7.12.39:

The Lion Has Wings . . . is now playing to packed and enthusiastic
audiences throughout Canada and is repeating in the Dominion the
triumphant success which it is enjoying in this country.

In Leeds, at the Paramount Theatre, *The Lion Has Wings* broke every
record and played to more people in one week since the opening of the
theatre. In Manchester it has been playing concurrently at three
theatres, the Paramount, Oxford Street, and Market Street theatres
where in spite of the concurrency it also broken all records.

On the general release last week nearly 200 copies of the film were
playing simultaneously in North London and the Provinces. This is
believed to be the largest number of copies of any feature film ever used
for general release.

The Lion Has Wings is being 'dubbed' for exhibition in France. This
French dubbed version will be ready for showing throughout France,
Belgium, Switzerland, and other countries in Europe where French
dialogue is more widely understood than English within the next week
or two.

Copies of the English version have been sent to France for showing to
the BEF.

Arrangements are also in hand for the showing of the English version
with subtitles in the languages of the country, in other European
countries, including Portugal, Holland, the Scandinavian countries,
Spain, etc.

Quotation from *Daily Telegraph* 23.12.39:

The first performance of the French-speaking version of *The Lion Has
Wings* was given in Paris tonight to an invited audience.

Sir Edward Villiers came over from London to represent the Ministry
of Information, and the British Ambassador, Sir Ronald Campbell and
Lady Campbell, were present, together with members of the Embassy
Staff. Gen. Bouscat, Chief of Staff of the French Army of the Air, and
other important French military and civil authorities also attended,
together with a number of French and British 'aces'. The latter were
given special leave.

Among the distinguished people who saw the film it was somewhat
touching to meet Mme Bleriot, widow of the first man to fly the Channel.
She was much moved when she saw the record of her husband's take-off
on that occasion and his landing near Dover.

The film was given an enthusiastic reception throughout, particularly the portion dealing with actual incidents of life in the Air Force.

The Lion Has Wings was distributed without bars; i.e. the distributors gave no guarantee that they would rent the film to only one cinema in each area. As a result 200 copies of the film were made instead of the usual seventy, and the film was shown by the Gaumont, Granada, Odeon, and County circuits and most of the independents. Only the ABC did not touch it.

The Lion Has Wings was the first film to be seen by the King and Queen after the outbreak of war.

16 *Let George Do It*

Mass-Observation was particularly interested in humour and its sources. This is demonstrated by the in-depth analysis of *Let George Do It* (1940). George Formby was the top British box-office star from 1938 to 1943 inclusive and the nature and structure of his films emerges from the analysis. The film was one of the most successful of 1940, outgrossing the Hollywood classic *The Grapes of Wrath* in its first month of release (August). The graphs and detailed response to laughter tables are omitted. The report was compiled by Len England and is dated 1 October 1940. It formed Mass-Observation File Report 435.

For a full discussion of the film and its role in wartime propaganda see Anthony Aldgate and Jeffrey Richards, *Britain Can Take It: The British Cinema in the Second World War* (Oxford, 1986), pp. 76–95.

Made at ATP Studios, Ealing
Produced by Michael Balcon
Directed by Marcel Varnel
Script by Angus MacPhail, Basil Dearden, John Dighton, Austin Melford
Length: 7,392 feet
Running time: 82 mins
Cast includes: George Formby, Phyllis Calvert, Garry Marsh, Romney Brent

Briefly the story is as follows: George is mistaken for a Secret Service agent and is sent to Bergen to find how the band leader, Mark Mendez, sends code messages to Germany. He gets the code but is trapped in a submarine with Mendez. He captures the submarine, and saves a ship from being sunk. (The story is given in greater detail in Appendix 1, which also contains a numbered list of the jokes observed.)

The method of observing the film is explained in Appendix 2.

Opinion of the film as a whole

Analysis was made of the Press reviews of *Let George Do It* (for list of papers consulted see Appendix 3) and of the opinion of the general public (see table).

	Press	Public	Men	Women
His best	24%	8%	17%	–
Very good	20%	23%	33%	16%
Amusing	36%	61%	50%	68%
Bad	8%	8%	–	16%
Not in good taste	12%	–	–	–

There is considerable difference between Press and public opinion, the Press – always considered to be antagonistic to George Formby – liking the film more than the general public. But only 8 per cent of Press and public alike think the film is bad, women seeming to dislike the film more than men. The Press comment occasionally on the bad taste of the film, in that it reveals the inefficiency of the British spy system in Norway.

Many of the press articles praise the film at length:

Formby fans will love it. It's cheerful, tonic, topical and British made (*Sunday Express*, 14.7.40)

Never mind the plot, but don your lowest and most receptive brow, cast your inhibitions to the winds, and enjoy fully a manifestation of that social quality which in no small measure represents what we are fighting to defend. (*Spectator*, 19.7.40)

I can sit through the film again and again just watching his artistry. Verdict o.k. (*Sunday Chronicle*, 14.7.40)

but the public was much more terse and less enthusiastic, e.g.:–

It was all a bit of a farce. (M 20 B)
It was an afternoon's entertainment. (M 20 B)
It was all right but not much more. (F 25 C)

Twenty-four per cent of the Press considered the film to be the best that George Formby has ever made; the only reference made to any other film of Formby's was in the *Sunday Express* to *Come on George*. But of the public only 8 per cent, a third of the Press figure, thought this film his best. Specifically asked what they thought his best film, the remaining 92 per cent answered

It's in the Air	46%
No Limit	19%
Trouble Brewing	9%
I See Ice	9%
(don't know)	9%

A further emphasis upon the difference between Press and public is shown in the fact that many critics admitted that they usually disliked George Formby – 'he's not my cup of tea' – but that they were won over by *Let George Do It*. Of the public, on the other hand, 86 per cent say that they like George Formby usually but only 72 per cent liked him in this picture. The Press, in other words, have become more favourable to George since this picture, while he has lost some of his popularity with the public.

The funniest sequence

There are five main comic sequences in *Let George Do It*: the cabin scene (jokes 10–13), the vamping (jokes 17–19), the bakery (jokes 23–7), the dream (jokes 31–8) and the submarine (jokes 41–50).

References to each of these sequences were extracted from the newspapers, and compared with the answer to Question 5 in the questionnaire (what do you think was the funniest part of the film?) and with the amount of audience response to each sequence as noted in cinema observation. In the table the sequence considered the most popular is regarded as 100 and others taken as a percentage of that figure.

	Press	Public (questionnaire)	Public (cinema)
Cabin	–	66	100
Vamping	33	–	82
Bakery	33	100	83
Dream	100	66	54
Submarine	66	100	80

There are the most striking differences here not only between Press and public but also between what the public laughed at at the time and what they said was the funniest sequence afterwards.

Audience response indicates that the cabin sequence was the funniest scene of all, but a much smaller number mentioned this scene in answer to a direct question, while the Press does not mention it at all. The dream sequence, on the other hand, is regarded as funniest of all by the Press (though some critics took objection to it), and as fairly funny by the public in answer to the questionnaire, but audience observation shows that the sequence was on the whole a failure and raised only half as many laughs as the cabin sequence. The vamping sequence raised more laughs than either the dream or the submarine but is not mentioned at all by people asked some days after they had seen the film.

The divergence between what people laughed at in the cinema and what they thought funniest afterwards can probably be explained as follows. In an unpopular sequence there might be one joke which was highly popular, and people mentioned the sequence considering only the one joke in it; for example, the loudest laugh for any joke in the picture was for George socking Hitler on the jaw and the Storm Troopers being delighted, but the rest of the dream sequence was not at all well received. Statistical analysis of audience reaction therefore puts the dream sequence at the bottom of the list. But some, remembering their delight at Hitler's defeat, thought in retrospect that the whole sequence was as funny as the one joke, and named that.

Variation between Press and public is explained by the fact that the attitude of the Press is distinctly that of the West End picturegoer. Even the film critics in the 'popular' papers selected as the funniest scenes those that were well received at the Empire and the Ritz, and ignore the jokes that caused much laughter in Fulham and the Elephant and Castle.

The jokes

Most popular joke

The ten most popular jokes in the film judged by audience response to the film are as follows:

1 (Joke 39;93 points) After George knocks Hitler out, the Storm Troopers cheer.
2 (Joke 10;87 points) George wraps petticoat round his head.
3 (Joke 12;86 points) George answers when Nielson knocks at his wife's door.
4 (Joke 19;85 points) George dislodges plaster in his fight with Iris and it falls on Nielson.
5 (Joke 29;85 points) 'She's got five children: it's all my fault.'
6 (Joke 49;83 points) George is shot out of a torpedo.
7 (Joke 50;83 points) George lands from the torpedo right into Mary's arms.
8 (Joke 18;80 points) 'Do you like One Night of Love?'
9 (Joke 27;80 points) The loaf containing the camera goes inside the ovens.
10 (Joke 24;78 points) George is swinging on a wire when it becomes electrified.

It will be seen in the first place that that no one joke has an overwhelming majority and that the big laughs are distributed fairly evenly throughout the whole film. Other points that emerge such as the lesser popularity of topical jokes and of spoken jokes will be discussed later in the report.

Jokes categories

The jokes in *Let George Do It* were divided into the usual Mass-Observation categories (see appendix 4). Twenty-five points were awarded to the most popular joke, 24 to the next and so on down the scale. The result of this analysis is as follows:

Ill-health	106
Sex	79
War, politics, etc.	55
Domestic affairs	44
Clothes	24
Money	13
Art	6
Lavatory	2
Domestic objects	1

Mass-Observation has done various other joke studies at times from 1937; the main studies have been of concert parties in Blackpool, of pantomimes, of music halls, and the analysis of a joke competition in the *Sunday Dispatch* (for further details see Appendix 4). Accepting the most popular category in each study as 100 and the others as a percentage of this figure, the results shown in the table are obtained:

Blackpool		*Music hall*		*Pantomime*		*Film joke**		*Formby*	
1 Ill-health	100	War	100	War	100	Ill-health	100	Ill-health	100
2 War	91	Sex	64	Clothes	55	Sex	55	Sex	72
3 Dom. affs	80	Ill-health	28	Sex	46	Dom. affs		War	51
4 Local	73	Dom. affs	24	Ill-health	34			Dom. affs	40
5 Sex	70	Clothes	23	Dom. affs	34	Art		Clothes	22
6 Dom. objs	58	Lavatory	18	Food	27			Money	11
7 Food	55	Sport	13	Live big shots	18			Art	5
8 Money	55	Dom. objs	11	Dead big shots	15			Lavatory	2
9 Art	55	Alcohol	10	Art	15			Dom. objs	1
10 Alcohol	53	Food	9	Dom. objs	11			Food	1

*The full report containing these figures is at the moment unobtainable.

In almost every case the most popular categories are the same, though the proportionate popularity varies considerably. In every medium, ill-health, domestic affairs and sex constitute three out of the five most popular categories, and in four out of the five mediums war is also among the first five. At Christmas, 1939, when the music hall and pantomime survey was made, the war was going well for Britain and war jokes were wildly popular – in each case they constitute nearly a third of the total number of jokes. In August, 1940, they are much less popular, but still get half as many references as the top category.

These comparative lists emphasise once more the connection of humour and cruelty. It is not simply that ill-health is the most popular category in three out of five mediums, but a breakdown analysis of sex jokes reveals that a great many of them are also concerned with abnormalities such as prostitution, illegitimacy, adultery, and so on.

Spoken jokes

To the fifty jokes observed in *Let George Do It*, the total response in points (see Appendices 2 and 11) was 2,642; this means an average of 52.8 for each joke, and of 2.4 for each joke at each performance.

Of the 50 jokes observed, 14 were spoken and the other 36 depended upon action. The table shows the response to each type.

	No.	Points	Average response for each perf.	Average response each joke each perf.
(Total)	(50)	(2,642)	(52.8)	(2.4)
Spoken	14	639	45.5	2.1
Acted	36	2,003	55.6	2.5

The difference here is not large, but it does serve to emphasise the fact that the cinema is not the right medium for verbal wit. Exactly the same conclusion was reached from the *Sunday Dispatch* competition where the number of verbal jokes mentioned was less than one in ten.

Topical jokes

In *Let George Do It* there are 11 jokes which depend for their humour on the topical situation (jokes 1, 7, 22, 31, 33, 34, 35, 36, 37, 38 and 44).

	No.	Points	Average response for each perf.	Average response each joke each perf.
(Total)	(50)	(2,642)	(52.8)	(2.4)
Topical	11	398	36.2	1.6
Non-topical	39	2,244	62.7	2.9

There is here a most marked preference for non-topical jokes; of the eleven topical jokes, only one (no. 38, Troopers Cheering at George knocking out Hitler) really succeeded at all, while the two least successful jokes in the film (nos 7 and 33, The Ministry of Information joke and the 'Ace of knaves – Adolf Hitler') are both topical references. On average, the topical joke is only a little over half as popular as the non-topical one.

Most of the topical references are in the dream sequence where George dreams that he goes over to Germany on a barrage balloon and knocks Hitler out. The Press, as a whole, regarded this as the funniest scene in the film, but there were some critics who considered it quite the reverse. Of the seven critics who referred to this scene, four were enthusiastic and three were hostile. Typical quotations:

The nightmare sequence is inspired. (*Sunday Dispatch*)

The only thing I didn't like in *Let George Do It* is the incident of the Hitler burlesque. Few of us to-day really think of Hitler as a funny man. It leaves a sour taste in what is otherwise a tonic picture. (*Observer*)

On this point press and public do agree, for almost the same proportion of 4 pro to 3 con appeared in the answers to the question 'What did you think of the scene with Hitler?'

	Press	Public
Like it	57%	58%
Dislike it	43%	42%

There is here a difference of only 1 per cent, and in each case nearly 50 per cent say that they dislike the sequence.

The story of *Let George Do It* is highly topical throughout: yet the evidence goes to show that the film succeeded in spite of its topicality and not because of it.

Difference in response to jokes: regional

In Appendix 5 graphs [omitted] indicate the varying response to the ten most popular jokes in the West End, semi-suburban area, middle-class suburb, working-class suburb, and provincial town. The only startling difference of opinion is over joke 49 (George being shot out of the torpedo) which gained an average laugh of only 2 in the West End but rose to 4.8 in working-class suburbs. Elsewhere the graphs show fairly steady curves with a rise in the volume of laughter in the suburbs.

It does seem, however, on further analysis that the West End prefers the more subtle wisecrack while the suburbs like the slapstick. The response to spoken jokes in the West End, for instance, is slightly higher than in the suburbs (2.3 as opposed to 2.1) and most of the spoken jokes are more subtle than the acted ones. On some occasions in the suburbs such remarks as 'She's got five children and it's all my fault' (joke 29), and the Neilson's insistence on one bedroom (joke 16) misfired entirely but in the West End these were two of the big laughter points.

The difference between semi-suburban cinemas (Dominion, New Victoria, Stoll), middle-class and working-class suburbs is almost entirely one of degree and will be discussed later in the report. For every joke except one (joke 12), the middle-class response is slightly higher than the semi-suburban, and the lower-class higher than the middle.

Provincial audiences seem to be even more fond of slapstick than suburban areas. The bakery sequence, for instance, where all the humour is derived from George being covered in dough is far more popular in the provinces than anywhere else. An even better example is provided by the dream sequence. It has already been noted that the most popular joke in the film was not George knocking out Hitler but the Storm Troopers being so delighted by their leader's defeat. In the provinces, however, this misfired while the actual KO was greeted with much laughter and cheers.

On the whole, however, the regional and class differences in humour are small, as other M-O studies have indicated. In Appendix 6 a graph [omitted] shows the response to the film in all five areas and it will be seen that the variation in response is small, even between West End and provincial.

Difference in response to jokes: sex

At some shows of *Let George Do It* representative counts of 50 people were made. Roughly the proportion of men to women was 40 to 54 in the afternoon (6 per cent children) and 52 to 48 in the evening. This difference serves in some degree to distinguish between the jokes that appeal to men and women.

In the following graph [omitted] total joke response at afternoon performances is indicated by a pencil line, and at evening performances by a dotted line. The almost exact parallels of the two lines indicate that there cannot be a great deal of difference between the tastes of men and women. This conclusion was also reached in the analysis of the *Sunday Dispatch* joke competition where it was found that the difference between the entries from men and from women was practically negligible.

General on jokes

All the material indicates the general similarity in joke material and joke response. The difference between the subject matter of jokes made at Blackpool in 1937 and in *Let George Do It* is small, while the response to any given joke does not differ greatly in class groups or in sex groups.

Spoken jokes were less well received than acted ones, and the topical references were not a success.

Miscellaneous on film

Songs

In *Let George Do It* there are four songs which occupy about twenty minutes, nearly a quarter of the running time. But each one of them has a place in the story and two of them are essential to the development of the plot. The response to these songs, on the whole, seems good.

Song	*Continuity*	*Response*
1 'Grandad's Flannelette Nightshirt'	George on a station waiting room sings, then makes a collection.	Fair popularity.
2 'Mr Wu is Cleaning Windows Now'	George sings at an audition for Mendez.	Well received; very loud laughter at line 'I've heard the rumours Girls go out without their . . . garters'.
3 'Count Your Blessings'	'Pep' song, sung on broadcast and containing code message.	Well received; frequent comment and humming.
4 'Ooh, Don't the Wind Blow Cold'	George sings this as he tries to escape from Mendez.	Little laughter but much interest.

In answer to the question 'Do you like George Formby singing in the middle of his pictures?':

Like them	45%
Like him singing but not these songs	20%
Dislike them	28%
No opinion	7%

His songs, then, are popular but these particular songs were not as much liked as some. Also if nearly a third of the audience dislikes George Formby singing it is surely excessive to devote a quarter of the running time to songs.

A small number (12 per cent) said that they liked the songs because they 'fitted in', and because 'they form a continuous sequence and are not forced in'. The fact that there was nothing incongruous in George bursting into song added to the pleasure.

Propaganda element

It has already been shown that 12 per cent of the Press considered *Let George Do It* to be in bad taste, and also to be bad propaganda; only one paper (*The Spectator*) thought that the film was good propaganda. The arguments against the film as propaganda were mainly these:

(a) The story concerns spying at Bergen when the audience knows that the German Fifth Column at Bergen was first-class.
(b) The British spy in one scene discloses all her plans to somebody who turns out to be a total stranger, then says 'What a colossal fool I've been.'
(c) The Hitler sequence is simply encouraging wishful thinking.

Specifically asked 'Do you think the film was propaganda?', 80 per cent of the public questioned said 'no', the other 20 per cent said 'yes' very doubtfully. Only one person considered it bad propaganda on the grounds that it was 'not pronounced enough to be effective'.

Method

The survey of *Let George Do It* provides a check on Mass-Observation method for observing films. In Appendices 6, 7, 8 and also on page 10 graphs [omitted] indicate the variation in response between

(a) afternoon and evening audiences.
(b) West End, semi-suburban, middle-class, working-class, and provincial audiences.
(c) the audiences at the same cinema at all four performances in one day.
(d) audiences in full and half empty cinemas.

Considering these individually:

(a) The two graphs are almost identical, the response at the evening performance being slightly higher than that in the afternoon. Nowhere is there a difference of more than one point between response at any joke in afternoon and evening.
(b) 4 of the 5 graphs on this chart show considerable similarity but the provincial audiences react differently; particularly jokes 37 and 49–50. The degree of response is greater, and the peaks of the graph higher, in working-class suburbs than in middle class, but the rise and fall is closely similar; it is a difference in *volume* only.

(c) The similarity between each of the four performances observed in one day is very marked. Nowhere is there a difference of more than one point.

(d) It seems that in a cinema that is crowded the audience is more willing to laugh, and less jokes are complete failures. The degree of response is therefore more even throughout the jokes. In an empty cinema the good jokes will still get good laughs, but the mediocre ones are more likely to fall.

All this tends to show that if a film is observed once or twice, a fair estimate of its general reception can be gained, and the main laughs, or the sequence that raises the most comment, will be discovered.

General conclusions

In brief the conclusions of the survey are these:

1 Press and public alike enjoyed *Let George Do It* but the Press was more enthusiastic about it than the public.
2 Press and public differ considerably in their opinion of the funniest sequence in the film; the public's idea of the funniest sequence when asked afterwards is not the same as when observed in the cinema.
3 The most popular jokes in the film are similar in their categories to those in other joke mediums.
4 Spoken jokes are less popular than acted ones.
5 The topical jokes in the film were not on the whole popular.
6 The difference in response to the film varies little from area to area but the broader jokes are appreciated more in the suburbs than in the West End, and more in the provinces than the suburbs.
7 The difference between the jokes liked by men and by women is small.
8 The songs in the film are popular.
9 The film is considered bad propaganda by the Press, but is not considered as propaganda at all by most of the public.
10 The survey proves that a fairly accurate impression of the way that an audience is reacting to a film can be gained from only one or two observations of the film.

Appendix 1: Outline of the story and list of jokes

Outline of the story

George is a member of the Dinky Doos concert party. He is mistaken for a British spy, who, as a ukelele player, is being sent to Bergen to spy on

Mark Mendez, a band leader. He arrives and with the help of Mary, a reception clerk in the hotel, discovers the code by which messages are sent to Germany. But he himself is found out and dosed with scopolamine, a drug which makes him tell the truth. After giving the game away he dreams that he catches Hitler single-handed. Then he escapes but lands up in a German submarine. He succeeds in warning the British ships, in making the Germans surrender the submarine, and finally is shot from a torpedo-tube straight into the arms of Mary on a British vessel.

The jokes

(First scene Mendez band; in the number 'Ooh, Don't the Wind Blow Cold' the ukelele player is shot dead; he was a British spy discovered by Mendez. Second scene a theatrical agency where a new ukelele player is engaged, also a secret service man. One man is sent from the agency to Dover to meet the agent, another to contact the Dinky Doos concert party)

1 The man to contact the Dinky Doos concert party says that he cannot go 'I've made arrangements. . . . It's my night for ARP.' The agent replies, 'Oh well, here's a quid. Take her with you.'
2 He arrives on the station in black-out. Asks station-master 'Where are the Dinky Doos?' Station-master: 'Second door on your left, sir.'
3 He then asks a woman, 'Are you a Dinky Doo?' The woman's husband replies, 'She is not. She is a respectable married woman.'
4 The agent finally finds the Dinky Doos. Shines his torch and illuminates George Formby's puzzled face.
5 The party link hands and go off. George links hands with the married couple (the Nielsons) by mistake. The husband tries to hit him but only knocks himself out.
6 In bar. George and the other Dinky Doos perform a conjuring trick by which George's ukelele turns into a nightshirt.
   (George sings 'Grandad's Flannelette Nightshirt'.)
7 The Dinky Doos are going by boat to Blackpool 'because the railways have all been commandeered by the Ministry of Information'.
   (George is mistaken for the secret service uke player and is put on the boat for Bergen.)
8 On the boat are Mr and Mrs Nielson. They want to share a cabin but the boat is too full. But it is finally arranged and a steward is told to inform Mr Nielson. This waiter has been badly tipped by Nielson so he decides to tell him 'in the morning'.
9 On deck George is looking under the weather.
10 He looks at his berth ticket upside-down and reads 9 instead of 6; 9 is Mrs Nielson's cabin. He goes in, without thinking douses one of her

petticoats in water, wraps it round his head and goes to sleep in the top bunk.

11 Mrs Nielson and George snore in harmony.

12 In the morning Mr Nielson knocks on the door to wake his wife. George answers. Mr Nielson nearly faints at the thought of a man in his wife's room.

13 He breaks down the door; in doing so he falls flat on his face. George walks over him into the corridor.

14 At the customs the inspector looks at a bag that is full of conjuring tricks. A cigar box turns into a flower pot and hits him.

15 Later he puts what he thinks to be a piece of tobacco in his mouth. George pulls yards of ribbons, sausages, etc. out.
(George gets to the hotel and is given an audition with the band, sings 'Mr Wu is Cleaning Windows Now'. He is given a message by Mary, the British spy-receptionist clerk, to meet her in room 64. This message is read by Mendez who sends Iris, a vamp, there first.)

16 Nielson arrives at the hotel and is insistent on one bedroom only.

17 George sees Iris the vamp and makes a bolt for the door.

18 Iris (referring to perfume) says 'Do you like One Night Of Love?' George calls for Moother.

19 George is finally chased under the bed and Iris's attempts to dislodge him dislodge the plaster of the room beneath, occupied by the Nielsons.

20 In his own bedroom Mary is waiting for George. She tells him of the existence of a music code by which Mendez broadcasts information to Germany. George says 'It's as plain as the nose on your face', then sees it is a rude remark.
(Mary tries to get George to help her after she finds that he is not a British spy, but he refuses.)

21 As he undresses he argues with himself, even while cleaning his teeth.

22 Then he thinks it would be nice to be 'Sir George Hepplewhite, VC'
(George goes to Mendez's room but is rebuffed. He returns and hunts for the code. Mendez returns and he hides under the bed.)

23 Mendez drops a coin under the bed. To prevent him looking under, George takes a coin of his own and puts it within easy reach of Mendez.
(George finds the plans and takes photographs of them. Unfortunately he drops the camera out of the window into a bakery.)

24 George swings out of the window on a wire. The wire becomes electrified and he drops into the bakery too.

25 Swinging down a chute after the camera he gets covered in flour.

26 Still in pursuit George gets into a vat and is churned up.

27 He watches the camera (inside a loaf) go inside the ovens.
(He escapes with the camera and he and Mary decipher the code. He sings 'Count Your Blessings'. Mendez's plan fails but Mendez is sure that George was the Betrayer.)

28 George, talking to Mary, pretends to be angry with her; when a stranger appears, George says he will report her to the manager. The stranger says 'I am the manager.'

29 George adds, to get out of the mess 'She has five children, I am responsible.'

30 George is taken by Mendez and is given scopolamine, which makes him tell the truth. Starts off with 'I hate the sight of you.'
(Afterwards he gives away vital secrets and is left in a stupor; he dreams as follows.)

31 Mendez and his friend appear with German hats. He shoots at them, their trousers fall down and reveal short pants with swastikas on.

32 He and Mary seek a marriage that 'is made in heaven' and arrive at the Pearly Gates.

33 He presents his cards, a pack of them, and is told that he has not got the ace of knaves – Adolf Hitler.

34 He goes off in a barrage balloon to find him, passing on the way a sign 'Blackpool 200 miles, Berlin 900 miles'.

35 He sees the Fuehrer ranting below him.

36 He shins down a rope and claims Hilter as his last 'Territorial demand in Europe'.

37 George knocks Adolf out with an uppercut.

38 The Storm Troopers go mad with joy at the decease of their Fuehrer.
(George wakes up again to find that Mary has boarded the ship 'Murrayfield'. He goes to play in the band.)
(The man next to him in the band tells him that it was in that very seat, and during that very number that the previous ukelele player was shot. George, to escape being shot, wanders about the floor while singing 'Ooh, Don't the Wind Blow Cold'. He tries each exit in turn but all are guarded by Mendez's men).

39 He swings on the chandelier to get away.

40 The chandelier crashes and he escapes.
(George escapes but hides in a boat in which Mendez goes out to a German submarine. George knocks out the pilot and follows Mendez aboard.)

41 He is called to. Answers 'Jawohl' in broad Lancashire.

42 Called again. Says 'Aye', then hurriedly adds 'Jawohl'.

43 Knocks out wireless operator and tries to contact *Murrayfield*. Gets soprano on the BBC.

44 Then gets Haw-Haw saying that the British Fleet has been sunk by Winston Churchill off Wigan pier.
(He finally contacts *Murrayfield* and gives warning. But the submarine has caught up with *Murrayfield* and is ready to fire torpedo.)

45 George jabs pilot with dividers causing ship to swerve.

46 Shot of submarine rocking violently.

47 The submarine rolls this way and that and finally turns a somersault.
48 George runs from Mendez and hides in torpedo tube. The door slams on him.
49 Somebody presses the torpedo firer and George is shot off.
50 He lands on an awning on the ship and falls at Mary's feet.

Appendix 2: Method of approach to survey

1 A list of fifty jokes in *Let George Do It* was compiled and sent to investigators and part-time observers. Instructions were given for method of observing the film (see Appendix 2a) and the response to each joke was put into one of five categories, numbered from (1) to (5), indicating the various degree of response.

   The film was observed 24 times, 21 times in various parts of London, once in Watford, once in Ipswich and once in Southport. In one London cinema the film was observed at all four performances given in one day. Note was taken of time of day, number of people in the cinema, weather conditions, and so on.

2 Analysis was made of Press reviews of *Let George Do It*, and a questionnaire was as follows:

   1 What did you think of *Let George Do It?*
   2 Do you like George Formby as a rule?
   3 Do you like him in this film?
   4 What do you think was his best film?
   5 What do you think was the funniest bit of this film?
   6 What did you think of the sequence about Hitler?
   7 Do you like George Formby singing in the middle of his films?
   8 Do you think this film was propaganda?
   9 (if so) Do you think it was good or bad propaganda?

(Analysis of the questionnaire is given in Appendix 9.)

Appendix 2a: Note to observers on *Let George Do It*

On the following pages there is a list of 50 jokes from the new George Formby, *Let George Do It*. Briefly, what we want to find out is what jokes are liked best by audiences in various parts of the country.

Probably the best method for you to follow is this:

1 Read through the following pages carefully more than once before you see the film, so that, when you do see it, you will know where the jokes come and what they are.

2 In the cinema, divide audience laughter response into five categories; consider as category (1) a laugh from a few people, (2) a laugh from slightly more, and so on up to (5) for a loud laugh from the whole audience.

3 Get down the audience response at the time. Write it down in a notebook. You can save yourself from writing over what you have already written by marking the place where you are in your notebook with your left thumb.

4 When you write up, put down the number only of the joke and the response to it by the side. If there was no laugh put down N. r. for No Response. If you missed a joke put down Missed.

e.g. Joke 1 Laughs (2).
e.g. Joke 2 Laughs (5).
e.g. Joke 3 N.r.
e.g. Joke 4 Missed.
e.g. Joke 5 Laughs (1).

5 As well as the joke response put in your report:

(a) The date that you went and the time of day; the name of the cinema; the price of your seat; the weather conditions.

(b) How the audience reacted to each of the four songs in the film; whether they started humming them, or laughed at them, or were bored by them, or whatever the reaction was.

(c) Any comments or opinions on the film overheard in the cinema, or outside, or collected afterwards.

(d) An account (or cuttings) of any local advertisement.

(e) If you are in the cinema when the lights go up, a count of 50 people divided into men, women and children.

Cinemas showing *Let George Do It* in your neighbourhood are: [names].

Appendix 3: Newspapers

Reviews from the following papers were used in the study of the film:

Daily papers
  Times
  Daily Telegraph
  Daily Express
  Daily Mail
  Daily Herald
  News Chronicle
  Daily Dispatch
  Daily Mirror
  Daily Sketch

Evening Standard
Evening News
Star

Sunday papers
Sunday Times
Observer
Sunday Express
Sunday Chronicle
Sunday Pictorial

Weekly papers
Jewish Chronicle
Time and Tide
New Statesman
Spectator
Illustrated London News

Yorkshire Observer
B.B.C. film talk

Appendix 4: Mass-Observation joke work

In analysing jokes Mass-Observation uses the following categories:

Domestic Affairs	Live Big Shots
Domestic Objects	Dead Big Shots
Food	War, politics, etc. (see note A)
Money	Law
Jobs	Science
Clothes	Education
Sex	Art
Ill-Health	Religion
Lavatory	Abroad
Alcohol	English Towns
Sport	Local

Note A: since September 1939 the 'War' category has been subdivided into a further 19 categories such as Army, Prices, Germany, etc.

The Mass-Observation studies referred to in the report are as follows:
(a) A study of 8 Blackpool concert parties made in the summer of 1937.
(b) A study of 8 London music halls made in January 1940.
(c) A study of London pantomimes made in January 1940.
(d) An analysis of a competition set by Moore Raymond in the *Sunday Dispatch* asking readers to submit what they thought to be the three

funniest scenes in talking pictures. To this nearly 700 answers were
received containing nearly 2,000 scenes.

Appendix 9: Questionnaire results

		Men	*Women*	*Total*
Q.1	(opinion of film)			
	His best	17%	–	8%
	Very good	33%	16%	23%
	Amusing	50%	68%	61%
	Bad	–	16%	8%
Q.2	(opinion of George Formby)			
	Like him	88%	83%	86%
	Dislike him	12%	17%	14%
Q.3	(opinion of George in this film)			
	Like him	76%	66%	72%
	Dislike him	24%	34%	28%
Q.4	(Formby's best film)			
	It's in the Air	46%	46%	46%
	No Limit	19%	19%	19%
	Trouble Brewing	–	19%	9%
	I See Ice	–	19%	9%
	(don't know)	19%	–	9%
Q.5	(best sequence)			
	Cabin sequence	20%	14%	17%
	Vamping	–	–	–
	Bakery	35%	29%	33%
	Dream	10%	29%	17%
	Submarine	35%	29%	33%
Q.6	(Hitler sequence)			
	Like it	60%	56%	58%
	Dislike it	40%	38%	42%
Q.7	(songs)			
	Like them	50%	40%	45%
	Dislike them	33%	23%	28%
	Dislike these songs	17%	23%	20%
	No opinion	–	16%	8%

Q.8   (propaganda)

Yes	25%	15%	20%
No	75%	85%	80%

(Of the 20% who considered the film propaganda, only one-fifth thought it bad propaganda.)

The Great Dictator

The Great Dictator was one of the most important films of the war. Any Chaplin film was an event. But *The Great Dictator* was more than an event. It was a landmark. It was Chaplin's first talking film. His two previous sound films, *City Lights* (1931) and *Modern Times* (1936), had been dialogue-less. It was also a major political statement. For it held up to ridicule the policies and person of Adenoid Hynkel, dictator of Ptomania, whose place is taken by his exact double, a Jewish barber. Chaplin played both roles, with Jack Oakie as a Mussolini figure (Benzino Napolini, dictator of Bacteria) and Henry Daniell as Garbitsch (Goebbels). Chaplin's wife Paulette Goddard played the heroine. The film contained the celebrated balletic sequence in which Hynkel played with a globe and it ended with a much-discussed four-minute speech direct to camera calling for humanity, co-operation and peace.

The original idea for the film was suggested to Chaplin by Alexander Korda and Chaplin began working on the script in 1938, completing it just before Britain declared war on Germany in September 1939. While he was still scripting, pressure was put on Chaplin to abandon the project. He recalled:

> I began receiving alarming messages from United Artists. They had been advised by the Hays Office that I would run into censorship trouble. Also the English office was very concerned about an anti-Hitler picture and doubted whether it could be shown in Britain. But I was determined to go ahead, for Hitler must be laughed at. Had I known of the actual horrors of the German concentration camps, I could not have made *The Great Dictator*; I could not have made fun of the homicidal insanity of the Nazis. However, I was determined to ridicule their mystic bilge about a pure-blooded Aryan race. . . . But I was determined to make it, even if I had to hire halls myself to show it.

The filming took place from September 1939 to the end of March 1940 and the film was finally ready for showing by September 1940. Even though Britain was at war, America was still at peace. Hollywood was largely keeping clear of anti-Nazi films and the Gallup poll showed 96 per cent of the United States' population opposed to America entering the war. It opened in New York on 15 October 1940 to mixed reviews and in London on 16 December 1940 to general and unreserved delight. The final speech was much praised and the Communist Party put it out as a pamphlet. George Orwell devoted a lengthy review to the film in *Time and Tide*.

Chaplin had invested 2 million dollars of his own money and two years' work in the film. It paid off, securing considerable box-office success in both Britain and America. It grossed 5 million dollars worldwide and *Kinematograph Weekly* recorded that it was the top-grossing American film in Britain in 1941 and second only to *Forty-Ninth Parallel* as the most popular film of the year. Although the M-O report (FR 764) is unsigned, it was probably the work of Len England. A letter from Arthur Calder-Marshall commenting on the report was attached to it and is also printed here. The report was dated 29 June 1941.

For the background to the making and reception of the film, see Charles Chaplin, *My Autobiography* (Harmondsworth, 1966) and David Robinson, *Chaplin: His Life and Art* (London, 1985).

On the censors' concern about the film, see *Historical Journal of Film, Radio and Television* 5 (1985), pp. 85–90.

I Preliminary

Produced and directed by: Charlie Chaplin
Distributed by: United Artists
Players: Charles Chaplin, Jack Oakie, Paulette Goddard, with Billy Gilbert, Henry Daniell, Maurice Moscovitch.
Length: 11,162 feet
Time: 124 minutes
Certificate: U

The purpose of the survey was to discover the effect of the film upon the general public, and the popularity of various jokes. The methods mainly used were direct observation of the film (in sixteen different places) and questionnaire.

II Pre-release material

Probably no other film ever had such a pre-release campaign as the Chaplin film. At least a year before the war broke out, it was reported that Chaplin was going to make a film in which he parodied Hitler, and 'Production No. 6' became part of general film gossip. The fact that Hitler's and Chaplin's fiftieth birthdays came within a few days of one another was boosted considerably by the press and frequent mention was made of the film. The film did go into production and the most elaborate precautions were taken to see that nobody got any inkling of what was going on. When it was shown in New York, the film critics were not too friendly, but much play was made in this country of Goebbel's attempts to belittle the film. He was said to have announced that it was playing to half-empty houses when in reality it was packing the Astor, one of the largest cinemas in New York. Rumours began to circulate about its coming to this country. Some of these said that it would not be shown until after the war, others that Chaplin was going to charge high prices on the *Gone with the Wind* line. Agitation was made for the quick release of the film, and it was even suggested that Chaplin himself should come over for the première. *Picture Post* ran a leading feature, a title page and an article by Rebecca West long before a single copy of the film came to this country, and both *Everybody's* and *Illustrated* showed many stills of the film. Highbrow weeklies, too, made a great fuss of it: *Sight and Sound* ran a complete article. *The Leader* could produce a reference to it on the front page with the assumption that all readers would have heard of the film, while *Lilliput* produced an abstruse joke on the connection of Hitler and Chaplin.

The first copies of the films sent to this country were sunk on the way. The second copies arrived safely, and the film appeared simultaneously at three different cinemas just before Christmas, 1940. This has only happened before in the case of *Gone with the Wind*. The wireless now took up the publicity, announced in its news bulletins that the Prime Minister and various other notables had seen one showing of the picture, while a special performance had been given at Windsor Castle to the King and Queen and the Royal Princesses. The postscript to the 9 o'clock news on the date of its première was devoted to interviews with people coming out of the cinema. Newspapers not only devoted complete film pages to the film, but also referred to it in leading articles, while the *Evening Standard* had a complete leader page devoted to it. Local cinemas showed trailers of the film urging people to see it in the West End; advertisements for restaurants used stills from the picture; two music hall comedians produced jokes on the film in the first week of its showing. The final speech controversy raged everywhere; Hannen Swaffer devoted his whole column to a verbatim reprint of the speech. Even five weeks after its première no paper missed more than a day or two without some reference to the film. Its banning in Argentina or showing in Mexico was considered news of some importance, while Chaplin's refusal to accept a film critics' award for the best male performance of last year created considerable comment in the British Press.

Not unnaturally all this 'ballyhoo' had its effect upon the public. All M-O film material points to the fact that only Charlie Chaplin – and possibly Norma Shearer – retain considerable popularity during long absences; in answer to the questionnaire at a late stage of the investigation 66 per cent of those interviewed said that they liked him. Any film of his was bound to have a good-sized reasonably enthusiastic audience. Yet *The Great*

Dictator became so well known that in December 1940, before any copy of it had arrived in this country, 90 per cent of a sample had heard of it, and 75 per cent wanted to see it. Even in January, when full information about the film was available, 57 per cent still wanted to see it. There is every evidence in M-O material to indicate that the average method for selecting a picture is to read the paper or take a friend's advice the same week as the film was showing.

Many of the people who so wanted to see the film were out of the run of the usual filmgoer; indeed, the very fact that 75 per cent of a sample questionnaire (not merely of film-goers) wanted to see it reveals that *The Great Dictator* was likely to appeal to a far wider audience than most films. There are many remarks of this nature:

> M 30 A: It'll be the first film I've seen for over two months. I've had no time to see films, but I couldn't resist the opportunity of seeing Chaplin again.

> M 40 C: I'd like to see it though I don't go as a general rule.

> M 60 D: I don't often go to the pictures but I'm going to see the new Charlie Chaplin.

The public, then, was very sympathetic to the film, even before its première. But the publicity did not stop when the film was shown. In the first place the critics praised it more unanimously than any other film dealt with by M-O, probably more than any other film in history. The critics' reaction will be dealt with in detail later, suffice it to say that the *Times* and the *Worker* agreed about the general excellence of the film.

The trade now took up the film again. Not a great deal of direct advertising was done, but a large portrait of Chaplin as Hynkel with the words 'The World is Laughing Again' appeared in various media from tube trains to sober weekly journals which have never carried film advertisements before. A four-sheet broadsheet was distributed at cinemas, rare in wartime. The film was given a simultaneous première at three West End cinemas – only *Gone with the Wind* had done this – and on release was shown in more than one cinema in the same area: *The Lion Has Wings* is the only precedent. It was, the public was told, the first film to beat the black-out, and took more money in the first week than any film since September. Its release was extremely rapid and the film was shown in small towns (which usually showed six-month-old pictures) less than six weeks after the English première.

Yet, despite all this, interest in the film very rapidly waned. The 75 per cent who wanted to see it in December had decreased to 57 per cent in January, and only 58 per cent actually saw it according to a questionnaire in March. Later still, an observer reports from Shrewsbury a direct antipathy to the film. People were going for preference to the other films showing in the town. No amount of publicity could counteract the majority opinion of the film that it was 'disappointing'.

III Public opinion of the film

While no comparable figures are available, probably [for] no picture in history has there been such unanimity of praise from the critics. All evidence – the ten best films of year, for instance – point to the fact that film critics rarely agree. Yet not a single English review is anything but favourable; e.g.

Chaplin's masterpiece. *New Statesman & Nation*, 21.12.40.

Towers above the general run of slick commercial production like a lonely peak. *Daily Telegraph*, 16.12.40.

Brilliant . . . a film to see and think about as well as like. *Daily Worker*, 12.12.40.

The wisest, wittiest, and most cunning film-work that Chaplin has ever done. It presents the comedian for the first time in his full stature as an artist. He might have waited all his life for this one film. *Observer*, 11.12.40.

Will rank among the greatest of film comedies. It is certainly Chaplin's greatest performance. *Sunday Dispatch*, 15.12.40.

The rebirth of political satire. *John O'London*, January 1941.

. . . just about the only good thing that has come out of this war. *Documentary News Letter*, January 1941.

Among the fifteen reviews analysed in detail there are unfavourable references in three only; all of them are to the speech.

The public's opinion was very different. There is a variation, as will be shown, between the opinions expressed by the public after seeing the film, and their actual reaction during the performance. Asked: 'What did you think of *The Great Dictator?*' 400 people replied as shown in the table.

	Men	Women	Total
Really good	46%	34%	40%
Quite good	23%	26%	25%
Disappointed	17%	18%	18%
Not much	10%	15%	12%
Nothing	4%	7%	5%

The emphasis here is not so much on the 40 per cent who liked it very much, but the one-fifth who *spontaneously* said that they were disappointed. Constantly, the same phrases are appearing:

M 20 A: A vague feeling of disappointment.

M 20 B: Frankly I was disappointed. I had heard so much about it and read so much about it in the papers that I expected a super good film and to me it seemed to be a very patchy comedy, not nearly so good as some of his earlier films.

M 35 C: It wasn't what the critics said it was.

M 50 D: My husband and I were very disappointed, we couldn't see anything to laugh at at all.

M 35 D: It was all right, but I'd been told of much more.

So much did this feeling spread that by the time it had been generally released people were expecting to be disappointed. An observer in Wellington, Shropshire, where it was released at the beginning of March, reports that people were generally saying that it was a flop, and were going to other films in preference.

There is every indication, however, that while people were sceptical after they had seen the film, actually during the film it was thoroughly enjoyed. The investigator who is responsible for the film work of Mass-Observation reports of the West End showing that:

The response was the best that inv. has ever seen to a film; not one sign of boredom noted anywhere throughout the whole two hours of the film. The film was clapped in the middle, noted only in feature films with such feature films as *The Lion Has Wings* and *For Freedom*.

Other showings note the same good response, and the joke chart indicates the same thing. Average response to each joke is a laugh for nearly half the audience (2.2) as opposed 2.7 for *Let George Do It*, a very popular film for which only fifty jokes were checked on. Very few jokes got no response at all.

IV The jokes

The biggest laugh

Here again there is a distinct variation between the opinion expressed as to the best bit and the actual observation at the cinemas. Observations show the most popular jokes to be as follows:

1 Charlie takes the pin out of a grenade and then drops it down his trousers by mistake (joke 8 – response 4.4)
2 Charlie, wanting to hide a coin in his pudding, swallows more and more (joke 66 – response 4.3)
3 Napolini eats mustard with food (joke 97 – response 4)
4 Hannah hits Charlie over the head with a frying pan by mistake (joke 30 – response 4)
5 Charlie, having eaten coins, hiccups and clinks (joke 67 – response 3.9)

All the jokes are slapstick, and all of them are in the usual Chaplin vein – the old Chaplin as many people refer to him. And it is important to note, though this will be referred to again, that none of the jokes are specifically topical though the most popular of all refers to a war incident.

Asked after they had seen the film what they thought the best part of the film, 400 people answered as follows. Infinitely the most popular part was the speech at the end, followed by the balloon dance; neither of these are humorous parts. Following in succession are these incidents:

Throwing food about (joke 94 – response 3.6)
(General) scenes as a soldier
Jack Oakie as Napolini

Two of these three incidents are nebulous and cannot be strictly compared, but those in the table are limited to one incident.

Joke	Incident	Popularity	Response
79	Train shunts up and down	4th	3
	Jews eating puddings	5th	(Not recorded)
17	Guy speech	6th	1.8
30	Hannah hits with frying pan	7th	4

Here only one joke occurs in both lists; the opinion of the film is entirely different after the public have seen it from that when they are actually watching it. It seems that the joke which causes howls of laughter at the moment of impact is not necessarily that with the most profound effect.

Topical jokes

Of the 100 jokes selected for special study, 50 were topical, and 50 were non-topical. The average response to topical jokes was 1.85 and to non-topical 2.35; there is a considerable variation here which seems to indicate quite clearly that not even Chaplin can get away with war jokes. George

Formby's *Let George Do It* showed the same point even more strongly with 2.9 response for non-topical jokes, and 1.6 for topical.

Spoken jokes

This is the first film in which Chaplin has spoken, and, apart from the speech at the end, talking does not seem to have increased his comic powers; the caricature of Hitler ranting is the only spoken joke that occurs in the top twenty, and this is no more speech than the song or the lecture oration in *Modern Times*. Spoken jokes get an average response of 1.4, while acted get 2.4. Here again there is an indication that film technique calls for an essentially visual approach. Even George Formby with his songs and wisecracks gets more laughs with acted jokes.

Categories

The jokes were divided into the various Mass-Observation joke categories: 100 points were awarded to the most popular jokes, 99 to the next, and so on. The results shown in the table were obtained:

Category	No. of jokes	Total points
War	41	1,970
Ill-health	28	1,876
Domestic objects	6	310
Domestic affairs	4	232
Clothes	5	218
Law	3	187
Jobs	4	171
Sex	3	137
Sport	3	78
Money	2	59
Lavatory	1	5¼

Though war jokes are nearly a third again as frequent as ill-health, there is only a very slight difference in the points scored by each. Here again there is indication of the unpopularity of war jokes.

V Regional variation

It was proved in the *Let George Do It* report that regional variation is very important in film observation. No detailed work was done on the subject in *The Great Dictator* survey, but by the few observations that were made it seems, as before, that the laugh variation is dependent purely on quickness of uptake. Thus in Streatham an audience laughs when Charlie loses his belt while flying upside down, while in Bermondsey there was no response till he actually falls. In Streatham the sight of Napolini spreading mustard on his strawberries gets a laugh; in Bermondsey there is a pause until he actually eats them.

VI The worst part

No particular part of the film caused particular dislike as will be shown from the following answers to the question:
'Which did you think the worst bit?':

Don't know	23%
None bad	20%
All bad	2%
None in particular	2%
Parts not mentioned more than once	30%

This, in all, accounts for 77 per cent of the answers. No single incident gained more than 5 per cent of the answers, 2 only (sic). Five incidents were mentioned more than once. These were:

Speech	5%
Buffet	5
Train	4
End	4
Balloon	4

Each one of these scenes is among the ten most popular portions of the film. No part of the film, therefore, caused any widespread dislike.

VII The speech

At the end of the film, Chaplin drops the part of the barber and becomes himself; for four minutes he speaks directly to the audience, appeals to the little man to fight against the machines. Chaplin, himself defending it, says:

To me it is the logical ending of the film story.

To me it is the speech that the little barber would have made – even had to make. People have said that he steps out of character. What of it? The picture is two hours and 7 minutes in length. If two hours and 3 minutes is comedy may I not be excused for ending my comedy on a note that reflects honesty and realistically the world in which we live, and may I not be excused for pleading for a better world.

To the critics this speech caused no little trouble: of the 100 per cent praising the film as a whole, only 40 per cent praised the speech. *The Times* equivocated, with 'the fitness of the last speech will excite the arguments of filmgoers for weeks to come'. Others became far more partisan:

> Pretty good stuff until the last mouthful when . . . soldiers are invited to turn their swords into ploughshares as though the war was not on. (*Everybody's*, 3.4.41)

> The oration is delivered with an eloquence and a sincerity that will hold an audience spellbound. (*Documentary Newsletter*, January 1941)

> Pity Charlie Chaplin makes that long speech. (*Evening Standard*, 14.12.40)

> An electrifying finale with a white-hot passionate burst of eloquence for democracy. (*Daily Herald*, 12.12.40)

> Though the speech was brilliant, it carries no idea not implicit in the film and only makes the propaganda obvious. (Matthew Norgate, BBC, 20.12.40)

> The moving speech . . . (*Daily Worker*, 12.12.40)

The text of the speech was printed in full in the *Daily Worker* (21.12.40), Hannen Swaffer's column in the *Daily Herald* (16.12.40), the *Documentary News Letter* (January, 1941), and was used as the bulk of a Communist leaflet headed 'You the people have the power'.

The public, on the other hand, was more enthusiastic about the speech than the film as a whole. Sixty-two per cent thought the speech really good, another 9 per cent liked it; only 40 per cent thought the film as a whole really good, and another 25 per cent quite good. Twenty-eight per cent or nearly a third thought it the best bit of the film. Typical comments:

M 20 A: Moving and sincere.

M 30 C: Marvellous.

F 35 D: All heart and soul in his speech.

F 40 D: The finest speech I've heard. None of our statesmen couldn't do it.

As opposed to the jokes, there is a similar reaction in and out of the cinema. At the West End audience, the speech was interrupted by 8 seconds applause, the longest noted in any feature film anywhere. At 50 per cent of the cinemas applause was heard in the middle of the speech as well as at the end.

It is to be noted that the public concerned itself with the *matter* of the speech, while the critics, with a few exceptions, concerned themselves with the relationship of the speech to the film as a whole. The basis of criticism was completely different.

VIII Propaganda value

The critics assume automatically that the film is both propaganda and good propaganda. Twenty-five per cent of the public on the other hand don't regard the film as propaganda at all. Of those who did think it propaganda, over 75 per cent thought it good as such.

IX Reason for failure

What is the reason for the comparative failure of this film? Partly over-propaganda. Exactly the same effect was noted to the film *Men of the Lightship*, 20 minutes long, but praised so highly that it was billed in some places as the main feature film. This publicity was more than the film could hold. Similarly with Chaplin's *Dictator*. From every source the public was told that this was one of the greatest, funniest, most important of all films. They were expecting miracles. And while they enjoyed the film while actually watching it, second thoughts showed that it wasn't quite so funny as they first thought; and they were disappointed.

There was, however, a far more important reason. Ever since the beginning of the war there has been a strong reaction against war films; it can be roughly said that no feature film with a war motif has been really successful, though some (e.g. *Convoy, Night Train to Munich*) have caused interest. The point has already been mentioned; non-war jokes received nearly 25 per cent greater applause than war jokes; war jokes though nearly double in number scored only slightly more points than ill-health jokes.

In January, before anything was known of the film, 40 per cent of women and 20 per cent of men questioned thought it wrong to laugh at Hitler; it was 'degrading', 'useless', was too serious to laugh at. Only 1 per cent more thought it good to laugh at our enemies. Though no such question was specifically asked in the late questionnaires, there is indication that the film was often regarded as 'bad taste', and, on the other hand, nobody refers to the film as enjoyable because it makes fun of the war.

Every sign points to the wartime cinema as essentially 'escapist'. Comedy is infinitely more popular than drama, and crazy unreal comedy more so than the spy-war brand. Even Chaplin could not break down this initial prejudice against his subject matter.

A third possible, though subsidiary, reason for the only partial success of the *Dictator* lies in the difference between this film and the usual Chaplin film. As has already been mentioned, Charlie Chaplin had a reputation which could survive years without making a film; he created a picture of himself as the little man with the bowler hat and a cane. The *Dictator* does not entirely agree with this picture, and there is constant reference to 'the old Chaplin' which the public liked better.

X Conclusions

The main conclusions of the report are as follows:

1 *The Dictator* had one of the largest publicity campaigns in history, and also one of the best press criticisms.
2 This publicity had its effects in that it created a large number of people wanting to see the film before it was released.
3 Expressed opinion of the public showed under half considering it really good.
4 The actual showing of the film showed a good response to the film.
5 The most popular jokes are slapstick; spoken jokes are more popular than [blank], non-topical than topical.
6 The speech was much more popular with the critics than the general public.
7 There is a strong variation between the direct response to the film and the opinion expressed of it afterwards.
8 Possible reasons for failure:

   (a) the very fact that it was a war film,
   (b) the over-publicity of the film,
   (c) the change from Chaplin's usual style.

Clanricarde Gnds

My dear Tom,

I'm returning the report on *The Great Dictator*, some of which I found very interesting, especially the relation of build-up to first and second thoughts on the film.

I am not quite certain of the analysis of the war and non-war jokes. For example, 3, Napolini eats mustard with food, is analysed as a non-war joke. It was in fact a slapstick joke, refurbished as a national joke. Most of the people to whom I talked, who liked that joke, appreciated the point that it was ENGLISH mustard and the success of the Libyan and Abyssinian campaigns at that time gave even greater topicality to it. One man told me, a commercial traveller in the Midlands, that it was the cleverest thing he had ever seen on the screen. It was a combination between a familiar slapstick device and a political analogy (the unsuspecting attitude of Napolini putting mustard on his strawberries being a good symbolisation of Mussolini entering the war in the expectation that Britain as well as France was going to collapse, and then finding that we were still going hot and strong).

This leads me to wonder whether the reason why topical war jokes are not appreciated on the screen is that the time taken in writing, shooting and projecting is so long that the jokes are no longer topical by the time that they reach the screen. This is backed up by the criticism, unmentioned in the report but frequently made, that the film would have been funny in the years preceding the war. The date of the film's conception was 1937 and the film as a whole was 1937 minded. That is to say, it was out of date even before it was shot.

The general war jokes which were more popular than topical war jokes according to this were probably more 'topical' also, by the time they reached the audience. The joke for example of the General, ordering his aide-de-camp who orders the Major who orders the captain who orders etc. until Chaplin has to do the jobs is one appreciated by all soldiers in the British Army; and it is 'topical' because it is still true when the audience sees it.

This seems again to be the question of the inability of crystallising emotions or humour round specific situations in a war of rapid movement which moves from phase to phase before the popular mind has had time to absorb the last phase.

Another aspect of the Napolini joke, to return to that, is the magic quality of the analogy; the irrefutable fact that Napolini eating mustard in large quantities will be very uncomfortable providing a reassurance that Mussolini is equally certain to catch it hot from us. The humour of the joke is thus partly the old slapstick incongruity and partly relief from anxiety. The early war scenes in the same way derive their humour more from the fact that they reassure the solider that shells are not such horrible things and express his own hatred of the officers above him as from any anti-German or anti-Nazi feelings they express.

The same lack of analysis occurs in relation to the final speech. After having established the fact that some critics disliked the final speech because it was not part of the whole film and the public was not bothered by this, the observer should have gone on to the much more interesting and fundamental point. Did the public like or dislike the speech because it was anti-Nazi or anti-war or democratic or pro-Jewish.

Having seen these categories, I feel that they are very inadequate. It is only when they are subdivided that any valuable conclusions can be reached. Any statistics about whether people like jokes about the war are valueless without further information about the different sorts of jokes about the war. When a man is confronted with a joke about the war and doesn't laugh, it is no evidence that he dislikes jokes about the war but only that he dislikes that sort of joke about the war.

See you soon,

Arthur Calder-Marshall

18 *Ships with Wings*

One of the most memorable sequences of films during the Second World War was the series of gritty, realistic, semi-documentary wartime dramas that came out of Michael Balcon's Ealing Studios. Balcon's decision to concentrate on that type of film was crucially influenced by the reception in certain quarters of *Ships with Wings*, which was premiered in November 1941 and went on general release in January 1942. Despite sequences shot aboard HMS *Ark Royal*, it looks today a highly romanticised and artificial tribute to the Fleet Air Arm. Its plot centred on a reckless, daredevil pilot, cashiered from the service for causing the death of the heroine's brother in a crash. He redeemed himself when war came by flying a suicide mission against an enemy-held island. With John Clements essentially repeating his role from *The Four Feathers* and Leslie Banks, the erstwhile 'Sanders of the River', playing the Admiral, the film looks back to the pre-war Imperial melodramas. With its phlegmatic, pipe-smoking officers, stiff-upper-lipped ladies and foreigners either sinister (Germans) or comic (Italians, Greeks), it is far removed from the down-to-earth realities of 'The People's War' that the Ministry of Information was making one of the main thrusts of its propaganda. Apart from that, with its host of very obvious model shots of ships, planes, even the island, it exudes an indelible aura of phoniness.

In general, reviews of the film were favourable, even enthusiastic, but it earned severe disapprobation in certain influential quarters which deeply affected Balcon. First of all, Prime Minister Winston Churchill decided that the final action sequence was a disaster for the Fleet Air Arm and would cause alarm and despondency. He wanted the film withdrawn. But after representations from Ealing, he agreed to leave the final decision to the First Sea Lord, who passed it. But the highbrow papers (*The Times, The Observer, The New Statesman*) mocked the film as outdated musical-comedy stuff. *The Daily Mail* ran an article by war correspondent Noel Monks saying the film was a disgrace and should be scrapped. *The Documentary News Letter* ran an editorial declaring: 'Films of this kind should not be made in wartime.' The burden of all the criticism was that the film lacked realism. So Balcon commissioned Tom Harrisson to report on showings of the film and to assess its propaganda value. At the same time, Harrisson was working for Admiral John Godfrey, Director of Naval Intelligence, and decided to do special samples of the reaction of naval wives to the film, as the Admiralty was worried about their morale. Mass-

Observation prepared no less than four detailed reports: File Reports 967 (11 November 1941), 1059 (28 January 1942), 1204 (12 April 1942) and 1218 (21 April 1942). The results show that the public in fact loved the film. Nevertheless, Balcon was so concerned about the criticism that he went ahead with a switch of production to the sober and earnest reconstructions of real-life episodes from 'The People's War' that were to earn Ealing critical plaudits. But it is evident from Mass-Observation's work that he did not do so because of the public's dissatisfaction with Ealing's gung-ho melodramas. We print the final M-O report, which summarised the previous three. Len England attached a memorandum which is also printed here.

This was not the first time that Ealing had consulted Mass-Observation. In 1940 they had asked for M-O's opinion on the viability of a proposed feature film *Battle for Britain* about German air raids. Mass-Observation advised against making it on the basis of their audience reaction tests and assessment of audience mood (FR 491). Len England reported to Sergei Nolbandov that any film about the war was liable to fail at that moment when a vast majority of the cinema audience was going 'to get away from it for a few hours'. Those war films which had been successful were divided into two classes, those portraying a phase of the war unknown to the mass audience (*Convoy, Contraband*) and those making fun of the war (*Laugh it Off, Pack Up Your Troubles*). Furthermore, air raid scenes were probably the most unpopular sequences in films. *Battle for Britain* was not made.

For a discussion of the place of *Ships with Wings* in wartime cinema, see Charles Barr, *Ealing Studios* (London, 1977) and Jeffrey Richards, 'Wartime British cinema audiences: The case of *Ships with Wings*', *Historical Journal of Film, Radio and Television* (1987), 129–41.

I Scope of report

This is the final report on detailed material collected in London, Edinburgh, Glasgow, Cardiff, Birmingham, Cheltenham, Bournemouth, Rochester, Chatham and Portsmouth, on the film *Ships with Wings*.

Investigations proceeded throughout the first four months of this year, and were made at different cinemas in all areas indicated.

Direct questioning was employed in this investigation, and a short questionnaire was asked outside cinemas showing the film *Ships with Wings*. Points investigated were whether or not people liked the film, and how it influenced their feelings as regards the Navy. Full details with illustrations on these points will be given on the following pages.

II General public reaction

In all the areas investigated, with both sexes and all classes and ages, this film has had an overwhelmingly good reception, and aroused a large amount of interest. Of the total sample, just under nine people in ten expressed some liking for the film, and six people out of ten stated that they liked the film particularly much, or used other very praising terms. A slightly larger proportion of women than men liked this film, and women were decidedly more praising in their comment on the film than men.

84% of men are favourable to the film
90% of women are favourable to the film
87% of both sexes are favourable to the film

A slight difference in reaction was observed between the four different areas studied:

82% were favourable to film in LONDON
85% were favourable to film in MERCHANT PORTS
88% were favourable to film in INLAND
93% were favourable to film in NAVAL PORTS

We thus find greatest approval of the film in those areas which are closely linked with the Naval tradition, and have probably better knowledge of Naval personnel and Naval affairs than the other areas investigated. London has the smallest amount of approval of the areas, probably because of the more sophisticated cinema audiences there.

The men interviewed in the four different areas differ little in reaction from each other. Thus:

82% of men were favourable to film in INLAND
84% of men were favourable to film in LONDON
86% of men were favourable to film in MERCHANT PORTS
88% of men were favourable to film in NAVAL PORTS

Women, however, varied more widely in their reactions to the film in the different places studied.

80% of women liked the film in LONDON
84% of women liked the film in MERCHANT PORTS
95% of women liked the film in INLAND
99% of women liked the film in NAVAL PORTS

We thus find women in Inland and to a slightly larger extent in Naval Ports more enthusiastic about the film than those in the other areas studied.

A small but definite and consistent class difference was found to exist as regards liking this film. Thus better-off people in all areas studied always like this film slightly less, and are more critical of it than the less well-off:

81% of AB class liked the film
89% of C class liked the film
90% of D class liked the film

The age differences were also studied and it was found that the younger age group approved of the film slightly more than the older generation:

89% of people of 35 and under liked the film
85% of people of 40 and over liked the film

From the above figures it will be seen how very widely the film appealed, and though there are small differences in sex, class and age, it can be stated that the film appealed to all to a very large extent.

III Types of approval

Though such a large number of people approved of the film, types of approval varied very widely and we find that we had to deal with three distinct types of praise and approval:

(a) those who approved of the film generally,
(b) those who approved of the film very much, and
(c) those who qualified their approval and mentioned particular parts of the film.

There was a very definite place difference in amount of *enthusiasm*, Naval Ports being most enthusiastic and London least so, with Inland and Merchant Ports occupying a midway position:

49% of LONDON people liked the film very much
53% of MERCHANT PORT people liked the film very much
70% of INLAND people liked the film very much
73% of NAVAL PORT people liked the film very much

Qualified approval was the same for all sexes, classes and ages – in each case 5 per cent.

Terms of approval varied enormously and illustrations could be given *ad infinitum*. Here we will give only a few of the most frequent ones (further material is available if required).

General approval terms were mostly short, and the same phrases occur over and over again:

F 20 B: It was alright.
F 35 C: It was quite good.
F 30 C: Not too bad.

F 60 D: Good.

M 20 B: Seen worse.

M 30 B: Average for that type of film.

M 25 C: Fairly good.

M 18 D: Not bad at all.

People who liked the film very much used a rather wider vocabulary to express themselves. Some people state how much they enjoyed seeing the film:

F 55 B: Wonderful film. I thoroughly enjoyed it. Yes, I thought it was wonderful.

F 30 B: I enjoyed it.

F 40 C: It was good. I liked it. It was propaganda really, wasn't it?

M 40 B: I liked it.

M 40 C: Jolly good. I liked it.

M 50 C: It was quite good. Full of excitements. That's my chief pleasure in the films.

M 50 D: I certainly did like it.

Others used very praising terminology in describing the film:

F 25 B: I thought it was very good.

F 45 B: Very nice.

F 20 C: Awfully good.

F 20 C: Fine.

F 25 C: Wonderful.

F 30 C: Grand.

F 30 C: Lovely.

F 30 C: Very interesting.

F 40 C: Marvellous.

F 40 C: Beautiful.

F 50 D: Splendid.

F 35 B: Better.

F 35 C: It was thrilling. I don't know how they make those pictures.

F 40 C: It was very good indeed. Makes you realise.

F 20 D: Oh, it was lovely, very good. I'm going to see it again.

F 25 C: It was a very good film.

M 35 C: I thought it a remarkably good film.

M 40 C: Jolly good.

M 45 C: It was a remarkably good propaganda film.

M 30 D: Really fine.

M 30 B: Very good entertainment.

M 60 B: An excellent film.

M 50 C: Jolly fine picture.

M 55 D: A very good thrilling film.

A few people qualified their approval, and the most often mentioned points are the good photography, the good acting, and admiration for the production of the picture. The photography was very much admired:

F 35 C: The photography was very good.
M 45 B: Splendid photography.
M 50 B: Good photography and very realistic.
M 60 D: It's a masterpiece of how they got the shots of the Navy.

The acting was commented upon:

F 50 A: . . . one of the best bits of acting I've seen.
M 40 C: I thought it a very wonderful film. Well photographed and well acted.
M 45 B: . . . good acting.

The production of the film was much admired:

F 40 C: One of the best pictures I've seen.
F 30 B: It was the best of its type I've seen. Better than the similar type of American film I saw recently.
F 55 B: Very nice – different to the rest.
F 45 C: I think it's the best I've ever seen.
F 60 B: They took a lot of trouble with it. It was very well done. You couldn't see that any of them were models.
M 30 B: It was realistic on fight conditions. It makes people realise there is a war on. It's jolly satisfactory and very realistic.
M 30 C: It was a decent film. The best British I've seen.

As will be seen from these quotations, the film appealed widely to different people for very varying reasons. The great mass of approval was emotional and not at all deeply thought out. The film appealed directly to people's feelings, the men were presented in a heroic setting and were made to perform heroic feats, and this went straight to the public's heart. People especially who had relations or friends in the Navy or in the Fleet Air Arm were interested and touched by the film.

Other points mentioned:

1 The film teaches you about what the Navy is doing.
2 The Fleet Air Arm is for the first time shown adequately, – some people say it shows they are better than the RAF.
3 It shows what an interesting life they have.
4 It makes you think about the sea.
5 It makes you feel proud of the Navy and our young men.
6 It makes you want to join the Navy (no less than 3 per cent made this spontaneous comment).

7 It makes you want to help the Navy, build more ships, save more, eat less, etc.

IV Unfavourable comments

There was very little unfavourable comment on the film, and only slightly over one person in ten of the whole sample was critical in any way. Men were more critical than women, as is usual in this type of investigation. The wealthier classes were rather more critical than those having less money:

19% of AB class were critical
11% of C class were critical
 8% of D class were critical

The two different age groups criticised to much the same extent, though the older age group criticised just slightly more. Criticism in the four areas investigated is naturally in inverse proportion to liking the film, and we thus get:

 6% of people criticised the film in NAVAL PORTS
11% of people criticised the film in INLAND
14% of people criticised the film in MERCHANT PORTS
16% of people criticised the film in LONDON

We divided the unfavourable comments into three groups:

1 Some people generally disliked the film, were bored by it, or disappointed because the film had not come up to their expectations.
2 Some people actively disliked something about the film, such as the story, the acting, etc.
3 Some people quite liked the film, sat through it, but came out with some definite criticism.

The differences in qualified criticism between the different areas studied are not very striking:

2% of people expressed qualified dislike in NAVAL PORTS
6% of people expressed qualified dislike in INLAND
6% of people expressed qualified dislike in LONDON
7% of people expressed qualified dislike in MERCHANT PORTS

The majority of the general criticism just expresses dislike without explaining itself much further:

 F 45 B: Glad, I didn't see it all.
 F 30 C: Got on my nerves a bit.

M 40 C: Not bloody much.

M 40 C: Not much.

M 60 D: I wasn't so struck with it as I might have been – it lacked something.

M 25 C: Bloody – I hate the sea or anything to do with it.

M 60 D: It seemed a bit overdone to me.

There were, however, a fairly large number of people who had gone to see the film with definite expectations and were *disappointed* by it:

F 25 C: It was not what I expected.

F 45 B: I was rather disappointed. I don't know that I liked it as much as I thought I was going to, and I don't know what it was about it.

F 55 C: I was disappointed.

F 40 D: I was disappointed. I didn't think it was going to be quite like that.

M 30 C: It didn't come up to my expectations.

F 35 C: I was a bit disappointed. I expected a bit more story in it. There wasn't enough.

M 45 B: I was disappointed. It was too stereotyped . . . it could have been made 100% more effective.

A few people stated that they disliked seeing the type of film, or were getting rather tired of them:

F 30 C: Getting rather tired of them.

F 30 B: I'm rather tired of these films.

M 50 B: I'm not too keen on this sort of thing myself, but I suppose it was good if you like that sort of thing.

M 30 C: God, I hate those films.

Qualified criticism varied rather widely, but there were several points which were disliked by more than one person, such as the absence of any story, the presence of a story and a love theme, the acting, the bogusness of the film, the longness of the film, and the obvious propaganda points in the film. Various other odd points were also mentioned.

The *love story* was disliked strongly by some:

F 35 B: I didn't think they were going to put all this soppy love into it.

M 45 B: It's a pity that there was any love element in this film.

The *lack of story* was commented upon, mainly by women:

F 45 D: Silly thing – no story.

F 45 D: A bit silly, not enough story for me.

M 45 B: The story was a bit played up in some parts.

It was complained that the film was nothing like *realistic* enough, and that things do not happen like it in the Navy:

> F 25 B: I think the professional actors spoiled the realistic scenes.
>
> M 20 B: It was alright but there were too many successes. Good photography but not realistic.
>
> M 18 B: Very funny, but quite unrealistic.
>
> M 65 C: It was alright, very good for the younger ones but us older ones who've been through it know a bit better. It never happens like in the film, not in real life.
>
> M 40 D: I've been in the Service myself; I know what it's really like.
>
> F 55 B: I'm not sure. It was too much of a mixture of reality and fancy. They didn't always seem to go together too well.

A minor but very definite complaint was about the *obviousness of the propaganda* in the film, and this was often strongly disliked where it was mentioned:

> M 45 C: Fed up with propaganda pictures.
>
> M 50 C: I don't think it is very good propaganda and that's what it is supposed to be.

The alleged *faking* of some of the scenes was occasionally commented upon, though only people 'in the know' seemed to have noticed this to any great extent:

> M 20 D: It's very good, but there is a bit too much model work in it. It's too obvious.
>
> M 50 B: Lousy. Biggest fake ever put before the public. I've just been telling the manager so.
>
> M 45 B: A lot of nonsense. That's what I thought of it. It wasn't clear, it doesn't go straight through – too much modelling too.
>
> M 25 C: Very good but some parts I didn't like. The faking was amateurish – nothing up to the American standard for fake photography. The bombing attack for example was most unconvincing.

The film was compared several times to *The Lion Has Wings*, *Convoy* and *Target for Tonight*, to the disadvantage of *Ships with Wings*:

> F 30 B: It was good, but I preferred the first one – *The Lion Has Wings*.
>
> F 45 A: Well, it's not as good as *Convoy*.
>
> F 40 C: It was very good, but not as good as *Target for Tonight*.

There was also an underlying feeling present in some people that it might not be a good thing to show that *kind of picture*:

> F 25 C: I thought it was very good. But I don't know if it ought to be

shown. It makes you rather worry when you see all the things you do.

F 45 B: Very good, but it must be a bit harrowing for some people.

It was also said by a few people that the film was rather *too long*:

F 55 B: A bit long drawn out.

A few felt that the whole picture was too *amateurish*:

M 40 C: Too amateurish.
M 40 C: Not much – too amateur – not enough punch.

And one or two persons felt it was a bad thing to show the film *after the 'Ark Royal' had been sunk*;

M 50 B: It would have been more appreciated and been better if the *Ark Royal* had not been sunk.

To sum up

There was really little tangible dislike of the film. Those people who seriously thought about the film when coming out of the cinema, mostly felt vaguely that there was something wrong with the picture, but often found it difficult to express themselves in so many words. This is perhaps best illustrated by the following remark made by an old sailor at Portsmouth:

M 40 B: I was rather disappointed. The photography was excellent – the ship itself. . . . I was in it before the war – it was good as far as the ship was concerned but . . .

It thus seems that the major feeling of dislike and criticism was one concerned with the unreality of the way the film treated the Navy, and some who had gone for the purpose of finding out what the Navy was doing, came away feeling that they had seen just 'another fairy-tale'.

Other points mentioned:

1 It makes you distrust the judgement of senior Naval officers.
2 It makes you feel naval pilots behave in a wild and silly way.
3 It suggests that the Fleet Air Arm are inferior to the RAF [comparison is often made here and at other points with *The Lion Has Wings* and *Target for Tonight*]. The film isn't fair to the Navy.

V The film as Naval propaganda

Everywhere the film was shown against a background of approval for the Navy itself. The four different areas studied varied very little in their general reactions to the Navy, though Naval Ports can be said to have been slightly more favourable:

72% of people were favourable to Navy in INLAND
74% of people were favourable to Navy in MERCHANT PORTS
75% of people were favourable to Navy in LONDON
81% of people were favourable to Navy in NAVAL PORTS

There are some slight class differences, the more moneyed classes being quantitatively less keen on the Navy than the poorer section of the population:

73% of AB class were favourable to the Navy
74% of C class were favourable to Navy
79% of D class were favourable to Navy

The age differences, also, are slight, though there is some indication that the older section of the sample has responded more readily to the 'propaganda' of the film than the younger generation:

73% of people of 35 and under were favourable to Navy
78% of people of 40 and over were favourable to Navy

Replies, though similar in context, varied a lot in phraseology. There were a lot of short, straightforward answers just praising the Navy:

F 40 C: Shows you what our men are like compared to the Huns.
M 20 B: Pretty efficient. The Italians haven't got much change.
M 40 C: They are doing a grand job.
M 45 D: I think they're doing all they can.
M 55 D: They do a fine job of work.

In a large number of people emotions and feelings were evoked *by seeing this film*. Pride in the Navy is mentioned by several; some people said the film made them more thoughtful than they had been hitherto about the Navy:

F 19 C: Proud that my boy's in the Fleet Air Arm.
F 40 D: Proud to be British.
F 65 D: Very proud of them.
M 25 B: I'm glad it's ours and not the Germans'.
M 60 B: Prouder every minute.
M 30 C: Proud of our oldest Service.
M 20 C: Proud – that's what we were meant to feel, I suppose.
M 60 D: Proud that they are doing so well.
F 65 C: I felt I ought to do something to help them.
F 18 D: Glad that I can save to help them a little.

F 50 D: That I ought to do all I can to help them.

F 25 C: Yes, it made you think that things have got to be done whatever the cost.

F 35 B: One's thoughts naturally turned to them.

F 30 C: It made you think of those fellows.

F 30 D: Grateful for what the Navy does.

M 55 B: Made you think something was worth while.

M 40 C: It did make you think of our Senior Service.

M 60 D: Makes one thing about them, you know.

Most of the qualified remarks also could be classed into groups. There were a small number of people who had relations or friends in the Navy, and *identified them with this film*:

F 30 C: I've got a brother in the Navy and I think they are fine.

F 30 C: Lovely, you see my husband is in the Navy.

F 40 C: Proud, I've a son in the Navy.

F 50 B: My son's there, so of course it made me think.

F 45 B: Made me feel glad that my husband is in the Navy.

F 50 D: Oh, my husband has been blown up three times.

Men, and particularly young men, after seeing the film *felt that they would like to join the Navy:*

M 25 C: It's a very good Service and I wish I had been in it.

M 25 C: I felt as though I'd like to join it when I saw it.

M 30 D: Wished I was in it.

M 55 D: If I were young enough I'd join it.

One young man who was just about to join the Navy was glad to see the film because he thought it told him *what he would be doing presently:*

M 20 B: Gave me an idea what I shall be doing presently.

The work of the Navy and Fleet Air Arm in the film was *admired* by some:

F 60 D: It's very patriotic, isn't it? You don't realise all those fellows are doing for you and this makes you see it better.

M 35 A: They do something at least – more than can be said for the Army.

M 40 C: I think they are even more heroes than the RAF.

M 20 D: The Fleet Air Arm is the finest branch of the Navy.

M 20 D: Well it shows you what they can do – I liked that best where he crashed the dam – I wonder how they do that?

M 20 C: The Fleet Air Arm are certainly doing their bit and keeping up very well.

VI Effect of film on Naval prestige

There is very little strong criticism of the Navy or the Naval treatment of the film. Firstly we find a number of people who definitely disapproved of the way the Naval theme was treated in the film. Some of these thought the picture which was given of the Navy false and resented this:

F 50 D: I don't think it was quite fair to them.

F 25 B: It was rather spoiled by putting it in that sort of film. I'd sooner see a straightforward instruction film.

F 35 B: All my feelings, if any, about it were smothered by the love theme in the film. Just like the cheap and nasty American thing.

F 50 B: It seemed to put the Navy itself into a bad light and made the Fleet Air Arm all important.

M 50 B: I think we appreciate the work they do without the film to help us.

M 50 C: I don't think it's a good idea putting them in films like this.

F 55 B: But really if they wanted to give you a realistic picture of what they are doing, they ought to have made a picture like *Target for Tonight*.

Then there were people who showed a definite resistance to any propaganda film, and stated that they were tired of seeing this kind of picture:

F 20 B: I'm so tired of this MoI type of film.

F 20 B: I'm so sick of these pictures; they leave me cold.

F 30 C: Left me cold.

A few said that after seeing the film they were glad they were not in the Navy, or their husbands were not in that Service:

F 45 C: I hate the sea.

F 30 B: Glad my husband isn't in it.

M 20 B: Thankful I'm not in it.

M 25 C: Glad I am not a sailor.

Some were again bored by the propaganda:

F 45 B: They are overdoing their propaganda – it's not necessary.

F 30 C: Just propaganda.

M 30 C: Propaganda, I suppose, you know.

And lastly, some people talked about the recent mishaps that had befallen the Navy in various theatres of war:

F 45 B: I think it's a pity there isn't more of it, then we wouldn't have
lost those two battleships.

M 40 C: Rotten, what's the good of the Navy when they can't stop the
Japs in Malaya.

M 28 D: After the propaganda and the Swordfish and what's
happened. . . .

The film has definitely influenced a few, mainly women, to feel more
about the Navy. Most are, however, in effect, already esteeming the Navy
and regarding *Ships with Wings* as fantasy, not fact.

VII Demand for more such films

A very small spontaneous demand was made for more films like *Ships with
Wings*. Most of this type of reply comes from London where about one
person in thirty said that he or she would like to see more pictures of this
type. In Inland and Merchant Ports about one person in a hundred made
this demand, but no one mentioned this at all in Naval Ports. This desire
for more films of this 'super-patriotic' kind comes from both sexes and all
classes equally. There are, however, a slightly larger number of *older
people* than younger people who feel the need for more films like *Ships
with Wings*:

M 30 B: I'd like to see more of these sorts of films.

M 40 B: I liked the film and would like to see more like it again.

M 60 A: . . . they ought to show more films like that, we don't get enough
of them.

M 30 C: I think some like that ought to be shown.

F 45 C: Lovely – it was a good picture – in fact, we could do with a few
more like that – have you seen it? It was a sensible picture
wasn't it?

VIII Summary

After studying the reactions of people all over the country in all sorts of
cinemas, after interviewing people who know nothing about the Navy,
have brothers or husbands or sons in the Navy, and after interviewing
men who are sailors themselves, or have spent a lifetime on the seas, we
come to the conclusion that the film had been a great success among all
sections and classes of people.

Nearly nine people in ten liked this film in some way. When we compare
this figure to other figures obtained at previous film investigations, this is

an exceptional standard. The film appealed to a wide public, and only the minority of 'sophisticated sections' of the population approved of it slightly less, or criticised it. Because of the film's emotional appeal, women were more taken with it than men, and the poorer sections of the people slightly more than the richer. People who lived in places with a Naval tradition liked the film better than those who had little intimate knowledge of the Navy. The film also had slightly more appeal for the younger generation who loved the battle-scenes and the excitement of the film generally.

In spite of the general appeal – and it was a kind of reaction which was emotional rather than 'thought out' – there was a considerable body of fairly well reasoned criticism. Perhaps the criticism most often made, and most deeply felt, was that though the film was nice and exciting, it did not correspond to facts in real life, and in effect was unrealistic. Probably, after thinking further about the film, more people would have felt this than did at the time of being interviewed. Some of the people who knew something about cinema technique complained of the model-work in the film, and thought this very badly done, e.g. the scene of the Italian island, and the bombing of the dam, as well as some of the flying scenes. It was regretted that actors rather than the 'real people' should have taken part in the film, and to a few the life on an aircraft carrier did not appear credible from the film scenes.

The film had had a large amount of advance publicity and many people went to the cinema with a fairly definite picture in their mind about what they were going to see. This, of course, sometimes led to disappointment, and some had a vague feeling of being let down. Some were also annoyed by the love story which had been imposed on the film, and felt that the film would have been far better, had it left out the more personal element which had nothing to do with the film, and was boring. On the other hand there also were complaints – from women only – that there was too little story in the film and that it was therefore dull.

Some women felt that it was not right to show this kind of picture at the present time when so many of the nation's young men are serving with the Navy, since their reactions and friends would worry more about them after seeing this film. The obvious 'propaganda' points were also disliked, and it was said that there was no need to have films to bolster up the Navy, already high in prestige.

But a large amount of the criticism is not as explicit as the above remarks might indicate. Many people feel that this film did not strike quite the right note, though being entertaining enough. The artificiality of some of the story gave people an underlying uncomfortable feeling, and some thought that the whole film was too much in the way of being a mixture between a fairy-tale and reality.

People were definitely stirred by it and moved, but this did not go deep. Many of the people who came to see this film, came *because* they liked the

Navy and had an interest in it. The film therefore, preached mostly to the already converted, and though it is likely that it succeeded in increasing those people's admiration for the Senior Service, this tendency was not strong.

The Navy was also little criticised, but there was again a definite body of opinion who felt that the film did not do the real Navy justice. It was said that no Naval officers would behave as did those shown on the street, and that the film was something of a caricature of the Navy. Several people mentioned that they thought it a mistake to put the Navy into this kind of picture, and contrasted *Ships with Wings* with *Target for Tonight*, stating that the latter gave a feeling of reality, while the former had little to do with Naval life.

To the more critical the film contained some bad points:

1 Aircraft carriers (from the film) seem like luxurious hotels, inhabited by officers who drink all day and discuss women. Most of them seem bored.
2 Admirals are amiable fathers whom one talks to quite naturally, and argues with about orders.
3 The officers' interests centre around the Admiral's family. The Admiral's son is treated preferentially.
4 Aircraft when landing near a fire, would in reality jettison their bombs before? Bombs have the unpleasant habit of going off when hotted to a certain temperature?
5 The bombing scenes of the island and the dam are obviously faked and so quite unreal. The island seems to be made of superior cardboard.
6 It is quite impossible to direct two aeroplanes locked together, and almost impossible to clash with another plane in mid-air at will.

These points could be enumerated at will, but the fact remains, that people did not notice them very much, anyway not before thinking more deeply about the film. They go to the cinema to be entertained, not to be educated. *Ships with Wings* entertained; it did not apparently educate. The film, therefore, was able to carry people along with it, over the logical bumps.

Memo on *Ships with Wings*

I have not seen this film, but I should say from experience of film observation that it is liable to be a fairly big success, however big the faults of production, etc., are. The reasons for my saying this are as follows:

1 It will almost certainly include technical details of which the audience was unaware. These will be not be rammed down their throats but presented quietly and unassumingly, so that the audience will think that they are clever in finding them out. Witness the similar effect of

the RAF operational room scenes in *The Lion Has Wings*, and the convoy details in *Convoy*.

2 There is the direct heroic motif in it, the one man who by his own effort can make a difference to the course of the war. There will be an inevitable tendency to put oneself in his place, and to get rid of the 'cog in the wheel' attitude. This motif would probably be stronger if the hero was not of the upper classes from the beginning.

3 The sentimental appeal of the *Ark Royal*. How strong this is, I don't know, but I should fancy that a little careful advertisement could make this interest considerable. This appeal was not, however, sufficient to make *For Freedom* (The *Graf Spee* battle) a success.

4 The bombing scenes and the general action. It is my personal opinion, substantiated fairly well, that what might be called the impersonal bombing scene is very effective, the personal one most unpopular. There is still great interest in, say, a building, or a lorry, or a dam being blown up for it is a very fine cinematic thrill. But there is great antipathy to people being blown up. A scene such as (I assume) the war scenes in *Sergeant York*, or the sea battle in *Convoy* are *not* popular because bombs and shells will be seen killing real people and everybody in the audience will think of some friend or relation in circumstances similar to those shown. I believe that all the scenes in *Ships with Wings* fall in the first class.

It is important to note the great similarity in story between *Ships with Wings* and ATP's earlier and very successful (except for battle scenes) *Convoy*. In this earlier film, the cad – once again played by John Clements – runs away with the captain's wife, but in the hour of need with the ship fighting a great battle against overwhelming odds he saves the situation and dies in the attempt.

19   Newsreel Content (28 January 1940)

There were five privately owned newsreel companies who between them reached the whole of the mass cinema-going audience. They came under government supervision at the outbreak of war. Although plans had been drawn up in peace time for the establishment of a Ministry of Information and the control of the news media, there was an initial period of confusion and misunderstanding during which the three armed services each maintained their own news censors and for a time the news censorship division was actually detached from the Ministry of Information. The situation was made worse by the MoI's first policy – to block the flow of news altogether. So the War Office banned all photography of military subjects and no filming of the departure of the British Expeditionary Force was allowed. This resulted in Britain losing the first round of the propaganda war. For while the Germans flooded the cinema screens of neutral countries with scenes of their victorious armies sweeping across Europe, the British could offer nothing in response. At home, the news ban had the effect, as Mass-Observation noted, of compelling the newsreel companies to resort to reconstructions and comedy inserts in the absence of authentic news footage. But the first head of the Films Division at the MoI, Sir Joseph Ball, was soon pressing for a change of policy and by January 1940 the Ministry was stressing that 'we need the co-operation of the newsreel companies more, possibly, than of any other part of the film industry. We are actively seeking their co-operation at the moment, because without it the distribution of favourable news is almost impossible.' The arrival of Sir John Reith, with his belief in 'news as the shocktroops of propaganda', as Minister of Information in January 1940, decisively completed the change of policy. The news censorship division was reincorporated in the MoI and a positive approach to propaganda evolved, what Nicholas Pronay calls 'propaganda with facts if not *the* facts, truth if not the *whole* truth'. There was comprehensive pre- and post-production censorship of the newsreels and the censors' aim was clearly stated in 1941 to be 'the translation as far as practicable of the Minister of Information's wishes in regard to propaganda into terms of moving pictures and commentaries'. There were official lists of banned topics and definite policies on, for instance, precisely how much bomb damage should be shown on the screen. According to J. C. Robertson, 'the evidence suggests that . . . the system evolved before the war and improved during its early stages through Sir John Reith's reorganization at the MoI proved effective right through to August 1945 despite a great increase in the amount of film censorship work after June 1941'.

Mass-Observation was interested both in what went into the newsreels and what the public attitude to them was. Len England prepared a report (FR 22), dated 28 January 1940, on the content of newsreels since the outbreak of war.

On the control of newsreels during the war see Nicholas Pronay, 'The news media at war', in N. Pronay and D. W. Spring (eds), *Propaganda, Politics and Film 1918–45* (London, 1982); and on film censorship in general, J. C. Robertson, *The British Board of Film Censors: Film Censorship in Britain 1896–1950* (London, 1985).

Subject matter

Naturally as soon as the war broke out the whole emphasis of newsreels became centred on war news; in the first six months, less than 15 per cent of their news has had no connection with war (see Appendix A) either in this country or in Finland. But the lack of activity after the collapse of Poland forced the newsreels to look beyond Europe for their shots. They could not indefinitely show sequences of the BEF on manœuvres or in their trenches, and by the middle of December the British Army in France began to fade from the newsreels; between the beginning of November and the middle of December seventeen observed newsreels contained shot of the BEF. Since that date there has been one.

At sea more was happening, but the difficulty here was to get action pictures; with the *City of Flint*, for example, the newsreels could do no more than take pictures of the stationary ship when she docked at Bergen, while when the *Rawalpindi* was sunk by the *Deutschland*, the newsreels showed shots of each ship firing their guns and cut them with one another. The same difficulty occurred with the work of the RAF. In both cases some attempt was made to enliven the sequences by the introduction of faked shots of submarines sinking or of air battles with the remark 'this is what it would have looked like'. On one occasion the audience laughed at an RAF fight and it seems that these reconstructions have been given up. But a dangerous precedent has been created in false news.

No shots of action on the Western Front were released until the 11 December and it was another ten days before action at sea was obtained. Neither of these sequences were more than a muddled picture of bombs dropping and shells firing – and the one of the navy was taken by an officer of the ship – the audiences were not impressed. But when, just before Christmas, the *Graf Spee* was scuttled, cameramen were on the spot and on 2 January newsreels contained a long sequence of the sinking battleship. At the end of it the audience at the Cameo, Charing Cross Road, as a rule most unresponsive, clapped loudly and even a fortnight later a suburban audience applauded.

But an event such as the scuttling of the *Graf Spee* was too rare for the newsreels to depend upon it for interest. When the Polish resistance was finally crushed and no activities on the Western Front were forthcoming, the newsreels turned elsewhere for shots of fighting. One long sequence dealt with the war in China and caused more comment than anything else in observed newsreels. For some time manœuvres in America were the mainstay; these were staged on a large scale with tanks being blown up, aeroplanes bombing ground troops, and above all a night attack with tracer bullets which the Gaumont British commentator admitted to be 'America's gift to the cinema, to make up for the war in Europe'.

Then on 30 November 1939, Russian troops invaded Finland, and there were immediate air raids. Since that date eighteen newsreels have been observed, and in thirteen of them shots of the war in Finland have been included with an average length of over two minutes. Six of these thirteen newsreels have caused comment, once the Finns have been applauded. This exceptionally high degree of response seems to indicate that the newsreels have been right in emphasising this element, but the number of people who in answer to the questionnaire said that they objected to war in newsreels, together with the 'God's and 'horrible's' of the comments, tends to indicate that they are not effective propaganda.

Here again, however, there is evidence to suggest that the newsreels have been 'reconstructing' events. Some of the shots, it is said, bear a marked resemblance to those of bombed Spanish towns; women supposed to be rushing to shelter in an air raid were laughing; of a picture of a burning village, the Pathé commentary said that it had been fired by the retreating Red army, while Paramount argued that the Finns had burnt it after them themselves.

Before the war, even in the last weeks of August, the only response to shots of soldiers was laughter. On not one occasion since the war has any soldier been laughed at with the exception of two French soldiers riding a tandem, a sequence that was intended to be funny. The Women's army has, however, created some amusement due in part at any rate to facetious remarks in the commentary; Universal, for instance, with shots of Land Army girls on a turkey farm produced remarks about 'nice birds'. On other occasions bad marching has produced titters.

Though there has been no laughter, there has been a good deal of clapping at the sight of soldiers and sailors. At the beginning of the war the sight of a sailor leaning out of a window was on one occasion sufficient provocation for general applause, while on another French troops marching were clapped. About 10 per cent of the appearances of allied forces have been greeted by clapping; otherwise they have been watched in silence.

Mention has already been made of the inclusion of faked news in newsreels. Yet another way in which the companies have tried to make up for the lack of any interesting information is by the introduction of items which are topical but have no direct news value. At the beginning of the war, for instance, the Crazy Gang became an admirable substitute for news. On one occasion Bud Flanagan portrayed a soldier in a dug-out dreaming of French girls and Blighty; on another, in an item called 'The Worst Wrestling Match', the Crazy Gang did a fight in slow motion. On this occasion no attempt at all was made to connect it to any item of news and the audience was at first mystified; a week earlier the Crazy Gang had been seen wrestling, but this time it was for the troops and soldiers were seen in the shots. Cartoons were used in short epilogues; in the same news as 'The Worst Wrestling Match' a cartoon addressed to Hitler pointed out that 'we've got the money, we've got the guns, so what are you going to do?' The next week Pathé included an illustrated poem on the value of 'Keep it Dark.' The inauguration of the keep-fit classes on the wireless prompted Universal to depict a fat woman trying to touch her toes, while Pathé has now instituted a whole series of 'Nasti News'. One was seen by an observer:

Lord Haw-Haw enters with large moustache and monocle. By his side is a 'lie-making machine'.	(laughs 1)
Remarks about Goering and his medals.	(laughs 2)
'Next Tuesday a British ship was sunk at Tiddley-winks on Spee.'	(laughs 2)
A man who has been painting a wall at the back turns round; it is Hitler.	(laughs 2)
He awards Haw-Haw with an Iron Cross.	(laughs 2)
'To facilitate scuttling, German ships are being made without bottoms.'	(laughs 3)
Fade-out with Hitler saluting.	(laughs 3)

It will be seen that there is a high degree of audience response to this comedy. At the 'Keep it Dark' sequence there was even some applause. And while this is not a post-war [i.e. wartime] development – it was used quite extensively by Movietone before the war – nevertheless in newsreels observed since the war, nearly 30 per cent contain a comedy.

Personalities

There follows a comparative table of the appearances of famous figures in pre-war and post-war [i.e. wartime] newsreels.

	Pre-war (12 newsreels)		Wartime (38 newsreels)	
	No. of appearances	*No. of times applauded*	*No. of appearances*	*No. of times applauded*
British politicians				
Anderson	3	0	0	0
Baldwin	5	3	0	0
Cecil	4	0	0	0
Chamberlain	10	1	4	2
Churchill	0	0	5	3
Eden	0	0	2	0
Lloyd George	5	(2 laughs)	0	0
Halifax	11	1	0	0
Henderson	8	1	0	0
Hore Belisha	3	0	6	3
Hoare	0	0	1	0
Simon	0	0	4	2
Runciman	1	0	0	0
Kingsley Wood	4	0	0	0
Total	54	8	22	10
Royal family				
The King	8	0	11	2
The Queen	5	0	11	3
Queen Mary	3	0	1	1
Duke of Kent	2	0	0	0
Duke of Gloucester	0	0	4	1
Duke of Windsor	0	0	8	6
Duchess of Kent	1	(1 laugh)	0	0
Duchess of Windsor	0	0	1	0
Total	19	1	36	13
Other figures				
Daladier	5	0	3	0
Hitler	0	0	1	0
Roosevelt	4	2	1	0
Stalin	0	0	2	0

It will be seen immediately that the emphasis in wartime news has shifted from personalities to events. The numbers of well-known people in thirty-eight newsreels observed since the war are hardly greater than the number in twelve pre-war newsreels. It has also shifted from politicians to royalty and within those groups from one figure to another. Finally, the audience now responds to different figures.

Before the war, the appearances of the King and Queen were less frequent than those of either Chamberlain or Halifax: since the war [started] both of them have appeared more than twice as often as anyone outside the royal family, and whereas on no occasion formerly were they applauded, now they have been clapped on 20 per cent of their appearances. The Duke of Windsor was not seen at all before the war, since he has appeared eight times and been applauded on six of them, or on 75 per cent of appearances. The Duke of Gloucester has not been seen at all before the war, though one of his four appearances since has been clapped.

Before the war, as has been mentioned, Lord Halifax and Mr Chamberlain were more frequently seen than any personality; since the War Lord Halifax has not been seen at all and Mr Chamberlain was not observed until three days before Christmas, while on his tour of the front. On this occasion he was not clapped, but after the resignation of Hore Belisha, when Mr Chamberlain was photographed making his Mansion House speech, he was applauded on two occasions though in both cases very feebly. Hore Belisha, on the other hand, has made six appearances since the war, four times before his resignation; on one occasion he was clapped. After his resignation he made two very brief appearances but each time he was immediately clapped. Mr Chamberlain, in brief, in two appearances of four minutes and three minutes, in which he made many remarks that caused clapping from his Mansion House audience, was applauded very feebly. Hore Belisha, in two appearances of half a minute, in which he did not speak a word, was clapped more vigorously.

Of other politicians the two that have made most appearances have been most clapped. Mr Churchill has made five appearances, including a five-minute reconstruction of a broadcast which constituted the entire news at the Gaumont, Haymarket, and on three occasions was clapped. Simon has made four appearances and was clapped twice; neither of these politicians appeared at all before the war.

On the other hand, there are many politicians as well as Halifax who have not appeared at all since the war. Sir John Anderson, Lord Baldwin (clapped on 60 per cent of his appearances pre-war), Viscount Cecil, Lord Chatfield, Lloyd George, Sir Neville Henderson, Lord Runciman, and Sir Kingsley Wood, none has appeared in observed newsreels since the war. Roosevelt who was clapped on two of his four pre-war appearances has been seen only once when the audience showed signs of boredom.

Military leaders have not been featured to any great extent. Lord Gort has made three appearances; on no occasion was he clapped and when he gave a Christmas message – 'the first time in newsreel history that a commander-in-Chief has spoken' as the Pathé Gazette announced – the only response noted by an observer was one woman who remarked 'silly, isn't it?'. Gamelin has made one appearance and Colonel Lane in charge of the Army Mail made an appeal at Christmas. A brief shot of the General who signed the Anglo-Turkish agreement was greeted with immediate, loud applause.

A sequence of the burial of the victims of the Munich bomb explosion, obtained through neutral countries, included a long shot of Hitler – there was no response at all. At the beginning of the Russo-Finnish war sequences of Stalin were included; at the Cameo, Charing Cross Road, one man called out something fairly loudly and another muttered 'Urcha'. At the Regal, Kennington, there was no response at all.

The appearances of the Crazy Gang have been mentioned before, but it is worthy of note that Gracie Fields has appeared as often. On none of her four appearances has she been clapped, but there has been general laughter at all her jokes. On each occasion she has appeared on the newsreel just after a broadcast, and every time she has been photographed actually entertaining the troops, not specially engaged by a newsreel company.

Summary of content

The newsreels appear to have well judged public taste. Since the war the public figures who have appeared most in the newsreels are those that have been most applauded. The shifting of emphasis from politicians to the royal family may indicate that the public now prefers the uninterfering royalty to troublesome Members of Parliament, though the popularity of Sir John Simon, even after the announcement of his war budget, is surprising.

In subject matter the tendency is directly on war themes, though until Russia's invasion of Finland there were few 'action' shots. Shots of the BEF were frequent until all aspects of their life had been exhausted, and much the same applied to the navy. Nevertheless the newsreels are very far from succeeding in making all their contents vital as the number of criticisms in the questionnaire on the grounds to 'no news' or 'repetition' show.

Finally, a new tendency is appearing to produce in newsreels both faked news and reconstructions of events that could not be filmed, and also comic interludes that have no direct connection with any item of news. This must be a direct consequence of the absence of news, or the difficulty of getting it, and while they are well received, they must be regarded as a dangerous inclusion. In their true form newsreels can be regarded as a record more accurate than any other, but once reconstruction or faking appears, their whole value is lost.

Other general tendencies

As well as the general tendencies in newsreels that have been noted under 'Subject matter', there are one or two general points that must be observed. Before the war the newsreels portrayed the official view of events on most occasions though at the time of the Munich crisis one of the companies was asked to withdraw a speech by Wickham Steed which was considered to be out of keeping with the Government's plans. Later, however, at the time of the film tax, the newsreels argued that they provided the Government with excellent propaganda free of all charge.

Since the war the newsreels have continued to contain much propaganda, a little too much, judging from the questionnaire. Shots of Dominion troops are almost invariably an excuse for the expression of patriotic sentiments, while even the arrival of Indian troops in France provoked the remark that India stands behind Britain as one man. Among the political figures on the screen, no Opposition speakers have been seen and no opportunity has been missed to pour invective on Germany or on Russia. The feature 'Keep it Dark', mentioned elsewhere, was an even more obvious case of propaganda.

But for all this the newsreels appear to have found a little more initiative in the war. At the resignation of Hore Belisha, Paramount came out openly on the side of the departing Minister, and in so doing reflected public opinion; 'so leaves one of our ablest men' ran the commentary. On this matter a question was asked in the House.

The same company, a few weeks previously, had provoked another Parliamentary question over their item on the return to this country of Miss Unity Mitford:

> Lord Denman described as a fake that part of the film showing battleships manœuvring, troops on parade, a strong force of police, a royal guard of honour, and aeroplanes flying in formation.
>
> To magnify Miss Mitford's return into a matter of national importance as this film seemed to do was really absurd. Far more objectionable than the pictures was the running commentary. The commentator proceeded to make rather cheap jokes at the expense of Lord Redesdale and his daughter.

In peace time no newsreel would have dared to express an unconstitutional opinion as strongly as this.

Another tendency that may be said to be due to the war is that which is producing 'horrific' shots. Before the war shots of the burning of the Graf Zeppelin were cut on the grounds that they were too horrible for the general public. Yet in one newsreel recently a whole series of shots showed dead Russians lying in the snow, and it was followed up almost immediately by a sequence on the Turkish earthquake which included a picture of a man pulling at a leg that was emerging from a shattered house. At both these shots there was considerable comment from the audience and at the second, a number of 'oh's, but there was no sign of any general revulsion, as there was at the first photos of the bombing of Helsinki, a sequence which little imagination was necessary to translate into an event which might happen to any member of the audience.

Questionnaire

Two hundred people, equally divided into class, age, and sex groups, were asked, among other questions, 'What do you think of the newsreels?' Their answers, in brief, can be classified as follows:

Like them very much	Like them	Doubtful	Dislike them	Dislike them very much	Don't know
24%	37½%	19%	12½%	2½%	4½%

This large majority who like the newsreels is fairly evenly distributed among all groups, as will be seen from the more detailed table.

	Like them very much	Like them	Doubtful	Dislike them	Dislike them very much	Don't know
Class B						
Men over 30	36%	44%	4%	8%	4%	8%
Men under 30	4%	24%	20%	44%	4%	8%
Women over 30	36%	44%	16%	–	–	4%
Women under 30	32%	32%	24%	12%	–	–

	Like them very much	Like them	Doubtful	Dislike them	Dislike them very much	Don't know
Class D						
Men over 30	36%	20%	24%	12%	–	8%
Men under 30	4%	48%	16%	24%	8%	–
Women over 30	32%	36%	28%	–	–	4%
Women under 30	16%	52%	20%	4%	4%	4%

It will be seen that the only group that shows any strong objection to newsreels are the men under 30 of the middle classes; men under 30 of the lower classes have no greater number among them who like the newsreels greatly, but practically half their number showed no objection to them. Not a single woman over thirty had any criticism to make of newsreels.

Of these two hundred people only sixty, or 30 per cent, gave any further comment. Nearly 10 per cent of these criticisms were on the grounds that the news was merely repetition:

They're pretty interesting except that the 'somewhere in France' descriptions of what is happening come over and over again. (Man, 20, working class)

They're good when you have only seen them once but after two or three times. . . . (Man, 20, middle class)

They are the same thing over and over again; but I suppose that it's all right for some people. (Man, 40, worker)

Even more complained that they contained much too much propaganda, men under 30 of the middle classes being particularly critical of this aspect:

I hate all propaganda of any kind. (Man, 20, middle class)

Well, for instance, they will show you the navy and they say 'isn't it superb?' and its object is to defend freedom while the German navy wants to destroy everything. And that's that. (Man, 20, middle class)

They are all right when they are not saturated with propaganda as they invariably are. (Man, 25, middle class)

There's much too much glorious Britain, triumphant Britain about them. (Man, 25, worker)

They are trying to boost the royal family. (Man, 40, worker)

Many complained of the lack of news:

They are all right most of them. There's not much news in them, of course. (Woman, 20, middle class)

I don't think they give very interesting news nowadays. (Man, 20, middle class)

Let's have real news. Same trouble as that of the press. (Man, 20, middle class)

Six per cent could not believe what they saw, even though a newsreel is supposed to consist entirely of photographic records of actual events:

I think the news reels are hooey, they tell you what is dished up every five minutes on the wireless, with the same Nazi planes crashing and our men not all coming back, but they don't tell you how many don't. I don't believe a thing, honestly. (Woman, 20, working class)

They only show the light side of war and the enemy trying to be destructive. (Man, 40, worker)

While one woman complained that there was not enough war pictures in the news, many others thought there was too much. This objection to shots of actual fighting is borne out by newsreel observations.

You get a lot of destruction in them and my lady doesn't like it. (Man, 40, worker)

It doesn't give me personally much pleasure to see bombs dropping and houses falling down. (Man, 50, middle class)

The bombing of Helsinki was a bit too realistic. It's all right showing war, I suppose, but that was a bit too much. (Woman, 20, working class)

Many people, on the other hand, added most complimentary remarks:

They are the most important part of the show, I go there for that. (Man, 50, worker)

They are interest number one for me. (Man, 50, middle class)

They are best of all sometimes. I go sometimes to see them. (Woman, 20, middle class)

I enjoy them, I wish they went a bit slower and were a bit longer. (Woman, 50, working class)

Despite the fact that many of the newsreels sequences are common to all five companies, five people mentioned the name of one particular reel that they liked or disliked. One man chose Paramount, another Pathé and GB, two more mentioned GB. One woman, on the other hand, said 'We always enjoy them, but I don't like the man with the too dramatic voice, you know the man I mean', presumably meaning Emmett of the Gaumont British.

In brief, over 60 per cent of the people questioned liked the newsreels, and, unlike those who said they liked *The Lion Has Wings*, many of them gave reasons or comments on their approval, one man going as far as to wish that the newsreels were a feature; that there is a genuine interest in them is borne out by the number who showed a preference for one newsreel in particular. Many of the criticisms, on the other hand, concern matters that are not the fault of the newsreels. The largest number of complaints was directed against the inclusion of too much war news; but a newsreel by its nature must be concerned with topicalities and therefore the war. Others argued that there was 'no news'; but this is due to the Censor not to the companies who would obviously be delighted if there was more news released to them.

Most of the remaining criticism was directed against the propaganda element in newsreels; this complaint appeared with equal regularity on *The Lion Has Wings* questionnaire where it was established that any propaganda to be successful must be concealed. The newsreels with their 'glorious Britain, triumphant Britain' are not masking their propaganda sufficiently to give it the most effect. It would be as well for the newsreels to remember in this connection that the only class of the public that shows any marked opposition is the men under thirty of the middle classes. Of these 48 per cent dislike the newsreels, half of them giving as their reason that 'there is too much propaganda'.

General conclusions

1 The newsreels are genuinely popular.
2 The newsreels have to some extent earned this popularity by discovering public opinion and altering subject matter to taste.
3 Emphasis has changed in wartime
   (a) the inclusion of faked news
   (b) the inclusion of 'comedies'
   (c) the inclusion of 'horrific'

4 Emphasis is now entirely on war matters.
5 Newsreels still contain much propaganda.
6 But this propaganda is a little too obvious.
7 The newsreels are developing character of their own.
8 General tendencies in newsreels are
   (a) the inclusion of faked news
   (b) the inclusion of 'comedies'
   (c) the inclusion of 'horrific'
9 Audience now applauds royal family more than politicians.
10 No longer thinks that soldiers are funny.

Appendix A: Content of newsreels (divided into subject matter)

	Pre-war	Wartime
Soldiers	7% of shots	71%
War (except soldiers)	21%	14%
Non-war	62%	15%

The emphasis has shifted naturally from non-war subjects to war subjects but there is also a shifting from the effect of the war on the private citizen to its effect on the soldier as soon as war is declared. The very small percentage of shots of soldiers pre-war may be due to the laughter caused by their presence.

Appendix B: Statements and criticisms (made by 60 out of 200 interviewed on newsreels)

| | Class B | | | | Class D | | | | Total |
	M.O.	M.U.	W.O.	W.U.	M.O.	M.U.	W.O.	W.U.	
Criticisms									
No news		3	1	2	1			1	8 (12%)
Restricted news		2			1			1	4 (6%)
Propaganda element	1	4			1	2			8 (12%)
Disbelief		1			1	1		1	4 (6%)

	Class B				Class D				Total
	M.O.	M.U.	W.O.	W.U.	M.O.	M.U.	W.O.	W.U.	
Repetition		1			1	3		1	6 (9%)
Too much war	3	1		2	1		1	1	9 (14%)
Too little war								1	1 (1½%)
Too short							3		3 (5%)
Too slow					1				1 (1½%)
Uninteresting		1							1 (1½%)

Comments

	Class B				Class D				Total
	M.O.	M.U.	W.O.	W.U.	M.O.	M.U.	W.O.	W.U.	
Look forward to them most of all		1		1	1		1		4 (6%)
Lot of news								1	1 (1½%)
Should be a feature						1			1 (1½%)
Educational								1	1 (1½%)

Liked particular one: Man over 30, B – Gaumont British
Woman over 30, B – Pathé and Gaumont British
Man over 30, D – Paramount
Woman over 30, D – Gaumont British
Disliked particular one: Woman over 30, B – 'man with dramatic voice'

Newsreel Report 2 (26 May 1940)

A second newsreel report (FR 141), dated 29 May 1940 and compiled by Len England, shows how the newsreels were responding to the course of the war. The report is prefaced by the statement:

> The following report is a rough one, one of the routine series of interim reports made by the observer in charge of film work, with the help of several other whole-time observers in London, checked by a number of part-time observers in the provinces. General points are made on pp. 11–13. In addition we would stress the suggestion that the effect of continuous atrocity newsreel sequences may in the long run tend to have a blunting effect on people's general level of reaction. Photographically, people are being mentally prepared for the worst?

Subject matter

On a previous report covering newsreels from the beginning of war until the end of January some emphasis was laid on the fact that newsreels were tending towards the inclusion of comedies, faked news, and reconstructions to make up for the absence of events in the European war. Yet although the period to the end of January was an arbitrary one, since that date there has been hardly one comedy or reconstruction in any of the fifty-six newsreels observed and no evidence has come to hand of any faking. Pathé Gazette continued with their 'Nasti newsreel' until the end of March but what had originally been a weekly feature was issued at irregular intervals, three weeks elapsing between nos 7 and 8; none of these were observed after January, but an observer was told that they had been a great success. In addition after the news of the invasion of Holland had come through, but before any pictures were available, use was made of old shots to decorate a commentary on the might of our navy, but no attempt was made in these cases to pretend as with earlier reconstructions, that this was the real thing. Finally, a George Formby visit to the troops had obviously been 'touched up' before being shown on the newsreels and additional scenes had been added. Yet, in the period September 1939 to January 1940, out of 40 observed newsreels 15 contained comedies or reconstructions; in the period February to May

1940, out of 56 newsreels observed at most two contained reconstructions or comedies with three additional 'Haw-Haw' items noted by an observer but not actually seen.

This disappearance was not due to an increase in the amount of available news; if anything the position grew worse and on 29 February a typical newsreel was as follows:

Canadian airmen arrive	70 ft
Evacuation of Finnish children	44 ft
'Bandy' match at Stockholm	48 ft
Red Cross boxing championships	62 ft
Cape Town Mayor's Fund	27 ft
Polish airmen inspected	27 ft
Belgians move forest	32 ft
The watch on the Rhine	47 ft
German plane down on east coast	29 ft
German ship seized by French patrol boat	40 ft
In the Maginot Line	107 ft
The Queen in Scotland	102 ft
U.S. Army Manœuvres	106 ft

This can hardly be called an inspiring collection of items, most of which run for less than half a minute and one of the longest of which consists of those large-scale American manœuvres which one commentator has already called 'America's gift to the cinema'.

The difficulty in obtaining news was not made easier by the decreasing interest in the war in Finland and, as will be seen later, in the royal family. It was mentioned in the first report that out of eighteen newsreels observed after the start of the Russo-Finnish war, thirteen had contained sequences of the fighting and on six occasions, or nearly 50 per cent, the Finns were applauded. Between February and the end of the war at the beginning of April, out of thirty-two observed newsreels only fifteen contained shots of Finland and [on] not one occasion was there any applause, indeed in the middle of March, an observer noted continual signs of boredom throughout a long and graphic sequence of air raid havoc; this, in Obs.'s opinion, was due to a feeling of 'we've seen this all before' as all shots, however well taken, of damaged streets and refugees bear great similarity to one another.

The gap created by the loss of the comedies has been filled by increased emphasis on Home Affairs, Sport, and Dominion Troops. The last of three categories gained a natural prominence as Expeditionary Forces arrived in France and Egypt and it was helped also by a great deal of material that was sent from Australia. The increased importance of the other two are less obvious.

Though the number of observed newsreels increased *slightly* in the second period, the number of items devoted to sport rose from 2 to 22 and to ARP and Home Affairs from 10 also to 22. It was not merely at the beginning of spring that sport became more popular; ice-skating, tennis (table), and rugby were observed in February and when at the beginning of April the Grand National was run, well over half of an eight-minute reel of Pathé Gazette was devoted to it. Such items were popular, table tennis and the Grand National causing a particular amount of comment.

Some of the sequences on Home Affairs were on agriculture, others on the collection of waste materials, one or two on souvenirs from German raids, in the shape of bullets, etc. The only considerable comment caused here was in one item on old iron with a humorous commentary in the style of Jack Warner with references to Blue Pencil and Bedstead-Cutter-Uppers; this caused the loudest laughter noted in all the observed newsreels.

The mainstays of the newsreels, the armed forces, still occupy by far the largest part of the total footage, though both Army and RAF have suffered a little at the expense of the Navy. To the Navy there is an exceptionally high degree of response, 21 out of 39, or 55 per cent, of its appearances being clapped. One reason for this is of course that until the invasion of Norway all the most important events in the war took place at sea. Between February and May the *Exeter* returned home, the *Altmark* was attacked, and later the *Cossack* returned home, the *Starfish* torpedoed a German cruiser, and finally the Navy sunk a great many ships in Narvik Fjord, an event recorded by cameramen on one of the vessels in the engagement; in addition the *Queen Elizabeth* crossed the channel and the *Queen Mary* began a mystic voyage. In the same period – no direct references to the RAF's part in Norway or Belgium have been observed – the Air Force performed a number of feats, in particular the bombing of Sylt, and were applauded on 6 out of 20, or rough 30 per cent of their appearances.

The Army until the invasion of Norway were forced to sit still and do nothing, and out of the 20 appearances made by it in newsreels not one was applauded; in fact the only response noted was boredom. When at last the Army did go into action, they were applauded loudly and all appearances since the middle of April have been applauded.

Personalities

A very much larger number of famous people have appeared in newsreels in the period from February to May 1940 than in that from the beginning of war to January. The table shows only those who appeared in the first period and takes no notice of those who were first seen in February or after.

| | 1st period | | 2nd period | |
	No. of appears.	Times appld.	No. of appears.	Times appld.
Chamberlain	4	2	1	0
Churchill	5	3	8	4
Eden	2	0	5	0
Hore Belisha	6	3	0	0
Hoare	1	0	0	0
Simon	4	2	2	0
The King	11	2	22	3
The Queen	11	3	22	2
Queen Mary	1	1	2	0
Duke Windsor	8	6	0	0
Duke Gloucester	4	1	0	0
Duchess Windsor	1	0	0	0
Gort	3	0	1	0
Gamelin	3	0	1	0
Daladier	3	0	2	0
Hitler	1	0	4	(2 laughs)
Roosevelt	1	0	5	1
				(1 boo)

In addition to these figures there have been seen in newsreels of the second period:

Lord Halifax	Lord Woolton
Kingsley Wood (2)	Duff Cooper
Stanley (2)	Duke of Kent (2)
Dorman Smith (4)	Duchess of Gloucester (3)
Sir John Reith	Princess Royal
Neville Henderson	Duchess of Kent
Walter Elliott (3)	Queen Wilhelmina

Both table and list exclude a great many 'miscellaneous' people; yet it will be seen at once that although the number of people observed is considerably higher the applause is very much lower. In the first period 65 appearances were made by these people and on 23 occasions were applauded, that is nearly 30 per cent of appearances. In the second period out of 100 appearances only 10, or 10 per cent, were applauded, 4 per cent of which were for Mr Churchill.

The percentage of royal figures seen to political figures is about the same but within those groups there has been much alteration. The Duke of Windsor, the most popular of royal figures, has not been observed once in the period. The King and Queen, while doubling their appearances, have been applauded only the same number of times, and the King is now slightly more popular than the Queen. The reason for the decline in the popularity of the King and Queen is, in Obs.'s opinion, due to the fact that they are always seen visiting factories, civic centres, or the King on his own awarding medals. Every sequence is similar to the last.

Of politicians Churchill is still easily the most popular figure though even he is applauded slightly less than before, while once in Manchester the only response was laughter at his hat. Mr Chamberlain, even before his resignation, was not seen at all, his only appearance being a brief glimpse in a composite shot of the new cabinet; this was seen in a West End cinema where there was no applause for anybody but Obs. was told that in a suburban cinema on the same day a shot of him at Munich in the film *For Freedom* was greeted with very loud applause.

Mr Dorman Smith, the late Minister for Agriculture, broke new ground by twice being interviewed on a farm. The opening shots would show him walking round a farm with the owner, then there would be a close-up of him leaning over a gate with the farmer telling him of his plans for the future of agriculture. This in Obs.'s opinion was highly effective, the usual method of interviewing being of a figure at desk, short and long shots being cut with one another.

The appearance of military leaders become even fewer. Of foreign leaders Roosevelt is now the most often seen, but while in March he was applauded, a speech of his in May was greeted with a shout of 'shut up'. Hitler was three times observed with Mussolini at their Brenner Pass meeting, but on no occasion was there any hissing, though laughs were caused, as usual, by the Heil Hitler salute. On a fourth occasion British Movietone News brought out a very short sequence of Hitler making 'funny faces' while speaking, but there was very little laughter; the probable reason is that it was shown just after the invasion of Holland; a time when Charlie Chaplin decided not to show his film *The Great Dictator* until after the war because 'Nobody is in a mood to laugh at Hitler now.'

Other people seen in newsreels range from Madeleine Carroll and Joe E. Brown to Tanner and Koht. Only two of these caused any response; there was applause when Lord Derby told the Canadian troops in England to give the Germans 'a hell of a time' and when Sir Ian Hamilton was seen at a Gallipoli celebration there was very loud spontaneous applause.

Summary of content

In the main the content of the newsreels has not altered greatly, the main change being that comedies and reconstructions have decreased, their place being filled with news of Dominion troops, Sport, and Home Affairs. The navy has slightly increased in number of appearances and heavily increased in popularity; the Army, on the other hand, until 'total warfare' began, was rarely seen and clapped only once.

In dealing with personalities, the newsreels seem to have lost some of their judgement of popular taste. The number of personalities seen has increased, though the applause given to them is very much smaller; the most popular figure of all, the Duke of Windsor, has not been seen at all during the period, while the King and Queen have been seen twice as often as before though the applause given to them remains the same. A very large number of politicians have been seen, but out of them only Mr Churchill has been clapped and even he slightly less often than formerly.

Later developments

Reference has been made before in this report to the change that took place in the content of newsreels when total warfare began. Before that date the reels were not of outstanding quality as was shown in the quotation of a typical reel for February. Mr Sidney Bernstein of Granada Theatres considered them to be so bad that he wrote to the *Kine Weekly* (18 April) as follows:

> Gerald Sanger, producer of British Movietone News, blames kinema exhibitors for the fact that newsreels are limited to nine minutes owing to lack of playing time and because exhibitors 'don't want to show them any longer'.
>
> This attack is grossly unfair for exhibitors are anxious to run longer newsreels provided the quality of their contents justifies such a policy. In fact it must always be the quality of newsreels that governs their length.
>
> If for no other reason longer newsreels would be welcomed because they would rate as a first-class box-office attraction.
>
> At the outbreak of war it was generally anticipated that newsreels would be an all-important factor in kinema programmes. That hope has not been fulfilled because of the quality of the newsreels which has not come up to expectations.
>
> We play all makes of newsreels and our experience has been that patrons have been disappointed in most of the issues shown since the outbreak of war.
>
> Frankly patrons so far regard war time newsreels as dull, and there is no excuse for dullness in any department of the business.

Mass-Observation investigation does not support the statement that patrons regard the newsreels as dull, but certainly the decreasing response to such items as fighting in Finland and the visits of the King and Queen indicate less interest. Confidence in newsreels was not re-established by their handling of the Parliamentary crisis that broke at the beginning of

May. On Tuesday evening it was known that Mr Chamberlain's cabinet was in a dangerous position, yet in the reels that were released on Thursday and which would not reach a final version until Wednesday evening contained no mention of such events. There could have been no question of the newsreels being full of other material, for the only topical matter in them was the return of British troops from Norway, though on the Friday or Saturday an extra hundred feet were added on a naval engagement in Norway. Nor could there have been any objection to the using of old material, of sequences from the library, as on the Monday over three minutes in most newsreels were devoted to such shots. At that moment Chamberlain had public sympathy – shown in the *For Freedom* incident already mentioned – and there seems to be no valid reason why such an opportunity as this was missed.

However, on Friday, 10 May, Germany invaded Holland and newsreels assumed a new importance and gained a new interest. Some first-hand material had come through from Norway, including an amateur sequence on the battle of Narvik Fjord, the burning *Graf Spee* had been shown just before Christmas and in November shells had been seen bursting in French villages; this – with the exception of news from Finland – was all the graphic war news that the newsreels had been able to capture in nine months of war. Now the cameramen wasted no time and by Monday, 12 May cinemas were showing shots of British troops in Belgium and air raid havoc. Since that date every reel has shown at least one action shot, either of a plane bombing a ship, the splashes of the bombs and the puffs of smoke of shells bursting round the plane clearly visible, or of planes being brought down, their flight to the ground being followed by the camera. As well, many pictures of air raid havoc have been shown, of the wounded and often the dead. A newsreel at the end of May, 1940 with rather more items than usual ran as follows:

Day of intercession in Paris
General Weygand takes over command
Holland evacuated during aerial attack
Dutch cruiser joins allied navy
Refugees arrive by the thousand
Evacuee children re-evacuated
British government swoops on aliens
London increases her defences
Nazis' murderous attacks on Red Cross ambulances
Blockhouses attacked from the Maginot Line
Aerial combat over France

There is now, as a rule, no need to include scrappy items such as these, but it will be seen that even when such a position does arise, the newsreels are still topical and concerned with important events. Out of these eleven items only one (blockhouses attacked on the Maginot Line) could have been old stock held over for a dull newsreel, while in two items (Holland evacuated and Aerial combat over France) shots of actual fighting and of planes being brought down were included, shots that had obviously been taken by professional cameramen with clear well-taken pictures.

Newsreels had now become 'an all-important factor', a point which the *Kine Weekly* acknowledged by devoting their main news page to the subject in an article headed:

BRINGING THE WAR HOME TO THE PUBLIC

Newsreels are Now Top of the Programme

[*later in article*] From now the newsreel will be of extreme importance and will have to be given a place of honour in the programmes of all classes of kinemas.

That the public will anxiously follow the swaying tide of our destinies on the screen is obvious, and exhibitors would do well to consider special exploitation for today's newsreels are 'top of the bill'.

Newsreels with such content have only been showing for a fortnight and it is too early to draw any general decisions from the audience response noted to them. But though the response has been very high almost invariably it has consisted of cries of 'oh' and other signs of horror. And an observer coming out of a cinema overheard this remark from an elderly middle-class woman:

Oh, I wish we'd missed the news. With the other two pictures I forgot all about the war for an hour or two, but those horrid pictures brought it all back. They showed you. . . .

A Mass-Observation questionnaire has already shown that war pictures are not popular and it may be that as the war becomes more violent the cinema will form one of the best mediums of escape; the news will immediately shatter any such illusions for no reel yet observed has shown any reticence over air raid havoc and has emphasised the dead bodies and the wounded, bleeding and sometimes even without an arm or leg.

If this is not so, if the public does enjoy such action scenes, a different danger will arise. One shattered building looks very much like all others, a long shot of a diving aeroplane is always the same. It has already been mentioned how audiences have tired of Finland shots and of the King and Queen, probably because of the similarity of all sequences, and the newsreels will now find it not easy to avoid the same apathy towards fighting nearer home.

General tendencies

It was mentioned in the previous report that almost unanimously the newsreels adopted the official attitude to the war, a dissentient voice occasionally coming from Paramount. In the period now under review there has been no major issue such as that roused by the Unity Mitford film and the only time that the Government has interfered was over one Norway sequence. The day that the withdrawal from Norway was announced, the reels were allowed to release shots of troops leaving for that country; this was considered impolitic and the Government succeeded in stopping the showing in some cinemas but not in others. (N.B. this version of the story is that given in some newspapers; others say that it was not Government officials but the cinema managers who thought the sequence unsuitable.)

There have been a few examples of criticism in the newsreels. Paramount introduced Dorman Smith by talking about the Government's 'almost suicidal policy of agriculture', while Pathé in showing lumps of shrapnel that had fallen in the streets of a south-east coast town 'supposed that somebody knew why the sirens hadn't gone off'. But on the whole the newsreels have consistently adopted the official attitude.

On the other hand there have been fewer examples noted of the wild patriotism in which Emmett excelled, though commentaries have become much more vigorously anti-German. The sequence already mentioned which contained various shots of Hitler speaking was headed 'This is the Madman' and finished with Leslie Mitchell of Movietone saying passionately, 'We must destroy him utterly.' But the response to shots of Hitler is not high, very little hissing or booing being heard. On another occasion there was a shot of some German prisoners being brought to this country; though the cinema was full only one woman hissed. Her companion turned to her and said 'It's not their fault.' The woman who had hissed, replied 'I suppose not, but why do they fight then?' These sentiments are very little different from some overheard at the very beginning of the war when two women agreed that German prisoners were 'poor devils'.

General conclusions

Before the invasion of Holland the newsreels, faced with an absence of interesting news, were filling the gap not with comedies and non-news material but with more sport and home affairs, but were failing to attract much interest. They were including more personalities when personalities were less popular, and missed at least one opportunity for topical news.

When total warfare began, however, the newsreels reacted well and produced action sequences rapidly; it is still too early to say what effect such pictures will have on audiences, although already they have raised a high degree of comment.

This interim report (FR 215), dated simply June 1940, points to some of the latest trends in newsreels and popular reaction.

Mention was made in the last report of the horrifying effect that some newsreel sequences had upon members of the audience. This effect is becoming more obvious. An observer in Streatham heard one elderly working-class woman say 'Gertie and I cried all through the newsreel. Those poor boys out there in all that. The pictures were terrible.' In a Watford cinema another observer heard one girl say to her friend 'I don't think they should show you this, do you? at shots of air raid havoc. In the *Picturegoer* (15.6.40) a letter was published as follows:

> There has been much criticism in the past on newsreels showing us the horrors of modern warfare in China, Spain, etc., and although we felt strongly about these presentations they did not strike near enough to make us protest publicly.
>
> But the war newsreel of to-day is horrifying us. This week we went to our local cinema to see *Adventure in Diamonds* and *Spats to Spurs*, a light programme calculated to make us forget what might be happening 'over there'. But did we enjoy our programme? No, because we viewed it through a haze of tears and the horrible quickening of nerves as we saw our boys moving up to the Belgian front.
>
> As the war continues in all its fury, are we to be subjected to further horror, are we to watch our husbands bombarded, are we to see the shattered limbs of our brothers lying on the battlefield, the anguished bodies of our sons carried in on stretchers? No, unless the film distributors realise that we cannot sit in a luxury cinema watching these ghastly things, unless they relegate the war newsreel to its proper place, the New Theatre, we will stay outside the cinema for the duration. This is our resolve and there are thousands of mothers and wives who feel the same.

A further letter commented on the same thing:

> Some of the recent newsreels have been in very bad taste; an outstanding example being the showing of dead bodies lying outside a bombed Belgian hospital. Cannot the censor prevent the issue of these

pictures which can only bring pain and suffering to those loved ones on active service. After all, we go to the cinema to be carried away from our troubles.

The main response to these shots continues to be a very high degree of comment and signs of horror at the most unpleasant shots. There is no indication in this that the shots are popular but they still constitute the bulk of newsreels and are accompanied by such remarks as 'There are other sights too grim to show you.'

To shots other than of air raids the response is increasing. In the British Movietone News, 13.6.40, an item called 'The Italian Assassin' began with close-ups of Mussolini. Obs. watched this reel twice and on each occasion there was an immediate and widespread outburst of hisses, boos, catcalls and laughs. Obs. has never seen this on any other occasion though twice at least the newsreels have contained shots of Hitler himself. The outcry lasted for nearly a minute on each occasion.

Response to political and military figures has increased; Reynaud, Weygand and Gort have been clapped every time they have appeared though none of the three has been applauded at all before the last two weeks. There has been very prolonged applause for Churchill every time, and at a West End theatre where response is usually very low a man called out 'Well done' when the Prime Minister appeared and clapping followed.

The royal family, however, receive less applause than before. The British Movietone reel mentioned above was observed with two very highly responsive audiences; the last item was a fairly long sequence of the King presenting medals at Buckingham Palace; the Queen was watching from the balcony. At the first showing of this the King was applauded for 2 seconds – Reynaud had received 5 seconds applause a minute before – at the second showing there was no clapping at all. On each occasion the shots of the Queen were greeted in dead silence.

The most important newsreel item in the last few weeks has been the Dunkirk evacuation; shots of this were obtained by cameramen on the spot, and by others lining the train route from the coast home. They could not, however, be released immediately and there was an opportunity by skilful cutting to exploit the dramatic possibilities of the situation. Paramount and Movietone in the main let the shots speak for themselves and did not give them much commentary; GB produced a patriotic commentary which will be mentioned further; and Pathé blended the shots into a sequence that gained a higher response of applause than anything else yet noted by an observer. The sequence began with soldiers marching into Dunkirk; then came a word of congratulation to the Navy and the Air Force for their assistance, this being illustrated with stock shots; the actual embarkation; then compliments to the French army, to the nurses and other women helpers, to the wounded, finally shots of the landing, the train journey, and a few words from the troops. The whole item lasted about four minutes; for nearly a quarter of that time, that is, a full minute, there was applause. Hitherto the loudest applause had been 10 seconds for the survivors of the *Altmark*.

Mention has been made of newsreel commentaries. Of late these have become more violent and more patriotic. The GB commentary mentioned above was to a musical background with the sound of bursting shells interrupting it regularly. Phrases from the commentary are as follows:

A miracle of fighting genius . . . most brilliant withdrawal in military history . . . the navy has earned our undying gratitude, the army is undefeated, its spirit unbroken, their courage brought them through unconquered . . . these shots taken entirely at random all show laughing faces . . . this is the epic of Dunkirk . . . no ship ever ran into such an inferno of hurtling steel . . . the name of Dunkirk will live for ever . . . one day the story will be told in full of these men who were saved to fight again . . . no man had thought of self.

Compare this with a few extracts from the Paramount commentary:

The BEF were brought from almost certain annihiliation . . . a surprisingly large number brought rifles with them . . . one look at them shows what they have been through . . . 900 vessels went to and fro in this amazing evacuation.

For the most part this commentary was simply a description of events, the extracts quoted are the only ones that contain high phrases or superlatives. Compare, for example, Paramount's 'one look at them shows what they have been through' with GB, 'these shots taken entirely at random all show laughing faces'.

Paramount, however, produces less factual commentary on other matters. On an air raid in France the commentary ran:

This is a page of German history written in blood and dust by the subhuman monster that is Hitler . . . hospital trains are his especial delight . . . not until Germany has suffered these horrors will she go down to terrible defeat.

Already in a previous report mention has been made of Paramount's anti-German commentary to shots of prisoners; on that occasion there was no sign of similar fury among the audience and it is still very infrequently that there is any hissing at shots of German prisoners.

There has, of course, been no criticism at all by any of the companies. Paramount mentioned 'the tea-party politics of the Chamberlain Government' but even this was in a speech lauding the present Cabinet.

At least two companies, in showing a sequence of Soho Italians leaving this country, laid emphasis on the fact that no anger should be shown against Italians leaving this country. British Movietone said 'for the first time we are at war with Italy. Those windows that have been smashed in Soho are probably the results of merely private grudges' while Paramount mentioned that the war 'was rough on Italians who had been living half their lives in this country'.

In short the main points in newsreels in the last few weeks have been these:

1 An increasing indication that the air raid sequences in newsreels are not popular.
2 An increasing degree of audience response to political and military figures though a marked decline in the response to royal figures.
3 More violent commentaries though most of the companies have not given way entirely to these.

Newsreel Report 3
(6 October 1940)

The last major newsreel report (FR 444), covering the period May – September 1940, compiled by Len England and dated 6 October 1940.

In the period under review, May to September 1940, exactly 100 newsreels were observed. Most of the observation was done in various parts of London, in Watford and in Northwood, but reports are also included from Orpington, Chelmsford, Ipswich, Birmingham and Southport.

Public opinion of the newsreels

Included in a Mass-Observation questionnaire in December 1939, and also in August, 1940, was the question 'What do you think of the newsreels?'. Briefly the results are as shown in the table (see also Appendix 1).

	Like them	*Dislike them*	*Doubtful*
1939	61½%	15%	23½%
1940	24½%	50%	25%

Percentage giving as their reason for dislike that the newsreels have 'no news':

1939	12%
1940	35%

It will be seen from these figures that the newsreels have lost a very considerable amount of their popularity in the last six months, and the number of those who actively dislike the reels has trebled and reached 50 per cent. In December nearly a quarter of the people questioned liked the newsreels immensely: 'They are interest number one', 'I go to see them.' In the following August less than 10 per cent of those who like them are really enthusiastic about the reels.

The reason for this decline in popularity is simply that the newsreels contain no news; 35 per cent of the 50 per cent who dislike them give this as a reason, and they come from both sexes and middle and working class alike. In December only 12 per cent criticised the reels on the grounds that there was no news, and these were almost all men under 30.

The attitude of the newsreels to the problem of news

The fact that the 'no news' complaint has strengthened so much between Christmas and Summer is made even more remarkable when the actual incidents of the war are considered. Between September and December 1939 the only major incident of the Anglo–German war was the capture of the *Graf Spee*; there was in addition the Russo–Finnish war. But between May and August 1940 the newsreels dealt with the following incidents among others:

The evacuation from Norway
The cabinet crisis, and Mr Chamberlain's resignation
The invasion of Norway and Holland
The Dunkirk evacuation
The collapse of France
Invasion preparations
The battle in the air
The entry of Italy into the war

There is surely more news of interest here than there ever was in peace-time.

The newsreels are not unaware of the position. Paramount, in showing the Italian version of an engagement in the Mediterranean which had come via America, said in its commentary 'Why leave all the propaganda to the enemy? Give British newsreels a chance to show America what the British navy is doing.' W. J. Gell, head of Pathé, in a statement in the *Kine* (22.8.40) said that newsreels could not be longer without becoming boring, as military and naval authorities refused permission to a great many shots. The blame is laid in the same quarter by the Ministry of Information (see 13th Report of the Select Committee of National Expenditure, page 8):

> The difficulty in obtaining newsreels lies not with the newsreel companies but with the fighting services from whom facilities are largely required. One of the functions of the Films Division is to obtain these facilities. Repeated requests by letter and telephone and in personal interviews have produced little result. The fighting services have in a general way declared their willingness to provide facilities but in practice few facilities have been obtained. . . . The Sub Committee feel that the fighting services have not fully appreciated the value of propaganda as an integral part of the war effort.

Efforts of the companies to meet the situation

Though the absence of news may be due in the main to the fighting services, the newsreels themselves can hardly be said to have made the best of what facilities they have. In the first place, they have not always seized the opportunities that they have had. For example, the cabinet crisis at the beginning of May reached its climax on Tuesday, 7 May, and must have been foreseen before this date. But the newsreels released on the Thursday of that week contained no reference to the crisis, while those of the following Monday consisted merely of shots of the cabinet drawn from old stock.

In the second place, there seems to have been very little effort by the newsreels to replace news by something more interesting. In the first months of the war when there was very little news, some of the reel was made up of reconstructed or faked news and some by the inclusion of comedies. The Crazy Gang appeared frequently and Pathé launched a highly successful series of skits on Lord Haw-Haw. The newsreels, in other words, were becoming more of interest shorts, but they were holding public attention.

There are now very few attempts at reconstructions, for the shots of the war that can be shown are good, many of them action shots of convoys being bombed, or of aerial battles. But there have been no comedies and little attempt to provide interesting material other than 'topical news'. But occasionally what is almost a short documentary has been included and sometimes a trailer with an appeal or advice. These two must be considered separately.

1 Documentary: The news of the Dunkirk evacuation was held up a little by the censor, and there was time for the newsreels to develop the shots by cutting into a well told story. Pathé in particular used this technique and built up the story of Dunkirk in a way that provoked very high audience reaction; each service was dealt with individually and the part that they played explained. This system of part news – part documentary was further exploited after the collapse of France. Gaumont, for instance, produced 'This Land of Ours', beginning with shots of English countryside and of English people enjoying themselves in peace time: 'we had hoped to enjoy these things in peace, the simple things'. But war comes and we must put our backs into the war as we did into sport in peace time. The item closed with a shot of the King decorating war heroes, thus bringing it up to date.

Pathé had an item 'The British Empire's Unity', showing troops from all parts of the Empire joined together with a common cord. Our own army and air force and navy; 'Often have we said in jest "Thank God we've got a navy", now we can say it in earnest.'

But this documentary idea was not long lived. It is possible that it was killed by the MoI shorts which were first introduced about this time (June – July).

2 At the end of the newsreels, trailers have been added giving advice about taking cover in air raids, covering Andersons with earth, looking out for Fifth columnists, and so on. Sometimes these have been carried by all reels with the same commentary spoken by the various commentators, or with the same pictures and a different commentary. Occasionally they have been included in the middle of the reel – an appeal for nurses in a Pathé reel, for instance – and there have also been a series of appeals for National Savings by such people as Patsy Hendren, Leslie Henson and Vic Oliver.

The most ambitious effort observed was Gaumont's 'You Have Heard of the Fifth Column – You Can Wipe It Out' which lasted about three minutes and warned the man in the street against lights being used for signalling, rumours being spread, photographs being taken, leaflets spread, German wireless listened to, cars left unattended, and so on. But, for the most part, such trailers last no more than half a minute and help only in a very small degree to solve the problem of 'no news'.

In the main the newsreels have been content to show what news they have unadorned. The following are some items which have been considered of sufficient general interest to merit inclusion:

Elephants in a USA zoo
Arrival of a USA ambassador in Australia
Croydon 'carrying on' after being bombed
Rioting in Mexico
Inspections of troops in USA
ATS Sports Day
Jewel sale at Christies
The Duchess of Gloucester inspects a Red Cross centre

These are not items chosen at random from particularly bad newsreels. The Pathé reel on Dunkirk, for instance, which was so exceptionally well received, lasted only for about 4 minutes and was preceded by:

River Plate heroes convalescing in South Africa
Park railings being used for munitions
War wedding of the Queen's cousin
The Duchess of Gloucester inspects a Red Cross centre
A special appeal for nurses

British Movietone News at the beginning of the Blitz preceded their pictures of bombed London with:

Britain's Day of Prayer

More Canadian troops arrive
Duchess of Kent visits a hospital
'Dead' Guard (V.C.) is prisoner of war
New Zealand band plays popular airs for Londoners
US ambulances for Great Britain

Occasionally a newsreel devotes the whole of its 9 or 10 minutes to one incident; Gaumont did it to some particularly fine shots of bombs falling round a convoy and an aerial battle ensuing, while Paramount devoted their first issue after the beginning of serious raids to describing the damage in an item entitled '45,000,000 Heroes Can't be Wrong'.

Audience reaction

Personalities

Though audience opinion of newsreels has declined, the amount of audience response to newsreels has increased. The table shows the response to the most important personalities in newsreels since the beginning of the war. The table is divided into three periods representing the following months:

Period 1   October 1939 to January 1940 (middle)
Period 2   January 1940 to April 1940
Period 3   May to September 1940

In the first column is the percentage of appearances of each character in observed newsreels; the second column indicates the percentage of their appearances on which they were applauded.

Figure	Period 1		Period 2		Period 3	
	apps	applause	apps	applause	apps	applause
King	27%	16%	44%	14%	46%	36%
Queen	27%	27%	44%	9%	24%	17%
Windsor	20%	75%	–	–	4%	75%
Churchill	10%	60%	16%	50%	14%	77%
Chamberlain	8%	50%	2%	–	4%	25%

The appearances of the King have steadily increased in number since the beginning of the war though in the first months of 1940 he was seen more often and clapped less frequently. But now he is more than twice as popular than at any other period of the war, and he appears far more often. The applause as well as being more frequent is also longer; on the occcasion of his last speech, as recorded by Gaumont, he was clapped for 17 seconds, the longest applause for one man ever noted in the cinema.

The Queen, on the other hand, though more popular than at the beginning of the year, is not as well received as she was in 1939 when she was the best liked of all the royal family. The emphasis has shifted from the Queen to the King; possibly this also indicates a shifting from a *personal* attitude to a *patriotic* one. In the early days of the war when there were fewer surface signs of patriotism, the Queen was most applauded as she was the member of the royal family most liked. Now the King is clapped, not so much as a man, but as a symbol of the country.

The Duke of Windsor retains his great popularity; the only occasions on which he has been seen this year are at his installation as Governor of the Bahamas, and of four renderings of this in the newsreels three were applauded. Once the reel was seen in a half empty West End cinema where response is usually very low; here he was applauded 7 seconds, a very long period.

Other members of the royal family have appeared occasionally but have not been applauded at all. The Duchess of Kent has made 7 appearances, the Duchess of Gloucester 3, and the Princesses 3; the Duke of Gloucester has not been seen at all and the Duke of Kent only three times.

Among politicians Churchill still remains easily the most popular. Though only appearing in 14 newsreels, he has been clapped in 11 of them; this makes a percentage of applause of 77 per cent a higher figure than for any other personality or even for any of the services.

Politicians have not been seen a great deal during the period under review; they have been seen *en masse* at the cabinet reshuffle and at a service at Westminster Abbey, but individually only six have been seen. Mr Chamberlain has been seen 5 times and been applauded once. Mr Eden has been seen 5 times and applauded twice – in the previous period he was seen 5 times but not applauded at all. The three Labour leaders, Attlee, Bevin and Morrison, have been seen but not applauded at all. Sir Archibald Sinclair has made one appearance.

There has been a surprisingly high response to foreign figures, just as there has been to foreign troops (see below). General de Gaulle alone of all personalities in newsreels has been applauded on every single one of his appearances (all made before the Dakar incident), while on 3 out of 5 occasions he was clapped for more than 5 seconds. Reynaud was well applauded on his only appearance, so was Heile Selassie. Leopold was cheered loudly at an appearance in May, and was equally loudly hissed when seen in September.

The only figure that has not appealed to the public imagination is Queen Wilhelmina of Holland. She has appeared more frequently than any other foreign ruler – 7 times – and on one occasion made a long speech, but has not been clapped at all.

Response to American personalities still remains very varied. In the earlier part of the year Roosevelt was hissed on some occasions and clapped on others, and there is still a divided audience when he appears. Willkie has always been received in silence.

Finally Hitler and Mussolini. In period 1 Hitler was seen once in the distance (a shot of the burial of the Munich victims) and there was no response. In period 2 he was seen 4 times and *laughed at* twice. In period 3 he has been seen 6 times, on 4 of which occasions he was hissed and the other 2 laughed at. In other words he has become a figure of much greater interest than before, but one that is not so easily laughed at. On every occasion the response was immediate and widespread.

Mussolini was not seen at all in newsreels – except for a brief shot at the Brenner pass meeting – until Italy's entry into the war. This shot was seen in three different cinemas and was invariably greeted with immediate and loud hissing. One inv. saw it on a Saturday night, and reports that he has never seen such an outburst in any London cinema; there were catcalls, boos, hisses from all parts of the cinema, though it was in a middle-class area where response is usually less vigorous.

The Services

During the first part of this year the activities of the Navy were the mainstay of newsreels, and were applauded on 55 per cent of their appearances. The RAF and the Army both appeared far less frequently but while the Army was not once applauded until the middle of April, and the beginning of land warfare, the Air Force was applauded on 30 per cent of its appearances.

Between May and September the percentage of appearances has altered little, but there is a considerable levelling in response to the various services. The Navy is still most frequently seen – in 59 out of 100 newsreels at least one sequence was concerned with the sea – but it was only applauded on 46 per cent of its appearances. The RAF, seen 45 times, was applauded 20 times, or on 44 per cent of its appearances, an increase of 14 per cent on the previous period. The Army has only been seen 29 times but has been applauded on 14 occasions, or on 47 per cent of its appearances.

There is now very little to choose between the forces; the lowest percentage of applause is 44 per cent, the highest 47 per cent. The Army distinguished itself at Dunkirk, and the Air Force in the aerial war of the last few months, and both services have increased their popularity. The Navy, on the other hand has had little spectacular to do in the last few months and has declined a little in popularity while still being applauded as much as either of the other services.

There has been a high response both to colonial troops and to foreign troops fighting for Britain. Australians, Canadians, New Zealanders have been applaused on 25 per cent of their appearances; the most popular of all Empire troops have been the Indians. Czechs, Poles, Frenchmen, Dutch, shown in training in this country, have been applauded on 43 per cent of their appearances.

The women's army is still laughed at and never applauded, except when an individual woman is shown having won a medal for gallantry. The LDVs have been clapped on only 3 occasions out of 15. The ARP services were laughed at until the beginning of the Blitzkrieg, but since then they have been loudly applauded. In exactly the same way were shots of all troops laughed at before the war broke out; first the Navy proved its worth and became popular, and then the Army and the Air Force. But until the beginning of August both the women's army and the ARP were always regarded as funny. The ARP has now joined the fighting services in being well applauded.

Air raid shots

In thirty-two observed newsreels, sequences of air raid damage have been included. For the first few months the shots were of damage in France and Belgium, and the main reaction of the audience was one of disgust and horror. Of the 16 shots of air raid damage shown between May and the middle of June, 8, or 50 per cent, were received mainly with exclamations of disgust. Comments overheard in the cinema, and letters to the *Picturegoer*, seem to indicate that the excessive and unpleasant reality of these shots was not at all popular; the attitude is summed up in the frequently heard remark 'I forgot all about the war until the newsreel came on, and that showed me all the horrors.'

Through July and August only a few air raid pictures were shown and most of these were in a rather facetious vein; a damaged pub with the locals playing darts in the ruins, for example. Then when the serious raids on London began air raids again filled the greater part of the news. This time, however, the pictures were not so terrifying; there were no action pictures of steeples crashing or bombs actually exploding; there was no emphasis on the suffering of the homeless and the refugees; above all, there were none of the pictures that had formerly caused most horror, those of dead bodies, or men and women armless or legless. Perhaps as a result of this toning down, perhaps because air raid damage is nothing strange these days, the pictures have been received in silence, often in bored silence.

This absence of horror is not limited to London which has experienced the Blitzkrieg. Reports from Watford and Southport also indicate that the reels have been received in silence with no expressions of disgust or repulsion.

Miscellaneous

Commentary

In the last five months the newsreel commentaries have become far more dramatic and emotionalised. Movietone produced a sequence in May containing nothing but old shots of Hitler with a vituperative commentary, and the same newsreel celebrated Italy's entry into the war in an item entitled 'The Italian Assassin' with similar abuse. All the shots of air raid damage in London are accompanied by such phrases as 'this cold blooded murderer', 'this damned assassin' and so on. Paramount showed shots of German prisoners with a commentary that argued that the people were as bad as their leaders; Movietone, on the other hand, in 'The Italian Assassin' was more tolerant:

> The King of Italy did not want to fight . . . [during shots of damage in Soho] For the first time we are at war with Italy. The windows smashed are probably the results only of private grudges. . . . It would be wise to treat the Italian navy seriously and many of their troops are good.

If abuse of the enemy has increased considerably, patriotic sentiments have doubled themselves. This began at Dunkirk which Gaumont news almost turned into a glorious victory, and was followed up in the patriotic shorts mentioned earlier. Gaumont finishes every reel with a Union Jack.

Criticism or satire is now less prominent than ever before. The only remark noted which could be called criticism was a reference in Paramount to the 'tea-party politics of Chamberlain' some weeks after Mr Chamberlain had resigned.

Propaganda element

One interesting point that emerges from the comparative questionnaires is a changing attitude towards the use of the word 'Propaganda'. In December 1939, 12 per cent of those asked their opinion of newsreels objected on the grounds that they were 'propaganda' on two or three occasions simply the word 'propaganda' was sufficient on its own to condemn the newsreels.

In August 1940, on the other hand, nobody objected to the newsreels on the ground that they were propaganda, but 7 per cent said that they were *good* propaganda. These were not enthusiastic over the point and nobody said that they liked the reels because they were propaganda; but this does seem to indicate a changing attitude towards the word.

General conclusions

1 The newsreels are losing much of their popularity, the reason being that they are said to contain no news.
2 The newsreels are aware of the position, but put the blame on to the Services.
3 But little attempt has been made by the newsreels to liven up their reels.
4 The royal family is increasing in popularity, the King is now more popular than the Queen.
5 Churchill is still highly popular and the only popular politician.
6 Foreigners who are helping Britain's cause are highly popular.
7 Hitler is being more seriously treated than before.
8 The Services are now about equally popular; ARP and foreign troops are also well received.
9 Shots of air raid damage, very frequent in reels, were received with disgust in April and May but in silence in September when air raids are known to the audience.
10 Commentaries have become more emotionalised.
11 The propaganda element in newsreels has become less unpopular.

Appendix 1: Questionnaire

Q. What do you think of the newsreel? (asked in December 1939 and August 1940)

	Men		Women		Total	
	1939	*1940*	*1939*	*1940*	*1939*	*1940*
Like them	54%	34%	70%	23%	61½%	24½%
Doubtful	20%	19%	25%	29%	23%	25%
Dislike them	26%	53%	5%	48%	15%	50%

	1939	*1940*
Dislike them on the grounds of 'no news'	12%	35%
Dislike them on the grounds of being propaganda	12%	–
Think they are good propaganda	–	7%

23   The Faking of Newsreels

Len England was particularly interested in the faking of newsreels and compiled this report (FR 16), dated 7 January 1940, on the subject. He took evidence from Sidney Cole, a leading film editor, trade unionist and associate editor of *The Ciné Technician*, Ralph Bond the documentarist and Christopher Brunel, son of the film-maker Adrian Brunel and a student of film propaganda.

The impression created by any film upon an audience is the result both of the actual photographs and of the sound and commentary. Both of these elements can be made misleading. In the question of newsreels, where a great deal of the sound is added from material in their libraries a completely false interpretation of the evidence can be conveyed. A picture of a burning building, for instance, may be accompanied by the sound of bombs exploding and by the commentator saying 'This is but one of many buildings which have suffered.' A further false impression may be gained if the building is photographed from many different angles with the result that it seems on first sight as if the shots are all of different buildings. The audience cannot concentrate at the same time on both commentary and pictures and the tendency is to merge the two together, believing the evidence of the eyes and therefore of the ears.

In this direction nothing can be proved as the details of how a newsreel is made are the closed secret of the newsreel companies. There are examples, however. The Gaumont British news (18.1.40, seen LE, Gaumont, Streatham) contained a shot of Indian troops in France and prefaced it with the words 'India stands with Britain to a man'. The Pathé Gazette (21.12.39, seen LE, Regal, Streatham) contained shots of a destroyer in action; obviously here there could have been no sound equipment and all the explosions and so on had been added later. The newsreel men in Finland naturally wish to travel light and carry no sound equipment (evidence: Ralph Bond) and so all the sound of these shots is superimposed. Some houses in Finland have been photographed from several angles to give the impression of several houses (evidence: Sidney Cole). Commentary gave the impression that a whole train load of Swedish volunteers was leaving for Finland; but an observer noticed women and children also in train and volunteers only in one part of it (Sidney Cole). One sequence of a burning Finnish village was syndicated to the newsreels and Pathé said that it had been fired by a retreating Red Army and Paramount that it had been set alight by the retreating Finnish army (evidence: Christopher Brunel).

In some cases the sequences show signs of being 'prepared'. A cameraman told an observer (LE, before special study) that a regiment of soldiers had been marched backwards and forwards over a hill for a whole morning for the benefit of a newsreel; on another occasion a tank was shot being loaded on to a ship for France, but as soon as the cameras had stopped it was taken off again as the ship was never able to carry such cargo. The evacuation of Dulwich College was taken; one boy walked in and out of a house many times before the newsreels were satisfied that the shots were sufficiently 'natural' (evidence: LE from boy at the school). An appeal by Madame Gripenburg contained the story of a woman in a fur coat coming to the door of the Embassy and handing in some money (Sidney Cole). The newsreels showed this scene meaning either that they knew before that the woman was coming or that they reconstructed it afterwards. Many of the shots of the Finns sniping released to all reels have been taken from a position in *front* of the Finns so that the cameraman must have been standing with his back to the enemy. GB (13.12.39, seen LE, Academy) showed shots of air raid havoc including women sheltering under a wall; some of them, however, were laughing and there were 'feet' walking about on top of the wall quite unconcerned; the shots in Pathé (8.1.40, seen LE, Brixton Pavilion) on the other hand showed the children crying as they went into shelters. In shots of action on the front (Paramount 30.11.40, seen LE, Astoria, Streatham) a cameraman focused the camera on a spot and a second later a shell burst right in the middle of the section covered. And finally in none of the action shots (except those at sea taken by naval officers) has the camera jolted or been out of focus.

A third method has been to 'reconstruct' events. British Paramount News (20.11.40) cut shots of crashed bombers with violent action pictures prefaced with some remarks such as 'this is what it would have looked like'; at Eros News Theatre, Piccadilly Circus, an observer heard one man say 'of course this isn't real' and at the Paramount, Tottenham Court Road the next day, some laughed at the sequence. The Cameo News (GB and Paramount) on 4.12.39 contained a sequence of a submarine being sunk after a depth charge had hit it. A GB news early in the war (seen LE privately) contained a shot of the Kiel ships being bombed before *The Lion Has Wings* did the same. GB News (1.2.40, seen LE, Gaumont, Streatham) contained description of patrol; only scenery was a tree, barbed wire and snow and the camera accompanied the patrol even when it inspected a blockhouse, presumably in enemy lines. The whole action took place in broad daylight. The commentary gave the impression by inference that this patrol was the actual one on which the first DSO (?) was awarded; it ran something like 'This is a patrol of one officer and three NCOs; Captain – won DSO on patrol.' Obs. knows this deceived at least one person.

It must be re-emphasised that nothing can be proved conclusively unless one of the newsreels makes a big mistake. All of the 'editing' is done by the newsreels in secret, and there can be no proof that sound track was added afterwards, that commentary was intentionally misleading, or that actions were posed or reconstructed.

24   Interview with Kenneth Gordon

Following up his interest in newsreel faking, Len England interviewed Kenneth Gordon, veteran Pathé newsreel cameraman, trade union activist and editor of *The Ciné-Technician*, the journal of the technicians' union, the ACT. The interview took place on 10 February 1940.

Obs. met Mr Gordon in National Trades Union Club, Little Newport St. He had forgotten appointment and had to be phoned. Mr Gordon a man about fifty, fat, red-faced, jolly.

(Obs. asked about faking in newsreels.) Every one of the news reels is misleading. The managing directors of all of them are just trying for knighthoods; Paramount is the only one that is at all intelligent.

Naturally they fake shots. In many cases it is quite impossible for the cameramen to rig up their cameras and I think it is legitimate to fake sometimes; you have to do a certain amount. Sometimes if a man poked his head up he'd be picked off. But he must illustrate his story somehow so he uses trickery. Some people – Ernest Brooke in the last war – have gone over the top with the troops but a normal camera person just couldn't do it. Of course you do occasionally get genuine shots. The Germans in Poland could take shots but the opposition was so little then. But in Finland you're not only fighting an enemy that is strong but you're doing it among the trees where you couldn't get real shots. And when they show you patrols going out on skis; well of course it couldn't be genuine because if the cameraman and the audience could see the Finns so could the Russians and that would be the end of the patrol.

(Obs. raised question of one house taken from four angles.) That always happens, it is only natural. The cameraman has got to make the most of his story. A journalist can add any amount to his story by descriptive writing; but a cameraman has only his pictures of the actual facts to show. So he makes as much of them as he possibly can.

(Question of Spanish shots being used.) I shouldn't think that that was possible. I think it is quite legitimate to use other shots of bombs dropping from an aeroplane; after all an aeroplane and a bomb are the same whether they are Greek, Armenian, Spanish or Finnish and it adds reality to the shots that otherwise couldn't be got. Remember that except

by a very big piece of luck the cameramen can only take the shots after they have happened.

(*Question of sound.*) That is a very complicated business. The men need great mobility and they obviously can't take sound shots. But some of the stuff from Finland was actually recorded.

(*Question of commentary.*) I am so fed up with listening to their propaganda and their pro-government stuff, ignoring the Labour of the country, that I just close my ears and don't listen.

The Gaumont British reel on the Heligoland raid is an excellent example of what you need. They showed the actual pilots returning from the actual raid, and gave you details of the bullet holes on the planes. All this was done some hours after they had returned for the first time but they were the real thing. Then they built the story up with montage of the bombs dropping on the ships in just the same way as a journalist would build up his story. They must get their story; they get what they can and build it up.

(*Gaumont British shot of patrol.*) They may have got the same patrol at a different place. Taken the actual people if necessary but done it behind the lines; that's where the commentary misleads you, but remember if it didn't it would rob it of its whole effect. Remember that this war is run by Lord Muddlecombe. There are so many rules and so many people that the newsreels are always in the wrong place at the wrong time. So they have to do the right thing. If the *Graf Spee* business had been in Scotland it would never have been on the newsreels, they wouldn't have got there in time. But in America as soon as they heard the news the aeroplane engines were warming up and they were off. The newsreels just have to reconstruct.

There have been two periods in newsreel histories. In the first place they fought each other so hard that Chicago racketeers weren't in it. Then they all decided to be friends, and they only sent one cameraman on any one job. And naturally they sent the cheapest and therefore the most useless man on the job. Even a weak man if he was up against somebody good would try his best; but when there is no competition there is no incentive and the results are lousy. What's one of the main causes is that we never have enough money; we are paid a ridiculous sum though it will have to go up some time soon. Universal is the cheapest news and they are all undercutting as well as trying for their knighthoods.

If you want any more details try Cummings of Paramount. He is a great enemy of me personally but he is the only man of them who has any intelligence.

25   Fifteen Ministry of Information Shorts

The Films Division of the Ministry of Information was hampered by lack of a consistent propaganda policy until 1940. The 13th Select Committee on National Expenditure reported in September 1940: 'The work of the Films Division in the home field has been largely ineffective through the lack of clearly defined objectives on the part of the Ministry.' In ten months, 17 out of 28 planned films had been scrapped because they had been overtaken by events. The confusion was due in part to the constant changes of personnel but this situation was resolved by the appointment in April 1940 as Director of the Films Division of Jack Beddington, formerly director of publicity for Shell. He remained in charge until 1946. The Films Division achieved a coherent approach to film propaganda during his tenure of office. The celebrated GPO Film Unit was taken over, renamed the Crown Film Unit and put to work. To meet the immediate propaganda requirements, a programme of five-minute films was inaugurated. Their aim, as Sir Kenneth Clark, Controller of Home Publicity at the MoI, declared, was 'to help people to remember government messages by putting them in dramatic form'. Dallas Bower was put in charge of launching the programme, and contacted an old associate, the director Thorold Dickinson. Dickinson assembled a team and put together the first five-minute film, *Westward Ho! – 1940*, reassuring parents about the need for and importance of the evacuation of children. Two weeks after shooting began, the film was premiered at the Dominion cinema, Tottenham Court Road. By 1942, eighty-six of these films had been made, a few by the Crown Film Unit but the majority by outside production companies. The films were distributed free to cinemas at the rate of one a week and included in the regular programme. Towards the end of 1942, the production of five-minute films was discontinued in favour of fifteen-minute films issued monthly, allowing a longer exploration of more complex issues. But the short message idea was continued in 'trailers' attached to the newsreels.

Mass-Observation was concerned to monitor the reception of these films by cinema audiences. The first report on fifteen MoI shorts and two GPO films was compiled by Len England and dated 16 October 1940 (FR 458).

On the MoI five-minute films see Frances Thorpe and Nicholas Pronay, *British Official Films in the Second World War* (Oxford, 1980) and PEP Arts Enquiry, *The Factual Film* (London, 1947).

Fifteen official MoI shorts, and two G.P.O. films released through the MoI, have been the subject of study. A general report on the whole 'short' situation is to hand this week.

The failure to advertise these official films was found to be a weakness, and lately the failure to show them. For instance, at six out of seven cinemas in Watford, and two out of three in Streatham, recently, the 'shorts' could not be seen at all. By the end of August a survey showed that 59 per cent of Londoners had seen and remembered something about Ministry 'shorts', and that of these nearly four liked them for every person who disliked them. This is a much *higher degree of popularity* than that enjoyed by newsreels, but it has not been wholly maintained. There has generally been a much higher degree of popularity and response from middle-class people than from working-class people (sex differences are very slight). This seems to derive *largely from the essentially upper- and middle-class attitude* of many of the films; this started with the original 'Careless Talk' films, in each of which the spy was a worker (barman, café proprietress, pub crawler), while in two of them the gossipers were working class, though in only one was the cast as a whole working class. The hero of one of these films, a factory scientist with a beautiful large house, is killed by the idiocy of a factory worker. The hero of another is a rich young airman; his fiancée lives in a luxury flat. This tradition has been maintained, though not to the same extent, in the later five-minute 'shorts'; Miss Grant and Miss Know All are ladies with large houses; while the working-class population of *Call to Arms* was really a joke, and repeatedly where working-class characters are represented favourably, they are not represented faithfully. It is interesting to notice that the most remembered and commented on feature of any film was Priestley's commentary to *Britain at Bay*; he provides a bridge [between] middle and working classes.

Another factor which seems to have led to the decline in intensity of interest is the lack of continuity or apparent theme sequence in the films from week to week. Several films were criticised for vagueness, e.g. *Seafort*, which was very puzzling: *Call for Arms, Yesterday Is Over Your Shoulder*, which had direct appeals for service without explaining clearly how or where to offer it. The *lack of humour* has also been a striking feature of many of the films; only four have made any real attempt to exploit humour, and in two of them mass taste has been considerably misjudged. Finally, the stressing of stars in some of the films has detracted from the feeling of reality upon which the success of such films largely depends; Stanley Holloway, Robertson Hare, Emlyn Williams, Dorothy Hyson, and so on, turning 'shorts' into rather vague and incoherent minor feature films.

If the Ministry had followed up every one of its films, with even quite simple research into mass criticism effect, the cumulative lesson might have been learned, and valuable adjustments made. As it is, the *ad hoc* and largely aesthetic approach still apparently prevails.

If we classify these films into 'short stories' and 'strict documentaries', and compare the observed audience response of the two main types, we find a consistently higher degree of response to the documentary; approximately one-eighth of response to the documentaries is unfavourable, whereas rather under a half of the response to the story films is unfavourable.

Roughly, this means that bad sequences in short stories really irritate people, while bad sequences in documentaries are not so likely to annoy, but, on the other hand, a short story which takes into account the other considerations, can be more successful than the documentary in arousing audience interest, and especially personal identification which is associated with probable definite action. The power of a purely documentary film to make people change their habits is doubtful. But here is a subject which vitally requires research. What is the *effect* of an MoI film like *Food for Thought*, in terms of actual increased economic cooking and intelligent dieting? This type of effect could easily be tested, and we hope to undertake such tests in the near future, but really it is the job for a special organisation working directly with film interests.

Details of films mentioned in report

1(a) Now You're Talking

Produced: John Paddy Carstairs (Ealing Studios)
Cast: includes Sebastian Shaw, Edward Chapman, Dorothy Hyson
Characters: An explosive expert; his wife; his assistant; factory hands; barmaid, lorry driver, timekeeper, constable, foreign agent, café proprietor, girl friend.

Story: Late one evening news comes through to an explosive laboratory that a special gun has been found on a German plane. The expert decides to work on through the night, though his wife is worried especially when she breaks a mirror. Alf, one of the factory hands, has to work late, unloading the plane, and sends words to his girl friend. This piece of information is overheard by the café proprietor who hands it on to an agent; the agent comes down, meets Alf when he comes off duty and pumps him. Discovers that only two people are at the factory, and wangles in, diverting the guards by getting a friend to drive past without headlamps blacked out. He leaves a bomb, the factory is blown up with the expert and the gun.

Next day in the pub, Alf, the cause of all the trouble, looks at a Careless

Talk poster and wonders who has given the game away.
Observed: LE, Regal, Streatham, 21.5.40.

(b) Dangerous Comment

Produced: John Paddy Carstairs (Ealing Studios)
Cast: includes Frank Lawton, Penelope Dudley Ward, Milton Rosmer.
Characters: Various Air Force officers, two girl friends; barman; pin-table lounger; German Chief of Staff

Story: A young officer who is doing a secret job is reprimanded for telling his father about it. The following story is told to point the moral:
An RAF raid was set for Bender Dam, and the man who was to run it is told at the last moment that somebody else is to take over. He goes off in a huff, tells his girl, who in turn tells her friend. Then the man takes over once again, and his girl is frightened and refuses to go to a party. The friend excuses her absence at the party by telling of the Bender Dam incident. This is overheard by the barman, who passes the news on to an agent in a pin-table saloon. But the police are on the track, and though the news gets to Germany, the British raid is cancelled and all is well.
But the officer who is being reprimanded is so delighted by the story that he goes straight out to tell his father! The superior says on the fade-out 'You see what we're up against.'
Observed: LE, Regal, Streatham, 3.6.40

(c) All Hands

Produced: John Paddy Carstairs (Ealing Studios)
Cast: includes John Mills and René Ray.
Characters: A sailor; his girl; a waitress; U-boat crew; an elderly country gentleman

Story A girl and her boy – a sailor – are meeting for the last time before he leaves in a little teashop. He has to go earlier than was expected. A waitress overhears this, and passes it on to another waitress, saying what a pity it is. This second waitress goes into a cinema and there under a seat passes a message on to someone sitting near her. He in turn passes it to a man in the country, who signals a message to a German U-boat. The ship on which the sailor was leaving is intercepted by the U-boat. The sailor goes down. Back in the shop the waitress who has been the cause of all the trouble says 'Isn't it awful? I wonder how it happened.' Fade-out on the Careless Talk poster.
Observed: LE, Eros, Piccadilly Circus, June 1940

2 (a) Britain at Bay

Produced: GPO Unit
Commentary: J. B. Priestley

Story: Shots of the English countryside, and a contrast between the peaceful life of this country and the war preparations of Germany. Shots of our Army and all forces ready and waiting to stem invasion.
Observed: LE, Empire, Leicester Square, 16.7.40; KM, Odeon, Sidcup, 17.7.40

(b) Albert's Savings

Produced: Merton Park Studios
Recited by Stanley Holloway

Story (acted): Albert turns out his money box to buy ice creams but the money is confiscated by his father to buy him a National Savings certificate. Albert is fired by the idea and starts to sell everything that he can lay his hands on, his father's pipe rack, his mother's stuffed birds, the stick with the horse's head handle. He buys the certificate but is found out, and is just about to be beaten for stealing when it is discovered how he spent the money. He is given a blessing instead.
Observed: LE, Astoria, Streatham, 17.8.40; LE, Regal, Streatham, 14.8.40; PM, Odeon, Ipswich, 12.8.40.

(c) Call to Arms

Produced: John Paddy Carstairs (Ealing Studios)
Cast: includes René Ray and Jean Gillie
Characters: Chorus girls; munition workers

Story Two of the girls of 'Non Stop Nudes' are full of their own petty grievances until they see a munitions girl faint in the streets due to overwork. This so impresses one that she goes to the factory the next day. Soon after the other one also turns up. Emphasis is laid on the dirty manual labour and the courage of the women. One evening as they are going home, an order for another two million bullets comes through. Without being told, the girls go to it. A final appeal to all to do this sort of work.
Observed: LE, Regal, Streatham, 23.7.40; GW, Odeon, Wealdstone, 26.8.40

(d) Food for Thought

Produced: Adrian Brunel (Ealing Studios)

Cast: includes Mabel Constanduros, Muriel George
Characters: Suburban housewives and householders

Story: A housewife gathers other householders in her road together and explains by the help of practical examples the values of various foods. The foods are shown and there is mention of what special qualities they have.
Observed: LE, Gaumont, Streatham, 31.7.40

(e) Miss Grant goes to the Door

Produced: Brian Desmond Hurst (D & P Studios)
Cast: Mary Clare, Martita Hunt, Manning Whiley, Ivan Brandt
Characters: Two elderly ladies in a country house; an LDV; a German officer masquerading as a British one

Story: Two ladies hear a warning in a country district and go down to their shelter. On the way, one goes to a room for her knitting and absently turns on the light. The other rushes to turn it off again, but both look in horror at the window where a man is looking in. He collapses outside the door. They bring him in, dead, and recognise his uniform as German. They go outside and hear the church bells ringing; invasion has started. Then an English officer comes to them, asking where Jarvis Cross is; but he says 'Yarvis Cross' and Miss Grant guesses that he is German. She holds him up with a revolver from the dead German, while her companion goes to the nearest LDV post, where a lecture is in progress on 'How to deal with parachute troops'. Meanwhile Miss Grant so far relents as to give the German a cigarette; as she hands it to him, he knocks her out. He goes to the garage, but finds the bike locked and the car without its distributor. As he runs out, he is caught by the LDV who on their way have blown up the canister containing all the Germans arms.
Observed: LE, London Pavilion, 7.8.40; LE, Gaumont, Streatham, 6.8.40; LE, Regal, Streatham, 8.8.40; JA, Carlton, Watford, 9.8.40; GW, Rex, Northwood Hills, 8.8.40; PM, Picture House, Ipswich, 10.8.40.

(f) Mr Borland Thinks Again

Produced: Paul Rotha (British Films)
Cast: includes Emlyn Williams and Beatrix Lehmann
Characters: Farmers; a sailor, son of a farmer; refugee Belgian boy; Ministry of Agriculture official

Story: A farmer refuses to believe in the value of silage though his go-ahead son on the farm, and his other son, a sailor home on leave, impress the necessity on him. He listens to a lecture and demonstration by an official but is still unimpressed. But when he returns and is talking to a

Belgian refugee boy, an aeroplane goes overhead and the refugee runs for cover, terrified. The thought that this might happen here strikes him so forcibly that he decides to build a silo straight away.

Observed: LE, Astoria, Brixton, 3.9.40; YS, Regal, Stockport, 4.9.40

(g) Salvage with a Smile

Produced: Adrian Brunel (Ealing Studios)
Cast: includes Aubrey Mallalieu, Ronald Shiner
Characters: A professor; a dustman; a housekeeper

Story: When the dustman comes to the professor's house, much to his astonishment he is invited in, and the professor explains to him what happens to the salvage that he collects. Bones are turned to glue and so on, paper into cartridge cases. The dustman in turn explains what is the best way to pack rubbish.

Observed: LE, Gaumont, Streatham 27.8.40; GW, Plaza, Regent Street 24.8.40

(h) Sea fort

Produced: Ian Dalrymple (Ealing Studios)

Story: A garrison in a fort at sea to ward off attacks by sea and air. A tour of the fort is made, and the men are shown on and off duty. A mock attack is made.

Observed: GW, Tatler, Charing Cross Road, 19.8.40; LE, Red Hall, Fulham, 19.8.40; LE, Gaumont, Streatham, 20.8.40; YS, Pavilion, Stockport, 22.9.40

(i) Westward Ho! – 1940

Produced: Thorold Dickinson (D & P Studios)

Story: Children getting ready to leave London. The train journey and arrival. The new homes at the reception area. Speakers from Norway, Belgium, Holland and France pointing out the value of evacuation from their own experience. A soldier says how happy he is that his child is safe.

Observed: LE, Astoria, Streatham, 11.7.40.

(j) Yesterday is Over Your Shoulder

Cast: includes Robertson Hare, Joyce Barbour

Story: A little town clerk reads an advert in a paper for technical schools to produce skilled labour. Being a handyman, he joins one and is taught

how to use highly skilled tools. As he works he sings 'Yesterday Is Over Your Shoulder' and one day Mr Bevin comes to watch him at work. When he returns home, his wife is shocked to see the respectable little clerk wearing a cloth cap, and swearing.
Observed: LE, Gaumont, Streatham, Sept. 1940

(k) Miss Know All

Cast: includes Martita Hunt

Story: A young girl's father goes to pick up her mother at a hospital, and does not return by the bus he was expected on. Miss Know All overhears a remark on the wireless about a hospital being hit, and jumps to the conclusion that it must be the local hospital and that father and mother are dead. This worries the girl. But when father returns quite all right with mother, he goes out and gives Miss Know All a piece of his mind for causing such trouble.
Observed: LE, Regal, Streatham, 21.9.40; NM, Stepney, 18.9.40

(l) Dover Front Line

Produced: GPO Unit

Story: Description of life in Dover with nobody worried by bombs and shells. The wardens and firemen. The balloon barrage men and the anti-aircraft batteries. The men and women in the streets taking shells near them calmly and complaining about the effect on their beans.
Observed: LE, Gaumont, Streatham, 8.10.40

3 (a) Squadron 992

Produced: GPO Unit

Story: First the training of balloon barrage men (main characters appear throughout, a Scotsman, a chauffeur, a commercial traveller, and so on). Then a barrage is sent to the Forth Bridge, and is set up. The men enjoy life and then one day the Germans try and bomb the bridge. They are chased by British fighters, and one is brought down just as a terrier catches a rabbit. The balloon barrage continues as usual.
Observed: LE Regal, Streatham, 5.7.40

(b) Men of the Lightship

Produced: Cavalcanti
Directed: David Macdonald

Story: The crew of the East Dudgeon lightship are due for relief. They go about their duties, laughing and joking. A mine is sighted and they go out and anchor it, but a destroyer comes and blows it up. Then, just before the relief ship, two German planes appear and start bombing them. They have to leave ship, the skipper wounded in the arm. They row all day and all night, and finally sight land. But they are too weak to prevent the boat turning over as it reaches the shore and all are drowned.

Observed: LE, London Pavilion, 7.8.40; GE, Studio Two, 14.8.40; LE, Gaumont, Streatham, 20.8.40

26   *You're Telling Me* Film Report

You're Telling Me was an MoI five-minute film, produced by Paul Rotha, about rumours. It showed how the incident of a small boy throwing a stone at a factory window was progressively exaggerated into the destruction of the factory. The report (FR 639) is dated 5 April 1941.

The MoI five-minute film *You're Telling Me* started distribution in mid-March, 1941. A small survey was made on some of its effects, mainly in the London area. No special validity should be attached to statistics in this report, and no comprehensive national survey has been attempted. This report is also necessarily hasty as the principal film investigator is being called up in the middle of it.

Audience response

The film was observed on a number of occasions by our standard methods. Altogether 14 response points were plotted. In two cases there was a hundred per cent response and the following list grades the responded-to sequences in order of response:

1 Scene in barber's shop where barber tells customer that his brother 'missed death by inches'.

2 In train, man telling owner of factory that the place has been blown to blazes.

3 Same conversation, 'killed every man on the night shift'.

4 End sequence: 'My name happens to be Harper'.

5 Waitress on telephone tells barber place was 'absolutely gutted'.

6 Secretary tells waitress factory is a terrible mess.

7 (Only non-verbal response) Face in chair changes to face in train.

8 'I don't think anyone invents them, they just grow.'

9 End conversation, Harper tells Smith the factory looks all right to him.

10 Jones to Brown in train, seeing broken window, assuming a bomb near.

11 Boy throws stone through window.

12 Remark on everybody liking to feel in the know.

The last five of these only obtained sporadic response, mostly in the form of occasional verbal comment. Two other points where response might have been expected – Mr Brown on the telephone and a rabbit pie discussion – hardly evoked any response at all.

Incidentally, one of the commonest types of overheard comment in the second week was when the film came on, thus:

Oh, I've seen this.
I've seen this before.
I've seen this one.
Yes, I've seen this, it's good. (various London cinemas)

Apart from this there was little spontaneous comment, and very little unfavourable, though one man at the point 'blown the place to blazes' exclaimed 'It's getting worse and worse.' (but he may have meant that the rumour was getting worse and worse).

In general, the response was definitely good as compared with the average film, especially the average five-minute film. But a large part of the response was laughter, and it is not certain how much of such laughter means the registration of a message about *rumour*. This will be discussed below. People were distinctly interested in the film, but also a considerable number of people are extremely critical now of all such films, are perhaps too aware of their propaganda background and MoI context.

People's criticism

The opinion of a reasonably representative sample of Londoners was collected in six widely separated boroughs during the end of March. As usual, great difficulty was experienced in finding out whether people had seen the film, because they did not remember its title and because they muddled it up with other MoI shorts, particularly other films on rumour. Thus 4 per cent were emphatic that they had seen the film, but when asked when they had seen it, said anything from one to six months ago. The majority who had seen it had seen it in the previous week. This makes the figures all the less reliable, but they nevertheless give an indication of the general atmosphere. It should be remembered that in direct interviewing people always tend to be more favourable to any form of status quo than in investigation by other methods, and the following figures must be qualified in this respect.

Of those who had seen it and were checked as having seen it:

78% were very favourable
6% were fairly favourable
16% were negative, not favourable or indifferent

The striking feature of the verbatim replies is the frequency with which different investigators in widely separate areas and on different days got the simple reply: 'Very good.' Compared with other shorts investigated, this may be regarded as an exceptionally high degree of approval, but approval of a superficial sort. However, such answers indicate that the film has left a pleasant memory even if nothing more definite than that. But *very few* people were able to indicate any specific reason why they thought the film was good:

It was jolly good – very sarcastic.
Oh very good – very instructive.
I thought it was good. Just how things would happen.

Less formal interviews were more revealing. The following three informal interviews give the atmosphere rather better:

1 *Inv.:*   What did you think of the MoI film *You're Telling Me?*
  M 20 D: It was good.
  Inv.:   Can you remember it clearly?
  M 20 D: Not very.
  Inv.:   Did you think it was better or worse than the usual MoI films?
  M 20 D: Not quite so good.
  Inv.:   Do you think it will make any difference to rumour-mongering?
  M 20 D: Yes.

2 *Inv.:*   What did you think of the MoI film *You're Telling Me?*
  F 50 B: A very good film. I think there ought to be more like it to stop
             people talking.

3 *Inv.:*   What did you think of the MoI film *You're Telling Me?*
  F 50 B: Better propaganda than most I have seen.
  Inv.:   Do you think it will make any difference to rumour-mongering?
  F 50 B: Well it's doubtful whether it will stop rumours.
  Inv.:   Do you think it got its points over?
  F 50 B: Yes, I think it did.

And here are five candid comments from working-class people:

Very funny but not much else.

I thought that the children were ever so good, but I didn't care about the rest, *men don't talk like that in trains*, at least not any that I've seen.

No, I didn't like it, things like that don't happen in our life. I think that all this business about rumours is a lot of madness.

Lousy, I don't like them sort of films much, no earthly use in them.

Good. These propaganda films, I think, are very interesting, they do make one realise what is happening and how a little thing like that rumour can do a lot of damage.

When we penetrate below the surface we come to the opposition that exists both against all *known* propaganda, and against especially any propaganda which asks people to do something unpleasant and implies criticism of British behaviour instead of boasts for it. People so need the dramatic at this time, and rumour is a form of dramatising the war. Anti-rumour strikes up against considerable unconscious resistances in consequence (for further theoretical discussion of this subject see Rumour reports).

Similarly, though people much enjoyed the film for the most part, when asked if in their opinion it would curb rumour-mongering, the majority replied NO.

People were also asked to compare this short with other shorts and say whether it was better or worse. Here opinion was distinctly in favour of this film, though some margin must be allowed for the fact that it will have been the latest MoI short that most of them have seen:

Well above the average of the usual MoI films.

One of their better efforts.

Definitely worse.

Better, the best I've seen.

Better than any others I have seen.

Slightly better than some of those that I have seen.

I have seen better ones, that one about the lighthouse for instance.

Funnier than some of the others.

Better than most.

Better than most we see.

Upper-class opinion was less favourable to the film than working-class opinion which has been the main comment so far quoted. Here are some typical comments of varying nature from upper-class people, male and female:

I thought that it was a very good propaganda film which was quite amusing to watch although it was rather blatant propaganda, the actors were all good and there was some nice touches in it such as the kids at the beginning.

Lousy. No real documentary value at all, *might have been made by an amateur.*

I enjoyed it and thought it quite amusing, though it was a bit laboured in parts.

Futile, I think all these propaganda films are a waste of time, no one pays any attention to them.

All right but I am not very keen on these sort of film, I thought that the idea was good and the steps by which the rumour was spread were very well chosen with perhaps just an eye for comedy.

Very good indeed, it seemed to me to be really effective propaganda, this sort of film is surely much better than the ones about salvage collecting and the terrible one on food.

Rather puerile, you know. I don't think that any film which is quite as obvious as that will really be of any propaganda use.

I suppose it was all right though I can't say that I paid much attention to it.

Summary of general opinion

General opinion can be summed up as largely favourable, but not for very specific reasons, whereas those who are unfavourable make definite points about the film. It is extremely probable that many of those who are favourable to the film have not taken it *very seriously.* This seems partly to be due to the amusing nature of the film itself, partly to the fact that the whole business of rumour cannot fully be dealt with by direct propaganda; and partly because all MoI shorts are widely regarded as 'propaganda' and looked at by a considerable number of people as kind of exhibition pieces, the pleasant sermon in the feature programme, the Two Minutes Silence after which you get back to making the armaments. Principal points of criticism are:

The film is *too* funny, considering the theme.
The dialogue, especially the train sequence, is unreal (working-class comment; note that the sequence is in a first-class carriage both ti nes).
The treatment was rather 'childish' (upper-class comment).
'It was rather blatant'; too clearly propaganda.
This film like anything else dealing with rumour doesn't really do any good.

Favourable comment was mainly based on the idea that:

The film was particularly well put together.
The sequence of events was natural and interesting.
It showed what really happened in real life.
It was amusing.

Whatever people *said*, and however they consciously reacted, it is certain that this film has revealed to many, whether they recognise it or not, more of the machinery of the rumour than they had seen before. Perhaps this effect would have been *increased* if the rumour had been based on a dramatic beginning, with a real bomb doing a small amount of damage (e.g. falling in wasteland by the factory); as it was, there was a feeling that such a lot of rumour would hardly develop so quickly *from nothing at all*. Ordinary people do not regard themselves as fools. There is therefore a tendency, noted frequently in MoI shorts (e.g. *Telefootlers, Goofer Trouble*) for the audience to regard the behaviour of the people on the screen as amusing but rather absurd and exceptional. The audience do not sufficiently identify themselves with the actual story, and do not feel that *they* would ever make such a mistake merely over a *stone*. Again, this situation might have been crystallised in the film if one of the characters had raised the issue on the screen, had said 'Oh, that's a rumour' and tried to refuse to pass it on, but being convinced against his better judgement that it was true.

Again, the rumour was not shown as having any bad effects, except temporarily alarming a waitress, who however compensated her distress by the satisfaction of spreading the rumour on a larger scale. No harm was done by the rumour spreading. If rumour is to be treated at this level, you have got to think about it and about the propaganda about it, just as clearly and fundamentally as if you were setting out to try to stop people telling dirty stories.

Finally, it was only by complete coincidence, the fluke of the rumour-spreader spreading the rumour to the owner of the factory, that the truth was revealed. While that shows up the rumour itself, it does not show people how to check on their own personal rumours. One of the main reasons why rumours are spread is because the people who spread them *genuinely believe them* and have not the faintest idea that they are spreading a rumour.

The opinion of managers

As usual, managers readily spoke for their audiences. They were especially ready to say which part of the film people laughed at or reacted to most, generally naming the very end, where Harper revealed his identity as the owner of the factory. As we have already shown, this is not confirmed by observation in the same cinemas.

We have not previously had occasion to interview managers about MoI shorts, so that we have no standard of comparison for this one. But we were impressed in a number of cases by the considerable *irritation* which quite a proportion of managers seemed to feel about MoI shorts in general. Nevertheless, managerial opinion tended to follow the lines of public opinion in being considerably approving of the present film. Perhaps the degree to which the opinion of managers reflects any real situation in the audience can best be indicated by quoting from three in News Theatres near to each other and with closely similar clienteles.

1 *Man.*: I thought it was silly all those people talking like that.
  Inv.: What about the audience?
  Man.: Oh, they laughed at it.
  Inv.: But weren't they meant to?
  Man.: Oh, they thought it was silly. They were saying 'Wasn't it daft?' as they came out.

2 *Inv.*: Could you tell me what was the reception like of the MoI film last week, *You're Telling Me*?
  Man.: Very good – really very good anti-jabber film shall I say because people see it and realise the ridiculous rumours put around by irresponsible people, who make rumours grow. (*He goes on to relate story of the film fairly accurately but with bits of home-made dialogue which were quite good. He seemed to fancy himself as the man who was not taken in by the rumour-mongers.*) Oh, yes it's a good one.
  Inv.: Did they laugh at all the film?
  Man.: Let me see now, the main bit they laughed at was where at the end the man says I am Harper.

3 *Inv.*: Could you tell me what sort of reception the MoI film *You're Telling Me* got last week?
  Man.: A good one. It definitely went home. That's why I call it good.
  Inv.: A better or worse reception than the other MoI films?
  Man.: Not worse for its class. Some create more interest than others.
  Inv.: Do you think it will affect rumour-mongering or not?
  Man.: Yes, I feel that in that one, I think it went home to a lot of people, because you do hear a lot of rumours – I heard from so and so, and so on.
  Inv.: Did it get many laughs?
  Man.: Well that sort of film would not get a definite laugh. Mostly I think when the man said he was Harper.

Children

Several observers report that where children were present at the showing of this film, they received it with particular interest.

Conclusion

For reasons beyond our control, we did not get adequate notice to make a full study of this film. And we have not had adequate time to write up this report and fully think out the points raised. A number of points and suggestions are made in the text, and further information and discussion can be supplied if required. We make no great claim for this report, but hope that it has some possible suggestive interest.

Preliminary Report on Opinion about Ministry of Information Shorts

Opinion was sought from the Mass-Observation panel of observers about the MoI shorts, which they considered the best and which the worst. A total of 142 answers were analysed, 75 from men and 67 from women. The findings were embodied in a report (FR 799), dated 24 July 1941.

1 General opinion of the films

In the previous month observers were asked for their general opinion of government advertising, and answers to the present question were analysed on the same basis. The table compares general opinion of MoI films with general opinion of government advertising as a whole. In both cases where no general opinion was given, but instances of good and bad were given, replies were entered in the 'mixed to fair' category. Similarly when no general opinion was given, but examples were predominantly good or bad, replies were entered in the appropriate group.

	Percentage expressing this opinion about:	
Opinion	*Govt advertising*	*MoI films*
Very good	3	4
Good	18	25
Mixed to fair	23	17
Bad	22	8
Very bad	8	2
Seldom notice any (for films: Leave little impression; forget)	18	7
Not seen any; don't go to cinema	–	31
No opinion, unclassified	8	6

Thus people's opinion of MoI films is very considerably higher than their general opinion of government advertising. A smaller proportion of those who see them are unimpressed or forget what they were about. On the other hand 31 per cent are not reached by the fims at all in this sample. Over and above this a considerable proportion have only seen one or two MoI films, either because they only visit the cinema occasionally or because these films have not been shown when they were there. Taking this into consideration, it seems likely that with present distribution and cinema-going habits these films impact on well under half of people as a continuing source of propaganda. Therefore their comparative success compared with other forms of propaganda is partly mitigated by the limited proportion of people who see them.

2 Praise and criticism

160 comments were made on about 50 different films; some of these were not in fact MoI films, though observers were under the impression that they were. In a few cases it was impossible to discover to which film observers were alluding. Without detailed acquaintance with the scenarios of each film it was found impossible to be certain in some cases that entries were made under the correct film, but where reasonable certainty was not possible comments were omitted from this analysis.

Though observers were asked which they considered best and worst of the films, only a minority felt qualified to say this. Analysis was therefore made of all favourable and unfavourable comment on individual films.

The ratio of praise to criticism was 96:66, i.e. roughly three appreciative comments on individual films for every two critical comments.

The most frequently praised films were:

London Can Take It	12 appreciations
Men of the Lightship	8
Dai Jones	6
Goofers	4
Eating out with Tommy Trinder	4
Merchant Seamen	4
Miss Grant goes to the Door	4
Channel Incident	4
Mobile Canteen	4

The most frequently criticised were:

Call for Arms	6 critical comments
Miss Grant Goes to the Door	5
Home Guard	4

Her Father's Daughter	4
Visit from Canada	4

The most frequently mentioned films were:

London Can Take It	12 mentions
Miss Grant Goes to the Door	9
Dai Jones	8
Men of the Lightship	8
Eating out with Tommy Trinder	7
Home Guard	7
Call for Arms	6
Christmas under Fire	6
Merchant Seamen	6

Thus *London Can Take It* was the most frequently commented on film, and received nothing but praise. *Men of the Lightship* also received only praise, while *Dai Jones* was praised six times and criticised twice. *Call to Arms* and *Her Father's Daughter* received nothing but critical comment. *Miss Grant Goes to the Door*, and *Home Guard*, though both aroused considerable interest, were both praised and criticised. Other films mentioned received praise and criticism in varying proportions.

The following films were mentioned by between three and six people and were *mainly praised* (if mentioned by three people only, only those films praised in all three cases are listed):

Christmas Under Fire
Mr Proudfoot Shows a Light
Ack Ack
Heart of Britain
Visit from Canada

The following film was mentioned by five people and was *mainly criticised*:

Words for Battle

It was found impossible to distinguish in observers' answers between *Any Old Iron* and *Salvage with a Smile*, but one or other of these films was referred to by ten people, six praising the film and four criticising it.

3 Producing units

Twenty-three of the films mentioned by observers were produced by four different units. The ratio of praise to criticism for each film produced by each of these units were added, giving the results shown in the table. Thus the Crown unit receives over four times as much praise as criticism.

Producing unit	Total number of comments on this unit's films	Ratio Praise	:	Criticism
Crown	47	4.2	:	1
D & P	38	.6	:	1
Ealing	10	1.0	:	1
Strand	14	1.0	:	1

28   Report on Ministry of Information Shorts

This massive report, dated 1 April 1942, was based on research undertaken between December 1941 and March 1942 (FR 1193). It followed the progress of four MoI shorts through the nation's cinemas, assessing the public's reaction and the effects of the films. The films were: *War in the East* (produced by Edgar Anstey), an account of the war in the Pacific with maps and diagrams; *Seaman Frank Goes Back to Sea* (produced by Derrick de Marney), which shows broadcaster Frank Laskier returning to work in the merchant service and appealing for more contributions to national savings; *Newspaper Train* (produced by John Taylor), showing how the newspapers were delivered during the Biltz; and *Rush Hour* (directed by Anthony Asquith), a dramatised anecdote urging shoppers to travel between 10 a.m. and 4 p.m. and not during the rush hour. The films are referred to by short names: *Pacific* (because they have miscalled the film *War in the Pacific*), *Laskier* (again due to a mistaken use of title, *Seaman Laskier Goes to Sea Again*; we have substituted *Seaman Frank*) *Newspaper* and *Shopping*. The report is prefaced by a statement:

> The object of this investigation was to find out what effects, if any, these films had. And in what ways, if any, this effect might have been increased, reduced or modified. Further, what lessons, if any, could be learnt from the detailed analysis of the impact of these four reasonably characteristic MoI films. We attempt in the report that follows to answer all these questions as fully and accurately as possible.

For reasons of length, we are only able to print the conclusions of this report. But it is interesting to observe the stress they lay on the need for information rather than exhortation and the demonstration of the success of the most informational of the films, *War in the East*. This conclusion coincides exactly with the approach that was now developing at the MoI, particularly since the arrival of Brendan Bracken in July 1941 as Minister. Dr Stephen Taylor, head of the Home Intelligence Unit, reported in October 1941: 'The British public as a whole shows a very high degree of common sense. Given the relevant facts, they will listen to and accept explanations when they will not accept exhortations.' On 10 April 1942, Bracken told the Cabinet: 'We must stop appealing to the public or lecturing at it. One makes it furious, the other resentful.' It is probably no coincidence then that the MoI five-minute films ceased in late 1942 and longer, more informational films took their place.

Part C   The effect of five-minute shorts

(In the previous part of this report we have dealt in detail with people's reactions to each of the four films. We have seen that *Pacific* was the most liked, *Newspaper* the least. We have noticed many gradations of opinion and many points of detailed criticism. We have not, however, attempted as yet to measure the actual *effect* of these films. The fact that people come out liking or disliking an MoI short is important, but it is not by any means the end of the story. Each of these films had as its purpose the modification of existing opinion or attitude on some one or more points. How far was this purpose achieved?)

XIV   General effect

It is clear from the material already given that two of the films, *Seaman Frank* and *Newspaper*, did not clearly get even their main purpose across to many people. *Shopping* and *Pacific*, especially the latter, were much more successful in this respect. In order to try and measure more carefully the degree to which the message or purpose of the film had penetrated, 632 interviews were made. About a third of these people remembered seeing each of these films, so that in each case we can compare about 200 people who have seen the film with 400 who have not seen it, on the point of knowledge which is a main message of the film. Slightly more women than men had seen the films, but the difference is in no case of major importance. The margin of comparison error is around 7 per cent. The figures that follow have no absolute validity; but are comparable within this sample, irrespective of its general validity, and can provide some indications of value.

Bearing these qualifications in mind, in the next Section each film is examined in turn on this basis.

XV   Effect of each film

(i)   Seaman Frank
Sixty per cent of the sample said that they were saving in some way. When the saving habits of those who had seen *Seaman Frank* are compared with the general average (see table), it appears that seeing *Seaman Frank* has not upped saving, or more precisely that in this case people who had seen the film were not thereby notably inspired to start saving if they were not already doing so. There is one important qualification here: it is possible that savers tend rather less to go to

cinemas than non-savers and therefore that anyway and irrespective of this film the proportion of non-savers among cinema-goers (and thus among those seeing MoI shorts) would be higher than in the general aggregate of the population, which includes some who save to the maximum rather than spend in wartime on any 'luxury'. But other studies do not suggest that this difference would in itself be considerable enough wholly to explain the situation indicated in the above table.

| | Percentage saying they are doing this | |
	Of the 632 sample	Of those who say they have seen the film
Saving	60	56
Not saving	38	40
Uncertain	2	4

It would, of course, be absurd to suggest that the film has actually made people less likely to save, though we have seen that it has irritated some people quite considerably. We have also seen that large numbers of those seeing the film did not appreciate that it was Savings propaganda, and in fact among D class (those who save least often) *nearly twice as many* thought it was propaganda for the Navy or Merchant Navy as thought it was propaganda for savings. The way in which the propaganda note was inserted at the end was indeed something of a weak anti-climax. It had a further serious deficiency from the *effect* point of view. *The appeal was primarily to the non-saver.* As other Mass-Observation studies, undertaken for the National Savings Committee, have shown, the great majority of those who can save are saving, and the main problem of Savings propaganda in 1942 is to increase the margin of savings among those already saving; this film made no real appeal to the person already saving. The people who think saving advantageous have always saved, and many others have been brought in for patriotic and other motives since the war. For more than two years there has been intensive savings propaganda. *Seaman Frank*, from this point of view, was little more than a drop in the ocean, and the drop does not seem to have rippled out to any visible extent.

(ii) Newspaper

Newspaper was the least liked and most disliked of the four films. Like

Seaman Frank, many people commented on its comparative obscurity, even while liking it. Only a little over a third had any clear idea of what the film was supposed to show. This relatively weak impact is reflected also in the present effect test. When the effect on people who had seen the film is compared with the general aggregate of the 632 sample, we find no appreciable improvement, on this evidence, among those who have seen it, as regards attitude to the job the newspapers are doing in wartime (see table).

Opinion of job	*Percentage of this opinion*	
newspapers have	*Of the 632*	*Of those who say they*
done in war	*sample*	*have seen the film*
Good	50	51
Bad	11	14
Indifferent	16	20
No opinion	25	15

Looking at these figures, and comparing the reactions to the Press of people who had seen the film to those who had not seen the film, we find that the film has not appreciably influenced these people in the 'right' way. Of the total, slightly more people who have seen the film think the newspapers have done a bad job and rather more are indifferent to the Press than of those who have not seen the film.

Taking error into account, we can conclude that this film has had no noticeable effect on the way people feel about the newspapers in wartime. From this point of view it appears to have been an almost complete failure.

It is not without interest to compare back the material from interviews made with those coming out of cinemas. Fifty-four per cent of those coming out of cinemas showing this film said the film made them feel in some way appreciative or favourable to the newspapers, as compared with 62 per cent who said it made them feel the same way about the railways. This further confirms the lack of precision in the film's impact.

(iii) Shopping

The way in which people enjoyed this film, but at the same time tended to treat it as something not to be taken very seriously, has been shown. The proportion of women shopping earlier or later than before the war among those coming out of cinemas, has also been touched upon. In the 632 study,

Personal shopping time compared with pre-war	Percentage of Women giving this reply	
	Of the 632 sample	Of those who say they have seen the film
Earlier	49	50
Later	7	5
Same	23	28
Uncertain	9	6
Does not apply	12	11

this question of earlier or later shopping was asked again, so that answers could be compared with those who had and had not seen the film (see table).

As with *Seaman Frank*, there may be a selective tendency among those who have seen an MoI film, in this case possibly due to women in cinemas being more likely to shop late. On the other hand, the bias might equally be in the opposite direction, and anyway so many women are cinema-goers that the tendency is not likely to be of predominant importance either way. Taking into account the detailed material already considered, it is difficult to doubt that in terms of actual *effect*, shopping was not – importantly – successful, and that the minority of women concerned personally with the propaganda message often did not identify themselves with the funny fat woman shopper, and did not feel that the moral of the film applied to themselves personally.

There is of course another question which was outside the scope of this enquiry: how many women actually do avoidable shopping late, and in what groups and in what localities are these unnecessary shoppers distributed? For ourselves, we would suggest that the answer to this question might have provided a more exact basis for the preparation of this film. In the course of the present investigation, we did contact and get detailed statements from forty-one shopkeepers in Luton, Maidstone and High Wycombe, and an equal number in London, after the completed showing in these areas of this film. All kinds of shops were investigated. The general conclusion – though we stress that no special study was made of this point – is that the volume of 'unnecessary' late shopping in these particular places during this period was inconsiderable, and according to some shopkeepers insignificant. For what it is worth, the information obtained from these shopkeepers may be of interest (see table).

Time at which shopkeepers say they do most of their trade	Percentage of shopkeepers naming this time
Before 11	13
11–1	20
1–4	33
Before 4, but no specific category within this	11
After 4	15
Uncertain, etc.	8

(A good deal of detailed comment from shopkeepers is available for illustration and documentation on this and a number of other points, if required.)

No shopkeeper noticed any effect which he could directly attribute to the *Shopping* film in his district. Twenty shops in High Wycombe were visited *before* the film was shown there, and then again afterwards. The same was done to six Maidstone shops. None of these shops noticed any change in shopping times and habits during the intervening period. Fifteen bus drivers and conductors and two inspectors were interviewed in the same way, with the same result. This does not mean that there had not been any effect, of a visible sort, though it does mean that there has not been an effect sufficiently large to be 'obvious'. (It should be added that the three provincial towns selected for study were ones where the film was fairly well shown, and where there is a notable shopping congestion, largely due to evacuation.)

(iv) Pacific
The previous three films have not shown any very noticeable effect on people's behaviour or attitude as regards saving, shopping and admiring newspapers. *Pacific* shows a clearer result (see table).

Opinion on possibility of bombing Japan	Percentage holding this opinion	
	Of those of the 632 sample	Of those who say they have seen the film
Very easy	2	0
Easy	10	8
Difficult	28	28
Very difficult	21	32
No idea	39	32

Thus those who have seen the film are in this case (alone of the four films) significantly 'improved' as regards the film's message. This improvement would be much greater if women were omitted, for among men the improvement is marked.

It can fairly be said, therefore, that this film had driven home its lesson more than the other three. But it must also be said that plenty of people came out of it misinformed on this particular point, which is reasonably representative of the specific points in the film. From this it seems, once more, as if a five-minute film cannot put across a lot to a lot of people at one time. Apparently, the most an average five-minute film can do, so far as the present study shows, is to put across a little to a lot, or a lot to a little. *Pacific* succeeded to some extent in both these ways, but might have succeeded still more if it had determined to go all out for either one of them. It would be absurd to expect that five minutes in the cinema could fundamentally educate millions of people ignorant since birth on the subject of Asiatic geography. A film which can do as much in this respect as *Pacific*, has done much. And as well as the particular effect, it has certainly had a general informative and educative effect which cannot be measured precisely. All four of the films have had some general effect, no doubt. All four have heightened people's awareness of some aspect of the war effort. But only *Pacific* has heightened it in any large way, in any one distinct direction. With diffidence we add our own belief, based on other studies, that it might be possible, by further developing the informative technique, to get across simple, essential information through the short film to larger sections of the community. To pursue this would involve studying other films, but from our own cruder studies of earlier MoI shorts we strongly suspect that the *informative film* which aims to impart facts is more likely, other things being equal, to succeed in its job than the more 'propagandist' film which seeks to alter behaviour, and usually appeals through the 'emotions'.

All this is a difficult subject, and it would probably in fact have been more profitable (though this could have hardly have been visualised before the investigation was initiated) to study each film by a standard procedure at its A and B showings, rather than to attempt to track each film through categories down to G. Much more might have been learned by studying thirteen films in thirteen weeks, and we should welcome the opportunity of doing this. We have, however, the advantage of having made a number of other film studies for commercial groups, and for our own purposes. We therefore approach the conclusions below, based on the material given above, with some confidence. Small private studies of the short *Arms for Scrap*, showing during the present study period and accidentally encountered (while looking for other films), suggests that this film too was rather in a *Seaman Frank* category of a diffuse effect, though its message was perhaps more clearly understood. Similarly, material (encountered during the investigation) on the short *Tale of Two Cities* suggests that this film was moderately effective, though people did not understand it clearly, and felt there was inadequate explanation. Many people were absolutely fogged after seeing the Leslie Banks poetry Savings short, *We Want More Ships*. But reaction to *100 Million Women* was overwhelmingly favourable, and this film moved people to a marked degree and gave them much information which interested them. Finally, the film *Builders* which came on just at the end of the investigation had a striking effect in the few cinemas where it was observed, received an exceptional amount of audience response and subsequent overheard comment: this film, like *Pacific*, broke away from the traditional format, and explained, did not exhort, did not tell the audience they ought to do anything, simply showed them a part of the war effort in an interesting, informative, informal way.

Part D Non-showing

(The frequent absence of any MoI short at cinemas observed proved to be a major complication in the present enquiry. As originally planned, this subject was to be included in the present report, but as this report is now lengthy, and as in fact this point was not one we were particularly asked to investigate (it was not visualised as important in planning the investigation from either side), we propose to submit a separate memorandum on this subject shortly.)

Conclusions and summary

1 The four films were studied in detail and reaction at all levels fully illustrated in the text.
2 The large majority of people say they like MoI films, but an appreciable minority are critical, especially of the film *Newspaper*.
3 Points of general criticism were the shortness of the films, lack of entertainment value, similarity of MoI shorts to each other, and unsatisfactory commentary.
4 The reception of *Seaman Frank* can be summed up as follows:
   (a) Most people liked this film, dislike coming mainly from B class.
   (b) Approval was coloured by disappointment, people expecting much from Seaman Frank Laskier, because of his broadcasts.
   (c) People, even those liking the film, were often puzzled as to what it was about, or not clear about it – especially the commentary, which was strongly criticised.
   (d) The sudden introduction of the Savings theme at the end was not

much appreciated, and most people simply did not realise that the purpose of the film was to encourage savings.

(e) More women thought it was to encourage appreciation of or recruitment into the Navy or the Merchant Navy than thought it was about savings, and this misunderstanding was even higher among D class people as a group.

(f) Broadly, the film commanded sympathetic and patriotic attention, but to some extent failed to satisfy initial interest or to crystallise out the feelings aroused.

(g) Incidentally, the propaganda message of the film at the end, rather weakly presented, was directed only at the person who was not saving *at all*, did not encourage those already saving to save more.

5 Reaction to *Newspaper* can be summed up as follows:

(a) This film was a flop, when compared with other MoI shorts.

(b) This was largely so because it failed to register clearly on people, to hold interest or show good cause for existing either as entertainment or as propaganda or as anything else.

(c) It was much the most criticised of the four films, especially among B class.

(d) As usual, some were enthusiastic, but most approval in this case was decidedly lukewarm.

(e) An exceptional number considered the film definitely bad.

(f) People disliked the American commentator, what they considered the confusion of the film, and many points of detail, of which people were particularly critical in the present instance.

(g) Many misunderstood the main purpose of the film, and many had no idea of what its purpose was, especially in D class. Many of those who liked the film had no idea that it was supposed to convey any serious message or information.

6 Reaction to *Shopping* can be summed up thus:

(a) This film appeals especially to women, unlike the other three.

(b) It is generally regarded as good entertainment, though there is also some very strong criticism of it.

(c) Because it was regarded as good entertainment, the film was liked more than if it had dealt with the same idea less amusingly. But its somewhat caricature comedy set up a certain amount of conflict about its propaganda aspect.

(d) A minority also felt that the entertainment value was poor in itself, though Muriel George's acting was generally admired. It was, however, essentially regarded as acting, not 'reality'.

(e) There is some uncertainty about whether the film was intended to enable shoppers to get home, or war workers.

(f) The film did not directly apply to a lot of the people who saw it, and even more did not make those to whom it did apply feel that it applied to them personally.

7 Reaction to *Pacific*, the most successful of the films, can be summed up thus:

   (a) This film was the most liked of the four, although it was the least cinematographic and traditional.

   (b) The map technique was generally approved, and there were signs that people would welcome more of it, especially if done a little more emphatically and vividly.

   (c) The film had its best reception from men and B class, its worst from women and D class. It definitely failed to get across to a good many females of the working classes.

   (d) People were thoroughly interested in the film, and glad of its facts, for which there is a much greater demand than has generally been appreciated by the MoI? Much of the criticism was offered because the facts were felt to be presented too quickly or confusedly.

   (e) Thus many came out, after seeing the film, still ignorant about principal points of fact dealt with and illustrated in it. This was particularly so, again, among women and working-class people.

   (f) This experiment appears to have been justified and to have scored a relatively high degree of success for this film, when compared with the other three studied. The imparting of facts in a five-minute film may be more suitable to this medium than the attempt to produce a change in habit or opinion of the sort attempted in the other films.

8 Up to p. 90, the report deals primarily with people's approval, disapproval, criticism and comment – actual audience reaction was very low on all four films. The last part of the report (Sections XIV and XV) attempts to indicate the effect of the films, which is of course in the end more important than the crude verbal reaction. There is evidently a considerable discrepancy, which has indeed been noted in the past with other such films, between liking the film and doing anything about it. People will say they have taken in the message, but many have only taken it in at a very superficial level.

9 The effect of *Seaman Frank* on savings seems to have been very slight, if not negligible, and this effect was further limited by the fact that the film appealed only to the non-saver.

10 The effect of *Newspaper* has been negligible, according to this evidence, as is indeed confirmed by the whole tone of comment and reaction all through.

11 The effect of *Shopping* has been small, though it has probably had some very slight effect.

12 The effect of *Pacific* has been considerable, and has appreciably

improved the knowledge of a minority. Its full effect was limited by the large amount of information given in a short time, which could not be taken in fully by a lot of people, especially less educated people.

13 Broadly, then, MoI films now command an extensive goodwill. The limitations on them are partly limitations of what can be done in five minutes in the entertainment cinema atmosphere. But there are also undoubtedly limitations within the films themselves, in lack of precise definition as to the purpose of the film, who it is aimed at, and whether or not the people at whom it is aimed can take it in. That is to say, from the point of view of public reaction, there is undoubtedly room for technical simplification, and more precise focus in the films studied. To take one small instance of the many referred to in the text, the commentaries in both *Newspaper* and *Seaman Frank* are such as to minimise the impact for large sections of the community, while the character acting of Muriel George, excellent dramatically though it may be is almost designed to obscure the reality message and purpose of this film?

14 *Pacific* was largely a success in terms of effect as well as opinion, because it made a compromise between being just another film and being something different, informational propaganda. This compromise, fully discussed in the text of the report, puts MoI shorts in a difficult position where they are always liable to be resented or rejected if they are too much propaganda, and loved but ignored as propaganda if they are too much entertainment.

15 From this study, and from material collected in other connections, it seems as if the strictly informational film has a particular function not yet fully exploited, whereas the film which attempts to influence habits in a straight propagandist way, like *Seaman Frank* or *Shopping*, may have a more limited use than has been supposed. There are several reasons which could be adduced for this, including the following:

   (a) People are increasingly tired of exhortations and requests and general propaganda, especially along familiar lines.
   (b) But people are hungry for more information, straight direction, understanding. And a great many people are ignorant about an enormous amount of things in the war which they are in fact ready to be very interested in. For instance, how does a submarine operate at sea? What is the function and scope of the dive bomber? What are the new hostels like for girl war workers? The life story of General MacArthur. What are the aptitude tests for the ATS? How is the Budget arrived at, and what is the relation between savings, taxes and undesirable spending? What are the peoples, provinces, importance and strategy of India? Where are the world's oil supplies, and why?

(c) Information is applicable to practically everyone in a cinema audience, whereas a great deal of the *Seaman Frank* or *Shopping* type of propaganda is only applicable to a minority.

(d) It is much easier to put across information, which does not require any positive behaviour effect, than to put across 'pep' and requests for changed behaviour. The short film offers a particularly suitable medium for giving information in ways which cannot be provided elsewhere (e.g. by radio or newspaper). Exhortations to change behaviour are given every day and in every way through other media.

16 After considering the hundred pages of evidence in this report, there seems some ground for suggesting that the MoI short might well attempt, experimentally, to be *less* ambitious in what it tries to do during five minutes. There are enormous vacua of ignorance and misunderstanding about great areas of the war, like EPT and Treasury control, the Civil Service and MI5, day nurseries and post-war economics, which people are thirsting to be told about. There is a whole group of themes around production and the results of production. Such material seems particularly suitable for film treatment, and it is not at present anyone's responsibility to impart it coherently to the mass of people.

17 The field material collected for this report all the way through suggests that people cannot take in much in five minutes. This is particularly so of those sections of the community which most need further instruction and energising for the war effort, namely women and D class. They like the films for the most part, and often like them most. But they least often get the point. The difficulty in presenting these films is, of course, that a film to please one section of audience may displease another. But any attempt to please everybody quickly is likely to fail, and there may be reasons for attempting a planned, and even long-term, impact on defined sections of the audience. Here, as elsewhere, there may be room for some further analysis of exactly what MoI films are trying to do and to whom.

18 All through this report we have treated each class group and each sex group on roughly equal terms. It should be stressed at this stage that the biggest sections numerically of the cinema audience are women and working-class people, and that for this reason the more critical reactions of B class, who know more and are more amenable to the last two years of propaganda anyway, may often be ignored. It could fairly be argued that the film is the medium by which material can be imparted to millions of those who least take in newspaper and radio material, and of whom almost a third read no newspaper and do not listen regularly to the radio.

19 People have got used to the five-minute short, accepted it and liked it,

but they do not appreciate, however, so to speak, that they are entitled to see one a week and to see one in every cinema in the country. There is no audience pressure on cinema managements to show a five-minute film, and frequently therefore they are not shown – this will be documented in the separate memorandum we are submitting on this subject. The whole question of making people more expectant of films, now that they have so much general goodwill, might be explored. An MoI short *about* shorts, how they are made, who makes them, how they are distributed, could indirectly deal with this point. The time may have come, too, when the subject is of sufficient interest and prestige to be dealt with in a BBC postscript, etc.

20 A further question arises in connection with the length of the films. The research material on many points indicates that people cannot take in much during the five minutes of a film, or rather that they cannot take in much of a serious message. But some of these messages could only with difficulty be made much simpler, and the question therefore arises whether five minutes is the right length of time. We have not been asked to investigate this point, only to report on four five-minute films. But at many points in the enquiry people have spontaneously mentioned this and suggested that the films could and should be longer. For what it is worth, in our own opinion, there is much to be said for having quite considerably longer MoI films, if that were possible, especially films of an informational type, dealing with subjects like war economics, news service, the integration of strategy, war production, and the many other things which are of general interest and which people need to know about even if the don't want to, though many do want to, consciously.

21 One other point should be made here. No informational film, however presented, is not thereby necessarily effective. *Newspaper* was an informational film, primarily; but it gave its information in an unprecise, 'over-intellectualised' way. The film may have been technically perfect from the film technician's point of view, but the only point of view from which these films can be examined logically, in the short run, seems to be their effect on the people for whom they are intended. At every point, we came up against this need for checking more closely against audiences, and especially for pre-analysis and pre-checking before the film format is finalised. We stress this with diffidence, because Mass-Observation is necessarily biased in making this point. But we venture to say that in our view there are few places where such checking is [more] necessary than in the often hurried making of films, which have to be prepared in a special atmosphere, and which have to be shown in every part of the country and to every sort of person over a period of nearly three months from the date of first showing.

It would be absurd to be dogmatic from a detailed study of only four pictures, and of course much can be learned by continuous study of film after film, a process of accumulation of knowledge and learning, which, after a few months, would probably produce certain subsidiary foolproof knowledge.

22 A final question arises. Is the present tendency in MoI films to have all the shape of a complete picture, a beginning and an end, a peak and valley graph trajectory, suitable to this length of time? Has the MoI film tended to follow, almost unthinkingly, the traditional pattern of longer films? To some extent we suspect that the answer to this is YES. And that a good many of the minor failures are due to this squeezing of a longer period into a short one, and the conforming to a pattern of documentary or feature development which is in fact impracticable in five minutes – impracticable that is, from the point of view of the audience.

23 It is this point of view of the audience with which alone this report has been concerned. In concluding it, we must emphatically state that nowhere do we intend ourselves to criticise these films, and that we are entirely ignorant of the technical and other considerations involved. We are doing no more than trying honestly to report what the people who see the films say about them, think about them, do about them.

24 Many other points are discussed in the text of the report. If it will be helpful to have any further summaries or memoranda or discussions based upon this report, we are readily at the service of those concerned in this matter.

Indexes

General Index

Entries referring to attitudes and opinions about films (e.g. accents, class in films, history films etc.) are brief. Further details can be obtained by reading the answers to the questionnaires (pages 32–136 and 220–91) and by consulting the film titles index for individual films.

Most journals and newspapers are subsumed under the entry Press, except for specific cinematic magazines.

Abercrombie, Mr, 5
accents, attitudes to, 39
Adams, Mary, 5–6, 11
adventure films, attitudes to, 34–6
advertisements, 39, 147–8, 211–12; lack of, 426
age of cinema-goers, 41, 42, 221
air raids, in films, 175, 181, 186, in newsreels, 416–17
Aldgate, Anthony, 299, 331
Allan, Elizabeth, 290
Allen, Chesney see Flanagan and Allen
American films, preferred by Bolton audiences, 13, 34, 39, 41–99, 101–35; see also Hollywood; individual films in film titles index
Anderson, Sherwood, 234
Anderson, Sir John, 146, 385, 386
Anstey, Edgar, MoI film by, see War in the East in film titles index
anti-war speeches, 181, 184, 186, 358–60
Arlen, Richard, 290
Arliss, George, 62, 75, 76, 276
Arnold, Captain Harold, 326
Arthur, Jean, 263
Askey, Arthur, 14
Asquith, Anthony, 13, 169; MoI film by, see Rush Hour in film titles index
Astaire, Fred, 94, 109, 273
attendance at cinemas, 12, 13–14, 33
audience response, 9, 24, 213–14; to Great Dictator, The, 354–63; to Let George Do It, 214, 348–9, 355; to Lion Has Wings, The, 178, 179, 182,

302–11, 355; to MoI shorts, 434–9, 442–4, 447–59; to newsreels, 389–93, 406–8, 409–10, 413–18; to Ships With Wings, 366–73, 377–9; see also Bolton; directive replies; men; women
Auer, Mischa, 193
Ausden, E., 217

Bacon, Lloyd, 224
Baillie, Sir Adrian, 145–6
Balcon, Michael, 145, 331, 364–5
Baldwin, Stanley, 162, 385, 386
Ball, Sir Joseph, 141, 381
Banks, Leslie, 290, 364, 446
Barbour, Joyce, 431
Barr, Charles, 365
Barrymore, Lionel, 294
Bartlett, F. C., 14
Beddington, Jack, 425
Beery, Wallace, 63
Bell, Oliver, 141
Benny, Jack, 228, 238
Bentley, Nicolas, 10
Bergman, Ingrid, 227, 253, 282, 285, 290
Bergner, Elizabeth, 273, 290
Bernstein, Sidney, 5, 169, 184, 400
Bevin, Ernest, 414
black-out, effect of, 129
Blore, Eric, 79
Board of Trade, 141, 142–3
Bogart, Humphrey, 224, 253
Bolton, survey of cinema-going in, 3, 4–5, 24–5; cinema managers, 27–31; questionnaire replies, 32–136; research programme, 21–6;

see also Crompton; Odeon;
  Palladium
Bond, Ralph, 419
Bower, Dallas, 425
Bowker, Eric, 325–6
Boyer, Charles, 94, 108, 276, 286
Bracken, Brendan, 12, 446
Brandt, Ivan, 430
Brassey, Sir Charles, 167
Brennan, Walter, 294
Brent, Romney, 331
British films: preferred by Bolton
  audiences, 13, 34, 39, 43–7, 53–4,
  57–64, 69–81, 89–94, 97–107,
  111–34; *see also* individual films in
  film titles index
Bromhead, Lt. Col. A. C., 141
Brontë, Emily, 256
Brook, Clive, 15, 144
Brunel, Adrian, 8, 299, 327, 429, 431
Brunel, Christopher, 8, 327, 419, 420
Buchanan, Jack, 59, 73, 84, 113
Bushell, Anthony, 328
Byington, Spring, 294

Cagney, James, 47, 110
Calvert, Phyllis, 331
Campbell, Sir Ronald and Lady, 329
Cantor, Eddie, 63; jokes by, 193, 194,
  195, 197
Carroll, Madeleine, 62
Carstairs, John Paddy, 431–2
cartoons, 3–6; *see also* Bolton;
  directive replies; Disney; *Donald
  Duck, Mickey Mouse*, and *Popeye* in
  film titles index
Cecil, Viscount, 385, 386
censorship, 141, 166
Chamberlain, Joseph, 175
Chamberlain, Neville, 175, 213; in
  newsreels, 162, 352, 385, 386,
  400–1, 403, 412, 415, 416, 419;
  portrayed in films, 303, 311
Chaplin, Charles, 143, 350, 399; jokes
  by, 192, 193, 194; opinions of, 56;
  see also Great Dictator, The, and
  Modern Times in film titles index
Chapman, Edward, 427
Chase, Charlie, 100
Chatfield, Lord, 386
Cherkassov, Nikolai, 290
children, effects of films on, 211, 297
Churchill, Winston, 154–5, 215, 364;
  in newsreels, 164, 167, 171, 385,
  398–9, 400, 406, 413, 414;

portrayed in films, 260
'Cinderella' stories, 297
Ciné-Technician, The, 299, 419, 422
Cinema, 140
Cinema Research Unit (CRU), 4
Clair, René, 288
Clare, Mary, 430
Clark, Sir Kenneth, 425
Clarke, D. K., 141
class, of cinema-goers, 7, 16, 221,
  313–17, 389–94, 437–8, in films,
  199, 293
Clements, John, 15, 364, 380
closures, cinema, 139, 146
Coburn, Charles, 294
Cochran, C. B., 210
Colbert, Claudette, 106, 188
Cole, Sidney, 419, 420
Colin, Jean, 144
Colman, Ronald, opinions of, Bolton
  audiences, 62, 108; Mass-
  Observation reports, 236, 246, 263,
  267, 268, 272, 274, 285, 290
comedies preferred, 8, 14, 17, 34–6,
  167, 175, 185, 186; in 'fade-outs'
  (rare), 201, 202, 203, 205; in family
  life films, 293–4; *see also* Bolton;
  directive replies; jokes; individual
  films in film titles index
competitions to encourage response,
  5, 33; 'fade-outs', 200–8, 214–15;
  jokes, 191–9
Constanduros, Mabel, 430
Cooper, Duff, 398
Cooper, Gary, 73, 135; jokes by, 192,
  194
Cotten, Joseph, 244, 283
Courtneidge, Cicely, 106
Coward, Noël, 15; *see also In Which
  We Serve* in film titles index
Crawford, Joan, 58, 212
Crazy Gang, 163, 168, 175, 178; jokes
  by, 192, 198; in newsreels, 384, 387,
  411
crime films, attitudes to, 34–6, 174
Crompton Cinema (Bolton), responses
  to films at, 5, 33–4, 35–6, 38, 39;
  men's, 59–69; women's, 70–6
Crosby, Bing, 224, 230, 238, 242, 247
Crown Film Unit (earlier GPO Film
  Unit), 6, 425
CRU (Cinema Research Unit), 4
Culver, Roland, 259

Daladier, Edouard, 385, 398

Dalrymple, Ian, 299, 431
Daniell, Henry, 351
Davenport, Harry, 294
Davis, Bette, 227, 233, 234, 253, 255, 275, 279, 285
Dean, Basil, 168
Dearden, Basil, 331
death *see* tragedies
Demarest, William, 294
DeMille, Cecil B., 135
Denman, Lord, 388
Derby, Lord, 399
Deutsch, Oscar, 5
Dickinson, Thorold, 425, 431
Dietrich, Marlene, 74, 79, 108
Dighton, John, 331
directive replies to Mass-Observation questionnaires on favourite films (1943), 220–91; men, 222–57; women, 258–89
Disney, Walt, 52, 82, 128, 155, 233, 241, 246; *see also Bambi; Dumbo; Fantasia; Reluctant Dragon; Victory Through Air Power* in film titles index
documentaries, 1, 14; *see also* GPO Film Unit; Ministry of Information
Documentary Newsletter, 1, 11, 209, 299, 354, 359, 364
Donald Duck, 59, 60, 124
Donat, Robert, 135, 237, 290
Douglas, Robert, 328
Downs, Johnny, 106
dramas and tragedies *see* tragedies
Drayton, Alfred, 145, 261
Dunne, Irene, 192
Duprez, June, 299, 327
Durbin, Deanna, 54, 222, 262, 281, 292

Eckman, Sam, 185
Eddy, Nelson, 41, 74, 111, 283
Eden, Anthony, 166; in newsreels, 166, 167, 385, 398, 414
effects of films, 296–8; *see also* Social Research
Elliott, Walter, 398
Embassy Cinema (Bolton), 27; manager of, 28–30
Emmett, E. V. H., 153, 392, 403
emotional films *see* sentimental
Empson, William, 3
England, Len, 6–8, 9–10, 168, 299; on audience preferences, 173–86; on cinema queue, 188–90; on effect of

war on film industry, 219–20; on family life and films, 292–8; on *Great Dictator, The*, 351; on joke competition, 191–9; on *Let George Do It*, 330–49; on newsreels, 382, 395–423
Evans, Clifford, 259
exhibition of films at beginning of war, 145–7

'fade-outs', 15, 200–8, 214–15; categories of, 201–4; dates of, 204–5; most popular, 200–1, 205–8
Fairbanks, Douglas, 203
faking newsreels, 419–23
fashion, effect of films on, 212, 297
Faye, Alice, 106
Field, Betty, 275
Fields, Gracie, 204; jokes by, 193, 196; opinions of, 41, 49, 59, 73, 83, 109, 168, 261; in newsreels, 387
Fields, W. C., 194
fighting sequences in films, 181, 182–3; *see also* war films
film industry and wartime, 6, 13, 140–5, 218–19
Film Weekly, 170
films *see* Mass-Observation
Films Division *see* Ministry of Information
Flanagan, Bud, 163, 384
Flanagan and Allen, 59, 238
Flynn, Errol, 62, 135
Fonda, Henry, 188
'forces' films *see* 'services' films
Ford, Richard, 5, 140, 145
Ford, Wallace, 135
Formby, George, 14, 144; jokes by, 193, 194, 195, 196, 198; in newsreels, 397; opinions of, 41, 46, 49, 59, 106, 109, 168, 244; *see also Let George Do It* in film titles index
Francis, Kay, 58
Fyffe, Will, 198

Gabin, Jean, 268
Gable, Clark, 107, 135, 297
gangsters *see* crime
Garbo, Greta, 74, 108, 135
Garson, Greer, 15, 16; opinions of, 261, 263, 267, 268, 272, 274, 275, 277, 280, 285
Gaulle, General Charles de, 213, 414
Gaynor, Janet, 62, 107, 110, 111
Gell, W. J., 410

gender differences *see* men; women
George, Muriel, 430
George VI and family, 213, 330, 352;
   in newsreels, 162, 165, 171, 185,
   385, 386, 396, 398–9, 400, 406, 411,
   413–14; portrayed in films, 303, 311
Geraldo, 144
Germany, films about life in, 174,
   175, 176, 180–1, 186
Gilbert, Billy, 351
Gillie, Jean, 429
Gleason, James, 294
Gloucester, Duke and Duchess of,
   166, 216
Goddard, Paulette, 350, 351
Godfrey, Admiral John, 364
Goebbels, Dr Joseph, 12, 148;
   portrayed in films, 144–5, 161, 350,
   352
Goering, Hermann, 164, 384
Gollancz, Victor, 2, 5
Goodman, Ezra, 143
Gordon, Kenneth, 8, 422–3
Gort, Lord, 165, 386, 398, 406
Goulding, Edmund, 205
GPO Film Unit (later Crown Film
   Unit), 1–2, 141, 155–6, 425
Grant, Cary, 192, 194
Grapewin, Charley, 294
Grayson, Kathryn, 290
Greene, Graham, 153, 154
Greenstreet, Sidney, 282
Gregson, Mr, 27–8
Grierson, John, 1
Grigg, Sir Edward, 141

Halifax, Lord, 385, 386, 398
Hall, Arthur, 33
Halliwell, Leslie, 3, 21, 27, 32, 40
Hamilton, Sir Ian, 399
Handley, Tommy, 14, 246, 274
Hardwicke, Sir Cedric, 246
Hardy, Oliver *see* Laurel and Hardy
Hare, Robertson, 261, 426, 431
Harker, Gordon, 136, 198
Harrisson, Tom, 1, 2, 4–8, 11, 12, 14;
   on *Lion Has Wings, The*, 299; on
   Ships with Wings, 364; on Social
   Research and film, 209–16
Haw-Haw, Lord, 384, 411
Hawks, Howard, 136
Hay, Will, 14, 171, 236; jokes by, 193,
   196, 198
Henderson, Sir Neville, 385, 386, 398
Hendren, Patsy, 412

Henreid, Paul, 253, 285
Henson, Leslie, 412
Hiller, Wendy, 267
history films preferred, 34–6, 40
Hitchcock, Alfred, 144, 225, 283
Hitler, Adolf, 148; in newsreels, 162,
   164, 171, 185, 384, 385, 387, 398,
   403, 407, 415; portrayed in films, 6,
   148, 153, 154, 157–61, 176, 178,
   181, 183, 219, 302–3, 315, 317, 323,
   334, 337–8, 344; *see also Great
   Dictator, The*, in film titles index
Hoare, Sir Samuel, 385, 398
Hobson, Valerie, 188–9
Holloway, Stanley, 426
Hollywood, effect of war on, 143–4;
   see also American films
Home Front, films about, 176–7, 186
Home Intelligence, 5–6, 10, 11–12,
   209
Hope, Bob, 224, 230, 238, 247, 268
Hore Belisha, Leslie, 385, 386, 398
Horton, Edward Everett, 79
Houston, Renée, 106, 193
Howard, John, 290
Howard, Leslie, 15, 220; opinions of
   (Bolton audiences), 62, 113;
   opinions of (Mass-Observation
   reports), 223, 234, 253, 256, 262,
   266, 267, 279–80, 288, 290
Howard, Sydney, 66, 73, 193
Hulbert, Jack, 84, 106, 194
Hull, Mr, 27, 28–9
humour *see* comedies
Hunt, Martita, 430, 432
Hunter, Ian, 107
Hurst, Brian Desmond, 145, 299, 328;
   MoI films by, 429–30
Huston, John, 289
Hyson, Dorothy, 426

industry, film *see* film industry

Jackson, Gordon, 259
Jannings, Emil, 251
Jeffries, Stanton, 325
Jenkins, Allen, 252
Jennings, Humphrey, 2, 3, 6, 7, 168,
   225
Johnson, Celia, 15
jokes, 191–9, 214; 'cinematographic'
   sequences, 198; comedians as stars,
   198; dates of, 196–7; in *Great
   Dictator, The*, 355–7; in *Let George
   Do It*, 333–9, 342–6, 347, 357;

nationality of films, 197; regional differences, 196; sex differences, 195–6; types of situation, 194–5; unintentional, 199; *see also* comedies
Jolson, Al, 51
Jones, John Martin, 4–5, 27; on Bolton investigation, 21–6
journals *see* press
Jouvet, Louis, 290

Kelly, Patsy, 71
Kennedy, Edgar, 55
Kent, Duke and Duchess of, 386, 398, 413, 414
Kinematograph Weekly, 220, 299, 402, 410
King, Sidney, 259
Kingsley Wood, Sir, 385, 386, 398
Knight, Esmond, 236, 253, 282
Knight, June, 109
Korda, Alexander, 144, 153, 173, 350; *see also Lion has Wings, The*, in film titles index
Korjus, Militza, 283
Kruger, Otto, 58
Kunz, Charlie, 210

Lake, Veronica, 297
Lamour, Dorothy, 62, 242
laughs *see* comedies; jokes
Laughton, Charles, 135, 136, 144, 290; jokes by, 192, 193, 194; opinions of, 222, 224, 226, 235, 246, 286
Laurel, Stan, and Oliver Hardy: jokes by, 192, 196, 197; opinions of, 41, 43, 47, 54, 59, 66, 73
Lawson, Wilfrid, 267, 294
Lawton, Frank, 428
Lee, Anna, 135
Legg, Stuart, 3–4
Lehmann, Beatrix, 430
Leigh, Vivien, 59, 277
Leopold, King of Belgium, 414
Levy, Louis, 64
Livesey, Roger, 275, 283
Lloyd, Harold, 194
Lloyd George, David, 162, 385, 386
Lockwood, Margaret, 268
Lombard, Carole, 94, 113
Lorre, Peter, 224
love *see* sentimental
Loy, Myrna, 55, 94
Lucan, Arthur, 14

Lukas, Paul, 253, 255, 295
Lynn, Ralph, 49, 197

McCurdy, J. T., 15–16
Macdonald, David, 432
MacDonald, Jeanette, 41, 42, 44, 62, 74, 75, 91, 109, 111
Mackay, Barry, 135
McLaglen, Victor, 62
McLaine, Ian, 6, 11
McLaughlin, Gibb, 328
MacMillan, Lord, 5–6
MacPhail, Angus, 331
Madge, Charles, 2, 3, 6
Mallalieu, Aubrey, 431
Malleson, Miles, 329
mangers, cinema, 27–31; on MoI shorts, 439–40
Manvell, Roger, 13
March, Fredric, 74
Marney, Derrick de, 328; MoI film by *see Seaman Frank* in film titles index
Marriott, Moore, 192
Marsh, Garry, 331
Marshall, Herbert, 62
Marx Brothers, 49, 71; jokes by, 193, 194, 195, 197
Mason, James, 14–15, 268
Mass-Observation: formation of, 1–3; *see also* Bolton; directive replies; Ministry of Information shorts; newsreels; wartime
Matthews, Jessie, 63, 79, 84, 96, 107, 135
Melford, Austin, 331
melodramas, 15, 30
men, reactions to films: Bolton questionnaire, 34–8, 41–53, 59–69, 77–105; 'fade-out' preferences, 202, 203, 206–8; *Let George Do It*, 332–3, 338; joke preferences, 195–6; *Lion Has Wings, The*, 312–23; Mass-Observation questionnaires, 222–57; MoI shorts, 436; newsreels, 389–94; *see also* audience response
Mickey Mouse, 43, 59, 60
Miles, Bernard, 259, 282, 290
military matters, in newsreels, 163, 164, 165; *see also* 'services' films; war films
Miller, Max, 196
Mills, John, 15, 135, 290, 428
Ministry of Information, 5, 10–13, 209–10, 299; censorship and

restrictions by, 139, 141, 145, 166;
    see also Home Intelligence
Ministry of Information shorts, 177,
    210; cinema managers on, 439–40;
    details of, 427–33; opinions of,
    434–40, 442–44; producing units,
    444–5; report on, 446–59; *see also*
    film titles index, in particular
    *Newspaper Train; Rush Hour;
    Seaman Frank; War in the East;
    You're Telling Me*
Mitchell, Leslie, 264, 403
Mitchell, Thomas, 253, 294
Mitford, Unity, 388, 403
MoI *see* Ministry of Information
Monks, Noel, 364
Montgomery, Robert, 58
Moore, Grace, 75, 109
moral objections, 28
morale, 6, 11–12, 15–16
Morrison, Herbert, 414
Moscovitch, Maurice, 351
Mullen, Barbara, 268
Muni, Paul, 136
musicals preferred, 29, 34–6, 40
Mussolini, Benito: in newsreels, 399,
    406, 415; portrayed in films, 350,
    362
mysteries, unpopular, 29–30

nature films, attitudes to, 34–6
Naughton, Bill, 3
Neagle, Anna, 62, 116, 125
newspapers *see* Press
newsreels, 8, 185, 186; in first three
    months of war, 162–7; 28 January
    (1940), 381–94; 26 May (1940),
    395–404; June (1940), 405–8; 6
    October (1940), 409–18; faking,
    419–23; personalities in, 162,
    385–7, 397–9, 413–5; prestige of,
    212–13
Newton, Robert, 15
Niemoller, Pastor, 175
Niven, David, 15, 144, 223; jokes by,
    192, 194
Nolan, Lloyd, 55
Nolbandov, Sergei, 365
Northwood, report from, 170–2
Nunn May, R., 141

Oakie, Jack, 350, 351
Oberon, Merle, 153, 167; in *Lion Has
    Wings, The*, 299, 304, 306, 318, 320,
    328, 329

observation, methods, 4, 9–10; reports
    see audience response
Odeon Cinema (Bolton), responses to
    films at, 4–5, 24–5, 32, 33, 34, 35,
    37–8, 39; men's, 76–105; women's,
    106–35
Oliver, Vic, 210, 276, 414
Olivier, Laurence, 13, 15, 261
organist, cinema, 32, 39, 83–4, 95,
    125
Orwell, George, 351
Ouspenskaya, Maria, 290

Paderewski, Ignace Jan, 135
Palladium Cinema (Bolton),
    responses to films at, 5, 24–5, 33–4,
    36, 38–9; manager of, 27–8; men's,
    41–53; women's, 54–8
Pallette, Eugene, 294
Palmer, Lilli, 290
patriotism, 167, 174; in 'fade-outs',
    203, 204
Payne Fund (USA), 211, 215
Pendleton, Nat, 78
personalities in newsreels, 162,
    385–7, 397–9, 413–15; *see also*
    individual names
Picturegoer, 7–8
Pidgeon, Walter, 15, 219, 285
Popeye, 43, 51, 60
Portman, Eric, 15, 282
posters *see* advertisements
Powell, Dilys, 13–14
Powell, Eleanor, 63
Powell, Michael, 12, 299, 328
Powell, Sandy, 174, 179
Powell, William, 55, 86, 94, 96, 192
preferences, film *see* Bolton; directive
    replies
Press, the, 28; on box-offices
    successes, 220–1; on cinema
    closures, 139; film reviews, 170; on
    Great Dictator, The, 351–3, 354,
    359; on *Let George Do It*, 331,
    332–3, 346–7; on *Lion Has Wings,
    The*, 297, 323–7, 329–30; and Mass-
    Observation, 1, 2, 7–8, 10–11; on
    newsreels, 218, 402, 405; on
    posters, 148; propaganda, 211–12;
    on *Ship With Wings*, 364; on
    wartime restrictions, 140, 143–4,
    146; *see also* competitions
Priestley, J. B., 287; commentary to
    MoI film, 426, 429
Pronay, Nicholas, 41, 381, 382, 425

propaganda, 12–13, 154–5, 167–8, 186, 211–12; captured German films, 10; *see also* Bolton, questionnaire; directive replies; Ministry of Information shorts; *Lion Has Wings, The*
Prouty, Jed, 294
Pudovkin, V. I., 290
Putti, Lya da, 251

questionnaires *see* Mass-Observation
Quota Acts (1927 & 1937), 142, 144

Radford, Basil, 193
Raft, George, 4, 136
Rainer, Luise, 285
Rains, Claude, 253
Randle, Frank, 14
Ray, René, 428, 429
Raymond, Jack, 136
Raymond, Moore, 7, 191, 200, 214
realism in films, 14, 15, 34–6
Redgrave, Michael, 221, 225, 268
regional differences and comedy, 196, 337–8, 358
Reith, Sir John, 6, 381–2, 398
Renoir, Jean, 290
reports *see* Mass-Observation
Reynaud, Paul, 406, 414
Ribbentrop, J. von, 148
Richards, Jeffrey, 41, 187, 299, 331, 365
Richardson, Ralph, 153, 167, 230; in *Lion Has Wings, The*, 299, 303–4, 306, 318, 320, 328, 329; opinions of, 236, 253, 282, 287
Robertson, J. C., 381, 382
Robeson, Paul, 48, 136
Robinson, David, 351
Robson, Flora, 305
Rogers, Ginger, jokes by, 192; opinions of, 94, 109, 224, 244, 252
romanticism *see* musicals; sentimental
Romero, Caesar, 106
Rooney, Mickey, 194, 244, 292
Roosevelt, F. D., 162, 385, 398, 399, 415
Rosmer, Milton, 328, 428
Rotha, Paul, 217, 264; MoI films by, 430, 434–40
Roy, Harry, 84
royal family *see* George VI
Runciman, Lord, 385, 386

Sabu, 135
Sanders, George, 263
Sanger, Gerald, 218, 400
Saville, Victor, 144
Scott, Randolph, 73, 290
scripts, film, 3
Selassie, Haile, 414
Selby, Hubert *see* organist
sentimental films: 'fade-outs', 201, 202, 203; family films, 295, 296–8; *see also* musicals
'series' of films *see* family life
'services' films, attitudes to, 174, 175, 176, 177, 178–80, 182–3, 186, 415–16; *see also* Bolton; directive replies; military matters; war films
sex differences *see* men; women
Shaw, George Bernard, 139, 168, 175, 240, 266
Shaw, Sebastian, 431
Shearer, Norma, 106, 205, 352
Shiner, Ronald, 329
Sight and Sound, 143–4, 218
Sim, Alastair, 79, 135
Simon, Michel, 290
Simon, Sir John, 385, 387, 398
Sinclair, Sir Archibald, 414
slapstick, attitudes to, 34–6, 39
Sommerfield, John, 3
songs, 297, 339–40; *see also* musicals
Sparkle, Ned, 196
speeches, anti-war, 181, 184, 186, 358–60
Spender, Humphrey, 3
spiritual films *see* uplifting
Spring, D. W., 41, 382
'spy films', 34–6, 148–52, 156–62, 174, 176, 177, 186; *see also* film titles index, in particular *Confessions of a Nazi Spy*
Stalin, Joseph, 260, 385, 387
Stanley, Oliver, 141–3, 144, 145
Stanwyck, Barbara, 58, 62
Stead, Peter, 41
Steed, Wickham, 388
Steinbeck, John, 223, 256
Stevenson, R. L., 227
Stewart, Binkie, 4
Stewart, Donald, 106
Stone, Lewis, 294
Stooges, The Three, 42, 55, 109
Street, A. W., 326
Streicher, Julius, 144–5
Sullivan, Francis, 144–5
supernatural 'fade-outs', 200, 202, 203, 205

surveys *see* Mass-Observation
Swaffer, Hannen, 352, 359

Taylor, Dr Stephen, 11–12, 446
Taylor, John, MoI film by *see*
   Newspaper Train in film titles
   index
Taylor, Robert, 297; opinions of, 54,
   108, 110, 235
Temple, Shirley, 69, 96, 292
themes, preferred, 173–87; pre-war
   films, 173–4, 176; wartime films,
   175–6; wartime shorts *see* Ministry
   of Information shorts
Thompson, Alex, 326
Thorpe, Frances, 425
Thurtle, Ernest, 13
Tone, Franchot, 58, 74, 135
Tracy, Arthur, 106
Tracy, Spencer, 74, 252
tragedies preferred, 34–5, 40; in 'fade-
   outs', 200–4, 205, 215; in family life
   films, 293, 295
trailers, attitudes to, 39
travel films, attitudes to, 34–6, 39
Trevelyan, Julian, 3
Trinder, Tommy, 14, 144, 259

United States, research on effects of
   films on children, 211, 215, 297; *see*
   also American films
'uplifting' endings, 200, 201, 202, 204

Varnel, Marcel, 331
Veidt, Conrad, 144, 188–9, 253, 282
Villiers, Sir Edward, 141, 329
volunteer film panel, 7–9, 211–12

Wakefield, Duggie, 196
Walbrook, Anton, 15, 233, 271, 275,
   276
Wallace, Nellie, 329
Walls, Tom, 49, 73
Walsh, Raoul, 135
Walton, William, 264
war films, attitudes to, 34–6, 39, 173,
   174–7, 186; *see also* 'services';
   military matters
War Office, 141
Ward, Edward, 210

Ward, Penelope Dudley, 428
wartime, cinema-going in, 6; first
   three months, 139–69; family life
   portrayed, 10, 192–8; and film
   industry, 218–19; hazards of Mass-
   Observation, 217; queue, 188–90;
   Social Research and, 209–16;
   volunteer reviewer's letter, 170–2;
   specific films *see* film titles index;
   see also directive replies; 'fade-outs';
   jokes; Ministry of Information;
   newsreels; themes preferred
Wartime Cinema Survey (1943), 221
Watson, Lucille, 290
Wayne, Naunton, 193
Welles, Orson, 221, 225, 244
Wells, H. G. *see Things to Come* in
   film titles index
West, Mae, 195
West, Rebecca, 352
Westerns, 34–6
Whiley, Manning, 430
Wilcox, Herbert, 144
Wilhelmina, Queen of the
   Netherlands, 398, 414–15
Willcock, H. D. (Bob), 10
Williams, Emlyn, 426, 430
Williams, Hugh, 282
Windsor, Duke of, in newsreels, 163,
   185, 385, 386, 398, 400, 413–14
Winninger, Charles, 294
Withers, Googie, 287
women, reactions to films, Bolton
   questionnaires, 34–8, 41, 54–8,
   70–6, 106–35; 'fade-out'
   preferences, 202, 203, 206–8; joke
   preferences, 195–6; *Let George Do
   It*, 332–3, 338; *Lion Has Wings,
   The*, 312–23; Mass-Observation
   questionnaires, 258–89; MoI shorts,
   436, 450, 454; newsreels, 391–6; *see*
   also audience response
Woolley, Monty, 222, 268
Woolton, Lord, 398
'Worktown' *see* Bolton
Wright, Teresa, 244, 283
Wyatt, Jane, 290
Wynyard, Diana, 144

Young, Loretta, 94

Index of Film Titles

Ack Ack, 444

Action for Slander, 40, 67; men's opinions of, 95, 96, 100, 104; women's opinions of, 117, 124, 132, 134

Action in the North Atlantic, 242, 253, 254

Adventure in Diamonds, 405

Adventures of Tartu, 221, 242

After the Thin Man, 55, 67, 82, 207

Albert's Savings, 429

Alexander Nevsky, 225, 286, 287

Alf's Button Afloat, 47

Algiers, 206

Alibi, 263

All at Sea, 179

All Hands, 428

All Quiet on the Western Front, 81, 144, 175, 182, 211; audience response to, 173, 183

All That Money Can Buy, 227, 228

Amazing Mrs Holliday, The, 228, 230, 262, 269, 288

Amphyitrion, 252

Andy Hardy Gets Spring Fever, 192, 197; other *Andy Hardy* films, 292

Angels with Dirty Faces, 207

Another Dam, 48

Anthony Adverse, 74

Any Old Iron, 444

Arabian Nights, 265

'Arf a Mo, 'Itler, 155

Arms for Scrap, 452

Ask a Policeman, 207

Assignment in Brittany, 268

At the Circus, 207

Awful Truth, The, 79, 114, 192, 197

Baroness and the Butler, The, 30

Bachelor Mother, 192, 196, 197

Bambi, men's opinions of, 220–1, 227, 229, 233–5, 241, 247, 250; women's opinions of, 259, 260, 261, 274, 275, 288

Bank Holiday, 238

Barretts of Wimpole Street, The, 73, 122, 207

Bataan, 227, 234, 247

Battle for Britain (not made), 365

Battle of Britain, 257, 281

Battle of Stalingrad, 225

Battlefields of Britain, The, 154, 168

Beau Geste, 174, 182

Bedtime Story, 260

Beloved Vagabond, 127

Ben Hur, 64, 90, 94, 104, 135

Betty, 114

Big Fella, 108, 136

Birth of a Nation, 211

Blue Bird, The, 283

Black Sheep of Whitehall, 235, 236

Black Swan, The, 221, 244, 246, 282–3

Black-out (later *Contraband*), 144, 169

Blockade, 202, 207

Blossom Time, 64, 135

Blossoms in the Dust, 232, 249, 268

Bluebeard's Eighth Wife, 30

Bombardier, 244

Bomber Command, 288

Brains Trust, 248, 250

Brewster's Millions, 227

Bride Came COD, The, 258

Bride Wore Red, The, 114

Brief Encounter, 13

Briggs Family, The, 175

Bringing up Baby, 207

Britain at Bay, 426, 429

British Agent, 175

Builders, 453

Café Metropole, 78, 84, 97

Call to Arms, 210, 216, 426, 446; narrative description of, 433

Call It a Day, 124

Camille, 72, 74, 75, 94, 108, 127

Captain Blood, 83, 121, 135

Captains Courageous, 76, 207

Cargo of Innocents, 235, 258, 280

Carnet de Bal, 170, 230, 250, 266, 284

Casablanca, men's opinions of, 223, 230, 231, 241, 244, 252, 253; women's opinions of, 266, 273, 276, 282, 286, 287

Catherine the Great, 126

Cavalcade, 63, 104, 144, 206

Cavalcade of the Navy, The, 155

Chain Gangs, 79

Chance of a Lifetime, 10

Channel Incident, 443

Charge of the Light Brigade, 40; men's opinions of, 46, 47, 60, 61, 68, 77, 78, 84, 90, 97; women's opinions of, 56, 107, 110, 120, 121, 128

Christmas under Fire, 444

Circus, The, 207

Citadel, The, 207, 299

Citizen Kane, men's opinions of, 223, 225, 227, 239, 242, 243, 244, 249, 250

City, The, 167

City of Flint, 382

City Lights, 350

Coal Face, 3

Coconuts, 50

Colonel Blimp see *Life and Death of Colonel Blimp*

Come and Get It, 77

Come on George, 332

Command Performance, 82, 106

Coney Island, 272

Confessions of a Nazi Spy, 174; audience response to, 156–62, 166, 180, 181, 182; narrative description of, 148–9, 180

Conquest of the Air, The, 153, 328

Conspiracy, 174

Contraband (formerly *Black-out*), 169, 175, 365; advertisement for, 188–9

Convoy, 15, 175, 360, 365, 372, 380

Count of Monte Cristo, The, 47, 62, 64, 126, 135

Counterfeit, 47

Covered Wagon, The, 73

Cowboy and the Lady, The, 192, 197

Crash Dive, 244, 275

Criminals of the Air, 86

Dai Jones, 444, 446

Dangerous Comment, 428

Dangerous Moonlight, 219; opinions of, 231–2, 233, 238, 259, 271, 276, 288

Dark Angel, The, 122

Dark Journey, 132

Dark Victory, 'fade-outs' in, 200, 204, 205, 206, 215

David Copperfield, 64, 67, 100, 122

Dawn Patrol, 'fade-outs' in, 204, 205, 206

Day at the Races, A, 56, 72, 74

Day on the Russian Front, A, 229, 247

Day Will Dawn, The, 275, 279

Dead End, 202, 207

Dear Octopus, men's opinions of, 229, 233, 234; women's opinions of, 260, 263, 268, 272, 283

Desert Victory, men's opinions of, 220–1, 225, 226, 228, 229, 235–45, 249, 257; women's opinions of, 220–1, 259, 260, 262, 264, 266, 267, 275, 279, 281, 283, 284, 288

Disraeli, 132

Divorce of Lady X, The, 30

Dixie, 242

Do It Now, 155–6

Dr Jekyll and Mr Hyde, 227

Dr Syn, 76

Dodsworth, 102, 132

Double Crime on the Maginot Line, 174, 179

Double or Nothing, 79

Dover Front Line, 432

Drake of England, 47

Dreyfus, 252

Drums Along the Mohawk, 188

Dubarry was a Lady, 263, 276

Dumbo, 225, 226, 264, 266, 282

Early Each Morning, 237 (CH)

Eating out with Tommy Trinder, 443, 444

Elephant Boy, 55, 74, 85, 109, 136

Enemy Agent, 174

Englishman's Home, An, audience response to, 177, 182; jokes in, 199; narrative description of, 150, 176, 177, 181–2

Equipage, L', 170

Escape to Happiness: family life shown in, 295; opinions of, 227, 251, 252, 253, 265, 276

Escape from Devil's Isle, 30

Espionage Agent, 150, 174

Eternally Yours, 204, 207

Everything is Rhythm, 84

Exile Express, 150–1

False Faces, 47

Fantasia, men's opinions of, 220–8, 235–7, 242, 250, 251; women's opinions of, 220, 262–6, 269, 274–7, 281, 283, 288

Farewell Again, 82

Farewell to Arms, 207

Few Ounces a Day, A, 10

Fifth Avenue Girl, 207

Fin du Jour, La, 229, 231, 238, 258

Fire Over England, 66, 77, 112, 124, 132, 153, 154; used in *Lion Has Wings, The*, 299, 316, 318

Firefly, The, 29

Fires Were Started, 225, 249, 257, 281, 284

First Days, The, 167

First of the Few, 13, 15; men's opinions of, 220–1, 223, 229, 233–4, 239, 242, 246–8, 256; women's opinions of, 220–1, 262, 264, 265, 269, 270, 279, 280, 284, 288

Five Came Back, 206

Five Graves to Cairo, 229, 231, 238, 258

Fleets In, The, 238

Flemish Farm, The, 248

Food for Thought, 427, 429

For Freedom, 355, 380, 399, 401; narrative description of, 175

For Valour, 49, 67, 135

For Whom the Bell Tolls, 15, 270

Foreman Went to France, The, men's opinions of, 224, 238, 240, 245, 248; women's opinions of, 259, 281

Forever and a Day, 242, 248

Forever England, 46

49th Parallel, 12, 15, 351; opinions of, 225, 229, 232, 281, 282

Four Daughters, 207

Four Feathers, The, 207, 279, 364

Fra Diavolo, 192, 197

Frankenstein, 77

Freedom Radio (formerly *This German Freedom*), 169

French Leave, 174

French Without Tears, 207

Frog, The, 124, 136

Frozen Limits, The, 163; audience response to, 178; jokes in, 192, 197, 198; narrative description of, 175

Fury, 202, 239

Gang Makes Good, The, 249

Gang Show, 106

Gangway, opinions of, 135; men's opinions of, 78, 89, 90, 93, 95, 101; women's opinions of, 107, 109, 116

Gap, The, 48, 153, 154; used in *Lion Has Wings, The*, 299, 316, 318, 320, 328

Garden of Allah, The, 74, 87, 108, 109, 112, 127

Gasbags (earlier *Siegfried Line*), 186

Gentle Sex, The, 13; men's opinions of, 220–1, 234, 237, 248, 250, 252, 256; women's opinions of, 220–1, 258, 260–7, 270, 275, 277, 278, 280–2, 286, 288, 289

Gentleman Jim, 249

George Washington Slept Here, 228

Gestapo (later *Night Train to Munich*), 186

Get Cracking, 244

Ghost Goes West, The, 294

Girl Must Live, A, 193, 197

Glass Key, The, 227, 238

G-Men, The, 47, 96

Go-getter, The, 91

Gone With the Wind, 15, 352; family life shown in, 294; men's opinions of, 220, 222, 227, 238, 240, 241, 243; women's opinions of, 220, 259, 261–4, 268, 269, 277

Good Earth, The, men's opinions of, 64, 68, 77, 83; women's opinions of, 75, 76, 122, 131

Goodbye Mr Chips, 148; 'fade-outs' in, 200, 204, 206, 215

Goose Steps Out, The, 229

Gorilla, The, 147

Grapes of Wrath, The, 239, 331; family life shown in, 294, 295, 296

Great Dictator, The, 9, 14, 15, 245, 264, 350–63, 401; Chaplin's speech in, 358–60; jokes in, 355–7; opinions of, 354–63; pre-release material, 351–4

Great Mr Handel, The, 251; Mass-Observation questionnaire opinions of, 242, 248, 256, 261, 271, 287, 289

Great Waltz, The, 207, 227, 285

Great Ziegfeld, The, 63, 72, 206

Greek Testament, 227

Green Eyed Woman, The, 238

Gunga Din, 174, 182, 204, 206

H.M. Pulham Esq., 227

Hamlet, 274
Hardies Ride Again, The, 193, 197
Heart of Britain, 444
Heaven Can Wait, 263; family life
  shown in, 294; opinions of, 233, 251,
  266
Hello, Frisco, Hello, 221, 232
Hell's Angels, 144, 175, 182; audience
  response to, 173, 183; jokes in, 199
Hellzapoppin, 245, 246
Henry V, 13
Henry VIII see Private Life of Henry
  VIII, The
Her Father's Daughter, 444
Here Comes Mr Jordan, 239, 256, 268
Here is Tomorrow, 237
History is Made at Night, 94, 96, 116,
  120
Holiday Inn, 256
Holy Matrimony, 230, 281
Home Guard, 443, 444
Hopalong Cassidy's Return, 46
Housing Problems, 3
How Green Was My Valley: family life
  shown in, 293–4, 295; men's
  opinions of, 227, 239, 240, 243, 245;
  women's opinions of, 270, 275, 280,
  283
Huckleberry Finn, 207
Human Comedy, The, 261, 286, 287
Hurricane, The, 30, 79, 207

I am a Fugitive from a Chain Gang,
  207
I Know Where I'm Going, 13
I Married a Witch, 226, 265, 268, 276,
  288
I Met a Murderer, 208
I Promise to Pay, 78, 96
I See Ice, 332
I Was a Captive of Nazi Germany,
  162, 174, 180–1
I Was a Spy, 173, 175, 182, 183
Idiot's Delight, 184
I'll Walk beside You, 280, 287
Immortal Sergeant, 262
In Old Chicago, 79
In This Our Life, 243
In Which We Serve, 13, 15; men's
  opinions of, 220–3, 226, 228, 229,
  233, 234, 238–51, 256, 257;
  women's opinions of, 220–1,
  258–62, 264–71, 276, 278, 280, 282,
  283, 285, 286, 288
Informer, The, 207

Invisible Man, The, 206
It Happened One Night, 119, 245
It's in the Air, 193, 197, 332
It's Love I'm After, 113
It's That Man Again, 248, 256

Jericho, 48, 108
Journey into Fear, 225, 230, 252, 256
Journey for Margaret, 282, 284
Juarez, 207
Jungle Book, The, 229, 265
Jungle Princess, The, 43, 55, 127

Katja, 280, 283, 284
Keeper of the Flame, 226, 260
Kid from Spain, The, 193, 197
King Kong, 43, 199
King Solomon's Mines, 108
King Steps Out, The, 56, 127
Kings Row, men's opinions of, 231–2,
  233, 247, 253, 254–6; women's
  opinions of, 269, 270, 275, 287
Knight Without Armour, 79, 104

Ladies in Retirement, 245
Lady Hamilton, 219, 265
Lady Vanishes, The, 193, 197
Lamp Still Burns, The, 221, 233, 248,
  288
Land of Promise, 237
Laugh It Off, 144, 169, 365; audience
  response to, 173, 178, 179
Law and Disorder, 176
League of Frightened Men, The, 71
Let George Do It, 9, 14, 210, 214,
  331–49; audience response to, 214,
  348–9, 355; jokes in, 333–9, 342–6,
  347, 357; narrative description of,
  175, 176, 341–2; Press reviews of,
  331, 346–7; songs in, 339–40
Let The People Sing, 240
Libelled Lady, 192, 197
Life and Death of Colonel Blimp, The,
  men's opinions of, 220–2, 225–32,
  238–40, 242, 244, 247, 250, 252,
  257; women's opinions of, 220–1,
  258, 260–5, 268, 270–7, 282–8
Lilac Domino, The, 109, 128
Lion Has Wings, The, 6, 9, 143, 144,
  155, 166, 167, 174, 175, 210,
  299–330, 380, 420; audience
  response to, 178, 179, 182, 302–11,
  355; comparison with Ships With
  Wings, 372, 373; 'fade-outs' in, 207;
  narrative description of, 152–4,

163, 183, 300–1; observers' reports, 302–11; Press reviews of, 323–7, 329–30; questionnaires on, 311–23, 392

Little Foxes, The, 233, 279

Little Friend, 252

Little Lord Fauntleroy, 67

Lives of a Bengal Lancer, 40; 'fade-outs' in, 204, 206; men's opinions of, 46, 47, 50, 60–1,77, 84, 85, 94, 135

Lloyd's of London, 47, 84, 97, 122, 135

London Can Take It, 443, 444

London Town, 10

Londoners, The, 316, 320

Lone White Sail, 263

Long Voyage Home, The, 225

Lost Horizon, 'fade-outs' in, 201, 204, 206, 215; men's opinions of, 61, 70, 83, 91, 96; women's opinions of, 71, 72, 75, 108, 120, 122, 127, 131, 132, 134, 258, 285

Love Affair, 208

Love From a Stranger, opinions of, 136; men's opinions of, 85, 96; women's opinions of, 107, 122, 123, 124, 132

Love on the Dole, 13; family life shown in, 294, 295, 296, 297

'M', 207

Madame X, 103

Madonna of the Seven Moons, 15

Magnificent Ambersons, The, men's opinions of, 220–1, 223, 227, 230, 242–4, 249, 252–6; women's opinions of, 220–1, 262, 270, 274, 277–8, 286

Magnificent Obsession, 74

Major Barbara, 175, 227, 240, 260

Major and Minor, The, 238, 244, 252, 269

Make Way for Tomorrow, 72

Malta Convoy, 272

Maltese Falcon, The, 244, 282

Man in Grey, The, 15, 221; men's opinions of, 226, 231–2, 242, 243; women's opinions of, 262, 263, 268

Man in the Iron Mask, The, 203, 207

Man Who Came to Dinner, The, 226, 239, 243, 245, 257, 281

Manhunt, 219

Manila Calling, 238

March of Time, The, 67, 168

Marie Antoinette, 205, 206

Marx Brothers Go West, 256

Mary Burns Fugitive, 47

Maryland, 283

Masquerade, 251

Mata Hari, 50

Mayerling, 207, 274

Maytime, 29, 40; 'fade-outs' in, 201, 206; men's opinions of, 56, 63–7, 69, 91, 95; women's opinions of, 71, 72, 74, 75, 127

Meanest Man in the World, The, 238

Men of the Lightship, 360, 443, 444; narrative description of, 432–3

Merchant Seamen, 443, 444

Millions Like Us, 13; family life shown in, 293, 294–5; opinions of, 238, 241, 263, 277, 278

Miracle of Morgan's Creek, The, 294

Miserables, Les, 64, 207

Miss Grant Goes to the Door, 10, 443, 447; narrative description of, 210, 434

Miss Know All, 430

Mission to Moscow, 221; men's opinions of, 229, 237, 238, 252; women's opinions of, 260, 262, 270, 272, 279, 286–7

Mr Borland Thinks Again, 430–1

Mr Bunting Goes to War, 242

Mr Deeds Goes to Town, 75, 245

Mr Proudfoot Shows a Light, 444

Mrs Miniver, 15–16; family life shown in, 293, 295; men's opinions of, 220–1, 228, 238–43, 247, 256; women's opinions of, 220–1, 258–62, 269–73, 276–7, 280, 281, 285, 288–9

Mobile Canteen, 443

Modern Times, 350, 357; 'fade-outs' in, 192, 193, 196

Monkey Business, 50

Moon is Down, The, men's opinions of, 223–4, 231, 246, 248, 256–7; women's opinions of, 289

Moon and Sixpence, The, 221; men's opinions of, 226, 240, 243, 245, 251, 252, 256; women's opinions of, 263, 269, 276

Moonlight Sonata, The, 88, 135

Moontide, 252–3, 268

More the Merrier, The, 263

Mother's Boy, 93

Mountain Justice, 79

Mountain Music, 50

Mountains Wait, The, 269

Mutiny on the Bounty, 40, 135–6;

men's opinions of, 49, 50, 62–3, 65, 66, 68, 82–5, 91, 96, 97, 99, 104, 135; women's opinions of, 72, 73, 122
My Friend Flicka, 279
My Gal Sal, 286
My Learned Friend, 247
My Man Godfrey, 79, 91, 113, 114, 124; jokes in, 193, 197
My Sister Eileen, 250

Nancy Steele is Missing, 56
Narrow Corner, The, 91
Naughty Marietta, 47, 74
Nero, 64
New Moon, The, 283
New Teacher, The, 265
Newspaper Train, 10, 453; opinions of, 446–7, 448, 454, 455, 456, 458
newsreels *see* general index
Next of Kin, The, 228, 240, 262, 282
Night at the Opera, A, 193, 197
Night Mail, 3
Night Must Fall, 42, 59, 73, 75–6, 127
Night Train to Munich (earlier *Gestapo*), 186, 360
Nine Men, 226, 243, 244, 247, 263
No Limit, 46, 332
North of Shanghai, 174
Nothing Sacred, 113
Now Voyager, 227, 243, 273
Now You're Talking, 427–8
Nurse Edith Cavell, 174; 'fade-outs' in, 207; narrative description of, 149, 182

Oh Mr Porter, 207
O.H.M.S., 46, 52, 135
Okay for Sound, 47, 59, 106, 120
Old Bones of the River, 193, 197
Old Maid, 207
Old Mother Riley Joins Up, 168, 179
100 Men and a Girl, 229
100 Million Women, 453
One in a Million, 108
One Night of Love, 67
One of our Aircraft is Missing, 231–2, 240, 282, 283
One Way Passage, 206
Only Angels Have Wings, 207
Operational Height, 237
Our Fighting Navy, 154
Our Soviet Ally, 246
Out of the Fog, 229
Over the River, 127

Pacific see War in the East
Pack Up Your Troubles, 365
Palm Beach Story, 226
Papageno, 250
Paris Calling, 273
Parnell, 108, 127
Passing of the Third Floor Back, The, 73
Pastor Hall, 175, 239
Penn of Pennsylvania, 219, 274
Penny Pool, The, 56
Peter the Great, 249, 250
Petrified Forest, The, 225, 234, 255, 258, 280, 289
Pied Piper, The, 226, 261, 268, 277, 279
Pimpernel Smith, 219
Pinocchio, 241
Plainsman, The, 47, 84, 208
Poison Pen, 207
Presenting Lily Mars, 260
Pride and Prejudice, 261, 286
Prince and the Pauper, The, 76, 108, 135
Prisoner of Zenda, The, 205, 206
Private Life of Henry VIII, The, 94, 135, 193, 195, 197, 252
Private Secretary, The, 61
Professional Soldier, 46
Professor Mamlock, 143, 174, 176, 245; audience response to, 180–1, 182; narrative description of, 180
Proud Valley, The, 13, 175
Pygmalion, 299; opinions of, 227, 241, 244, 260, 266–7

Q Planes, 150, 206
Quai des Brumes, Le, 268
Quality Street, 122
Queen Christina, 94, 135; 'fade-outs' in, 201, 204, 206, 215
Queen of Hearts, 193, 197
Queen Victoria, 226
Quiet Wedding, 244, 259

Raiding Air Fighters, 155
Rainbow on the River, 108, 127
Random Harvest, 15; men's opinions of, 220–1, 225, 235, 236, 240, 242, 243, 246, 247, 256; women's opinions of, 220–1, 258, 263–9, 272–6, 281, 284
Rebecca, 15, 238, 244, 279
Reluctant Dragon, The, 241, 283
Remarkable Andrew, The, 279

Rhodes of Africa, 94
Rio Rita, 234
Road Back, The, 81
Road to Morocco, men's opinions of, 224, 238, 247, 252; women's opinions of, 259, 264
Road to Moscow, 230
Robin Hood of Eldorado, 47
Roi S'Amuse, Le, 251–2
Roman Scandals, 193, 197
Rosalie, 29
Rose Marie, 47, 110
Ruggles of Red Gap, 74, 224; 'fade-outs' in, 207; jokes in, 192, 195, 196
Rush Hour (Shopping), 10; opinions of, 446–7, 449–50, 454–5, 456–7
Russian Fairy Tale, 260

Said O'Reilly to MacNab, 198
Salute John Citizen, 270, 272, 293
San Demetrio – London, 13
San Francisco, 40; 'fade-outs' in, 204, 206; men's opinions of, 51, 80, 93; women's opinions of, 54, 56, 288
Saratoga, 77
Savage with a Smile, 444; narrative description of, 431
Scarface, 124, 136
Scarlet Pimpernel, The, 228, 242, 253, 255
Sea Fort, 426; narrative description of, 431
Sea Hawk, The, 219
Seaman Frank Goes Back to Sea, 10, 452; opinions of, 446–8, 449, 453–4, 455, 456–7
Secret journey, 151
Secret Mission, 279
Sergeant York, 380
Seventh Veil, The, 15
Shadow of a Doubt, 263; men's opinions of, 243, 244, 247, 257; women's opinions of, 262, 277–8
Shadow of the Wing, 299
Shall We Dance, 127
Shining Victory, 277–8
Shipbuilders, The, 295
Ships With Wings, 9, 14, 219; report on, 365–80
Shipyard Sally, 202, 206
Shopping see *Rush Hour*
Siege of Leningrad, 284
Siegfried Line, The (later *Gasbag*), 175, 186
Sign of the Cross, The, 135, 206

Silent Battle, The, 184
Silent Village, The, 245, 256, 273
Silver Fleet, The, men's opinions of, 230, 231–2, 235, 236, 252, 253, 256; women's opinions of, 282, 286–7
Sing As We Go, 261
Singing Fool, The, 32, 51
Sixty Glorious Years (spliced into *Queen Victoria*), 289
Sky's the Limit, The, 113, 273
Slight Case of Murder, A, 193, 197
Slightly Dangerous, 294
Smashing the Spy Ring, 151
Smilin' Through, 96; 'fade-outs' in, 201, 204, 205, 206
Snow White, 4, 61, 199, 207
So Proudly We Hail, 244
Somewhere on Leave, 234
Son of Monte Cristo, 219
Song of the Forge, The, 126
Sons of the Sea, 175
Sorrel and Son, 64, 67, 135
Souls at Sea, 48, 61
South Riding, 238
Soviet Russia at War, 264
Spats to Spurs, 405
Spies of the Air, 177; narrative, 174, 177
Spies at Work, 174
Spy in Black, The, audience response to, 177; 'fade-outs' in, 204, 206; narrative description of, 149; poster for, 147–8
Spy for a Day, 174, 179
Squadron 992, 432
Squadron Leader X, 228, 268, 275
Stagecoach, 208
Stalingrad, 226, 237, 238; see also *Battle of Stalingrad*
Stalingrad Fights, 263
Stanley and Livingstone, 207
Star is Born, A, 40, 48; 'fade-outs' in, 204, 206; men's opinions of, 78, 93, 95–9; women's opinions of, 107–11, 116–22, 127, 133
Stars Look Down, The, 13, 208
Stella Dallas, 40; 'fade-outs' in, 202, 207; men's opinions of, 87, 89, 95, 97, 100, 103; women's opinions of, 108, 110, 113, 116–22, 127–34
Storm in a Teacup, 124
Stormy Weather, 248
Story of Louis Pasteur, The, 131, 136
Story of Stalingrad see *Stalingrad*
Story of Vernon and Irene Castle, The, 201, 206

Stradivarius, 274
Strange Incident, 225
Strawberry Blonde, The, 253–4
Street Singer, The, 51
Student Prince, The, 114
Such Men are Dangerous, 251
Suez, 206
Sullivans, The, 293
Sun Never Sets, The, 174
Sunny, 95
Suvorov, 259

Take My Tip, 106, 110
Tale of Two Cities, A, 64, 67, 73;
    'fade-outs' in, 200, 202, 204, 205,
    206, 215
Tale of Two Cities (short), 456
Tales of Manhattan, men's opinions
    of, 224, 225, 228, 231, 239, 246, 247,
    248, 251; women's opinions of, 263,
    265, 266, 280, 286
Talking Feet, 108
Tarakanova, 256
Target for Tonight, 218, 222, 269,
    283, 288; comparison with *Ships
    With Wings*, 372, 373, 376, 379
Tartu see *Adventures of Tartu*
Tarzan Triumphs, 232
Telefootlers, 439
Television Spy, 174
These Three, 251
They Came to a City, 287
They Died with Their Boots On, 228
They gave Him a Gun, men's opinions
    of, 43, 48, 64, 69; women's opinions
    of, 56, 74
They Made Her a Spy, 151–2
They Met in the Dark, 242
They were Sisters, 15
Thin Man, The, 67, 89, 114, 119
Things to Come, 63, 175; audience
    response to, 173, 182, 183, 184;
    'fade-outs' in, 202; opinions of, 250,
    274; narrative description of, 182
Think Fast, Mr Moto, 61
Thirteenth Chair, The, 51
39 Steps, The, 62, 74
This England, 9, 219
This German Freedom, 144, 169
This Gun for Hire, 227
This Happy Breed, 13, 15; family life
    shown in, 294, 297
This Land is Mine, 226, 260, 286, 287
Those Kids from Town, 228

Three Comrades, 200, 201, 204, 215
Three Smart Girls, 54, 102, 134;
    family life shown in, 294
Three Smart Girls Grow Up, 207
Three Stooges, The, 86
Thunder Afloat, 174, 185
Thunder Rock, men's opinions of,
    220–1, 224–7, 237, 239, 242, 243,
    249, 250, 252, 256; women's
    opinions of, 220–1, 273, 274, 281,
    284, 286–9
Thunderbirds, 284
Thursday's Child, 249, 256, 281, 294
Tivoli, 67
Tobruk, 272
Tommy Atkins, 173, 179
Tomorrow We Live, 234, 261
Top Hat, 56
Top of the Town, 48, 106
Topper, 198
Tortilla Flats, 239, 250, 252
Tovarich, 208
Traitor Spy, 174, 183
Trapped in the Sky, 151, 174
Trouble Brewing, 332
Two Yanks In Trinidad, 288

Under the Red Robe, 85
Under Two Flags, 174
Underworld, The, 250, 259
Up Periscope, 246
Up for the Cup, 66, 193, 197

Vanessa, 76
Vanishing Virginian, The, 287
Variety, 251
Victoria the Great, 40; men's opinions
    of, 49, 62, 64, 78, 82, 83, 86, 87, 90,
    91, 94–9, 104; women's opinions of,
    71, 106–11, 116, 119, 120, 121,
    125–34; spliced into *Queen Victoria*,
    289
Victory Through Air Power, 227, 230,
    273–4
Viennese Nights, 95
Visit from Canada, 447
Viva Villa, 47

Wake Island, 242, 244
War Against Mrs Hadley, The, 228,
    242, 286
War in the East (Pacific), 10, 446–7,
    451–3, 458
Watch on the Rhine, men's opinions

of, 222, 230, 247, 252, 253, 255, 257;
women's opinions of, 258, 275, 283,
285
Waterloo Bridge, 144, 175, 182
Way Ahead, The, 13
Way to the Stars, The, 13
We Dive at Dawn, men's opinions of,
246, 256; women's opinions of,
265–8, 276–8, 286
We Want More Ships, 453
Weaker Sex, The, 257
Wee Willie Winkie, 127
Went the Day Well?, 269, 273, 281,
286
Westward Ho! – 1940, 431
When Tomorrow Comes, 206
When We Are Married, 245, 283
When We Build Again, 237
Where's That Fire?, 171, 208
White Angel, 97
Whoopee, 193, 197
Who's Your Lady Friend?, 101
Wicked Lady, The, 15
Wings Over Empire, 155

Wings of the Morning, 109
Winterset, 202
Woman Chases Man, 78
Women, The, 207
Women Aren't Angels, 261
Words for Battle, 444
World of Plenty, men's opinions of,
243, 244–5, 250; women's opinions
of, 264, 272
Wuthering Heights, 'fade-outs' in,
200, 204, 206, 215; opinions of, 250,
256, 262–3, 265, 276

Yankee Doodle Dandy, 226, 243, 264,
274, 276
Yesterday is Over your Shoulder, 426,
433–4
You Can't Have Everything, 47
You Can't Take It With You, 294
You Only Live Once, 48, 56, 207
You were Never Lovelier, 226, 272
Young Mr Lincoln, 207
Young Mr Pitt, The, 235, 237, 264
You're Telling Me, 217, 434–40